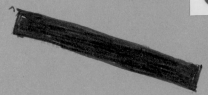

labor economics

SECOND EDITION

by

HERBERT G. HENEMAN, Jr., Ph.D.

Professor of Economics and Industrial Relations
Chairman, Industrial Relations Department
University of Minnesota

and

DALE YODER, Ph.D.

Professor of Industrial Relations
Director, Division of Industrial Relations
Stanford University

SOUTH-WESTERN PUBLISHING COMPANY

Cincinnati   Chicago   Burlingame, Calif.   Dallas   New Rochelle, N.Y.

P21

PREFACE

You, with this book in your hands, may reasonably doubt the importance of examining its Preface. What can a preface add to what you could learn from the Table of Contents? Why should you be concerned with the authors' profession of purposes and hopes, or their expressions of appreciation, or their inevitable declaration of responsibility?

Possibly the best preface for any book is its table of contents, which outlines the coverage of subject matter and suggests the rationale of order and continuity. The table of contents that follows this preface displays in gross perspective what the authors have done. It identifies the seven parts of the book and thus suggests intended breadth and balance. You can note that we have avoided any singular or particularistic slant. This is not simply the economics of labor marketing, or of collective bargaining, or of employment security. Neither is it simply a union or employer or government approach to current labor problems.

Chapter titles may suggest the authors' determination to stress system, concepts, process, theory, and policy. They distinguish major subsystems in labor marketing, employment, collective bargaining, and economic security. They may, however, fail to document this revision's reduction of descriptive, factual material to the minimum required for analysis and understanding of relationships and processes. Indeed, this second edition appears to be more bulky than its predecessor. Added pages are largely attributable, however, to new, more readable and pleasing typography and many additional tables and charts.

Chapter titles can only hint at our increased emphasis on theory as the tie that binds facts together and gives them meaning. Greater emphasis on theory seems to us timely and essential. As relevant information accumulates and the pace of change accelerates, theoretical frameworks and structures take on added importance. Without the rationale of theory, students are likely to become lost in a maze of data. Only theories can give meaning and suggest relevance and relationships. Fortunately, today's better qualified faculty members and more sophisticated students are ready to understand and undertake such abstraction, analysis, and synthesis. Students can be encouraged to think in terms of models that can accommodate future developments and translate new problems into meaningful patterns. We conclude that the usual undergraduate course should by no means be restricted to the description of historic change and superficial discussion of current problems. Its major contribution can and should be the development of analytical interest and competence in the labor economics area.

New chapters on productivity, industrial relations systems, labor markets, leisure, and economic growth express our recognition of the changing responsibilities assigned to the labor economics course. In part these changes involve significant innovations in the cultural setting and environment of our own industrial relations system. Heightened public interest and concern are symbolized by such legislation as the Manpower Training and Development Act and by institution of the annual *Manpower Report of the President*. Such changes prescribe specific attention to international comparisons of industrial relations systems and to the role of human resources in economic growth and development.

Numerous conference discussions of changing course responsibilities have been helpful in this connection; individual suggestions have also had an obvious impact.

The Table of Contents cannot make it clear that the authors see the labor economics course as the most useful and promising avenue of approach to a broad range of problems involving the conservation and development of human resources through employment. That ubiquitous area of problems is of prime interest and concern in all modern economies, from the least developed to the most mature; many such problems express universal social and political ideals. On this account, the labor economics course must be recognized as an important part of the preparation for sophisticated citizenship as well as elementary in the continuing education of professional and business leaders.

Similarly, the Table of Contents cannot explain that this text in itself is only one part of the programmed introduction to labor economics contemplated by the authors. Text discussions and analysis are supplemented by analytical review questions for each chapter. Short case problems in most of the chapters help students relate concepts and analysis to current issues and thus introduce added meaning, reality, and tangibility. An instructors' manual has been prepared to help the instructor bridge gaps between text and questions and case problems. Several hundred objective questions, tied to the individual chapters, are available from the publisher.

Only a detailed, page by page study can demonstrate the high value we place on criticisms and suggestions from our academic colleagues who have used the first edition.

The same thoughtful, detailed study will clearly indicate the extent to which we have directed attention to significant research. Footnotes offer more than a thousand selected references. They have been incorporated not simply to give credit but also to suggest the potential contributions of and need for more research. At the same time, these specific references should be helpful in encouraging students to undertake fascinating excursions and studies beyond the scope of the text.

Finally, this preface is important to the authors because it permits acknowledgement of their indebtedness to colleagues who have helped to make this second edition possible. That list includes Miss Georgianna Herman, Professors Thomas Mahoney, George Seltzer, Cyrus Smythe, and John Turnbull of the University of Minnesota, Professor John P. Troxell of the Stanford University Graduate School of Business, Professors Einaar Hardin and Winston Oberg of Michigan State University, and Professor Herbert Parnes of Ohio State University.

For secretarial assistance, we express our appreciation to Miss Jean Ross at the Stanford end of our axis and, at the Minnesota pole, to Miss Donna D'Andrea, Mrs. June Jarpey and Mrs. Marjorie Whitehill.

Major shortcomings must be charged to the authors. We made the critical decisions; opinions, unless otherwise credited, are ours. We will appreciate criticisms and suggestions, for we shall keep on seeking more perceptive approaches to this dynamic, fascinating field. Meanwhile, we hope this edition will help both faculty members and students to achieve broader perspectives combined with deeper insights.

Herbert G. Heneman, Jr.

Dale Yoder

CONTENTS

Chapter   Page

PART III — COLLECTIVE BARGAINING: POLICY, PRACTICE, PROBLEMS

PART IV — EMPLOYMENT: GOALS, THEORY, AND PROBLEMS

Chapter   Page

PART V — THE COMPLEX ROLE OF WAGES

HUMAN RESOURCES AND LABOR PROBLEMS

The modern world faces many problems arising from man's industrial and technological development; unemployment; the obsolescence of skills; lack of work opportunities for the aged, young people, and minority groups; individuals' difficulties in adjusting to rapid change; the necessity of improving personnel practices; and the uncertain future of underdeveloped areas, to name but a few. All of these relate to the efficient use of resources in modern society, particularly human resources. . . .

Human resources are the key to economic development. . . . how people think about work, and what they consider to be important goals in life, will determine whether their country will develop or not. The notion that material resources are the key to development is fallacious.[1]

WORK AND WORKING RELATIONSHIPS

Industrialized societies around the world have long recognized that working relationships are the source of many of the benefits and satisfactions their citizens regard as essential and, at the same time, are the setting for some of the most persistent social problems. Less developed nations, with economies in various stages of industrialization, are similarly concerned with both the potential benefits of working relationships and the difficult issues that arise in and are created by the relationship described as "employment."

[1]Eli Ginzberg, "Man and His Work." Reprinted by permission from the *California Management Review*, Volume V, Number 2, Winter, 1962, pp. 21–28. Copyright 1962 by The Regents of the University of California.

In even the simplest and least advanced economies, work is recognized as inescapable. The basic subsistence requirements of human beings cannot be met without effort. As populations grow, pressures for work and the benefits it creates become greater. Both "developed" and "immature" national economies recognize that the combination of human and physical resources is essential to the continued development of their economies. The principal overt manifestation of continued economic development is rising scales of living. Better food, improved housing, expanded educational opportunities, and increased leisure are some of the tangibles which are identified with increased productivity of workers. Economic growth and development also involve many changes which are noneconomic in character, such as national pride, recognition in associations of nations, and cultural accomplishments. The fruits of continued economic development are achieved through work or employment which combines human and other resources in the production and distribution of goods and services.

Worker Commitment and Organization

Effectiveness in work requires *work commitment* from individual workers; that is, the individual worker must recognize a responsibility to perform assigned tasks, he must be where the work is to be done, and he must accept directions about when and how to do the work. For workers born in industrial societies, this commitment is almost automatic; they do little more than to follow traditional patterns. In economies that are in the process of industrialization, commitment may be a problem. Workers whose experience is limited to rather primitive agriculture may not adjust readily to the new and different patterns of jobs, responsibilities, and restraints imposed in the changing economy.[2]

---

[2]For a basic reference, see Wilbert E. Moore and Arnold S. Feldman (eds.), *Labor Commitment and Social Change in Developing Areas* (New York: Social Science Research Council, 1960). See also Robert L. Aronson, "Labour Commitment Among Jamaican Bauxite Workers," *Reprint Series No. 108* (New York State School of Industrial and Labor Relations, June 1961), pp. 156–82. According to Moore and Feldman, "Commitment involves both performance and acceptance of behaviors appropriate to an industrial way of life." In other words, the fully committed worker accepts the norms of both the new, productive organization and its new, accompanying social system. This adjustment is not solely to new job assignments and ways of doing work but includes new residential patterns, ways of assigning status, political orientation, and social goals.

Labor force commitment is essential in any division of labor, for the reliability of each of the parts is imperative if the whole is to operate successfully. In many so-called underdeveloped countries workers are not used to an industrial way of life and may have

To make work effective also requires organization for work, for to only a limited extent can workers make their contribution alone. Most workers must join large or small combinations with leaders, managers, rules, and systems. Many workers perform tasks that are in themselves small and specialized. Their assignments must be timed or synchronized with those of other workers. Someone must oversee and direct their collaboration, and orders must be given, accepted, and carried out. Work thus creates a maze or fabric of relationships with other workers, associates, superiors, and subordinates. These relationships of employment are widely described as "industrial relations."

Worker Attitudes Toward Work

In addition to contributing to the total productivity of the society, work is also the means by which workers achieve personal objectives. The range of these personal work objectives is wide, and effective utilization of human resources must take this range into consideration.

Many workers regard work as a "necessary evil," for they think of it as something to be done as an indirect means to desired ends rather than as a source of direct and immediate satisfaction in itself. They work because they have to in order to gain other personal objectives,

---

little or no experience with such institutions as money and credit arrangements, mutuality of contract obligations, and many other systems that accompany industrial life.

Generally, the types of economic change sought by underdeveloped countries require not only changes in the basic economic system but also changes in the social system. Manpower performance requires acceptance of and commitment to these changes; hopefully, understanding of changes is also achieved. As changes come, adjustments are needed in: (1) the work place; (2) the market system, including both labor and commodity markets; and (3) the social structure. In essence the new industrial worker is confronted with novel personal behavior and patterns of social activities. Not all such adjustment takes place in factories, for additional banks, stores, transportation systems, and government services provide examples of concomitant developments to which individuals in an emerging industrialized society must adjust.

Modern industrialization and development in an underdeveloped area, as noted elsewhere in this volume, can "telescope" many years of technical research and development by borrowing technological and economic innovations from existing highly developed countries. These do not have to be "invented" anew. Attempts to graft on to an existing social structure, however, require a radical personal and social transformation; and it is a moot question as to how this process can not only be "telescoped" but also be made to mesh with the technological shortcuts.

It is obvious that social institutions must have acceptance and support of the people involved. This is no less true of the labor forces in newly emerging industrial economies in which many persons will encounter a wholly new concept — that of employment and all of its direct and side effects upon their lives. How this transformation is effected to yield commitment is crucial to the success of industrialization for emergent economies.

There are lessons for already developed industrial economies in the process which takes place in emergent economies, for industrial and economic transition appears to be never-ending — it leads to persistent change. Quite simply stated, present highly industrial economies also must be alert to maintain labor force commitment during the technical strains and stresses which occur in the technological revolutions at hand and ahead.

such as being able to buy some of the goods or services they want. The work objectives of other workers relate to status desires, for the individual's social position in a system of human relationships is importantly influenced by his occupation.[3]

Still other workers have work objectives which are broader than those relating to earning a living or achieving status. Many workers expect their jobs to involve a contribution which they, as well as their employer, regard as worthwhile. They may be interested, as Doherty has put it, in accomplishment as well as function.[4]

Effective utilization of human resources must also take into consideration the fact that personal work objectives change. For example, *automation*, as the current form of persistent technological change, affects attitudes toward and expectations from work Among other things, the concept of work as an inevitable burden loses some of its supporting arguments as a result of automation. In noting that automation changes values, Jacobson and Roucek observe that each step toward automation is also a step toward emancipation from the rigors of a "no work, no eat" value system.[5]

Efforts by workers, unions, managers, and society to avoid the waste inherent in such practices as restrictive work rules, featherbedding, and labor hoarding must take into consideration the variety of these personal work objectives and the fact that they are not static. Groups also differ in their interpretations of the purpose of work (e.g., employers may emphasize the goal of productivity while employees may emphasize the goals of high wages, economic security, or job satisfaction).[6]

Societal Attitudes Toward Work

The effort to achieve effective utilization of human resources gives rise to many questions which must be faced and answered by all societies. Who will be expected to work, and who shall be excused or prevented from working? Who is to decide what tasks deserve highest priorities and rewards? How shall those who are expected to work be encouraged or required to do so? What about those who do not want

---

[3]See Edward Gross, *Work and Society* (New York: The Thomas Y. Crowell Company, 1958), pp. 6–10.

[4]Robert E. Doherty, "Waste Not, Profit Not," *Reprint Series Number 115* (New York State School of Industrial and Labor Relations, 1961). Original in *The Commonweal*, Vol. 75 (December 1, 1961), pp. 250–52.

[5]Howard B. Jacobson and Joseph S. Roucek (eds.,), *Automation and Society* (New York: Philosophical Library, Inc., 1959).

[6]See Howard M. Vollmer, *Employee Rights and the Employment Relationship* (Berkeley: University of California Press, 1960).

to work? How shall tasks be allocated among workers? How shall leaders, directors, and bosses be identified? Who is to decide how much work will be expected by each worker? How shall workers be encouraged to meet these expectations?

At least as important are other questions about what shall be done with the results of work. How shall these benefits be allocated and distributed? To what extent shall each worker participate in the benefits made possible by economic activity and continued economic development?

Some questions which may be less obvious are also important. For example, who has the responsibility for training and retraining workers? How shall a society support the worker for whom no work can be found? How much concern should be felt for worker interest in and satisfaction from work?

Societies have not followed a uniform pattern in the answers they give to these questions. On the contrary, answers show a wide range of diversity. In some primitive societies, for example, women are the principal workers. In some modern societies assignments to workers are made by public agencies which tell each worker what his task will be. Some societies have proposed to distribute the benefits of work "to each according to his need." Others have sought to relate benefits to contributions.

Such variations reflect the basic ideologies and philosophies which are inherent in the culture or the hierarchy of values held by dominant political groups. Answers express prevailing attitudes toward such values as individual freedom and human dignity, as well as attitudes toward living and working conditions. Answers are also expressive of differences in theories, that is, tentative explanations of individual and group behavior. Thus, one society may assign leadership or management in work on the basis of a theory that leaders are born to lead while another society encourages competition for leader jobs on the theory that "the cream will rise to the top."

Answers to questions such as those posed in preceding paragraphs receive continuing attention in the pages that follow. Attention is directed to these questions and to the effectiveness of such answers as have been developed, particularly in the United States and in other industrialized nations whose philosophies idealize political and economic freedom. The major objective is to discover both the contributions and the shortcomings of current answers and of proposed alternative solutions.

Although there are many different attitudes and practices with respect to work and working relationships in modern societies throughout the world, there are many similar attitudes and practices among Western industrialized nations. The European Social Charter,[7] which is largely concerned with public employment policy, is one evidence of common objectives among the societies of Western industrialized nations. Article 1 of this document is concerned with the right to work. The parties "accept as one of their primary aims and responsibilities the achievement and maintenance of as high and stable a level of employment as possible with a view to the attainment of full employment." They "undertake to protect effectively the right of the worker to earn his living in an occupation freely entered upon." This article also provides for free public employment services for all workers, with appropriate vocational guidance, training, and rehabilitation. Other goals include "just conditions of work," including safe and healthy working conditions, fair remuneration, the right to form and belong to unions and to bargain collectively, protection of young workers and employed women, vocational guidance and training, social security, medical assistance, rehabilitation for the disabled, and special protections for migrant workers and their families.[8]

Employment Goals in the United States

In the United States attitudes toward work are the subject of frequent discussions. Many of them have been written into public policy through legislation on hours, working conditions, child labor, social security, and collective bargaining. Citizens of the United States are generally agreed on several major goals:

1. We regard work as distinctly respectable. Indeed, we think that working for a living is the natural and appropriate status for adults who are able and available to work. We really mean what we say about the dignity of labor. (It should be understood that this is a somewhat new and novel point of view. In most earlier societies work was widely regarded as degrading, and workers were those who had been born under such unfortunate circumstances that they could not avoid work.)

---

[7]The European Social Charter was prepared by the Council of Europe, an advisory group on social, economic, legal, cultural, and scientific matters which was founded in 1949. Each of the following fifteen nations has one minister on the Council: Austria, Belgium, Denmark, France, Great Britain, Greece, Iceland, Ireland, Italy, Luxemburg, Netherlands, Norway, Sweden, Turkey, and West Germany.

[8]"The European Social Charter and International Labour Standards: I," *International Labour Review*, Vol. 84, No. 5 (November, 1961), pp. 462–77.

2. We want all workers to have the best jobs they can handle or perform; the jobs best suited to their interests, abilities, and skills; the jobs in which they can gain the greatest satisfaction, work with the greatest enthusiasm, and earn the largest economic return.

3. We want all workers to have steady jobs with a minimum of involuntary idleness, a maximum of economic security, and the opportunity to develop potential skills to the highest degree possible.

4. We desire that the income from work be shared in such a manner that poverty and economic hardship will be continually reduced. There is particular concern for the so-called masses of workers who have only recently, in the long period of history, been permitted a share in life's luxuries.

5. We intend to use every available resource to encourage the persistent growth of the economy so that it can provide choices of jobs and can support advances in living scales for all citizens.

6. We believe that workers should have the right to join unions and to bargain collectively about working conditions and relationships.

7. We believe that the society must maintain the freedom of choice of each individual worker, for we want no system of assignments or totalitarian direction of workers. Thus, we regard as a dominant goal the protection of the freedom of each worker to make his own decisions, to enter or leave the labor force on his own initiative, to choose the job he prefers, and to leave that job when he wishes.

The principal barrier to the attainment of these goals, or at least the major impediment to continual progress in these directions, is ignorance and lack of understanding. True, a large amount of reasonably accurate information about workers and working conditions is available for use in assessing the progress which has been made toward goals. In addition, there is growing understanding of the processes that must be utilized to achieve further progress. However, additional reliable information must be secured with respect to the factors that affect the creation of jobs, the individual selection of jobs and careers, the stability of employment, and the distribution of rewards for working.

WORKERS, JOBS, AND INDUSTRIAL RELATIONS

Some 75 million people in the United States, about 43 percent of all citizens, are workers; and of the adults 14 years of age and over, 58 percent hold jobs. Workers hold more than 30,000 different jobs, and in each recent year they have been paid more than two thirds of our total national income for their personal participation in employment.

Workers include men and women; young and old; beginning (threshold) workers and old timers; native born and foreign born; city dwellers and farmers; proprietors and tenants; owners and hired help; highly skilled and common labor; and employers, employees, and self-employed. All have one common characteristic — they all hold or are looking for jobs. These workers create, collect, sell, trade, and deliver all sorts of goods and services.

The workers who hold the more than 30,000 different jobs in the United States have varying responsibilities for filling or creating jobs. The largest class of workers is made up of *employees*, those who work for others. Other workers have created their own jobs and are thus *self-employed*. The group of self-employed workers includes such workers as physicians, lawyers, farmers, and television repairmen. Still other workers own businesses in which they require help. They hire workers to join their work teams and thus become *employers*.

Other workers, described as *managers*, may find it difficult to think of themselves as falling clearly into any of the above three groups. They serve as personal representatives of owners in directing the activities of many large firms and public agencies. In their jobs they may represent several thousand stockholders or several million citizens. These managers frequently think of themselves as employers, for they hire many other workers to help them.

Nonworking Workers

At any particular time some workers may not be working. For some of them this idleness is a matter of satisfaction, for they are on vacation. Still others among those not working have been laid off. They have been released from their usual jobs because their help is not currently needed. Some of those not working are idle because of illness. Most of those who have been laid off or who are ill regard this situation as temporary.

The group of nonworking workers always includes many others who have no present work connections. They are between jobs. Some are unemployed because they want to change their work and have, on their own initiative, quit jobs they held. Some want jobs similar to their former work but in another part of the country. Some want different kinds of jobs. Some simply want to change employers or to change from being an employee to work in which they will be self-employed or will employ others to work with them. Others have been discharged from their jobs. The work they were doing may have been completed or eliminated by new machines, changed production procedures, or the fact that consumers have ceased to buy what these workers produced. Some of them did not do their work in a manner satisfactory to those for whom they were working.

In addition to workers who are or are not working, the population includes almost 100 million others who are not seeking work. These are the very young and the very old, those disabled by illness or accident, and the housewives and mothers who must remain at home.

Work-Centered Living

For most adults work occupies more of their time than any other activity. Their home and family life and their program and system of living are built around, shaped by, and integrated with their jobs. They plan every week, month, and year by close reference to the present and prospective future of their work. They time their meals, arrange for family outings, schedule their vacations, move from city to city, borrow and save, buy and sell, and educate their children all in terms of what their job responsibilities require and what their present and prospective job earnings permit.

Every member of the household is keenly aware of the importance of the jobholders' jobs. All arrange their lives about the requirements of these jobs. Working and planning for work are matters of concern to both parents and children. Babies, barely able to frame one-syllable words, are queried about what occupation they plan when they "get big." To an impressive degree the whole of life is job-centered, work-oriented, and focused on employment. As students of this field have frequently observed, the most important effect of work is probably not the material values it makes possible but, rather, the pattern of life it prescribes for people.[9]

Employment Relationships

A society that devotes so much of its time and thought to working, and especially to working in large teams of workers, creates many social or interpersonal relationships that are job-connected. When

---

[9]One of the most interesting pictures of work as a system of living is that presented by Daniel Bell in his "Work in the Life of an American," which is Chapter 1 in William Haber and others (eds.), *Manpower in the United States* (New York: Harper and Brothers, 1954), pp. 3–22.

Friday worked for Robinson Crusoe, their working relationships were fairly simple. In our society, however, the simple relationship of one employer and one employee is rare. One employer may employ hundreds or thousands of employees. One employee may work for several employers in the course of a single day or week. Working or employment relationships may bind an employee to millions of other employees, for employees may form unions with thousands of members all of whom are drawn together by their similar jobs and employment problems. Where employees have joined a union, relationships with the union may exist for both the employee and the employer. Working also creates relationships between one employer and other employers which may result in associations of employers.

Job-connected relationships have become so numerous and so complicated that a special name has been coined for them. These relationships are called *industrial relations*, by which we mean the relationships growing out of and associated with working or employment. Industrial relations means *employment relationships*.

LABOR PROBLEMS

Employment relationships, like all other relationships, are the setting for personal and social problems. People who have little trouble getting along by themselves find that living or working with others is more complicated. Employment relationships raise questions that individuals answer in different ways, so these contacts and associations are not always harmonious and agreeable. Thus, working together often necessitates cooperation and collaboration among individuals with different values and viewpoints. For example, the plant manager in Milpitas, California, may see things quite differently from his opposite number in Detroit; and the Peoria local of the plasterers' union may oppose a change sponsored by the Milwaukee local of the same union.

Participants in employment relationships face a wide range of activities in which they must work out mutually satisfactory arrangements. Such arrangements have implications (1) for attaining the social ideals and objectives already outlined and (2) for determining the part that individual workers are to play, their responsibilities, opportunities, privileges, contributions, and economic rewards.

Workers differ in their opinions about which arrangements best assure progress toward accepted social and personal objectives. One worker, for example, feels that fair wages are best insured by a system of employer-union bargaining. Another prefers to go it alone and to handle his own wage negotiations. One thinks that promotions should be closely related to length of service — seniority. Another thinks that promotions should be based strictly on merit. One worker thinks that progress is speeded by having public agencies play a more active part in regulating employment. Another wants government to leave more room for individual decisions and the determination of working conditions by employer-union bargaining.

Employment relationships also result in differences of opinion between employers and employees. An employer, for example, may seek to limit labor costs and wages at levels that he regards as reasonable and right. At the same time, some of his employees may want higher wages and greater security because they regard these conditions as reasonable and right. An employee may be a union member and zealously try to strengthen the union while his employer regards the suggestion of added authority for the union as a threat to his management, prestige, and profit. An employer may want to hire only the best, most productive, and most cooperative employees and to release those who are less efficient and who, in his opinion, fail to deliver a fair day's work. Employees, on the other hand, may expect their union to protect them from discharge even if they are not as productive as the best or most efficient employees.

Ideals vs. Reality

The complicated differences of opinion which exist in employment relationships create special social problems which are commonly described as labor problems. *Labor problems* represent conflicts of social reality with social ideals in situations surrounding or rising out of employment. Involuntary unemployment is an excellent example, for most people agree that those who want to work and are capable of working should have jobs. When people who want to work cannot find jobs, their idleness is widely recognized as a labor problem.

In a discussion which defines labor problems, it should also be noted that references are frequently made to *the labor problem*. This term has been used as a convenient designation for a sort of synthetic problem, a composite of all less-than-ideal working relationships. It is also frequently used to describe the users' "pet peeve" with respect to labor — some particular condition to which he objects.

Labor problems change with the passage of time. In earlier periods, for example, the unemployment of children was regarded as a problem; the employment of children was approved. Children were farmed out to employers who were regarded as benefactors of both the children and the public. Later, concern about child labor resulted in the enactment of both federal and state legislation to curb it. There are, of course, many other examples which illustrate that labor problems change. For several years immediately after 1900, the inrush of foreign labor was regarded as a serious labor problem which threatened the earnings and employment of native workers. Long hours of work were widely regarded as a labor problem until comparatively recently. The growth of unions has sometimes been described as a labor problem, for this historic expansion occasioned frequent conflict and violent struggles between employer associations and labor organizations.

Major Problem Areas

Five labor problem areas presently occasion wide public concern, for society has clearly failed in each of these areas to attain accepted social goals.

Industrial unrest and labor-management conflict. Most strikes, lockouts, and all extended struggles between employers and unions are regarded as somewhat objectionable, particularly if they occasion public inconvenience and hardship. Work stoppages in the basic industries and those that endanger public health or safety are of special concern, as are conflicts that involve violence and interfere with the maintenance of law and order.

Unemployment and underemployment. Most of us are immediately concerned when large numbers of workers cannot find jobs. We regard national levels of unemployment in excess of about 6 percent of the labor force as representing an emergency, and we are similarly concerned about local or regional unemployment. We are also concerned with the application of human resources in ways that fail to develop and use the greatest skills and potentialities that workers possess. Such *underemployment* is evident in some part-time work and in discriminatory employment practices that relegate foreign-born or certain racial and religious groups to limited types of work. A similar problem exists in the inadequate vocational guidance and improper initial placement of younger workers who, as a result, may never have an opportunity to develop valuable aptitudes. Underemployment also results from discrimination against older workers.

Inadequate wages. While we are not in entire agreement as to what we regard as standard or substandard wage rates, we are concerned about wages and earnings that fail to provide a comfortable living and that force workers and their families to depend on public aid. Further, we expect the earnings of workers to eliminate such conditions as "slum" housing, underprivileged children, and other handicaps associated with poverty.

Inadequate economic growth. Our citizens are increasingly concerned about working arrangements that appear to retard continuing economic growth. Working relationships that preclude continued advances in technology, prevent workers from performing a reasonable amount of useful work, or seem likely to induce rapid inflation are regarded as socially objectionable.

Other economic insecurity. We regard as serious problems the threats of interruptions in work, earnings, and income and the hazards to family scales of living that may be occasioned by illness, accident, or enforced retirement.[10]

Many specific, more sharply defined problems attract attention from time to time. For example, we are concerned when workers are being prepared for jobs that have vanished by the time they are ready to work or when workers are dissatisfied or frustrated by jobs and working conditions. We object to labor hoarding, featherbedding, and other practices that keep workers from doing a full day's work. We object to employers who act in a dictatorial manner with favoritism and prejudice playing a prominent part in working relationships.

Solutions for Labor Problems

The perfect solution to any labor problem is its elimination through the achievement of related social objectives. Solutions usually evolve and develop in a series of steps or stages. They take shape through experimentation and the gradual accumulation of knowledge and understanding. They grow as learning takes place from study and experience with temporary, expedient adjustments. Learning results from the sometimes makeshift arrangements fashioned by a conciliator or mediator, an arbitrator's award, or a stopgap agreement

---

[10]For a specific analysis of labor problems in one industry, see Eli L. Oliver, "Labor Problems of the Transportation Industry," *Law and Contemporary Problems* (Duke University School of Law, Winter, 1960), pp. 3–21.

whittled out as a last-minute compromise to prevent a strike. Further insights may be gained from a temporary truce negotiated by a union's business agent and some firm's labor relations director. Learning results from experience with supplementary unemployment benefits negotiated as one step toward the stabilization of employee income and economic security; it results from legislation forbidding closed or union shop agreements; it results from innovations that automatically adjust wages to costs of living or which advance wages to compensate for increasing output. In other words, partial solutions for labor problems develop bit by bit as forward steps are taken toward the outcome desired. Sometimes, of course, temporary expedients and experimental ventures are ill-advised and turn out to be backward or sideways steps rather than advances toward desired goals.

Understanding Working Behavior

Why do workers — employers, employees, and the self-employed — behave as they do? Why does their behavior create or contribute to the situations we regard as labor problems? What factors explain the conflict of employers and unions or the waste of some human resources in unemployment? Why are not all wages living wages? Why does not our system provide greater economic security? What and where are the roots of our labor problems?

Answers to all of these questions are somewhat obscure because working relationships involve the complex interaction of a variety of variables. Moreover, analyses of problems must cut across the usual departmental and disciplinary lines which divide, classify, and catalog knowledge about why people act as they do; for the behavior of employers and employees is not explainable in terms of known principles in a single social science or discipline. What men and women think and do about working is not simply explained as an expression of biological needs or a pattern of inborn instincts or reflexes. Neither is it simply an economic response which is explainable in terms of labor demands and supplies and material rewards for working. Rather, what workers do and think and say must be traced in part to basic physical and psychological needs; economic objectives; the conservative influence of culture, custom, and tradition; political attitudes and beliefs; and other less obvious conditioning factors.

Sound, step-by-step advances in the solutions of labor problems come slowly, but progress can be speeded by (1) encouraging widespread interest in and understanding of what is already known about industrial relations, (2) maintaining an experimental viewpoint, and (3) engaging in intensive, codisciplinary research which is designed to add to our knowledge and understanding.

LABOR ECONOMICS

This book is designed as an introduction to employment relationships through the avenue of labor economics and, as such, is not a comprehensive, codisciplinary analysis of all the behavior of work. It provides an economic interpretation of employee relations which directs attention to processes by which human resources are developed, allocated, applied, and conserved.

The approach of economics to employment relationships and problems is useful in explaining a fairly wide range of employment behavior, for one primary and almost universal reason for working is economic — the desire and need for income. The labor economics approach is also useful because of the extensive array of economic facts with respect to employment which has been collected, analyzed, and maintained over a long period of time. Data on hours, rates of pay, earnings, wage structures or relationships, employment and unemployment, union membership, strikes and lockouts, industrial accidents and illness, labor mobility and turnover, and other employment conditions are readily available as a basis for economic analysis.[11]

Economics has been defined as "the science that describes and predicts the behavior of several kinds of economic men — notably the consumer and the entrepreneur."[12] *Labor economics* is that section of economics that focuses attention on the development, application, and conservation of manpower or human resources as contrasted with other material resources. Labor economics is especially concerned with questions about how consumers and entrepreneurs make decisions that require or prevent the development and employment of worker resources, how workers themselves make such decisions, and how the mechanism of price is used to implement these decisions.

Economics provides a point of view or frame of reference for the systematic analysis of resource development and application. The

---

[11]For an excellent discussion of the limitations of an approach through a single discipline, see Kenneth E. Boulding, "Economics as a Social Science," *The Social Sciences at Mid-Century* (Minneapolis: University of Minnesota Press, 1952). For an illustration of another approach, see John B. Knox, *The Sociology of Industrial Relations* (New York: Random House, Inc., 1955).

[12]Herbert A. Simon, "Theories of Decision-Making in Economics and Behavioral Science," *The American Economics Review*, Vol. 49, No. 3 (June, 1959), pp. 253–54.

general nature of economic analysis has achieved popular recognition in the adjective "economical." The term implies care, saving, and frugality with respect to the use of resources. From its beginnings economics assumed that individuals and groups wish to conserve their resources and to use them frugally and with maximum effect.

Utilization and waste. With the avoidance of waste as an assumed objective in all economic behavior, economics studies the processes in which resources are discovered, developed, allocated, utilized, and in all these processes, conserved. Resources include whatever is usable and is in limited supply. The behavior to be explained involves the activities in which people discover, develop, allocate, and combine resources, principally through the mechanisms of exchange and price. As a discipline economics undertakes a systematic description and analysis of the processes in which resources, including the work of people, are combined to satisfy demands for material goods and services.

Following the established pattern of science, economics describes, measures, and explains the behavior with which it is concerned. It notes types of and patterns in economic behavior. It has developed a growing kit of yardsticks or scales with which to measure or quantify various types of economic behavior. It has, for example, measures of employment, unemployment, wage rates, earnings, and income. At the same time, it seeks explanations of economic behavior in relationships with other conditions or factors.

Models and relationships. Economic analysis provides *models* that describe *sequential relationships* in which variables consistently follow one another. Thus, when national production and income are expanding, employment tends to move toward higher levels. Again, wars have consistently been followed by periods in which strikes are unusually numerous. Changes in wage rates, during most of our history, have simulated but lagged behind changing patterns of consumers' prices. Economic analysis also notes *functional relationships* that suggest how (but not why) the variables in these sequential relationships are associated. Analysis notes consistent patterns of covariation and correlation and may describe, for example, the historic pattern of increasing leisure in which working hours have been reduced by about one third of the contemporary increase in man-hour productivity. Prediction is possible on the basis of verified functional relationships even though no real explanation of the association is known. Hazards in such forecasts should be clear, however, for patterns may change without warning.

Economic analysis is particularly interested in *causal relationships* that provide knowledge of the "why" in observed behavior. For example, the stated causes of strikes are known, and the generally depressive effects of extensive unemployment are understood. For many other suspected causal relationships, *theories* have been developed as reasonable and plausible explanations advanced in the absence of demonstrated understanding. These theories are of great value in continued progress toward fuller understanding, for they permit the construction of models and suggest relationships for further study. *Models* identify significant variables and illustrate the processes in which they are influential. They focus attention on the most important and basic relationships while, at the same time, suggesting what may be modifying conditions and factors.

The search for knowledge in labor economics must recognize the newness and experimental nature of our system of employment relationships. The goals which are proposed — the dignity of work and workers, rising living standards for all, the abolition of poverty, assurance of a high degree of economic security, and others — are goals which no earlier society has attained. Thus, in a very real sense the society pursuing such goals is embarked on a new, high road. In such a venture it is imperative to maintain a willingness to modify and experiment, to recognize the limitations of tradition and folklore based on earlier experience, and to seek to maximize knowledge of verifiable facts and demonstrable interrelationships. Such a program needs to foster and facilitate (1) the wide acceptance of present knowledge and (2) the rapid discovery of added knowledge.[13] In recognition of these

---

[13]The individual desirous of keeping abreast of current developments in the labor or industrial relations field should have access to at least a few periodicals. For this purpose a minimal list would include: *The Industrial and Labor Relations Review*, published quarterly by the New York State School of Labor and Industrial Relations, Cornell University, Ithaca, New York; *The Monthly Labor Review*, published monthly by the Bureau of Labor Statistics, U. S. Department of Labor, Washington, D. C.; *Labor Law Journal*, published monthly by Commerce Clearing House, Inc., 214 N. Michigan Ave., Chicago 1, Illinois; *Labor*, a national weekly newspaper published by 15 railroad labor organizations, 401 Third St., N. W., Washington 1, D. C.; *The Federationist*, published by AFL-CIO, AFL-CIO Building, Washington 1, D. C.; *Personnel*, published bimonthly by the American Management Association, 330 W. 42nd St., New York 26, New York; various publications of the Employee Relations Division, National Association of Manufacturers, 2 East 48th St., New York 17. For a more comprehensive list of related publications see "Manpower Management Five-Foot Shelf," *Bulletin 19* (University of Minnesota Industrial Relations Center, 1956).

For reference purposes the following are some of the more recent books in the field: Arthur D. Butler, *Labor Economics and Institutions* (New York: The MacMillan Company, 1961); Sanford Cohen, *Labor in the United States* (Columbus, Ohio: Charles E. Merrill

needs, this book is dedicated to presenting (1) an organized introduction to what is known about economic behavior in employment and (2) numerous sharp reminders of the serious gaps in our knowledge.

ANALYTICAL REVIEW QUESTIONS

1. How is work related to economic growth?
2. What would you describe as some noneconomic evidence of national development?
3. What is commitment to work and is it a one-sided type of commitment?
4. How does work commitment lead to industrial relations?
5. List several important questions that societies must answer to assure adequate supplies of workers.
6. Show that modern societies differ in their answers to these questions.
7. What is meant by ideologies, philosophies, and values?
8. How do our theories affect work, working relationships, and the waste of human resources?
9. Is work a necessary evil for some or all workers?
10. List five expectations you have with respect to any job you would accept.
11. How are job expectations related to featherbedding?
12. How does automation change values?
13. Illustrate the status implications or connotations of several jobs in a single industry.
14. How can the status of jobs be influenced by control of entry to them?
15. What is the purpose of the European Social Charter?
16. From your own experience or reading, cite some evidence to justify listing each of our manpower goals.
17. What types of additional information do we need to help us attain these goals?
18. How has work modified or shaped your daily living?
19. What is meant by nonworking workers?
20. What is meant by labor problems, and why do they change from time to time?
21. Comment on the concept of "the labor problem."
22. Cite examples of our expedient approaches to solutions for labor problems, and explain why they should be regarded as experimental.
23. What are the distinctive characteristics of the labor economics and co-disciplinary approaches?
24. How do you distinguish sequential, functional, and causal relationships?

Books, Inc., 1960); Richard A. Lester, *Economics of Labor* (New York: The Macmillan Co., 1964); Chester A. Morgan, *Labor Economics* (Homewood, Illinois: Dorsey Press, 1962); Melvin W. Reder, *Labor in a Growing Economy* (New York: John Wiley and Sons, 1957); Lloyd G. Reynolds, *Labor Economics and Labor Relations* (4th ed.; Englewood Cliffs, New Jersey: Prentice-Hall, Inc., 1964); L. Reed Tripp, *Labor Problems and Processes* (New York: Harper and Brothers, 1961); Paul E. Sultan, *Labor Economics* (New York: Henry Holt and Company, 1957).

25. How would you define economics, and why was it historically described as "political economy"?
26. What is a model, as the term is used in economics?
27. List what you regard as the major labor problems of our times.
28. List five questions for which you expect answers from your study of labor economics.

Case 1-1

FAMILY ALLOWANCES

Assume that you have been out of school for three years. You have always had an interest in politics and are now active in one of the local party organizations. Several members have proposed that the state should introduce a system of compulsory "family allowances" which would require that employers pay supplements in addition to regular wages and salaries to all employees who have more than one dependent. These supplements would provide specified amounts for each additional nonworker. Proponents of the idea point to the fact that such allowances are an established practice in a number of foreign nations in Europe and South America.

• Relate this proposal to what you understand to be established economic goals in our society. Make up your mind where you will stand on this proposition and prepare an outline of the arguments you will present in the next class period.

Case 1-2

KEEPING THE UNION OUT

Assume that after graduation you get a job in the personnel department of a young but growing manufacturing concern. You like the work and contemplate a career in the industrial relations field. About three months after you start, you have lunch with the executive vice-president and get into a discussion about some local union organizing activities. He expresses the opinion that efforts will soon be made to get your employees to join a union and explains that the firm's policy is to prevent unionization. He says the "old man" — the president and major stockholder — is not against unions in general but that he is violently opposed to having to deal with a union within his own firm. The president feels that union membership would prove the ingratitude of employees for all he has done in building up the business and providing good wages and steady employment. The vice-president suggests that if you want to keep your job you had better help in seeing that no union gets the right to bargain for your employees.

• How will this conversation affect your attitude toward your job? Is such a policy or attitude "un-American" or is it entirely appropriate under these circumstances? Prepare a short outline of your position to which you can refer if you are called upon to discuss this problem in the next meeting of your class.

Case 1-3

PROS AND CONS OF STRIKING

Miss Sarah Lampland is now an airline stewardess. She graduated from college two years ago. Recently, when the pilots on that airline were on strike, she returned to the campus for a visit. She has created a good deal of controversy by her discussion of the strike.

She is an active member of the union of airline stewardesses. She is fully aware the pilots struck only after prolonged negotiations. Because the airlines and their employees are subject to regulation under the Federal Transportation Act, several attempts were made to mediate the dispute. A fact-finding commission made a formal investigation and reported its findings and recommendations. Although these recommendations were accepted by management, they were not acceptable to the union. Thereafter, the intention to strike was clearly stated by the union. The strike came in midwinter when air traffic was at its peak.

A few days after the strike was called and when it became apparent that no rapid settlement was in prospect, the airline laid off many of its employees, including ground and maintenance crews, office and sales workers, and stewardesses. Miss Lampland is one of those thus forced out of work. She is currently drawing unemployment benefits.

She argues that the action of the pilots in striking to gain their demands is contrary to fundamental American ideals, goals, and objectives with respect to work and working relationships. Although she insists that she is a firm advocate of unions, she feels that the pilots have placed themselves and the labor movement in the position of opposing the public interest. She points to the obvious waste of human resources in the resulting unemployment. She argues that the pilots' action, in view of their impressive salaries, labels them and their union as selfish rather than considerate and mindful of the best interests of the country. She believes that such a strike is a likely source of inflation and hence a hazard to the welfare of all citizens.

A senior student, the daughter of a pilot on another airline, has taken sharp issue with Miss Lampland. She argues that the pilots' strike is entirely consistent with American ideals. The pilots have every right to strike, she says, if they cannot negotiate a satisfactory contract with their employers. They are free men; to require them to work under any other circumstances would, in effect, restrict their freedom. She suggests that, as a high-salaried group with a good deal of economic power or leverage, they have an obligation to set an example for weaker unions. She points to the public policy statements in the National Labor Relations Act and the Labor Management Relations Act as specifically justifying such action as a means of balancing the power of employers in our free enterprise system. She argues that the threat of strikes like this is essential to insure an adequate share of income for the wage and salary workers of the nation. She insists that salary increases are a result, never a cause, of inflation.

• Assume that you may be called on to evaluate these arguments in the next class session. With whom will you agree? If you think any important arguments have been omitted, be prepared to advance them. If you cannot agree with either side, be prepared to advance your own proposal for handling such controversies in a manner consistent with established American ideals. You may find it helpful to read the policy statements in the laws to which your fellow-student refers.

MANPOWER AS A RESOURCE

In 1962 Congress passed the Manpower Development and Training Act. This Act required the President, for the first time, to submit an annual Manpower Report to the Congress. In this epic document, submitted in March, 1963, President Kennedy wrote:

> Manpower is the basic resource. It is the indispensable means of converting other resources to mankind's use and benefit. How well we develop and employ human skills is fundamental in deciding how much we will accomplish as a nation.
> The manner in which we do so will, moreover, profoundly determine the kind of nation we become. . . .[1]

The present chapter is concerned with a description of our manpower resources: who they are, how many they are, where they work, what they are doing. It is concerned only briefly with wasted manpower resources since that is discussed in detail in Chapters 14, 15, and 16. Emphasis is given to the dynamic aspects of our manpower resources, for in a free enterprise economy workers have freedom to work or not to work — to change jobs. Employers are free to hire, fire, and lay off.

This chapter has two major purposes: (1) to present information about manpower resources and (2) to note the continuing change in the allocation of our manpower. Such information is an essential and basic background for everything else that is discussed in this book.

---

[1]*Manpower Report of the President*, (Washington 25, D.C.: United States Government Printing Office, March, 1963), p. xii.

Throughout the chapter one assumption is evident: of all a nation's resources, its people are at once the most valuable, complicated, and changing. Human resources are the most valuable because they are the major source of economic growth. However, the determination of how human resources may be utilized optimally is difficult, for the participation and contribution of individuals are subject to wide variations and constant changes. The effective application of human resources requires foresight and planning. Such foresight and planning must be based upon wide understanding of the numbers and types of people available now and in the future and an understanding of the major variables affecting the choices of jobs and the work opportunities available to individuals.[2]

POPULATION

Total population is the basic reserve from which manpower resources are drawn; it sets an outside limit. While it is true that in no nation does all of the population work, in some nations the population is almost equivalent with the labor force, except for the very young, the very old, and the sick and disabled.

World Population

The world population now numbers over three billion persons. In 1950 it was about two billion. It is estimated that 25 percent of all those who ever lived are alive today. The United Nations Population Commission has predicted a world population of seven billion by the year 2000. As can be seen from these figures, the population of the world is growing at an increasing rate. Such growth has tremendous implications for labor economics. Work must be organized to produce food, clothing, and shelter; educational opportunities must be expanded; and new social rules and institutions must be provided.[3]

---

[2] See Eli Ginzberg, *Human Resources: The Wealth of a Nation* (New York: Simon and Schuster, 1958), Chs. 1 and 2.

[3] The Asian continent represents the dominant factor in world population and labor force. Asia has more than half of the world's population, a population growth rate of 2.2 percent per year, and accounts for 65 percent of the world's population growth. From 1960 to 1987 it is expected that the growth in population in Asia alone will exceed the entire 1960 population of the rest of the world. About two thirds of the Asian labor force is in agriculture. The 1960 annual labor force increment was 16 million persons, a figure expected to increase dramatically each succeeding year. The process of economic development requires that all or most of this increase be channeled into nonagricultural sectors of the labor force. See "The Population and Labour Force of Asia, 1950–80," *International Labour Review*, Vol. 86, No. 4 (October, 1962), pp. 348–67.

The problem of providing jobs can be illustrated by reference to India. From 1961 to 1966 new labor force entrants will number 17 to 18 million. However, provision must

Population of the United States

The population of the United States is roughly 6 percent of the world's population; thus, the United States has 6 percent of the world's most basic resource. Population growth has been uneven in the United States, as can be seen in Table 2-1 below. It should also be noted that proportions of youngsters and oldsters vary through time.

Table 2-1

TOTAL POPULATION OF THE UNITED STATES AND POPULATION UNDER 10 YEARS AND OVER 65 YEARS — 1910 AND 1940–60

Year	Total Population (in millions)	Under 10 Years		65 Years and Over	
		Number (in millions)	Percent of Total[1]	Number (in millions)	Percent of Total[1]
1910......	92.0	20.4	22.2	3.9	4.3
1940......	131.7	21.2	16.1	9.0	6.9
1950......	150.7	29.4	19.5	12.3	8.1
1960[2]	179.3	39.0	21.8	16.6	9.2

[1]Based on unrounded figures.
[2]Includes Alaska and Hawaii (totaling 860,000 in 1960).

Source: *Manpower Report of the President* (Washington 25, D.C.: United States Government Printing Office, March, 1963), p. 10.

Immigration

Today the population of the United States is largely native-born. When the country emerged as a nation, and much of the time thereafter, manpower resources were in critically short supply; and it was necessary to import labor, including slaves and indentured servants. Free labor in the form of immigrants was used more commonly in the North, although at the time of the Revolution 15 percent of the half-million Negroes in the United States were in the North.

As the exploitation of natural resources required more and more manpower, especially skilled manpower, and as slavery and indentured servants disappeared, immigration increased rapidly. By 1900–1914 one million or more immigrants came to the United States each year. Before 1900 most of the immigrants came largely from Northern Europe; after 1900 proportions from Southern and Eastern

---

also be made for the 7½ to 8 million unemployed in 1961, thus requiring 25 to 26 million new jobs. Some idea of the magnitude of this task may be inferred from the difficulties the United States has in providing 1 to 1½ million new jobs each year despite our vast economic resources. See "The Forty-Fifth Session of the International Labour Conference," *International Labour Review*, Vol. 84, No. 5 (November, 1961), p. 329.

Europe increased steadily. Most immigrants were of working ages and came for the purpose of securing a job. In 1921, with a sharp depression and a rise of nationalism in the United States, rigid quotas were set and have been enforced since then. In 1910 foreign-born and their children made up over 45 percent of our labor force. By 1950 they accounted for less than 10 percent.[4] Since the 1930's immigration has averaged considerably below a quarter-of-a-million persons per year. Immigrants admitted to the United States in the fifteen-year period, 1947–1961, totaled 3.5 million. Whereas earlier immigrants were predominantly unskilled or semiskilled, one third of the immigrant workers entering the country after World War II had professional, technical, or skilled-occupational experience. Only about 10 percent have been unskilled.

Before World War II immigrants tended to represent young age groups; recent immigrants are somewhat older. In the 15-year postwar period, 40 percent of the male immigrants were in the 25–44 year age group.[5]

LABOR FORCE

Not all of the population works at any given time nor is the entire population available for work. This can be illustrated by data for the United States, as shown in Figure 2-1.

Definition of the Labor Force

Who are those who are not in the labor force in the United States? Essentially, the labor force excludes all of those who are under 14 years of age, not working, and not seeking work. Conversely, the labor force includes all of those 14 years and over who are working or seeking work.

In this country only a fraction of those who could hold jobs do so. Homemaking, the activity of the housewife, is not regarded as working in the sense of holding a job — it is not "gainful" employment. Some

---

[4]For an excellent discussion, from which the above is abstracted, see Sanford Cohen, *Labor in the United States* (Columbus, Ohio: Charles E. Merrill Books, Inc., 1960), pp. 2–27.

[5]Data from Frank L. Mott, "Manpower and Immigration," *Manpower Report* (United States Department of Labor: Office of Manpower, Automation and Training), No. 4, November 20, 1962. Immigration is a source of labor supply in other countries, as well as in the United States. Western European nations have a severe labor shortage, a shortage so severe that in some cases it hampers economic growth. Some two million Europeans work in a Western European country other than their own. The migrants are concentrated in a few countries — West Germany has over 700,000 working in-migrants, Switzerland has 650,000 (about one fourth of the total Swiss labor force), followed by France, Sweden, United Kingdom, and Benelux. Italy is the largest source of out-migrants, followed by Spain, Greece, and Portugal. For the most part these are not permanent migrations —

citizens have accumulated sources of income that make it unnecessary for them to work. Some are ill and cannot work. Several million are, at any particular time, unemployed and seeking work.

Adults, 14 years old and over, working or seeking work make up what is described as the *labor force*. This labor force includes two major divisions: the civilian labor force and the armed forces. The civilian labor force may be divided to distinguish between: (1) the *employed*, those working or only temporarily away from their jobs at any particular time, and (2) the *unemployed*, those who are not working, are on indefinite layoff, or are looking for work.

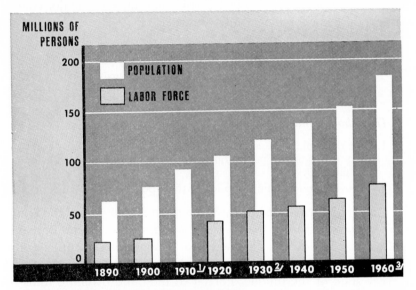

[1]Comparable labor force estimate not available.
[2]Data prior to 1930 are decennial census figures. Beginning 1930, labor force data are annual averages and population figures are estimates, including Armed Forces abroad, as of July 1 of each year.
[3]Includes Alaska and Hawaii.

Figure 2-1
TOTAL POPULATION AND LABOR FORCE — 1890-1960

Source: *Manpower Report of the President* (Washington 25, D.C.: United States Government Printing Office, March, 1963), p. 9.

---

usually they involve work permits of one year or less and in effect provide seasonal employment opportunities, although many of the immigrants do remain permanently. The exporting country benefits from alleviation of unemployment or underemployment, improved balance of payments from money sent home, and newly acquired skills that represent an upgrading of the labor force when the migrant returns home. See "The Worker Goes Abroad," *OECD Observer*, No. 2 (January, 1963), pp. 16–17.

All persons 14 years of age and over in the noninstitutional population who are not included in the armed forces or the civilian labor
force may be regarded as *labor reserves*. This group includes students,
housekeepers, those who are retired, and others who are voluntarily
idle. It may be noted that these potential or reserve human resources
exclude the institutional population. These are the inmates of penal
institutions, homes for the aged and infirm, and hospitals. In recent
years this excluded group has averaged about one million persons in
the "14 and over" age group.

The relationship of the total labor force to population may be
clarified by Figure 2-2 on page 28, which also indicates major changes
in our total labor force over a 64-year period.

Sources of Labor Force Information[6]

There are two basic sources of labor force information: household
data and establishment data.

Household data. Household data are provided by:

1. The decennial census of population which gives the only complete count of the population and is used as a benchmark for
   sampling surveys.
2. Monthly and annual sampling of the labor force (MRLF).

Current information on employment, unemployment, and related
data are compiled from the *Current Population Survey* of the Bureau of
the Census. This survey, conducted each month, is a scientific sample
of 357 sample areas comprising 701 counties and independent cities
in every state of the union. Forty-two thousand dwelling units are
visited, and interviews are made at 35,000 households containing over
80,000 persons age 14 years and older. In 1964 a sampling ratio of
1 in 1,380 was used. Findings are released by the United States Department of Labor in the MRLF, *Monthly Report on the Labor Force*. The
MRLF household data are the only regular monthly data on the
entire labor force and the so-called *labor reserve*. The regular MRLF
survey is supplemented by special studies and reports on such subjects
as dual job holding, educational level and labor force status, labor
force status of married women, high school drop-outs, annual personal and family income, and many other subjects. Annual reports

---

[6]For an excellent technical analysis of our labor force measurements, see the so-called
"Gordon Report," formally known as: President's Committee to Appraise Employment
and Unemployment Statistics, *Measuring Employment and Unemployment* (Washington, D.C.:
United States Government Printing Office, September 27, 1962).

summarizing the MRLF's are also made, along with technical releases about conceptual and methodological problems.

Establishment data. Establishment data, collected by the Department of Labor with the assistance of State Employment Security Agencies or State Departments of Labor, are based on monthly payroll reports. They provide current information by industry and by geographical location on wage and salary employment, hours, earnings, and labor turnover in nonfarm establishments. The data exclude unemployed, self-employed, proprietors, unpaid family workers, farm workers, domestic workers in households, and military personnel.

The sample of 120,000 reporting units consists of heavy representations of the largest establishments in each industry with a considerable representation of smaller establishments as well. For example, the samples cover 16 percent of all employees in service establishments, 19 percent in wholesale and retail trade, 21 percent in construction, 66 percent in manufacturing, and 100 percent in federal government. Almost 25 million employees are included in the payroll reports, thereby permitting more detailed releases about employed persons than does the MRLF. A seasonally adjusted series also is prepared, and results are published by the Department of Labor each month in the MRLF and in *Employment and Earnings*.[7]

Labor Force Participation Rate

Figure 2-2 shows year-to-year changes in what is called the *labor force participation rate*. It is a percentage representing the proportion of the noninstitutional population 14 and over that is in the labor force, either working or seeking work. It includes both civilians and the Armed Forces.

The participation rate is an important measure of human resources, for it describes the proportions of adults who are self-supporting and who must support the rest of the population. In 1963 when the labor force numbered approximately 75 million, each worker, on the average, supported approximately 2.5 people. A participation rate of 0.50 would mean that only half of those over 14 were working and that the other half over 14, together with the more than 40 million under 14, must be supported by this working group.[8]

---

[7]For a technical discussion of the methodology used, see John P. Wymer, "The Revised and Expanded Program of Current Payroll Employment Statistics," *Employment and Earnings*, Vol. VIII, No. 5, Annual Supplement Issue (November, 1961), pp. v-x. See also any current issue of the MRLF or *Employment and Earnings*.

[8]The relation of working age population to dependents is described by *dependency ratios*, defined as: the number of persons dependent on every 100 persons age 15–64 plus

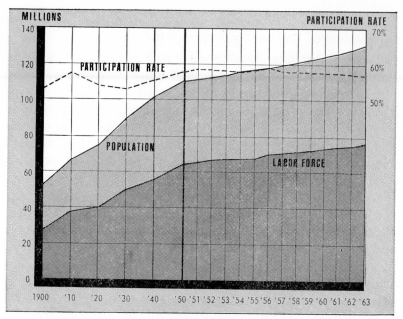

Figure 2-2

**POPULATION 14 YEARS AND OVER, LABOR FORCE,
AND PARTICIPATION RATE — 1900–1963**

Sources: Gertrude Bancroft, *The American Labor Force* (New York: John Wiley and Sons, 1958), pp. 28 and 202; Bureau of the Census, *Annual Report on the Labor Force, 1957, Series P-50*, No. 85 (June, 1958), p. 3; Bureau of the Census, *Monthly Report on the Labor Force, Series P-57*, No. 197 (December, 1958), p.1; *Manpower Report of the President* (Washington 25, D.C.: United States Government Printing Office, March, 1964), p. 195.

What is the normal participation rate? Why is not this participation rate constant and even throughout the 64 years for which data are shown? Why do larger proportions participate at some times than at others? What level of participation can be expected in the years ahead? How may forecasts be made of the probable size of future labor forces?

---

those 100 persons. The population of working age is defined as those 15 through 64 years of age.

In Asia, for example, the population of working age varies from 50 to 70 percent of the total population, with an average of 57 percent. About three fourths of the Asian population of working age is in the labor force. About two thirds of the Asian labor force is in agriculture, one fifth in services, and one eighth in industrial activities.

It is customary in international comparisons to compute ratios of economically active population to total population. ("Economically active population" is roughly comparable to our definition of the "labor force.") In Asia these ratios vary from 28 to 53 percent, with a weighted average of 42 percent. Social customs concerning economic participation of females vary greatly among Asian countries. Thus, female participation rates vary from 51 percent in Thailand to 4 percent in Pakistan. See "The Population and Labour Force of Asia, 1950–80," *International Labour Review*, Vol. 86, No. 4 (October, 1962), pp. 357–61.

Several factors affect this participation rate. The sex distribution, marital status, and age of dependents of the 14 and over group are all influential. Customs, conventions, and traditional hiring practices have a direct effect on the numbers who seek employment. For example, the practice of refusing employment to older persons may lower the participation rate by causing many elders to give up attempts to get jobs and to withdraw from the labor force. Discrimination in employment may similarly affect potential women workers, as well as members of various racial, national, and religious minority groups. All such influences increase the economic burden and responsibilities of those who hold jobs. On the other hand, a rising rate may be indicative of several types of participation that are questionable in terms of public policy. For example, youngsters 14 to 18 years of age may be working or seeking work instead of going to school.

Over the years the participation rate has shown the influence of these and other factors, with fluctuations from about 53 percent to 63 percent. Such provisions as pensions and retirement programs have affected this rate, as have changing customs with respect to education, jobs for women, and other variations in hiring practices. Participation may also be influenced by current employment, hours, and earnings of labor force members. When employment and wages are at high levels, some potential or reserve workers who would otherwise remain outside may be encouraged to join the labor force. On the other hand, if wages are low or jobs are scarce, these reserves may not try to work. To further complicate these relationships, when unemployment is widespread and earnings show sharp reductions, some *secondary workers* — wives, children, and others — are likely to seek work to supplement the earnings of usual breadwinners. As a general rule, the rate appears to decline as local wage levels rise over a period of time. It may also be reduced, in spite of secondary additions, when income and employment are sharply curtailed in a period of business recession.[9]

The *Annual Report on the Labor Force*, released by the Bureau of the Census, regularly notes the level and any evident trends in the participation rate. The rate has been rather stable at about the 58 percent level in recent years. Durand's study of earlier data indicates that a participation rate of about 58 percent has been normal in

---

[9]See Clarence D. Long, "The Labor Force and Economic Change," Chapter 13 in R. A. Lester and Joseph Shister, *Insights into Labor Issues* (New York: The Macmillan Co., 1948), pp. 329–55.

this country since before the turn of the century.[10]

Movement into and out of the Labor Force

Annual average participation rates are deceptive in that they tend to obscure the dynamics of labor force movements — into and out of the labor force, from employment to unemployment, job shifts, and many other changes. In 1961, for example, the labor force averaged 74.2 million in total with a civilian labor force of 71.6 million. However, during 1961, 82 million persons were in the labor force, and 80 million of these persons actually worked sometime during the year.[11] (As previously noted, the labor force has grown since 1961; it was over 76 million in 1964.)

Seasonal Variations in the Labor Force

The number of persons in the labor force, employed and unemployed, shows substantial variations from month to month (these are called *seasonal variations*). Thus, for example, in 1962 the total labor force in June was 6 percent higher than in January. The change in the civilian labor force from May to June represented a 3 percent increase in a single month. The labor force begins each year at its lowest point, and expansion normally appears in March. After a short plateau through April, the major seasonal growth takes place in May and reaches a peak in July and August. The decline begins in September and continues through December.[12]

---

[10]See John D. Durand, *The Labor Force in the United States, 1890–1960* (New York: Social Science Research Council, 1948), pp. 17–20.

[11]Carl Rosenfeld, "Work Experience of the Population in 1961," *Monthly Labor Review* (Washington, D.C.: Bureau of Labor Statistics), Vol. 85, No. 12 (December, 1962), pp. 1347–58. Forty-three million held full-time, year-round jobs in 1961, i.e., only slightly more than half of all workers held full-time jobs throughout the year. Fifteen million persons were unemployed sometime in 1961, about a million more than in 1960. Five million had two or more spells of unemployment. Almost 2 million of the unemployed did not work at all during the year. Almost 6 million had been out of work for 15 weeks or more, and half of these had sought work for more than 6 months.

Year-round, full-time workers increased very little from 1955 to 1961 although the labor force increased by 5 million in the same period. Less than 10 percent of the increase in jobs occurred among full-time workers.

The number of unemployed women increased faster than men in 1961, but the proportion of unemployed workers continued to be greater for men than for women.

Of 32 million persons employed part-time at sometime during 1961, almost 11 million gave inability to find jobs as the main reason for not working all year.

[12]Since 1955 labor force component estimates (for unemployment and employment) have been available with an adjustment that attempts to eliminate the portion of the variation due to seasonal influences in order to try to show the influence of more basic trends. In effect this adjustment is an approximation based on the average of past experience, even though the current year's seasonal pattern seldom resembles the average of past seasons very precisely. Thus, for example, unemployment in June is always up

Labor Force Age Distribution

The age distribution of the labor force in 1890 and 1963 is shown in Figure 2-3. The labor force, like the population, is growing older. There have been sharp declines in proportions of younger workers, 14 through 34 years of age; and there have been sharp increases in proportions of older workers, 35 through 64 years of age. The proportions of workers 65 years of age and over have remained about the same. These changes reflect the increasing life span of the population

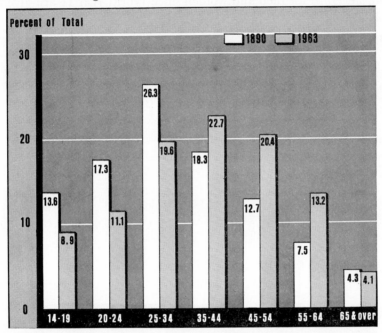

Figure 2-3
AGE DISTRIBUTION OF THE LABOR FORCE — 1890 AND 1963

Sources: Gertrude Bancroft, *The American Labor Force* (New York: John Wiley and Sons, 1958), p. 35; *Manpower Report of the President* (Washington 25, D.C.: United States Government Printing Office, March, 1964), p. 196.

sharply over unemployment in May; and this is due, in part, to the influx of students into the labor market. If this customary May to June seasonal effect created by students can be eliminated from the estimates, a better idea of whether total unemployment is increasing or decreasing more than "normal" can be obtained. Unfortunately, however, seasonal adjustment factors are not precise.

For seasonal measures of the labor force, unemployment and employment, see the monthly releases of the Department of Labor or the annual *Economic Report of the President* — e.g., see *The Economic Report of the President, 1963*, p. 195. For a discussion of procedures used to adjust for seasonality, see M. S. Raff and Robert L. Stein, "New Seasonal Adjustment Factors for Labor Force Components," *Monthly Labor Review* (Washington, D.C.: Bureau of Labor Statistics), Vol. 83, No. 8 (August, 1960), pp. 822–27 and United States Department of Labor, *Reprint No. 2349*, 1960.

plus the influx of older women to bolster the older groups. In addition, more time spent in school, early marriages, and more time devoted to child rearing among young women has lowered the proportions of younger women in the labor force.

Labor Force Sex Distribution

Figure 2-4 shows *proportions* of men and women in the labor force, which should not be confused with participation rates. Labor force *participation rates* for men and women since World War II are given in Table 2-2.

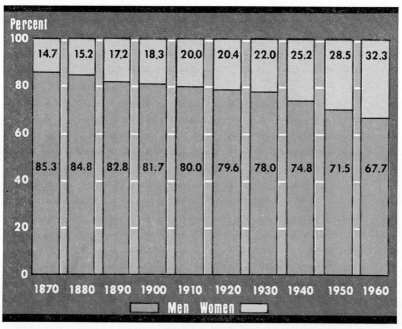

Figure 2-4
CHANGING SEX DISTRIBUTION OF THE LABOR FORCE — 1870–1960

Sources: Gertrude Bancroft, *The American Labor Force* (New York: John Wiley and Sons, 1958), p. 137; *Manpower Report of the President* (Washington 25, D.C.: United States Government Printing Office, March, 1964), p. 196.

Perhaps the most striking labor force trend in recent years is the greatly increased participation of women, especially those between 45 and 65 years of age; and it is expected that this trend will continue. While women account for one third of the labor force, they have made up about three fifths of the gain in the labor force from 1947 to 1963. (From 1947–1963 women in the labor force increased by 8.2 million, men by 5.9 million. Participation rates for women increased in the period 1947–1963 from 31 percent to 37 percent; male rates declined from 84 percent to 79 percent.)

Table 2-2
LABOR FORCE PARTICIPATION RATES
BY SEX AND AGE — 1947, 1955, and 1963

Sex and Age	1947	1955	1963
Male			
All males	84.4%	83.6%	78.8%
14–19 years	54.2	49.5	43.5
20–24 years	84.8	90.8	88.3
25–34 years	95.8	97.7	97.3
35–44 years	98.0	98.1	97.6
45–54 years	95.5	96.5	95.8
55–64 years	89.6	87.9	86.2
65 and over	47.8	39.6	28.4
Female			
All females	31.0	34.8	37.0
14–19 years	31.6	29.9	28.4
20–24 years	44.9	46.0	47.6
25–34 years	32.0	34.9	37.2
35–44 years	36.3	41.6	44.9
45–54 years	32.7	43.8	50.6
55–64 years	24.3	32.5	39.7
65 and over	8.1	10.6	9.6
Total participation rate — Male and Female	57.3	58.7	57.3

Source: *Manpower Report of the President* (Washington 25, D.C.: United States Government Printing Office, March, 1964), p. 196.

The recent rise in women's employment has been almost entirely concentrated among married women. From 1947 to 1963 the number of married women in the labor force increased from 7.5 to 14.1 million; this was 53 percent of total labor force growth.[13] In Table 2-2 note the dip in women's participation rates in the 25–34 age group, the so-called child-rearing years. Notice also that the highest participation rate in 1963 is in the "new grandma" group, 45–54 years, where about half are in the labor force.

---

[13]While the proportion of single women was about the same in 1960 as in 1940, their participation rate has declined from 45 to 43 percent.

Married women are more likely to be part-time workers than married men. One in 10 of the married women in the labor force in any month was not in the labor force in the previous month, a ratio 10 times as great as that for married men.

Nonwhite married women have higher participation rates than do white married women. Among single women, however, white women have higher participation rates than do nonwhites.

Several factors explain the increased participation of women in recent years:

1. Movement from rural to urban areas where job opportunities are larger.
2. Advances in the mechanization of household implements reduces the time needed for household chores.
3. Rising levels of education qualify more women for work outside the home.
4. Changing economic pressures on the family and changing social attitudes toward married women.
5. More two-car families simplifies the problem of women getting to work.
6. Greater availability of part-time jobs.
7. Growing concept of two careers — one before raising children, a dropout period while raising them, and an "emancipation period" after they are grown up.[14]

In Table 2-2 note the following with respect to men: the youngest (14–19 years) and oldest (65 and over) age groups showed the sharpest declines; the 20–24 year group increased its participation rate by about 4 percent; over 90 percent of the men from 20–64 are labor force participants.

Some of the factors affecting male participation rates are:

1. Movement from farms to cities. On farms there are lots of job opportunities for young boys and unskilled workers; in the city there are fewer job opportunities for these groups.
2. More young men are getting more education in order to get jobs later.
3. A substantial number of unskilled, untrained boys in the 14-19 year age group drop out of the labor force after failing to find jobs.
4. For older men illness and lack of job opportunity play major roles. The 60–64 age group shows declines which, in part, are attributable to the "early" retirement offered by the Social Security Act and private pension plans.

Labor Force Race Distribution

Negroes comprised 14 percent of the population of the United States in 1930, 10 percent in 1940 and 1950, and 11 percent in 1960.

---

[14]Thomas Mahoney in a study of why married women work in St. Paul, Minnesota, found that past employment experience and family income were predictive of labor force participation for married women under 30. Over 30 years of age, family income is not predictive; size of family is positively predictive for this group, and past work experience is a very important predictor. In short, most older married women in this study apparently work because they have found it a satisfying experience rather than because of economic need. See Thomas A. Mahoney, "Factors Determining the Labor Force Participation of Married Women," *Industrial and Labor Relations Review*, Vol. XIV, No. 4 (July, 1961), pp. 563–77.

Seventy-three percent of the Negro population are urban residents. There has been a levelling tendency in labor force participation rates classified according to race. For males, white participation rates are 81.0 percent and for nonwhite, 79.1 percent. For women, white participation rates are 35.0 percent and for nonwhite, 45.8 percent. A decade ago the participation rate was 32.6 percent for white females and 44.9 percent for nonwhite.[15]

Education and Labor Force Participation

Education has an important influence on the labor force participation rate; there is a marked increase in participation rates associated with higher educational levels. This is especially true for women and older workers.

For women who have not completed high school, the participation rate is 32 percent; for college graduates, 53 percent. A greater proportion of better educated women work whether or not they have children. In part this may reflect greater job opportunities for those with more education.

Those with more education tend to remain in the labor force longer. There is a disproportionate number of part-time and unemployed workers among the less well educated. In 1960 the median school completion of employed workers was 12 years and only 10 years for the unemployed.

Quality of the Labor Force — Education and Training

Education is obviously important in terms of occupational structure. Eighty percent of employed college graduates hold either managerial or professional positions. Forty-two percent of men who fail to complete elementary school are employed as laborers or semiskilled operatives as compared with 23 percent for those who complete high school (but not college).[16]

---

[15]Work-life expectancy increased for nonwhites by almost four years from 1940 to 1955; this reflects a decline in mortality rates in middle-aged nonwhites. (Work-life expectancy increased only 1.6 years for whites in the same period.)

[16]The median income of male college graduates in 1961 ($7,400) was $2,350 higher than for male high school graduates. Male high school graduates earned $1,600 more than those not going beyond grade school. Obviously such differences reflect differences in opportunities and natural abilities and are not just a function of education.

Since 1940 there has been a 70 percent increase in the proportion of workers who have completed four years of high school or more. The proportion of workers completing four years or more of college almost doubled in the same time period, up from 6 to 11 percent. The rise in educational attainment is greater for men than for women.[17]

Manpower, as is true of most other natural resources, is not economically very valuable in its raw form; it must be refined and developed. About one fourth of the population is attending school for the purpose, at least in part, of getting ready for the labor force. The most striking educational gain since World War II is in higher education. The gain in the number of men completing college is especially impressive—women apparently prefer husbands to diplomas, for they still lag in this regard.

In addition to education and training in school, it is estimated that industry spends an amount almost equal to its profits after taxes (some $25 billion a year) for training after employees have entered the labor force. Nor is the end in sight, for higher and higher skill levels are needed. Retraining needs to be expanded. Almost 5 percent of the labor force (over 3 million people) are *functional illiterates* (those with less than 5 years of school), and they have a difficult time in the labor market.[18]

High school dropouts have also had a difficult time in the labor market. In June, 1959, 1½ million graduated from high school; one half of these enrolled in college in the fall, 54 percent of the boys and 39 percent of the girls. Nine tenths of the boys and three fourths of the girls who did not go on to college entered the labor force; 10 percent of the nonworking girls were married by fall and 10 percent went into nursing and vocational schools. Dropouts from high school were almost the same in number as high school graduates who did not go on to college (800,000). There were twice as many nonwhite as white dropouts. Half the young women dropouts were married. Both the young graduates in the labor force and the dropouts had much higher

---

[17]College enrollments are expected to more than double by 1975; see *U. S. News and World Report* (January 21, 1963), p. 61.

Year	College Enrollment
1962	4.2 millions
1965	5.2 millions (est.)
1970	7.3 millions (est.)
1975	8.6 millions (est.)

[18]In 1890, 90 percent of the Negro population was illiterate as compared with 5 percent in 1960. In 1961, 95 percent of the nonwhite and 98 percent of the white children aged 14–15 were in school.

rates of unemployment in October of the same year (1959) than the average for the labor force as a whole. Fifty percent of the high school graduates had clerical, office, and sales jobs as compared with only six percent for the dropouts.[19]

There is an occupational hierarchy in terms of education. For example, in 1962:

1. The average professional and technical worker had at least a college degree.
2. The average clerical worker, sales worker, manager, and proprietor had at least a high school degree.
3. The average service worker, semiskilled operative, craftsman, and foreman had some high school education.
4. The average laborer, farmer, and domestic had only elementary school training or less (eighth grade or below).[20]

Unemployed in the Labor Force

As noted earlier, the labor force is made up of (1) those with jobs, including the self-employed, and (2) those unemployed. In recent years almost 95 percent have had jobs and only about 5 percent have been unemployed.[21] However, the rate of unemployment has increased, as can be noted in Figure 2-5. Although not shown in the chart, average duration of unemployment is also increasing. An

---

[19]Sophia Cooper, "Employment of June 1959 High School Graduates, October 1959," *Monthly Labor Review* (Washington, D.C.: Bureau of Labor Statistics), Vol. 83, No. 5 (May, 1960), pp. 500–506.
    Since 1957 both employed and unemployed have increased their educational levels sharply. Indeed, in 1962 unemployment was no more heavily concentrated among the less educated than it was in 1957, five years before. However, the gap in employment remains fairly steady, as is indicated by the following analysis:

PERCENT NOT FINISHING HIGH SCHOOL

Year	Employed	Not Employed	Gap
1957	52%	71%	19%
1959	49%	69%	20%
1962	45%	63%	18%

Education is important in a brainpower economy. However, educational advances alone cannot guarantee jobs. Educational attainment and job opportunities must advance together if serious imbalance is to be avoided. See Denis F. Johnston, "Educational Attainment of Workers, March 1962," *Monthly Labor Review* (Washington, D.C.: Bureau of Labor Statistics), Vol. 86, No. 5 (May, 1963), pp. 504–15.
    [20]Arnold Katz, "Educational Attainment of Workers, 1959," *Monthly Labor Review* (Washington, D.C.: Bureau of Labor Statistics), Vol. 83, No. 2 (February, 1960), pp. 113–22.
    [21]Unemployment rates are generally higher for Negroes than whites, and in economic downturns unemployment increases twice as rapidly for nonwhites. Generally, unemployment rates for nonwhites are about double those for whites; part of the reason lies in the higher proportions of nonwhites with lesser occupational skills.

examination of Figure 2-5 reveals that after each of the post World War II recessions unemployment declined. However, after each of the recessions, unemployment was not reduced as much as had been the case following the preceding recession. Unemployment did not drop below 5 percent from 1957 until July, 1964.

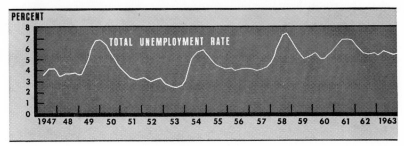

Figure 2-5
SEASONALLY- ADJUSTED UNEMPLOYMENT RATE — 1947–1963[1]

[1]Seasonally adjusted, based on quarterly averages.

Source: *Manpower Report of the President* (Washington 25, D.C.: United States Government Printing Office, March, 1964), p. 16.

THE EMPLOYED

This section of the chapter deals with the 95 percent of the labor force that is employed. Unemployment is such a serious problem that it receives special attention in Chapters 14, 15, and 16, plus numerous references elsewhere.

The employed may be classified (1) by source of compensation, (2) by industry, and (3) by occupation. Changes in employment distributions within each of these categories demonstrate the dynamic nature of the economy and the labor force.

Employed Persons by Compensation Source

There are four major compensation source categories: (1) employers, (2) wage and salary earners, (3) self-employed, and (4) unpaid family workers.

Employers, or "job-givers," play a crucial role in the economy. It is essential to have sufficient demand for labor, especially in times like the present when there is a rapidly increasing number of job seekers.

Typically, employers are business concerns, many of which are corporations (about 500,000 firms are corporations). There are 4½ million business concerns in the United States, and 75 percent of these business concerns have fewer than four employees. However, these smaller firms employ only 1 out of every 16 employees. Conversely, the 25 percent of firms with four employees or more account for 15 out of every 16 employees.

In terms of numbers of businesses, excluding farms, almost 45 percent are in retail trade, 18 percent are in services, 11 percent are in construction, 7 percent are in wholesale trade, and 7 percent are in manufacturing. Only 10 percent of all manufacturing firms have 100 or more employees, but these bigger firms employ three fourths of all employees in manufacturing.

Wage and salary workers (employees) have become the largest component of the labor force. Both self-employed and unpaid family workers have declined as a proportion of the total labor force. One hundred years ago a majority of our labor force was self-employed (largely in agriculture), but today this proportion is 1 in 8.

Shifts in employed persons among various major compensation sources are shown in Table 2-3 which summarizes experience since World War II.

Table 2-3
EMPLOYED PERSONS BY COMPENSATION SOURCE — 1947, 1955, AND 1963

Class of Worker	Millions Employed			Percent of Employed		
	1947	1955	1963	1947	1955	1963
Wage and salary workers	45.0	51.8	58.8	78%	82%	85%
Self-employed workers	11.0	9.6	8.6	19%	15%	13%
Unpaid family workers	2.0	1.8	1.4	3%	3%	2%
Total	58.0	63.2	68.8	100%	100%	100%

Source: *Manpower Report of the President* (Washington 25, D.C.: United States Government Printing Office, March, 1964), p. 197.

In Table 2-3 note both the absolute and relative increase in wage and salary earners since World War II. Note also the decline in the self-employed. Although not shown in Table 2-3, only about 10 percent of nonagricultural workers are self-employed, and self-employment among these workers occurs in a wide variety of occupations. The largest share of the self-employed is in trade and service industries, but the number of self-employed professional workers is growing — from 11 percent of all self-employed in 1948 to 15 percent in 1961.

The self-employed work longer hours — 8 hours more per week than wage and salary workers in 1962. Their employment is more stable; unemployment is much less extensive than among other employees; and, if professionals are excluded, wages are lower.[22]

Employed Persons by Industry

As society becomes more affluent, demands for goods grow less rapidly than demands for various kinds of services. Indeed, with all of the mechanical marvels in today's homes, a prospective husband should check his bride-to-be to make sure that she has a plumber's license, an electrician's license, and so on. In the United States during the decade of the 1950's, service-producing industries passed goods-producing industries as the major source of employment. This can be observed in Table 2-4.

The change in growth rates among industries can be seen in Figure 2-6 on page 42. Note especially that while total nonfarm employment increased at an annual average rate of 1.9 percent during the first decade (1947–1957), from 1957–1963 the growth rate was only 1.4 percent. Growth rates are highest in: (1) state and local government, (2) services, and (3) finance, insurance, and real estate. Negative growth rates are found in: (1) mining, (2) agriculture, (3) transportation and public utilities, and (4) manufacturing. Thus, increasing employment tends to characterize the service producing industries, and declining employment is found in goods producing industries. Table 2-5 shows that this trend is expected to be continued through 1975.

Despite declines in manufacturing employment from 1957 to 1963, manufacturing is still our largest employment sector, followed by trade, government, and services.

Public employment. Throughout the past half century one of the most impressive trends in the labor force is the rising proportion of public employees. In round numbers approximately nine million civilian workers, in over 100,000 governmental units, plus three million in the military services are government employees. In terms of civilian

---

[22]John E. Brugger, "Self-Employment in the United States, 1948–1962," *Monthly Labor Review* (Washington, D.C.: Bureau of Labor Statistics), Vol. 86, No. 1 (January, 1963), pp. 37–42.

Table 2-4

PERCENT DISTRIBUTION OF EMPLOYMENT
BY INDUSTRY DIVISION — 1947, 1957, AND 1963

Industry Division	1947	1957	1963[1]
Total[2]...................	100.0	100.0	100.0
Goods-producing industries....	51.3	45.9	41.2
Manufacturing............	29.8	29.0	27.4
Durable goods...........	16.1	16.7	15.4
Nondurable goods.......	13.7	12.4	12.0
Mining..................	1.8	1.4	1.0
Construction.............	3.8	4.9	4.8
Agriculture..............	15.8	10.5	8.0
Service-producing industries...	48.7	54.1	58.8
Transportation and other utilities................	8.0	7.2	6.3
Trade...................	17.2	18.4	19.2
Finance, insurance, and real estate..................	3.4	4.2	4.6
Service and miscellaneous...	9.7	11.4	13.4
Government.............	10.5	12.9	15.3
Federal................	3.6	3.7	3.7
State and local.........	6.9	9.1	11.6

[1]Preliminary.
[2]Represents wage and salary employment in nonfarm industries based on employers' payroll data, plus total employment in agriculture based on household survey data.

Source: *Manpower Report of the President* (Washington 25, D.C.: United States Government Printing Office, March, 1963), p. 17; *Manpower Report of the President*, 1964, pp. 19 and 197.

workers, this represents an increase of more than 200 percent since 1920. More than two thirds of the total is accounted for by state and local agencies. The largest segment of this total is in education, followed by national defense, hospitals and health services, highway departments, the postal service, and general administration. Workers in education now number more than three million.

One half of the public employees are employed by local governments, federal governments have one third, and state governments have one sixth. In the last three decades employment in local governments has more than doubled, state employment is up four-fold, and federal employment is up five-fold. Public employees made up 9.9 percent of all nonagricultural wage and salary earners in 1929, and this percentage increased to 16 percent in 1960. From 1929 to 1960 the civilian labor force increased by 43 percent while government employment increased 178 percent.

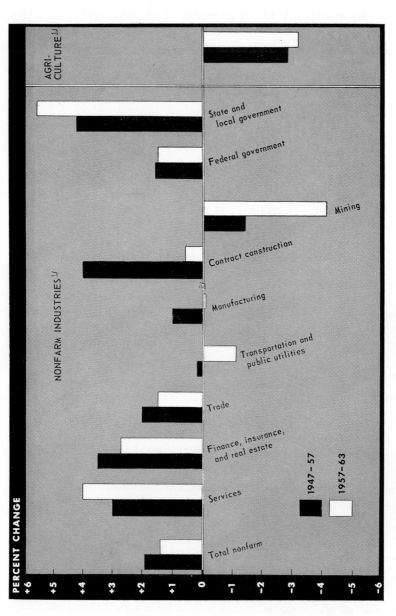

Figure 2-6

ANNUAL RATES OF EMPLOYMENT GROWTH BY INDUSTRY — 1947–57 AND 1957–63

[1]Employment represents payroll employees in nonfarm industries and total employment in agriculture.
[2]Less than 1/10 of 1%.

Source: *Manpower Report of the President* (Washington 25, D.C.: United States Government Printing Office, March, 1963), p. 18; *Manpower Report of the President*, March, 1964, p. 19.

Table 2-5

NONAGRICULTURAL WAGE AND SALARY WORKER EMPLOYMENT BY INDUSTRY DIVISION — 1960 TO 1975

Industry Division	Employment (in millions)			Percent Change, 1960–75
	Actual	Projected		
	1960	1970	1975	
Total..........................	54.3	67.7	74.2	37
Service-producing industries............	34.0	43.7	48.8	44
Wholesale and retail trade............	11.4	14.0	15.6	37
Government.......................	8.5	11.5	12.8	51
Service and miscellaneous............	7.4	10.2	11.9	61
Transportation and public utilities.....	4.0	4.4	4.5	13
Finance, insurance, and real estate.....	2.7	3.5	3.9	44
Goods-producing industries............	20.4	24.0	25.4	25
Manufacturing.....................	16.8	19.2	20.3	21
Contract construction...............	2.9	4.0	4.4	52
Mining...........................	.7	.7	.7	....

Note: Individual items may not add to totals because of rounding.

Source: *Manpower Report of the President* (Washington 25, D.C.: United States Government Printing Office, March, 1963), p. 95.

The upward trend in public employment is more rapid than the growth of population. In part the upward movement is clearly related to demands for higher attainment in formal education. At the same time, larger proportions of older persons look to public agencies for support and assistance (instead of to their families). Urbanization creates problems that require public attention to building codes, sanitary facilities, and police and fire protection. Meanwhile, increasing research (in both physical and social sciences) and highly expensive exploration are met through public agencies.[23]

[23]Daniel H. Kruger, "Trends in Public Employment," *Proceedings of the Fourteenth Annual Meeting, Industrial Relations Research Association* (December, 1961), pp. 354–66.

The federal government is the largest "consumer" in the market. In 1962 the federal government spent $115 billion. The federal government, through its spending allocations, affects the size and location of labor forces in the various states. Almost one fifth of all personal income comes from federal spending. Such spending, however, is not spread evenly from state to state. Sixty-one percent of federal spending that can be allocated by states goes to 13 states, while the remaining 37 states get 39 percent. California gets $10 billion, New York $6 billion, and Texas $4 billion. At the other end of the scale, Vermont gets $114 million and Delaware $145 million.

Because the states vary substantially in their personal income, federal payments have a differential effect on each state's economy. In Alaska and New Mexico federal payments constitute almost one half of all personal income, while in Delaware only 10 percent and in New York only 13 percent of personal income comes from federal spending.

Thus, the federal government through its allocations has become a major determinant force in labor force allocation; it is a tremendous factor in business development

Agricultural employment. The most impressive declines in employment have occurred in agriculture. From 1947 to 1962 farm employment declined 3 million, or 200,000 per year. Early in our history agriculture accounted for 90 percent of all employment. By 1910 only 30 percent were in agriculture, and by 1962 about 8 percent were so employed.

An agricultural labor force of 5 million feeds and clothes a nation of 190 million people and produces impressive surpluses in the process. As is noted in the next chapter, productivity gains in agriculture have been double those in other industries. Rural areas have served as the source of most of our industrial manpower resources. In a sense, the farms have been factories producing not only food and fibre for export but also human beings for export to manufacturing, trade, service, government, and all other labor forces. This out-migration from agriculture to other industries has helped make possible the great economic expansion and growth of the United States.

Not quite 15 million people live on farms (about 8 percent of the population). Forty-five percent of all farm people are under 20 years old, but these young people tend to move off the farms as they get older. There are relatively few young adults on farms (only 25 percent of the farm population is in the 25–44 year age group). In spite of the small percentage of the population which lives on farms, agriculture has excess manpower resources. That there is a serious underemployment problem in agriculture is evidenced by the fact that a hired farm force of about 4 million persons is tied up doing the equivalent of about 1.2 million year-round jobs. Although there is an excess of manpower resources, many individuals remain on the farm because of lack of job opportunities elsewhere.[24]

---

and job creation. States can and do compete for government contracts. So-called "normal" labor market allocation does not apply in these cases; in many cases political considerations may be paramount. Further, employment standards including wages may be affected in the states, with spillover to industries not otherwise directly affected by government spending. See *U. S. News and World Report* (November 12, 1962), p. 78ff. See also *Business Week* (November 3, 1962), pp. 56–60.

Special notice should be taken of the impact of defense spending on employment. One of every ten dollars produced in goods and services is spent in national defense. Nearly 1 of 10 in all workers is employed by the defense establishment and defense industries. Eighty-six percent of all federal government purchases for goods and services is for national defense. Thus, disarmament would call for massive retraining, relocation, and creation of more job opportunities which would probably be largely concentrated in the civilian-public sector of the economy. See *Quarterly* (New York: Carnegie Corporation), Vol. X, No. 2 (April, 1962), pp. 6–8.

[24]See Committee for Economic Development, *An Adaptive Program for Agriculture*, 1962, pp. 32, 59–60. See also *Employment Security Review* (Washington 25, D.C.: Bureau

About 500,000 farm workers are migrants.   Half are between
14–24 years of age, three fourths are male, and a high proportion are
Negroes and Mexican in origin. (About one half of the migrants are
imported foreign workers.) Migrants tend to follow streams of job
opportunities, e.g., harvesting from Texas to the Great Lakes. Travel
patterns of seasonal migratory agricultural workers are shown in
Figure 2-7. Migrant workers averaged about $6 per day in 1958 and

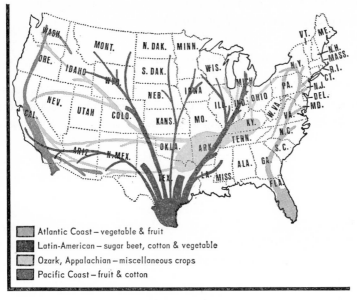

Atlantic Coast — vegetable & fruit
Latin-American — sugar beet, cotton & vegetable
Ozark, Appalachian — miscellaneous crops
Pacific Coast — fruit & cotton

Figure 2-7

TRAVEL PATTERNS OF SEASONAL MIGRATORY
AGRICULTURAL WORKERS[1]

[1]The map shows the northward migratory movement. This is reversed as the crop
season ends in the northern States and the workers drift back to home base — for many of
them, southern California, Texas, and Florida.
    Source: Lucile Petry Leone and Helen L. Johnston, "Agricultural Migrants and
Public Health," *Public Health Reports*, Vol. 69, No. 1 (January, 1954), p. 5.

of Employment Security), Vol. 29, No. 1 (January, 1962), p. 3.
    Farm workers are, in a sense, the real "forgotten men" in the American labor force.
They are excluded from most of our protective labor legislation. Job opportunities and
demands for their services are declining. More than half of all farms now employ no paid
workers.   Individual worker productivity, with modern agricultural equipment, has
increased rapidly; it was four times as great in 1960 as in 1910.
    Employment is seasonal, with peaks of unemployment in the winter. The general
level of unemployment throughout the year is higher than for nonfarm workers. Average
hourly earnings are low; in 1960 farm workers throughout the nation averaged 82 cents
per hour (compared with $2.29 for manufacturing workers) and $6 per day. Hourly
earnings have increased from about 53 cents in 1947 to 82 cents in 1960. Annual earnings
are comparatively low, averaging approximately $1,000 in 1959. Hourly rates are lowest
in East South Central states and highest in the Pacific region.

averaged only $710 that year for 119 days of farm work. Unemployment rates for migrants are very high—41 percent in 1959 with an average unemployment duration of 20 weeks.

Health, house, sanitation, and schooling facilities are usually substandard for these workers and their dependents. Two thirds of migrants' children are in school grades below normal for their age. Many of these escape from the migrant into the industrial labor force, but they face severe unemployment prospects because of their lack of vocational and educational preparation.[25]

Employed Persons by Occupation

Workers are now employed in a wider range of occupations than ever before in the history of the United States. Some occupations are professional, some managerial, some highly skilled, some semiskilled, and some unskilled. Perhaps the best way to get an overview of the wide range of jobs held by workers today is to thumb through the *Dictionary of Occupational Titles* which lists and briefly describes some 30,000 jobs.

The range and variety of skill requirements are directly related to a basic and primary problem with which labor economics is concerned — the effective application and utilization of human resources. The demands for various skills should provide the opportunities necessary for full utilization of all workers in the labor force. If the skill requirements of available jobs do not fit the pattern of skills possessed by workers, many workers will be employed in jobs which do not utilize their capacities to the fullest. For example, the employment of a skilled carpenter as a watchman represents a waste of skill. At the same time, effective application of human resources requires appropriate training

---

[25]Louis Levine, "The Migratory Worker in the Farm Economy" (U.S. Bureau of Employment Security, May 4, 1961). (Mimeographed.)

Domestic migrant workers are augmented each year by about 250,000 to 350,000 foreign workers, mainly Mexican *braceros*, although others come in from the British West Indies, Japan, Canada, and the Philippines. Imported workers are assured, by federal regulation, such benefits as health and accident insurance, standard housing and transportation, and guaranteed work. These regulations do not apply to domestics. See "The Migratory Farm Labor Problem in the United States," *Senate Report No. 1098* (Washington, D.C.: United States Government Printing Office, 1961).

Legislative proposals in recent years have sought to change some of these distinctions by bringing migratory workers under the coverage of the National Labor Relations and the Fair Labor Standards Acts and by regulating the employment of domestic migrants as employment of *braceros* is now regulated. (Public Law 78 prescribes rules for minimum wages, housing, transportation, subsistence payments, and emergency medical care for *braceros*.) In addition, proposed laws could provide training and retraining aid for migrants. See *Monthly Labor Review* (Washington, D.C.: Bureau of Labor Statistics), Vol. 85, No. 10 (October, 1962), pp. iii–iv.

to insure the development of needed skills in workers who have the necessary aptitude and potential for developing those skills.[26]

Data with respect to the changing occupational structure in the United States are shown in Table 2-6 and indicate that:

1. Total employment increased by 14 percent from 1950 to 1960.
2. White-collar jobs increased by 28 percent, whereas manual (or blue-collar) jobs increased by less than 6 percent.
3. In 1960 white-collar jobs (43 percent of employment) exceeded manual jobs (39 percent).
4. Agricultural employment declined over both decades; the acceleration of the trend is emphasized by the drop of 41 percent from 1950 to 1960.
5. Professional and technical jobs were the fastest growing occupational group in the decade 1950–1960 (up 47 percent).
6. Service jobs increased by 26 percent in the decade 1950–1960.
7. Clerical jobs increased 34 percent from 1950–1960; this, however, was a lesser rate of increase than the 59 percent growth from 1940–1950.
8. Craftsmen and foremen increased at a 12 percent rate from 1950–1960.
9. Operatives (semiskilled) increased by only 6 percent during the period from 1950–1960 (less than the rate of increase in total employment).
10. Laborers decreased 9.6 percent in the decade of the 50's.

In summary, lesser skilled jobs, such as laborers and farm laborers, actually decreased from 1950–1960. Semiskilled jobs increased at a slower rate than the average of all employment. Craftsmen and foremen increased at about the same rate as all employment. White-collar and service jobs increased much more rapidly than the average, with professional and technical jobs showing almost a 50 percent increase in the 1950–1960 decade.

As a society moves from "brawn-power to brain-power," more and more professionals are needed. The fact that we more than doubled our professional labor since 1940 is of crucial importance in using our manpower resources effectively. Future utilization and growth plans will require even greater increases in this vital segment of our labor force.[27]

---

[26]The recent shortage of engineers may be due in part to the inefficient utilization of those who are employed. See the following sources for discussions of such problems: National Manpower Council, *A Policy for Scientific and Professional Manpower* (New York: Columbia University Press, 1953) and A. J. Jaffee and Charles D. Stewart, *Manpower Resources and Utilization* (New York: John Wiley and Sons, 1951).

[27]Negroes have raised their occupational levels appreciably in the last two decades. In 1960 one fourth of working white males, but less than 7 percent of the Negroes, were

Table 2-6
UNITED STATES OCCUPATIONAL STRUCTURE — 1940–1960

Occupational Group	1960		1950		1940		Percent Increase	
	Number (in thousands)	%	Number (in thousands)	%	Number (in thousands)	%	1940–1950	1950–1960
All civilian employed.....	64,639	—	56,435	—	45,070	—	25.2	14.5
All with occupations reported...............	61,456	100.0	55,692	100.0	44,652	100.0	24.7	10.3
White collar workers......	26,588	43.3	20,819	37.4	14,676	32.9	41.9	27.7
Professional and technical	7,232	11.8	4,921	8.8	3,580	8.0	37.5	47.0
Managers, officials, and proprietors (nonfarm)...	5,410	8.8	5,037	9.0	3,634	8.1	38.6	7.4
Clerical...............	9,306	15.1	6,954	12.5	4,382	9.8	58.7	33.8
Sales.................	4,639	7.5	3,906	7.0	3,081	6.9	26.8	18.7
Manual workers........	23,746	38.6	22,437	40.3	16,394	36.7	36.9	5.8
Craftsmen, foremen......	8,741	14.2	7,821	14.0	5,171	11.6	51.2	11.8
Operatives.............	11,898	19.4	11,180	20.1	8,080	18.1	38.4	6.4
Laborers (nonfarm and mine)...............	3,108	5.1	3,436	6.2	3,143	7.0	9.3	− 9.6
Service workers..........	7,171	11.7	5,708	10.2	5,292	11.9	7.9	25.6
Nonprivate household....	5,445	8.9	4,297	7.7	3,200	7.2	34.3	26.7
Private household.......	1,726	2.8	1,411	2.5	2,091	4.7	−32.5	22.3
Agricultural............	3,950	6.4	6,728	12.1	8,290	18.5	−18.8	−41.3
Occupations not reported..	3,184	—	743	—	418	—		

Source: United States Census Data reported in *Monthly Labor Review* (Washington, D.C.: Bureau of Labor Statistics), Vol. 85, No. 11 (November, 1962), p. 1211.

Table 2-6 shows that despite the white-collar revolution, operatives still constitute the largest single occupational grouping of jobs in the United States. Clerical and professional jobs are gaining in importance and threaten to pass jobs held by craftsmen and operatives in the years ahead. The sharp decline in proportion of jobs in agriculture is especially noteworthy; however, agriculture still outranks unskilled nonagricultural labor in proportions of jobs in the occupational structure of employment in the United States.[28]

---

in professional and managerial occupations. Negroes are continuing to gain in these jobs at a faster rate than whites. Government employment opportunities have been a notable cause of this increase. Negro employment in unskilled jobs has declined markedly.

[28]Special note should be made of the fact that in 1960 census enumerators did a very poor job, for they did not secure usuable occupational information for over 3 million jobs. Errors in a complete enumeration or census by highly unskilled interviewers probably exceed the sampling errors obtained in the MRLF, which uses skilled, experienced interviewers.

A similar trend may be noted in manufacturing where production workers are declining and nonproduction workers are increasing. In 1947 one employee in six in manufacturing was in a nonproduction occupation. By 1957 the proportion was one in four and is continuing to decline.[29]

Men and Women's Jobs

The proportions of men and women in the various occupational groups are shown in Table 2-7. Higher proportions of men have jobs as: operatives, managers, officials, and proprietors; craftsmen and foremen; and laborers and farmers. Jobs in which there are higher proportions of women include clerical, private household, and service workers. The most distinctive occupational class for men is operatives; for women the most distinctive job class is clerical.

Table 2-7
PROPORTIONS OF MEN AND WOMEN BY OCCUPATIONAL GROUP — 1963

Occupational Group	Men		Women	
	Number (millions)	%	Number (millions)	%
Professional and technical............	5.3	11.7	3.0	12.8
Farmers and farm managers..........	2.3	5.0	0.1	0.4
Managers, officials, and proprietors....	6.2	13.7	1.1	4.8
Clerical............................	3.1	7.0	7.2	30.7
Sales..............................	2.6	5.6	1.7	7.2
Craftsmen and foremen..............	8.7	19.2	0.2	0.8
Operatives........................	9.0	19.9	3.5	14.9
Private household...................	—	—	2.3	9.8
Service workers.....................	3.1	7.0	3.6	15.3
Farm laborers and foremen..........	1.5	3.2	0.7	2.9
Laborers (except farm)..............	3.5	7.7	0.1	0.4
Total..........................	45.3	100.0	23.5	100.0

Source: *Manpower Report of the President* (Washington 25, D.C.: United States Government Printing Office, March, 1964), p. 199.

[29]During the 1950's occupational structures in the United States changed markedly from region to region and state to state. Rates of total employment growth were greatest in the Mountain, Pacific, and South Atlantic regions, while five Central states suffered actual losses in numbers employed. Operatives increased markedly in importance in the Central states, which reflects the continuing industrialization of that area. Professional and technical workers tended to increase most rapidly in the Pacific region. In general, however, regional occupational profiles showed more similarity in 1960 than in 1950. Since all regions are becoming less specialized and more balanced in their occupational structures, the prospects are that regions will continue to change in the same direction in the 1960's. See Stella P. Manor, "Geographic Changes in United States Employment from 1950 to 1960," *Monthly Labor Review* (Washington, D.C.: Bureau of Labor Statistics), Vol. 86, No. 1 (January, 1963), pp. 1–10.

A LOOK AHEAD

Population and Labor Force Changes in the 1960's

It is predicted that the following changes will occur in the American population and labor force in the 1960's:

1. Total population will be 208 million in 1970; it was 190 million in 1963.
2. Persons reaching age 18 will average 2.75 millions in the first five years of the decade; in 1965 this will increase dramatically to 3.75 millions (the result of the sharp increase in births in 1947).
3. Because of increased education, the typical labor force entrant in the 1960's will be at least a high school graduate (although 2.25 million will not go beyond grade school in the 1960's and 5.5 million will have only some high school).
4. In terms of labor force changes:
   a. The labor force will increase from 73.5 million in 1960 to 87 million in 1970.
   b. Retirement and death will decrease the labor force by 15 million; 26 million new-entry young people will enter the labor force, as will 3 million adult women some of whom will be reentries.
5. Nineteen million young people began their careers in the decade of the 1950's; 26 million will do so in the 1960's. By 1970 there will be 3 million new, young entrants a year. It should be noted that while there will be an extra one million young workers a year from 1965 on, the private economy produced only 185,000 additional jobs in each of the years from 1957 to 1962.
6. In the decade of the 1960's, there will be major changes in the age distribution of the labor force. Although there will be little change in the 35–44 age group, there will be increases of:
   a. 6.5 million in the under 25 age group.
   b. Almost 2 million in the 25–34 age group.
   c. 5.5 million in the 45 and over age group.[30]

Changing Occupational Distribution

Projected changes in employment by occupational group from 1960 to 1970 are shown in Figure 2-8. Laborers will not increase, and farm occupations will show a decline. All other occupational groups are expected to increase, with professional, clerical, and service showing the largest increases. Note the relatively lower growth among managers and sales workers in the white-collar group and the lower growth among craftsmen, foremen, and operatives in the blue-collar group.[31]

---

[30]Ewan Clague, "Demographic Trends and Their Significance," *The Changing American Population* (New York: Institute of Life Insurance, 1962).

[31]For a good discussion see George W. Hardbeck, "Occupational Trends in the United States," *Labor Law Journal* (May, 1962), pp. 361–63. It should be noted that

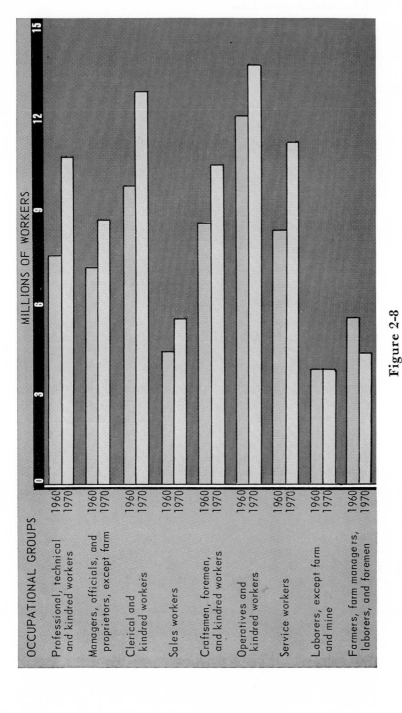

Figure 2-8

EMPLOYMENT IN MAJOR OCCUPATIONAL GROUPS — 1960 AND PROJECTED 1970

Source: United States Department of Labor, Bureau of Labor Statistics, Chart 2114, 1963.

Growth in Professional Jobs

From 1950 to 1960 employment in professional and related work increased from 4.9 to 7.2 millions. By 1975 persons in these jobs should number 12 millions. In 1950 one of twelve civilian labor force members was in a professional or related job, and in 1960 the corresponding ratio was one of ten. By 1975 the ratio is expected to be one of seven.[32]

In addition to considering new job entrants, the computation of total professional needs must take into consideration the fact that turnover will require many replacement entries. For example, two million new teachers will be needed as replacements between 1958 and 1975, about five times as many as are needed to staff new positions.[33]

Manpower Problems

The following items from the 1963 *Manpower Report of the President* provide an excellent summary of some of the major problems which exist in connection with manpower resources:

1. Employment has grown rapidly in the United States since the end of World War II, but the labor force has grown at an even faster rate.

2. Unemployment, consequently, has also risen.

3. The very sharp rise in long-term unemployment is of particular concern.

4. In need of special attention are the serious and intractable unemployment problems of: (a) young people, (b) older workers, (c) nonwhite workers, (d) workers attached to declining or unstable industries, (e) those located in depressed areas, and (f) unskilled workers generally.

5. All of these developments reflect the need for more jobs — for expanded employment.

6. Meanwhile, there have been serious problems of displacement within the labor force (changing occupations and industries) and consequent reemployment problems.

7. At the same time, current shortages of qualified personnel exist in many professions and specialized occupations.

----

while there are regular series on labor forces and labor supplies, there are no comparable series for labor demands. This represents a major deficiency in labor market information, and a regular series of total unfilled job openings would be most helpful. Present public employment service lists of job openings include only those registered at these agencies.

[32]Helen Wood, "What's Ahead for College Graduates," *Occupational Outlook Quarterly*, Vol. III, No. 4 (December, 1959), pp. 3–9.

[33]*Ibid.*

8. Worker mobility, while substantial in the United States, is inadequate for effective matching of men and jobs.

9. Basic dimensions of our future manpower problems are the unprecedented increase in the labor force in the 1960's and the radically changing patterns of labor force growth.

10. Future productivity gains, added to the growing labor force, accentuate the employment problem. Enough jobs must be created to replace jobs lost through automation and to meet the needs resulting from labor force growth.[34]

Qualitative Manpower Resource Outputs

As has been stated repeatedly, manpower is a raw resource. Sheer numbers of people are of little economic consequence in a modern industrial economy.

An *optimum labor force* is frequently described as the number of workers that can, with existing physical resources, maximize the goods and services available to all. A smaller force would be unable to develop and utilize the full potential of the society. A larger number would create lower, less effective technical coefficients in combinations of workers and physical resources, i.e., less efficient capital-worker ratios.[35]

The concept of an optimum labor force is useful in suggesting the importance of these coefficients or ratios, but it should be recognized as a gross concept involving many significant intrinsic variables. It directs attention to one important goal — efficient combinations of resources at a particular point in time. It may provide a yardstick for evaluating policy on immigration, emigration, hours of work, or child labor. On the other hand, several other objectives may be as important.

An optimum labor force, for example, is not the same as an optimum population. For the latter the commonly used criterion is per capita income. Population could vary with no change in numbers

---

[34]*Manpower Report of the President* (Washington 25, D.C.: United States Government Printing Office, March, 1963), pp. xv–xvi, 3–8.

Those who have read Chapter 1 of this book will recognize that the *Manpower Report of the President*, excellent and needed as it is, deals primarily with only limited facets of manpower problems — essentially it deals with problems of employment and unemployment. In this book many other problems are covered, such as labor-management relations, wage policies, economic security, and many others.

[35]This is, of course, the concept that economists call the *production function* which defines or specifies the amount of output that can be produced by each set of inputs, or factors of production. At any one time there is always a maximum-optimal combination of inputs that yields highest output.

of labor force members. An increase in population would then mean reduced per capita income. However, if the labor force grew as population expanded, changes in per capita income would depend on the marginal contribution of added workers. Similarly, effects of reduced population on per capita income would hinge on any possible concomitant change in capital-worker ratios. It should also be noted that changes in either labor force or population, or in both, could be counter-balanced by changed working hours or improved methods of combining resources.

Aside from problems of national defense, the optimum is perhaps best measured by the rate of economic growth, with associated rises in real incomes; for this criterion suggests that quality rather than quantity of the labor force is the mark of the optimum. As will be noted in later chapters, a major source of growth is the rising productivity of workers, and a major factor in that rise is their educational level. Perhaps, therefore, the best measure of the optimum labor force is that of annual increases in labor productivity. When that indicator turns down, it could mean that numbers are exceeding the economy's current capacity to prepare them for work.

Education, training, and health programs can increase the quality of manpower inputs. Of vital consequence are the resultant outputs — the production and the productivity of manpower resources. Hence, the chapter which follows discusses productivity and especially manpower productivity.

ANALYTICAL REVIEW QUESTIONS

1. Why is manpower described as the *basic* resource?
2. What are the implications of population growth for economic problems?
3. What age groups in the United States population are growing most rapidly in absolute terms? In relative terms?
4. How do post World War II immigrants to the United States differ from those prior to that time?
5. Why is labor force commitment essential in any division of labor?
6. How do household data on employment and unemployment differ from establishment data?
7. How is the "labor force" defined?
8. Can both employment and unemployment increase in the same month? What would the effect be on the size of the labor force if this happened?
9. What is the labor force participation rate? Are members of the armed forces excluded from this computation? What has been our typical participation rate in recent years?

10. What factors tend to increase the participation rate? To decrease it?

11. How many people move into and out of the labor force in a year? During what months is the labor force at its highest level? Lowest level?

12. What has happened to participation rates of married women in recent years? Which age groups of married women show increasing participation? Which show decreasing participation?

13. What factors help account for the increase in women's labor force participation? For decline in men's participation rates?

14. How is education related to labor force participation? How is education related to occupational structure?

15. What proportion of our employed are wage and salary workers? Are self-employed professional workers increasing or decreasing?

16. What industries offer the largest volume of employment? Are service-producing or goods-producing industries growing at the fastest rate? In what sections of the United States do we find the greatest percentage increase in nonagricultural employment?

17. How does the growth in public employment compare with population growth? In what sectors do we find most rapid growth in public employment (a) in absolutes and (b) in percentages? Why is public employment increasing?

18. How does the federal government affect labor force allocation?

19. How many migrant farm workers do we have in the United States? What are their principal problems?

20. How can skilled workers be underemployed?

21. What major occupational groups show a growth rate in excess of 20 percent from 1950 to 1960? What is the fastest growing occupational group? Are semiskilled jobs keeping pace with the average growth rate of all jobs? What occupational group provides the most jobs?

22. Are proportions of nonproduction workers in manufacturing increasing or decreasing?

23. What three occupational groups employ the most women? The most men?

24. How many young people will begin their labor force careers in the decade of the 1960's? How many will enter each year in the 1970's? What will happen to numbers of persons in the 35–44-year-old age group in the labor force during the 1960's?

25. What occupations offer the best employment opportunities in the coming decade?

26. What is meant by an "optimum labor force?" Is this the same as an "optimum population?" Why or why not?

27. How is "labor productivity" related to "optimum labor force"? Why is the concept of optimum labor force important?

Case 2-1

LEISURE AT 55

You are asked to evaluate a proposed bill to be introduced in the federal Congress. It would permit all male and female workers to retire at age 55 and, if they are eligible for federal pensions, to draw full pensions thereafter. It would, in other words, simply reduce the age requirement for such pensions. The bill has been widely discussed, with opponents generally holding that the nation cannot afford it, that it would greatly increase total pension costs, and that it could be financed only by higher taxes.

• Analyze the proposal in terms of its effects on participation rates and supplies of labor. Prepare an outline of your position on the question and be prepared to present an organized argument supporting your position in the next class session.

Case 2-2

MORE VOCATIONAL TRAINING?

Your home city must provide additional high schools to take care of the rapidly growing teen-age group. The question of bond issues for such physical facilities as are needed has been submitted to citizens in two elections. In both, authority to issue the bonds has been voted down. A citizen's committee is now carrying on a compaign to get a favorable vote in the next election.

The local taxpayers' association has issued a public statement in which it is argued that one major reason for failure to give public authorization for the bond issue is the failure of existing high schools to "prepare children for useful jobs." The association says that if the Board of Education will guarantee that new schools will be used to give vocational training — in agriculture, plumbing, sheet-metal working, automobile repair, and other similar fields — the bond issue will be approved. The association argues that at least half of all high school students should be directed into these vocational curricula.

The Central Labor Union has issued a statement denouncing this proposal on the ground that such a program would lower wages for present workers in these fields.

• You have been invited by the Junior Chamber of Commerce to discuss this issue. Your assignment here is to be prepared for the next class with a less-than-500-word press release summarizing your position and the points you will make.

PRODUCTIVITY

> I say we will beat you, and beat you with better organized pro-
> duction. . . . Capitalism can be conquered only by higher produc-
> tivity of labor. And this can be achieved only through automation
> and mechanization. . . . The most important task now is to reach
> the American level of production and overwhelm them in the field
> of economic competition.[1] — Soviet Premier Nikita Krushchev

In the previous chapter attention was directed to those who do
the work in society — who they are, where they are, and what they are
doing. These people work to produce and consume goods and services
which in turn satisfy their wants and needs. In our society the efficiency of their efforts and the reward for their work are at least partially determined by their productivity.

Productivity is a matter of wide interest and concern in all modern
societies. This chapter begins with a discussion of concepts of productivity and why it is used as a criterion in industrial relations and labor
economics. This discussion is followed by a section on measurement
of productivity, a section on actual productivity attainments, and
finally a brief discussion of problems encountered in using productivity
as a yardstick in industrial relations.

---

[1]Speech at Split, Yugoslavia, United Press International dispatch, *St. Paul Pioneer
Press*, August 25, 1963, Section 2, p. 14.

CONCEPTS RELATED TO PRODUCTIVITY

Work is a vital force in any society. It is seldom if ever an end in itself — instead, it is a means to an end or, more specifically, to numerous ends. Work may be viewed as an *economic force* concerned with effort and toil and the use of physical and mental energies to produce goods and services. Work may be viewed as a *social institution*, including status and authority systems and social values. Work may be viewed from an *engineering* or efficiency approach; thus, for example, engines do work and transform energy with varying degrees of efficiency. *Psychologically*, work may be viewed as a means of satisfying certain personal needs. Indeed, work can be viewed from many other viewpoints as well, including those of health and religion.

All of these viewpoints are significant and important. However, in this text major emphasis is given to economic aspects of work and, in that context, essentially to production and productivity. Within the framework of productivity, special attention is given to labor productivity because it is the basic yardstick for decision making in labor marketing. It is essential to understand some of the basic theories and facts about labor productivity as a foundation for many of the other subjects dealt with later in the text.

Wants, Needs, and Utilities

Humans use goods and services to satisfy many, but not all, of their wants. In fact, one definition of a *good* is anything that can satisfy a need or want. Some goods are practically unlimited and may be obtained without effort. Others are scarce and must be obtained through effort (or money) — these are *economic goods*. Most goods that we want are economic goods, including services. In economics production has reference to the want-satisfying properties of an object or service rather than its physical property. This want-satisfying effect is called a *utility*; production is thus regarded as the creation of utilities.

In psychological terms utility roughly corresponds to needs satisfaction. The economic term "wants" is equivalent to the psychological term "needs." One of the basic purposes of work (if not the most basic) is to satisfy needs or wants. These may be individual, group, corporate, national, or some other set. One simple classification of basic individual needs is that modeled after Maslow. He postulates classes of needs which, in general, form a hierarchy from lower to higher as follows:

1. Physiological (e.g., hunger, sex, thirst, etc.).
2. Safety (e.g., freedom from murder, accident, robbery, etc.).
3. Esteem (e.g., self-respect, respect of others).
4. Self-actualization (i.e., to be able to realize one's potentials).
5. Knowledge and understanding per se.[2]

Although some people differ, most individuals tend to satisfy these needs in ascending order. That is, they pay first attention to physiological needs; and when physiological needs are satisfied, they give attention to safety needs, and so on up the hierarchy. As lower order needs are satisfied, higher order needs become motivations. In essence, Maslow's classification provides for the concept of goals as a framework for the study of individual motivation. Although the subject of motivation will not be pursued at this point, it should be emphasized that people's goals reflect their needs or wants, that satisfaction of many of these needs require goods and services, and that goods and services require production. Typically, goods and services may appear to satisfy desires primarily on the lower end of the hierarchy. However, note that broiled hummingbird tongues in vintage wine may satisfy esteem as well as, or perhaps better than, physiological needs and goals. A college education, which is an economic service or good, may help satisfy goals of self-actualization and knowledge and understanding.

Needs and wants are almost limitless. When individuals satisfy those on the bottom rung of the ladder, most of them move up to the next rung, and ever onward and upward. Needs can be acquired; they are not all innate. However, the realities of life soon teach us that while needs may be unlimited, the stock of goods and services is relatively limited or scarce. Life also teaches that it is desirable to allocate these limited resources in a manner which maximizes need-gratifications at the least cost. Thus, individuals work to produce goods and services economically so that the goods and services may be consumed to satisfy a maximum number of their needs and wants. This is the picture of productivity as it concerns the individual.

Social Needs and Production

Man lives in a society — in groups. Hence, his needs must be

---

[2]A. H. Maslow, *Motivation and Personality* (New York: Harper and Brothers, Inc., 1954); and A. H. Maslow, "A Theory of Human Motivation," *Psychological Review*, Vol. 50, 1943, pp. 370–96.

gratified with consideration given to the needs of his fellowmen. Certain collective decisions must be made by any society, including:

1. What should be produced?
2. How can these goods and services be produced most efficiently?
3. How will the total output be divided? Who gets what and how much?
4. How should resources be used? Should they be used up now? Should some be conserved for future use?
5. How can all of these problems be resolved simultaneously and still retain enough flexibility to meet changing needs and circumstances?

All of these questions must be resolved in a setting of scarce resources. To take just one example at this stage: Larke predicts that in the decade ending in 1966 the needs for goods and services in the United States will increase by 40 percent, but the labor force will increase by only 14 percent.[3]

Group decisions are required to answer these economic questions in any society; different societies utilize different solutions to these same problems. The results of these decisions are not always satisfactory. Thus, for example, in Russia some consumer goods are so shoddy that people do not want them. In the United States much of our manpower resource is wasted through unemployment and underemployment. No economic system is perfect nor can any economic system escape having its ultimate yardsticks in human values. However, several principles hold true for any economic society:

1. One cannot consume that which is not produced.
2. Goods and services are more valuable the more closely they approximate consumers' needs and wants.
3. The output of goods and services can be increased by using more resources or by using existing resources more efficiently.

It is important to recognize the crucial role of productivity and the need for more efficient utilization of resources.

Basic Determinants of Productivity

What are the determinants of productivity? Basically, they include the following:

---

[3] A. G. Larke, "Human Relations Research: Academic Wool Gathering as Guide to Increased Productivity?," *Dun's Review and Modern Industry*, Vol. 68, No. 1 (July, 1956), pp. 42–44.

1. Quantity, quality, and location of natural resources.
2. Quantity and quality of human resources, including managers, professionals, technicians, and entrepreneurs, as well as the labor force generally.
3. Quantity and quality of capital stock.
4. The capital-labor ratio.
5. State of technology, including innovation, research, and development.
6. The size of the economy.[4]

Of these determinants of productivity, the quality of human resources, the state of technology, and the labor-capital ratio are probably the most important in terms of their long-run impact. Working conditions, human effort, human relations, and type of supervision are probably of lesser importance in their influence on productivity.[5] On the other hand, groups of employees and individuals can and do cooperate or resist in attempts to maintain and improve productivity. As will be noted later, industrial unrest, bogeys, and union policies and attitudes are also powerful determinants of output in the short run.

Productivity: An Economic Yardstick

Productivity decisions are basic in any kind of economic system — free enterprise, state controlled, or a mixed economy. In a *free enterprise economy* profits act as both a spur and a yardstick for productive efforts. The entrepreneur combines resources in response to consumer demands to create economic utilities. In a dynamic economy he innovates, takes uninsurable risks, and experiments with different combinations of production factors and techniques. In general, his demand for any factor of production depends upon its productivity. The very dynamics of an enterprise economy leads to uncertainty and risk, to loss as well as profit. The entrepreneur must be able to respond to economic ballots of consumers in the form of the prices they are willing to pay for the goods and services he produces. His is a complicated

---

[4]For more detail see C. R. McConnell, *Elementary Economics* (New York: McGraw–Hill Book Company, Inc., 1960), pp. 358–79; Lloyd Reynolds, *Labor Economics and Labor Relations* (3rd ed.; Englewood Cliffs, N. J.: Prentice-Hall, Inc., 1959), pp. 453–58; J. Harvey Dodd and Thomas J. Hailstones, *Economics: Principles and Applications* (4th ed.; Cincinnati: South-Western Publishing Company, 1961), pp. 45–66.

[5]Robert A. Sutermeister, *People and Productivity* (New York: McGraw-Hill Book Company, Inc., 1963), pp. 1–16.

role because of the complexity of market forces. A market economy leans heavily on specialization (including division of labor) and a system of exchange. Specialization is an important means of increasing productivity; but even between and among specialized resources, the entrepreneur experiments and substitutes more productive factors for less productive ones. Labor is almost always used in every combination of factors. Various kinds and grades of labor are competitive and hence capable of substitution of one for another. In a market economy an almost countless or infinite number of decisions interact to match production and distribution, prices and costs. The consumer may not be aware of his influence in a market economy. Thus, for example, few if any housewives when purchasing a loaf of bread instead of a can of beer think, "I am casting an economic ballot for the employment of millers rather than brewers"; but that is precisely what they are doing.

In a *state-controlled economy* government experts plan output and distribution. Market forces and the price system are not controlling, and economic decisions reflect political goals and decisions.[6] However, even here productivity is an essential consideration or yardstick. No political system, per se, is a substitute for higher output in a society where consumers' economic wants are important.

In the United States we have a mixed economy; some production is determined by market forces and some by political decisions. Production of compact cars versus big power-equipped cars is a market decision decided by consumer preferences. On the other hand, a decision to build a new school is essentially political. Note, however, that each of these decisions is concerned with productivity as defined above. Both reflect peoples' values which, in turn, reflect their needs, wants, and ethical systems.

Take certain fundamental ethical or belief systems, for example. If I grow apples on my apple tree, I am entitled to use them because I produced them. If Tom and Bill mow George's lawn (for which they receive $1.00) and if Tom mowed three fourths and Bill one fourth, we think it only fair that Tom get 75¢ and Bill 25¢. Note that we use *relative output* or relative contribution to production as a yardstick for determining the proceeds of that production. We pay in part according to productivity or contribution.

We could, and do, also distribute the proceeds of production according to *need*. The prevailing current ethic in the United States

---

[6]The Russian system of decision making is discussed in the next chapter.

seems to favor paying according to productivity as the more important yardstick. However, we are a generous people and do distribute much of our production (about one fifth) on the basis of need. Thus, for example, many forms of so-called economic security fall into this category, and the concept of a "needs" test is long and well established in certain types of social service work.

Although need is an important criterion, need does not create effective demand. Furthermore, an employer who pays his employees wages and salaries far beyond the value of their output will go broke and will have to go out of business. Also, a society that encourages wage increases that exceed productivity will have to contend with problems of inflation. An economic system that does not facilitate shifting resources to more productive uses as judged by consumer demands is inefficient and runs grave risk of unrest, decline, and even revolution.

A nation's strength is measured by the criterion of production. The United States is the world's dominant single power; with only 6 percent of the world's population, the United States produces 38 percent of the world's goods and services, or real income. At the same time, there are writers who question our very affluence and what it might be doing to the vitality of our people. Some say we produce too much. Some say the United States produces too much of some things and not enough of others. For example, we are said to be deficient in the arts, humanities, education, churches, and other cultural values.

Productivity: A Yardstick for Decision Making

Productivity is used as a yardstick of equity in many decisions concerning labor and employment. It is used as a basis for decision making:

1. By the individual:
   a. What occupation shall I pursue?
   b. Do I get a fair wage for my efforts?
   c. Shall I change jobs?
   d. How can I raise my standard of living?
2. By the firm:
   a. What kinds of people shall we hire?
   b. How much shall we pay for various jobs?
   c. Which employees shall we promote, transfer, lay off, or rehire?

     d. What kind of wage and salary system shall we use?

     e. How can we provide incentives and motivation?

     f. What resources should we try to substitute for labor? When and where? Can we substitute less expensive for more expensive labor?

     g. How can we reduce labor costs?

     h. How can we afford to give more leisure to our employees?

     i. How can we increase productivity?

3. By the union:

     a. What productivity measures shall be the basis for our wage demands?

     b. How can we reduce hours of work?

     c. How can we reduce unemployment and underemployment?

     d. Do we want increases in money wages or real wages, or in some other condition?

4. By society:

     a. How should we allocate, utilize, conserve, and develop our manpower resources?

     b. What is a fair basis for settling labor-management disputes?

     c. How shall we distribute relative shares of gross national product (or national income) to the various factors of production? How shall we distribute national income to non-workers versus workers?

     d. How can we protect the purchasing power of those on fixed incomes?

     e. How shall we pay government employees whose product does not pass through normal market channels (does not meet a profits test)?

     f. How can we prevent wasted manpower resources?

     g. How can we meet competition in foreign trade?

     h. How much manpower can we afford to have in our military establishment?

     i. How can we increase our economic growth rate?

     j. How much and what types of education do we need?

     k. How much should we spend for health and medicine?

     l. How can we protect the value of our money?

     m. How can we maintain or raise our standard of living?

The above questions are illustrative, not exhaustive. Although these questions may appear quite dissimilar, they have one common feature — productivity is a yardstick used in every one of these decisions. Generally, it is not the only criterion, but often it is the most important single criterion.

Distribution of Productivity Gains

One of the interesting and important policy questions with respect to productivity is: Who should get the proceeds from increased productivity? If wage increases exactly equal labor productivity gains, the extra spending money (added wages) and the extra supply of goods and services will balance out, and prices will remain stable. If productivity increases and wages remain stable, prices will tend to fall since the same amount of money will be available for an increased amount of goods and services.[7] If prices fall and wages remain stable, the benefits are distributed to all consumers. If the productivity increase is passed on in the same proportion to wage earners alone, however, they benefit while other sections of the consuming public do not. Who should get the benefit?

Unions argue that since the increase in productivity is an increase in labor productivity, they should get the benefits. However, as is discussed later in this chapter, it is very difficult, if not impossible, to measure labor productivity accurately.

Productivity is the relation between input and output. It could be measured in ergs, in tons, or in many other ways. In the United States we usually measure productivity as a ratio between physical product and man-hours worked. In one way the choice of man-hours in this index is unfortunate because many people regard the increase in output as being caused by labor — and this is not necessarily so. Indeed, improved management, machines, and methods are as likely to be the cause of increased productivity as are the added efforts of labor. Labor is seldom used alone but instead works jointly with capital, and the product of each is practically indistinguishable. Hence, capital seeks and gets a share out of higher productivity also, although it is equally difficult to decide the exact proportion of increased productivity attributable to capital.

The subject of investment technically lies outside of our subject area, but the crucial effects of both private and public investment upon productivity must be heavily underscored. Private expenditures for new business plant and equipment increase technological efficiency and productivity. Give an employee better tools and he will be more productive — a man with a shovel cannot compete with a man with a bulldozer. Public expenditures for schools and health programs also are important because they increase the quality of the labor force and make it more productive. A nation without engineers and doctors cannot compete on even terms with a nation that has them. The two factors of better plant and equipment and better quality of employees are related, for in many cases the use of more complex tools requires

---

[7]This might have an undesirable national income, full employment effect since investment is usually curtailed when prices are falling.

better educated employees. Neither alone would be sufficient.[8] Thus, it is practically impossible to determine who deserves to get the benefits of increased productivity on the basis of who caused the increase.

This much is sure: unless capital also shares in the distribution of productivity gains, workers stand to lose by having their standard of living frozen, for they will not get better tools and equipment. Workers should be especially interested in seeing that there is a sufficient reward to capital to provide them with better tools, increased productivity, higher wages, and adequate jobs.

Effects of Technological Change

The effects on productivity of technological change are complex, difficult to assess, and subject to much argument. Logical analysis is complicated by the number of factors or variables that affect employment levels; empirical findings are meager and subject to severe limitations because the data usually are incomplete and do not account for all of the major sources of variation. Hence, it should be realized that there is no simple answer to such questions as "Does technological change cause unemployment?"

In general, effects of technological change depend upon the nature of the new machines, whether they are *complementary* or *supplementary* to labor. If complementary, new machines tend to increase labor's absolute real income and its proportionate share. If machines are supplementary (substitutes for labor), then the effect is to increase the supply of labor units to be combined with the complementary factors. Insofar as capital for labor-substitute machinery is withdrawn from that for machines complementary to labor, the productivity of all labor is reduced. The reader is warned that these tendencies presume a high degree of flexibility in the combination of men and machines. If the technical coefficients are fixed and inflexible (the machines permit little variation in the number of men used), then the extent of these effects is reduced.

If the technological change is accompanied by a reduction in prices and employment and wages remain constant, living standards and real wages increase. Indeed, this has been the greatest cause underlying our increased standard of living. Technological changes are generally greatest in times of war and prosperity and in industries

---

[8]See the excellent discussion by Arthur R. Upgren and Maynard Krueger in "Economics in Everyday Life," University of Minnesota Industrial Relations Center *Bulletin 20*, June, 1958.

that are expanding. Technological changes affect resource allocation substantially. In general, it is the long-run forces, such as population growth and higher living standards, rather than technological change per se that expand an economy. In the long run purchasing power can be expanded and maintained only through increased productivity, that is, through expanding the labor force and/or expanding the output per worker.

Hypothetical case. Some basic ideas about the effects of technological change may be gathered from the simplified analysis that follows. First, though, it should be noted that there are many types of technological change, some *capital saving* and some *labor saving*. Only laborsaving improvements resulting in decreased labor requirements per unit of output are considered here. Laborsaving improvements result in the same product being turned out with less labor or in more product being produced with the same amount of labor. In either event less labor goes into each unit of product, and the efficiency of labor is said to be increased according to our usual method of computing labor productivity.

The short-run effects of a laborsaving technological change (assuming no great changes in consumer demand or secular inflation) can be illustrated by considering a hypothetical case. The basic data for this hypothetical case are shown in Table 3-1.

Table 3-1
EFFECTS OF LABORSAVING CHANGES — 50 PERCENT SAVING

	Product Demand			Employment in Firm	
Demand Situation	Sales and Production	Price and Cost Per Unit	Income and Costs	Man-Hours Per Unit	Total Man-Hours
1. Before change	500 units	$1.00	$ 500	1.0	500
2. Inelastic demand change	550 units (10%)	.80 (25%)	$ 440	0.5	275
3. Elasticity: unity change	625 units (25%)	.80 (25%)	$ 500	0.5	313
4. Elastic demand change	1,500 units (200%)	.80 (25%)	$1,200	0.5	750

It is assumed that there is a savings of 50 percent in the amount of labor used in producing each unit of output. The key to understanding the effect of this change on employment lies in the changes in *product demand* (watch this closely). Line 1 shows the situation before the technological change: 500 units were produced and sold at a price of $1 per unit. A competitive situation is assumed; hence, the price includes normal returns to other factors, that is, a normal profit. In this situation it takes 1 man-hour to produce each unit of product, and there are 500 total man-hours of employment. Assume now that: (1) a laborsaving improvement cuts the man-hours needed for a unit of product to 50 percent of the previous time, or one-half hour (0.5), as shown in the next-to-last column; (2) there is a reduction in price of the product from $1 each to 80¢ each. (The price does not drop by 50 percent even though labor requirements and labor costs drop by this amount; for other costs involved do not drop, and some costs, such as capital costs, may increase.) Effects of three different cases of product demand are given on Lines 2, 3, and 4 of Table 3-1.

The employment effects can be judged by references to the elasticity of the demand curve for the product made by the firm. *Elasticity* is defined as the proportion between the relative change in price and the relative change in quantity taken.[9]

With inelastic demand, the percentage increase in quantity taken is less than the percentage drop in price. This is illustrated on Line 2 of Table 3-1. The price dropped from $1 to 80¢, a drop of 20¢. This drop could be considered a 20 percent decline in price if $1 were used as the base. It is generally considered preferable, however, to compute elasticities using the smaller of the values involved in a price change as the base (and similarly the lesser quantity in the case of quantity changes).[10] The two values involved in the price change in the present situation are $1 and 80¢; since 80¢ is the smaller value, it will be used as the base. Thus, the proportionate change in price is 20¢ divided by

---

[9]Note that the reduction in price is assumed to be on the *same* demand curve; the price reduction should be regarded as sliding downward and to the right on the existing demand curve. The price cut should not be regarded as part of a *new* demand curve and schedule of prices and quantities. It should be noted that in analyzing effects of elasticity of demand, consumer preferences and income are regarded as fixed or unchanging. In real life situations they do change, however, and any adequate examination of the effects of technological change should take account of such variations.

[10]See Kenneth E. Boulding, *Economic Analysis* (rev. ed., New York: Harper and Brothers, 1948), p. 132. Other methods of computing elasticity could be employed, but the particular method or formula used is not basic to the present example. The student would be able to observe the same basic tendencies regardless of which of several basic elasticity formulas was used.

80¢, or 25 percent. The quantity taken by consumers increased from 500 units to 550 units, or 10 percent (the percentage increase is obtained by dividing 50 units by the base of 500 units since 500 is smaller than 550). These percentage changes are shown in parentheses in Columns 2 and 3 of Table 3-1.

Elasticity is said to be unity (or one) when the percentage change in price and the percentage change in quantity taken are equal. This is illustrated on Line 3 of Table 3-1. Price declines 25 percent from $1 (before the change) to 80¢ (20¢ divided by 80¢). The quantity taken rises by 25 percent from 500 to 625 units.

Elastic demand is defined as a situation where the percentage increase in quantity taken is greater than the percentage decrease in price. Price dropped from $1 to 80¢, a 25 percent decline. Quantity increased from 500 units (before the change) to 1,500 units, an increase of 1,000 units or 200 percent.

Next, consideration is given to the employment effects following the technological change in each of the three situations in the hypothetical case. Where demand for the product is inelastic (Line 2), 550 units are sold. Since labor requirements are reduced by 50 percent (due to the technological change) and it takes only 0.5 man-hours to produce one unit of product, it will require only 275 man-hours of labor to make the 550 units ($550 \times .5 = 275$). Total man-hours needed by the firm therefore declined from 500 before the change to 275 after the change.

Where elasticity of demand for product is unity (Line 3), man-hours of employment dropped from 500 before the change to 313 after the change. With product elasticity greater than unity (Line 4), output rose to 1,500 units and employment increased to 750 man-hours.

All of the above refers to employment effects within the firm where the technological change was made. There may be additional employment effects in other firms. Originally consumers spent $500 on the product (Column 4). In the inelastic demand situation (Line 2) they would spend only $440 for the product and would have $60 left over. If they save and do not invest this amount, there is no additional employment effect. If they spend it elsewhere, however, demand curves for other products should be affected (move up and to the right); and if those firms expand output to meet the increased demand, employment should expand in those firms. Whether it will expand sufficiently to absorb all of the displaced manpower depends upon elasticity of demand, proportion of labor costs to total costs in those firms, and other factors.

Change in elasticity of demand for product. In the hypothetical case if the product demand increased by only 45 percent (instead of 200 percent as in the third case shown on Line 4 of Table 3-1) with the same price cut of 25 percent, only 725 units would be sold with employment at 363 man-hours. If the product demand increased by 100 percent (with price cut still 25 percent), 1,000 units would be produced and total man-hours would be 500 as in the original example before the technological change.

In the example of elastic demand (Line 4), while employment increased in the original firm, employment may decrease in other firms. At the old price of $1, consumers spent $500 on this product (Column 4); presumably they would spend $1,200 at a price of 80¢, an increase of $700. Unless they spend the added $700 from money saved and hoarded or unless this $700 is financed by an expansion of money or credit, presumably they will reduce their demands for other products by $700. Thus, employment may be expected to fall in other firms (whether it will decline by the same number of man-hours depends upon elasticity of demand in other firms, their proportions of labor costs to total costs, etc.). If the product demand curve is more elastic in the present firm where the added $700 is spent and labor costs are a higher proportion of total costs than in other firms, then the reduction in employment elsewhere may be less than the added employment in the firm where the technological change took place.

Table 3-2
EFFECTS OF LABORSAVING CHANGES — 30 PERCENT SAVING

Product Demand				Employment in Firm	
Demand Situation	Sales and Production	Price and Cost Per Unit	Income and Costs	Man-Hours Per Unit	Total Man-Hours
1. Before change	500 units	$1.00	$ 500	1.0	500
2. Inelastic	550 units	.80	$ 440	.7	385
3. Elasticity: unity	625 units	.80	$ 500	.7	438
4. Elastic	1,500 units	.80	$1,200	.7	1,050

Change in labor efficiency. In the hypothetical case shown in Table 3-1, it was assumed that the labor savings per unit of output were 50 percent. Somewhat different employment effects (in the firm) would result if a different percentage of increase in labor efficiency were assumed. This is illustrated in Table 3-2.

The first four columns of Table 3-2 are the same as in Table 3-1. Since Table 3-2 assumes a 30 percent laborsaving improvement, this changes the man-hours per unit of output in Column 5 to .7 instead of .5 as in Table 3-1. Total man-hours (Column 6) then change as shown. Line 2 of Table 3-2 shows 385 total man-hours (550 units times .7 man-hours). Total man-hours on Lines 3 and 4 are computed in the same manner. Note especially that the elasticities of demand for product have not been altered. In Table 3-2, however, total man-hours are increased in all cases over those shown in Table 3-1 (Lines 2, 3, and 4). This stems from the fact that a smaller increase in labor efficiency due to the technological change is assumed (only 30 percent labor saving per unit).

The two examples (Tables 3-1 and 3-2) above may be summarized as follows. Whether or not a laborsaving technological change accompanied by a price cut will displace labor within a firm depends upon several factors. Two of these factors have been illustrated: (1) elasticity of demand for the product and (2) extent of labor saving brought about by the change. Without specific knowledge of changes in these factors (and others beyond the scope of our present elementary analysis), it is impossible to state conclusions about the effects of labor-saving technological changes upon employment levels. It should be apparent from the examples given that such generalizations as "employment will remain the same if elasticity of demand for the product is unity" may be inaccurate. Prediction of employment effects must be based upon precise knowledge of elasticity of demand for product and/or the percentage of labor saved by the technological change. In Table 3-1 (50 percent labor saving), 313 man-hours were employed where demand had elasticity of unity, a decline of 187 hours from the situation before the technological change. In Table 3-2 (30 percent labor saving), 438 man-hours were used in the elasticity of unity example, a decrease of 62 man-hours over the original situation before the technological change.[11]

---

[11] This occurred when the elasticity of demand for the product was held constant. Different man-hour totals would have been obtained had product elasticity also varied.

Effects of technological change when prices are not reduced.   The example in Table 3-1 assumed that a portion or all of the savings from the technological change were passed on to customers in the form of reduced price for the product. Suppose that prices are not reduced and that the entire saving goes into added profits. This would not necessarily reduce employment levels if the firm would spend all of the money or if the government would confiscate the added profits and use them to provide more public services, thereby increasing employment. Added profits could be used for added investment in plant and equipment which might result in added production capacity. Hence, it might be assumed that employment would rise since labor is needed to build the new capital equipment and to man the new equipment. Unfortunately, this may only be a short-run effect since extra plant and equipment requires added consumption (or customers) to keep it busy. Little if any sustained effect upon consumption would be expected where the entire savings goes into higher profits and more investment if this does not materially increase consumer demands and spending for goods and services. If, on the other hand, the added profits are spent regularly by employers on additional goods and services and they do not save any more than before, the effects would be to add to employment (the effects would be about the same as when there are price cuts on the product as the result of laborsaving improvements). Employment in the firm would tend to fall, but in the elastic case employment would increase somewhat in other firms.

Labor mobility.   The importance of labor and other resource mobility in adjusting to technological change can hardly be overstressed. Without mobility of jobs, skills, etc., effects upon employment could be undesirable. (See Chapter 6.)

Percentage of labor costs to total costs.   It is sometimes said that when the proportion of labor costs to total costs is small, labor displacement effects are slight and are less than when the proportion of labor costs is high. In some cases this is an obvious truism. In a plant using 500 man-hours per month, a laborsaving improvement of 10 percent cuts man-hours by 50; whereas, a similar improvement in a plant using 500,000 man-hours reduces man-hours by 50,000. In absolute terms the effect is less on the plant with a smaller number of man-hours used, but in relative or percentage terms the initial employment effect is the same regardless of the labor cost proportion.

However, in a firm with a small proportion of labor costs, the firm may be less inclined to lay off help since not much would be saved in this way. In addition, it may be inconvenient to lay off employees where crew requirements are relatively fixed; that is, one cannot lay off one eighth of a man on this machine and one seventeenth on another machine. When firms do not lay off employees as a result of laborsaving improvement and if output remains the same, it is apparent that labor costs are increased. Total costs may decline if the new method is more efficient, but they will not decline as much as they would if the surplus labor were not carried. In a long-run, competitive situation it would not be possible to carry extra help in this manner. In a monopolistic situation such help can be carried at the expense of monopolistic profits.

The effects of (1) proportion of labor saved and (2) elasticity of demand for product are much more important determinants of employment effects than percentage of labor costs to total costs. It should be obvious that a monopolistic firm could carry extra help (that would otherwise be displaced by the laborsaving device) out of monopoly profits in the case of a relatively large saving in labor per unit of output or in the case of an inelastic demand for the product. The absolute costs may appear less formidable to the firm, and they may be more likely to absorb the small added labor costs out of monopoly profits. The likelihood of this happening does not appear to be great, however, since little purpose would appear to be served by introducing a laborsaving device and then refusing to take advantage of the reduction in labor costs. It is more likely that the new device would have to cut other costs over and above labor costs if a firm were to act in this manner; for example, the device might be both labor saving and capital saving.

The capacity of firms with a low proportion of labor costs to absorb displaced employees from other firms undergoing technological change is distinctly limited. In many cases firms with a low proportion of labor cost act as if their demand for labor is highly inelastic.

MEASUREMENT OF PRODUCTIVITY

Concepts with respect to productivity do not supply complete answers to such basic questions as: How can we produce more? How can we produce goods and services that will better satisfy our needs?

Who should get the proceeds from increased productivity? These are complex questions, and their answers require complex solutions. It should be apparent at this stage of the discussion, though, that productivity is a very important criterion in decision making. Thus, we need to know how productivity is measured and how well we measure productivity.

Productivity measures are not readily available for all sectors of the economy. They are very crude, and they abound in approximations and "guesstimates." They represent the joint contribution of many factors of production, and it is almost impossible to attribute or allocate productivity gains to one factor of production, such as capital or labor.

Production and Productivity

Production is a quantitative measurement; *productivity* is a qualitative measurement. Production is a gross measure of output (e.g., the number of automobiles produced in a certain time period). Productivity measures output per unit of input (e.g., the number of bricks layed per man-hour worked). Sometimes great confusion and conflict stem from confusing these two related but different concepts.

A simple hypothetical example will illustrate the difference between production and productivity. Suppose two workers produce 40 boxes per day. Now suppose a third worker is added and production increases to 60 boxes per day. There is no question that production has been increased, for we can count the boxes they made; but what of productivity, i.e., output related to input? Productivity remained unchanged — two workers produced 20 boxes per worker per day; three workers also produced 20 boxes per worker per day. If, however, through improved production techniques, or any other means, production of these three men is increased to 90 boxes a day, or 30 per man per day, then productivity is increased at the same time. It should be noted, however, that productivity can increase while total production falls, or production can increase while productivity declines.

Productivity is usually defined as "output per man-hour, quality considered." Assume that the boxes the hypothetical workers made would last for two weeks. Now assume that better boxes can be made so that they last for six weeks. Assume further that each man still makes 20 boxes per day (of the new improved quality). Has productivity increased? The answer is "yes," by conventional definition.

As shown below, this qualitative improvement concept in productivity measurement is fairly easy to deal with conceptually, but it is difficult to deal with operationally.

There are two basic ways to get more output: (1) by using more input and (2) by obtaining more output per unit of input, i.e., using input resources more efficiently. Obviously, both methods can operate simultaneously. If three men can produce 90 boxes a day and 150 boxes a day are needed, by hiring two more men (and using more materials, etc.) output can be expanded. However, because resources are scarce, there are limits as to how much expansion can be accomplished in this manner. In a market economy increased efficiency in the use of resources is a prime goal.

Gross National Product

It is important to a society or nation to know how much it produces. It is also important to measure changes to see if they are in the desired direction and amount. *Gross output* is an important determinant of a nation's standard of living and welfare. Knowing gross output, it is simple to obtain another vital measure, *per capita output*, or the amount of production per person in the economy. Unless total output grows faster than population, per capita output can decline, as it did in India in the early 1960's.

Generally, the measurement, *Gross National Product (GNP)*, is used as our overall quantity yardstick of output. GNP is the current market value of all the goods and services produced in a given period of time, e.g., a year. It includes activities of government as well as private business. Note that GNP is not stated in physical units (so many sheep plus so many hi-fi sets, etc.). This is too cumbersome to combine and total. Instead, it is customary to use the money value of all these goods and services (in 1963, for example, our GNP was $585 billion). It is customary also to distinguish four major classes of components.[12] In 1963 these were:

1. Personal consumption	$373.2 billion
2. Private domestic investment	82.3 billion
3. Net exports of goods and services	4.4 billion
4. Government consumption	125.1 billion
Total	$585.0 billion

---

[12]There are two methods of computing GNP: (1) the expenditures method, of which this is an example, (2) the charges against GNP, including income, depreciation, and

Our GNP increased from $518 to $585 billions from 1961 to 1963. Government purchases of goods and services increased from $8 billion in 1929 to $125 billion in 1963. Such indicators or yardsticks are obviously useful in appraising a nation's economy. Thus, for example, our GNP decreased from $365 billion in 1953 to $363 billion in 1954, not a very healthy record of performance, although small changes in GNP may reflect deficiencies in data and methodology.

The GNP reflects changes in price levels; refined GNP series are available that use constant dollars (i.e., take account of price variations).[13] Also, more detailed breakdowns are available (e.g., by type of product, type of income, and others). Much of the discussion and controversy concerning growth rates in an economy (see Chapter 25) is concerned with GNP. Obviously, if we were to put our unemployed to work, we could increase our quantity of output, or GNP; but this would not necessarily increase our productivity.

It is notable that, despite recent growth in GNP, employment has failed to expand or grow at a rate equal to the growth of GNP. This gap in rates is largely due to increasing productivity. It raises the question of job opportunities very sharply, for as stated in the previous chapter, the labor force is entering a period of unusual growth. The disparity between growth in GNP and in employment can be observed in Figure 3-1.

Sources for Productivity Measures and Their Limitations

Ideally, our national productivity series would be obtained by asking all plants, stores, enterprises, governments, etc. that produce goods and services to send their figures to Washington to be summated.[14] In practice it is not that simple. In real life firms do not keep records in the way economics textbooks assume that they do.

taxes. Both methods give the same total. The second method is discussed in Chapter 18 in connection with distributive shares and income payments. For a brief basic discussion of these methods see J. Harvey Dodd and Thomas J. Hailstones, *Economics: Principles and Applications* (Cincinnati: South-Western Publishing Co., 1961), pp. 505–30.

[13]See any recent *Economic Report of the President* and *Annual Report of the Council of Economic Advisers.*

[14]For details of changes in productivity see John W. Kendrick, *Productivity Trends in the United States* (New York: Princeton University Press for the National Bureau of Economic Research, 1961). In 1962 output indexes were shifted to a new standard reference year, 1957–59 = 100. Also, data for Hawaii and Alaska were included for the first time. See "Indexes of Output Per Man-Hour for Selected Industries, 1939 and 1947–61," *Annual Industry Series* (Washington, D.C.: Bureau of Labor Statistics, October, 1962); Sylvia B. Gottlieb, "Output per Man-Hour in the Private Economy, 1947–63," *Monthly Labor Review,* Vol. 87, No. 4 (April, 1964), pp. 429–30.

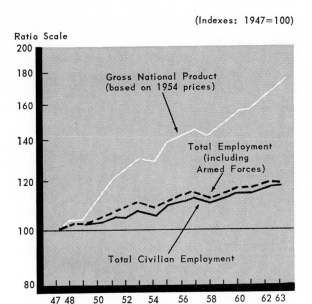

(Indexes: 1947=100)

Figure 3-1

GROSS NATIONAL PRODUCT AND EMPLOYMENT — 1947–1963

Source: *Manpower Report of the President* (Washington 25, D.C.: United States Government Printing Office, March, 1963), p. 77; *Manpower Report of the President*, 1964, pp. 195 and 262.

Productivity measures are seldom employed at the company, division, plant, and department levels in American industries. Instead, business firms continue to rely upon such historic criteria as production, profitability, or unit cost. Management's limited use of productivity measurement as a tool may result from general lack of concern with productivity measures or from the technical difficulties involved.[15]

According to John Kendrick and Daniel Creamer, if one can assume that firms make proper adjustments to existing market forces, the most important ingredient for their future success is the pace of their technological progress as reflected in real costs. *Real costs* involve the relationships of the physical volume of inputs to outputs, adjusted for price.

---

[15]John W. Kendrick and Daniel Creamer, "Measuring Company Productivity," New York National Industrial Conference Board *Studies in Business Economics No. 74*, 1961, p. 3.

In the long run firms typically buy and sell in competitive markets at similar prices. Hence, their internal efficiency, or productivity, is their basic reason for success or failure. In the short run an inefficient firm may make profits because of unfilled consumer demand or market shelters (e.g., tariffs). In the long run such special circumstances may change. Knowledge of internal efficiency is, therefore, an essential guide to company health and growth. Such knowledge is also an important factor in internal control and budgeting. Knowledge of productivity is essential in monopolistic as well as competitive situations.

Basically productivity is a physical phenomenon. It is essential to separate price and quality components of value, and it is important to separate classes of inputs (e.g., labor in man-hours, capital per man-hour, etc.). Care must be taken, for example, not to impute productivity increases when the reason for added output is due to increased plant utilization. In addition, changes in price levels for either inputs or outputs should not obscure the basic nature, meaning, and measurement of productivity changes.[16] Generally, constant dollars are used as the common denominator of measurement.

One of the great difficulties of productivity measurement is that of making adequate allowances for "quality" changes (e.g., changes in comfort, safety, or style). New products, or products changed in form and design, may give the consumer added utility. Thus, for example, how does one equate the physical output of a transistor FM radio with the older, crystal head phone sets of a previous generation? Also, what about innovations such as color TV? With what previous products should these be compared to measure efficiency in uses of our resources?

Labor inputs also differ through time. Can constant man-hours adequately reflect differences in education and health from one generation to the next? In addition, how about relative contributions of direct and indirect labor — how is the addition of a personnel manager in a staff position reflected in labor output? Obviously, refined measures of labor and other inputs should be used in productivity measurement.

Unfortunately, as noted above, few firms have such detailed data readily available. This means that government data reflects the "averaging" and "estimating" of the data firms are able, or willing,

---

[16]*Ibid.*, pp. 6–14.

to supply. This is true of both output and input data. Thus, for example, few firms readily separate and identify product outputs in physical terms. Usually these specifics are obscured in aggregates called "value of production," "value added by manufacturing," and similar terms. For many service and government establishments, estimates of productivity are barely "guesstimates" at best. Further, problems arise in combining productivity estimates from different economic sectors (e.g., manufacturing, trade, and agriculture). As a result, there are nothing but estimates of productivity for the United States economy as a whole.

The basic limitations in productivity measurements stem from the fact that they are generally unavailable at the source (e.g., in the individual firm, as discussed above). It should be obvious that even a government agency cannot, through statistical manipulation, turn such inadequate source materials into precise, meaningful measurements. At best productivity measures reflect general tendencies within a range of possible values. This does not mean that they are not useful, but it does mean that they should be used properly (i.e., paying attention to their concepts and methodology). Using current productivity measures to "umpteen" decimal places is silly at best.

Solomon Fabricant illustrates many of these points.[17] In a research study by the National Bureau of Economic Research, the question was asked, "What has been the average rate of growth in the Nation's productivity for the period 1947–57?" The answer depends upon which series of measurements is used; Fabricant cites answers ranging from 3.4 percent to 2.0 percent per annum. Without specification of its content the word "productivity" can mean more than one thing.

Conceptually, productivity is a ratio of output to input. A *productivity index* is the ratio of such a measure for one time period relative to another. In these comparisons definitions are of utmost importance. For example, does input mean simply the sum of all man-hours worked, or does it mean a weighted sum that counts hours of skilled work for more than hours of unskilled work?

---

[17]Solomon Fabricant, "Which Productivity? Perspective on a Current Question," *Monthly Labor Review*, Vol. 85, No. 6 (June, 1962), pp. 609–13. For a similar discussion see, "New Fuel for an Old Fire: How Fast is Productivity Gaining?" *Business Week* (January 16, 1960), pp. 22–23. See also Solomon Fabricant, *Basic Productivity Change* (New York: National Bureau of Economic Research, *Occasional Paper No. 63*, 1959), pp. 29–37.

The productivity index must be appropriate for the purpose in mind. In the analysis of changed output, for example, change in total quantity of inputs used as well as changes in productivity must be considered. In wage analysis, negotiation, or determination, the appropriate concept is not output per unit of total input. Instead, it is output per man-hour, or better yet, output per weighted man-hour.

The Bureau of Labor Statistics publishes two annual output-per-man-hour indexes:

1. *Physical output* per man-hour. This relates production in physical units to man-hours of production workers.
2. *Net output* per man-hour. This deals with the relationship between value added (at constant prices) and all persons engaged in production (proprietors, unpaid family workers, and employees).

The BLS is very careful to point out the limitations of these data:

1. They do not measure the specific contribution of labor, capital, or any other factor of production. These changes may and do reflect the joint impact of:
   a. Technological improvements.
   b. Rate of operation.
   c. Changes in integrated processes.
   d. Skill and effort of the work force.
   e. Efficiency of management.
   f. Status of labor relations.
2. They do not represent a true cross section of the American economy's performance:
   a. The indexes for separate industries should not be combined to provide an aggregate.
   b. Whole areas are left out (e.g., the government sector).

It should be noted that the output concept used is comparable to that of GNP (i.e., gross value of final goods and services produced excluding intermediate products). Two separate series are available using two different labor inputs:

1. Payroll hours — from establishment data (these are hours paid for, not worked).
2. Hours worked — from sample surveys of household data.

Neither the manpower nor the output components reflect changes in the qualitative aspects of labor (and other) inputs, and they do not reflect the qualitative aspects of output.[18]

---

[18]See Jerome A. Mark, "Industry Indexes of Output per Man-Hour," *Monthly Labor Review*, Vol. 85, No. 11 (November, 1962), pp. 1269–73.

Two additional difficulties in connection with using productivity indexes should be observed. First, choice of a base year for the index can have an effect upon the trend. Second, available price indexes (used to provide constant dollar terms) do not cover all goods and services and have many other limitations, as is indicated in Chapter 19.

Productivity Attainments

In the United States from 1909 to 1963, the average annual gain in output per man-hour was 2.4 percent. After World War II (from 1947–1963), the average gain was 3 percent. From 1960 to 1963 the average gain was 3.6 percent.

Total private output increased even faster than productivity from 1947–1963, but employment expanded much less rapidly. This is shown in Figure 3-1, on page 77, and in more detail in Figure 3-2 on page 82.

Figure 3-2 shows output by major sectors in the private economy. Note that agriculture has the sharpest annual gain in productivity (about 6 percent), and that nonagricultural industry is up only 2.4 percent per year.

Table 3-3 classifies major industries in terms of their average annual increase in output per man-hour from 1947 to 1962. The top portion of the table shows annual average increases over the 15-year period; the bottom portion shows increases for the period 1957 to 1962. In the latter period agriculture, mining, transportation, and communications had increased over 3.5 percent. Construction, trade, services, and finance-insurance-real estate had annual increases under 2.5 percent. As shown in Chapter 2, trade, finance, and services are the sector in the private economy with the most rapid employment growth. In short, we are expanding private employment opportunities in industries with lower than average annual productivity increases.

Figure 3-3 shows changes in productivity and employment for selected industries. It should be emphasized that these employment figures are for production workers only. Substantial increases in employment of nonproduction workers are not reflected in this chart.

Some industries have had substantial gains in man-hour output (e.g., synthetic fibers, cigars, and petroleum refining). Steel and glass containers are examples of less than average productivity gains. Notice that for some industries more than one output series is used.

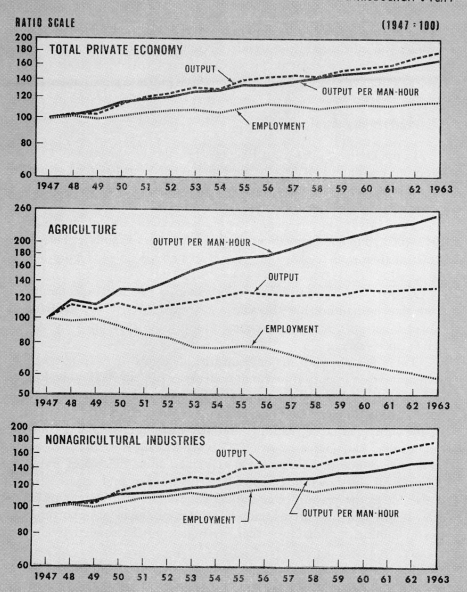

Figure 3-2
INDEXES OF OUTPUT, EMPLOYMENT, AND OUTPUT PER MAN–HOUR
FOR THE TOTAL PRIVATE ECONOMY — 1947–1963[1]

[1]1963 data preliminary.
Source: *Manpower Report of the President* (Washington 25, D.C.: United States
Government Printing Office, March, 1964), p. 48.

Table 3-3

APPROXIMATE PERCENT CHANGE IN OUTPUT PER MAN-HOUR, BY INDUSTRY — 1947 TO 1962[1]

Industry	Average Annual Increase		
	Under 2.5 percent	2.5 to 3.5 percent	Over 3.5 percent
	1947 to 1962		
Agriculture............................			x
Mining...............................			x
Manufacturing.........................		x	
Construction..........................	x		
Trade................................	x		
Finance, insurance, and real estate..........	x		
Transportation........................		x	
Communication and public utilities..........			x
Services..............................	x		
	1957 to 1962		
Agriculture............................			x
Mining...............................			x
Manufacturing.........................		x	
Construction..........................	x		
Trade................................	x		
Finance, insurance, and real estate..........	x		
Transportation........................			x
Communication and public utilities..........			x
Services..............................	x		

[1]These estimates of output per man-hour are based in part on estimates of output (GNP) published by the U. S. Department of Commerce in *Survey of Current Business,* September 1963. Exact averages are not shown because the output figures will be bench-marked next year to the 1958 input-output table and are, therefore, still preliminary. 1963 data are not yet available for these industry groups.

Source: *Manpower Report of the President* (Washington 25, D.C.: United States Government Printing Office. March, 1964), p. 49.

For example, railroad transportation is fifth from the top in terms of car miles and eighth from the top in terms of revenue traffic. In only three industries did production workers increase in numbers employed. The chart does not show gain or loss in total output for each industry; coal mining and railroad transportation both showed sizable gains in productivity despite sizable declines in output.

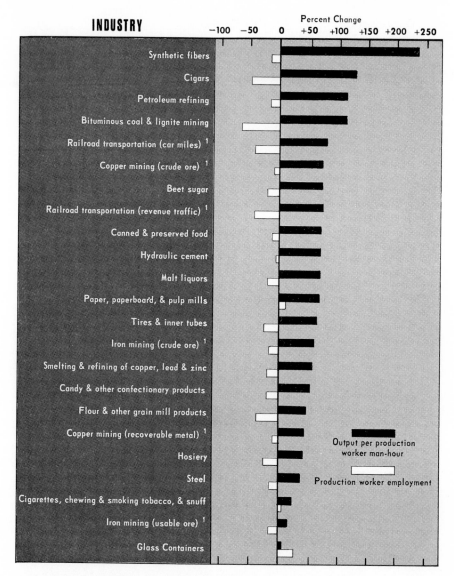

¹Terms in parentheses indicate the measure of output used in the index.

Figure 3-3
OUTPUT PER MAN-HOUR AND EMPLOYMENT OF PRODUCTION
WORKERS FOR SELECTED INDUSTRIES — 1947–1960

Source: *Manpower Report of the President* (Washington 25, D.C.: United States Government Printing Office, March, 1963), p. 71.

Output and Productivity Growth

Given that two of our major goals are to increase output and to increase productivity, what makes them increase? There is no simple answer to this question; instead, growth represents a complex of factors in different combinations in different industries. It has already been noted (p. 80) that the BLS productivity data do not directly measure such things as technological improvements, rate of operations, changes in integrated processes, changing levels of skills and effort in the work force, efficiency of management, and the status of labor relations. Instead, these get measured indirectly. In general, growth comes from more efficient use of existing resources, increases in resources, more capital, and improved methods. Definitive data are not available to measure the impact of all of these, but some evidence is available concerning better utilization and improved quality of our manpower resources, the role of increased investment per worker, effects of research and development, and percent of plant capacity being utilized.

Improved utilization of manpower. The massive shift of manpower resources out of agriculture into more productive industries and the increase in educational attainments of the labor force have already been described in Chapter 2.

Increased investment per worker. There has been a sharp increase in average investment per job (i.e., plant, tools, and equipment for each worker). On the average investment per job was: $14,000 in 1951, $17,000 in 1956, and $24,000 in 1961.[19] There are, of course, wide variations in investment per worker from industry to industry. In the petroleum industry, for example, the average investment was $62,000 in 1961 as compared with $37,000 in 1951.

It is apparent that to create 1,000,000 new jobs investment of approximately $24 billion in plant and equipment will be needed. Currently there is much debate over how and who shall make such investment, as will be noted in Chapter 25.

It is generally assumed that United States growth and productivity rates are roughly one half of those in the Soviet Union. Francis

---

[19]Malcolm S. Forbes, "Jobs Cost Money," *Forbes*, Vol. 90, No. 8 (October 15, 1962), p. 11.

Bello argues that since productivity is the responsibility of the government in Russia, but is not in the United States, perhaps we need to have some government agency officially responsible for maintaining desired rates of productivity.[20] It is instructive to compare changes in output and investment as Bello has done in Table 3-4.

Table 3-4
CHANGES IN INVESTMENT PER WORKER IN PLANT AND EQUIPMENT AND CHANGES IN OUTPUT PER WORKER — 1929–1960

Per Worker	Percent Change Per Year			
	1929–1947	1947–1954	1954–1960	1947–1960
Investment per worker	0.0%	3.5%	1.9%	2.7%
Output per worker	1.5%	3.3%	2.1%	2.8%

Source: Francis Bello, "The Technology Behind Productivity," *Monthly Labor Review*, Vol. 85, No 8 (August 1962), p. 866.

Although *investment per worker* (the value of business capital stock) did not increase from 1929–1947, output increased 1.5 percent per year. Obviously, more plant and equipment per worker per se were not the reason. Methods improvement, better personnel programs, improved quality of the labor force, and better quality of plant and equipment were probably largely responsible for the increase. During the 1947–1954 period output did not rise as fast as investment per worker, but output exceeded investment in the 1954–1960 period. Presumably, the 1954–1960 capital outlays were more efficient.

Expenditures for new plant and equipment in the United States increased from $21 billion in 1947 to $39 billion in 1963. The stock of *capital equipment* (the portion of capital stock most closely related to output per worker) rose at an annual rate of 5.4 percent from 1947–57 but declined to 1.3 percent from 1957–1962. The annual increase in *plant* per worker averaged about 1 percent per year from 1947–1962. In recent years the bulk of investment in capital stock has gone for replacement and modernization of facilities (two thirds); only one third of the new investment has been allocated to expansion of facilities.[21]

Effect of research and development. The question of how much more and better tools add to increased productivity is, of course,

---

[20]Francis Bello, "The Technology Behind Productivity," *Monthly Labor Review*, Vol. 85, No. 8 (August, 1962), pp. 865–67.

[21]*Manpower Report of the President* (Washington 25, D.C.: United States Government Printing Office, March, 1964), p. 51.

"a tough nut to crack." The payoff for research and development
(R & D) is hard to determine because R & D may be used to gain
efficiency or to alter existing products to please consumers (e.g., to
make paper milk cartons instead of glass bottles). No one knows for
sure how much of the money spent for R & D is for efficiency and how
much for style changes.

In 1959, for example, the National Science Foundation reported
that private industry spent about $0.9 billion on R & D and the gov-
ernment about $0.6 billion, for a total of 1.5 billion in new technology
directly applicable to productivity. (This includes machinery, computers, new processes, measuring instruments, etc.) But note that the
private R & D investment is less than 0.2 percent of the GNP and less
than 10 percent of the $11 billion spent on advertising in the United
States. As Bello points out, it may be astonishing that American
business finds it profitable to spend $11 on advertising for every 90
cents spent on research to raise productivity.

This is not to say that advertising is unproductive, of course.
It does, however, raise real and difficult questions about the rational
proportions between the two expenditures, particularly when we live
in a world where other industrial countries place different and higher
values on increasing the rate of productivity increase. Those who have
a blind faith that research and development (R & D) activities
necessarily pay off in increased productivity should note, though, that
little or no relation can be demonstrated between R & D expenditures
and various measures of economic growth.[22] Since the 1920's in the
United States, R & D expenditures have increased sharply while
output per man-hour has maintained about the same rate of increase.
In the last decade R & D expenditures have been increased at record
rates while the rate of increase in output per man-hour has slumped.
The same conclusion is reached if we relate R & D increase to increases
in GNP.

While such evidence holds for the economy as a whole, it may be
true that individual companies have gained from R & D; and it is
certainly true that whole new industries have arisen through R & D.

Percent of plant capacity utilized. The percent of plant capacity
being utilized also can and does affect productivity measures. Fixed
costs have to be recouped against output. When a plant is running

---

[22]See Robert A. Solow, "Gearing Military R & D to Economic Growth," *Harvard
Business Review*, Vol. 40, No. 6 (November–December, 1962), pp. 50–51.

below capacity, costs per unit of output tend to be higher. When output increases again, costs tend to go down and, apparently, productivity goes up. This is due to volume of production and is called *volume productivity;* sometimes this is distinguished from changes in *real productivity* (i.e., where volume of operation is constant).

Labor Costs

Labor costs are similar to productivity measures. They represent wages and salaries (or total compensation including fringes) per unit of output produced. Employers are very much interested in labor costs, probably more so than in wage rates. Thus, if wages increase 10 percent and output 20 percent, labor costs decline. Employers are concerned about labor costs of their competitors, both here and abroad. There is, however, some misunderstanding that tends to equate hourly wage rates with labor costs. This type of misunderstanding on the part of employers, unions, employees, and the public comes to the fore in discussions of international trade and how "cheap foreign labor will take our business and jobs away from us."

PRODUCTION AND FOREIGN TRADE

In the last decade United States exports have exceeded imports by about $5 billion annually. At the same time, hourly wage rates in the United States are much higher than in any other country — 2 to 4 times higher than in Northern Europe and still higher in comparison with Japan and Italy. These two facts present an apparent paradox.

However, a brief analysis of some of the determinants of foreign trade can help clarify the situation.[23]

1. Some trade reflects geographic advantage. Malaya and Bolivia export tin. Iceland has to import coffee and cotton. In these types of trade, labor cost is not a major consideration.
2. Some trade reflects better engineering. We thought some British airplane engines exceeded ours in performance and quality, and we imported them. Again, labor cost was not the definitive yardstick.
3. Some trade flows occur without direct reference to producer's costs. Advertising, service, political arrangements, and preferential trade treaties provide examples.
4. Finally, a great volume of trade flows on the basis of cost as reflected in price.

[23]See William C. Shelton and John H. Chandler, "The Role of Labor Cost in Foreign Trade," *Monthly Labor Review,* Vol. 86, No. 5 (May, 1963), pp. 485–90.

With respect to Item 4 above it must be remembered that labor cost is only a part of total costs and that the latter is definitive in trade flows. Further, while hourly wage rates may seem to be important per se, they are not; for they tell only half of the story. The other half of the story is what labor produces an hour — output per hour of labor input, or productivity. If nation A pays $3.00 per hour for workers producing commodity X and each worker turns out six units in an hour, labor cost per unit (not per hour) is 50¢. If nation B pays $1.50 per hour to workers producing commodity X and each worker turns out two units per hour, then labor cost per unit in nation B is 75¢.

In general, each country can produce some goods at greater comparative advantage than can other countries. With respect to labor comparisons, it is the ratio of hourly wages to labor productivity which affects foreign trade flows. This ratio is called *unit labor costs*.[24]

NOT BY BREAD ALONE

Later in this volume we will encounter productivity again and again in discussions of wage policies and plans; wage theories; real wages and living standards, employment, unemployment and underemployment; inflation and price stability; leisure and the shorter work week; social and economic welfare policies and programs; labor force allocation and occupational distribution; unrest and conflict; and in many other places. In all of these areas labor productivity is a crucial criterion or yardstick. It should be emphasized again that it is not

---

[24]For a technical and applied discussion see William C. Shelton and John H. Chandler, "International Comparisons of Unit Labor Cost: Concepts and Methods," *Monthly Labor Review*, Vol. 86, No. 5 (May, 1963), pp. 538–47.

See also N. Arnold Tolles and Betti C. Goldwasser, *Labor Costs and International Trade* (Washington 6, D.C.: Committee for a National Trade Policy, 1205 Connecticut Ave., N. W., 1961). The principle of comparative advantage or comparative costs should be especially noted. It is economically sound for each nation to specialize in production of goods and services in which it has the maximum comparative advantage (in production) or has the minimum comparative disadvantage. In many cases, however, production decisions are based upon political policy rather than economic considerations. J. Harvey Dodd and Thomas J. Hailstones, *Economics: Principles and Applications* (4th ed.; Cincinnati: South-Western Publishing Co., Inc., 1961), pp. 741–44; Campbell R. McConnell, *Elementary Economics* (New York: McGraw-Hill Book Co., 1960), pp. 44–48, 665–66; G. L. Bach, *Economics* (3rd ed.; Englewood Cliffs, New Jersey: Prentice-Hall, 1960), pp. 686ff. For a series of studies on United States employment and foreign trade by the Bureau of Labor Statistics, United States Department of Labor, see: "Domestic Employment Attributable to U.S. Exports," January, 1962; "Employment in Relation to U.S. Imports," 1962; "The American Worker's Stake in Foreign Trade," 1962; and "The Relationship Between Imports and Employment," April, 1962; John H. Chandler and P. C. Jackman, "Unit Labor Costs in Eight Countries Since 1950," *Monthly Labor Review*, Vol. 87, No. 4 (April, 1964), pp. 377–84.

the only yardstick used, even though it is one of the principal economic criteria. Other economic forces such as supplies and demands (which are themselves related to productivity) are also important. Other so called noneconomic considerations are also important. Productivity is objective; often people are not.

It is well to keep in mind that maximum productivity is certainly not the only goal of individual workers, firms, or economies. At particular times and in certain circumstances, it may not be given top priority. In the convenient and indefinable "long run," it may have to take second or third place in goals.

Simon has suggested that a concept of *satisficing* may be more realistic than maximizing for defining the profit goals of the firm.[25] A somewhat similar relationship of personal aspiration to attainment may be realistic for many workers at all levels. For many rank and file employees, maximizing earnings may be secondary to maximizing the sum of job satisfactions. Maximizing productivity may, in this situation, fall fairly low in the hierarchy of goals. In the worker's view, its relationship to earnings (a secondary objective) may be involved and complex if not actually negative. He may see earnings as likely to be increased by reducing his production. Dubin has described the persistent and generally unrecognized significance of indifference to output.[26]

Nor do all employers favor productivity as a yardstick for wage determination. The Chamber of Commerce of the United States has argued strongly against productivity wage increases and urges reliance upon "market forces" instead.[27]

ANALYTICAL REVIEW QUESTIONS

1. How do economic concepts of work differ from sociological concepts of work?
2. How is economic utility related to psychological need satisfaction?
3. What is Maslow's hierarchy of needs? What is its significance?
4. What collective decisions concerning production must any society make?
5. What are the two basic means of increasing the output of goods and services?

---

[25]Herbert A. Simon, "Theories of Decision-Making in Economics and Behavioral Science," *American Economic Review*, Vol. 49, No. 3 (June, 1959), pp. 262ff.

[26]Robert Dubin, *Human Relations in Administration* (2nd ed.; Englewood Cliffs, New Jersey: Prentice-Hall, Inc., 1961), pp. 61–62.

[27]See *Productivity and Wage Settlements* (Washington 6, D.C.: Chamber of Commerce of the United States, 1961).

6. What are the basic determinants of productivity? Which three are the most important?
7. How are profits related to production?
8. How is specialization related to productivity?
9. Contrast determination of what will be produced in a market economy versus a state-controlled economy.
10. What are the two basic concepts underlying distribution of goods and services?
11. What kinds of decisions are made by a firm that utilizes productivity as a yardstick?
12. In what ways does a society use productivity in its decision making?
13. Why must a firm or society use productivity as an economic yardstick?
14. Why is it difficult to determine the productivity of any of the factors of production separately (e.g., labor, or capital)?
15. How is productivity related to price levels?
16. How is productivity defined? How is productivity different from production?
17. Why is it necessary to give capital some of the returns from increased productivity?
18. Why does it make a difference if new machinery is labor complementary or labor supplementary?
19. What is meant by fixed technical coefficients?
20. Do technological changes per se raise living standards and employment levels? Why or why not?
21. How is product demand related to the employment effects of increased productivity?
22. How is elasticity defined?
23. Define: (a) elastic demand, (b) inelastic demand, (c) unit elasticity.
24. In general, given a laborsaving technological change, would you expect employment effects to be greater in a firm with elastic or inelastic product demand? Why?
25. How does the extent of labor saving brought about by technological change affect employment?
26. When the proportion of labor costs to total costs is small, what are the likely employment effects of technological change? Why?
27. Can production increase without a change in productivity? How is this possible?
28. How does the definition of productivity take care of variation in quality of output?
29. Why is gross output an important concept? What do we call the measurement of gross output in the United States?
30. What are the basic components of GNP?
31. Which has been growing at a faster rate, GNP or employment?
32. How does percent of plant utilization affect productivity?
33. What is a productivity index?

34. Differentiate physical output per man-hour from net output per man-hour.
35. What are the major limitations of the BLS productivity series?
36. What two different labor input concepts are used in labor productivity measurement? How are these defined?
37. What sectors of our economy enjoy the greatest annual productivity gains?
38. What makes output and productivity grow?
39. What has happened to average investment per worker in the United States? Does increased investment per worker by itself cause output per worker to increase?
40. Are increased expenditures in research and development accompanied by similar increases in productivity? Why or why not?
41. How are labor costs computed? Is this the same concept as productivity? Why or why not?
42. How can a country with high labor costs compete with a country with lower labor costs?

INDUSTRIAL RELATIONS SYSTEMS

The term "industrial relations systems" may be used to connote two somewhat different sets of ideas. First, it may be used to describe relationships between and among persons at work — relations between those who manage and those who are managed, union members and their agents, white-collar workers and blue-collar workers, etc. These relations are institutionalized or systematized to permit and facilitate day-to-day working relationships. Such systems may be formal or informal, as in the case of compensation systems and grievance systems. They are part and parcel of the day-to-day operations of an organization or enterprise and may be called *operational industrial relations systems*.

The second usage of the term "industrial relations systems" is concerned with the ideas and the logic of employment relationships. The focus is on explanation and understanding, not description. The approach is that of abstraction and determination of relationships, i.e., conceptualization. Thus, this second approach may be said to be concerned with *conceptual industrial relations systems*. For purposes of study, it is desirable to emphasize and call attention to the differences between these two kinds of industrial relations systems — the operational (or real world) and the conceptual (abstract).

Conceptual systems serve the important function of helping to explain operational systems. Conceptual systems facilitate understanding of employment behavior and processes. They emphasize the "why" of employment relationships and thus aid in theorizing and generalizing. They help make sense and order out of a myriad of facts by specifying and calling attention to important variables and relationships.[1]

In this text both conceptual and operational systems are discussed. It is important that the student should grasp: (1) how conceptual systems can facilitate understanding of operational systems and (2) relationships between the two types of systems. It is the aim of the present chapter to clarify the nature of these two approaches and to amplify their meaning. Such explanation is provided at this point in the text to help the student have a better and easier understanding of the topics in the subsequent chapters. As will be noted later in this chapter, and throughout this book, there are many kinds of industrial relations systems — some general, and some partial, i.e., of narrower scope. Throughout most of the book a particular partial system, that of labor economics, will be stressed. At the present moment, however, a wider framework will be employed, and several examples of other approaches and systems will be given.

CONCEPTUAL SYSTEMS

A general model of the field of industrial relations would include the following major sets of variables:

1. Employment goals (public and private) — their nature, development, modification, and effectiveness.

2. Relationship of employment goals and processes to other economic, technical, social, and personal goals.

3. The social and technological setting or climate of industrial relations and its impact upon employment goals and processes, and vice versa.

4. The nature and character of human resources, individual and group.

5. Organizations of human (and other) resources to attain economic, social, and personal goals with optimal efficiency.

6. Plans, means, and techniques for maximizing usefulness of human resources (e.g., policies, programs, and practices).

7. Modifiers, restraints, and reinforcers of employment behaviors including both structures (e.g., unions) and processes (e.g., social interaction).

---

[1]Important in the sense that they provide explanation and hence knowledge and understanding.

If we measured all of the sets of variables suggested above, the result would be a massive collection of facts. Actually, we would be overwhelmed by our collection and would find it difficult to give meaning to the facts. Hence, we seek to sort out the most relevant and consequential and set aside those of lesser importance. This is the process of *abstraction* and *generalization*. The purpose of classification, abstraction, and analysis is explanation, or understanding. We are greatly aided in this endeavor by theorization.[2]

Theories. Theories are the crucial link between the conceptual or abstract world and the real life world. They are the bridge between logic and reality. Theories are of major importance in explanation and understanding. All theories try to explain something — a phenomenon or event or relationship between variables. A theory proceeds from specified assumptions or postulates, specified variables and their relationships, to hypothesized results, i.e., what we set out to explain. At the risk of oversimplification, a theory may be said to be "good" or satisfactory if it permits accurate predictions — if it does not it is "not good." A "good" theory possesses the following characteristics:

1. Addresses itself to some question, i.e., attempts to answer or explain something.
2. Includes a statement of assumptions (if) and the consequences derived from those assumptions (then).
3. Is based on logical reasoning; its conclusions are deduced logically from its premises.
4. Is tentative and provisional, admits the possibility of acceptance or rejection.
5. Is testable or verifiable through observation and measurement in the real world.
6. Permits the statement of clear-cut hypotheses between and among its variables.

---

[2]For general background see: A. C. Benjamin, "Some Theories of the Development of Science," *Philosophy of Science Journal*, University of Missouri, Vol. 20 (July, 1953), pp. 167–75; Herbert Feigl and May Brodbeck, *Readings in the Philosophy of Science* (New York: Appleton-Century-Crofts, Inc., 1953); Herbert Feigl and Wilfred Sellers, *Readings in Philosophical Analysis* (New York: Appleton-Century-Crofts, Inc., 1949); Carl G. Hempel, "The Theoreticians' Dilemma," in *Minnesota Studies in the Philosophy of Science*, Vol. II (Minneapolis: University of Minnesota Press, 1958); O. Hillis Kaiser, *An Essay on Method* (New Brunswick, N.J.: Rutgers University Press, 1952); Sherman Krupp, *Patterns in Organization Analysis: A Critical Examination* (Philadelphia: Chilton, 1961), especially Chapter 4, "The Boundaries of a Theory"; Arnold M. Rose, *Theory and Method in the Social Sciences* (Minneapolis: The University of Minnesota Press, 1958); Bertrand Russell, *Human Knowledge* (London: George Allen and Unwin, Ltd., 1948). For an excellent treatise on how to dissect theories, see William K. Estes, Kenneth MacCorquodale, *et. al.*, *Modern Learning Theory: A Critical Examination of Five Examples* (New York: Appleton-Century-Crofts, Inc., 1954). See also the references in Appendix A, pp. 785–86.

Hypotheses. A hypothesis is part of a theory but not a whole theory in itself. The theory predicates the variables and relationships specified in the hypothesis; the hypothesis is a tentative explanation of relationships between and among a more restricted number of variables. The proof of a hypothesis lies in data from the real world. In short, a hypothesis is a proposed link between theory and fact.

Models. A model is an expression of a tentative explanation. It is an abstract generalization of a set of variables and their specified relationships. A model, unlike a theory, does not need to be defined in such a way that it can be tested through observation and measurement or experimentation.

Many models are limited in what they seek to explain. They might seek to explain wage rates, wage levels, layoffs, productivity, job satisfaction, occupational status, labor force commitment, or collective bargaining outcomes. Indeed, this book is filled with models, although they are not always explicitly identified as such.

Systems. A conceptual system is a group of assumed relationships combined to form a whole and to operate in unison. It has, as principal features, order and balance. Since models are generally limited deliberately and since we know that all segments and areas of industrial relations are related, the search for understanding may combine models. This offers the possible advantage of a more generalized explanation. When only a few models are combined, they may form a *partial system.* Thus, for example, a partial system in industrial relations might seek to explain occupational status and authority systems and careers. No partial model deals with all of the variables and outcomes of employment behavior and industrial relations, even though each partial system is complex and thorough in itself. If all significant

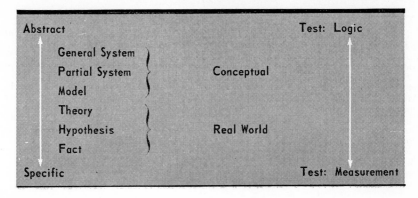

major variables in industrial relations were accounted for in one grand, overall combined model, we would have a *general industrial relations system*.

Thus, we have a *hierarchy of explanation* from the general to the specific. Systems are the most general, facts the most specific. (See illustration at the bottom of page 96.)

Variables and Relationships

Employment relationships are those that determine, or result from, employment behavior. In the real life world employment relationships are those relationships that exist among people who work. In conceptual thinking, however, it is customary to define relationships as the connection between and among variables.

A *variable* is something that changes or is capable of being changed. A variable may be conceptual and not capable of objective measurement; or it may be operational and hence measurable. It is useful to classify variables into *independent*, or those which are assumed to "cause" change, and *dependent*, those which are assumed to "result." Take some simple examples:

Independent	Dependent
Amount of rainfall	Height of corn
Amount of national income	Aggregate level of employment
Incentive wages	Productivity

In these simple hypotheses the arrow is used to denote the direction of the change. A useful hypothesis is one that not only says two variables are related but also shows the direction of the relationship. Take labor turnover as an example:

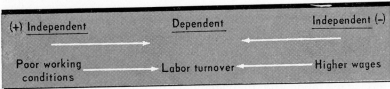

(+) Independent	Dependent	Independent (−)
Poor working conditions	Labor turnover	Higher wages

The diagram says that poor working conditions will cause turnover to increase (+) and higher wages will cause turnover to decrease (−). Note how the hypothesis specifies the predicted effect of the independent variable upon the dependent. In some theories prediction of order or process may be more appropriate than prediction of direction. The required explanation may specify a time sequence, or sequence of events that must follow in order. A simpler form of relationship between variables is called *association*; this does not imply cause and effect. Instead, association is concerned with consistency of the relationship. *Correlation* is an example of known consistency, without specification of a causal relationship as a necessary requirement. Such relationship is *functional* and is useful in prediction and control. In association relationships, dependent and independent variables often are not labelled as such.

Sometimes other variables come between independent and dependent variables — these other variables may be called *intervening variables*. For example, take the relationship:

Independent	Intervening	Dependent
Incentive wages ⟶	Labor union ⟶	Output

This says that, while higher wages generally raise output, if there is a labor union involved this may change the results from what would be expected if no labor union were present. Intervening variables are also known as *moderating variables*.

Goals and Hierarchies of Goals

Dependent variables may be goals which may be classified in several dimensions:
1. Long-run versus short-run.
2. Change versus stability or equilibrium.
3. Individual versus group.

There is, however, no common hierarchy of goals or objectives in industrial relations. Goals may have different priorities in an affluent, industrialized society as opposed to an emerging industrial society in one of the developing countries. Those playing different roles in our society (e.g., labor and management) may place different priorities on goals. This fact may, and does, lead to conflict not only in goals per se but in means as well.

To make a complete catalogue of the employment goals and objectives which may be regarded as dependent variables in industrial relations would be an imposing if not impossible task. To clarify the concept, however, several illustrations follow:[3]

SELECTED DEPENDENT VARIABLES OR GOALS

A. Society[4]
1. Adequate supply of labor skills — quantity and quality.
2. Adequate demand for labor — full employment and high purchasing power.
3. Well-functioning labor markets — to effectively match labor supplies and demands.
4. Highest possible productivity of the labor force.
5. Effective rules for working relationships, conflict avoidance and reduction.
6. Industrial peace.
7. Reduction and alleviation of economic insecurity.
8. Higher standards of living.
9. Effective meshing of industrial relations systems with economic, political, and social systems.
10. Sufficient deferred consumption to provide adequate capital and growth.

B. Associations of Firms
1. Commonality of wage rates, labor costs, and conditions of employment.
2. Mutual "protection" devices.
   a. Strike insurance.
   b. Labor legislation.
   c. Antipirating agreements.
3. More effective bargaining power.
4. Favorable socio-economic-political climate.
5. Commonality of industrial jurisprudence.

C. Associations of Unions
1. Higher wage levels.
2. Job security — control of technological progress and work rules.
3. Favorable socio-economic-political climate.
4. More job opportunities, reduced unemployment.
5. Social insurance.
6. Labor legislation.
7. Mutual protection, including strike benefits.
8. Greater bargaining power.
9. Shorter hours.

---

[3]The assistance of Roberta J. Nelson and David Selby of the University of Minnesota Industrial Relations Center in helping to provide examples of models and partial systems is gratefully acknowledged. Examples of goals of individuals have been provided in the first portion of Chapter 3.

[4]Chapter 1 of this book discusses social goals and objectives in the United States in more detail.

D. Business Organizations
1. Lower labor costs.
2. Greater productivity.
3. Skilled labor force.
4. Control over work assignments, speeds, and conditions of work — flexibility in job assignments.
5. Adequate wage level and structure.
6. Extra reward for extra output and effort — merit concept.
7. Reduction in turnover, absenteeism, tardiness, strikes, and lockouts.
8. Job satisfaction for employees.

E. Informal Work Groups
1. Mutual protection and assistance.
2. Mutual determination and provision of job satisfactions, outputs, and work speeds.
3. Mutual reward and status systems.
4. Informal communications system.
5. A united front against formal authority system.
6. Informal leadership and friendship structures.

If there is a most important single general goal for industrial relations in modern society, it probably is efficiency in the use of human resources. Here we are using efficiency as a common denominator for many types of efficiencies — in attainment of psychological and social goals as well as economic. Thus, there can be efficient ways of satisfying personal needs; attaining job satisfaction, status, and occupational hierarchies; rule making; and many others. Labor economics emphasizes the use of human resources in the production and distribution of goods and services in which the economically efficient use of human resources is a major criterion of decision-choice. This is essentially what was discussed in Chapter 3 on productivity.

Alternative Approaches to Industrial Relations

Few investigators seek to study the entire gamut of industrial relations because of the vast number of variables involved (with attendant complexity of relationships) and because their interests lead them to particular areas of study — they try to explain more limited sets of relationships with fewer variables.[5]

---

[5]For basic references that illustrate a variety of approaches, see: Chris Argyris, *Understanding Organizational Behavior* (Homewood, Ill.: Dorsey Press Inc., 1960); Peter M. Blau and Richard W. Scott, *Formal Organizations* (San Francisco: The Chandler Publishing Co., 1962); John Dunlop (ed.), *The Theory of Wage Determination* (London: MacMillan

A brief catalogue of systems. Industrial relations frameworks, theories, and systems tend to fall into a dichotomy: (1) those focusing upon internal organizational factors (e.g., unions, business firms, etc.) and (2) those focusing more broadly upon external or environmental factors, largely institutional. Gerald G. Somers describes some of the more common approaches to industrial relations systems as follows.[6]

The development of the labor movement approach (*Commons and Perlman and the Wisconsin School*). This approach raises questions as to how and why unions come into being, what programs and ideologies they have.

The causes of industrial peace and conflict approach. Here labor economists tend to emphasize market forces and power relationships while psychologists and sociologists stress needs and drives of individuals and the interactions of individuals and work groups.

The human relations approach. This approach emphasizes small group behavior and tends to ignore external environmental forces.

The web of rules approach. Here market forces, power relationships, and technology are related to interactions of workers, management, and government agencies. This approach is not strongly concerned with personality, human relations, motivation, and small group actions.

Co. Ltd., 1957); Walter Galenson and Seymour M. Lipset (eds.), *Labor and Trade Unionism* (New York: John Wiley and Sons, Inc., 1960); Robert Dubin, *The World of Work* (Englewood Cliffs, N.J.: Prentice-Hall Inc., 1958); Arthur M. Ross, *Trade Union Wage Policy* (Los Angeles: University of California Press, 1948); Morris S. Viteles, *Motivation and Morale in Industry* (New York: W. W. Norton Co., 1953); William Foote Whyte, *Men at Work* (Homewood, Ill.: Dorsey Press and Richard D. Irwin, 1961).

See also Reinhard Bendix, *Work and Authority in Industry* (New York: John Wiley and Sons, Inc., 1956); Frederick Hertzberg, Bernhard Mausner and B. B. Snydermann, *The Motivation to Work* (New York: John Wiley and Sons, Inc., 1957); Abraham Maslow, *Motivation and Personality* (New York: Harper and Brothers, 1954); Douglas McGregor, *The Human Side of Enterprise* (New York: McGraw-Hill Book Co., Inc., 1960); George B. Strother (ed.), *Social Science Approaches to Business Behavior* (Homewood, Ill.: Irwin-Dorsey Series, 1962); James G. March and Herbert A. Simon, *Organizations* (Pittsburgh: Graduate School of Industrial Administration, Carnegie Institute of Technology, 1958); R. V. Presthus, "Toward A Theory of Organizational Behavior," *Administrative Science Quarterly*, Vol. 3, No. 1 (June, 1958), pp. 48–72; Talcott Parsons, "Suggestions for a Sociological Approach to the Theory of Organizations," *Administrative Science Quarterly*, Vol. 1, Nos. 1 and 2 (June and September, 1956), pp. 63–85 and 225–39; Leonard Sayles, *Behavior of Industrial Work Groups* (New York: John Wiley and Sons, Inc., 1958); Ralph M. Stogdill, *Industrial Behavior and Group Achievement: A Theory* (New York: Oxford University Press, 1959) — good in use of input and output variables. See also references in footnote 2 on p. 58 in Chapter 3 of the present volume.

[6]Gerald G. Somers, "The Labor Market and Industrial Relations Research," in *Essays on Industrial Relations Research — Problems and Prospects* (Ann Arbor: The University of Michigan and Wayne State Institute of Labor and Industrial Relations, 1961), pp. 45–72. In the same volume see also William F. Whyte, "Needs and Opportunities for Industrial Relations Research," pp. 1–18; Robert L. Aronson, "Research and Writing in Industrial Relations — Are They Intellectually Respectable?", pp. 19–44; George Seltzer, "The Labor Relations Climate — Its Nature and Significance," pp. 73–102.

The exchange approach. Somers argues that a central unifying focus in industrial relations can be found in a fifth approach, one that he calls "the theory of exchange." He says "the heart of industrial relations is in the worker and his interactions with other workers and management at the work place."[7] All of the relevant factors in employment behavior on the job and all of the relevant influences that flow out of employment filter through the worker at his work place.

The division of labor and its counterpart, exchange, is essential to the interaction process. Somers refers to exchange not only in the economic sense but also in the sociological and psychological sense. Thus, for example, social conformists and deviates are determined by their conceptions of desirable exchange relationships. Group equilibrium relates costs and rewards in exchange; individual employment behavior results from balancing and weighing of costs and rewards.

Exchange can be the unifying interaction framework not only within the work-place but without as well. Thus, for example, market forces and bargaining power involve exchanges.

To Somers the exchange framework makes possible a unification of partial industrial relations systems into a general system. It can link the labor movement, peace-conflict, human relations, and web of rules (or economic environmentalists) into a unified general theory.[8]

The social processes approach. The industrial sociologist is concerned with work viewed as social processes.[9] Employment relationships are an important part of man's social life. Edward Gross defines work relationship as "one in which persons perform activities which are

---

[7]See Gerald G. Somers, *op. cit.*, p. 59.

[8]All interactions between parties to the employment process (individuals and groups) can be viewed as balancing costs and rewards (or gains). Both costs and rewards are probably composites but are the resultants of exchange. Perceived costs and gains and attempts to influence power and bargaining power are part of the interaction process. Thus, exchange provides a nexus between external environmental changes and internal plant behavior, since exchange involves social and psychological as well as economic values. Theoretically, an industrial relations equilibrium would be reached when all parties involved have optimally maximized their actual or potential exchanges, i.e., costs and rewards are in balance. It is doubtful if this equilibrium would ever occur in the real world, of course; but as a theoretical construct, an abstract system of this type may help one's understanding by providing a general, unified system of industrial relations.

[9]"Work" means different things to different people. To the physicist work is measured in foot-pounds or ergs. It is a definition of what happens when force moves through distance. Work is a generalized concept, including nonhuman energy as well as human. To the biologist work is a human activity involving use of muscles and nerves, chemical changes, and cell activities. The psychologist looks upon work as a task or series of tasks to be done. The economist is more interested in the purposes and effects of work rather than the physical processes involved; he is concerned with efficiency of labor inputs and outputs in cost terms. See Edward Gross, *Work and Society* (New York: The Thomas Y. Crowell Company, 1958), pp. 6–11.

designed to achieve objectives usually assigned by others. The activities that they perform are called 'work'." Gross defines the framework of working relationships as consisting of:

1. The institutional system.
2. The status and authority system.
3. Careers.

The *institutional system* includes the work complex (how work is related to other institutions, e.g., family and community), the work structure (division of labor and specialization), and the economic structure.

Occupations have important and complex interrelationships. *Status* refers to a social location within a system of human relationships and includes economic factors, power, and prestige. Occupation is an important status determinant. Control of entry into occupation and control of teaching and learning are powerful factors. The concept of *career* and the factors that influence career patterns are related concepts. Within the formal work group informal specialization and informal work groups are powerful forces. Work organizations are systems that relate division of labor and authority to accomplish formally recognized ends. Industrial sociologists are more concerned with how workers "get along" with each other than with their outputs of goods and services.

The work adjustment approach. Some scholars are concerned with attempting to reconcile apparent disparities between and among goals. They start with a familiar concept — that employment does not mean the same thing to all people; employment goals differ because they reflect different needs of employees, employers, and the public. Thus, for example, employers may emphasize the goal of productivity; employees, the goal of job satisfaction. Obviously, disparity in goals must be recognized and adjusted — balanced out — in a satisfactory system of employment relationships.

H. M. Vollmer, for example, describes an employment action as "effective" if it represents achievement of organization goals; it is said to be "efficient" if it achieves a desired organization end and simultaneously satisfies the interests and needs of the individual employees in their collective endeavor. Hence, relationships between employee and managerial "rights" are crucial in achieving such balance.[10]

---

[10]Howard M. Vollmer, *Employee Rights and the Employment Relationship* (Berkeley: University of California Press, 1960).

England, Lofquist, Dawis, and their associates at the University of Minnesota Industrial Relations Center have developed similar concepts. They use "work adjustment" as the ultimate, integrating criterion in the employment relationship. *Work adjustment* involves balancing of two sets of subcriteria, "satisfaction" and "satisfactoriness." *Satisfaction* is the work adjustment viewed by the individual employee — *job satisfaction* is a common term for this phenomenon. *Satisfactoriness* is the employer's judgement of the employee's performance toward attaining the organization's goals. It includes the concept of productivity but is broader than that, since few organizations have productivity or efficiency as a sole objective. In a free economy both employer and employee enter voluntarily and can withdraw from the employment relationship. Their employment behaviors are evaluated in terms of their own yardsticks, and future behaviors reflect these evaluations. Continued association in the employment relationship requires continuing adjustment of these two sets of employment values. Work adjustment is therefore an equilibrium-type concept.[11]

In brief, at any point in time, an individual's work adjustment is defined by his concurrent levels of satisfaction and satisfactoriness. Satisfactoriness is a function of the correspondence between an individual's set of abilities and the ability requirements of the work environment — provided that the individual's needs correspond with the reinforcer system of the work environment. Satisfaction is a function of the correspondence between the reinforcer system of the work environment and the individual's set of needs — provided that the individual's abilities correspond with the ability requirements of the work environment.

Satisfaction moderates the functional relationship between satisfactoriness and the correspondence of the individual's ability set with the ability requirements of the work environment. Satisfactoriness moderates the functional relationship between satisfaction and the correspondence of the reinforcer system of the work environment with the individual's set of needs.

The probability of an individual being forced out of the work environment is inversely related to his measured satisfactoriness. The

[11]See Robert E. Carlson, Rene V. Dawis, George W. England, and Lloyd H. Lofquist, *The Measurement of Employment Satisfaction* (Minneapolis: University of Minnesota Industrial Relations Center, Bulletin 35, May, 1962), pp. 4–5. For more details see *A Definition of Work Adjustment* (Minneapolis: University of Minnesota Industrial Relations Center, Bulletin 30, May, 1960).

probability of an individual voluntarily leaving the work environment is inversely related to his measured satisfaction. Tenure is a function of satisfactoriness and satisfaction. The correspondence between the individual (abilities and needs) and the environment (ability requirements and reinforcer system) increases as a function of tenure.[12]

The interaction of social and technical processes approach. Some scholars regard industrialization as both a technical process and a corollary social process. Employment relations and processes are viewed as a portion of social relations and processes. John Dunlop defines an industrial relations system as ". . . an analytical subsystem of an industrial society on the same logical plane as an economic system, regarded as another analytical subsystem."[13] He points out that economic and industrial relations systems overlap and at the same time have different scopes. To Dunlop an IR system is not just a subsidiary part of an economic system, nor of a social system, nor of a behavior system; it uses different methods of investigation, different tools, and different theories. In fact it is ". . . a distinctive analytical and theoretical subject matter . . . a genuine discipline."[14]

Dunlop distinguishes three sets of relationships in industrial relations. These are:

1. The relation of the IR system to society as a whole.
2. The relation of the IR system to the economic system.
3. The internal relations within the IR system.

Three sets of "actors" are involved in the system: (1) managers, (2) rank-and-file employees, and (3) government agencies. Essential in the setting of industrial relations are:

1. Technology and working environment.
2. Market restraints.
3. Power relations.

From all of these relationships stem sets of rules for work and employment.[15]

---

[12]From Rene V. Dawis, G. W. England, and L. H. Lofquist, *A Theory of Work Adjustment* (Minneapolis: University of Minnesota, Industrial Relations Center, *Bulletin 38*, January, 1964), pp. 10–11. See also, R. E. Carlson, *et al.*, *The Measurement of Employment Satisfactoriness* (University of Minnesota, Industrial Relations Center, *Bulletin 37*, December, 1963); and R. E. Carlson, *et al.*, *The Measurement of Employment Satisfaction* (University of Minnesota, Industrial Relations Center, *Bulletin 35*, May, 1962).

[13]John Dunlop, *Industrial Relations Systems*, (New York: Henry Holt and Company, 1958), p. 5.

[14]*Ibid.*, p. 6.

[15]*Ibid.*, see pp. 7–17; 380–89. Each group of actors has common beliefs, or an ideology which defines the place and role of all actors. These ideologies tend to: (1) bind together

Dunlop's concept of an industrial relations system as a group of rules and relationships was expanded by Kerr, Dunlop, Harbison, and Myers. They became interested in industrial relations in different countries.[16] They were concerned with similarities and differences between and among industrial relations systems in various countries. Dunlop had argued that the central task of industrial relations was to try to explain the rules. Kerr, *et. al.*, started out with hypotheses concerning power relationships among parties to the industrial relations system but returned to the study of the nature of rules and who makes them as more important questions.

The setting for their study was economic growth and development, essentially industrialization. Their focus was upon the structuring of the labor force, i.e., relations between the manager and the managed. They noted in their studies that every industrial relations system had a "web of rules" and rule makers — the *managerial* elite. Thus, industrialization leads to industrial relations, ideologies develop, the actors develop rules, occupational hierarchies emerge, and all of this is an on-going process.[17] They point out that "There is a world-wide contest going on over industrial relations systems no less than over economic systems.[18]

---

the members of each group, (2) differentiate the groups, or (3) separate the groups. All groups may hold a common ideology (e.g., belief in the free enterprise system). This ideology induces them to attempt to find agreements for work relationships. The interaction of the actors, given their common ideology plus their different ideologies and contexts, produces rules which serve the interests of the parties. These rules are the result of compromises reached through exchange of values.

Dunlop's system is dynamic. Because the actors, ideologies, and contexts vary through time and space, rules must be varied accordingly. Dunlop suggests that the best way to study industrial relations is by comparing working rules in similar industries. He suggests three categories of rules:

1. Procedures for making substantive rules.
2. Substantive rules.
3. Procedures for administering or changing the rules.

He suggests comparing these rules among different firms in one industry or among similar industries in different countries — or in the same industry or firm at different times. Thus, the historical context provides a means of comparison, of studying the effects of differing contexts and ideologies upon rules.

Dunlop holds that the main outlines of a national industrial relations system emerge at an early stage of economic development. (Here he is using system in the operational as well as conceptual sense.) It is the process of industrialization, with its economic development and its corollary development of working rules, which shapes and changes the industrial relations system.

Dunlop concludes that three groups of rules may be found in all (operational) industrial relations systems. These are:

1. Procurement of a labor force.
2. Compensation and wages.
3. Procedures for settlement of disputes over existing rules.

[16]See Clark Kerr, John T. Dunlop, Frederick H. Harbison, and Charles A. Myers, *Industrialism and Industrial Man* (Cambridge: Harvard University Press, 1960).

[17]Note that this emphasis is similar to that of the industrial sociologists (e.g., the work of Gross discussed above).

[18]Kerr, *op. cit.*, p. 234.

Kerr, *et. al.*, lay out three interdependent functions that any industrial relations system must perform. These are:

1. Define duties, responsibilities, power, and authority of employees, managers, and the state.
2. Control and keep dislocations, frustrations, and protests of the parties within tolerable limits as industrialization rolls along.
3. Establish a web of rules, both substantive and procedural.[19]

They regard the future of industrial relations as pluralistic industrialism (sharing of rule making) with "bureaucratic gamesmanship"[20] as the *modus vivendi*. They predict that pluralistic industrialism will never reach equilibrium because of varying pressures for uniformity and diversity in rules in response to technological change and all its concomitants.[21]

BACK TO REALITY: OPERATIONAL SYSTEMS

At the outset of this chapter it was noted that industrial relations systems and their components could be either conceptual or operational, abstract or "real world," and that theories supplied the bridge between the two kinds of systems. The previous portion of this chapter has been concerned with attempting to make clear the meaning and nature of conceptual systems of industrial relations and to give some illustrative examples. The remaining portion of the chapter provides some examples of operational, real-life, partial industrial relations systems.

The term "system" will now be used in its more conventional sense, that of an orderly sequence or method of doing things. Thus, a grievance system consists of a certain order of steps or sequences of events. There are many operational industrial relations systems including selection systems, compensation systems, and bargaining systems.

These operational systems stem from goals and related problems. They differ in different parts of the world — they may even differ in

---

[19]Clark Kerr, John T. Dunlop, Frederick H. Harbison, and Charles A. Myers, *Industrialism and Industrial Man* (Cambridge: Harvard University Press, 1960), pp. 234–35.
[20]*Gamesmanship*, at the risk of oversimplification, may be defined as not only taking advantage of the rules of the game but also using the rules forcefully to attain objectives and gain advantages.
[21]Kerr, *op. cit.*, p. 296. For an interesting attempt to test the Kerr, *et. al.*, hypotheses, see Robert J. Alexander, *Labor Relations in Argentina, Brazil and Chile* (New York: McGraw-Hill Book Co., Inc., 1962).

different parts of the same nation. Thus, for example, executive compensation systems usually differ from those for rank-and-file employees. For those of us in the affluent society of the United States, it is well to remember that our type of problems and our industrial relations are unique — not common or universal.

Operational systems differ through time and place. Today's compensation system in the United States is different from that of a generation ago. The Russian compensation system is different from that in the United States. However, despite apparent differences, operational industrial relations systems may have certain similarities, as we have noted in the brief discussion of Dunlop, Kerr, *et. al.*, above.[22]

Manpower Planning

Asia has her manpower problems, Russia has hers; the United States has manpower problems, and so does every society. Some of these problems are similar from one nation to another — few are completely unique. Many countries have different goals, although most industrialized nations have great similarity of goals. There is more dissimilarity, however, in the ways various societies attempt to attain their goals — to prevent and alleviate manpower problems. Or put succinctly, different nations have different operational industrial relations systems.[23]

No one has undertaken a complete cataloguing of these differences. At this point the discussion will illustrate briefly the Eastern European industrial relations system, which is not a private enterprise market system, and then briefly give attention to planning in Western Europe, which is partly a market and partly a state system. These examples will be used: (1) to differentiate these industrial relations systems and (2) as a basis for comparison with the United States system which is still essentially a market system. The next two chapters on labor markets will discuss more fully how industrial relations systems reflect economic, social-political systems.

---

[22]For an interesting discussion of comparative operational industrial relations, see Charles A. Myers, "The American System of Industrial Relations: Is it Exportable?", *Proceedings of the Industrial Relations Research Association* (December 1962), pp. 2–14.

[23]Cf. R. P. Billimoria, "The Pattern of Labor-Management Relations in India," *International Trends*, C10S, Symposium B11, Paper No. B11b, 1963.

Manpower planning in Eastern Europe. In the Soviet Union and Eastern European countries, manpower planning is an integral part of the systems of general planning. Manpower planning reflects a network of decisions by public authorities on the volume, methods, and composition of production; the disposal of output; and price fixing.[24] While other countries allocate resources through the market system, Eastern European economies lay out detailed production tasks for various economic units (regions, industries, and enterprises) and allocate their resources to achieve this production. In short, manpower allocations are budgeted in detail. Actually, availability of resources, human and material, is a starting point for fixing production targets. Four levels of planning are involved:

1. The nation.
2. The region.
3. The industry.
4. The individual enterprise.

More careful planning in recent years stems from a lack of labor reserves. Since World War II, such sources as women, older workers, and surplus farm labor have been absorbed; reduced birth rates stemming from World War II casualties have left a gap in the "normal" supply of threshold workers. With emphasis upon increasing economic growth and its attendant rising labor productivity, very careful utilization of manpower resources is essential. It should be noted that "planning," as used by Eastern Europeans, has two component meanings: (1) a blueprint for action and (2) the action itself. In their practice these functions are inseparable.

There are two kinds of plans: "informative indicators" which are not binding and "directive indicators" which are binding; the former are used for guidance in fulfilling the latter. The degree of concreteness of plans varies — in general, plans are more concrete the lower they are in the economic hierarchy and the shorter the time span under consideration.

There are three major levels of planning agencies:

1. The central planning bodies which work out plans from instructions received from the Council of Ministers (central government) and the Central Committee of the Communist Party.
2. The regional economic councils.
3. The local industries and enterprises.

---

[24] Abstracted from "Manpower Planning in Eastern Europe," *International Labour Review*, Vol. LXXXVI, No. 2 (August, 1962), pp. 95–127.

Planning involves a continuous flow of information and directives from one level to another The basic concept underlying these processes is the "balance." A *balance* contains a statement about the future availability of some resources (e.g., manpower) and a list of intended "uses" of the resources. Planned availability and planned use must always be in balance. Balances are of two types: (1) planning and (2) achievement. Planning balance sheets lead to achievement balance sheets which, in turn, lead to new planning balance sheets, etc.; this is done vertically and horizontally in terms of economic units. Major tasks include consolidation and elimination of inconsistencies.

The Labor Plan. The overall State Plan of Development of the National Economy includes manpower balances, and these relate to the Labor Plan. The Labor Plan is a group of mutually interdependent plans for labor productivity, manpower allocation and utilization, and wages.

A typical yearly Labor Plan would include:
1. Total annual wages fund.[25]
2. Total labor force.
3. Manpower requirements to be provided by interregional transfer.
4. Rate of growth of labor productivity.

These are obligatory directives. Noncompliance brings economic sanctions (e.g., lower wages and other punishment). It should be noted that the wages fund includes a "premiums fund," i.e., incentive production bonuses. Every enterprise has a labor and wages department (like an Industrial Relations or Personnel Department).

Labor productivity planning is of the greatest importance; it is crucial at the local enterprise level. Divergences between planned and actual productivity are carefully noted and accounted for, and plans are made to overcome any obstacles that stand in the way of achievement. Special teams of workers, technicians, and economists go over divergences by individual departments and shops within an enterprise.

Planning of the number of workers needed is the most important portion of manpower planning at the local level.[26] Manpower balances at higher levels are prepared primarily on a regional basis

---

[25]See "Wages Fund" wage theory, pp. 578–79 of this text.

[26]In brief, an estimate is made of the average number of hours a worker will work per year, after deducting planned holidays, "planned" absences, etc., to arrive at the "planned real fund of working time." Average hours are then revised against "output norms" (based on either time study or past performance). Next an adjustment is made for expected or "planned" increases in labor productivity. Then the necessary labor inputs for each

(province, region, or republic) and include a consolidation of collective (or public) and private sectors (e.g., some agriculture is still on a personal or private basis). It should be apparent that the collective sector gets top priority on resources. Special manpower balances are also drawn up for skilled occupations, young persons, and graduates of university and technical schools.

All of these balances have to be in alignment and this is no mean task. Plans to use additional manpower resources may be denied at higher levels, and sources of supply may be under- or overestimated. Each change in any balance is immediately translated in imbalance on many other manpower balance sheets. Actually, at any moment, the concept of complete general balance is a theoretical abstraction, much like the concept of general equilibrium in economic theory.

Manpower distribution. As manpower requirements change, so does manpower distribution. Such shifts may involve:

1. Sectors (state, cooperatives, private industry).
2. Industries (e.g., manufacturing and agriculture).
3. Geographic areas and other divisions of the labor force.[27]

Distribution and redistribution of the labor force is accomplished through shifts (or mobility) and channeling of new entrants. A crucial channel is the vocational training system; 50 percent of all placements are made through this medium. Plans are made for needed workers, training requirements are set, and graduates of training programs are distributed by sector, region, industry, and enterprise. Participants are recruited from youths and persons of all ages, largely from the country areas. Most of the recruits are in the so-called State Labor Reserve System made up of a wide net of residential training schools.[28]

Next in order of importance is the Organized Recruitment of Workers System which accounts for 44 percent of all placements in the Soviet Union. Here experienced workers are offered one- to

---

product are determined; these are called "norm-hours" and are calculated and checked by occupation and wage group as well as in product terms (i.e., more "balances"). By adding together all norm-hours for all products, the production plan and staffing requirements for the individual establishment are determined. These estimates are made quarterly and are adjusted for turnover and new production needs.

[27]It should be noted that the Soviets do not have a labor force concept similar to ours— indeed, the division between the labor force and the rest of the population is very unclear (at least to outsiders).

[28]It should be emphasized that in the Soviet Union there is no compulsory drafting of labor reserves into the labor reserve system. Instead, "volunteers" generally exceed quotas. It is apparent why this is so since job openings in individual enterprises are reserved for those who go through the vocational training systems that make up the State Labor Reserve System.

three-year contracts; and upon completion of their contracts, they may have a permanent job or return to their previous place of residence. Seasonal industries and interindustry and interregional transfers rely heavily upon this system. Here again "volunteers" provide the needed cadres of workers. Resettlement and newly cultivated areas make up the remainder of formal state recruitment.

However, increasing use is being made of so-called "free recruitment," i.e., individual enterprises going out and recruiting as they do in the United States. In Czechoslovakian industry, for example, free recruitment accounts for around 70 percent of accessions. Such firms use essentially the same techniques as those employed in the Western industrial countries.[29]

Planning for specialists (e.g., engineers, teachers, etc.) is more complicated in that it involves longer "lead-time." In industry, ratios of staff specialist to total personnel are determined. For social welfare occupations, specialists to population ratios are set (e.g., number of doctors per 10,000 population). These plans are translated back into university and technical school student enrollments. Flexibility in distribution of these graduates is facilitated through provision of state scholarships which stipulate that such scholarship recipients will take whatever posts are allocated to them for three-year terms.

The right to work and layoff. The Soviet Constitution guarantees the right to work to all citizens. Hence dismissal of employees is no simple matter and is based upon detailed statutory regulation. A fall in the volume of work, for example, is not a valid reason for discharge. Certain offenses may be grounds for discharge (e.g., criminal acts). Some employees enjoy superseniority (e.g., expectant mothers, employees on military leave, and union officials). In all cases dismissal must have approval of the local union, and management has no appeal. Nor can higher union bodies or the courts overrule the union local. However, this right apparently does not apply in connection with reduction in manpower requirements according to production plans ordered by economic agencies above the plant level.

As part and parcel of work guarantees, it should be emphasized that the Soviet Union does not have unemployment insurance and, hence, loss of a job leaves the worker with no social insurance. Loss of a job also affects housing, food, and other necessities of life. In case of unlawful dismissal, managers are held personally liable for damages,

---

[29]At the present time Western scholars are not fully aware of how free recruiting is balanced against state-provided labor reserves and the Organized Recruitment System.

even if the dismissal took place at the request of the union. Alleged illegal dismissals are referred to arbitration, i.e., a hearing by the joint works committee (equal number of union and management representatives). Their decision must be unanimous. Failing that, or in an appeal from their decision, the worker can take his case to the courts.[30]

Labor mobility. Under Stalin Russian workers could not change jobs without government permission. In 1960 freedom of job movement was instituted. By 1963 it was estimated that at least one third of Soviet workers had changed jobs at least once (or more) from 1960–1963. On the average it took twenty days to find a new job, a serious loss in man-hours.[31]

Manpower planning in Western Europe. As in the case of Eastern Europe, Western Europe's industrial relations systems reflect their own goals, problems, resources, and cultures. Thus, Western Europe's manpower planning is different from Eastern Europe's, and both are different from manpower planning in the United States. The European Social Charter, described in Chapter 1, represents an interesting and perhaps vital experiment in attempting to find an international industrial relations system.

European business, labor, and government are experimenting with economic planning. Such planning seeks to regularize and strengthen private investment, not simply by forecasting but by controlling it. This is done allegedly without infringing on the right of private business to make its own decisions. Such planning also seeks to coordinate government and private policy for growth and ties in public investment, taxation, and monetary policy with private planning.

The French Patronat, dominant French employer association, has pushed hard for such planning in France. Other countries have had similar experience, and a Common Market planning association is under way. Under the French 4-year plan an overall expansion of gross domestic production is specified, investment and consumption rates are set, and the increase is allocated to appropriate industrial sectors. The planned increase in production then is related to increases in jobs, such increases matching the total expected growth of the labor force. Detailed projections of spending by every industry and government agency are allocated to new plant and equipment,

---

[30] Abstracted from "Dismissal Procedure III: U.S.S.R.", *International Labour Review*, Vol. LXXX, No. 1 (August, 1959), pp. 73–87.

[31] *U.S. News and World Report*, May 6, 1963, pp. 46–47.

research and development, education, housing, highways, and other investments. Basically, the plan uses an input-output system which shows how much every industry must buy from and sell to every other industry if the plan is to be realized.

Increasingly, government, labor, and business leaders in the United States are watching these European developments and raising questions concerning the desirability of similar voluntary coordinated planning for growth in the United States.[32]

This chapter has emphasized that conceptual systems are abstractions that can be useful to the student in facilitating his study and to the scholar in his research. The major focus in this book is on *employment processes*; the major task of this book is to facilitate their understanding. Familiarity with both conceptual and operational systems is essential to this end. This approach is illustrated in the next two chapters dealing with labor markets. Chapter 5 presents a conceptual approach to labor markets; Chapter 6 is concerned with operational labor markets and some of their major institutions. Unlike the present chapter, which is broader in scope, the balance of the book will emphasize a labor economics approach.

ANALYTICAL REVIEW QUESTIONS

1. How do operational systems differ from conceptual systems? How are they related?
2. What distinguishes a partial system from a general system?
3. What major sets of variables are included in a general model of the field of industrial relations?
4. What is the purpose of classification, abstraction, and analysis?
5. What function do theories perform?
6. What are the major components of a theory?
7. What is a hypothesis? How is a hypothesis related to a theory?
8. What is a model? How does it differ from a theory?
9. What is meant by a "hierarchy of explanation"? How are logic and measurement used as tests?
10. What is a variable? How are independent variables different from dependent?
11. What makes a hypothesis useful?
12. What purpose is served by the concept of intervening variables?
13. What are some different dimensions of goals?

---

[32]"Europe Charts Its Business Future," *Business Week*, April 7 1962 pp. 80ff. Gosfa Rehn, "Manpower Adaptability and Economic Growth," *OECD Observer*, No. 1 (November 16, 1962), pp. 14–18 (available OECD, Chateau de la Muette, Paris 16ᵉ). Such joint planning is somewhat like the "Codes" under NRA in the 1930's in the United States.

14. What are some of the goals of informal work groups?
15. How does the "web of rules" approach differ from the "exchange" approach in classifying industrial relations systems? What is the alleged advantage of the exchange approach?
16. What is meant by the term "social processes approach"?
17. How does Gross define the framework of working relationships?
18. What is the difference between "effective" and "efficient" employment actions? How is this different from "satisfaction" and "satisfactoriness"? How do these concepts relate to work adjustment?
19. Why is work adjustment an equilibrium concept?
20. What three groups of rules may be found in all operational industrial relations systems according to Dunlop?
21. How is industrialization related to a "web of rules"?
22. What are some examples of operational industrial relations systems? Are such systems common or universal?
23. How does manpower planning in Soviet Russia differ from manpower planning in the United States?
24. What are the major components of a Soviet State Labor Plan?
25. Why is the concept of manpower "balances" important in a planned economy?
26. In the Soviet economy how is vocational training related to manpower planning and labor force distribution?
27. How does manpower planning in Western Europe differ from manpower planning in Eastern Europe?
28. What kinds of employment policy are laid out in the European Social Charter?
29. How are employment processes related to industrial relations systems?

Case 4-1

A "DO IT YOURSELF" MODEL

Construct a model of employment effects of a labor supplementary technological innovation to be introduced in a manufacturing plant. Obviously the firm's employment level will be the dependent variable. Be sure to show independent variables (new machines and processes would be an example) and intervening variables (worker resistance and union attitudes would be examples). Be sure to show for each variable the expected or anticipated effect on the employment level, i.e., whether it would tend to increase it or decrease it. Specify any conditions essential to the operation of your model (e.g., nature of the product demand curve). One procedure might be to draw three columns: (1) independent variables, (2) intervening variables, and (3) the dependent variable. Put appropriate variables in each column. Then draw a rectangular "box" around each. Show relationships by connecting those boxes that contain *related* variables; connections might be made by a line with an arrow denoting direction of the relationship. Then indicate above the line whether or not the expected relationship is positive or negative (+ or −).

Thus, for example, such a model might look somewhat like one of the following:

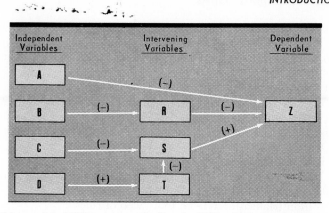

In this model, "C" causes a decline in "S" which in turn causes an increase in "Z."

Another arrangement might be:

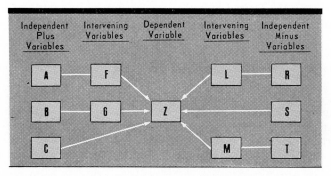

Note that plus independent variables are those that cause an increase in employment level, and minus variables cause a decrease.

• Bring your model to class and be prepared to: (1) reproduce it on the blackboard, (2) defend your choice of variables, and (3) defend your specification of relationships.

Case 4-2

MACHINES OR JOBS

You are the business agent of Local 606. The company proposes to install new machines that will cut labor requirements for your union members by 20 percent. Management proposes to cut the price of the product 10 percent and you are sure that this will increase demand for the product by at least 50 percent. Several key members of the union policy committee suggest resisting introduction of the new machinery by having the members restrict output on the new machines. What advice would you give these committee members? What plan of action would you lay out for your union and how would you attempt to "sell" it to the members? What arguments would you use?

• Write up your program and bring it to class.

LABOR MARKETS: CONCEPTUAL

Labor markets are important components of industrial relations systems, both conceptual and operational. In general, labor markets are the meeting places of the many forces affecting man in the working phase of his life. There are many kinds of forces: social, psychological, political, and economic, to name a few. Because economic factors are so important, they receive special attention here. Further, emphasis is on economic forces within a free society. This chapter deals with the concept of labor markets, with some illustrative data on labor mobilities and job shifts.[1] The next chapter discusses real-life labor market operations including employment processes, job facilitating agencies, and major institutions affecting labor market operations.

ECONOMIC ROLE OF LABOR MARKETS

Labor markets provide the principal means of access to jobs in a free society. People who want to work find and choose among various jobs in labor markets. Employers find the men and the women for their jobs in these same markets. Labor resources are disposed or allocated to the work to be done through the labor marketing process.

---

[1]The best brief single summarization and analysis of these areas is contained in the excellent critical study: Herbert S. Parnes, "The Labor Force and Labor Markets," in H. G. Heneman, Jr. *et. al.* (eds.), *Employment Relations Research* (New York: Harper and Brothers, 1960), pp. 1–42.

This process and the complex of individual labor markets in our society play a major part in determining which jobs we take and many of the conditions under which all of us work.

Several of our major labor problems are closely related to this process of labor marketing. If the marketing processes operate smoothly and if supplies of and demands for labor are balanced with prompt agreement on price, those who want jobs find them. Those who seek help get it. On the other hand, if job-seekers in a particular market are more numerous than jobs, potential job-holders may face a delay in finding employment, for they may have to enter other markets. In some markets jobs may go unfilled; in others, people who want to work may not find jobs. Moreover, what takes place in labor markets influences the conditions of work. The labor marketing process largely determines wages, hours, and economic security.[2]

Labor marketing has not always played such an important economic role, and it is by no means equally influential in all modern societies. When medieval rulers and their royal associates wanted particular services performed or goods produced, they did not hang out help wanted signs or advertise employment opportunities. Neither did they normally offer premium rates, bonuses, longer vacations, or other fringes to entice manpower into shortage occupations. They did not publicize employee swimming pools, clubhouses, or opportunities to buy the employer's stock at cut-rate prices. Their subjects faced no free choice among thousands of different jobs.

Much of the work to be done was performed by slaves. In this country white as well as Negro slaves were sold at auction. While some slaves were sold in markets, most people were born into their jobs. In many societies the son of a serf was born to serfdom. Jobs were filled by closed social systems that provided labor supplies from generation to generation. Only a select few were permitted a choice of work.

Labor marketing achieved wide acceptance when limited numbers of artisans gained their freedom. These craftsmen — workers in leather, in armor, and in merchandising, for example — sold their services for wages. Even then, however, the markets for their services were not entirely free. Prices on services as well as on goods were regulated, in part by church doctrines of "just price" and

---

[2]For an interesting and informative picture of local labor markets, see Irving Sobel and Richard C. Wilcock, "Labor Market Behavior in Small Towns," *Industrial and Labor Relations Review*, Vol. 9, No. 1 (October, 1955), pp. 54–76.

subsequently by royal edict and legislative action. Free marketing of people's services has been largely a development associated with industrial capitalism. It has become a common practice only since the Industrial Revolution. Experience is thus restricted to a comparatively recent period of history.

Free labor markets are by no means universal throughout the world today. They occupy a much less important place in economies that make arbitrary allocations of manpower to various jobs or allow only the members of specified classes to hold various assignments. Traditions that close doors to essential education and training frequently limit the free marketing process. In addition, slave labor still exists. A United Nations and International Labor Office report in May, 1953, found systems of forced labor maintained in the Soviet Union and four other iron-curtain nations and in two territories in Africa.[3]

In our society the allocation of human resources through labor markets is an impressive part of all economic activity. On the average, Americans in the labor force change jobs about once every 4 years. While most of these changes are made by a small proportion of the labor force, this means more than 15 million annual sales for our labor markets. In addition, many more workers get promotions and wage increases because of recognized market demands for their services.[4]

References to the concept of a hypothetical national labor market or simply to *the* labor market can be somewhat misleading, for they refer to a sort of mythical composite of thousands of markets. They cannot be realistically combined, for each has its distinctive supplies of and demands for labor. For example, there is a supply of first-class machinists and of unskilled labor in a particular locality, and there are demands for specialty salesmen, hotel cooks, and electrical engineers. Most employers do not have simple demands for labor. Their demands are for telephone operators, drop-forge crewmen, radio technicians, and chicken pickers, to cite a few examples. Very few jobs are available for raw labor; most jobs require some training or experience.[5]

---

[3]For details, see "The Extent of Forced Labor in the World," *Monthly Labor Review*, Vol. 76, No. 9 (September, 1953), pp. 944 ff.

[4]For greater detail on the use of these markets in our economy, see Gladys L. Palmer, *Labor Mobility in Six Cities* (New York: Social Science Research Council, 1954).

[5]For further discussion of this point, see Gordon F. Bloom and Herbert R. Northrup, *Economics of Labor and Industrial Relations* (Philadelphia: Blakiston and Company, 1950), p. 265, and Lloyd G. Reynolds. *The Structure of Labor Markets* (New York: Harper and Brothers, 1951), p. 42.

Sometimes it is said that the local labor market is tight or loose. What is meant is that, in general, jobs are plentiful or scarce. However, while jobs for unskilled labor may be scarce, jobs for electronic engineers may be far more numerous than available supplies. Some local markets may be tight, with apparent shortages, at the same time that other local markets have supplies of labor in excess of demands.

Some markets are much more obviously and tangibly defined than others. For example, in metropolitan areas most of those who want jobs as construction laborers go to union offices for them. Other markets are less formal. For example, the market for salesmen may be relatively unorganized and dispersed, with no central compilation of jobs or available workers. Because so many labor markets are informal, without a special market place and procedure, the whole concept of labor markets is sometimes described as a convenient and useful abstraction — a concept.

FUNCTIONS OF LABOR MARKETS

The essence of the marketing process is the balancing or equilibrating of supplies and demands through adjustments in prices. In economic terms the purpose of labor marketing is the creation of such utilities as may be derived from the direction or control of labor services at a particular time. Things — goods and services — change hands in all markets. Ownership, possession, or control is transferred, and new owners or possessors or users pay for the advantage they have gained.

Market Models

Economic analysis of pricing generally refers to models of markets, which are more or less simplified outlines of the principal variables and relationships that characterize the marketing process. Essentials in every market are buyers and sellers and prices. Buyers make bids or offers. Sellers follow the same pattern. These two parties get together to an extent that results in a transfer of possession, use, or control and a market price to be paid in this transfer.

Although all markets are similar in these characteristics, they differ in many others. As noted, some may be narrowly limited, in terms either of numbers of buyers and sellers or the area in which they operate. There is, for example, the market for fresh eggs in Gibson City, Illinois, or the market for water boys at a rural circus.

Some markets, at the other extreme, are worldwide, like the market for cotton or wool or wheat. Some markets involve direct, face-to-face negotiations. Others work through an extensive mechanism of exchanges, wire services, and brokers. In some markets the pricing mechanism operates with great speed, as in the betting windows for tickets on the third race at Oaklawn Park, Arkansas. In others pricing may be slow and apparently awkward, as in the home real estate market in the village of Falcon Park. Some markets operate most of the time; others are active only for a few days of each year. Some markets deal in futures. What is bought and sold may not exist at the time of the transaction.

Some markets are highly competitive with numerous buyers and sellers, while others are restricted or controlled. Control of supplies or demands offers opportunities for profit. Fortunes have been made and lost when individuals have cornered the wheat market, for example. *Monopoly,* in which a single seller controls supplies, and *monopsony,* in which a single buyer controls demands, are frequent market phenomena.

Economic analysis of labor marketing frequently finds models helpful in explaining the labor pricing process. A basic model describes a market operating under conditions of perfect competition. According to its assumptions, buyers and sellers act as informed, independent individuals. They enjoy perfect mobility, moving into and withdrawing from this market at will. They have an inclusive knowledge of the conditions in related markets, so that they can and will act wisely in the exchanges they make. Other models introduce modifications involving various degrees of imperfect competition, including monopoly and monopsony.

The assumptions of this abstract model do not fit the realities of most markets. Perfect mobility, for example, is seldom if ever achieved, and perfect knowledge is less than likely. Because markets seldom if ever fully meet these specifications, some critics object to the use of such simple models on the grounds that they are unreal and therefore misleading. Use of simple models is justified, however, not because they explain precisely what takes place in any particular labor market, but because they help to explain the basic tendencies in all markets. They focus attention on the major variables. Certainly the simple competitive model is not realistic for many markets, for their processes do not precisely duplicate its assumed conditions. But use of the simple model can explain continuing tendencies in such situations — tendencies that are widely influential and generally present. It can focus attention on what may be regarded as basic processes better than a more realistic model would. Use of similar models for this purpose is well established in the older physical sciences. Physics has long used a similar model to illustrate tendencies described as the law of falling bodies. In geometry, as Professor B. E. Goetz has noted, a major portion of the analysis depends on imaginary models that are impossible in real life.[6] The straight line, which has no width, is a simple illustration, as is the point, which has no dimensions other than zero. He notes that Euclid defines 23 such useful terms, all of them strictly imaginary.

At the same time, it is important to recognize limitations on the usefulness of these models. Since they do not precisely replicate existing markets, they do not justify firm conclusions as to what happens or will happen in any specific market. Since they illustrate general tendencies, conclusions can be stated only as likelihoods and probabilities. They are like the law of falling bodies, which should not be assumed to justify the conclusion that all bodies will or do fall at its specified rate.

Allocation of Labor

In our system, with its emphasis on a minimum of dictation and a maximum of freedom for individuals, labor marketing exerts a powerful influence on the whole broad field of employment relationships.

Labor markets largely determine where each member of our labor force works. Workers select the labor markets in which they will shop, the kinds of jobs in which they are interested. Prices bid for their services are important factors in this choice. Employers decide how much and what kinds of help they need and enter markets for these kinds of services. Wage rates influence their decisions as to what kind and how much to buy. If more help is needed to man our service stations and beauty parlors, we get these additional workers in large measure by making more attractive offers in appropriate labor markets. Similarly, if less manpower is needed in managing or financing or mining, shifts away from these jobs are effected through comparatively less attractive wage offers.

We expect this marketing process to push and pull our present and future workers to the jobs in our economy in which they are

---

[6]See his fascinating essay on "The Usefulness of the Impossible," in the *AAUP Bulletin*, Vol. 42, No. 2 (Summer, 1956), pp. 275–87.

most needed. As a broad, general principle, we want to maximize each worker's contribution, and we expect the labor marketing process to work toward that objective. This is in sharp contrast to other systems that assign or direct workers to industries and jobs. The importance of this difference is readily grasped by comparing our market allocation of workers with the draft of manpower for military duty in which we assign duties, telling workers where they shall serve and what they shall do.

While we have in several periods of national emergency considered drafting for nonmilitary jobs, in peacetime we depend on labor marketing to move workers to the jobs that will best meet our demands for goods and services. This marketing process has the major responsibility for distributing some 75 million workers among more than 30,000 different jobs, on the farms and in the cities, in hundreds of industries, throughout the length and breadth of the nation. The process is complicated by the fact that individual consumers constantly change their demands — shopping for two tricycles and a home this week, an automatic washer and a camera next week, a fly-swatter and a new car the next.

Pricing Human Services

Allocation and pricing are the two sides of the same coin. The labor marketing process sets the prices on various types of human services by balancing demands and supplies in each market. The resulting wages include many considerations in addition to the formal wage rate or salary. Some of these common additions — life insurance, pensions, hospitalization, premium pay for overtime and holidays, unemployment insurance, sickness benefits, and many others — are widely described as *fringes*. They generally add about 25 percent to the dollars and cents of formal wages and salaries.

Labor markets for various types of labor establish both dollar wage rates and salaries and the range and quality of fringe benefits. Millions of workers formally enter these markets, some of them several times each year. For other millions current market prices — the going wage or salary — are the major factor in setting compensation. This market-value yardstick is applied to all types of workers, from unskilled labor to corporation executive. Markets create wage and salary structures, made up of the rates of compensation for related jobs, which we shall consider in greater detail in Chapter 18.

TYPES OF LABOR MARKETS

Many types of labor markets may be conceived of, and for a variety of reasons differentiation is essential. Consider the following examples:

Type of Market	Examples
1. Geographical.	(New York City; Minnesota)
2. Occupational.	(Agronomists; typists)
3. Industrial.	(Steel; agriculture)

Each of these major types may be broken down into more specific operational markets. Often these types are combined (e.g., market for truck drivers in the iron mines of Northern Minnesota). Some markets reflect differences such as age, sex, or race (e.g., old men's jobs, lady wrestlers, or "jobs for colored"). The essential difference in each type of labor market is the group of workers being considered — that provides the definition of the type of labor market.

ESSENTIALS IN LABOR MARKETS

Although labor markets are directly comparable in many ways to markets for other types of resources, the labor marketing process also has some unusual characteristics. Most labor markets are less formal and tangible than grain markets or stock markets or retail stores and shops. They show no such year-round, continuous activity as the local grain exchange, or the Board of Trade in Chicago, or the New York Stock Exchange. Buyers and sellers do not usually come together to sell their services the way farm produce is sold in many community marketing centers. Rather, an informal local market for carpenters is maintained by the officers of their union and local contractors. Representatives meet and negotiate wage rates and fringes annually. The local market for unskilled labor operates through relatives and friends, the public employment offices, the employment divisions of local firms, and the newspapers of the locality. Markets for some of the higher skilled trades may be established and maintained through interstate clearance in the public employment service or classified advertisements in trade and technical journals. Markets for corporate managers and executives and their professional staff — accountants, designers, industrial relations directors, and others — are provided by management associations, newspapers, private employment offices, and special "executive search" divisions of consulting firms.

Despite this tendency toward informality, several characteristics are common to all labor markets. All deal in crudely measured units of labor. All include *labor supplies* — personal services offered for hire. All include bidding employers, who thus create *demands* for *labor*. All establish *prices*, called *wages* or *salaries*, for the services in which they deal. Many of them operate in a fairly narrow region or locality, usually described as a *labor market area*.

Units of Labor

Labor markets deal in several different units or measures of human services, none of which is rigorously uniform. The usual unit for production workers is the man-hour, but many markets set prices on units produced, using piecework or incentive wage plans. For salaried workers the common unit is the month or the year. Salesmen may earn a commission based on the dollar volume of sales. Professional workers may be paid fees for each service or job. The lack of uniformity in each of these units is notable.

Labor Supplies

Labor markets are distinguished and may be identified by their supplies — the types of services in which they deal. They include, for example, markets for plumbers, for morticians, and for common labor. Supplies of labor are not, at any particular time, readily interchangeable among these markets. Plumbers do not enter the market for dental technicians, secretaries, professors of physics, or airline pilots. Supplies for many markets must be qualified by training, skill, and experience. Cairnes[7] described this characteristic of labor market supplies as involving "noncompeting groups." He thus called attention to the difficulty of quickly substituting supplies of labor available in one specialized market for supplies of labor in another. Although there may be substitution over a period of time, at any specific time there is no single supply of labor.

Of what does the labor supply in any particular market consist? How can it be measured or quantified? In the simplest description, labor supplies are regarded as numbers of workers available for hire. This gross appraisal is subject to numerous limitations and requires

---

[7]John Eliot Cairnes. For details, see his *Some Leading Principles of Political Economy Newly Founded* (London, 1874).

a number of refinements to make it at all accurate and realistic. What is actually bought and sold is some measure of the workers' interest, energy, and skill.

In some markets that establish wage rates based on the number of units produced, an attempt is made to measure these contributions rather exactly. What is most commonly offered for sale, however, is hours of service in which this interest, energy, and skill are applied. The most common unit in labor markets is thus the man-hour, although many markets for salaried workers deal in the man-month or the man-year.

Not all the possible man-hours of all the individuals who may enter a labor market are available for hire. On the contrary, individuals normally reserve about two thirds of the hours in each day and one or two full days in each week for rest and nonworking activities. Some individuals may wish to reserve more. Others may be willing to work more but only at premium rates of pay. Hence the simple economic model of a market regards available supplies of labor at any time as being somewhat flexible or variable, depending on the price or wage. In graphic form, the schedule of quantities available at various prices becomes the familiar supply curve. It indicates smaller quantities of work-hours offered at comparatively low prices and increasing quantities at higher rates. In the typical chart of the market model, it appears as an upward-sloping line from left to right.

Factors affecting supplies. What are the principal factors affecting the supply of labor in a market? Among the most important are eight, including:

(1) *Population.* The influence of birth rates and death rates creates a basic supply with something in the nature of outside or gross limits on all individual market supplies.

(2) *Participation rates.* As noted in Chapter 2, family circumstances, age, custom, and other conditions combine to determine what part of the total population will enter the labor force and seek work. Participation appears both as a cause and a result of going wages, for both low earnings and relatively high bids for workers may bring added supplies into labor markets.

(3) *Skill, experience, and other job requirements.* Entrance into most markets requires special qualifications. As frequently noted, few jobs

are adapted to raw labor. Essential preparation may require special aptitudes and training, guided experience, and combinations of these qualifications. For example, most engineering jobs require at least four years of college. Supplies of electricians are limited in many localities by requirement of an extensive apprenticeship. College professors, physicians, and several other professional workers must have had approximately 20 years of formal schooling before they can become a part of the labor supplies in these markets.

Since preparation for participation is frequently an extended process, the decision making of vocational choice plays an important part in determining supplies in many markets. We know comparatively little about what actually takes place and why particular choices are made. We usually assume that a powerful influence is exerted by the prospective income from various types of work. Supplies in many markets are unquestionably restricted because relatively few workers are willing to undertake long and perhaps expensive periods of education. Family tradition and social pressures and prestige may play important roles.

Employer hiring policies may play an important part in limiting supplies. Discriminative practices expressed in demands for labor — directed against older workers or members of minority groups or maintaining unnecessary skill or educational requirements — may reduce supplies.

(4) *Opportunities for training.* Supplies may be limited because relatively few workers can acquire specified education and training. This effect is common in the markets for highly skilled workers. Supplies of physicians have been restricted on this account. Provisions for apprenticeship in many skilled crafts impose rigorous limitations on supplies.

(5) *Mobility.* Market supplies are directly conditioned by the mobility of labor force members, that is, their versatility and ability to move into a variety of markets for which they are qualified. Several types of mobility may be noted, including: (a) *geographic* — the potential for shifting about from one locality for another; (b) *occupational* — the possible adaptability to a variety of skill and experiential requirements; (c) *industrial* — possible changes of industry; (d) *employer* — degree of attachment to an individual firm; and (e) *labor force* — representing movement into and out of the labor force. Labor

mobility has been the subject of extensive study in recent years.[8]

It is apparent that many factors condition labor mobility. Some of them are in effect barriers or frictions in the marketing process. Ignorance of market conditions is one such friction. Inability or unwillingness to travel is another complicating factor. Many employees limit their mobility because of attachments to a single employer or to their home community. Others find their mobility restricted by family attachments. Husbands cannot move because their wives are working, and wives cannot take a better paying job at a distance because husbands do not want to leave their employment.

As noted, some barriers are introduced by employer hiring practices that discriminate on the basis of age, sex, nationality, race, or religion. Others may be interposed by unions that limit numbers of apprentices or maintain exclusive jurisdictions and limit union membership. On the other hand, both unions and employers may increase worker mobility. Unions may supply their members with important facts about labor markets and assist in training apprentices. Employers may advertise jobs and provide opportunities for experience and training that permit employees to enter additional labor markets.[9]

Labor mobility in the United States is much greater than in the older European nations. Their systems of training as well as the more rigid social stratification tend to restrict transfers and shifts. In several nations, of which Japan is a notable example, traditional employer

---

[8]For a discussion of these characteristics of the labor force and their influence on labor supplies, see Herbert J. Parnes, "Research on Labor Mobility," *Bulletin 65* (New York: Social Science Research Council, 1954); *Labor Mobility and Economic Opportunity* (New York: Technology Press and John Wiley and Sons, 1954); and Gladys L. Palmer, *Labor Mobility in Six Cities* (New York: Social Science Research Council, 1954). For reports on occupational mobility, see Maurice C. Benewitz, "Migrant and Non-Migrant Occupational Patterns," *Industrial and Labor Relations Review*, Vol. 9, No. 2 (January, 1956), pp. 235–40; also his "A Study of Labor Mobility for St. Paul, Minnesota," *Labor Law Journal*, Vol. 7, No. 11 (November, 1956), pp. 690–712; Leonard P. Adams and Robert L. Aronson, *Workers and Industrial Change*, Vol. 8, Cornell Studies in Industrial and Labor Relations, New York State School of Industrial and Labor Relations, 1957; Vincent F. Gegan and Samuel H. Thompson, "Worker Mobility in a Labor Surplus Area," *Monthly Labor Review*, Vol. 80, No. 12 (December, 1957), pp. 1451–56; Robert C. Stone, "Factory Organization and Vertical Mobility," *American Sociological Review*, Vol. 18, No. 1 (February, 1953), pp. 28–35; A. J. Jaffe and R. O. Carleton, *Occupational Mobility in the United States* (New York: Kings Crown Press, 1954); W. Lloyd Warner and James Abegglen, *Occupational Mobility in American Business and Industry* (Minneapolis: University of Minnesota Press, 1955); Richard A. Lester, *Adjustments to Labor Shortages*, Princeton University Industrial Relations Section, 1955; Donald J. Bogue, "Residential Mobility and Migration of Workers," in William Haber *et al.* (ed.), *Manpower in the United States* (New York: Harper and Brothers, 1954), Chapter XI; and William H. Miernyk, "Inter-Industry Labor Mobility: The Case of the Displaced Textile Worker" (Boston: Northeastern University Bureau of Business and Economic Research, 1955).

[9]Howard D. Marshall has considered the pros and cons of unions in their relationship to labor mobility in his "Unions and Labor Mobility," *Labor Law Journal*, Vol. 7, No. 2 (February, 1956), pp. 83–97.

attachments make workers immobile. In Japan, when a worker is hired as a permanent employee, he is expected to remain with the same employer for his entire career.[10]

(6) *Alternative uses of time.* Each individual worker presumably weighs the value of his hours devoted to other than working activities against the income to be earned by working. He thus creates some sort of subjective schedule of personal hours and wage rates. He weighs the disutility of each added hour of work against its utility for leisure, public service, and other nonemployment uses.

(7) *Organization of buyers and sellers.* Just as large employers or associations of employers may influence supplies in a particular market by their hiring practices, organized employees may exert a powerful influence by maintaining specified selling practices. They may, if they are permitted to negotiate a closed-shop agreement, allow only union members to enter the market. If they maintain a union-shop requirement, supplies are thereby limited to those willing to join the union. If the market is one in which only skilled craftsmen are qualified, a union of employees may set up tests of requisite skill, frequently requiring completion of a multiyear apprenticeship.

Most common among the changes introduced by worker organizations is that in which a single, uniform price or wage rate is specified. This standard rate or *scale* may create a distinctive labor supply schedule. At rates lower than the scale, if the organization dominates supplies, no hours are offered. At the wage rate fixed by the scale, the entire supply (with the possible exception of hours that are available only at premium rates) is available. The supply curve becomes, strictly speaking, a point in the usual chart, although it may be easier to visualize as a horizontal line parallel to the base.

(8) *Job opportunities.* When job opportunities are scarce, workers may withdraw from the labor force. Availability of welfare payments and social insurance may facilitate this process. On the other hand, when job opportunities are plentiful, some workers may seek second jobs and other persons may enter the labor force to "cash in" on good times and the ready availability of extra income in the form of jobs. Thus it can be seen that labor supply is not independent of demands for labor.

---

[10]Margot Jeffrys has reported on mobility in two English communities in *Mobility in the Labor Market: Employment Changes in Battersea and Dagenham* (London: Routledge and Kegan Paul, Ltd., 1954).

Demands for Labor

Every labor market is regarded as including a *demand schedule* for the services represented by labor supplies. It is composed of the bids or offers of potential employers for the services of potential employees. The most common unit is the man-hour of work. The simple labor market model assumes that each employer has in mind a schedule of his own demands. That schedule proposes to offer several prices, depending on the quantity of services each will buy. His minimal requirements must be hired, even at what he may regard as a relatively high price. He can and will hire more if they can be had at somewhat lower prices. Each employer is assumed to have considered alternate uses of his resources — the possible purchase of machines, new plant facilities, and other changes — as substitutes for man-hours in this market.

The sum of these individual employer schedules creates the market demand schedule. It represents the bids of all employers in the market for various quantities of services at specified prices or wage rates. In the usual chart of the model, it appears as a downward-sloping line, indicating that a relatively high price is offered for what employers regard as minimal quantities of services and that added quantities will be hired if they can be bought at lower rates.

Factors affecting demands. What are the major factors that influence the shape and the location of employers' demand schedules? What are the determinants of employers' bids in the labor marketing process? The answer is not simple, mainly because any attempt to trace these factors back to their sources carries the investigation far outside the labor marketing process. We can, however, note several factors of proximate significance.

(1) *Employers' estimates of consumer demands.* For many labor markets, this factor is the greatest influence. Most labor markets are characterized by what are usually described as *derived* or *indirect* demands. Offers of employment are made because employers think they can make a profit by producing goods and services that others will buy rather than because employers want these services to satisfy their own needs. The original sources of demands for labor are frequently not as evident as these sources may be in commodity markets, because their influence has to filter through several intervening stages or processes. Demands for labor arise, in the first

instance, from the desires of consumers to purchase goods and services. These primary demands must be communicated and translated for many types of labor through an extended labyrinth of retailers, wholesalers, transporters, and manufacturers. Buyers in labor markets want what these working hours can contribute to some product or service that these buyers expect to sell. The local canning factory wants women to inspect corn that will be canned and sold to a grocery chain. A machine tool company wants men to build stamping presses that will be sold to automobile manufacturers, who will in turn use the presses to make auto parts to be assembled by other employees and sold by other employers and their employees. Even the local barber or beautician hires barbers, not to cut his or her hair, but to cut hair for customers who will pay the proprietor.

This complicated chain of demands, although it also affects many commodity markets in our round-about economy, is particularly important in labor markets. It makes errors in forecasting ultimate sales easier and more serious. Mistakes in translating ultimate consumers' demands into jobs can occasion economic losses, unemployment, waste, and personal hardship.

(2) *Elasticity.* Estimates of probable consumer demand require appraisals of the influence of product prices on demands for these products. Buyers must consider the elasticity of product demands, that is, their sensitivity to changes in price. For some products small variations in price may have little effect on purchases; for others, price differences may occasion drastic variations in quantities consumed. If employers can afford to sell the product at a relatively low price, because the price of labor is also low, that fact may justify buying more hours of labor. If they must pay more for labor, and if that means they must ask a higher price for the product, then quantities of labor to be sought may be reduced.

(3) *Labor costs.* The impact of elasticity in product demands on labor markets is directly influenced by the relative importance of labor costs. Some industries, like transportation and manufacturing, have relatively high labor costs. Their type of operation makes the expense of hiring workers a major element in total costs. Employers in certain other industries, like the petroleum extractive group, have comparatively low labor costs and a very large capital investment per worker. In such industries the price of labor is less critical.

(4) *Productivity of workers.* Hourly wage rates provide only a crude measure of labor costs, which are also directly affected by the productivity of workers. Productivity is influenced not only by the tools, equipment, and management or leadership available to employees, but also by their interest and attitudes as well. Hence demands for labor must involve an estimate of the effectiveness or productivity with which it will be employed and the contribution it can be expected to make.

(5) *Organization and monopsony.* Demands for labor may also be shaped and modified by the organization of employers for the purpose of presenting a unified front in labor markets. They may broaden eligibility for employment in some markets, thus facilitating the participation of cheaper foreign or migratory workers, as in certain markets dealing in agricultural labor.

While much is known about the volume and characteristics of labor supplies, knowledge of labor demands is more limited. Only gross figures on job openings are available, and relatively little is known about factors influencing changes in demands for labor. Such information is needed for occupational forecasting, training, and retraining. It is needed so that supplies may be balanced with demands. At present our sights are so blurred that we do not hesitate to spend billions hoping to create demands for labor, but we have not seen fit to spend millions in an attempt to gain knowledge and understanding with respect to quantities and qualities of labor demands and underlying influences and causal factors. Yet this is precisely the type of information needed in community development projects, retraining programs, and other attempts to increase employment.

Pricing

Like other markets, those in which the services of people are bought and sold establish prices. The simple model of labor markets deals in what are assumed to be homogeneous units, each interchangeable with all others. It establishes a price for units of labor in that market. The pricing process is the subject of further and more detailed discussion in later chapters on wage theory.

Labor Market Areas

While some labor markets are national or international in scope, many others are limited and defined not only by the types of labor in which they deal but also by the territory they serve. They may be conveniently identified with a particular community. For many purposes it is helpful to describe labor markets, in terms of their location, as *labor market areas*. At least two yardsticks have been used to set the boundaries of labor market areas. The most common, basing these limits on hiring and job-seeking practice, achieved wide acceptance during World War II. The War Manpower Commission described local markets as the geographic areas within which workers with fixed home addresses usually sought employment and employers looked for potential employees.

This definition noted that labor market areas vary by industry and occupation, so that "there are usually several interrelated occupational and industrial labor markets within a common geographic area." The United States Employment Service now uses a similar definition, regarding such a labor market area as one in which "workers can change jobs without changing their residences" and consisting of "a central city or cities and the surrounding territory within a reasonable commuting distance." The Bureau of Employment Security reports each month on employment and prospective employment in some 150 areas.[11] Each area is classified in the bimonthly report in terms of its current and prospective employment as related to labor supplies. Six classes of local labor markets are identified, including:

	Description	Unemployment Rate
Group A	Overall labor shortage	less than 1.5%
Group B	Low unemployment	1.5 to 2.9%
Group C	Moderate unemployment	3.0 to 5.9%
Group D	Substantial unemployment	6.0 to 8.9%
Group E	Substantial unemployment	9.0 to 11.9%
Group F	Substantial unemployment	12% or more

Figure 5-1 on the following page shows the locations of 60 percent of the areas included in these reports and their classification at the time of one such report.

The second common yardstick for defining labor market areas was used by the War Labor Board in its administration of the World War II Wage Stabilization Program. It emphasizes the similarity of existing wage or salary patterns in each industry. The labor market for each industry extends to the limits within which wage patterns are uniform. Thus, the Chicago labor market for the steel industry includes the city of Chicago plus several suburbs to the south of the

---

[11]See, for an interesting report on current practice, James H. Thompson, "Commuting Patterns of Manufacturing Employees," *Industrial and Labor Relations Review*, Vol. 10, No. 1 (October, 1956), pp. 70–80.

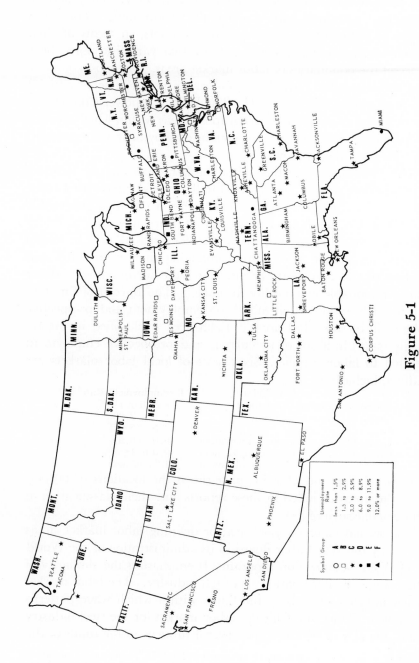

Figure 5-1

CLASSIFICATION OF SELECTED MAJOR LABOR MARKET AREAS ACCORDING TO RELATIVE ADEQUACY OF LABOR SUPPLY — MARCH, 1964

Source: United States Department of Labor, *Area Labor Market Trends*, March, 1964, pp. 9-11.

city. It does not include northern suburbs, because different wage levels prevail in these areas.[12]

Institutional Labor Markets

Geographic labor markets, or labor market areas, are very limited in their conceptual usefulness because such areas may not be clear-cut, and because factors other than location are generally more important in labor marketing. Labor market areas overlap, change, and generally operate without reference to political divisions or units. Instead, it may be more insightful to define labor markets in terms of their "institutional rules." These webs of rules, as noted in the previous chapter, affect entry, movement within, and withdrawal from labor markets and thus define labor markets more sharply for purposes of explaining such processes as labor allocation and wage determination.[13]

Orme W. Phelps has produced a "structural model" of institutional labor markets.[14] He describes five major types of institutional labor markets: (1) private employees outside of business (e.g., housemaids, farm labor); (2) nonunion employees of small firms; (3) government employees; (4) nonunion employees of large firms with formal personnel policies; and (5) union members. The first two are "unstructured," i.e., institutional rules are weak. The latter three are "structured," i.e., institutional rules are strong and influential. There has been an increasing number of empirical studies using this or a similar framework and, as noted in the preceding chapter, institutional markets are central factors in several industrial relations systems.[15]

DISTINCTIVE FEATURES OF LABOR MARKETS

Labor markets have, as noted, many characteristics that are common to all markets. They also have some distinctive features.

---

[12]For further discussion of local labor markets, see William Goldner, "Spatial and Locational Aspects of Metropolitan Labor Markets," *American Economic Review*, Vol. 45, No. 1 (March, 1955), pp. 113–28.

[13]See Clark Kerr, "Labor Markets: Their Character and Consequences," *American Economic Review*, Vol. 40, No. 2 (May, 1950), pp. 278–91, and his "The Balkanization of Labor Markets," in E. Wight Bakke (ed.), *Labor Mobility and Economic Opportunity* (New York: John Wiley and Sons, 1954), pp. 92–110.

[14]See Orme W. Phelps, "A Structural Model of the U.S. Labor Market," *Industrial and Labor Relations Review*, Vol. 10, No. 3 (April, 1957), pp. 402–23.

[15]For an excellent study of the first type of institutional labor market (structureless, farm labor) see Lloyd H. Fisher, *The Harvest Labor Market in California* (Cambridge, Mass.: Harvard University Press, 1953), p. 9.

Among those that deserve special mention are: (1) their special personal and social importance; (2) the perishability of labor; (3) the problem of defining and measuring units; (4) the frequent failure of labor markets to establish a uniform price; and (5) the usual absence of market reporting.

Social and Personal Impacts

Our special social concern about the smooth functioning of labor markets is evident and understandable, mainly because frictions in these markets may readily occasion unemployment, with accompanying personal distress and hardship. Unemployment has an impact on the families of workers and on the communities in which they live. It may affect political attitudes. It may encourage workers and their families to advocate revolutionary social, political, and economic change. The stability of a social order may be seriously threatened if labor markets fail to facilitate regular and satisfying employment.

This distinctive feature of labor markets arises in part because they are the only markets in which what is sold must be personally delivered and made useful by the seller. The farmer who sells his wheat can send it to the elevator in the care of his hired man. The employee who sells her services as a secretary, on the other hand, must be present in person to deliver them. If you could buy the physician's skill without the necessity for his personal attention or the housepainter's talent without his having to climb the ladders, labor markets would be much more directly comparable to commodity and other markets. Professor Kenneth Boulding has emphasized this personal characteristic of labor markets in his statement that "the labor market is like the marriage market," because buyers and sellers form habits of accommodation to each other that are not readily broken.[16]

We have recognized this distinctive personal importance of labor marketing in public policy and legislation. We have created public agencies to facilitate labor marketing, notably our nationwide system of public employment offices. We have laws that apply only to labor markets — laws requiring that employers negotiate with unions when a majority of employees want to bargain collectively and other laws limiting job offers to women and children and licensing private

---

[16]For a stimulating discussion of these differences see Boulding's analysis in David McCord Wright (ed.), *The Impact of the Union* (New York: Harcourt, Brace and Co., 1951), p. 254 ff.

employment agencies. The Clayton Act of 1914 declares that "The labor of a human being is not a commodity or article of commerce" (Section 6), thus seeking to differentiate labor markets from all others. The general rule of *specific performance* by which parties to a contract are required to carry out these agreements does not apply to contracts for labor. Such a rule applied to labor, it is held, would permit the equivalent of slavery through contract.

Perishability and Waste

Another distinctive characteristic of labor markets is the high level of potential perishability or waste in unsold services. When workers are unemployed — for whatever reason — much of their potential contribution is irretrievably lost. The worker, unable to effect a sale of his services at a satisfactory price, cannot simply turn off his power and save his strength to be sold at a later date. This differs from the situation in many commodity markets, in which delayed sales need occasion little or no actual waste of resources. This highly perishable nature of labor gives a special atmosphere of urgency to labor markets.

Lack of Standard Unit

Labor markets differ from commodity markets in that they deal in a variety of loosely defined and unequal units. In most commodity markets the unit exchanged is simple and clearly defined. Coal, for example, is sold by the pound or ton, wheat or corn by the bushel, and perfume by the dram or ounce. Markets may recognize several grades, maintaining individual markets for grades A and B or large and small sizes; but they transfer fairly objective measures — pounds, dozens, tons, bushels — of a verifiable standard item.

As has been noted, hours of work may be quite different in quality and quantity of contribution. Even if compensation is based on output, variations in quality, spoilage, and waste may occur. What the employer buys and the employee sells is not a simple, uniform unit of service.

What many employers hope to buy and think they are buying is enthusiastic participation in the work-team's job and the loyalty of workers. They may seek to buy prospective development and improvement and potential for leadership and promotion, with an interest in advancement. They may regard part of the pay for new employees as an investment in training and experience. The employee, in the same market, may expect much more for his services than the price represented by the wage rate. He probably wants stability and security in employment. He may want an opportunity to be trained and developed and promoted. He may expect to be paid more after he has worked 6 months or 1 year or 5 years, even if he is doing the same job. Other employees may expect privileges such as coffee breaks, discounts on products, convenient leaves of absence, and others. They may count on benefits such as sick leave, insurance, private pensions, and hospitalization. On the other hand, some employees want the highest possible take-home pay, attaching less value to long-term opportunities or supplementary benefits.

Because the sale of services involves so many considerations not spelled out in units of work — many of them unmentioned and existing only in the minds of buyers and sellers — misunderstandings and sharp differences of opinion easily arise.[17]

Absence of Uniform Price

Another characteristic in which labor markets differ from many commodity markets is their frequent failure to establish a common, uniform price. In commodity markets establishment of such a market price has long been recognized as one means of identifying markets. In many labor markets, however, workers receive a range of wage rates. Numerous wage surveys report these differences.

Several reasons explain this characteristic of labor markets. In part, this range of rates results because employees regard money wages as only a part of their compensation for work, being supplemented by various employee benefits and services. Other conditions may be regarded by employees as more important than the wage rate. Real or imagined chances for advancement and an employer's policy of promoting from within may assume important proportions in the minds of some employees. Some employers have more local prestige than others. The people with whom an employee works may make a difference. Studies of the reasons given by workers for leaving and changing jobs list a wide range of nonwage conditions that employees describe as being important to them.[18] The range of

---

[17]Many suggestions have been made for a standard unit of work. Perhaps the most common proposal is that which contemplates measuring units of human energy. Philip H. Wickstead proposed using a foot-pound but recognized the difficulty of measuring foot-pounds involved in writing. See his *Common Sense of Political Economy* (London: The Macmillan Co., 1910). For a suggestion of the opportunities for further research, see David Cox and K. D. M. Sharp, "Research on the Unit of Work," *Occupational Psychology*, Vol. 25, No. 2 (April, 1951), pp. 90–108.

[18]For studies of why workers change jobs, see Charles A. Myers and W. Rupert Maclaurin, *The Movement of Factory Workers* (New York: John Wiley and Sons, 1943); Lloyd G.

rates paid in some markets is attributable in part to the fact that these markets operate periodically, at widely separated times, rather than continuously. Also, individual rates may be adjusted for length of service or merit. The limitations of communication and market knowledge also facilitate variations in wage rates. A notable trend toward less dispersion is apparent in many markets in which frequent wage surveys are undertaken and those in which employees sell their services through unions.

Limitations on Market Information

Unlike the situation in many commodity markets, the facts about labor supplies, demands, and current prices are generally not widely publicized. Few regularly published reports describe conditions in labor markets. Financial and commodity markets are usually described daily in newspapers.

LABOR MARKET DYNAMICS

Simpler conceptual models of labor markets are static, i.e., they deal with forces at rest or in equilibrium. Through definition they specify very limited changes in variables, define constants, and exclude many dynamic considerations. Admittedly, real life, operational labor markets are not static and are constantly changing. Modern analysis seeks to formulate models that involve more dynamics.

The concept of dynamics involves movement and change. Thus, in labor markets attention is directed to variables in the conceptual model. We can attempt to measure and analyze these forces inferentially by reference to movements of the participants in labor markets, those who are in the labor force. Such movements can be described in the aggregate, or *macro* sense (e.g., large groups of employees), or in the *micro* sense (i.e., small groups of employees or individuals).

Job Shifts and Labor Mobilities

Chapter 2 noted the importance of geographic shifts in population. In 1960 there were 159 million persons 5 years old and over in the United States. Almost half, some 75 million, had changed residence since 1955 — i.e., in a five-year period. One fifth changed

Reynolds and Joseph Shister, *Job Horizons* (New York: Harper and Brothers, 1949); Charles A. Myers and George P. Shultz, *Dynamics of a Labor Market* (New York: Prentice-Hall, Inc., 1951).

counties within a state. While job changing was only one of the causes of movement, it was a very important influence.[19]

In another type of change, 8 million workers changed employers in 1961. They changed jobs for a variety of reasons, as shown in Figure 5-2. Thus, older men and women were more likely to lose their jobs than younger people. For both men and women those 18–54 were more likely to gain a better job as a result of the shift. Women changed jobs for "personal" rather than "economic" reasons more frequently than men. Different age and sex groups had differing propensities to shift jobs, as shown in Figure 5-3.

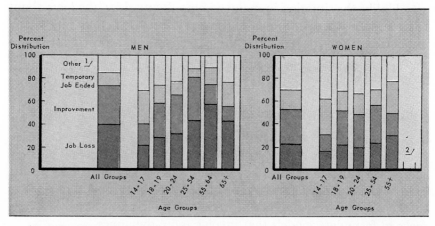

[1]Includes illness, household or school responsibilities, fired, retired, miscellaneous, and reason not reported.
[2]Small number of job changes by women over 65 included with age group 55 and over.

Figure 5-2
JOB CHANGES, BY REASON FOR CHANGE — 1961

Source: *Manpower Report of the President* (Washington 25, D.C.: United States Government Printing Office, March, 1963), p. 58.

Overall, men were more likely to change jobs than women. Older persons were less likely to change than younger workers. Nonwhite men had a higher rate of job change than did white men; but white women had a higher rate of job mobility than nonwhite women. Persons who made several job shifts in 1961 were more likely to be unemployed than those who made only one job shift. The decreasing job mobilities of older workers, especially those over 54 years of age, is in part a reflection of lack of job opportunities and will be discussed

[19]See *Manpower Report of the President* (Washington 25, D.C.: United States Government Printing Office, March, 1963), p. 55.

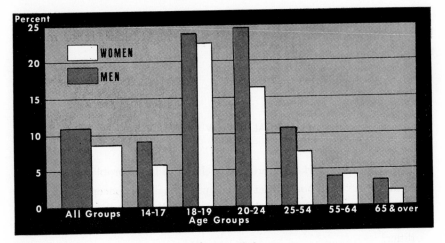

Figure 5-3
PERCENT OF PERSONS CHANGING JOBS, BY AGE AND SEX — 1961[1]

[1]Persons 14 years of age and over who changed jobs, as a percent of those who worked in 1961.

Source: *Manpower Report of the President* (Washington 25, D.C.: United States Government Printing Office, March, 1963), p. 59.

in more detail in Chapter 24. Note, however, that for workers 25 years and older, mobility rates are less than half of those for the 18-24 year old groups.

Job shifts within occupations also show differentials. Thus, in 1961 the rates of job change for selected major occupational groupings were:

Professional and Technical.............	1 in 12
Managers, Officials and Proprietors......	1 in 20
Clerical and Sales....................	1 in 10
Skilled.............................	1 in 7
Semiskilled Operative.................	1 in 7
Laborers (nonfarm)...................	1 in 8

In terms of industry, and by sex:

	Men	Women
Agriculture................................	1 in 11	1 in 20
Construction..............................	1 in 4	—
Manufacturing.............................	1 in 10	1 in 12
Transportation and Public Utilities............	1 in 12	1 in 11
Trade....................................	1 in 7	1 in 8
Service...................................	1 in 8	1 in 11
Government...............................	1 in 16	1 in 14[20]

[20]*Ibid.*, pp. 61 and 192.

The following chapter is concerned with operational labor markets, including employment processes and institutions, labor market frictions, and labor mobilities.

ANALYTICAL REVIEW QUESTIONS

1. How are labor marketing processes related to labor problems?
2. Is the term "the labor market" used operationally or conceptually? Why?
3. What are the major economic functions of labor markets?
4. What characteristics do labor markets have in common? How do they differ?
5. What is meant by the term "controlled" labor markets? Give examples.
6. What justifies the use of simple conceptual labor market models even though they seldom correspond fully with real life operational labor markets?
7. How and why do labor markets allocate labor?
8. What do we seek to maximize in the labor marketing process?
9. How is allocation related to pricing?
10. Give examples of different types of labor markets. How are they differentiated?
11. What is meant by "noncompeting groups"? What is the significance of this concept for labor marketing?
12. How do we measure labor supplies? What problems do we encounter in attempting to quantify such measurement?
13. What is the shape of the typical, simple labor supply curve?
14. What factors affect labor supplies? How can employer hiring practices affect supplies?
15. What are the principal types of labor mobility?
16. What is meant by the term "frictions" in the labor marketing process? Why is this concept important?
17. How do the concepts of "utility" and "disutility" affect labor supplies? What do these terms mean in labor marketing?
18. What is a standard wage rate or scale? What kind of supply curve does this produce?
19. How do job opportunities affect labor supplies?
20. What is meant by the concept that labor is a derived demand?
21. What factors affect labor demands?
22. How are labor market areas generally defined?

23. What are "institutional" labor markets?

24. How do "structured" and "unstructured" institutional labor markets differ? List three types of structured labor markets.

25. What are the distinctive features of labor markets?

26. How are differences in employer and employee expectations related to lack of a standard unit of labor supply?

27. Why do labor markets frequently have a range of wage rates?

28. Are operational labor markets dynamic or static? What evidence supports your position?

29. What groups in the labor market are most likely to make job shifts?

30. How is frequency of job shift related to unemployment?

31. In what occupational groups are job shifts most frequent?

32. In what industry group are job shifts relatively most frequent? In what industry group do women make relatively the most job shifts?

LABOR MARKETS: OPERATIONAL

Chapter 5 has suggested what may be regarded as major variables in labor marketing and has described a model of the labor market. This chapter considers the realities of modern labor marketing. It emphasizes the institutional setting of labor markets in our industrial relations system, and it directs attention to the way workers find jobs and employers find workers.

THE EMPLOYMENT PROCESS: BACKGROUND

The *employment process* consists of matching job requirements and the vocational assets and liabilities of persons in the labor force. Seventy-five million people in the labor force must be distributed in 30,000 different types of jobs, in proper quantities, and at the right time and place. Each employee has a unique combination of aptitudes, interests, abilities, and personality factors. Each job requires a unique combination of employee traits and involves a unique combination of skills, duties, and responsibilities.[1]

Employment may be likened to an engine — an engine that keeps society moving. But no engine realizes its ideal maximum power.

---

[1] See Helen Wood's "Trends in Specialization of Occupational Requirements," (pp. 103–16) and Gladys L. Palmer and Ann R. Miller, "The Occupational and Industrial Distribution of Employment, 1910–1950" (pp. 83–102), both in William Haber *et al.* (eds.), *Manpower in the United States: Problems and Policies* (New York: Harper and Brothers, 1954).

Some of the fuel is wasted completely; gasoline spilled on a filling station driveway is a commonplace sight. This is much like unemployment — manpower resources that are not used at all. Not all of the gasoline that goes into the firing chambers is fully utilized. The same situation holds for employment where countless people are working at jobs that do not fully utilize their optimal capacities. In employment processes the complete waste of manpower through unemployment is more obvious and well known. That subject will be discussed in Chapter 14. The more subtle or disguised unemployment, utilizing only part of an employee's capacities, will be discussed in Chapter 15.

Just as a car can use too much gas (overutilization) or not get the full impact of what it burns (underutilization), so our human resources can be wasted through improper utilization and misallocation. Today's motors are more complex and require a higher, richer grade of gasoline than in the past; today's technological society also requires a higher, richer grade of human resources. Today's 300-horsepower engines are much more complex and more difficult to keep in proper adjustment than the old Model T's of a few years back. Today's labor markets also reflect the complexity of the times and require more complex and intricate adjustment.

The biggest single source of power loss in an engine is friction. The greatest losses of manpower resources are also caused by frictions — *labor market frictions*, defined as the impairment of manpower mobilities.[2] Ignorance, home and family attachments, faulty vocational guidance, institutional barriers such as employment hiring restrictions, union jurisdictional and seniority requirements, and discrimination

---

[2] The basic references on labor mobilities are: Herbert Parnes, *Research on Labor Mobility: An Appraisal of Recent Findings in the United States* (New York: Social Science Research Council, 1954); and Gladys L. Palmer, *Labor Mobility in Six Cities* (New York: Social Science Research Council, 1954). Findings of the latter work are summarized briefly in Charles A. Myers, "Patterns of Labor Mobility," in William Haber *et al.* (eds.), *Manpower in the United States* (New York: Harper and Brothers, 1954), pp. 154–65. Three fifths of all workers in the six-city survey had worked for more than one employer during the decade of the 1940's and only 30 percent of the men and 17 percent of the women had been employed continuously by the same employer during the decade. Over half of the job shifts were "complex," involving changes in employer, industry, and occupation. But reasons underlying these dynamics remain obscure. Myers emphasizes that much more research needs to be done in the "why" of labor mobility, especially the "pushes" and "pulls" of employment.

See also the section on "Mobility of Industry and Labor in the United States" in *Proceedings* of the Industrial Relations Research Association (December 28–30, 1953), pp. 202–33, containing papers by Seymour L. Wolfbein, Meredith B. Givens, Walter Isard, and L. Reed Tripp. Also Joseph Shister, "Labor Mobility: Some Institutional Aspects," in *Proceedings* of the Industrial Relations Research Association (December 28–29, 1950), pp. 42–49.

because of age, sex, race, color, creed, and national origin are examples of labor market frictions that "gum up the works" and keep the employment mechanism from delivering fullest efficiency.

INSTITUTIONAL FACTORS IN BEHAVIOR

The behavior of workers cannot be understood without reference to and appreciation of the major traditions that shape their working behavior. What workers do in getting, holding, and performing jobs would be as meaningless and mystifying without reference to the principal institutions that shape employment as the behavior of teams in a football game to a newcomer from Mars.

All the behavior of employment relationships would presumably be different, for example, if workers were assigned to their jobs by such traditions as are inherent in a caste system. It would require quite different explanations if the institution of slavery maintained master-slave relationships among workers. In our society the traditional institutions are quite different from the caste system or slavery, but they are nonetheless important and influential. Our working relationships and behavior follow patterns defined by the free-enterprise, capitalistic traditions of our economy and by the processes of labor marketing and collective bargaining. We need to note the outstanding characteristics of this institutional framework and the major traditional patterns of thinking and acting that are associated with them.

Our everyday usage defines an *institution* as a system of established, customary, or traditional practice. One major clue to an explanation of human behavior is the institutional setting in which the behavior occurs. We may not be what we are because of our institutions, but we definitely do what we do in large measure because of them. If, therefore, we seek to understand the behavior of work, one important key is a clear view of relevant institutional patterns and practice.

Concepts and Patterns

Institutions, large and small, have been created and developed to accomplish various purposes. They have, therefore, built-in concepts, ideas, and goals. Thus, the custom of paying wages is a way of compensating some workers and of getting people to take jobs. It is an accepted way and a means of attaining an objective of obvious importance. Because such a practice has proved that it works, the tradition has acquired prestige, sanction, and acceptance.

The influence of such institutions is most apparent in their prescription of approved patterns of thinking and acting. Much if not
most of our day-to-day activity, on the job as well as in other situations, conforms to these accepted patterns. We act as we do because
it is "the thing to do." Thus, institutions may create and maintain
a subtle type of social control by specifying behavior patterns that
have wide, uncritical acceptance.

These patterns of acting and of thinking are especially influential
because it is generally easier to follow them than to think through
some other answer. It is generally less trouble to conform than to
deviate. Moreover, these traditional patterns may have powerful
social sanction and approval so that anyone who proposes or introduces a different pattern may be regarded with suspicion as a radical.

Institutional Structures or Systems

The behavior of work is a complex expression of numerous institutional patterns. The concept of political democracy, for example,
exerts an influence on employment, and working behavior is in some
degree expressive of patterns defined by our churches, families, and
schools.

Detailed patterns of practice in employment relationships can be
conveniently grouped about the principal economic institutions with
which they are associated. Thus, the central institutional structure
that directly shapes employment behavior is what we usually call the
free-enterprise system. Another important part of the traditional
structure of our economy is the system of free labor markets upon
which we depend for the disposition or allocation of human resources,
that is, workers. Another cluster of traditional practices is associated
with our system of collective bargaining, in which groups of employees
negotiate with individual employers or employer associations to establish mutually acceptable working conditions.

The free-enterprise system. The free-enterprise system sets the
prevailing patterns in buying, selling, allocating, combining, and using
our resources. It has been described in other terms as the individual
enterprise, private profit, price, venture, and competitive system. Its
distinctive concept and purpose is the idea of permitting workers of
all kinds to venture and shape their own economic destinies within
limits set principally by the prices they can get for what they do. It is
an enterprise system because each worker ventures; that is, he takes a

chance with his personal services and other resources he may control. It is a price system in that resources, including human resources, are exchanged and thus allocated largely through marketing and pricing.

Some critics have argued that only a small portion of all workers are enterprisers. They identify the practice of enterprising exclusively with employers and owners of material resources. Actually, in terms of what they have to venture, many workers take as much of a chance and risk at least as much of what they have in their choice of jobs and of training for jobs.

The distinctive purpose of the system is the satisfaction of material wants through voluntary or free participation in work. As a general principle, it proposes to create and maintain such economic activity as free people, by their own wishes, are willing to carry on, allowing individuals to play whatever roles appeal to them. This is in sharp contrast to earlier systems that limited access to some jobs to those of royal blood or in which economic activity was planned, scheduled, and regulated to increase the wealth of a prince or a state. It is quite different from a system that says: "These jobs must be done, and *you* must do them." The system leans heavily on consumers as the ultimate pricemakers, who thus determine the reward for various accomplishments. It proposes to control economic activity primarily through the mechanism of markets.

One major incentive in this free-enterprise system is the possibility of profit. Participants are encouraged to venture because of this possibility. Free enterprise describes the purpose of this institutional system in almost exactly what these words imply. It prescribes a wide area of freedom in enterprise, liberty to take chances, to try the untried, to experiment, to do what one thinks best. It means that if someone wants to promote a rocket excursion to the moon rather than to assemble bodies in the local Chevrolet plant, that is his privilege. Of course, he may go broke trying; that is his choice and his problem.

Private industrial capitalism. Closely associated with the traditions of the enterprise system are those of the private ownership of capital. The central idea of private capitalism holds that productive tools and equipment may be privately owned; they are personal property. *Capital* is the term that is broadly used to describe material resources that are combined with human resources to produce goods and services for consumers. More particularly, the term includes the plants, machines, facilities, and equipment used in large-scale production. *Industrial capitalism* refers to the application of capital resources in large-scale business enterprises or industries, such as factories, mills, or vast transportation systems. For that reason, industrial capitalism is often described as *the factory system*.

The introduction of industrial capitalism initiated far-reaching changes in a wide range of traditional employment behavior. The home, which had been the workshop in the handicraft system, gave way to the mill and factory. Workers moved toward the workplace, instead of the earlier practice in which work was taken to workers who lived in or near the home of the master craftsmen. The system thus encouraged urbanization of the labor force.

At the same time, the new system tended to reduce the importance of skill and craftsmanship. This same change created new job opportunities for unskilled women and children. Large proportions of all those employed in the early factories were composed of these secondary workers. The new system of industrial capitalism tended to magnify cycles of employment and unemployment. It provided mass employment; but when the factories shut down, mass unemployment also appeared. Economic insecurity of workers was increased, compared to that prevailing under both the agricultural era and the handicraft stage.

Business organization. As industrial capitalism developed, it modified the whole traditional structure of business. As capital requirements increased, individuals found it necessary or advantageous to join with others to provide capital. Thus, the partnership, the corporation, and the bank became major capital-suppliers. In large measure they replaced the individual master craftsmen and the small shop-owner. Business leadership and direction passed into the hands of bankers, corporate boards, and corporation executives. Stockholder-owners were separated by a vast social distance from the workers who used their capital. An impersonal "legal person" became the employer — the company, the railroad, or the corporation. Owners changed daily as stocks were bought and sold in security markets. Some workers became the paid, professional managers for the absentee stockholders. Others became employees of the new business structures.

New roles for workers. The combination of private ownership and industrial capitalism specialized a group of financial workers who make it their function to encourage saving and to mobilize and invest their own savings and those of others. It created a group of proprietors, owners, employers, and managers, who use their own capital and that of others to provide stores, mills, factories, railroads, power plants, and other businesses. It developed a vast army of employees, who sell their services for wages and salaries to employers.

Those who now play these roles tend to act out these new and different parts. Proprietor-employer-managers emphasize the necessity for minimizing costs, getting highest prices, and maximizing profits. To that end, they propose to expand or restrict operations and employment, with estimates or forecasts of profits a major consideration in these changes. They may expect to employ the numbers and types of workers they require when they need them and to be absolved of responsibility for them when they are not needed.

Employees in this free enterprise system are expected to act in a manner dominated by their desire to maximize their personal returns. In general, they seek the highest wage available to them, subject to other considerations they may regard as controlling. In accordance with the traditions of the system, they can feel free to leave one employer to work for another they regard as more promising. They may conserve their strength, doing only as much as they have to or as they feel is appropriate under the circumstances as they see them.

Agency management. Industrialization has resulted in more large scale organizations, private and public. Fewer owners manage their own businesses — instead they hire managers to act as agents of the owners, i.e., agency management. Ownership through stockholding in private enterprise has become more diffuse and widespread. Likewise, managers of big public organizations may be regarded as agents of the public.

Agency managers are hired managers (employees) and typically are not dominant owners. As their duties and responsibilities become more complex, these managers have become more professional. They have more graduate and postgraduate training. They exercise a form of team leadership not unlike a college football coach, with a premium on delivering victories. The institution of agency management places heavy emphasis upon effective and satisfying employment of human resources. It is significant that both agency managers and union leaders are increasingly sensitive to employee needs and perceptions.

Free labor markets. The same changes that brought about the shift from merchant to trader and then to industrial capitalism also introduced the system of free labor markets. In terms of its viewpoint and philosophy, the institution of free labor marketing is as distinctive and as radical a change from earlier practice as the enterprise economy.

Workers exercise choice in the jobs they seek and accept and in the conditions under which they work. No authority can say: "Wait a minute, you've been assigned to coal mining," or "You are barred from certain jobs." One who has long been an unskilled employee may prepare himself and try for a job as a semiskilled technician. A union officer may enter a market for managers. A student whose father is an unskilled laborer may enter markets for engineers, lawyers, or physicians. Jobs are offered, services are tendered, and the work of people is exchanged at various prices.

With some restrictions, human services are bought and sold, shifted from one job to another, and thus assigned throughout our complex economy by this marketing process. Some controls are imposed — for example, by child labor and minimum wage laws and by licensing requirements for certain professional groups. For the larger part of the labor force, however, these markets are the means by which workers get and change jobs.

Brief mention should be made of the open-class social system that reinforces the free labor marketing process and encourages greater labor mobility with frequent job changes. Workers find an added incentive to shop around in job markets in the hope that they can improve their social status by finding and holding better paid jobs. This open-class social system characteristic of our society is also somewhat distinctive. In many other societies social status and acceptance are largely determined by birth and family; social classes are sharply defined; citizens do not cross lines.

In contrast, our society has tended to identify social status with economic status. Workers may improve their social status simply by "making good," that is, by their economic success. While other considerations also carry varying degrees of prestige, income is a major factor. Levels of occupational income come as close to class marks as any prevailing in our society. Hence social acceptance and recognition are closely associated with occupations, and freedom to change jobs is a matter of social as well as economic concern. The open-class social system thus reinforces our traditional support for free labor markets.[3]

---

[3]Actually, of course, job selection is influenced by many considerations. See, for interesting studies of first jobs and careers, Reinhard Bendix, Seymour M. Lipset, and F. Theo-

Collective bargaining. Another institution deserves special mention as a part of the current cultural and traditional background of industrial relations, for it exerts a powerful influence on the behavior of workers in our economy. Its traditional practices affect both labor marketing or allocation and day-to-day working relationships on the job. The institution is *collective bargaining,* which means group negotiation and administration of working conditions.

In collective bargaining unions are authorized by employees to act for their members in dealing with potential employers. Labor organizations or unions negotiate with employers to establish *labor contracts* or *collective agreements.* Such contracts or agreements specify wages, hours, and numerous other working conditions. They may indicate, for example, how employees get promotions, what conditions justify discharge, who loses his job first in periods of layoff, who is called back first, who gets a pension and how much, and what benefits — hospitalization, insurance, housing, loans, etc. — shall be available to employees. Unions also speak for their members in disputes over contract provisions and argue for them when they have grievances. They present a united front for their members when issues arise between these employees and their employers.

In collective bargaining unions of employees always represent individual workers. Employers may bargain as individuals, or they, too, may join with other employers in an employer association.

Collective bargaining, like the other institutions described in this chapter, is relatively new, but it has become an institution of major influence as economies were industrialized. The first unions appeared as what were known as yeomanry guilds in the declining years of the handicraft system. Unions appeared as the overt form of a worker protest movement generated by the process of industrialization. Employer associations frequently followed to mobilize the opposing strength of employers.

Collective bargaining prescribes a wide range of behavior patterns that are prominent in current industrial relations. Most spectacular is the strike, but the practices of day-to-day union-employer relationships are even more important for our purposes. Many employer and employee attitudes and activities would mean little without reference to the purpose and the traditional patterns of collective

dore Malm, "Social Origins and Occupational Career Patterns," *Industrial and Labor Relations Review,* Vol. 7, No. 2 (January, 1954), pp. 246–61; Seymour M. Lipset, "First Jobs and Career Patterns," *American Journal of Economics and Sociology,* Vol. 14, No. 3 (April, 1955), pp. 247–61.

bargaining.   Negotiating sessions, ultimatums, *rounds* of wage increases, pattern bargains that replicate key agreements in other
employment, grievance procedures, labor arbitration, and many other
common practices are associated with this institution.   The attitudes
of employees that explain their willingness to accept a standard wage,
to insist on seniority rights to jobs and overtime, to refuse to cross
picket lines, to maintain *union jurisdictions* (which define certain jobs
as belonging to members of a particular union) — these and many
others are most readily explained in terms of the traditions of unionism
and collective bargaining.   Although only a fourth of our workers
belong to unions, the influence of collective bargaining extends
throughout all employment relationships. Chapters 7 through 13 give
detailed attention to unions, employer associations, and collective
bargaining.

THE OPERATIONAL EMPLOYMENT PROCESS

Preceding pages have briefly described the major institutions that
shape employment in our type of economy.   Attention turns next to
the actual process of job-getting and holding and changing, i.e., to
the operational employment process.

Choosing an Occupation

There is abundant evidence that the employment process in the
United States does not function with 100 percent efficiency.   Labor
turnover, grievances, unrest, accidents, unemployment, and underemployment are symptoms of imperfection in labor marketing. Frequently the causes of such malfunctioning may be traced back to the
fact that people seek, or get into, the wrong jobs.   They do not choose
their occupations wisely.

As shown in Chapter 2, more and more jobs require lengthy and
specialized formal training.   The vast majority of today's jobs require
a high school education. An increasing proportion require a four-year
college degree, and the demand for professional graduate training is
gaining by leaps and bounds.   The most important single pre-
employment problem faced by an individual, therefore, probably is
in the area of selecting the proper amount and type of education.
This requires a long-term forecast of job opportunities; an assessment
of the individual's aptitudes, interests, and personality; and a careful
equating of these two sets of factors.

The average individual does not equate his vocational assets and job demands by himself. Few if any of us are able to make such appraisals correctly; hence we seek *vocational guidance*. Vocational guidance can be informal and nonprofessional or it can be formal and professional. Informal, nonprofessional guidance comes about most frequently through self-appraisal and through the advice of friends and relatives. Indeed, much vocational guidance comes too late, that is, after the person has entered the job market. Here he (in effect) offers his haphazardly trained and developed resources in an attempt to fill whatever jobs require the resources that he brings to the labor market. The labor market entrant in this situation is likely to go from firm to firm, usually seeking advice about job openings from friends, relatives, and neighbors. The latter probably have more knowledge of job openings than does the job applicant, but their labor market and employment knowledge is apt to be limited and distorted.

Because occupational and geographic mobility of labor force members may exert a powerful influence on worker productivity and contribution, many studies have sought to discover factors that appear prominent in occupational choices. Several of them conclude that one significant clue to this choice is the occupation of fathers — sons tend to select occupations at a similar or higher level than their fathers.[4] When children enter occupations higher or lower in skill requirements than their parents, this is known as *vertical mobility*.

The schools also enter into the vocational guidance process in varying degrees and with substantial variability in their effectiveness. Some schools, usually the larger city schools, have formal vocational guidance programs that help young people find their proper niche. Others, usually smaller rural schools, do not have adequate staffs or resources to provide professional guidance. Hence, the future labor market entrant may be operating in an aura of ignorance and wishful thinking. Jobs have very definite emotional and prestige, as well as economic, attributes.

Matching Men and Jobs

Employment consists of matching men and jobs, but that is not all. Unless the matching is done accurately, inefficient production will

[4]See A. J. Jaffee and R. O. Carleton, *Occupational Mobility in the United States* (New York: King's Crown Press, 1954); Seymour Martin Lipset and Reinhard Bendix, *Social Mobility in Industrial Society* (Berkeley: University of California Press, 1959).

result. Optimal productivity depends upon equating job requirements and the capabilities of those who fill jobs. When a person is placed in the wrong job, misplacement occurs. No one knows the amount of misplacement in our society.

Each job has a unique set of worker requirements, although some jobs overlap in requirements. Those that overlap extensively are called *job families*. Each individual has a unique combination of brains and brawn — of personality, physique, aptitudes, abilities, and interests. One entire field of psychology is concerned with individual differences.[5] Job requirements can be measured through *job analysis* (study of jobs), and employees can be measured and appraised in terms of their corresponding specific vocational assets. Through vocational guidance people can be prepared to enter occupations suited to their personality, abilities, aptitudes, and interests. Through *differential placement* in the employing organization they can be placed selectively in jobs commensurate with their talents.

The results of improper matching of men and jobs show up in labor turnover, lowered productivity, industrial accidents, low employee morale, absenteeism, and other employment problems. Many, if not most, of these problems originate in improper placement. Our loose hiring procedures increase our proportions of employees who quit their jobs and who are low producers. In some cases we hire persons underqualified for their jobs, and in others we hire people who are overqualified.

In practice placement is difficult because accurate placement requires measurement and research, experimentation, and scientific method. This means that vocational guidance and placement are tasks for professionals even as is medicine. Unfortunately, most guidance and placement are done by rank amateurs. Occupations have prestige as well as monetary values; far more high school students desire to enter the professions than have the personal capacities required for success in professions.

Parents and friends may do a poor job of vocational guidance because they misjudge the child's aptitudes, ability, and temperament. They may have faulty information about job requirements. They may try to realize their own thwarted vocational status and

---

[5]Some basic references on individual differences include: Leona E. Tyler, *The Psychology of Human Differences* (New York: Appleton-Century Co., Inc., 1947); Anne Anastasi, *Differential Psychology* (New York: The Macmillan Co., 1958); and James S. Jenkins and D. G. Paterson, *Studies in Individual Differences: The Search for Intelligence* (New York: Appleton-Century-Crofts, 1961).

prestige aims through the child or seek to perpetuate a family employment tradition. Employers also aid and abet the problem of employment misfits. All too frequently they overemphasize past experience
as a hiring criterion. They may seek to judge a job applicant's abilities,
interests, and potentials on the basis of subjective impressions. Employers may misuse personnel measuring instruments such as psychological tests. They may not utilize realistic, objective job specifications
and may set artificial hiring limits based on age, sex, race, education,
appearance, and other factors that may not be related to job success on
the specific job for which they are hiring.[6]

It should not be assumed that all hiring mistakes concern
threshold or entry employees on their first job. Most employees can be
expected to change jobs through labor turnover, promotion, and
transfer; hence, professional vocational guidance and selective placement policies and techniques must be brought into play throughout
an employee's vocational career. Both jobs and people change through
time to further complicate the guidance process. Vocational guidance
must be a continuing process.

Choosing the Right Employees

On the demand side, employers should seek the best-qualified
employees on the basis of objectively determined job requirements.
The study of jobs is known as *job analysis*. Through job analysis we
obtain specific information about job duties and requirements and
the characteristics of employees needed to meet such duties and requirements. Employing organizations with industrial relations departments usually make such objective appraisals both of jobs and of
candidates for employment.[7] Through the process of *selective* or *differential placement*, employers place candidates in jobs for which they are
best suited. Differential placement in a firm is the counterpart of vocational guidance in the school or employment agency. It is based
upon psychological and physical examinations and objective job analysis. It permits and facilitates optimal allocation, use, development,
and conservation of manpower resources.

---

[6]Probably the best single reference on employee selection and placement is C. Harold
Stone and W. E. Kendall, *Effective Personnel Selection Procedures* (Englewood Cliffs, New
Jersey: Prentice-Hall Inc., 1956.)

[7]Some evidence of the growth of personnel and labor relations jobs is provided by the
1960 United States census of population, which shows an increase of 87 percent since 1950,
up from 52,000 to 98,000 in 1960.

Unfortunately, many employers do not have professional manpower management staffs. Such firms are apt to base their hiring requirements and decisions upon prejudice and opinion. They may tend to overemphasize educational and experience requirements. They may have prejudices and hiring restrictions with respect to age, sex, or race.

The "Pushes" and "Pulls" of Employment

People enter the labor market for many and diverse reasons. Some people quit school because they do not like school. Others lack financial resources to continue their education even though they and society could profit by their further education. The underutilization and waste of our manpower resources through educational dropouts is great. Many drop out of school because they become discouraged or lack motivation. Some drop out through the *push* of economic need — for example, to support a family. Others enter the labor market through the *pull* of economic desire — perhaps they desire a hot rod with duals, four-barrel carburetor, and all the trimmings. Often the urgency of the push or the pull, plus labor market ignorance, causes them to take the first job that comes along — or at least one for which they are not best suited. This results in an economic waste and misapplication of human resources that we have called underemployment.

It is unfortunate that once in the labor market these people tend to stay there — going through a series of poor placements in response to new pushes and pulls in their lives. The average worker changes jobs once every 3.2 years. Ex-employees may have quit, been fired, or laid off. Regardless of the reason, if they were misplaced, they now have a chance for proper placement. But most people find new jobs by going to firms "cold" or upon advice of job openings from friends and relatives.

How People Get Jobs

The worker's view of job opportunity does not resemble the concepts of economic men who allegedly seek to maximize their wages. Job-seeking activities by the typical worker are largely a product of his environment. Ignorance of labor market conditions, immobility, and the customs of his group exert tremendous influence on his labor

market behavior. He may get his knowledge about jobs and job opportunities from his associates, a classic case of the "blind leading the
blind." Opportunity is of prime importance: he "hears" that they're
hiring at Swift's, or he knows of several plants where he can leave an
application. Many employers also rely heavily upon this form of behavior and, instead of seeking out qualified applicants, wait for them
to show up at the factory gates.

In good times most job changes are due to quits; in bad times most
job changes are due to layoffs. Workers leaving jobs voluntarily quit
for many reasons other than economic reasons. In general, men quit
more often for economic reasons, whereas women quit more frequently for personal reasons. Unsatisfactory working conditions and
unsatisfactory supervision bulk larger than wages in the reasons for
leaving jobs for both men and women. In a very large proportion of
cases, employees quit a job without having a job offer elsewhere. In
short, most people do not quit their jobs for the pull of a better job,
but quit instead because of the push of disagreeable (to them) features
on their present jobs.

Job satisfaction surveys show that male employees report the
following features of jobs as most important to them (ranked in order
from most to least important): (1) job security, (2) opportunity for
advancement, (3) type of work or nature of job, (4) pride in work, and
(5) pay and co-workers (tied for 5th place). Women like to be different and they rank (1) type of work, (2) security, and (3) advancement,
in that order.[8]

The importance of interests in job satisfaction may be inferred
from studies that show that the likelihood of being dissatisfied with
one's work is only about one third as great for those who go into a line
of work consistent with their interest test scores as for those who do
not.[9]

Most workers face multiple careers involving: (1) preparation for
a job (for example, formal education), (2) securing the first job, (3) securing additional jobs, and (4) retirement. In many cases the cycle
is interrupted by exit from the labor force for a period of time (for
example, a woman leaves to have and raise a child and then returns to
the labor force).

---

[8]See Clifford E. Jurgenson, "What Job Applicants Look for in a Company," *Personnel Psychology*, Vol. 1, No. 1 (Winter, 1948), pp. 433–45.

[9]G. Frederic Kuder, "A Rationale for Evaluating Interests," *Educational and Psychological Measurement*, Vol. 23, No. 1 (Spring, 1963), p. 5.

The implications of such motivation for optimal manpower allocation, utilization, and conservation may not be apparent. Mobility of labor is vital to a healthy, dynamic economy. But mobility has two aspects: (1) quantitative and (2) qualitative. The qualitative aspect is far and away the most important in a complex technological society that requires increasing amounts of brain power and decreasing amounts of brawn power. This accounts for public policy designed to ensure appropriate utilization of manpower. Public education and compulsory school attendance, child labor laws, and public employment services attest to the fact that modern societies cannot afford to leave the operation of their labor markets to chance.

JOB-FACILITATING INSTITUTIONS

People seek and obtain jobs in various ways, utilizing institutions ranging from highly informal to more structured or formal. These job-facilitating institutions include gate hiring facilities, union hiring halls, school guidance services, and private and public employment agencies. Each of these institutions facilitates job-getting and job-giving, albeit with varying degrees of effectiveness. Labor supplies and demands are typically filtered through one or more job-facilitating institutions.

Gate Hirings

Most employees begin their job-seeking at the company gate, either sent by friends and relatives or on their own volition. Here they are screened and evaluated by the personnel department in larger companies or by line management in smaller companies. They are usually accepted or rejected in terms of a specific job for which they apply. In more enlightened companies selective placement is used, and the candidate may be referred to other jobs in the company for which he has suitable vocational assets. He is developed or trained for his new job, although such training is usually of short duration. (Those who have the capacity to finish college and do not are not likely to find a company that will send them to college.) After being on the job, they may be transferred or promoted; or they may quit or be laid off, in which case the employment process starts again.

Union Hiring Halls

In some industries the selection process is done by unions. Employers needing help contact the union business agent who sends out a "qualified" employee. This is done in such industries as construction, printing trades, and the maritime industries. Unions usually do not have adequate measurement devices for appraising the potential talents of workers, and thus they may help to misallocate manpower resources through a series of subjective impressions. In highly skilled trades requiring apprenticeship, public policy recognizes this possible misallocation, and apprenticeship standards are recommended by the government in cooperation with employers and unions.

In the case of employees selected by either unions or employers, it is frequently asserted that there is no need for scientific selection procedures; that water will seek its own level; and that good employees will "make out" on their own efforts and poor ones will not. Such arguments have some merits, for "trial by fire" is essential in many jobs. But these arguments overlook the costs of labor turnover if the employee quits or is laid off. They overlook the waste through low production of misplaced employees. Where such an employee can survive the probationary period and has seniority and other forms of union-provided security, he can become a permanent misfit and low-grade producer.

School Guidance Services

As noted, many schools and colleges provide student personnel services that provide several types of guidance, including vocational guidance. Students are measured in terms of aptitudes, abilities, interest, and temperament and are counseled and trained to prepare them for appropriate vocational careers. Cooperative work-study plans help acquaint the student with the "taste" of work. Many schools run placement services, and employers frequently consult such sources in their quest for job applicants. Sometimes scholarships are available for further development of students with special talents, and the student guidance and personnel service also may play an important role in the employment process.

Employment Agencies

Some employees and employers seek the help of specialists in the marketing of labor, that is, employment agencies. Most private employment agencies charge a fee, whereas public employment services do not. The rationale behind a public employment service is that society loses when manpower resources are idle or misdirected and, conversely, that society gains when manpower resources are utilized properly. Public employment services deal with employment problems like public health agencies deal with health problems.

Private employment agencies. Public employment services arrange only a small proportion of the total number of placements and job changes. Perhaps as many shifts are handled through private employment offices, including those operated by individual firms, by associations of employers, by fraternal associations and churches, and by individuals who maintain them as private business enterprises.

Most of these private employment offices are limited in the geographic scope of their activities. They register applicants for local jobs only, having no facilities for clearing with other localities. In recent years, however, some private agencies have expanded, opening offices in several communities. Also, some local offices have, for many years, acted as recruiting agencies for employers in distant localities. For the most part, however, private employment agencies have concentrated their efforts on local jobs and applicants.

Private employment services have encountered serious criticisms. For many years they operated without public regulation. However, serious questions arose in the minds of many citizens with respect to the propriety and the practices of some private, fee-charging agencies. Some of the early private fee-charging services gave out misleading information on the jobs they sought to fill, charged what were regarded as exorbitant fees, discriminated against racial and other minorities, connived with employers to cause rapid labor turnover and thus increase their fees, and indulged in other objectionable practices. As a result, most states now regulate the activities of such agencies. In some foreign nations they are prohibited.

Fourty-four states, the District of Columbia, and Puerto Rico have laws regulating private employment agencies. The more comprehensive laws include the following features:

1. Requirement of a license and surety bond.
2. Regulation of placement fees.
3. Prohibition of undesirable practices.
4. Standards for records and reports.
5. Requirement for posting of license, fee schedule, and copy of the law.
6. Provision for administrative authority to make rules and enforce the law.

Coverage of these laws varies from state to state. Most states set standards that must be met before a license will be issued. Private agencies may charge an applicant a registration fee, placement fee, or both; 16 states prohibit registration fees. Placement fees are regulated in only 16 states; 10 states limit maximum placement fees. Typical sliding scales (based on earnings) range from 10 to 60 percent of the first month's salary, usually paid by the applicant.

Prohibited practices include: (1) misrepresentation of jobs, (2) splitting fees, (3) sending applicants without job orders, (4) sending applicants to places where a labor dispute exists, (5) sending applicants to illegal establishments, (6) sending minors to illegal occupations, (7) inducing employers to discharge or employees to quit, (8) using misleading name for the agency, and (9) making false entries in their registries. Penalties for violation include revocation of license, fines, and jail sentences.

The 4,500 private, fee-charging employment agencies provide a major share of all assistance in finding both jobs and personnel. Their 20,000 employees are more numerous than the staff of the United States Employment Service and the related state employment services. Private employment agencies have shown a sharp growth in the last two decades, about 250 percent, and this has been accomplished despite greatly expanded and improved public employment service activities during the same period.[10]

Regulation of private agencies cannot legally go to the extent of prohibiting them or regulating their fees. These two types of legislation have recently been held unconstitutional (in Washington and New York cases).

Many private employment agencies now provide excellent service, both to employers and to applicants. They do collect fees which are usually paid by those for whom they find jobs. On the other hand, they frequently provide extensive service to registrants, including testing and vocational guidance in addition to referrals.

Public policy today regards the private employment services as a desirable part of our total job-finding and recruiting facilities. No effort is made to route all applicants through the public offices nor to require the registration of all jobs in these offices, although the latter frequently undertake campaigns to encourage employers and employees to make more use of their services. Private fee-charging

---

[10]Abstracted from E. U. Fierst and William Lawson, "State Laws Regulating Private Employment Agencies," United States Department of Labor *Bulletin 209*, January, 1960.

agencies play an important part, however, in recruitment and placement, especially for clerical, technical, and professional jobs.   In
many cases they serve a valuable recruiting, testing, and screening
function, especially for small employers with nonprofessional employment departments.

Public employment offices. To help job hunters and employers in
getting together, a federal-state, nationwide system of public employment offices is maintained in the United States. Overall supervision
of the service is performed by the United States Employment Service,
which is in the Bureau of Employment Security, Department of Labor.
Cooperating state employment services maintain local offices in all
states.

In many areas the service provides specialized divisions for agriculture, for veterans, and for clerical, technical, and professional
placements. It may offer the services of its staff to aid employers in
improving personnel management, including the testing of applicants.
It may provide vocational counseling for registrants. State employment services handle all claims for unemployment insurance. At the
federal level the Bureau of Employment Security directs campaigns to
encourage the selective placement of handicapped workers, improve
the placement of older workers and minority groups, and control the
temporary admission of foreign workers in agriculture. In World
War II the entire system was federalized and became the operating
division of the War Manpower Commission.

Public policy with respect to employment offices has undergone a
number of changes.   In our early history private offices provided
practically the only job-finding assistance.   Later, cities and states
established public exchanges, and, still later, the federal government
joined in the maintenance and encouragement of a nationwide system
of public exchanges.

Expansion of these public agencies was indicative of a growing
public opinion that, in an economy as vast and complicated as ours,
there is a social responsibility for assisting workers to find the best
possible jobs and for aiding employers in getting help when and where
it is needed. This conviction has become stronger whenever widespread job scarcity or labor scarcity attracted public attention.
Depression and war have been the major occasions for expansions in
public employment services.

The present federal-state cooperative system was created by the
Wagner-Peyser Act of 1933. In 1935 the Social Security Act added

powerful incentives for developing state systems of unemployment insurance. The act specified that benefits must be paid through public employment offices. Thus, the federal-state system assumed the dual role of matching people and jobs, on the one hand, and administering unemployment insurance, on the other.[11]

In the present system states operate approximately 2,000 full-time local offices plus another 2,000 part-time itinerant offices, the latter open for one or two days each week. Offices are maintained by all fifty states, the District of Columbia, Puerto Rico, and the Virgin Islands. Federal funds for administration by each state are provided—without matching by the states — contingent upon compliance with standards established by the federal agency.

Under the federal-state system, the major peacetime activities of the United States Employment Service may be outlined as follows:

1. Development, maintenance, and administration of standards of performance for state systems as a basis for determining their eligibility to receive federal funds.

2. Maintenance of interstate clearance in which needs for labor and employment opportunities in one state are communicated to offices in other states.

3. Provision of dependable urban and rural labor market information on both a local and a nationwide basis. For this purpose, as already noted, major labor markets are regularly classified on the basis of current and prospective demands for and supplies of labor.

4. Maintenance of a continuing program of research designed to improve all the operations of local services and national clearance and to form a sound basis for necessary legislative changes.

5. Publication of the monthly *Employment Service Review*, reporting labor market conditions and the activities of cooperating state and federal services.

State employment services have the following major responsibilities under the present system:

1. To provide an effective referral service in major labor markets and thus to facilitate the balancing of labor supplies and demands. In this function the local offices register, interview, test, and counsel applicants for jobs; accept and classify requisitions for workers from employers; and refer suitable applicants.

---

[11]For an informative history of the United States Employment Service, see "The Public Employment Service System, 1933–1953," *Employment Security Review*, Vol. 20, No. 6, June, 1953 (entire issue). For more detail on the federal-state system of employment offices see William Haber and Daniel H. Kruger, *The Role of the United States Employment Service in a Changing Economy* (Kalamazoo, Michigan: W. E. Upjohn Institute for Employment Research, February, 1964). For an international comparison of public services, see E. Wight Bakke, *A Positive Labor Market Policy* (Columbus, Ohio: Charles E. Merrill Books, Inc., 1964).

2. Receive, investigate, and pay claims for unemployment insurance benefits.
3. Gather and release local labor market information; reporting employment conditions, wages, and earnings; and forwarding this information to the United States Employment Service. For this purpose local offices generally prepare and release a monthly newsletter summarizing important changes during the preceding month and providing detailed statistics.
4. Assist employers in improving their use of such techniques as job analysis, testing, counseling, training, and others.
5. Assist communities in planning employment for the future, maintaining appropriate training and retraining programs, and creating new and better employment opportunities.
6. Give special attention to problems of veterans, the aged, youth, and to the selective placement of handicapped workers.

Both federal and state employment services face difficult problems. Only a small portion of all job openings are reported to these services. Some employers are opposed to the public agencies as a matter of principle, holding that they tend to destroy private enterprise in this field. In some localities many employers favor private employment offices, rather than public agencies, for all but the least skilled jobs. In some communities public employment offices are regarded as sources for only the least marketable applicants. Discrimination on the basis of race, nationality, or religion cannot be practiced or facilitated by these offices, a policy that interferes with their use by some employers. Public offices cannot refer strikebreakers. These restrictions, although they may be justified by national public policy, limit use of the services in some localities.

The changing nature of the placement activities of the public employment service may be illustrated by the following figures for the period 1955–1959:

1. Professional and managerial placements — increased from 99,500 to 147,000.
2. Clerical and sales placements — increased from 730,000 to 835,000.
3. Skilled placements — increased from 312,000 to 335,000.
4. Semiskilled placements — increased from 733,000 to 802,000.
5. Unskilled placements — declined by 171,000.

Unemployed workers account for only 20 percent of employer hires or accessions, new entrants and reentrants for another 20 percent, and 60 percent are the result of job changes without any significant period of intervening unemployment.

The public employment service is strengthening its services to the employed and to brainpower jobs. It is not concerned only with unskilled unemployed, despite a common conception to that effect.[12] However, as a result of the fact that the public service makes a substantial portion of its placements from among those already employed, private agencies have sharply opposed such alleged "unfair competition."

Fair Employment Practices Commissions

Fair employment practices (FEP) laws, ordinances, and commissions seek to prevent discrimination. Such policies are intended to aid the community by promoting general welfare through improved utilization of manpower resources and reduction of unrest. They seek to provide each individual with job opportunity and equality on the basis of merit rather than prejudice.

For the employer they seek to expand his labor market in terms of increasing the supply of qualified employees, to facilitate use of the most qualified employee on every job, to give meaning to and gain acceptance of a free enterprise philosophy for employees as well as employers, and to add to the buying power of the community, thereby expanding the employer's market. For the employee, FEP aims at safeguarding the philosophy and practices of equality of opportunity, eliminating restrictive practices, providing the right to work at a job of his own choosing, and preserving the dignity of the individual.

Most FEP ordinances cover relations between and among employers, workers, unions, and employment agencies. They are administered by commissions representing the public interest who serve generally without compensation. Complaints are referred to a paid staff member, who investigates the case and attempts conciliation where warranted or dismisses the case where the facts do not bear out the allegations. These efforts are generally undertaken on a confidential, not public, basis. If conciliation efforts fail, the case is

---

[12]William Haber, "The U.S. Employment Service in a Changing Economy," *Studies in Unemployment*, U.S. Senate Special Committee on Unemployment Problems, *86th Congress, 2nd Session* (Washington, D.C.: U.S. Government Printing Office 1960), pp. 283–309. See esp. pp. 298–99. For a significant set of proposals to strengthen and improve the quality of the operations of the public employment service see E. Wight Bakke, *A Positive Labor Market Policy* (Columbus, Ohio: Charles E. Merrill Books, Inc., 1964). See also, William Haber and Daniel H. Kruger, *The Role of the United States Employment Service in a Changing Economy* (Kalamazoo, Michigan: W. E. Upjohn Institute for Employment Research, February, 1964).

generally referred to the commission, which attempts further conciliation and, if that fails, may hold public hearings and present the case to the courts. Some FEP commissions lack enforcement powers; under many ordinances, however, discrimination is a misdemeanor and is punishable by a fine and/or imprisonment (usually up to $100 and/or 90 days).

Most FEP commissions seek to prevent rather than to penalize discrimination. They emphasize educational activities and provide employment codes such as those relating to the nature of items admissible on application forms or blanks. Contrary to general impressions, FEP commissions do not confine their efforts to discrimination in hiring. Instead they deal with all phases of employment, including promotion, layoff, discharge, training rights, and many others. They can and do deal with discrimination by unions and public agencies as well as by employers. Usually they deal with discrimination based on race or color, creed or religion, and national origin. In some cases age discrimination is prohibited also.

Federal FEP

In July, 1964, Congress passed the long-debated Civil Rights Bill. This Civil Rights Act of 1964 includes a fair employment practice (FEP) section. Effective date of FEP provisions was set at one year following date of passage. Initial coverage is for firms in interstate commerce with 100 or more employees; after one year, those with 75 or more; after two years, those with 50 or more; and after three years, those with 25 or more. Discrimination in employment on the basis of race, religion, color, sex, or national origin is forbidden.

Enforcement on a voluntary basis is sought through a federal Equal Employment Opportunity Commission. This agency would enter a dispute only after appropriate local and state FEP commissions have exhausted their efforts. Where voluntary efforts do not bring a resolution, the person claiming discrimination can bring civil suit.

The Attorney General may sue for injunctions where he finds reasonable cause or belief that there is "a pattern or practice of resistance" to the employment rights promised by the act. He may request a court of three judges in a federal district court to hear the case, and the court is required to expedite the case. Appeal from the decision of this court is made directly to the United States Supreme Court.

Since almost all of the existing FEP commissions were in the North, the federal FEP is having its greatest impact in the South. It will take several years to establish major administrative rules and to provide court interpretations that "spell out" rights, obligations, and operational requirements and procedures under the act.

LABOR MOBILITIES

In the abstract model of the labor market, pricing is assumed to equilibrate demands and supplies. As earlier sections of this chapter indicate, however, both demands and supplies are dependent variables, being influenced by various institutional and personal characteristics. Such modifiers create frictions in the actual marketing process, and they impose constraints on the mobilities of workers.

Effective use, maintenance, and development of manpower resources occur largely on the job. Adequate employment processes, policies, techniques, and instruments are essential to the functioning of labor markets — individual, local, regional, and national. When employment functions are being performed properly, we tend to approach the most effective use of our manpower resources. When marketing fails to balance demands and supplies, human resources are wasted through unemployment, underemployment, and overemployment. Labor mobilities are essential adjustment mechanisms in a dynamic economy.

Variables Associated with Labor Mobilities

Since World War II there have been numerous studies of labor mobilities, their characteristics and correlates. Most of these have been studies of local labor markets. Few of these studies have had a common framework in terms of design and workers studied. Most of them have emphasized labor supplies rather than labor demands (or both). Most of them have contrasted differential demographic features of mobile versus nonmobile workers. Few studies have dealt adequately with motivational factors.

These local labor market studies have the advantage of digging deeper into situations where fewer rather than more variables are involved. Hence they explain and predict these specific market situations better than would generalized explanations for the United States as a whole, for example. They have the disadvantage, generally, of not being additive and, hence, it is very difficult to generalize about the characteristics of mobility.

Herbert S. Parnes, however, has summarized these studies.[13] The general picture that he draws suggests duality of job attachment. There is a considerable segment of the labor force with stability of job attachment; another sizeable segment is flexible, or mobile.[14] In some years total job separations approach half of the job total. However, the number of workers who separate is always smaller than the total number of jobs from which they separate. This is because of *recidivism*, i.e., a minority of job changers account for a disproportionate share of job changes.

Most job changes are complex in the sense that they involve three types of mobility simultaneously, i.e., change of employer, occupation, and industry. Within a single decade in one large study, one third of the workers changed industry (broadly defined), and one third of the men and one fourth of the women also changed from one major occupational group to another. Geographical mobility is less than occupational or industrial. Many workers have strong attachment to home ownership and have personal ties to their community, and these factors apparently outweigh economic considerations in their mobility.

There is an inverse relationship between mobility and age. If labor force participation is held constant, there appear to be no sex differences in other types of mobility; however, since women do move into and out of the labor force more often, their actual mobility rates are higher than men's. Nonwhites apparently are more mobile than whites. Married men are less mobile than single men; married women are more mobile than single women. Available evidence of the impact of unionism on mobility is inconclusive.

Of considerable interest to the labor economist is the question of the "rationality" of job-changing decisions. Do workers know of, and analytically consider, alternative job opportunities? In general, they do not. Most "quits" are made before the worker has another job lined up. Wages are the dominant factor in but a minority of job changes. However, in good times wages and economic considerations appear to be more important than in bad times. For those who do

---

[13]Herbert S. Parnes, "The Labor Force and Labor Markets," in H. G. Heneman, Jr. *et al.* (eds.), *Employment Relations Research* (New York: Harper and Brothers, 1960), pp. 16–30.

[14]For details see Gladys Palmer, *The Reluctant Job Changer* (Philadelphia: University of Pennsylvania Press, 1962).

have another job before they quit, economic considerations are more important than for those who do not. Workers typically just do not shop for jobs to find the best one — instead they take the first "satisfactory" job.

Labor Mobility in Northern Europe

Gladys Palmer found significant national differences in worker attitudes toward changing jobs in Northern European countries as compared with the United States. They apparently express significant differences in patterns of worker aspirations and expectations and in perceptions of the prestige associated with various occupations. In England, for example, many factory workers are resigned to the same long-term occupation; their satisfaction with work tends to increase with age. In Denmark more than half of a stratified sample of workers in various occupations indicated that, if given a choice, they would prefer their present jobs to any others. This level of satisfaction appears higher than is typical of similar occupational groups in the United States.[15]

Labor Mobility in the Soviet Union

In the Soviet Union (and Communist China) prices play an important role in the guidance of economic activity. But in the Soviet Union prices are not an autonomous force determining production, resource allocation, and consumption. Instead, prices are manipulated by the central authorities as one of various instruments used to accomplish planned goals.

There is freedom of occupational choice, and money-wage differentials are a principal mechanism for distributing the labor force. In the Soviet economy differences in compensation reflect the value of labor services rendered. Workers are not paid simply according to need. Instead, unequal monetary compensation is the basis of production incentives.

It should be noted that Soviet prices and wage rates do not reflect independently determined opportunity costs but, instead, reflect planner's preferences formulated on the basis of political as well as economic considerations.[16]

---

[15]See Gladys L. Palmer, "Contrasts in Labor Market Behavior in Northern Europe and the United States," *Industrial and Labor Relations Review*, Vol. 13, No. 4 (July, 1960), pp. 519–32.

[16]Morris Bronstein, "The Soviet Price System," *American Economic Review*, Vol. LII, No. 1 (March, 1962), pp. 64–99.

This chapter includes a discussion of the nature of institutions and especially the "economic" institutions of free enterprise, free labor markets, and collective bargaining. The discussion of collective bargaining is intentionally brief, for its importance in our society requires a more thorough and penetrating treatment. To set the stage for a more extensive discussion of collective bargaining, it is necessary to have a fuller understanding of labor movements which are the subject of the next chapter.

ANALYTICAL REVIEW QUESTIONS

1. What is meant by the term "employment process"?
2. How is manpower wasted in real-life employment processes?
3. What is meant by "underutilization"? Why is this an important concept?
4. What is an institution? Why is an understanding of labor market institutions important?
5. How does free enterprise affect labor marketing? Do employees take risks in such a system?
6. Could free enterprise operate without free labor markets?
7. How did industrial capitalism affect employment behavior and employment relationships?
8. How and why did industrial capitalism create new roles for workers?
9. In what sense are free labor markets "free"?
10. How is social status related to economic status in our society?
11. What do we mean by "collective bargaining"?
12. What were yeomanry guilds?
13. What evidence shows that labor markets do not operate at optimal efficiency?
14. Where do most labor market entrants get vocational guidance?
15. What is vertical mobility?
16. What are job families?
17. What is differential placement? Why is this concept important to labor marketing?
18. Why may parents and friends do a poor job of vocational guidance?
19. How do employer hiring requirements affect optimal manpower allocation?
20. What are threshold workers? Why is proper placement for them important to society?
21. What is meant by the "pushes" and "pulls" of employment?
22. What does underemployment mean in an economic sense?
23. How do most employees get jobs?

24. What are some principal reasons why employees quit their jobs?
25. What factors in job satisfaction do employees consider as most important to them? Do women and men have the same preferences?
26. Why is the qualitative aspect of labor mobilities important for manpower allocation and utilization?
27. What is the rationale behind a public employment agency?
28. What practices of private employment agencies are generally prohibited?
29. What are the major responsibilities of state employment agencies?
30. What are the advantages and disadvantages of local labor market studies?
31. What is meant by "duality of job attachment"?
32. In what sense are most job changes "complex"?
33. Are workers generally "rational" in their job changes? What evidence can you give for your answer?
34. How does labor mobility in Northern Europe differ from that in the United States?

Case 6-1

HELP WANTED — HIGH WAGES!

As personnel director of a large insurance company you are concerned with two facts: (1) your labor turnover rates are much higher than those of your competitors and (2) you cannot seem to get enough job applicants of the quality you want. Your wage rates are equal to any in your community or industry.

• Prepare a proposal for a research program to investigate this situation.

Case 6-2

GUIDANCE FOR THE PTA

You are a member of the Mahoney Township High School Board. You have been asked to speak at the PTA on the need for an expanded program of vocational counseling and guidance.

• Outline your speech.

Case 6-3

AN UNFAIR COMPETITION AGENCY

Willy England works for the state employment service. One night at a personnel association meeting he is taken to task by Ernie Cole, co-owner of a private employment agency. Ernie accuses Willy of working for an outfit that violates all concepts of free enterprise, that is, a public-supported competitor of his private agency.

• What arguments, if any, can Willy employ to justify the existence of his state employment service? Bring your outline to class.

LABOR MOVEMENTS

Anybody who wants to understand the labor movement had better start with the object itself in all its historical complexity and the multiple contradictions and defects of its present position. He had better not start with a preconceived notion of what a labor movement, considered as an instrument for attaining the ideal society, ought to be. An example of the latter approach is the complaint of a liberal intellectual, disillusioned with unions, who declared that government intervention must increase because "collective bargaining has failed to solve the labor problem." Indeed it has failed — and in a free society there can never be any "solution" to the labor problem, the price problem, the investment problem, or the woman problem.[1]

Much of the behavior of many participants in employment — including employers, managers and supervisors, and rank-and-file employees — is conditioned, influenced, and sometimes specified in detail by the customs and traditions associated with collective bargaining. In terms of the rapidity with which its influence has grown, the practice of collective bargaining is one of the most significant factors in modern employment relationships. This chapter provides an introduction to collective bargaining and to organizations of workers for bargaining purposes. The chapter begins with definitions of several terms. Attention is then directed to the background of historic labor movements and to theories about why unions have appeared and persisted.

Collective bargaining practices do not directly determine the working conditions of most employees in this country, for only a

---

[1]Max Ways, "Labor Unions Are Worth the Price," *Fortune* (May, 1963), pp. 108 ff.

minority of all employees is included in the membership of unions or in the bargaining units for which unions act as agents. In some other nations, however, the membership of unions represents a larger proportion of all workers. In this country the influence of union bargaining extends far beyond the employment of union members. Conditions established by bargaining are widely accepted and enforced in other employment. Workers who are not members of unions are granted similar adjustments in wages, hours, and other working conditions. The terms of bargained agreements tend to become standard practice throughout the industries and occupations in which they appear. Many of the vacation and other benefits enjoyed by supervisors and managers, for example, can be rather directly traced to the similar provisions negotiated by unions for rank-and-file employees.

The tradition of the *dignity of labor*, so frequently emphasized today, has been encouraged by the development of unions. As Lederer[2] notes, ancient and medieval societies held no such traditions. Primitive peoples relegated work to slaves captured in wars and to women. Laborers in most ancient societies included a small number of free artisans together with many slaves. General contempt for slaves often extended to the artisans. In medieval European feudalism, idleness (of the aristocrats) was noble; peasants, city workers, and small traders were "coarse" and regarded with contempt. When *guilds* appeared, they gained respect for the professional and skilled crafts represented by their membership; but all other wage earners were regarded as lowly, to be scorned.

The basic notion of the dignity of labor for the masses of common, nonprofessional, unskilled labor developed much more recently. The labor movement, emerging in early stages of industrialization, fought for improved status and prestige for wage earners. The traditions of that continuing struggle are a major factor in all employment today.

The term "labor movement" means a continuing association of workers — limited to employees — for the purpose of improving the status and lot of workers. A movement is an organized effort to achieve common or group goals. Unionism or organized labor constitutes such a movement. Labor movements have had as one principal objective the further organization of unions. Another basic goal has been to gain public support and both economic and political conces-

---

[2]Emil Lederer, "Labor," *Encylopedia of the Social Sciences* (New York: The Macmillan Co., 1937), Vol. 8, pp. 615–20.

sions for workers. Movements have frequently enlisted the cooperation of political and other leaders, including intellectuals who were
neither laborers nor unionists but who believed in the justice of labor
movement objectives.

DEFINITIONS

(1) *Collective bargaining* is called that because it is group bargaining. One or both bargainers — employees and employers — act
through associations. The term is contrasted with individual bargaining in which employees act individually in dealings with managers
and employers. The idea of bargaining as used in the term "collective
bargaining" is not unusual or distinctive. It means to haggle, to bid,
to offer, to negotiate in a sale or transfer — in this case the transfer
of services or work for wages. In collective bargaining a group of employees and an employer or group of employers negotiate about and
haggle over and ultimately agree upon the terms under which the employer or employers will offer and the union of employees will accept
employment.

(2) *Unions* are long-term or permanent associations of employees,
formed and maintained for the specific purpose of securing concessions
from employers by bargaining with them and policing and enforcing
such bargains. Their continuing character is stressed because they
are not single-shot, temporary groups. Rather, they and their members propose a continuing relationship with employers in which the
union will act as the agent for its members. Their action is not merely
that of bargaining for a contract. In addition, they propose to represent members in seeing that the contract is fulfilled, observed, and
carried out in the process of *contract administration.*

Bargaining is concerned with working conditions, many of which
may be determined in negotiation by employers and employees.
A union of employees may represent only those in a single shop or those
of a single employer. The same organization may, on the other hand,
represent employees in many such units. The organization may bargain with a single employer, or with several, or with an association of
employers. The essential condition is that a group of employees
negotiates as a group through an agent — their union — that is a
continuing organization.[3]

---

[3]See, for more detail, Harold W. Davey, *Contemporary Collective Bargaining* (2d ed.;
Englewood Cliffs, New Jersey: Prentice-Hall, Inc., 1959); Edwin F. Beal and Edward D.

(3) *Employers' or employer associations,* as the term is used in collective bargaining, are organizations of employers formed and maintained for the principal purpose of dealing with unions, most commonly for negotiating working relationships with employees. It should be noted that some types of employer associations are formed for other purposes. Trade associations, for example, may emphasize the promotion of industry products, securing favorable legislation, and gaining tariff protection or other favors from government. These organizations are employer associations, but they may devote little or no attention to dealing with unions of employees. The National Association of Manufacturers and the Chamber of Commerce of the United States are also employers' associations, but their programs extend well beyond the field of employment relationships. Neither of them is directly involved in the negotiation of labor agreements, although both have taken an active part in promoting or opposing legislation on collective bargaining.

(4) *Collective agreements* are the labor contracts or agreements negotiated in collective bargaining. They are signed statements that indicate what each of the parties can and will do to make the cooperation of employers and employees effective. In earlier periods, when agreements were less complicated and included fewer detailed provisions, some of these contracts were unwritten. Today, a collective agreement may deal with a wide range of subjects, from absenteeism to pensions and wages, and may be typed or mimeographed or printed as a booklet. Figure 7-1 illustrates the coverage of one such contract.

The collective agreement records what the employer and the union have agreed to in their negotiations. For example, the contract may provide that employees shall be paid at twice the regular hourly rates for Sunday work. It may list the rates of pay for all jobs. It may specify that employees shall be eligible for promotion on the basis of seniority and ability or that the employee with greatest seniority is entitled to a tryout in a vacancy. It may say that if the union and the employer disagree about how to settle a grievance, an outside arbitrator shall make a final and binding decision which both parties agree to accept. The agreement, in effect, is a contract between the parties; but it is also a special kind of contract because it concerns work, the services of people. It is the major guide and rule book on

Wickersham, *The Practice of Collective Bargaining* (Homewood, Illinois: Richard D. Irwin, Inc., 1963).

INDEX

Title	Page
Bulletin Boards	23
Business Representatives	4
Call-In Time	11
Classifications-Occupations	26
Coverage	2
Dues Check-Off	3
Duration	24
Grievance Procedure	21
Holidays	13
Hours	5
Insurance	18
Labor Grades	5
Lay-Off	19
Leadman	10
Maternity Leave	16
Medical Leave	15
Military Leave	16
National Security	24
New Occupations-Classifications	13
Overtime	11
Personal Leave	16
Preamble	i

INDEX

Title	Page
Probationary Period	18
Qualification Period	10
Recall	20
Recognition	1
Rights of Management	24
Safety Committee	23
Safety	23
Seniority	18
Set-Up Man	10
Shift Bonus	10
Shifts	5
Shop Stewards	4
Sick Leave Pay	17
Trainees	9
Union Shop	2
Upgrading	10
Vacations	14
Wage Rates	26
Wage Reopening	25
Wage Review	12
Work Day	4
Work Week	4

Figure 7-1

INDEX OF A LABOR CONTRACT

employment and working conditions during its term, which is most commonly 2 or 3 but may be only 1 or as many as 5 years.

The *term* of the agreement refers to its length or duration. In some European nations custom has developed an open-end contract that continues in effect until it is superceded by a new agreement. In this country the term is usually specified, and great pressure may develop when negotiation of a new contract nears the expiration date.

Recent years have been marked by a trend toward longer terms for these agreements. Employers generally seek longer agreements as a means of assuring uninterrupted employment and providing a basis for forecasting labor costs. Unions are usually reluctant to make these longer commitments, unless they include a *reopening clause* permitting negotiated changes in wages, fringe benefits, or other conditions.[4]

---

[4]Since World War II American agreements have shown a distinct tendency away from traditional 1-year terms. At the same time, the dates of terminations, traditionally concentrated in the spring of each year, have become more diverse. In 1961 only about 8 percent of all agreements were for one year, and about 5 percent were for more than one but less than two years. Nearly 40 percent were for two years, 30 percent for three years,

(5) *The bargaining unit* is the particular group of jobs covered by a collective agreement. A bargaining unit might include all jobs and employees of the Whirlwind Propeller Corporation. More commonly, however, an agreement for production workers would not include salaried office employees or supervisors and managers. Groups of skilled employees may be regarded as separate units, with one unit of tool and die workers, another of electricians, and another made up of the remaining production employees. Again, salesmen may be organized as a separate unit.

The bargaining unit fixes the boundaries within which employees negotiate as one group. Units were, in earlier periods, determined by bargaining. The question as to what constitutes a proper unit was so frequently a matter of controversy between employers and unions that federal legislation (The National Labor Relations Act of 1935) created the National Labor Relations Board and authorized that Board to decide questions of this kind when employers and employees could not agree. The jurisdiction of the N.L.R.B. is limited to interstate industry, but state agencies in several states have similar authority for intrastate industries.

(6) *Bargaining agents* are the unions that represent employees in each bargaining unit. Thus, Local 304 of the International Association of Machinists may be the bargaining agent for all machinists or all production employees in the Twin City Arsenal. A store's salespeople may constitute a bargaining unit, and their bargaining agent may be a local, single-firm union known as the Federation of Bloom Employees.

Unions become bargaining agents for the employees they represent in many ways. Sometimes an existing national or local union organizes the employees and is thus selected as their agent. In other situations employees organize themselves or ask the help of a union of similar employees in their initial organization. They designate their newly created union as their agent.

Conflicts frequently arise out of rivalry among unions that want to be bargaining agents for particular groups of employees. To settle these issues, bargaining agents for employees in interstate industries

---

and 10 percent for more than three years.

Meanwhile, in 1961, June was the month of most terminations, with April, May, August, September, and October also prominent in this respect. A portion of the older pattern remains; few agreements expire in winter months and in July. See "Major Union Contracts in the United States, 1961," *Monthly Labor Review*, Vol. 85, No. 10, 1962, especially pp. 1140-41.

may be certified by the National Labor Relations Board. For intra-state employment, several states provide similar certifications by a state labor board or other agency.

The certified bargaining agent is the union that has been granted the legal right to bargain for employees in a particular unit. Members may change unions by following decertification procedures specified by federal and state agencies. A union may be certified as the bargaining agent for a group when a majority of employees wants the union to represent them. Similarly, a union may lose its right to such certification if a majority of employees opposes its continued authorization. Public agencies conduct elections and examine membership or authorization cards as a basis for certification or decertification.

(7) *Negotiation* is the phase of collective bargaining in which the parties try to arrive at an agreement that will guide their relationship for a specified period of time. To negotiate means to discuss and talk over as a means of coming to an agreement. Negotiation of collective agreements is a process that frequently attracts wide popular attention, because disagreements are aired, strikes and lockouts are threatened, and public officials — conciliators, mediators, governors, secretaries of labor, and even presidents — may intervene before an accord is reached. Negotiation is thus the spectacular phase of collective bargaining.

Negotiation may be a brief or a lengthy process, but it usually requires a long period of preparation in which both parties determine what changes are desired and collect and organize information and arguments to bolster their demands. In most negotiations unions appear as the moving parties. They make most of the proposals for changes. However, a trend is apparent in which many employers are becoming positive rather than negative bargainers. They take the initiative in suggesting changes rather than merely opposing union proposals. Employers introduce their own demands — and not merely for trading purposes. They prepare to support these proposals, sometimes with *bargaining books* which are carefully documented manuals for their bargaining representatives.[5]

(8) *Contract administration* is the day-to-day application and interpretation of collective agreements. For example, an employee in the delivery service of a large department store may not have received

---

[5]The National Industrial Conference Board reports that 97 of the 213 firms included in one of their studies use such bargaining books. See Zoe Campbell, "The Use of Bargaining Books in Negotiations," *Management Record*, Vol. 19, No. 4 (April, 1957), pp. 118 ff.

payment for what he regards as overtime. He tells his union's business agent who may or may not agree with the employee's interpretation of the contract. If he does agree, the business agent takes it up with the employer. The foreman or the labor relations director of the company and the business agent of the union may work out a satisfactory interpretation of relevant contract provisions. They may not be able to agree, in which case the complaint — now put in writing and known as a *grievance* — is discussed by other employer representatives and union officers and may ultimately be submitted to an outside, neutral arbitrator for final decision.

Immediately after a new contract is signed, careful interpretations of each clause are prepared by many employers and given to all supervisors to aid them in administering the contract. Union officers and staff assistants may prepare similar guides for their members.

Some — perhaps many — of these administrative activities must be carried on day after day throughout the term of the agreement. New problems appear — situations that are not covered by the agreement. Provisions of the current contract may not work out as planned. They may have effects that were not anticipated. One or both parties may be anxious to change the contract. The parties can do so at any time if they agree upon these changes. But if only one party wants the change, evidence is collected and arguments prepared for the next period of negotiation.

BACKGROUND OF LABOR MOVEMENTS

A tendency for employees to get together to deal with employers is apparently almost as old as free employment. Historians ascribe the first organizations of employees to the simple shops in which several paid helpers worked under the direction and leadership of a single owner or proprietor. Formal unions and labor movements have their beginnings in the process of industrialization that has, to a greater or lesser degree, affected all economies. Unions were not characteristic of agricultural societies in which landowners maintained large estates manned by slaves and serfs. Slaves do not form unions.

When economies begin the process of industrialization, a new class of nonagricultural workers is essential. Such employees are usually recruited from the ranks of agricultural labor. They give up their places in agriculture seeking a greater degree of freedom, independence, and economic compensation. Reinhard Bendix has studied this process in which the nonagricultural work force is created during the process of economic development.[6] He concludes that in the early stages of industrialization, the new managers are usually little concerned about labor-management relationships. They are faced with difficult financial and public relations problems. New industrial workers are forced to make difficult adjustments in their commitment to industrial employment. They gradually accommodate themselves to the discipline of factory work, but they lose some security and develop dissatisfactions that cause them to tend to withdraw effort and efficiency. They are likely to be dissatisfied with both their material income and their jobs in the new relationship.

This process creates what Bendix calls a "revolutionary potential." Employers are regarded with favor by the general public and tend to appeal to the public for support in struggles to retain their managerial authority and power. Revolution materializes if the new classes of managers and employees are unable or unwilling to compromise. The greatest hazard of revolution, according to Bendix, occurs at the inception of industrialization. This conclusion contradicts that of Karl Marx, who regarded revolution as inevitable in the later stages of industrialization.

Early unions appear as expressions of employee dissatisfaction and protest. Their development and activity in later years of industrialization are shaped by the treatment they receive and the status they are accorded.

In relatively underdeveloped nations in which industrialization has only begun, a major goal of new unions is the development of competitive nationalism. They may be regarded as essentially political organizations, dealing with broad social problems rather than narrower economic issues in wages and other working conditions. Their goals are improved education, housing, and living scales to be attained through rising levels of productivity.[7]

The importance of protest and a sense of social injustice as a basis for unionism deserves special emphasis, for it is more pervasive

---

[6]For interesting details of his analysis, see his *Work and Authority in Industry* (New York: John Wiley and Sons, 1956). See also Clark Kerr, John T. Dunlop, Frederick H. Harbison, and Charles A. Myers, *Industrialism and Industrial Man* (Cambridge: Harvard University Press, 1960), especially Part II.

[7]See Everett M. Kassalow, "Union Organization and Training in Emerging Labor Movements," *Monthly Labor Review*, Vol. 85, No. 9 (September, 1962), pp. 1010–13.

than the simpler struggle to counteract the power of employers with which Americans are familiar. The American concentration on economic objectives is not the typical pattern. In less developed nations, unions tend to express the broader dissatisfactions of workers who have found themselves committed to new, different working conditions including new status and impersonal employment relationships in recently urbanized societies.

The Guild System

Unions in this country and those of western European nations date back to the stage of industrialization generally described as the guild system, to which frequent reference has already been made. As the medieval agricultural system of large manorial estates gave way to the handicraft system of home workshops in western Europe, these guild organizations developed and gained wide acceptance. Two types are usually distinguished, one composed of shopkeepers or retailers and known as *merchant guilds* and the other made up of handicraft workers and called *craft guilds*. Craft guilds included three types of members. Those older craftsmen in whose homes the work was performed were the *masters*. They employed other craftsmen on a day-wage basis who were known as *journeymen*, a title reflecting the French term for "day." Masters also employed *apprentices*, young aspirants to the craft who worked for their board and room while they were learning the trade. When they had served an apprenticeship, they became journeymen. They could then work for wages in the same shop or in other shops, and when they had accumulated sufficient capital, they could set themselves up as masters.

Expansion of trade and introduction of early factories tended to disrupt the guild system. Some masters became industrialists, expanding their shops and creating small factories. Others could not secure the necessary capital and either made a precarious living in competition with the new factories or became dayworkers. The need for greater capital handicapped journeymen who wished to establish themselves as masters. At the same time, masters frequently combined to restrict the numbers of new establishments.

In this situation *journeyman* or *yeomanry guilds* were formed — associations of independent dayworkers created to secure better working conditions by negotiation with the masters. Not all early unions developed out of these journeyman guilds, but the latter are legitimate forerunners of present-day unions and what are widely described as labor movements.

Labor Movement Objectives

In the early years of labor movements, they frequently engaged in spectacular activities, attracting wide attention. Beginning in 1811, for example, employees in weaving and the manufacture of hosiery and lace in England undertook a campaign to publicize what they regarded as deplorable working conditions. Known as the Luddites, they formed mobs and destroyed machines and mills, protesting against new laborsaving machinery. Fourteen leaders of this movement were executed in 1813. Another early English phase — the Chartist movement — attracted wide attention from 1832 to about 1848. Members demanded a whole charter of reforms, including universal suffrage, equalized political representation for areas in which employees were concentrated, abolition of property requirements for voting, and others. Somewhat the same objectives motivated another phase of the movement, the so-called Junta, which was prominent in Europe for several years after 1850. In 1864 the International Workingmen's Association was established, with headquarters in London, as the first socialist international in the labor movement.[8]

While political activities and programs of early labor movements attracted wide popular attention, many local unions of employees proposed less drastic but more immediate changes in the working conditions of their members. These activities occasioned the resentment of employers. In England legislation sought to restrict the organization and the usual activities of unions. A series of *Combination Acts* (the last one passed in 1824) made it illegal for such employee organizations to solicit members, make demands on employers, or attempt any form of collective bargaining. Although this attitude changed, unions did not formally secure legislative approval in England until passage of the Trade Union Act in 1871.

In the United States unions were not expressly forbidden in these early years. On the other hand, formal approval of collective

---

[8]For a description of the Luddite and other similar movements, see Simon Rottenberg, "Wage Effects in the Theory of the Labor Movement," *Journal of Political Economy*, Vol. 41, No. 4 (August, 1953), pp. 346–52. For more detail, consult "Labor Movement," *Encyclopaedia of the Social Sciences*, Vol. 7, pp. 682–96.

bargaining as a matter of general public policy was delayed until the National Industrial Recovery Act was passed in 1933.[9]

Foreign Labor Movements

The American labor movement is by no means typical of those throughout the world today. Indeed, modern American unions have frequently been described as unique in their concentration and emphasis on economic goals. Most foreign labor movements are more concerned with and more active in politics.

Further, the newer unions of less developed nations have proposed distinctive programs. They have provided many of the leaders of emergent nationalism. Unions have appeared as semipublic agencies which work with government to achieve political reforms. They have sought to enlist all citizens who share their political views rather than to develop occupational or industrial fraternities. They have emphasized educational objectives, with political education given top priority.[10]

In the Soviet Union the labor movement is constrained by a rigorous "Labor Code." Local bargaining, generally on an annual basis, is subject to ratification by political authorities. After such approval and formal registration, agreements have the force of law. They cover wages (including bonuses), production standards, provisions for change, safety and health, allowances for housing, schools, and hospitalization. Local disagreements are settled by public authorities. Strikes and lockouts are proscribed.[11]

Foreign labor movements are changing. Ross has noted a shift in influence within the British labor movement from central organizations to the local level.[12] In the years since World War II, unions have moved out of their earlier, defensive position. Prosperity has permitted numerous employer concessions in "workshop regulations."

[9]For more on the early history of collective bargaining, see Vernon H. Jensen, "Notes on the Beginnings of Collective Bargaining," *Labor and Industrial Relations Review*, Vol. 9, No. 2 (January, 1956), pp. 225–34.

[10]See Bruce H. Millen, *The Political Role of Labor in Developing Countries* (Washington, D.C.: The Brookings Institution, 1963). See also William H. Friedland, "Unions and Industrial Relations in Underdeveloped Countries," *Bulletin 47*, New York State School of Industrial and Labor Relations, January, 1963; Lester N. Trachtman, "The Labor Movement of Ghana," *Economic Development and Cultural Change*, Vol. 10, No. 2 (January, 1962), *Reprint No. 127*, New York State School of Industrial and Labor Relations. For an international view of collective bargaining, see Adolf Sturmthal (ed.), *Contemporary Collective Bargaining in Seven Countries* (Ithaca: Cornell University, 1957).

[11]See G. K. Maskalenko, "Collective Agreements in the U.S.S.R.," *International Labor Review*, Vol. 85, No. 1 (January, 1961), pp. 18–29.

[12]Arthur M. Ross, "The New Industrial Relations in Britain," *Report No. 192*, University of California Institute of Industrial Relations (Berkeley), 1962.

On the other hand, employers are accustomed and strongly attached to bargaining through associations. Local bargaining is achieving added acceptance, however, and could require drastic changes in British unions; the whole system of shop stewards may be revised, as may the traditional bargaining units.

Meanwhile, somewhat similar changes are occurring in West Germany. Unions seem to be moving in a direction that may make them more like American unions. Throughout Europe employer associations like Italy's *Confindustria* are struggling to maintain their powerful influence, in part by maintaining employee representation plans, in part by resisting government intervention, in part by encouraging interunion rivalries. Nevertheless, a movement away from the political-economic orientation of labor movements is evident, as is a trend toward plant rather than industry-wide bargaining.[13]

In Sweden collective bargaining is both highly organized and stable. Blue-collar workers are organized in the Swedish Confederation of Trade Unions (called L.O.) and white-collar workers in the Central Organization of Salaried Employees (T.C.O.). Professional workers have their own unions. Most major employers are in the Swedish Employers Confederation (S.A.F.). Negotiations are highly centralized at the industry level. In no other country is such a high proportion of workers organized.

Swedish labor legislation places few restrictions on unions and does not require compulsory arbitration in collective bargaining of new agreements. Interpretations of agreements are arbitrated by Labor Courts; conciliation (but not arbitration) for unsuccessful negotiation is provided by the state. Both labor and management strongly oppose government participation beyond consultation in the collective bargaining process. Sweden does not even have minimum wage laws. The system of collective bargaining and wage determination, while centralized and responsible, is definitely voluntary.[14]

Labor movements have created and maintained international associations and alliances. As will be noted in the chapter that follows, many American unions have locals and members in Canada, Mexico, and Central America. American unions have been prominent in many international associations of unions in particular industries. One example is the Miner's International Federation which

---

[13]See Arthur M. Ross, "Prosperity and Labor Relations in Western Europe: Italy and France," *Industrial and Labor Relations Review*, Vol. 16, No. 1 (October, 1962), pp. 63–85.

[14]See "Wage Negotiations and Wage Policies in Sweden: I," *International Labour Review*, Vol. 80, No. 4 (October, 1959), pp. 319–30.

represents 2.6 million union members in the mining of coal and ore in 31 countries. It is one of 18 International Trade Secretariats in the United Nations. The United Mine Workers of America has been active in the Federation since 1904.[15]

Socialist and communist unions have created international federations to gain power and encourage growth. Other unions, less interested in political action, have established competitive international associations. As early as 1864, an International Workingmen's Association was established as the "center" of socialist unionism. It is frequently described as the first socialist international. A second was created in Paris in 1899, and a third, the Communist International, was established with headquarters in Moscow in 1919. French unionists in the late 19th century developed a special viewpoint, called *syndicalism*, which proposes a society organized around autonomous associations of worker-owners in various industries. Advocates of Marxian theory have tried to use unions as steppingstones toward the classless society. They have sought to point the programs of international associations of unions in this direction, placing major emphasis on political action rather than on collective bargaining. Objection to this theory of unions and to such programs explains the American Federation of Labor's refusal to join and the Congress of Industrial Organizations' withdrawal from the World Federation of Trade Unions in 1949. It was also the major reason for the formation of the International Confederation of Free Trade Unions in 1949. AFL-CIO is a member of ICFTU.[16]

THEORIES OF LABOR MOVEMENTS

Since so much of the behavior of labor marketing and employment is now shaped by unions and collective bargaining, the philosophy and programs of the labor movement and of individual union

---

[15]See *International Miner's Federation* (Washington, D.C.: Bureau of International Labor Affairs, Department of Labor, 1963).

[16]For more on international variations in collective bargaining, see *The Trade Union Situation in the U.S.S.R.* (Geneva, Switzerland: International Labour Office, 1960); Dorothea De Schweinitz, "Consultation and Negotiation in Swedish Factories," *Monthly Labor Review*, Vol. 83, No. 10 (October, 1960); Miles E. Galvin, "Unionism in Latin America," *Bulletin No. 45* (1962); and William H. Friedland, "The Industrialization of Labor Protest in Tanganyika," *Reprint Series No. 123* (1961), both from the New York School of Industrial and Labor Relations of Cornell University; Bernard Karsh and Solomon B. Levine, "Present Dilemmas of the Japanese Labor Movement," *University of Illinois Bulletin*, Vol. 60, No. 17 (September, 1962). See also, A. M. Whitehill, Jr., and Shinichi Takezawa, "Cultural Values in Management-Workers Relations: Japan — GIMU in Transition," *Research Paper 5* (Chapel Hill, N.C.: University of North Carolina, School of Business Administration, March, 1961).

organizations are of special interest and import. Why have labor movements appeared, and why do they continue? Why have employees joined unions in the past, and why do they join today? What characteristics of employment relationships explain the emergence and development of unions?

Several theories of labor movements — explanations of union membership and of the policies and practices of unions — have received wide attention. A brief outline of the most prominent of these theories should be helpful in understanding the behavior of unions and their members.

Any survey of such theories should note that each explanation speculates about the particular actions and expressions of unionism that are regarded as most distinctive; and since various stages in the history of labor movements have emphasized varying purposes and objectives, impressions are likely to be dated. Also, labor movements have not been single-purposed.

It is inevitable that theories suggest possible prediction and control through appropriate courses of action. They may be advanced for that purpose. Their authors may regard them as arguments for particular courses of social or political action. A theory that explains the labor movement largely as a protest against the introduction of new machines, for example, might be interpreted to mean that unions will increase or become more demanding in a period of rapid technological change. It may also imply that more unions and union members will appear if society encourages continued mechanization. On the other hand, a theory that explains unions as the result of agitators and demagogues and propaganda might be advanced to justify legislation limiting the activities of such leaders.

Theories could be outlined simply by reference to their chief spokesmen, as the Marxian theory, the Webb theory, or the Hoxie theory. It may shorten this outline without serious loss of perspective, however, to note five major types of explanations. They include:

1. Revolution theory.
2. Industrial democracy theory.
3. Business unionism theory.
4. Psychological theory.
5. Great man theory.

Revolution Theory

Without question the leading spokesmen for revolutionary theories of labor movements were Karl Marx and Friedrich Engels, although they enlisted many prominent followers who have advanced similar explanations. Perhaps the classic expression of revolution theory is that found in the *Communist Manifesto* written by Marx and Engels in 1848.

Marxian thinking links unions and international associations of unions with what Marx regarded as an inevitable social revolution, inseparable from industrialization, that will destroy existing social, political, and economic order and substitute a new classless society. Marx and Engels were confirmed believers in an economic interpretation of historic changes. In their viewpoint the basic force that causes all societies to be constantly changing is economic. They regarded the Industrial Revolution, which marked the end of a predominantly agricultural society and the introduction of factories and industrial capitalism, as a major phase or step in this transition. This change destroyed the earlier manorial system with its serfs and slaves. It created the *bourgeoisie* — industrial capitalists and factory owners — and the *industrial proletariat* — employees in mass production. Followers of Marx concluded that further change, which they regarded as inevitable, would eliminate these classes. Although the economy of industrial capitalism is dominated by the bourgeoisie, the latter are, according to Marx, creating their own gravediggers. Marx held that further change would inevitably involve the elimination of capitalists and the ultimate establishment of a social and political order in which the masses would rule themselves, and all wealth and capital would be their property.

Unions, in this view, are a device through which members of the wage-earning proletariat mobilize their forces for these anticipated changes. They are necessary in the existing, intermediate stage to reduce the intralabor competition of wage earners who would otherwise underbid each other and fight among themselves. Marx regarded unions as helpful as a means of supporting wage rates, but their major significance was as a step toward international organizations of the proletariat. "The real fruit of their battle lies . . . in the ever-expanding union of the workers." Come the revolution, Marxians have long argued, international associations of unions will spearhead the revolt and insure domination of the new order by the masses. Unions will then have served their purpose, since no such organizations will be needed in the classless society.[17]

---

[17]For details of the Marxian view, see *Karl Marx, Selected Works*, prepared by the Marx-Engels-Lenin Institute in Moscow (New York: International Publishers, 1936); the

This revolution theory of the labor movement has many advocates in the world today. They have long been active not only in nations dominated by Communists but in several international associations of unions.

Industrial Democracy Theory

Sidney and Beatrice Webb, who were late nineteenth century English economists, Fabian Socialists, and public officials, are the best known exponents of what may be called the industrial democracy theory of unions.[18] The Webbs made a long, detailed study of English unions, including their stated objectives and their usual policies and practices. They concluded that unions arose out of the "definite separation between the functions of the capitalist *entrepreneur* and the manual worker." This, they explain, is most readily observed in the factory. They noted, however, that unions in trades carried on exclusively by hand labor and in which workers no longer had responsibilities for buying and selling preceded factories by a full century. In England "the pioneers of the Trade Union Movement were not the trade clubs of the town artisans, but the extensive combinations of the West of England woolen-workers and the Midland framework knitters." These workers became concerned when new processes and widening markets threatened a downward leveling of wages. Their primary purpose in organizing at that time was to obtain government protection against unemployment and reductions in earnings. In that objective they were thwarted by the superior political power and influence of capitalist employers who effectively prevented public intervention.

Unions are a means of introducing democracy into employment relations, according to the Webbs, who concluded that unions must be developed to insure the protection of employees' interests both on the job and in political circles. Unions would thus maintain a system of industrial democracy paralleling and strengthening political democracy.

A similar analysis has been provided by another English Fabian, G. D. H. Cole.[19] Cole sees unions, and particularly large, industry-

---

Communist Manifesto is available in Karl Marx and Friedrich Engels *Communist Manifesto: Socialist Landmark* (London: George Allen and Unwin, Ltd., 1948).

[18]Their books, *The History of Trade Unionism*, first published in 1894, and *Industrial Democracy* (1897) have long been required reading for any extensive study of labor movements.

[19]His best known statements appear in his *The World of Labour* (London: George Bell and Sons, Ltd., 1931).

wide organizations of employees, as preliminary and intermediate steps toward what he called the "guild." The latter would include all the "producers" when the socialist state is established. In that system the state will be the employer. Meanwhile, unions serve the purposes the Webbs described as means of providing a temporary system of partial industrial democracy.

It is interesting that a somewhat similar idea of unions as means of democratizing employment relationships has also been emphasized by the late American economist, Sumner H. Slichter.[20] No socialist, he pointed to the control of working conditions as the major explanation of unions. Employees as individuals may find it impossible to obtain and evaluate labor market information. Further, they cannot exert an effective influence on working conditions because employers do not find it profitable to cultivate the satisfaction of individuals and minorities among their employees. In this situation unions provide a means of matching employer power, and collective bargaining develops mutually determined rules of the game that constitute a system of what Slichter calls "industrial jurisprudence." These rules, like the laws of a democratic society, protect individual members against arbitrary action and give them added security.

Business Theory

Slichter's explanation could also have been classified as a business theory of unionism. Business theories stress union membership as a matter of sound day-to-day business policy and practice for employees. They discount the importance of such long-term ultimate and drastic changes in society as those predicted by Marxists. They emphasize the immediate advantages of collective action in dealing with employers. Many of the prominent spokesmen of this viewpoint are Americans, and several of them have been American union leaders.

Samuel Gompers, first president of the American Federation of Labor, regarded unionism as an immediate protective device and unions as business representatives of their members. Gompers objected to any notion of unions as primarily reformist or revolutionary agencies. "Our great Federation," he said, "has uniformly refused to surrender this conviction and to rush to the support of any one of

---

[20]For one of his many statements of this viewpoint, see Sumner H. Slichter, *Modern Economic Society* (New York: Henry Holt and Co., 1931), pp. 655–57. For a later statement, see his *The Challenge of Industrial Relations* (Ithaca: Cornell University Press, 1947).

the numerous society-saving or society-destroying schemes which decade by decade have been sprung upon this country." Rather, in Gompers' view, unions increase the wage earner's earnings, reduce his hours, enforce safety measures, and protect the employee from the "tyranny" of employers. At the same time, according to Gompers, unions strive to "enrich, enlarge, and magnify humanity" through their day-to-day action in behalf of members.

Adolph Strasser, long a representative of the Cigar Makers and another early AFL leader and spokesman, bluntly denied that the union members for whom he spoke thought in terms of "ultimate ends." In his opinion unions plan their courses from day to day, "fighting for immediate objects."[21] Several other leaders of American labor might also be cited as exponents of this viewpoint. John Mitchell, one-time president of the United Mine Workers,[22] emphasized the primary importance of collective bargaining as a means of gaining concessions from employers. He proposed "prudent business methods" for unions, was emphatic in renouncing long-term revolutionary or reformist motivations, and was outspoken in his opposition to concepts of an inevitable class conflict. Furthermore, Mitchell stressed the "sacredness of contracts" between unions and employers. It was Mitchell's opinion that no fundamental antagonism between laborer and capitalist was justified because of their joint interest in prosperity.

One of the best-known statements of this viewpoint is that of Selig Perlman.[23] Perlman emphasizes the bargaining setting in labor markets in which he sees wage earners as having long been at a disadvantage. Employees have recognized this handicap, which they view as a limiting of their opportunities to improve their status and living scales. Unionism appeals because it offers a means of satisfying the desire for more opportunity. The fundamental urge or need behind unionism is the wage earners' "consciousness of the scarcity of opportunity." Perlman sees unions as opportunistic — not revolutionary. Their ultimate objective is to increase economic opportunities for their members.

Wage earners, according to Perlman, have always been and must be at a disadvantage in bargaining because they compete with each

---

[21]For more of his viewpoint, see J. B. S. Hardman, *American Labor Dynamics* (New York: Harcourt, Brace and Co., Inc., 1928), pp. 99–101.

[22]See his *Organized Labor* (Philadelphia: American Book and Bible House, 1903) and *The Wage Earner and His Problem* (Washington: P. S. Ridsdale Company, 1913).

[23]Selig Perlman, *A History of Trade Unionism in the United States* (New York: The Macmillan Company, 1937), pp. 265 ff.

other.   Collective bargaining permits them to "ration" job opportunities and thus to prevent individuals from appropriating more than their rightful share.   This purpose of unions may easily be misunderstood or overlooked by casual observers because their stated objectives fluctuate with varying phases of the business cycle.   In periods of falling prices and declining profits, programs emphasize ultimate goals and political action.   When prices and profits rise, programs concentrate on immediate gains, proximate "betterments" within the limits of the wage system.[24]

Psychological Theory

The term "psychological" is used here more in its popular than its scientific sense.   Exponents of psychological theories see union membership as a means of satisfying several basic needs, drives, appetites, or wishes of individual employees.   In their view men and women join labor movements as a means of expressing or filling a broad range and hierarchy of fundamental human needs.   According to this viewpoint, membership offers much more than economic or business advantages, for, in addition, unions create a feeling of fulfillment, security, protection, and strength.   Members feel that they can speak and act with greater assurance and less fear of consequences.   The union provides a channel of upward communication and expression not controlled by management and not limited to favorable reactions.   It relieves the anxieties of wage earners.   It permits them to satisfy needs for recognition and appreciation, to develop and express their personal aptitudes and interests.

Carleton H. Parker is widely regarded as an early exponent of this school.   As Parker viewed industrial employment, working conditions and relationships create a state of "psychic ill health" among wage earners.   Employment produces "obsessions and thwartings" by blocking expressions of what Parker regarded as sixteen basic human instincts that "insistently demand" gratification.   This "repression" results in "perverted compensations," of which wandering, drinking, family desertion, strikes, violence, sabotage, and other forms of sublimation or substitution are examples.   The repressed wage

[24]See Philip Taft, "On the Origins of Business Unionism," *Industrial and Labor Relations Review*, Vol. 17, No. 1 (October, 1963), pp. 20–38. See also Ralph and Estelle James "Hoffa's Leverage Techniques in Bargaining," *Industrial Relations*, Vol. 3, No. 1 (October, 1963), pp. 73–93; for a mathematical analysis, see Carl M. Stevens, *Strategy and Collective Bargaining Negotiation* (New York: McGraw-Hill Book Company, Inc., 1964).

earner is frustrated and unstable. His behavior expresses what Parker called a "definite industrial psychosis" and a "stereotyped mental disease." Unions arise because they offer a promise of release, expression, security, and satisfaction.[25]

Another and more recent expression of a similar view is provided by Golden and Ruttenberg. Golden was an officer of the Steelworkers Organizing Committee and the United Steelworkers of America. Ruttenberg was head of the United Steelworkers Division of Research. They suggest that modern unions are created and supported because they fill psychological and social as well as economic needs of employees. Workers join to maintain their personal pride and dignity. Unions provide a means of combating the arbitrary use and abuse of managerial authority. Union membership is a means by which wage earners find "direct satisfaction in their daily jobs for economic, psychological and social needs."[26]

Professor E. Wight Bakke is another who concludes that employees regard unions as means of reducing frustrations and anxieties and of facilitating achievement of "standards of successful living." Unions, according to Bakke, provide opportunities for prestige and status, as well as for increased "creature comforts and economic security." They appeal to employees as promising aids in the achievement of wage earners' basic, long-term personal goals.[27]

Perhaps the most careful and detailed statement of this "human needs" viewpoint is that presented by Robert F. Hoxie. An American professor of economics and a lifelong student of unions, Hoxie saw American unions as springing from the "common needs and problems of the wage-workers." On the surface, unions are obviously functional; they are a means of propagating a viewpoint and putting the group's program into effect. These immediate programs vary from group to group and time to time, reflecting the environment and the "temperament" of their members.[28] Union objectives and programs can be classified to identify major types of unions. These types are not mutually exclusive or "pure" but represent differences in functional emphasis.

---

[25]See Carleton H. Parker, *The Casual Laborer and Other Essays* (New York: Harcourt, Brace and Company, Inc., 1920), pp. 161 ff.
[26]Clinton S. Golden and Harold J. Ruttenberg, *The Dynamics of Industrial Democracy* (New York: Harper and Brothers, 1942).
[27]See E. Wight Bakke, "Why Workers Join Unions," *Personnel*, Vol. 22, No. 1 (July, 1945), pp. 37–47.
[28]For greater detail, see his *Trade Unionism in the United States* (New York: D. Appleton-Century Co., Inc., 1921), pp. 56–67.

Hoxie regarded *business unionism* as the predominant functional type in this country. As noted, it proposes programs designed primarily to advance the day-to-day economic interests of union members. In contrast, what he described as *uplift unionism* emphasizes a wide range of social reforms, for example, changes in public education, taxation, and economic security. A third functional type — *revolutionary unionism* — proposes drastic political change, replacing the existing social system and relocating centers of power and authority. A final, fourth type — which he called *predatory unionism* — is essentially exploitive and might be described as "racketeering." In that type corrupt leaders use their unions for personal gain, sometimes in collusion with employers.

Great Man (Agitator) Theory

From their earliest days unions have appeared to some observers as the creations of discontented individuals who were, at the same time, effective leaders. No single statement of this viewpoint deserves special mention, but it has many exponents in our society today. It can be called the agitator theory, for it concludes that unions are the result of agitation by a few strongly motivated individuals. The theory holds that men join unions primarily because they are "talked into" it. Their action is the result of persuasion, possibly combined with threats and coercion.

Current Studies

Such an outline of possible explanations is mainly useful in emphasizing the variety and range of reasons for the inception, growth, and persistent activity of labor movements. As may be noted, these types of explanations are by no means mutually exclusive. Each of them, however, adds something to the others. Each may be right as to the major or principal explanation of unionism at certain times and under particular conditions. Together they provide a number of keys rather than one single and universal explanation.[29]

---

[29]For an analysis of the emergence of unions in recently industrialized economies, see Clark Kerr, Frederick H. Harbison, John T. Dunlop and Charles A. Myers, "The Labour Problem in Economic Development," *International Labour Review*, Vol. 71, No. 3 (March, 1955), pp. 3–15. See also Philip Taft, "Theories of the Labor Movement," *Interpreting the Labor Movement*, Industrial Relations Research Association, 1952, pp. 1–38.

Several recent studies of the reasons why employees join and form and support unions in this country provide added insights with respect to questions about the "why" of union membership. In many of these studies, union officers and members have been questioned. They have been asked why members join and continue to support their unions. The studies seek information on what members regard as the most important values of unions now, in the present setting.

These studies have not resulted in additional distinctive theories of unionism, but they have revealed the interest of members in business unionism, political action, the handling of grievances, and many other current union policies and practices. They show that members continue to join and form unions for many different reasons. Some members have a strong belief that it is an unfair contest that pits individual employees against employers who have much greater economic strength. They idealize a labor movement that will fight for the little fellow. Other unionists feel a personal need for the union to give them security and status in working relationships. Many indicate a predominant interest in the economic gains they ascribe to concerted action, while some emphasize the union's protection against unfairness, favoritism, and arbitrary action on the part of employers. A relatively small proportion reports joining or retaining membership because of contract requirements and personal pressures.

No simple tabulation of findings in these studies is justified, for they are not designed to be formally additive. They have not asked precisely the same questions nor do the respondents represent a carefully selected sample of all union members. Further, the studies report on "stated" reasons for participation in union activities. Some real and important reasons may be overlooked because investigators fail to probe sufficiently broadly and deeply. On the other hand, the studies clearly evidence the broad appeal of unionism and its real or assumed value as a means of satisfying a wide variety of employee wants and needs.[30]

---

[30]For more on these recent studies see: Hjalmar and Ruth A. H. Rosen, *The Union Member Speaks* (New York: Prentice-Hall, Inc., 1955); Walter Uphoff and M. D. Dunnette, "Understanding the Union Member," *Bulletin No. 18*, University of Minnesota Industrial Relations Center, June, 1956; Jack Barbash, "How and Why Unions are Organized," *Labor Unions in Action* (New York: Harper and Brothers, 1948), Chapter II; Joel Seidman, Jack London, and Bernard Karsh, "Why Workers Join Unions," *Annals of the American Academy of Political and Social Science*, Vol. 274 (March, 1951), pp. 75–84; Arnold M. Rose, *Union Solidarity* (Minneapolis: University of Minnesota Press, 1952); Leonard Sayles and George Strauss, "What the Worker Really Thinks of His Union," *Harvard Business Review*, Vol. 31, No. 3 (May–June, 1953), pp. 94–102, and also their *The Local Union: Its Place in*

Labor movements have provided no simple, completely satisfactory solution to the social and economic problems of industrial employment. They have, indeed, introduced many new problems. Understanding them requires perspective; they have emerged as efforts and attempts to satisfy a wide range of human needs. They have fashioned their programs according to priorities in these needs as perceived by their members and leaders. Sometimes top priorities have been given to economic problems and at other times to social or political expressions. As movements mature priorities change.

Labor movements today reflect these needs and the constraints of societies of which they are a part. American unionism, the subject of the next chapter, is by no means typical. Indeed, it is in part the subject of a chapter because it is distinctive in its goals, policies, and programs. In Chapter 9 attention is directed to the common policies and practices of American unions. Then, in Chapter 10, attention shifts to the role of employers and employer associations in collective bargaining.

ANALYTICAL REVIEW QUESTIONS

1. (a) What is meant by the dignity of labor? (b) How is this related to modern collective bargaining?
2. (a) What is the term or duration of most American collective agreements? (b) What is the economic significance of the trend toward longer agreements?
3. (a) What is the difference between bargaining units and bargaining agents? (b) How is each determined?
4. How are labor movements and collective bargaining related? How are they distinguished?
5. Collective bargaining does not end with the signing of a contract. What happens after the contract is signed, and why is this part of the collective bargaining process?
6. Why are unions likely to be politically oriented in newly industrialized nations?
7. What was the major difference between merchant guilds and craft guilds?
8. (a) What conditions tended to disrupt the guild system? (b) What effects did this have upon occupational mobility?
9. (a) What three types of members were found in craft guilds? (b) Who were in the yeomanry guilds? (c) With whom did this latter group negotiate?

the Industrial Plant (New York: Harper and Brothers, 1953). See also Mark Perlman, *Labor Union Theories in America* (White Plains, New York: Row, Peterson & Co., 1958); "The Theory of the Labor Movement Reconsidered: A Symposium," *Industrial and Labor Relations Review*, Vol. 13, No. 3 (April, 1960), pp. 334–97; Sydney Lens, *The Crisis of American Labor* (New York: Sagamore Press, 1959).

10. What were some of the basic goals of labor movements?

11. What is the significance of such activities as the Luddites, the Chartist movement, and the Junta?

12. In what ways are American unions not typical of unions in most other nations?

13. What are the major types of changes in European labor movements?

14. Why have not American unions shown more leadership in international associations of unions?

15. What five major theories of labor movements can be identified?

16. (a) Differentiate the bourgeoisie from the proletariat. (b) With what theory of the labor movement is this concept associated? (c) Who were its principal exponents?

17. In the Marxian philosophy unions would ultimately disappear. (a) How and why? (b) How would they be helpful in an intermediate stage of revolution? Why?

18. Does socialist unionism emphasize political or economic action?

19. (a) Describe the industrial democracy theories of the Webbs and G.D.H. Cole. (b) Contrast their viewpoints with the industrial jurisprudence or industrial democracy concepts of Sumner Slichter.

20. How is the business theory of unionism related to today's collective bargaining behavior?

21. Did the early AFL leaders emphasize long-run or short-run objectives? Why?

22. (a) Explain the "business" theory of labor movements. (b) How does the concept of opportunity fit in this theory? (c) What is the role of "job rationing"?

23. (a) What is meant by the statement that workers join unions for psychological as well as economic reasons? (b) What do we mean by psychological and social needs? (c) How are these needs related to collective bargaining behavior?

24. What is meant by Hoxie's viewpoint that unions are functional?

25. Describe the great man (agitator) theory of unionism. (b) Do agitators create or reflect unrest?

26. Do current studies of why workers join unions suggest a new theory of the labor movement? Why or why not?

Case 7-1

WHITE-COLLAR UNIONS

Assume that you have taken a job in the sales organization of a relatively small casualty insurance company. The firm has 350 employees, most of them women employed in bookkeeping and other clerical work in the home office. You work out of that office.

You have attracted the attention of the top management by the excellence of your sales record. They apparently regard you as a "comer" in the organization. You have heard through the grapevine that at least one of them has suggested that you are the executive type. You have been asked whether you would like to be sent to one of the university executive development programs, such as are offered at Harvard, Stanford, and many other institutions.

Yesterday you were invited to lunch with the executive vice-president. After lunch, he asked you what you thought about the probable unionization of their white-collar employees. After a little discussion, he made a request that you think the matter over and tell him what, in your opinion, the firm could do to make a union unnecessary from the standpoint of employees. You have been thinking about the various theories of unions and labor movements. You realize that you must take a position on the basic question: should the employer try to avoid organization of these employees?

• Your assignment, and it is really a difficult one, is to prepare a short outline summarizing what you would say to the executive vice-president. Be prepared to discuss that outline in class.

Case 7-2

A RIGHT-TO-WORK LAW

George England was the president of the Central Labor Union in a medium-sized industrial community. The state employer association had been campaigning for a "right-to-work" law that would make it illegal for an employer and a union to negotiate a union shop in which all employees would be required to join the union. The state legislature would meet the following January. In September the following editorial statement appeared in the local evening paper:

> "The CITIZEN has decided to support efforts to get a right-to-work law in our state. The decision has not been casual or thoughtless. We are convinced that several thousand of our state's citizens have become union members only because they have to join. It is our opinion that, at the present time, union shop requirements in contracts negotiated by employers and unions have been responsible for half the present membership of this state's unions. We have ourselves forced several employees to become union members in spite of their reluctance to join.
>
> We think that unions served a worthwhile purpose in earlier periods when most production workers were not well educated and could not know how to protect their own rights. We think unions may have been necessary when employers could be arbitrary because workers had no protection against unemployment and dependent old age. Today, however, we conclude that unemployment insurance and public pensions have largely eliminated the hazards of employment. We conclude further that unions are becoming less valuable with the passage of time and the growth of social legislation. Hence union shop provisions that require membership are in effect creating an artificial support for unions. In short, we think they are on the way out and should be allowed to go that way.
>
> On the other hand, of course, we have full respect for the opinions of those who hold a different opinion. We think that those who want to be union members should have that American right . . .

• Members of the Central Labor Union are much concerned about the effect of this editorial on members of the legislature. They feel that George, as president, should reply. Your assignment is to prepare a draft of a "Letter to the Editor" he might send to the newspaper and to be prepared to read and defend that letter in the next class.

UNIONS IN THE UNITED STATES

The general thesis in Chapters 8, 9, and 10 holds that the philosophy and practices of unionism and collective bargaining are a major variable influencing working conditions and employment relationships in all industrialized economies. At the present time some 17 to 18 million Americans are members of unions. Approximately 80 percent of them belong to a single major federation — the American Federation of Labor-Congress of Industrial Organizations. For most of these union members, negotiated agreements specify many of the conditions under which they work. As of 1961, an estimated 150,000 collective bargaining agreements were in force providing representation for more than 16 million union members. Somewhat more than half of this coverage was provided by 1,733 agreements, each representing more than 1,000 employees. In this group more than 60 percent involve single employers; the remainder represent groups of employers.[1]

As has been noted in Chapter 7, however, the influence of unions and of these collective agreements extends far beyond the ranks of union members. Negotiated terms and traditional practices associated with union membership shape current employment relationships outside the scope of existing contracts. Many of these practices are accepted by employers and employees who do not bargain collectively.

---

[1] "Major Union Contracts in the United States, 1961," *Monthly Labor Review*, Vol. 85, No. 10 (October, 1962), pp. 1136–41.

Unions and their members influence legislation and the actions of administrative agencies, including conciliation and mediation services, labor relations boards, and administrators of unemployment insurance and old age assistance.

HISTORIC DEVELOPMENT OF UNIONS

The historic development of unions in this country may for convenience be divided into three major periods. The first, beginning even before the nation was founded and extending approximately to the middle of the 1800's, was characterized by the organization of local craft unions. A second phase, dating roughly from 1850 to 1865 or the close of the Civil War, was marked by the organization of national unions in the major skilled crafts — stonecutters, hatters, iron workers, and others. A third period, that of federation, was initiated by the organization of the National Labor Union in 1866 and culminated in the merger of the AFL and CIO in 1955.[2]

Local Craft Unions

Small local unions were formed during colonial times, and effective local unions were reported in the earliest years of the new nation. Throughout the first half of the nineteenth century, local organizations operated largely as independent units and were limited almost entirely to the skilled crafts — leather-workers, printers, shipwrights, carpenters, and other building craftsmen. A shoemaker's guild was chartered by the Massachusetts Bay Colony as early as 1648, and an organization of coopers is reported at about the same time. Ship calkers were organized in 1700. Employed printers organized in New York in 1776. Shoemakers in 1792 and leather workers in 1794 formed local unions in Philadelphia. Shipwrights formed a local in New York in 1803. Carpenters as well as sailors were organized in New York in 1806.

Members of these early unions formed their associations primarily to enforce demands for improved working conditions, including higher

---

[2]See Leon Litwack, *The American Labor Movement* (Englewood Cliffs, N.J.; Prentice-Hall, Inc., 1962); Joseph G. Rayback, *A History of American Labor* (New York: The Macmillan Company, 1959). For a critical view of historic accounts, see Maurice F. Neufeld, "The Sense of History and the Annals of Labor," *Proceedings, Industrial Relations Research Association,* (14th Annual Meeting) 1961, pp. 214–26.

Questions have been raised about many historic explanations of union emergence and growth. George Brooks notes that explanations of the historic behavior of both unionists and industrialist employers may not represent the real reasons. Historic explanations, to be dependable, must be more penetrating, analyzing the processes underlying leader decisions, relationships, and influence. See his "The Relevance of Labor History to Industrial Relations," *Proceedings, Industrial Relations Research Association,* 1961, pp. 206–13.

wages and shorter hours — generally the 10-hour day and the 60-hour week.   Some strikes were called, and in a few instances unions organized boycotts in which they refused to patronize employers who opposed bargaining with their associations.   Some of the locals endorsed political reforms — abolition of imprisonment for debt and of required service in the militia, establishment of free public schools, tax and monetary reforms, immigration restriction, and the regulation of monopolies.   After the War of 1812, many of these locals joined with similar groups in other crafts to form city centrals or city federations.

National Unions

Several crafts were successful in combining locals to form embryonic national unions in the years just preceding the Civil War. Typographers created a national union in 1850, stonecutters in 1853, hatters in 1854, and a combination of molders, machinists, and blacksmiths was effected in 1857.   The Civil War increased demands for labor, forced employers to bargain, and thus encouraged unions. Some 32 national unions had been formed by the end of the war period.   Among the strongest, in addition to those already mentioned, were the Brotherhood of the Footboard (locomotive engineers), the Knights of St. Crispin (shoemakers), cigar makers, bricklayers, and carpenters.

Federation

In 1866 the first successful attempt to unite these varied crafts in a single, national organization resulted in formation of the National Labor Union.   It was created by the association of several city centrals and local federations of craft unions.   John Silvis, an officer in the iron molders' union, led the movement, which also sought to encourage a variety of cooperative business ventures by local unions.   This attempt at federation was short-lived.   Its local units, the city centrals, did not agree upon national issues.   Many of the cooperative ventures were unsuccessful.   The national organization lasted only a few years, but many of its locals joined a new association, the Knights of Labor.

Knights of Labor.   This organization started in and spread out from Philadelphia, beginning with a local of garment cutters in 1869.   At first known as the Industrial Brotherhood, its original member unions were locals in the Philadelphia area.   It became a national organization in 1872, at which time it also assumed the Knights of Labor title. Membership expanded slowly during the depression of 1873, in which many of the national craft unions had difficulty maintaining their unity. By 1878 only eight of these nationals continued.

The Knights welcomed locals in all crafts. In addition, the organization encouraged formation of noncraft locals to include employees in all but a few excluded occupations — saloonkeepers, gamblers, lawyers, physicians, bankers, and stockbrokers. Power in the organization was highly centralized; the supreme council could order district and local units to comply with national policies and programs. Because of this centralized control and the encouragement of both craft and noncraft members, this phase in the development of the labor movement is often described as that of *amalgamation*.

In some respects the Knights of Labor operated as a secret fraternity. Local meetings were conducted with extensive ritual. Public statements were signed with a symbol — five asterisks. Many nonmembers feared the organization as a threat to local and national government. The danger that it might seize control is said to have been discussed in several presidential cabinet meetings. The Knights engaged in a number of large, successful strikes which increased their prestige and influence.

Nevertheless, the organization lasted only a few years. Its decline is traceable to defeats in several major strikes, the organization's failure to develop a deep and continuing acceptance of common interests among its members, and dissension with respect to political objectives. Strikes, even when they were successful, were frequently costly and necessitated heavy levies on members. Many members objected to the highly centralized authority in the organization. The Knights of Labor lasted out the century, but it ceased to exert any great influence after 1890.[3]

American Federation of Labor. In 1886 some 25 craft unions, led by Samuel Gompers and Adolph Strasser of the Cigar Makers Union, formed the American Federation of Labor. It began as a loose federation of sovereign national craft unions. Prominent among the basic policies of the new organization was voluntary association and the autonomy of member nationals. The Federation did not deal

---

[3]For more detail on the Knights of Labor, see Norman J. Ware, "Knights of Labor," *Encyclopedia of the Social Sciences*, Vol. XIV, p. 387.

directly with individual members of local unions or with local unions that were members of affiliated nationals.

The Federation structure combined features of our colonial Confederation, the British Trade Union Congress, and the United States Government. National and international unions became the principal voting members. Their voting strength was weighted according to the numbers of members they represented and for whom they paid a per capita tax to the Federation. The Federation avoided interference in the affairs of its member unions, although it did try to settle disputes among them. It provided national representation before legislative bodies, helped members in their organizing campaigns, and encouraged popular acceptance of the union label.

Membership in unions affiliated with the Federation grew slowly and with several serious setbacks during the first 50 years of its life. The general course of that growth has been charted in Figure 8-1.

The Federation was created as a voluntary association of national unions whose members were for the most part skilled craftsmen. Some member unions also included semiskilled and unskilled workers within a particular industry. For example, the United Mine Workers represented various employees in coal mining — miners, carpenters, mule drivers, electricians, and others. Unions of craftsmen, however, held major power in the Federation. Its organizing activities were concentrated largely on the expansion of membership among craftsmen. When semiskilled machine operators were organized, they were generally expected to join a member craft union whose membership specifications permitted their admission. As the years passed, a growing minority of member unions proposed the expansion of organization on an industry basis rather than a pure craft basis.

Critics of the pure craft basis for union membership pointed to the fact that rapid technological change in American industry was creating a growing group of semiskilled, machine-tending employees. Mass production industries were employing ever larger numbers and proportions of all workers. Employees in these industries could not qualify for membership in unions that specified long periods of apprenticeship. They did not want to join unions in which most of the members were skilled craftsmen. They identified their interests with industrial unions made up of other semiskilled or unskilled workers like themselves, preferably those in the same industry.[4]

---

[4]In some usage, craft unions were described as "horizontal," while industrial unions were regarded as "vertical." This usage is unfortunate, for the term "vertical" is also

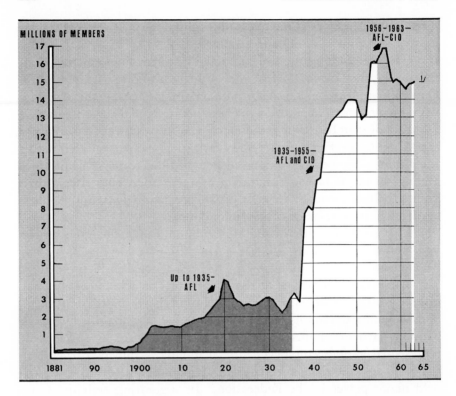

Figure 8-1

MEMBERSHIP OF UNIONS AFFILIATED WITH AFL-CIO — 1881–1963

Sources: Annual reports of AFL-CIO and United States Department of Labor, *Directory of National and International Unions in the United States, 1963, Bulletin No. 1395* (May, 1964).

Within the Federation a sharp difference of opinion developed. Several national unions favored an active organizing campaign to create new industrial or industry-wide unions and to admit such unions to the Federation. Other member unions opposed both the organizing of industrial unions of nonskilled workers and the admission of such industrial unions to the Federation. The issue was the subject of heightened attention when wages fell and unemployment increased in the 1930 depression.

---

used to describe unions, like that of the carpenters, that enroll employees in all stages of the processing of raw materials.

The three arguments most frequently advanced by those who advocated organizing industrial unions held that:

1. Membership of affiliated unions was declining as craftsmen were being replaced, in the changing economy, by semiskilled machine-tenders in the mass-production industries.
2. Industrial workers offered their services in competition with those of skilled craftsmen. Their products entered the same consumer markets as those of craftsmen. Hence, unorganized industrial workers created a direct threat to the wages and other working conditions of skilled workers.
3. The political power and influence of unions could not be effective as long as they represented only a minority of wage earners. The Federation could not "speak for labor" if it excluded industrial workers.

The principal arguments of Federation members who objected to the admission of noncraft workers and unions may be outlined as follows:

1. Numbers of industrial workers were so large that they could hold the major voting power in the Federation if their national unions were granted full and equal membership in the Federation.
2. Industrial workers have less bargaining power than craftsmen. Their inclusion in the Federation would probably pull the wages of craftsmen downward, and their presence would diffuse and reduce the bargaining power of the crafts.
3. Admission of industrial unions would create serious conflict within the Federation. The jurisdictions of many older AFL unions would have to be narrowed or they would be violated by those of the newer industrial unions.

Congress of Industrial Organizations. For several years those who favored a strong organizational campaign among industrial workers tried to secure favorable action by the Federation. Finally, on March 10, 1935, eight international unions withdrew from the Federation and created a new Committee for Industrial Organization. These founders included unions of coal miners, mine and smelter workers, typographical workers, clothing and garment workers, and those in textiles, oil, and the millinery industry.

The new CIO, financed by gifts from these older unions, undertook a vigorous organizing campaign in steel, rubber, flat glass, automobiles, and other mass production industries. On November 14, 1938, in a constitutional convention, a permanent organization known as the Congress of Industrial Organizations was formed. At its founding the new Congress included 41 national and international unions and organizing committees, and 675 directly affiliated local unions representing 4,037,877 individual members. This new organization remained an important part of the American labor movement until it was reunited and merged with the AFL in December, 1955.

The CIO was responsible for one of the most dramatic and dynamic phases in the history of the American labor movement. It introduced and developed many viewpoints, policies, and practices that were new to the traditions of the American Federation of Labor. Basic to all of them was the general policy of welcoming semiskilled and unskilled workers into the member unions of CIO. The Committee for Industrial Organization created a new era of dynamic organizing activity. It added a youthful militance and enthusiasm to the ongoing labor movement. Its leaders, generally younger than their AFL counterparts, were also more venturesome and aggressive.

CIO policy continued the central focus on business unionism, but it also placed greatly increased emphasis on political action. Policies favored more centralized control by national unions than had been traditional in the voluntary federation of sovereign national unions that made up the AFL. CIO undertook a continuing campaign to win popular understanding and support for the labor movement.

To implement these policies, CIO created its national organizing committees, which acted in lieu of national unions in holding new locals together during the preliminary organizing campaigns. CIO also established its Political Action Committee (PAC), endorsed individual political candidates, and undertook strenuous campaigns to "get out the vote." It took a positive position in favoring social legislation designed to improve workmen's compensation, unemployment benefits, and old age pensions, and to enforce minimum wage and maximum hour provisions. It initiated several new bargaining tactics, including *sit-down* and *slow-down strikes*, both of which were designed to compensate for the reduced bargaining strength of non-craft workers.

Most important, CIO demonstrated that strong, effective unions could be built around semiskilled and unskilled members on an industry rather than a craft or occupational basis.

The CIO organizing program in the 1930's has been described as the "turning point for American labor."[5] It gave new life and vigor to the labor movement and, as Galenson puts it, "The entire social

---

[5] Walter Galenson, "1937: The Turning Point for American Labor," Reprint from *Festskrift Til Frederik Zeuthen* (Berkeley: University of California Institute of Industrial Relations, 1959). See also his *The CIO Challenge to the AFL* (Cambridge: Harvard University Press, 1960).

structure of the country, its basic power relationships, were altered fundamentally over the brief span of six months."

AFL-CIO. After twenty years of separate and frequently competitive operation, the AFL and CIO concluded an agreement to combine in December, 1955. The new organization brought the national and international craft and industrial unions that were members of AFL and CIO together "under one roof."

The merged federation involved some compromises in the differing viewpoints of the former AFL and the CIO. The CIO emphasis on the organizing of industrial workers, however, was not lost in the merger. Also, the CIO position with respect to the importance of political action and the values to be gained from favorable legislation and friendly administration was accepted with little or no modification in the combined AFL-CIO. The relationship of member unions to the AFL-CIO, however, shows evidence of compromise, with a somewhat greater concentration of authority and more critical scrutiny of the actions of member unions than was characteristic of the AFL. Creation of the AFL-CIO special committee on the ethical practices of unions and their members and adoption of the Federation's code of ethics represent combinations of divergent philosophies with respect to the central responsibility for the behavior of members. Other policies of AFL-CIO and the programs advanced to carry out these policies are described in detail in Chapter 9.[6]

Union Membership Changes

Figure 8-2 provides an overall view of the growth of labor union membership in this country from 1897. The upward trend is apparent, as is the very rapid rise since 1933. Membership expanded most rapidly in the decade from 1935 to 1945, increasing from 3.5 million in 1935 to 14.5 million in 1945. Union membership amounted to 7 percent of the labor force in 1930 as compared with 22 percent in 1945 and about 25 percent in 1957. As a proportion of nonagricultural

[6]This historic review is necessarily brief. The interesting story of early union development is told in more detail in Mary R. Beard's *A Short History of the American Labor Movement* (New York: Harcourt, Brace and Co., Inc., 1920). Later history — 1916–1952 — as seen by a union journalist is reported in Edward Keating's *The Story of "Labor"* (Washington: Rufus H. Darby Printing Company, Inc., 1953). See also Kenneth McCartney and John G. Turnbull, "The Novel in the Study of the American Labor Movement," *Journal of Higher Education*, Vol. 24, No. 1 (January, 1953), pp. 5–12; Vernon H. Jensen, "The Beginnings of Collective Bargaining," *Industrial and Labor Relations Review*, Vol. 9, No. 2 (January, 1956), pp. 225–34. For details of the American Federation of Labor and the Congress of Industrial Organizations merger, see Arthur J. Goldberg, *AFL-CIO; Labor United* (New York: McGraw-Hill Book Co., Inc., 1956).

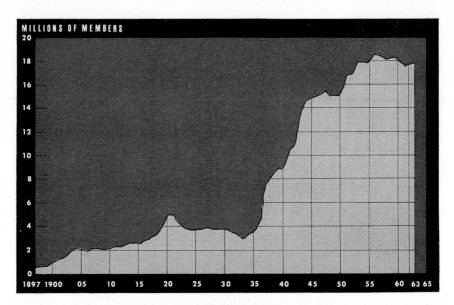

Figure 8-2
MEMBERSHIP IN AMERICAN UNIONS — 1897-1963

Sources: United States Department of Labor, *Directory of National and International Labor Unions in the United States, 1957, Bulletin No. 1222* (November, 1957), p. 8 and *BLS News Release*, No. 6026, December, 1963, corrected to January, 1964; United States Department of Labor, *Directory of National and International Labor Unions in the United States, 1963, Bulletin No. 1395* (May, 1964).

employment, membership increased from 12 percent in 1930 to approximately 33 percent in 1957. An intensive analysis, undertaken by Irving Bernstein, found that membership grew from 3 percent of the civilian labor force in 1900 to 26.8 percent in 1953.[7] Bernstein concludes that major factors explaining the long-run trend in membership are (1) expansion of the labor force, (2) wider social acceptance of unionism, (3) greater homogeneity among workers, and (4) extension of *union security* or required membership provisions. Some critics of his analysis suggest that the influence of cyclical change deserves greater emphasis. They find that changes in cost of living and in industrial production appear to be significantly and positively related, with a one-year delay, to union growth.[8]

[7]See his "Growth of American Unions," *American Economic Review*, Vol. 64, No. 3 (June, 1954), pp. 301–18.
[8]For details, see Harold W. Davey, Edgar M. Jones, and John Monroe, "The Growth of American Unions: Comment," *American Economic Review*, Vol. 65, No. 3 (June, 1955), pp. 389–90. The *Directory of National and International Unions in the United States, 1963* (*Bulletin No. 1395*, Bureau of Labor Statistics, May, 1964) provides the following estimates:

The peak of membership in national and international unions was reached in 1956, with about 17½ million members. Since that time membership has shown some decline, suggesting that some new factors may be exerting an influence. This plateau has been widely discussed and frequently cited as evidence that unions face a significant decline in power and influence. Some observers attach similar significance to the fact that reported membership, calculated as a percentage of all nonagricultural workers, reached a peak as early as 1945.

Speculation about the implications of recent declines is complicated by the limitations of all membership reporting. Current reports have benefited from federal legislation that requires unions to report their finances, but that requirement is most effective with respect to unions affiliated with AFL-CIO. Numerous local, unaffiliated unions face no such requirement. In addition, some evidence suggests the growth of bargaining associations, large and small, that do not regard themselves as unions but serve similar purposes. They are notable, for example, among white-collar scientists, engineers, and teachers. It is not at all impossible that such associations may be growing in numbers, membership, and power.

Unions affiliated with AFL-CIO reported some 15 million members in 1962. Current estimates indicate approximately three million unionists in unaffiliated unions. The largest of the unaffiliated is the Teamsters with approximately 1½ million members.

Present membership shows heavy concentration in manufacturing, construction, transportation, service industries, and government. Union membership varies from region to region and state to state, depending principally on the industrial activities of various localities. North Central, Western, and Northeast regions include large numbers and proportions of union members. The Mountain states and the South show much less penetration.[9]

	Percent of Labor Force	Percent of Nonagricultural Employees
1956	24.8	33.4
1957	24.6	32.8
1958	23.9	33.1
1959	23.8	32.1
1960	23.3	31.4
1961	22.0	30.1
1962	22.2	29.7

[9]For details see H. M. Douty, "Collective Bargaining Coverage in Factory Employment, 1958," *Monthly Labor Review*, Vol. 83, No. 4 (April, 1960), pp. 345–49 and H. P. Cohany, "Union Membership, 1958," *Monthly Labor Review*, Vol. 83, No. 1 (January, 1960), pp. 1–9.

Not all members of the labor force can be regarded as eligible for union membership. Farmers, proprietors, managers, most professional groups, and family workers are generally excluded in calculations of *union potential*. Solomon has estimated the union potential as including 72.5 percent of the labor force in 1950 as compared with his estimates of 49.0 percent union potential in 1900 and 64.5 percent in 1930. He concludes that the union potential is not likely to grow beyond 80 percent of the labor force.[10] An area of recent rapid growth is that of white-collar workers who now represent more than a third of this potential.

STRUCTURE OF THE AFL-CIO

In the American labor movement since the Civil War, major power and authority have centered in the national and international unions. The American Federation of Labor was founded on a philosophy of *voluntarism* with respect to the participation of member unions. The Congress of Industrial Organizations, while somewhat more centralized, preserved most of the autonomy of these national organizations. The merged AFL-CIO continues this pattern, although the Federation has used its right to exclude or expel as a means of eliminating what are regarded as Communist-dominated internationals, or, as in the case of the Teamsters, unions whose leaders have failed to meet required ethical standards as interpreted by the Committee on Ethical Practices.

The national unions are, however, the heart and center of AFL-CIO. All the rest of its somewhat complicated structure leans heavily on these nationals and internationals. Figure 8-3 outlines these organizational relationships.

Officers. The AFL-CIO has a president and a secretary-treasurer, an executive committee of 8 members, and an executive council composed of the president, the secretary-treasurer, and 27 vice-presidents. These officers administer the policies established by its constitution and conventions and direct the organization in the periods between conventions. The convention — held every other year — is the basic policy-making agency in the AFL-CIO.

---

[10]Benjamin Solomon, "Dimensions of Union Growth, 1900–1950," *Industrial and Labor Relations Review*, Vol. 9, No. 4 (July, 1956), pp. 544–61. For details on distribution of union membership among the states, see Leo Troy, *Distribution of Union Membership Among the States, 1939 and 1953* (New York: National Bureau of Economic Research, 1957).

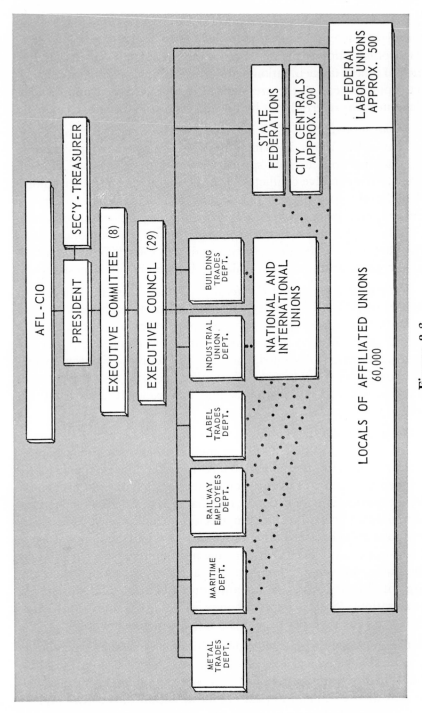

Figure 8-3

ORGANIZATIONAL STRUCTURE OF THE AFL-CIO

An additional agency known as the General Board of the Federation might have been included in the chart. Its membership represents a combination of the members of the Executive Council plus one principal officer of each national and international union. The Board meets upon the call of the president at least once a year and decides policy questions referred to it by the officers or the Executive Council.

Departments. AFL-CIO has established six departments. They represent subdivisions in which national unions having common problems may join to give special attention to matters of mutual concern. They resolve conflicts of jurisdiction among member unions and undertake special programs to advance their interests. Not all member unions belong to these departments. Departmental affiliation is voluntary. An international or national union may join more than one department. These departments maintain some 925 local departmental councils in the cities in which their membership is most active.

National and international unions. These are the principal members of AFL-CIO. They are national or international unions (internationals are so-called because they have locals in Canada, Mexico, or Central America) that maintain membership in the central federation. As noted, they are the sources of power in the federation, for they hold most of the voting strength, they charter and can revoke charters of their locals, and they can withdraw from the federation if they wish.

State federations. Within each state, locals of national unions that are members of AFL-CIO are invited to join state federations, which are chartered by the national AFL-CIO. These organizations assist member unions in working on their special statewide problems. They focus attention, for example, on what are regarded as inadequate unemployment or workmen's compensation benefits or objectionable restrictions on collective bargaining, such as might be imposed by a right-to-work law. They represent member unions before legislative committees and state administrative agencies, including those in charge of old age assistance, unemployment benefits, and workmen's compensation. State federations may assist in organizational campaigns and provide other similar services for member unions.

City centrals. Within individual cities member unions may form city centrals or city federations, which are also chartered by AFL-CIO. Their activities are similar to those of the state federations, except that their focus and impact are local, within the community.

Local unions. These are the basic units in the labor movement. At the time of the merger in 1955, AFL unions represented some 50,000 locals and CIO some 10,000. Some 500 *federal labor unions* are affiliated directly with AFL-CIO.

Locals are, except for federal labor unions, chartered by their nationals and internationals. They carry on the regular business of negotiating, settling grievances, administering agreements, and assisting members in their employment problems. Their members elect officers, employ business agents, and select delegates to state and national conventions. Their activities make up the grass-roots base of the American labor movement.

Federal labor unions. Some locals, as has been noted, are not members of any international. They may be newer locals, recently organized and as yet not affiliated with an international. In some cases, however, these locals have long maintained their federal status, preferring to be affiliated directly with the central federation. Many of these locals have been established by organizational campaigns in which several international unions have joined forces.

The overall organizational structure sketched in Figure 8-3 identifies the position of each of these subdivisions in the organization. Solid lines in the figure represent required relationships, while dotted lines indicate that participation is voluntary.[11]

Committees and staff. The range of AFL-CIO interests and activities is suggested by its standing committees and staff specialists. Standing committees advise the officers on civil rights, community services, economic policy, education, ethical practices, housing, international affairs, legislation, political education, public relations, safety and occupational health, social security, veterans' affairs, and research. The staff of the Federation includes specialists in accounting, civil rights, community services, education, international affairs, legislation, the library, organization, political education, public relations, purchasing, social security, and research.

UNAFFILIATED UNIONS

Throughout the years many local unions have remained independent and some national unions have not affiliated with any federation or congress. Other national and international unions have

---

[11]For details, see Maurice F. Neufeld, "Structure and Government of the AFL-CIO," *Industrial and Labor Relations Review*, Vol. 9, No. 3 (April, 1956), pp. 370–90; Philip Taft,

moved in and out of the AFL and the CIO. Several, including those regarded as Communist-dominated, have been expelled. The Mine Workers joined and left both the AFL and the CIO and are presently unaffiliated. The Teamsters were expelled from AFL-CIO in 1958, thus adding a million members to the ranks of unaffiliated unions.

For many years the most prominent independent unions were the "Big Four" of the railroad brotherhoods, including locomotive engineers, firemen and enginemen, railroad trainmen, and conductors. The firemen and enginemen and the railroad trainmen are now affiliated with AFL-CIO, joining 14 other unions in that industry. Largest numbers of independent unions are in manufacturing, transportation, and government.[12]

Some unaffiliated locals are company-wide, including only the employees of a single firm or plant. In earlier periods, especially in the period of the National Recovery Administration immediately following the depression of 1929–1932, many employers encouraged the organization of such locals. When employers aided in their organization and support, they were described as *dependent* or *company unions* or as *employee representation plans*. Some independent unions, while they have not joined AFL-CIO, have been associated in smaller federations. The largest of these associations — the Confederated Unions of America and the National Independent Union Council — merged in March, 1963 to form the National Federation of Independent Unions.

In recent years local, independent unions have probably increased in numbers. Their members, estimated as from 2 million to 3 million, include more than 10 percent of the national total. They are particularly attractive to white-collar, technical, and professional workers.[13] Their future is uncertain. Shostak has studied the independent, single-firm union and concludes that their prospects are unfavorable. He notes that "the independents have no appeal in industries characterized by horizontal job mobility or joint employer action, and the independents cannot match such features of the major

The Structure and Government of Labor Unions (Cambridge: Harvard University Press, 1954). See also Joan G. Kilpatrick and Miles C. Stanley, "Handbook on Central Labor Bodies," *West Virginia University Bulletin*, Series 64, No. 4–6 (October, 1963).

[12]See, for the interesting history of one of the most prominent of these unions, Reed C. Richardson, *The Locomotive Engineer, 1863-1963* (Ann Arbor: University of Michigan Bureau of Industrial Relations, 1963).

[13]Leo Troy, "Local, Independent and National Unions: Competitive Labor Organizations," *Journal of Political Economy*, Vol. 68, No. 5 (October, 1960), pp. 487–506; H. P. Cohany and J. Neary, "Unaffiliated Local and Single Employer Unions in the United States, 1961," *Monthly Labor Review*, Vol. 85, No. 9 (September, 1962), pp. 975–82.

unions as vast research facilities, large treasuries, considerable political influence, and the like." Hence, "There is likely to be a decline in the total number of such unions and in the membership they represent."[14]

On the other hand, many local and regional organizations that call themselves federations, associations, and organizations, generally avoiding the "union" designation, are effectively representing their members in something very much like collective bargaining. Federations of engineers, scientists, and teachers are prominent among these groups. They may be the means by which collective bargaining is extended to white-collar workers who do not find a typical union or affiliation with a federation of crafts and industrial workers attractive.

UNION LEADERSHIP

In this country union leadership generally comes up through the ranks; thus, most unions are led by former rank-and-file members. At mid-century presidents of unions in the AFL were, on the average, 55 years of age while those of the CIO averaged 42 years, according to a study by Mills. Of the total group 22 percent had some college education, 41 percent attended high school, and 36 percent were formally educated only in grammar schools.[15]

Top officers, even in the larger national and international unions, are paid salaries much smaller than those of corporation presidents in major business firms. In 1960 salaries of international union presidents ranged from about $10,000 to $72,000, with Harry Bridges of the Longshoremen at the bottom of the list and James Hoffa at the top. George Meany, as President of AFL-CIO, received $42,692. All such salaries are supplemented by expense accounts. All are small when compared with the salaries of corporate officers, which ranged up to more than $600,000.[16]

---

[14]Arthur B. Shostak, *America's Forgotten Labor Organization*, Industrial Relations Section, Princeton University, 1962, esp. pp. 127–29. See also Julius Rezler, "Labor Organization at Du Pont: A Study in Independent Local Unionism," *Labor History*, Vol. 4, No. 2 (Spring, 1963), pp. 178–95.

[15]Mills studied many other characteristics of union leaders. See C. Wright Mills, "A Who's What of Union Leadership," *Labor and Nations*, Vol. 1, No. 3 (December, 1945), pp. 33–36 and his *The New Men of Power* (New York: Harcourt, Brace and Company, 1948). For other interesting studies of union leaders, see Robert L. Kahn and Arnold S. Tannenbaum, "Union Leadership and Member Participation," *Personnel Psychology*, Vol. 10, No. 3 (Autumn, 1957), pp. 277–92; Bernard Karsh, Joel Seidman and Daisy Lilienthal, "The Union Organizer and His Tactics: A Case Study," *The American Journal of Sociology*, Vol. 59, No. 1 (July, 1953), pp. 113–22; George Strauss, Leonard R. Sayles, and Risha Sayles, "Leadership Roles in Labor Unions," *Sociology and Social Research*, Vol. 38, No. 2 (November–December, 1953), pp. 96–102; Glenn W. Miller and Edward J. Stockton, "Local Union Officer — His Background, Activities and Attitudes," *Labor Law Journal*, Vol. 8, No. 1 (January, 1957), pp. 28–38.

[16]See *U.S. News and World Report*, July 10, 1961, p. 90 and May 13, 1963, pp. 63–65.

Current leadership of American unions has been criticized both for its lack of dedication and zeal and for autocratic action. American unions have intentionally avoided any close affiliation with or leadership by nonmember intellectuals. Their earlier struggles with "captains of industry" may have encouraged if they did not actually require dictator leaders. Modern leaders still have to gain and hold their positions by participating in the internal union political process. At the same time they must conform to the modern view of leader obligations in what is often described as a "fiduciary" type of leadership.

AFL-CIO has sought to prevent racketeering leadership; its Codes of Ethical Conduct prescribe democratic control and prohibit conflicts of interest. The quality of leadership varies widely both at local and national levels. Few leaders have evidenced the ingenuity necessary to extend organization into the growing ranks of white-collar workers.[17]

UNION FINANCES

Union programs are costly, and union business is big business. Income is derived principally from dues, initiation fees, and special assessments, although some unions have profitable investments as well. Annual dues total more than $600 million of which about one half is retained by locals; the other half is forwarded to the internationals and to various levels of federations, city and state. The AFL-CIO receives a portion of this income in the form of "per capita taxes" amounting to 4¢ per month per member.

Dues average about $3.00 a month. They range from $1 to $25 a month, the highest being those of airline pilots. Initiation fees are usually from $2 to $5, with the lowest reported charges being 65 cents and the highest $250. Both dues and initiation fees are higher in craft unions than in industrial unions.

Complete information with respect to union finances is not available, but 1958 federal legislation — the Landrum-Griffin Act (with subsequent amendments) — has required more public accounting than ever before for larger, nonlocal unions. A *Fortune* estimate in 1962 listed as the five wealthiest unions the Ladies Garment Workers, the Brotherhood of Electrical Workers, the United Mine Workers, the

[17]See Jack Barbash, *Unions and Union Leadership* (New York: Harper and Brothers, 1959). See also his "The Leadership Factor in Union Growth," *Monthly Labor Review*, Vol. 86, No. 2 (February, 1963), pp. 133–36.

Amalgamated Clothing Workers, and the Teamsters in that order. Automobile Workers, Machinists, and Steelworkers would have been in this top-level list if they controlled negotiated pension and welfare funds.

The *Fortune* report concludes that unions control assets of about $4.5 billion, including some $1.5 billion in general funds, $500 million in welfare funds, and $2.5 billion in union-managed and jointly trusteed pension funds.[18]

Union funds are invested in a wide range of securities, from government bonds to banks (Amalgamated Clothing Workers), apartment houses (ILGWU, Electrical Workers, Painters, Milliners), home mortgages, corporate bonds, and common stocks. One Teamsters pension fund includes investments in resorts, hotels, gambling casinos, and a variety of business ventures.[19]

The United States Department of Labor has provided the graphic outline of union revenues and the services provided by unions for their members shown as Figure 8-4.

WHITE-COLLAR UNIONS

The immediate future of union power is closely related to organizational success among white-collar workers. Blue-collar occupations — the historic source of union membership — have become a smaller proportion of the labor force, and their rate of increase is lower than that of white-collar employees. To maintain their influence in the future, unions must make themselves attractive to growing numbers of white-collar workers.

In recent years unions have undertaken continuing campaigns to extend their membership among white-collar employees. It is estimated that some 14 million white-collar salaried workers may reasonably be regarded as potential members, including clerical and office workers, employees in retail and wholesale establishments, and government employees. More than 2.5 million of these employees are already represented by a variety of unions.

The appeal of union membership for such employees has increased as their historic advantage in salaries has declined or disappeared. Average earnings of organized craft and production workers

[18]"Labor's Capitalists," *Fortune*, November, 1962, pp. 153 ff.

[19]For details on current union income, by source, see the annual reports of the *Bureau of Labor Management Reports*, Department of Labor. Data refer to unions covered by the Landrum-Griffin Act.

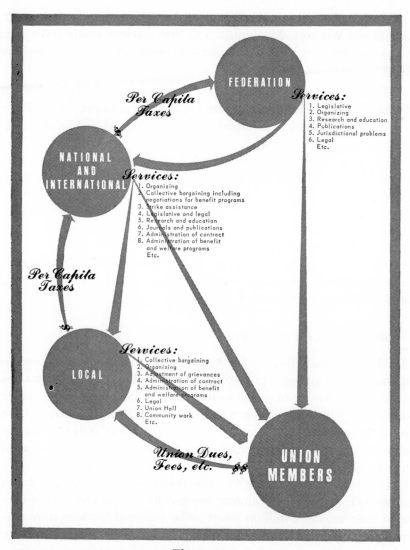

Figure 8-4

MAJOR SERVICES OF LABOR UNIONS AND SOURCES OF REVENUE

Source: United States Department of Labor, Bureau of Labor Statistics.

have overtaken and passed those of many office occupations. Many types of fringe payments which formerly were exclusively available to office workers have been extended to hourly-rated workers. In current practice employers frequently negotiate benefits with union members, after which similar provisions are made applicable to office jobs.

In spite of the resulting economic pressure toward forming and joining unions, the organization of white-collar workers encounters powerful resistance. Office workers are generally less willing to be standardized than production workers. Many office workers place a high value on opportunities for personal anvancement which, they feel, might be jeopardized by collective action. Union membership may be regarded as occasioning some loss of social status and prestige. Such attitudes are especially important among the growing numbers of technical and professional employees — engineers, for example.

Office workers who have joined unions have sometimes become a part of the bargaining units that include production workers. In this situation they are represented by industrial unions. Others have joined the Office Employees International Union. Retail clerks are represented by five affiliated and several independent unions.

Many managers are convinced that white-collar workers will continue to resist organizational drives. A study by the University of Michigan found that 57 of the 85 managers who responded believe that white-collar workers are "basically different." Differences, as these managers see them, make the white-collar workers more individualistic, independent, loyal, intelligent, informed and aggressive, and closer to management in thinking.[20]

Obstacles to the spread of unionization among these workers, according to the same survey, include the "negative status symbol phenomenon" of union membership, jurisdictional and other internal union conflicts, the heavy proportion of women among white-collar workers, and a trend toward smaller bargaining units based on automation. Factors encouraging unionization include poor supervision, defective salary administration, unsatisfactory benefits and services, and poor communications. The absence of formal grievance procedures may be closely related.

Union membership among public employees — federal, state, and local — is frequently regarded as setting an example for white-collar workers. Organization of teachers, for example, has been cited as an opening wedge for unionization of other clerical and office employees. Unions of federal employees were encouraged by the President's *Executive Order 10988* (1962) which restated the right of employees to bargain collectively through unions that could become sole bargaining representatives. At the federal level about 800,000 of the

---

[20]Clark C. Caskey, "White Collar Employees — A Union Dilemma and a Management Challenge," *Management of Personnel Quarterly*, Vol. I, No. 3 (Spring, 1962), pp. 10–13.

2½ million eligible employees were union members in 1963, principally in the National Federation of Federal Employees. Another quarter million state and local employees were organized, mainly in the American Federation of State, County, and Municipal Employees.

The scope of bargaining for public employees is more restricted than that required for private employment. Bargaining is restricted to conditions not set by law. Working conditions other than wages and hours have been negotiated, as have grievance procedures. Governments resist the right to strike for public employees on grounds of interference with public health, safety, and welfare and also because stoppages challenge the sovereignty of the public agency.[21] Further, civil service concepts generally do not embrace bilateral policy determination and may reject the propriety of using economic force to determine working conditions in public employment. Public employees generally are denied the right of arbitration with compulsory award as the final step in the grievance procedure.

Union members include both men and women. Union expansion into white-collar occupations tends to increase the proportions of women, who now make up about one sixth of the total union membership in the United States.

American unions have developed distinctive policies for advancing the general acceptance and practice of business unionism, and they have learned to depend on a wide range of programs designed to implement these policies. In the chapter that follows, attention turns to these policies, programs, and practices of labor organizations in the United States.

ANALYTICAL REVIEW QUESTIONS

1. (a) How many union members are there in the United States? (b) What proportion are they of the labor force? of those eligible for membership?
2. What effects do unions have upon employment conditions for nonunion members?
3. What were the principal objectives of the first unions in the United States?
4. What effect did the Civil War have upon formation of unions?
5. What policies of the Knights of Labor tended to encourage amalgamation of unions?

---

[21] See Arvid Anderson, "Labor Relations in the Public Service," *Labor Law Journal*, November, 1961, p. 1075.

6. What factors seem to account for the disappearance of the Knights of Labor?

7. (a) What were the two basic policies of the American Federation of Labor in its formative years? (b) How have these policies affected 20th century unionism in the United States?

8. How did technological developments help set the stage for the Congress of Industrial Organizations?

9. (a) What arguments were advanced in favor of admitting industrial unions to the AFL? (b) What arguments were offered in opposition?

10. (a) In what decade did American unionism experience its greatest growth? (b) What are some of the reasons for this?

11. Union growth has not maintained the 1935–1945 rate since World War II. What reasons might help explain this situation?

12. In what industries is union membership concentrated? Can you give any reasons to account for these varying proportions?

13. (a) In what regions of the United States is unionism strongest? (b) Where is it weakest?

14. Where is major power and authority centered in American trade unions?

15. What roles are served by state labor federations?

16. From what source do local unions get their charters?

17. What trends in the personal characteristics of union leaders are notable?

18. (a) Where do unions get their funds? (b) What proportion of dues, on the average, is retained by the locals?

19. (a) How much are average monthly union dues? (b) How much are average initiation fees?

20. (a) Have white-collar workers earned as high a percentage of wage increases as blue-collar workers in recent years? (b) What effect would you expect this to have upon their desire for union organization? (c) What actually has happened with respect to white-collar union membership? (d) What factors appear to account for this anomaly?

21. What is the status of unions of government employees?

Case 8-1

TO JOIN OR NOT TO JOIN

Assume that you are a white-collar worker in an insurance company office. You have been reasonably pleased with your experience in the firm, but some of its policies and practices do not seem either sensible or entirely fair. You have been quite honest in saying so in friendly conversations with fellow workers and with the supervisor in your department. You have been employed two years and appear to have a good chance for continued promotions.

For several months you have been receiving what you regard as propaganda literature from a local union of white-collar employees. You have had pamphlets on the advantages of belonging and some rather violent tirades against employers. You have glanced at them, not taken them very seriously, and thrown them in the wastebasket. Meanwhile, the grapevine has frequently brought you rumors that some of your fellow employees are members of that union.

Last Monday evening two representatives of the union, a man and a woman, called on you in your home. They asked you to sign an application for membership. They were quite polite and courteous about it. They made no bitter charges against your employer, although they did express the opinion that you could not expect a fair deal without an active union and collective bargaining. You found nothing they said with which you strongly disagreed, and you said you would think it over.

• They are due to come back for your answer tonight. Set down on paper the considerations that should lead you to the right answer. First list what you may reasonably expect to gain or accomplish by joining. Then, in a parallel column, list what you might lose. Be prepared to justify your decision in class.

Case 8-2

COMMUNIST DOMINATION — SYMPTOMS

Your next-door neighbor has given you something to think and worry about. He is a very friendly, cooperative person, a long-time employee of a local manufacturing firm. Usually, his viewpoints and moods are cheerful and pleasant. The other evening, however, he came into your house and asked if he could talk to you privately for a while. He closed the doors, pulled down the blinds, and proceeded to unload his troubles and suspicions. He is completely convinced that Communists have gained control of his local union. He thinks that they want to provoke a long strike. He says that the union is changing in character, that he doesn't care to go to the meetings any more, that he is personally afraid to say what he thinks, and that he is seriously considering looking for a job elsewhere.

He has come to you because he trusts you. You gave him the idea when you indicated a few days earlier that you were taking a course in this field. Now he wants your considered counsel.

• Think it over and prepare some notes for a further private conference with him. List the questions you think he should ask to discover whether Communists are in control. Then, first, assume that you conclude he is wrong in his suspicions, and list your advice to him. Then assume you conclude he is right about the situation, and list your suggestions.

UNION POLICIES AND PROGRAMS

Preceding chapters have discussed the emergence, growth, and persistence of labor movements and the organizational structure and membership of American unions. In this chapter attention is directed to the policies that guide unions in the United States and to the major programs through which unions seek to carry out these policies.

Policies are generally accepted and agreed upon courses or intentions. Policy declares what a group or association proposes. Policies are, therefore, closely related to ideals, goals, and objectives. They indicate the general direction to be followed in working toward accepted goals. Thus, one widely accepted union policy proposes to work for continually higher earnings for members.

Programs are plans for action to be taken, presumably to implement policies. Each such program may include a range and combination of specific practices. Thus, a program of negotiation (implementing the general policy of collective bargaining) may include such practices as convening negotiating committees, sending notices of demands to be made, refusing to work without a contract, asking the assistance of the conciliation service, proposing the arbitration of unsettled issues, and perhaps striking if disagreements appear to warrant such drastic action.

Practices often include *procedures*, which are established patterns of acting. Thus, practice may specify the procedure of written ballots in union elections or the procedure of opening each union meeting with the reports of standing and special committees.

BUSINESS UNIONISM

Basic to most of the policies of organized labor in the United States is the general philosophy of business unionism. Most of the policies of American unions involve the intention to achieve immediate economic gains for their members. Secondary interest in *uplift* or *reformist unionism* encouraged union concern about social reforms and what may be described as a liberal political viewpoint. Similarly subordinate is the general policy of seeking to elect and cultivate friendly legislators and public administrators.

For "business" purposes American unions have proposed to extend and strengthen their organizations. They have repeatedly stated their intention to organize the unorganized. On the other hand, while they have sought additional members, they have not generally tried to develop a class consciousness among employees. Business unionism is realistic in recognizing the comparatively high mobility of American manpower — its tendency to change employers, jobs, and status. Class consciousness and dedication to any radical program are difficult when today's automobile worker may be a used-car salesman tomorrow and a dealer next year. Hence, union policy has generally emphasized the attainment of specific economic objectives — higher wages, shorter hours, union security, the protection of workers' rights in jobs, political influence, and public support. Policy statements often reiterate continuing interest in the dignity of labor and the inalienable rights of free men, but the influential union programs are generally "bread and butter" programs.

Wages and Hours

As business unions, American labor organizations have consistently sought to raise wages. Their persistent wage policy was stated by Samuel Gompers in a word that has since become the classic answer to what unions want in wages. Gompers explained that they want "more." In general, and with few exceptions, the stated intention has been to get increased wage rates and earnings.

Everyone knows that unions propose rising wages for their members. But that general policy may, at one time, propose higher rates of pay and at another time forego a wage increase in order to maintain employment levels. Union policy presumably proposes something approximating a long-term maximization of total member income. To that end a union may, at one period, prefer relatively small gains for large numbers of members to the much greater possible increases available through sharp restrictions on membership. A union may conclude that more members mean more power in future bargaining.

Union policy must consider possible effects of wage increases on the employment of members in each bargaining situation. It must evaluate the likelihood of employer action designed to find substitutes for the services of union members. It must consider member appraisals of what their union has done for them as compared to the accomplishments of other unions. Perhaps the top priority is given to preserving and perpetuating the union. Secondary priorities emphasize maximum wages (and wage supplements or fringes) and maximum membership as a symbol of power and influence.

In day-to-day experience these policies encourage unions to oppose wage reductions even more strongly than they fight for increases and to protect the jobs of members even more strongly than they campaign for new members. Similarly, day-to-day policy relates wage objectives to the militancy and resistance of employers, the stage of the business cycle, and current public policy, i.e., determined control of inflation.[1]

Union policy on hours has been closely related to wage policy. In general, unions seek shorter hours; they hold that "whether you work by the hour or the day, decreasing the hours increases the pay." They have proposed reductions in hours as means of spreading the work among members when employment is scarce. They have sought premium pay for overtime, in part as a work-spreading measure. In most situations, however, unions have sought fewer hours per day and per week, with no reduction in weekly earnings. Indeed, reductions in hours of work have been used to increase weekly earnings, for by reducing the daily or weekly hours for which regular wages are paid, additional overtime with premium rates has been required.

Participation in Management

Although many managers may think unions want to take over the reins of management, union policy has usually tried to avoid union

---

[1] For much more detail, see Albert Rees, *The Economics of Trade Unions* (Chicago: University of Chicago Press, 1962), pp. 52 ff.

responsibility for managerial decisions. Unions and their members, with few exceptions, want to negotiate with managers about conditions affecting employees but not to become managers. They object to unilateral decisions on working conditions affecting their members. On wages, hours, overtime, seniority, promotions, pensions, benefits, and many other considerations, unions insist on their right to join in decision making.

Unions have forced the widening scope of collective bargaining which has inevitably increased their responsibility for management decisions. They have argued that unions must insure consideration of members' interests in all decisions that affect these interests. Some unions have sought a voice in decisions about changing products, moving plants to other locations, farming out production, layoffs, shutdowns, product pricing, investment, borrowing, new plants and equipment, and the levels of dividends. In some cases unions argue that such intervention is necessary because employers show little responsibility for employee interests or are unable or unwilling to protect these interests. In others, they express grave doubt about the skill and competence of managers and conclude that policy requires added and broader participation by union representatives. It is notable that the most extensive excursions of unions into what is sometimes described as the area of *management prerogatives* have appeared in those industries in which firms frequently find themselves in economic distress and business failures are numerous.[2]

Union Responsibility and Security

Most unions propose to be responsible. They intend to fulfill, carry out, and perform the agreements they negotiate. They regard themselves as responsible agents of their members. They propose to police their agreements and insure that both employers and employees observe their provisions.

Unions cannot insure responsibility, in the opinion of many union leaders, unless they can depend on continued union membership and a degree of central authority to parallel their responsibilities. They cannot be responsible if members may join or leave the union at will. Enforcement of collective agreements is also impossible, in this

---

[2]See Paul V. Johnson, "Decision-making Under Collective Bargaining," *Monthly Labor Review*, Vol. 80, No. 9 (September, 1957), pp. 1059–63; also Willard A. Lewis, "Collective Bargaining — The Management Setting," *Labor Law Journal*, Vol. 13, No. 6 (June, 1962), pp. 411–24.

view, if a large portion of the work force is not bound by such agreements. Individual employees, if not required to be members in good
standing in the union, may refuse to follow contract provisions. Other
employees, although benefiting from union activity, may refuse to
support the union. These "free riders" can create dissatisfaction
among union members who may also refuse to continue their support
of union activities. For these reasons unions propose *union security*, in
which all employees are required to become and to remain union
members or to support the union.

In earlier periods union security was generally described as involving *recognition* of a union. Negotiation and practice developed a
number of patterns, ranging from no recognition to complete acceptance of the union as the only authorized agent for all employees. The
most important of these patterns can be readily identified in current
employment. They include:

Open shop. Unions are ignored and no distinction is made by the
employer between union members and those who are not members.
Management deals with each employee on an individual basis and
recognizes no union as representing any of its employees.

Bargaining agent for members. In this relationship a union of
employees is accepted as representing only those employees who are
members. The union is not regarded as speaking for other employees
in the same shop or bargaining unit. The employer thus maintains his
freedom to deal with other employees as individuals.

Sole or exclusive bargaining agent. When so recognized, the union
is accepted as the agent for all employees in the unit. While there is no
requirement that all employees join the union, the organization negotiates for all employees, including nonmembers.

Preferential shop. The union is recognized as the sole bargaining
agent, and the employer agrees to hire union members if they are
available and to give first chance for employment to union members.

Maintenance of membership. All employees who are or who become members of the union on or after a specified date must remain
members in good standing for the full term of the agreement. This
form of union security achieved wide usage during World War II as a

compromise when unions demanded and employers opposed a requirement of union membership by all employees if a majority approved. Provisions generally include an *escape period* in which union members can resign if they wish.

Agency shop. All employees in the bargaining unit pay dues to the union although they do not have to join it. This arrangement is sometimes called the *Rand Formula*, having been specified by Judge Rand as a part of the settlement of the Canadian Ford Motor Company strike of 1945.

Union shop. All employees in the bargaining unit must be or become members of the union. Management is permitted to hire nonunionists, but when they are accepted as employees (at the end of the probationary period) they must join the union.

Closed shop. Only union members may be hired. Management may hire all employees for the bargaining unit through union offices, and the union may undertake to supply such numbers as may be needed. Employees must maintain their union membership in good standing. In the United States the closed shop for most interstate industries was outlawed by the Labor-Management Relations Act of 1947. It is permitted in some industries, notably construction and printing.

Checkoff. The checkoff is a supplement to these security provisions in which the employer deducts union dues (and sometimes initiation fees and assessments) from paychecks and remits these collections to the union. The *compulsory* and *automatic checkoff* compels union members to allow employers to collect these deductions. The *voluntary checkoff* requires that individual members personally authorize such deductions. Authorizations are generally revocable on 60- or 90-day notice to insure their voluntary nature. The checkoff is frequently combined with other forms of union security.[3]

---

[3]The most common form of union security is the union shop, presently included in 53 percent of current agreements, according to a 1964 Bureau of National Affairs survey of 400 contracts. An additional 14 percent provide a modified union shop; the most common modification requires that all employees join except those who were employed before the agreement was negotiated. Eight percent of the agreements specify the agency shop, and eight percent provide maintenance of membership. Eighty-three percent include the checkoff.

It is worth noting that union security is a much more prominent issue in this country than in most European nations. Unions in Europe have not emphasized this policy.[4]

Union Jurisdictions

As a matter of policy, American unions have usually sought to define jurisdictions in a way that will minimize overlapping and conflict. Each union has staked out its claims with respect to those eligible for membership or jobs under its control. Claims have been defined in several ways. They were first based on craft and geographic area. Later, industry was sometimes substituted for craft, and nationals and internationals extended their geographic coverage across the nation and into Canada and Mexico.

The American Federation of Labor long sought to prevent interunion competition by prohibiting *dualism*. It refused membership in the Federation to an applicant union whose jurisdictional claims were regarded as infringing on those of any member union. The same policy is common among state and local federations.

In spite of these policies, conflicts of jurisdiction have created continuing problems. Technological changes in building, for example, have raised issues between carpenters, metal workers, and electricians. When the CIO was formed in 1935, jurisdictional arguments were increased, for the industrial boundaries of CIO unions crossed many craft union lines. No single, central federation was available to bring the AFL and CIO rivals together. Merger and formation of the AFL-CIO in 1955 has not eliminated these frictions.[5]

Arguments over which union has the exclusive right to organize employees in certain jobs have frequently led to interunion *raiding* in which one union has sought to enroll the members of another and to gain acceptance as the certified bargaining agent for them. Prevention of jurisdictional disputes and raiding is a major responsibility of the departments in AFL-CIO. After experience with several special boards, AFL and CIO joined in creating the Industrial Union — Building Trades Accord in 1958. Conflict between AFL-CIO unions

---

[4]Michael Dudra, "Approaches to Union Security in Switzerland, Canada, and Columbia," *Monthly Labor Review*, Vol. 86, No. 2 (February, 1963), pp. 136–38.

[5]For details of a classic struggle of this type, see Harriet D. Hudson, *The Progressive Mine Workers of America: A Study in Rival Unionism*, University of Illinois Bureau of Business Research, 1952.

and unaffiliated unions — especially those expelled from AFL-CIO — remains a continuing problem.[6]

Union Fraternity and Democracy

Unions have grown from small, fraternal associations, generally composed of skilled craftsmen, into million-member, semipublic organizations. Their traditions, extending back to the fraternal guilds, are not readily adapted to their new size and status. In some cases traditional practices have facilitated undemocratic manipulation, the exclusion of minority groups from membership, or labor racketeering in which unions are captured by individuals or cliques who use organizations for personal gain.

Policies designed to strengthen the bargaining power of unions may limit member control of locals and internationals. One example involves the use of *trusteeships;* to insure local compliance with the programs of the international or compliance with an unpopular contract, the international may remove local officers and place the local in trusteeship, thus gaining control of members and financial resources. Other traditional practices were designed to prevent internal dissension and criticism and thus to present a united front in relationships with employers and the public. In some unions rules severely penalize any member found guilty of criticizing union officials. Members may have to stand trial before the officials they criticized.

Some unions have been reluctant about relinquishing centralized control and encouraging more democratic practice lest the actions of certain locals weaken the bargaining position and influence of the national organization or of other locals. They have, with understandable reason, feared that small, special-interest groups might gain control of locals and, through them, of the national organization. The success of Communist groups in thus achieving a dominant position in several unions has justified some such concern.

Many local unions that try to assure democratic procedures encounter serious difficulties in trying to maintain the active participation of members. One of the most perplexing problems is that of getting members to attend union meetings. This problem is complicated by the fact that some locals with several thousand members cannot provide physical facilities for regular meetings of the full membership.

[6]For an excellent summary, see Mark L. Kahn, "Recent Jurisdictional Developments in Organized Labor," Chapter 1, in Harold W. Davey, Howard S. Kaltenborn, and Stanley H. Ruttenberg (eds.), *New Dimensions in Collective Bargaining* (New York: Harper and Brothers, 1959).

Most but not all unions are now democratic in their acceptance of members. A strong trend in that direction has been reemphasized by public demands for integration in unions as well as in schools and employment. Several unions have established special tribunals composed of neutral third parties to hear the claims and protect the interests of individual members. The Public Review Board established by the UAW in 1957 is a well and favorably known example. Its seven members have staff assistance and are granted authority to make final and binding decisions.[7]

Many of the practices that formerly interfered with democratic controls have been eliminated by recent legislation. Some former election procedures tended to perpetuate control by individual officers or executive committees. Elections could be postponed. Similarly, constitutions could only be amended by conventions, which might not be convened. In some cases such conventions also provided the court of final appeal for member grievances.[8]

Union Political Policy

In the early years of the 19th century, American unions frequently championed political reforms. Later, both the National Labor Union and the Knights of Labor were active in politics. For both, the experience was costly, for it created internal dissension and diverted the attention of members from organizational and other problems facing their unions. This experience unquestionably influenced the American Federation of Labor in its determination to avoid political action. For many years the AFL refused all political affiliations and commitments. The Federation's political policy was described simply as "rewarding labor's friends and punishing its enemies." Partisan politics could not be brought into AFL conventions because they were specifically barred by the AFL constitution. Its leaders frequently opposed such legislation as that fixing

---

[7]See "A More Perfect Union: The UAW Public Review Board: Why, What, How," Detroit; UAW Publications Department, undated; see also David A. Swankin, "Union Disciplinary Powers and Procedures, (I. Grounds for Trial of Members and Local Officers)," *Monthly Labor Review*, Vol. 86, No. 2 (February, 1963), pp. 125–32.

[8]On these points see Philip Taft, *The Structure and Government of Labor Unions* (Cambridge: Harvard University Press, 1954); Glenn W. Miller and J. E. Young, "Member Participation in the Trade Union Local," *American Journal of Economics and Sociology*, Vol. 15, No. 1 (October, 1955), pp. 18 ff; Joel Seidman, "Democracy in Labor Unions," *Journal of Political Economy*, Vol. 41, No. 3 (June, 1953), pp. 221–31; Seymour Martin Lipset, Martin Trow, and James Coleman, *Union Democracy* (Glencoe, Illinois: The Free Press, 1956).

minimum wages and maximum hours on the ground that workers could protect their interests better by joining unions and negotiating terms of employment than by legislative action. The Federation did, however, approve formal lobbying activities in 1895 and moved national headquarters to Washington, D. C. in 1897, in part to facilitate closer relationships with legislators.

Opposition to radical changes. The American labor movement has included some members who have favored creation of a labor party and government ownership and socialization of industry, although advocates of these developments have represented distinct minorities. In the early years of the nation, local unions advocated reforms that were then regarded as radical, such as free public schools, the abolition of imprisonment for debt, and the removal of the poll tax. As the nation and the labor movement matured, however, the most prominent and powerful unions came to oppose radical changes.

In part, this characteristic of American unions is attributable to their generally unsatisfactory experience with a variety of labor parties and reformist and revolutionary unions. By the time the American Federation of Labor was established in 1886, its leaders were firmly committed to a pragmatic approach, which saw special labor parties and socialistic reforms as threats to union power and success. Smaller groups of socialist workers (The Socialist Labor Party, The I.W.W., The Communist Trade Union Unity League, and others) were formed from time to time; their life was generally short and their influence small.

Walter Galenson has explained the nonpolitical, nonsocialist policies of American unions in terms of several distinctive characteristics of both work and workers in this country, including a comparatively high scale of living, rapid change in social status and in economic and political power, an impressive rate of economic growth, and the absence of any pervasive class consciousness, prevented in part by racial and national divisions among workers.[9] Socialism was regarded as a "foreign" idea and program. Class consciousness was reduced by early American unions whose membership included the aristocracy of skilled workers. Unions thus exerted a divisive influence within the total labor group by representing a special subclass of craftsmen rather than all wage earners.

---

[9]Walter Galenson, "Why the American Labor Movement Is Not Socialist," Reprint from the *American Review*, Vol. 1, Winter, 1961 (Berkeley: University of California, Institute of Industrial Relations, 1961).

The two-party political system has operated in the same direction. The open-class system and relatively high mobility of American workers have prevented solidarity in voting and discouraged worker hopes of electing their own members to high office. Labor has sought influence within existing parties rather than outside them because unions could not reasonably hope to establish a labor-oriented society by political action. American unions have been conservative also because their members have achieved notable gains in economic security and personal protection against arbitrary action through the collective bargaining process. On the other hand, American unions have become increasingly active in politics in the present century.

CIO and AFL political action programs. From its inception the CIO proposed an aggressive program of political action. In 1943 its leaders formed the CIO Political Action Committee headed by Sidney Hillman, president of the Amalgamated Clothing Workers, to "conduct a broad and intensive program of education for the purpose of mobilizing the five million members of CIO and enlisting the support (of other unionists) for effective labor action on the political front." In 1945 state and local political action committees were organized. These committees endorsed and recommended candidates, published and circulated literature dealing with candidates and legislation, publicized what they regarded as the antilabor viewpoints and actions of some politicians, and organized campaigns to get out the vote.

Meanwhile, AFL leaders had concluded that their members must have more influence in legislative chambers. In 1947, after the enactment of the Taft-Hartley Act, the Federation established Labor's League for Political Education (LLPE), which encouraged state and local political committees and activities and followed the pattern of CIO-PAC, although generally with greater restraint. Both political arms of organized labor urged union members to support, by their endorsements and financial aid, candidates who were regarded as friendly to labor. International unions were asked to make voluntary contributions to these political action committees.

Following the merger of the AFL and CIO, popular discussion frequently debated probable effects on the political influence of organized labor and the possibility of an American labor party. The merged AFL-CIO formed a Committee on Political Education, generally described as COPE, to carry on the earlier activities of CIO-PAC and AFL-LLPE.

So far as labor domination of politics is concerned, it is noteworthy that union members frequently disagree with leaders when they enter the polls. On the other hand, union support has unquestionably been decisive in many local elections. Unionists have not contributed heavily to labor's political action committees. In general, union members, although loyal and cooperative in the "business" of their organizations, apparently consider much more than friendliness to unions as an essential qualification for public office.

A labor party? The possibility of a third labor party in the United States has long been discussed. An American Labor Party, operating somewhat successfully in New York after 1936, did not spread to other parts of the nation. That experience coincided with the earlier and similar experience of the United Labor Party of 1886 in Illinois, the Union Labor Party in Wisconsin in the same period, and later labor parties in New England, Colorado, and elsewhere. An American Labor Party, representing 15 state labor units, held a national convention in Chicago in July, 1920. Renamed the Farmer-Labor Party, it continues only as the Democratic-Farmer-Labor Party in Minnesota.

Both the CIO and the AFL have avoided third-party movements. Samuel Gompers and William Green, former presidents of the AFL, repeatedly expressed opposition to such a movement. Sidney Hillman, former chairman of CIO-PAC, expressed his opinion that such a third party would divide rather than unite the "forces of progress."

International Union Relations

Especially since World War II, American unions have sought to aid and cooperate with the labor movements in other non-Communist nations. As noted, they were represented in the International Federation of Trade Unions from 1910 to 1923 and from 1937 to 1949. The CIO joined the World Federation of Trade Unions in 1945. In 1949 both AFL and the CIO became affiliated with the International Confederation of Free Trade Unions, as did the United Mine Workers. Both AFL and CIO have maintained offices in Europe and have assisted in organizing workers there and in Central America. Some fifty American unions have developed affiliations with their counterpart organizations throughout the world. According to a published statement by the President of AFL-CIO in May, 1963, that body has spent 23 percent of its income on the development and aid of foreign unions in postwar years.

COLLECTIVE BARGAINING PROGRAMS AND PRACTICES

Preceding sections have explained union policies — the accepted courses and intentions of unions. To effect and carry out policies, American unions have developed numerous practices and programs. Basic to most of them is the practice of negotiating bilateral agreements with employers. American unions have also developed and supported a wide range of "worker's education" programs designed to help members improve themselves and increase their influence in public affairs. The remainder of this chapter outlines these major activities or programs.

Negotiation and Contract Administration

Most of the programs of unions are directly related to the business unionism that has been distinctive in the American labor movement. They seek to advance the economic status of union members by influencing the operation of labor markets, wages, and working conditions on the job. In labor markets these programs may seek to affect both demands for and supplies of labor. Most of them, however, center about the general practice of bargaining collectively rather than as individual employees.

Through negotiation and contract administration, unions wield a powerful influence in creating the rules of the game in day-to-day employment. Negotiations cover a wide range of working conditions and relationships. The breadth of this bilateral rule-making is evident from a list of the most common subjects in negotiated agreements and includes union security, rights of union representatives, grievances, organizational activities and dues collection in the plant; management security and rights; wages, hours, overtime, holidays, rest periods, vacations, leaves of absence, absenteeism, tardiness, seniority, disciplinary action; pensions, insurance, hospitalization; probation, retirement, transfers, layoff, recall, promotions, strikes, and lockouts. This is not by any means an exhaustive list.

In the process of negotiation, unions study their experience under current agreements, note new developments in other employment, canvas the wishes and suggestions of their members, create negotiating committees, designate their "bargainers," present demands to employers, consider counterproposals, arrive at tentative agreements, and submit these proposed terms to union members for ratification. They may employ skilled and experienced negotiators, or negotiation may be undertaken by a committee of local officers and rank-and-file members. They may encounter difficult issues, threaten to strike, call in mediators or conciliators, or agree to arbitrate unsettled issues.

Control of Labor Supplies

To strengthen the union's influence, it usually seeks to control supplies of labor available to employers. Such programs begin with efforts to insure that most or all employees will be available only on terms established jointly by negotiation. To that end various types of union security are negotiated, as are standard rates of pay. A *union scale* is established, setting minimum rates at which members can be employed. Other practices insure the maintenance of union jurisdictions by agreement with employers and other locals or internationals so that no "outside" substitute employees are available. These practices may be supplemented by restrictions on entrance to the union, which may admit only a predetermined number or may refuse admission to workers who have not successfully completed a specified apprenticeship.

The union thus seeks a monopolistic control of the labor supply. Achievement of that end is a major factor in the union's influence. A union that fails to achieve a degree of control must, therefore, be regarded as relatively ineffective. Further, it cannot be expected to balance the economic power of the employer in negotiation.

Restriction of Output—Work Rules

Sometimes restrictions on numbers are supplemented by limitations on the output of individual workers. Unions may set limits, pars, bogeys, or quotas on the amount of work each employee will perform. Such practices may specify how many bricks may be laid per day or how wide a paintbrush may be used. They may provide penalties to be assessed against members who exceed these quotas. In other situations they may create work rules that force the employment of more workers than are needed. In some restrictive practices union rules may force employers to hire standby teams in addition to workers already on the job, as when a traveling show must employ local musicians in addition to those who accompany the cast.

On the railroads, and in some other industries, such practices are widely known as *featherbedding*. They include "full-crew rules" that require employment of additional workers not actually needed to operate trains under normal circumstances and regulations that force employment of a second crew or shift after only a few hours' work by the first crew.

In general, work rules are developed to protect the employment security of union members. They set production quotas, require "full crews," or prevent the employer from contracting for work to be done elsewhere in order to provide added employment for union members. As a result, work rules may be relaxed when jobs are plentiful.

All such practices tend to force the underutilization of labor. At the same time, they require more than optimum amounts or proportions of labor. Their influence is widely assumed to increase costs to consumers. However, while this result is to be expected if employers are competitive, in which case output falls and prices are forced upward, they may not have this effect when the employer is a monopolist. In that case the added costs may be paid from profits.

Since restrictive work rules are designed largely to increase employment security, they may be eliminated by negotiated substitutes such as early retirement and dismissal compensation. Profit sharing may also discourage such restrictions.[10]

The Strike

The most drastic control of labor supplies is that exerted in a strike. The strike is generally a last resort on the part of a union, a tactic to be avoided as long as possible. It is a powerful and many-sided weapon. It can create hardships for nonparticipant third parties, as well as for employers and for union members themselves.

Strikes take many forms, as will be noted in Chapter 13. All, however, limit or reduce the labor available to the employer. Modern unions try to reduce the hardships imposed by strikes on their members; they provide *strike benefits*. Benefits range from $5 to $50 per week and may be calculated as flat rates, or they may vary according to the member's need as indicated by his dependents. Benefit provisions generally specify a one-week waiting period and require that

---

[10]See Edward Reighard, "Work Rules Under Profit-Sharing," unpublished thesis, Stanford University, 1963; Norman J. Simler, "The Economics of Featherbedding," *Industrial and Labor Relations Review*, Vol. 16, No. 1 (October, 1962), pp. 111–21; Paul A. Weinstein, "Featherbedding: A Theoretical Analysis," *Journal of Political Economy*, Vol. 68, No. 4 (August, 1960), pp. 379–87; Ivar Berg and James Kuhn, "The Assumptions of Featherbedding," *Labor Law Journal*. Vol. 13, No. 4 (April, 1962), pp. 277–83; Paul Jacobs, "Dead Horse and the Featherbird," *Harper's Magazine*, September, 1962 (Reprint No. 190, University of California Institute of Industrial Relations, Berkeley, 1962); Margaret K. Chandler, "Competition Between the Inside and Outside Labor Force for the Work of the Industrial Firm," *Proceedings of the Fourteenth Annual Meeting*, Industrial Relations Research Association, 1962, pp. 334–45.

recipients be available for picket duty. They are paid only for strikes authorized by the international union.

Boycotting and Picketing

Another important tactic, long used here and abroad, is the boycott. Unions may boycott an employer who refuses to conclude a collective agreement or to meet their demands, that is, they may refuse to have other business relationships with him. If he is a seller of goods, for example, they may refuse to buy. In the *primary boycott*, only members of the union that is involved in the dispute join in the agreement not to patronize the offending employer. Thus, for example, members of a retail clerks' union may boycott a local super-market with which they are in dispute. They may picket it or parade before it, carrying "We Don't Patronize" banners. In the *secondary boycott*, union members engaged in a dispute with an employer secure the cooperation of third parties who are not directly involved in the dispute. They might, for example, secure an agreement by all unions in a local federation that their members would not patronize the employer. Again, unionists in a factory in Wisconsin, in dispute with their employer, might be joined by other unionists throughout the country who would refuse to buy or install the products of the employer. It is generally observed that a primary boycott is usually ineffective, but a secondary boycott can exert tremendous economic pressure.

Picketing involves the provision of union representatives who parade, carry banners, and otherwise call public attention to a union criticism of or dispute with an employer. Such representatives maintain a *picket line* and try to persuade members of other unions, customers, and patrons not to cross that line. Members of associated unions may refuse to cross or go through picket lines if the picketing has been approved by a local central labor union or city federation.

Protection of Members

Among the most important union programs are those that provide day-to-day status, security, recognition, and protection for members. Unions offer opportunities for recognition and social advancement. Aspiring members can serve on committees, hold local offices, become "wheels" in the local and international.

At the same time, local union action is designed to give members an added feeling of security and protection. Unions, by their negotiation of seniority provisions, may assure systematic consideration of long service in time of layoff and recall to work after layoff. They provide a spokesman for dissatisfied employees. They protect members who complain or criticize from recrimination by supervisors or managers.

A major practice is intervention by the union to prevent discrimination, arbitrary discharge, or other penalties. This service alone, insuring the individual worker that he will not be penalized without cause, has been frequently described as the greatest single reason why members join.

Grievances

Negotiation generally establishes a formal procedure for the settlement of grievances. When an employee "grieves" — meaning that he feels he has been improperly or unfairly treated — he may immediately bring his union into the situation. If he prefers, he may first discuss the matter with his supervisor; but the union representative or shop steward may be asked to be present in even this earliest statement of dissatisfaction. If the supervisor is unable to make a mutually satisfactory adjustment, the usual procedure is to file a formal statement of the grievance, putting the complaint in writing for further consideration. Detailed procedure thereafter varies, but it always provides for several steps or stages, in each of which the grievance is reviewed and attempts are made to find a satisfactory settlement. One step or stage may involve discussion by a grievance committee representing both the employer and the union. Another step may bring the matter before a representative of the international union and the industrial relations director of the firm. In a final step the matter may be submitted to arbitration before a neutral arbitrator for final and binding decision.

Personal Services

To make the bonds of unionism stronger, unions may provide assistance in meeting the personal problems of members. While these services may not be directly involved in negotiations, they tend to hold members together and prevent defections in times of strife. They thus strengthen the control by union officers and help to insure union responsibility and the performance of contracts.

Many locals have promoted credit unions that make small loans to members. Some locals have developed programs of counseling, with professional counselors to advise members on health problems and on financial, housing, and other personal and family problems.

Many unions — especially those in the railroad industry and older craft unions — maintain an extensive system of financial aids and fraternal benefits for members and their families. Death benefits and life insurance are common, and assistance in old age, sickness or other disability, and unemployment are also important. Some unions maintain homes for retired members. Some have their own medical, health, and hospitalization provisions. Health centers with medical, dental, and optical services are provided by local unions in several areas.

Unions as Salesmen

Demands for labor are derived; some union programs are designed to increase product demands and thus create more work. Plasterers, for example, have widely advertised the advantages of plaster walls over types of dry-wall construction. Electricians, painters, plumbers, and other crafts have sought and secured building codes that necessitate more of their services. They have also campaigned for licensing legislation designed to restrict the competition of amateurs and support demands for craftsmen. In several cities unions have sought local legislation forbidding public purchase of products — streetlight poles, for example — produced by the employees of unorganized firms.

Union Labels

Older AFL unions have long taken the lead in a movement to create demands for member services and to promote solidarity in union ranks by popularizing the union label. The idea is to encourage members as well as consumers outside the labor movement to ask for goods and services identified by the registered mark of union workers. At the same time, the label serves to remind members of the fraternal nature of their unions. Such labels may be placed on products — hats, shoes, cigars, cigarette packages, and published material of all sorts — or they may identify an establishment — a bar, restaurant, or meat market, for example. Union conventions frequently hold a union-label roll call, asking members who are wearing union-label hats, shoes, and suits or who are smoking union-label cigars or cigarettes to stand and be counted. The label is said to have been started by cigar factories in California in 1875. The union label trades are represented by a department in AFL-CIO.

Unions in Business

Some unions have gone into business on the theory that they could better serve their members by providing union-owned retail stores, bakeries, laundries, undertaking and funeral parlors, mines, farms, factories, housing, life insurance companies, and banks. Unions have operated labor banks since 1920 and life insurance companies since about the same time. Among the most extensive housing programs is that of the Amalgamated Clothing Workers, which has built and operated apartments in New York City since 1927. In part, such ventures have appeared desirable for the productive investment of union funds. The United Mine Workers provides an excellent example, however, of extensive investment in business without assuming managerial responsibility.

There is no uniform pattern of success or failure in these business ventures. Some appear to have been well planned and well managed. In others unions have taken heavy losses. In some cases, as in the felt hat industry, unions have provided capital as a means of keeping firms in business. Most unions now avoid direct business ownership or management, but many unions have invested in corporate securities.

American unions face an increasingly important and difficult investment problem as their assets continue to grow. Pension and welfare fund reserves have come to involve impressive totals. Senate investigating committee hearings in 1956 and 1957 directed public attention to the hazards in the careless administration of these funds. Several international unions have sought safe, productive investments in insured home mortgages or those guaranteed by the Veterans' Administration. Others — the International Brotherhood of Electrical Workers and the United Mine Workers are examples — have created their own insurance companies which maintain continuing investment programs.

Research and Publications

To aid in effective negotiation, many national unions and some state and city federations provide research directors and assistants.

These staff members, professional economists, and others study experience under existing contracts, make comparisons with other unions and industries, prepare materials for negotiations, analyze the financial reports of business firms, draft legislative proposals, and otherwise aid officers and members in carrying out union policy.

AFL-CIO and international unions maintain public relations offices, provide news releases, and publish their own journals and newspapers to keep members informed.

Workers' Education

Workers' education programs, carried on and supported by local unions in many localities, help members to continue learning and provide additional orientation in the goals, achievements, and current programs of the labor movement. They also give special attention to the preparation of leaders for unions. Courses generally include parliamentary procedure, labor economics and labor problems, union history, labor's political program, conference leadership, and a wide variety of cultural subjects. These education programs may be offered by special labor schools or local high schools, colleges, and universities.[11]

Multi-Employer Bargaining

To widen the range of union controls over labor supplies, some unions have encouraged *master contracts* in certain localities and industry-wide bargaining in several industries. Under provisions of master agreements, all or most of the employers in a locality agree to meet the same minimum terms in employing union members. For example, construction contractors are faced with a single supply of local carpenters, bricklayers, plasterers, and other craftsmen. In industry-wide bargaining the entire labor supply for an industry may be represented in negotiations by a single union.

Master contracts are well established in local collective bargaining practice. The idea that all contractors in a locality should be expected to pay the same minimum rate for carpenters, for example, now meets with little criticism or opposition. Employers have in most cases accepted the practice as economically sound and desirable. The idea of

---

[11]For a detailed picture of these programs of workers' education see Caroline F. Ware, *Labor Education in Universities* (New York: American Labor Education Service, 1946); also her "Trends in University Programs for Labor Education," *Industrial and Labor Relations Review*, Vol. 3, No. 1 (October, 1949), pp. 54–69; also Jack Barbash, *Universities and Workers' Education* (New York: Harper and Brothers, 1955); also Joseph Mire, "Training for Executive Staff in Labor Unions," *Monthly Labor Review*, Vol. 85, No. 3 (March, 1962), pp. 261–63.

a single labor market for a particular craft in one locality tends to give stability to labor costs and removes a source of competitive advantage. In many localities employer cooperation in local labor markets has been traditional. Employers have sometimes cooperated in providing a single employment office. Those with responsibility for hiring have found it convenient to keep in touch with others having similar responsibilities in competing firms. In such cases a master agreement does little more than to formalize practice developed in day-to-day experience and balance the union's economic power with that of employers.

Industry-wide bargaining is similar, but it generally extends over a much wider geographic area and thus exerts a significantly greater influence on the whole national economy. In a common form a union deals with all or a majority of employers who form an industry bargaining committee or association for that purpose. In one variation a national union bargains with one or more of the largest employers. The resulting agreement becomes a pattern for contracts with other employers. This practice was common in the basic steel industry until recently and remains the established procedure in the automobile industry. The practice is sometimes said to involve power centers in which *key bargains* are generated, followed by *satellite bargains* with smaller employers in the industry. The satellite bargains imitate the general pattern established in the key bargain, but they may involve concessions or variations to fit special economic problems of the smaller firms.

Industry-wide bargaining is much less common in this country than in several foreign nations. In England and Sweden, for example, master agreements set the rules for most employment. In this country, although such industry-wide agreements have become more common in the past twenty years, they have been formally administered in only a relatively small number of industries.

Association bargaining on an industry-wide basis has attracted wide attention and created some popular concern. It is sometimes argued that it threatens the existence of smaller firms on the assumption that they may be marginal as to profit. Legislation has been introduced in Congress to restrict the area of such bargaining, one bill limiting the area to a 100-mile range. The propriety of industry-wide bargaining is also challenged by those who fear more serious strikes with greater hazards to the public interest and welfare as a possible outcome.

On the other hand, unions — and employers also — may be expected to work toward more multi-employer bargaining. Unions tend to adapt their programs to the patterns of competition in the industries represented by members. When several firms compete in the same product markets, unions are under pressures from both members and employers, demanding that the rules and conditions of employment be made uniform.

There are other reasons for expecting multi-employer bargaining — both at the local level and at the industry level — to become more common in the future. One such reason is the fact that older industrialized economies have moved in that direction, as already noted. Another is the increasing complexity of negotiations which puts the small, individual employer at a distinct disadvantage as compared with large firms or large unions. A third reason is the growth in influence of industry-wide national unions, a trend that creates pressures for similar matching employer organizations. Still another is the current trend toward more positive employer negotiation. Associations can probably make much more effective presentations of employer demands than most individual firms can. Such a change may well necessitate greater public intervention and regulation, in part to protect the public interest in possible industry-wide strikes and in part to prevent unreasonable demands by union or employer associations.[12]

CHANGING EMPHASES IN UNION GOALS AND TACTICS

Has collective bargaining become obsolete and unsuited for a modern industrial economy? Is it on the decline? Many recent critics of traditional union policy and practice suggest that unions must change if they are to survive. Technological change has reduced the numbers of craftsmen and is eliminating many of the occupations that have provided large numbers of union members. Traditional union practice provides no satisfactory solution to the growing problem of unemployment. Union-sponsored apprenticeship programs cannot

---

[12]For an interesting discussion of advantages and disadvantages in industry-wide bargaining, see W. Ellison Chalmers and Scott MacEachron, "Master Agreements in Collective Bargaining," University of Illinois *Bulletin*, Vol. 47, No. 22, November, 1949; see also Milton Derber, *Labor Management Relations at the Plant Level Under Industry-Wide Bargaining* (Urbana: University of Illinois Institute of Labor and Industrial Relations, 1955); and Gerald G. Somers, "Experience Under National Wage Agreements," *West Virginia University Business and Economic Studies*, Vol. 2, No. 4 (June, 1953), pp. 82 ff. For a case study, see Mitchell O. Locks, "The Influence of Pattern Bargaining on Manufacturing Wages in the Cleveland, Ohio Labor Market, 1945–50," *Review of Economics and Statistics*, Vol. 37, No. 1 (February, 1957), pp. 70–76; also Walter H. Carpenter, Jr. and Edward Handler, "Small Business and Pattern Bargaining," *Management Research Summary* (Washington, D.C.: Small Business Administration, June, 1961).

provide an adequate answer to growing demands for continuing training and retraining. International competition, the balance of international payments, national defense, and popular demands for rapid economic growth require sophisticated wage policies and have encouraged governmental intervention to restrict strikes and specify "guidelines" for wage increases. Bargaining has been the subject of tightening public regulation so that its scope, content, and procedure are largely prescribed by administrative agencies. Many of the historic programs of American unions are either outdated or greatly restricted. Union membership tends to become less attractive when union action is thus constrained.

Union members and leaders have recognized these changes. In part, their reaction has been to try to conserve the gains of the past. To that end some unions have given major attention to preservation of restrictive work rules, opposing changes that reduce numbers of jobs. Unions have undertaken organizing campaigns among white-collar workers, but traditional union practices are not appealing to many office workers, teachers, and technicians. The tendency to look backward has, in itself, alienated much popular support for unions; to many nonmember citizens, it suggests a reactionary rather than a crusading, forward-marching, socially-concerned movement.

Many union leaders are convinced that "old style" collective bargaining must change. Public opposition to major strikes has encouraged both unions and employers to experiment with third-party participation in bargaining. In one form neutrals join with company and union representatives in year-round discussions of differences. They assist in gathering and analyzing relevant data and defining issues before actual negotiations begin. In another form employee committees meet with managers to find immediate solutions to day-to-day problems. Their activities resemble the long-established practice in several European nations where *shop committees* representing employees supplement formal negotiation and contract administration with continuing discussions of employment problems. Before enactment of the National Labor Relations Act in this country, somewhat similar "employee representation plans" were common. In wartime special "labor-management committees" performed a similar function, but most of them disappeared immediately after the war.

Recently, in the basic steel industry, a Human Relations Committee was established following a long dispute and strike in 1959–1960. The committee includes representatives of eleven companies and the Steelworkers Union. Approximately 100 technical specialists are assigned to work with the committee, which considers problems and makes recommendations to both parties without committing either. When members cannot agree unanimously on recommendations, the committee defines the issues in detail, leaving decisions to formal bargaining.[13] In 1963 General Electric and the International Union of Electrical Workers announced a similar program.

Meanwhile, some union leaders foresee the need for a sharply revised union philosophy and a revised, "creative" approach to collective bargaining. They propose to widen the perspectives of unions, turn their attention on to such popular goals as rapid economic growth, general rather than union-member economic security, increasing productivity, effective international competition, and social welfare. They suggest that white-collar workers, including "intellectuals," will be interested in such goals which can also anticipate wide popular support.

Paul Jacobs, who concludes that traditional collective bargaining in the United States has reached and passed its maximum and is proving less and less adequate in meeting current worker needs, suggests several future changes. Most important, he concludes, is the necessity for greater emphasis on unions as political institutions. Although some improvement may come from continuous, year-round bargaining coupled with active third-party participation in such on-going negotiation, the major change must place less emphasis on economic power and more on political action.[14]

There is little disagreement among students of the American labor movement on the inevitability of significant change in both goals and tactics. American unions must change; major speculation concerns the probable nature of changes. In one careful analysis Jack Barbash concludes that the decisive influencing variables include the pattern of cyclical fluctuations in business, unions' political effectiveness, managerial success in finding satisfactory substitutes for unions among white-collar and professional workers, union experience in organizing

[13]See Joseph A. Beirne (President of the Communications Workers), *New Horizons for American Labor* (Washington: Public Affairs Press, 1962); see also George Strauss, "The Shifting Power Balance in the Plant," *Industrial Relations*, Vol. I, No. 3 (May, 1962), pp. 65–96; Solomon Barkin, "The Decline of the Labor Movement," (Santa Barbara, California: Center for the Study of Democratic Institutions, 1961).

[14]Paul Jacobs, *Old Before Its Time: Collective Bargaining at 28* (Santa Barbara, California: Center for the Study of Democratic Institutions, 1963), esp. pp. 45, 46; see also Jack T. Conway, *Ideological Obsolescence in Collective Bargaining,* (Berkeley: University of California Institute of Industrial Relations, September, 1963), 13 pp; also *Labor Looks at Labor* (Santa Barbara, California: Fund for the Republic, 1963); also Joseph Shister, "The Outlook for Union Growth," *Annals of the American Academy of Political and Social Science*, Vol. 350 (November, 1963), pp. 55–62.

and holding membership among public employees, and the sensitivity of unions and their members to the need for changing goals that match environmental changes.[15]

This chapter has given attention to major programs through which unions seek to carry out their policies. The next chapter notes the role of employers in collective bargaining and the policies and practices of individual employers and their associations.

ANALYTICAL REVIEW QUESTIONS

1. (a) Why do unions want to "organize the unorganized"? (b) What economic considerations are involved in this policy?
2. American unions have consistently emphasized economic objectives. What are some of their principal economic goals?
3. (a) Do unions interfere with employers' responsibility to manage business? (b) In what areas do they object to unilateral management decisions?
4. (a) What do we mean specifically when we say most unions propose to be responsible? (b) How is this related to their demand for union security?
5. What do we mean by union recognition?
6. What are the major forms of union security? Define each.
7. What is the difference between an agency shop and the sole or exclusive bargaining agent type of security?
8. (a) What type of union security includes an escape period? (b) Why is this form of security a compromise?
9. (a) What do we mean by dualism? (b) What is the economic significance of jurisdictional disputes?
10. What factors may impede union democracy?
11. Why are union leaders concerned with problems of membership participation?
12. (a) Do all unions have open membership? (b) What, if any, restrictions are most common?
13. How are international and local union officers elected?
14. (a) What was the major political policy of American labor prior to the formation of the CIO? (b) What is the current political policy of American labor and how is it implemented?
15. Why hasn't America had a third major political party, that is, a labor party?
16. Have American labor unions favored substantial government intervention in economic activity? Why or why not?
17. Labor's principal economic aims seek to increase members' income. (a) What does this mean? (b) Give specific practices. Why are these important?
18. How do unions seek to provide members with status, security, recognition, and protection?

---

[15]"The American Labor Movement," *Reprint Series No. 36,* University of Wisconsin, Industrial Relations Center, 1963.

19. What economic significance do the following have: (a) bogeys, (b) featherbedding?
20. (a) What are the intended economic objectives and consequences of master agreements? (b) What is the meaning and significance of satellite bargains?
21. What are the principal arguments offered for and against industry-wide bargaining?
22. (a) In what ways have unions sought to increase or maintain demands for labor? (b) Are such increases usually aimed at increasing aggregate demand for labor?
23. How have unions sought to help employers lower labor costs and increase efficiency?
24. Why does the increase in union welfare funds create an economic problem?
25. (a) What are goals of workers' education programs? (b) What subjects do they stress? (c) Why is workers' education important in a democracy?
26. What major accomplishments can be credited to third-party participation in collective bargaining? (Suggestion: Consider the steel industry experience, but look for other examples.)
27. What seem likely to be the most important variables in shaping future trends in the policies and practices of American unions?
28. What changes do you anticipate in the philosophy of the American labor movement?

Case 9-1

UNION-MANAGEMENT COOPERATION

The Spherical Tank Company has a labor contract that provides a union shop and a checkoff of union dues. Recently the firm has received a formal notice from the local union asking that one employee, John Ryerson, be discharged for failure to maintain his membership in good standing, specifically for being delinquent in the payment of union dues. Examination of the firm's records indicates that dues for Ryerson were deducted and forwarded to the union in each recent month.

Since cooperation between the firm and the union has generally been friendly and relationships are congenial, the director of industrial relations took this matter up with the business agent suggesting that the notice might have been sent by mistake. The business agent explained that the local had formally passed a motion, several months before, increasing dues from $2.00 to $2.50 for members who missed a regular meeting and whose absence remained unexcused. Notice of the action was sent to all members. Ryerson has three months of unexcused absences. The Union has concluded, therefore, that he is no longer a member in good standing. It is no secret that many members have been irritated by other actions on his part in which he appeared to be little concerned about the interests of the local.

• (a) Would you advise the employer to comply with the union request? (b) Should the employer assist the local in its efforts to improve attendance at local meetings? (c) Should the employer discuss the situation with Ryerson? (d) Should the employer try to act as a mediator or an arbitrator in seeking a settlement of the differences between the union and this particular member?

EMPLOYER POLICY IN LABOR RELATIONS

Bargaining always requires at least two parties. Collective bargaining is no exception to this rule. Preceding chapters have outlined the objectives, policies, and major practices of unions in collective bargaining. In this chapter attention is directed to a second party — the employer and his bargaining associations. Subsequent chapters will note the policies and practices of a third, but increasingly active participant — the public, as represented by various federal, state, and local agencies.

Employers in this country have shown wide diversity in their attitudes toward unions and the negotiation and administration of collective agreements. They have been less willing to play a uniform role than the employers of Sweden or England, for example. Further, the role of those we describe as employers is complicated by the fact that many of them — and a steadily increasing proportion — are themselves employees. In corporate business the employer is the firm, but the personification of the firm in employment relationships is its management. Managers are employees of the firm at the same time that they are employers, acting for the firm in dealing with other employees.

MANAGEMENT OBJECTIVES

Management's view of and approach to collective bargaining are shaped by the objectives and goals of the firm and its managers.

Goals — both those of firms and of individual managers — have attracted increasing attention and comment in recent years. The concept of short-term profit as the persistent and highest and overriding goal is clearly unreal. Moreover, it is clear that many goals — both those of managers and of the organizations they lead — involve more than economic considerations. Economic goals may be regarded as prerequisites to other objectives. Studies of organizational goals frequently give top priority to the perpetuation of the firm or to its continual expansion, growth, and influence. Other goals that may have high priorities include the development and protection of the corporate image, demonstration of a high concern for the public interest, and setting an example of the advantages of free enterprise in world markets. It is evident that such a range of goals may involve varying degrees of incompatibility among them.

Some individual managers may give top priority to the protection of their own economic security — the retention of their jobs. At the same time, perhaps the most common management goal is that of retaining a broad sphere of freedom for managerial decisions, variously described as "elbow room," "management prerogatives," and freedom for flexibility in strategy and tactics. That policy may prescribe opposition to encroachments by unions or government. The whole question of value hierarchies and managerial ethics has obvious implications for management policy.[1]

How such personal and organizational goals are translated into policy on labor relations is affected by varying characteristics of the firm, the industry, and the economy. If *labor costs* are relatively unimportant, for example, bargaining and union influence may be regarded rather casually. If *profits* are persistently high, fear of or resistance to bargaining may be minimized on that account. The *level of competition* in the industry may be influential; collective bargaining may be encouraged as a means of eliminating competitive advantage. Policy may change with changes in the phase of the business cycle; the economic outlook or forecast may make a big difference. Labor relations policies are also influenced by time-to-time fluctuations in the priorities given to various goals.

---

[1]See, for excellent discussions of goals and philosophy, William T. Greenwood, *Issues in Business and Society* (Boston: Houghton Mifflin Company, 1964); Joseph W. Towle and others, *Ethics and Standards in American Business* (Boston: Houghton Mifflin Company, 1964).

MANAGER THEORY AND POLICY

For many firms — and most large business organizations — the managers create employer policy. Classic analysis of corporate organization often describes management policy as the creation of the proprietor or a board of directors elected by stockholders. Owners or stockholders may sometimes establish and determine policy, which is translated into appropriate action through the programs and practices developed by hired managers. In practice in large corporate enterprises, however, questions of policy in dealing with employees rarely get a prominent place or even mention on the agenda for a stockholders' meeting. In most firms, labor policy, as a part of total policy, is a creation of managers rather than of owners. In large corporate business the myth of stockholder policy making is largely dispelled. The real policy makers are usually the paid, semiprofessional managers.

Managers' policies with respect to relationships with employees and with unions representing employees tend to reflect their attitudes toward those who work for and with them and toward the duties and responsibilities of management. Management policies or intentions change as these attitudes change. When managers assume that unions are revolutionary and threaten to destroy firms and established government, policy is likely to propose that unions be attacked and destroyed. When, on the other hand, managers see unions as essentially labor marketing organizations, then policy may propose to get the best possible deal in bargaining with them. Or managers may see unions as means of equalizing and stabilizing labor costs and propose to collaborate with them for that purpose. The major clues to management policy on collective bargaining, therefore, are the managers' theories of management.

Changing Management Theory

Managers' theories of management — the explanations they give themselves to interpret the behavior of workers and of working organizations — have changed and are changing. These theories or explanations of working and management relations have a dominant influence on policy because they shape managers' perceptions and prescriptions. Managers see problems in terms of their theories. They propose policies and programs that are consistent with these theories.

One major area of management theory is concerned with variations in the zeal, enthusiasm, effectiveness, and effort with which employees perform assigned tasks. Explanations of such variation are described as *motivation* or *work theory*. Historic work theory regarded workers as essentially incapable of directing themselves, keeping busy, or providing their own guidance and drive. In terms of such theory, managers concluded that they must make all decisions and provide detailed supervision and direction to get reasonable effort and performance. Managers must provide suitable rewards or penalties; otherwise workers would do little. Subsequent work theory emphasized the major influence of economic rewards; to assure effort and enthusiasm, managers offered piecework pay or bonuses for superior contributions. Modern work theory is more complicated. It explains workers' job performance in terms of a complex of needs to be satisfied on the job, including needs related to physical comfort, social acceptance, and self-expression.

Other major areas of management theory provide explanations of organizational behavior and administration or leadership. Theory in these areas has changed with time. Modern theory of organization as a management tool emphasizes the importance of small groups and individual participation as clues to organizational effectiveness. It also stresses the importance of organizational goals and the identification of individual goals with those of the organization.

In administration, modern theory places a high priority on specialized competence as a key to effective leadership in work. It sees administration as requiring more than personal magnetism or *charisma*; the effective manager must have special knowledge and skills, which are presumably the contributions to be made by modern management education.[2]

Theories prescribe policies and programs, and changing theories suggest changing policies and programs. "Theory bridges" relate philosophy to policy and policy to program. Managers have changed their perceptions of unions and collective bargaining as their theories of work, organization, administration, and of unions (see Chapter 7) have changed. As a result, some employers and managers encourage collective bargaining and participate in it with enthusiasm, while some

[2]For more on changing theory in management, see Douglas McGregor, *The Human Side of Enterprise* (New York: McGraw-Hill Book Company, Inc., 1960); Rensis Likert, *New Patterns of Management* (New York: McGraw-Hill Book Company, Inc., 1961); Sidney Mailick and Edward H. Van Ness (eds.), *Concepts and Issues in Administrative Behavior* (Englewood Cliffs, N.J.: Prentice-Hall, Inc., 1962); Saul W. Gellerman, *Motivations and Productivity* (New York: American Management Association, 1963); Dale Yoder, Raymond E. Miles, Lawrence McKibbin, Robert E. Boynton, and George W. England, "Managers' Theories of Management," *Journal of the Academy of Management*, Vol. 6, No. 3 (September, 1963), pp. 204–11; Dale Yoder, *Personnel Management and Industrial Relations* (5th ed.; Englewood Cliffs, N.J.: Prentice-Hall, Inc., 1962), Chapters 4–7 and the references cited there.

oppose any dealings with unions. Many employers object to collective bargaining and criticize it but accept it as inevitable — a necessary evil. Many employers have joined employer associations to match the organized strength of employees with organized employers. Still others have gone it alone, sometimes expressing frank criticism of the attitudes and practices of employer associations.

Current Policy

Historically, the first employer reactions to collective bargaining were distinctly negative and critical. Most employers did not welcome unions. Many still express satisfaction that their employees have never been organized or that they have won an election in which employees voted not to have a union represent them. On the other hand, many employers now insist that they would not go back to the earlier system of individual bargaining if they could. Perhaps the most common current attitude is one of tolerating unions while insisting that they limit the range of their demands and their "interference" in management.

Employer reactions to collective bargaining express a variety of attitudes that are largely shaped by the employer's theories of management and his image of the manager's part or role in business. The most common policies may be outlined as follows:

Protection of profits. Many employers see their primary function as that of trying to make the business as profitable as possible. They oppose unions if they conclude that unions threaten profits by demanding too much for employees. On the other hand, in some situations employers welcome an industry-wide union that standardizes wage rates, forcing competitors to pay uniform wages and thus protecting their competitive position.

An employer-manager may regard himself as an employee and continually on trial. He may feel that his own security depends largely on his continued success as measured by profits. If unions make his management less profitable, he may lose his reputation as a manager. He may therefore be concerned about his personal security and apprehensive about union "interference" for this reason.

Protection of management rights and prerogatives. The manager may regard himself as the guardian and trustee of employer rights to manage. He may see a union's demands to share in the determination of working conditions as an invasion of the area of rights and privileges associated with ownership and property, of which he is the protector and defender. He may be determined to shield the prerogatives of management from any encroachment by unions.

Employers frequently emphasize their responsibility as decision makers and express concern lest unions interfere in this function. Unions, on the other hand, may question the competence of some managements and try to secure joint decision-making responsibility. For example, an employer may feel that he should advance those he regards as the best men, while a union may insist that seniority have major influence in such promotions. Again, a union may protest the decision by managers to close down a plant or to transfer work to another locality. On the other hand, some employers have sought the aid of unions in making decisions, welcoming the collective determination of policy on a wide variety of organizational programs.

Many employers have quite seriously and conscientiously regarded themselves as the "great white father" so far as their employees are concerned. In their own viewpoint they have been thoughtful, considerate, and generous. They have given their best, worked long hours, and developed ulcers and high blood pressure, in part at least, for the benefit of those who have worked for them. They are apt to regard the fact that employees form or join a union as a personal insult and rank ingratitude. Employers may also fear that they will lose face in their own circles if employees are organized. They may be unfavorably compared with other employers who have never had a union.

Retention of employee loyalty. Employers and managers who recognize the importance of employee identification with the employer's goals have frequently opposed unions on the ground that they tend to destroy loyalty to the employer. Employers have assumed that effective participation in the work of the firm necessitates loyal employees who regard the employer as their benefactor and who appreciate what he has done and is doing for them. From their viewpoint, unions align employees against their employers, developing and maintaining critical employee attitudes incompatible with unquestioning loyalty to the employer. Evidence of this result is by no means clear. Some studies of employee attitudes indicate what is sometimes described as *dual allegiance*, in which employees most loyal to their union are also most loyal to the firm.[3]

---

[3] See, however, George W. England, "Dual Allegiance to Company and Union," *Personnel Administration*, Vol. 23, No. 2 (March–April, 1960), pp. 20–25.

Cooperation for mutual advantage. In some situations employers have welcomed unions and the help of union officials in management. Unions may know how to get competent professional and technical guidance and may be willing and able to provide such assistance. Unions may be helpful, also, in interpreting managerial problems to employees. They can stabilize and equalize wage rates and labor costs among competing employers. In particular cases unions have unquestionably meant the difference between profit and loss, continuing in business or failing. In a few instances they have provided essential capital for modern equipment. In systems of union-management cooperation, unions have gained security and special concessions in return for their help.

Many managers assume that unions offer a means of satisfying employee needs not readily attainable in any other way. They conclude that modern, large-scale industry creates needs for association and negotiation that can best be satisfied by unions. Accordingly, they welcome unions as helping to assure better working relationships and more effective workers.

No simple generalization can accurately synthesize these current policies. Any average must obscure important deviations. On the whole, however, it can be said that unions have by no means achieved general, enthusiastic acceptance by today's managers. Perhaps the most common attitude is one that accepts unions, negotiates agreements, and maintains effective working relationships with unions but fears their further inroads into what the employer regards as areas reserved for and essential to managerial decision making. Many employers who hold this viewpoint accept the general principle of collective bargaining as sound public policy. They are willing to concede that unions can and do benefit their members and may provide a desirable balance of economic power in our type of economy. But they suspect union officials of empire building, of seeking new worlds to conquer. Many managers conclude that unions are really unnecessary if management is competent. They see unions as developing out of and living on management mistakes.

Dynamic Labor Relations Policy

Few managers have maintained a constant policy on relationships with unions over any long period. Indeed, policies in many firms appear to follow a common pattern in which several stages can be identified.

In the first stage, which may be described as one of *resistance to unions*, employers object to bargaining, openly express their bitterness against union intrusion, and frequently refuse to recognize unions and their leaders. In this stage a wide variety of antiunion practices may appear. Employers may refuse to hire union members, or they may discharge employees they suspect of joining. The employer may affiliate with antiunion associations or threaten to go out of business or to close his plant if employees seek to bargain through a union. This is the stage of bitter struggles, free-for-all battles between union members and managers or plant guards, driving organizers out of town, and similar conflict.

A second stage, *toleration*, which has been variously described as "containment" and "defensive endurance," frequently follows. In this stage the employer decides he cannot eliminate unions, so he will have to live with them. That does not mean he has to like them. He concedes limited rights, meets and bargains within limits, but tries to prevent unions from gaining any added influence. This is the stage in which union officials are treated with calculated coolness and employers insist on the letter of the law so far as union observance of the contract is concerned. Union representatives may not, for example, be permitted to visit members during working hours or perhaps not on the firm's property. This has sometimes been described as "arm's length" bargaining.

In a subsequent stage, described variously as *collaboration* or *acceptance*, unions are taken for granted and collective bargaining becomes the established pattern. Employers in this stage may be critical of certain union policies or actions, but they raise no serious question about the regular and permanent participation of unions in both negotiation and contract administration. A considerable range of working conditions is regarded as appropriate for joint or bilateral determination.

A fourth stage of *union-management cooperation* may develop. In this stage unions are not only recognized but welcomed. They become joint managers in a wide area of employment relationships. They may take major responsibility for safety and accident prevention, increasing productivity and output, and other similar managerial functions. This stage has not been widely achieved nor has it developed uniformly. It represents, however, a most interesting experiment — one that deserves careful observation and appraisal.

Studies of such programs should be multiplied so that we can better judge both their promise and their limitations.

Employer action has shown as much variety as these various and changing policies would suggest. To keep unions out, pitched battles and violence have sometimes appeared. Some employer programs have sought to make employment so attractive that employees would have nothing to gain by organizing. Employers have sometimes organized *dependent unions* of their own employees. They have instituted grievance procedures to be sure that employee dissatisfaction is minimized and complaints receive prompt attention. Some employers have tried to buy the loyalty of employees by their generosity. Some have maintained a consistent practice of equaling or bettering what other employees have negotiated.

Many employers whose employees are represented by unions have negotiated *management security* clauses insuring the employer's freedom to act in various areas. Some have undertaken extensive in-plant training programs to acquaint employees with managerial and economic problems and thus influence both employee attitudes and union demands. Others have welcomed unions and have sought to find a mutuality in their interests and those of the union.

INDIVIDUAL EMPLOYER PROGRAMS

Current management policy has encouraged two somewhat distinctive but inevitably related types of programs. On the one hand, employers have provided specialists in labor relations to negotiate with union representatives and to provide expert assistance in day-to-day contract administration. At the same time, employers are giving much more attention to their own professional competence in manpower management. Most large firms employ labor relations directors and personnel managers to provide leadership in these programs.

Labor Relations Programs

Activities in labor relations are concerned with (1) contract negotiation and (2) contract administration. Labor relations staff members are specialists in dealing with employees as union members and with representatives of unions. They have found many of their activities prescribed or limited by law (see Chapters 11 and 12) and must, for that reason, keep informed on legislative changes, the rulings of administrative boards such as the National Labor Relations Board, and on arbitration awards (see Chapter 13).

The labor relations staff takes the lead in negotiations and in preparing for negotiation, making studies of current experience, and planning the presentation of demands and the replies to union demands. Labor relations staff members also provide expert assistance in interpreting contract provisions and settling grievances. They prepare cases for arbitration and represent management in arbitration hearings.

The work of labor relations staff members has increased as many employers have developed what is called *positive bargaining*. In earlier practice, because unions made most of the demands, the employer's part appeared to be one of being negative. In many cases demands that were refused a year or so past were later accepted, so that employers seemed always to be opposing what came to be accepted. In more recent practice many employers have changed this situation by carefully analyzing the operation of existing agreements, noting changes that appear desirable, and presenting their own demands in subsequent negotiations.

This change has familiarized union representatives with current problems as they appear from the point of view of managers. It has tended to break down the attitudes of "arm's length" bargaining which sought to exclude union discussion of managerial problems.

Manpower Management Programs

The labor relations staff may be a part of a larger industrial relations or employee relations staff division. In current practice the average firm employs one employee relations staff member per 125–135 employees. It has what is called a *personnel ratio* of about 0.75, which means that the total industrial relations staff includes three fourths of one staff specialist for each 100 employees in the organization. Recently, average firms have been spending annually about $90 per employee for these industrial relations staff services.

Industrial relations department members assist other members of the management in the development and formulation of policies for guidance in their relations with employees and organizations of employees. They plan and help in the administration of a wide range of programs to implement these policies and to improve the recruitment and selection of workers, their development and training on the job, and their motivation to do the best job possible.

In the industrial relations department the two most common subdivisions are those usually described as personnel and labor relations.

The personnel subdivision assists in relationships with employees as individuals; for example, in recruitment, testing, interviewing, counseling, employee appraisals, and others. The labor relations subdivision assists in relationships with groups of employees, particularly employer-union relationships.

In its staffing activity management recruits and selects personnel and promotes transfers, demotes, and terminates. In part, as a response to union programs designed to protect employees against arbitrary discharge and to enforce seniority in promotions, layoff, and recall, employers today give much greater attention to staffing problems. Under labor contracts, employment is much more "for keeps" than it was before these agreements became common. Modern employer practice begins with careful *job analysis* designed to find out precisely what each job involves and what personal qualifications are required. On the basis of job analysis and work measurement or time and motion study, it determines working standards and creates *staffing tables*. Job analyses also provide clues to the types of aptitudes and skills to be sought, and modern selection programs use interviews, tests, probation, and other techniques to appraise these qualifications.

Training or *development* is an impressive management function in many firms and agencies. New employees are trained for the jobs they are to take. Experienced employees are trained for promotion. Many employees and managers must be retrained to prepare them for changes in jobs. Both employees and managers may become obsolete as a result of new technology and new knowledge affecting their jobs.

Training and development programs begin with vocational counseling and guidance at the time of selection and employment. Thereafter, employers provide what may become very extensive training and development programs, with courses and classes and counseling and guided experience for all types of employees from the simplest job training on rank-and-file jobs to executive development programs for middle management. These activities are designed to improve the utilization of manpower and to develop the highest skills and abilities.

Managers recognize that modern industry provides few jobs for "raw" or common labor. They know that jobs in their organizations require special skills and that such skills are likely to be scarce and in strong demand. At the same time, they seek to impress employees with management's interest in their long-term welfare. They have in effect urged employees to regard the employer as their agent in the application of employee skills and effort. They have promised to coach the employee, to make him an "All-American" in the work team. They have adopted a policy of *agency management*.

Many industrial relations or manpower management programs are designed to provide effective incentives for all members of the working organization. The range of such programs has increased as modern work theory has suggested the broad scope of on-the-job motives and needs.

Most obvious among incentivation programs are those that provide financial incentives. Modern wage and salary administration seeks to provide effective wage rates combined with bonuses and premiums and with an almost endless variety of employee benefits and services, many of them commonly described as *fringes* (see Chapter 18). It creates wage and salary structures with labor grades based on a process of job rating or job evaluation. It seeks to assure fairness in pay among jobs, relating wages and salaries to contributions.

In addition, and related to these financial incentives, current practice may maintain a system of *personnel appraisal* or *personnel rating*. In that procedure each individual is appraised at regular intervals to provide a basis for salary adjustment or promotion. Such *merit* or *proficiency rating* seeks to establish the comparative value and performance of employees and sometimes to provide estimates of their potential abilities as well. The employee or manager may be counseled on his rating in an effort to help him improve his competence and contribution.

To encourage employee interest and identification, employers have developed programs that encourage employee participation in decision making. They create employee *suggestion systems* that provide prizes and rewards for ideas on how to do the job better. They train supervisors and managers to use *consultative management*, bringing members of their work crews into discussions about how best to accomplish their objectives. They undertake employee *morale* and *attitude surveys*, in which employees are encouraged to air their criticisms and express their opinions. They expect such participation to cause employees to identify themselves with the employer, to feel themselves a part of the team.

Many firms and public agencies expect their industrial relations executives and departments to supplement these essential "bread and butter" personnel and labor relations activities with other programs designed to improve both organization for work and administrative practice. Departments suggest, plan, and assist in experiments with new organizational arrangements. They may, for example, develop greater decentralization or reduce the number of layers of supervision and management. They may experiment with a variety of styles of administration. They may test new theories and develop creative approaches to old problems, such as staffing, recruiting, or bargaining.[4]

EMPLOYER ASSOCIATIONS

Associations of employers have existed as long as unions, but they have not produced spectacular movements comparable to the historic Luddites or the more recent multimillion-member labor organizations in this country and abroad. They have not developed international organizations with programs comparable to those of international labor organizations. They have often sought to gain popular cooperation and support, and they have invited outsiders — intellectuals or others — to join them in organized movements for this purpose.

Employers have formed associations to deal with problems of employee relationships since the early days of capitalism. Indeed, the domination of the guilds by masters, who held major authority, created a type of employer association before organizations of journeymen became common. As the Webbs noted in their study of British unions, employers appealed for political aid when the earliest durable organizations of wage earners appeared among woolen workers and knitters. Craft guilds served as employer associations in the American colonies, representing master cordwainers, carpenters, tailors, hatters, and others. They sometimes sought the assistance of the courts to restrict the activities of early unions.

A major reason why employer associations have attracted less popular attention than unions is the fact that they have not been nearly as numerous nor enlisted as many members. Historical records indicate their existence in all industrialized nations but provide no accurate counts of their numbers. In part, that is because employers have formed organizations for many other purposes, so that their programs in the area of employment relationships are somewhat obscured.

---

[4]For additional examples see the files and current issues of *Personnel* published by the American Management Association, 1515 Broadway, New York, and of *Personnel Administration* published by the Society for Personnel Administration, 1221 Connecticut Avenue, N.W., Washington, D.C. See also Robert E. Finley (ed.), *The Personnel Man and His Job* (New York: American Management Association, 1962).

No inclusive count of these organizations in the United States is available, either for the past or for the present time. In England, Sweden, and other western nations, contract negotiation by nation-wide associations of employers is an established practice. In this country, association bargaining plays a comparatively minor role. Industry-wide bargaining has become increasingly common, but it is not the most frequent pattern. Within localities master contracts have also achieved wide acceptance in the building trades, trucking and hauling, and some clerical and sales operations. Throughout the country local associated industries, employers' committees, and similar organizations have been formed to help members in negotiations in a wide variety of industries. The National Association of Manufacturers has encouraged the development of these associations and maintains a continuing relationship with many of them and with various state-wide employer associations and state associations of manufacturers. In addition to these specialized organizations, several thousand trade associations also give more or less attention to the labor problems of their members.[5]

It is estimated that there were more than 5,000 employer associations in the United States in 1962 — two or three times as many as there were 50 years ago. Over one fifth of all collective bargaining units were multi-employers, and they included more than 40 percent of all workers under union agreements.[6]

Some associations are small, local, independent associations that may be confined to a single industry. Others include large numbers of employers from many localities and a variety of industries. Some associations, generally described as *trade associations*, are industry-wide and represent employer combinations for a variety of purposes in which employment relationships may play a minor part. Several nationwide associations, with members from different localities, industries, or types of business — like the National Association of Manufacturers or the Chamber of Commerce of the United States — carry on a multidimensional program in which labor relations is but one of many interests.

These local, regional, industry-wide, and national associations vary also in their approaches to collective bargaining. Some of them

---

[5]Students may gain a more realistic understanding of collective bargaining by visits to the local offices of unions and employer associations. Their officers, managers, or business agents generally welcome an opportunity to describe programs and activities, exhibit copies of current contracts, and explain current issues in negotiations.

[6]K. M. McCaffree, "A Theory of the Origin and Development of Employer Associations," *Proceedings, Industrial Relations Research Association* (December, 1962), p. 56.

give major attention to current bargaining with unions of employees. They represent their members in such negotiations. Others are primarily concerned with the formation of public opinion and legislation on labor relations. They conduct no direct negotiations with unions but concentrate on releasing news stories and editorials designed to secure popular support for the employers' viewpoint and on lobbying in local, state, and federal legislative chambers.

Theory of Employer Associations

Most theories of employer associations hold that the associations developed to counteract and counterbalance the power of unions; that employees have formed unions, so employers have been forced to follow this example. It should be noted, however, that employer associations did not wait for the expansion of unions in England. Bonnet concludes that they have not always followed wage-earner organization in this country. He notes that they have appeared whenever a group of employers became convinced of values to be gained through united action on labor questions. He points to the organization of master shoemakers in colonial Massachusetts in 1646 as an example. Their purpose was presumably to secure legislation fixing wages and requiring seven-year apprenticeships. Bonnet also notes that employers in southern states organized associations in the textile industry where employees were "wholly unorganized."[7]

Any theory of such associations must recognize the fact that their purposes have included much more than merely negotiating with unions. Early associations sought political favor; more recently, associations have worked to protect members against public regulation and to secure the advantages of "fair trade" legislation that would prevent price-cutting.

On the other hand, many of these associations have been principally concerned with employment and demands for labor. They have sought to increase the power of employers in labor markets, in part by presenting a united front and maintaining a monopsony — a single inclusive control of demands for labor in individual labor markets — and in part by gaining political concessions and exerting political influence.

[7]Clarence E. Bonnet, "Employers' Associations" in the *Encyclopedia of the Social Sciences* (New York: The Macmillan Co.), Vol. 5, pp. 509–12. See also M. W. Alexander, "Employers' Associations in the United States," *International Labor Review*, Vol. 25, No. 5 (May, 1932), pp. 605–20. For a description of local associations and their programs and a useful bibliography, see William H. Smith, *Local Employers' Associations*, Institute of Industrial Relations, University of California (Berkeley), 1955.

From an economic viewpoint the employer association appears as an expression of what may be described as the *theory of countervailing power* designed to develop a monopsony to oppose a monopoly. Associations seek to limit and balance or overcome the market advantage of the organizations of employees with which they must deal. It is notable that few employer associations operate in labor markets in which employees are not organized. Insofar as associations have been authorized to act as agents in bargaining and in the administration of collective agreements, they mobilize buyers and thus present a mutually acceptable demand schedule.

Some of them have been created to fight unions and others to contain or restrict union activities by legislative action. Some associations may have appealed to members as offering a means of preventing employer-union conflict by creating a balance of power. By pitting organized strength against similar organization on the other side, they appeared to some to assure a sort of armed truce that could prevent disastrous conflict.

Observers have frequently noted the tendency of employers to identify their interests with those of consumers and to regard their struggle as essential to protect the public. Employer associations have frequently expressed this viewpoint and obligation. Other associations have frequently described their major objective as that of rescuing individual employees from the tyranny of unionism.

Types of Associations

In a study of historic and current associations in the 1920's, Bonnet concluded that most of them fell into two general types, based on the attitudes of their members and the functions of the organizations. He called the two *negotiatory* and *belligerent* associations.[8] Negotiatory organizations have as their major purpose the development and maintenance of collective agreements with unions. Their activities center about this objective; they keep in touch with contract changes and innovations, prepare materials for negotiation, and represent employers in the actual negotiating sessions. In contrast to these negotiatory associations, other organizations have been formed to combat unionism. These *belligerent* associations launch a variety of attacks on unions. They try to discredit unions and their leaders, to reduce their influence, and to prevent their spread.

---

[8]Clarence E. Bonnet, *Employers' Associations in the United States* (New York: The Macmillan Co., 1922), pp. 13 ff.

Bonnet concluded that the trend at the time he wrote (1922) was toward negotiatory associations. He pointed to the fact that most of the European associations started out as belligerent organizations but had become negotiatory. In the current scene in this country, practically all associations have to emphasize negotiation. Their members expect them to do so. Public policy favors and encourages negotiation and prohibits many of the earlier practices of belligerent employer associations.

Negotiatory associations include two major subtypes. One of them confines its activity strictly to representing members in bargaining. These *bargaining* associations help and may represent members when contracts are to be renewed or created. They may maintain a staff of skilled negotiators for this purpose. During the intervals between negotiations, each employer carries on the necessary activities of day-to-day contract administration. He makes decisions on contract applications and interpretations. His authority in such matters is not lessened by his membership in the association, which may be described as strictly negotiatory and advisory.

In contrast, the second type of negotiatory association emphasizes *administrative* functions. Organizations not only represent employer members in negotiating contracts; they also represent both members and the association in all interpretive or administrative decisions and actions. An important portion of the employer's authority or sovereignty in labor relations is transferred to the association. The organization maintains a staff of specialized contract administrators as well as negotiators. Grievances may not be settled by the individual employer; they become a matter of concern to all members of the association. Members of the association staff may step in to require an employer member to interpret and observe the contract their way. Such administrative associations have been most common on the West Coast.[9]

Historic Practices

The most spectacular activities of employer associations were belligerent and are now largely matters of history. They involved

---

[9]For details on the activities of administrative associations, see Clark Kerr and Lloyd Fisher, "Multiple-Employer Bargaining: The San Francisco Experience," in Richard A. Lester and Joseph Shister, *Insights into Labor Issues* (New York: The Macmillan Company, 1948), pp. 25–61, or their "The Administrative Employers' Association" in E. Wight Bakke and Clark Kerr, *Unions, Management and the Public* (New York: Harcourt, Brace and Company, 1948), pp. 346–50; see also Gerald Somers, "Pressures on an Employers' Association in Collective Bargaining," *Industrial and Labor Relations Review*, Vol. 6, No. 4 (July, 1953), pp. 557–69.

direct action to weaken and undermine unions and to enlist popular support in campaigns against labor organizations and their programs. Many of these tactics are now outlawed. They are of interest, however, because the memories of these campaigns and attacks still remain and influence current attitudes and behavior. They help to explain present-day union members' concern about union security, the right to strike, unfair labor practices, "slave labor" laws, and other phrases and slogans that still arouse tempers and raise blood pressures in the industrial relations arena.

In the early years of many employer associations, they sought to weaken unions and to arouse public fear and concern about them. One of the most interesting practices involved union spies. Employers sought the services of detective agencies, whose members infiltrated unions, frequently became officers, and made regular reports of union plans to employers. These spies helped to break strikes and provided information that could be publicized to create distrust among union members and concern and fear among citizens everywhere. In 1936, according to the staff of the National Labor Relations Board, some 200 agencies were furnishing from 40,000 to 50,000 spies.[10]

Associations sometimes encouraged the establishment of employer-dominated or dependent unions to prevent organization of the employees by outside unions. They maintained blacklists to prevent the employment of wage earners who were regarded as troublemakers and organizers. They supported war chests contributed by members to assist member firms in strikes. They arranged for producing goods a member could not deliver because of a strike of his employees. Some of them provided armed guards and *flying squadrons* of strikebreakers, who sometimes encouraged violence in order to show the need for their services. In other situations employer associations undertook the destruction of unions through disastrous strikes. The American Railway Union, for example, was greatly weakened by a lengthy strike against the Pullman Company in 1894 in which the Railway Managers' Association played an important part.

---

[10]For interesting reports of these activities, see Clinch Calkins, *Spy Overhead, the Story of Industrial Espionage* (New York: Harcourt, Brace and Co., 1937); or Pearl L. Bergoff, *I Break Strikes* (New York: Robert M. McBride & Co., 1936); or Sidney Howard, *The Labor Spy* (New York: Republic Publishing Company, 1924); or Leo Huberman, *The Labor Spy Racket* (New York: Modern Age Books, Inc., 1937). For a more prosaic report, see the published testimony in the twelve *Reports of the Senate* (La Follette) *Committee on Education and Labor* (Washington, D.C.: Government Printing Office, 74th, 75th, and 76th Congresses, 1936–1938).

Early employer associations did not often appeal for direct popular participation in their battles with unions. Rather, they sought to place unions and union leaders in an unfavorable light and to create a receptive attitude toward employer viewpoints and activities. Associations did, however, cultivate the favor and cooperation of local newspapers, bankers, and courts. In the United States they encouraged use of court orders to forbid labor mass meetings, parades, picketing, and other union tactics. They tried to popularize the idea that the right to carry on a business is a property right that must be protected by law. Another program encouraged employers to require that all employees sign *yellow-dog* or *ironclad contracts* of employment, in which they stated that they were not and would not become union members while working for the employer and agreed that violation of this contract justified dismissal.

In 1902 associated employer associations sought popular participation through their American Anti-boycott Association, and in 1903 the National Association of Manufacturers created the Citizens' Industrial Association to develop a nationwide, grass roots campaign against unions. Citizens of all callings were encouraged to join. Local *citizens' alliances* established a national legislative agency known as the National Council for Industrial Defense (later known as the National Industrial Council) in 1907.

In 1919, immediately after World War I, employers again sought to enlist the participation of citizens in a gigantic campaign to establish the *American plan* of open-shop, nonunion employment. Citizens were encouraged to patronize nonunion employers, to aid in breaking strikes, to act as strikebreakers, and to urge antiunion legislation. The movement had a considerable measure of success. Many industries that had been operating under collective agreements dropped them, and union membership suffered a sharp decline. In meat packing, in the maritime industries, in the building trades, and in many local plants throughout the nation, unions lost their bargaining rights.

These are, it must be clearly understood, programs of yesteryear. However, they, like historic riots and violence associated with unions, are an essential part of the traditional background of modern collective bargaining. Both employers and employees still remember these belligerent days. Many unionists suspect that employer associations still seek to weaken if not to destroy unions. Some employers are suspicious or convinced that union leaders are revolutionists at heart.

Modern Practice

Today's employer associations are negotiatory. They have been created and are maintained to assist members in collective bargaining relationships. Local associations provide a valuable assistance to members, especially small firms, by maintaining a staff of professional negotiators who keep abreast of developments and offer expert assistance in both negotiation and administration.

Many local associations provide dependable information that unquestionably reduces controversy and facilitates understanding if not agreement. Associations conduct wage and salary surveys, maintain a running check on negotiations, disputes, mediation, arbitration, and the action and rulings of state administrators and agencies. Many of them arrange for lectures and educational courses for their members. They have attained acceptance in their communities as providing a needed and constructive service.

Statewide and national associations join these local organizations in elections and legislative campaigns. They have been ardent advocates of right-to-work laws that make compulsory union membership illegal in 20 states (see Chapter 12). They have worked to secure tighter public control of the boycott and of picketing. They have generally opposed the extension of minimum wage legislation and the increase of specified minimum rates. Some associations have been active in policing the rules with respect to unemployment compensation benefits. In general, they have sought to prevent further public regulation of collective bargaining. However, some associations appear to approve proposals to bring unions under the provisions of anti-trust laws, to require compulsory arbitration of unsettled disputes, or to establish a system of labor courts.

Future of Employer Associations

In this country only a small fraction of all employers holds or has held membership in employer associations. That fraction is smaller than the proportion of wage earners who are union members. It is smaller than is typical in most industrialized nations. On the other hand, although detailed statistics are not regularly available, membership appears to have grown and to be growing. It seems likely that this trend will continue, for these organizations can exert a significant economic and political influence.

Just as unions control supplies of labor in labor markets, employer associations can be effective marketing agencies on the demand side.

In the absence of such associations, unions can concentrate bargaining power on individual employers, force major concessions, and then use these advances for leverage in bargaining with other buyers. This is the widely known practice of *whipsawing*.

In the past, individual employers have resisted appeals to join employer associations for several reasons. One explanation for this distinctive American individualism is the long-established tradition of independence that characterizes many employer-owners and managers in this country. To many of them, this personal independence and freedom is a matter of great personal importance. They reject suggestions that they should delegate any portion of their authority or initiative to gain added bargaining power in their relationships with employees.

Many employers may see a high degree of mutuality in the interests of employers and employees. They oppose both unions and employer associations as tending to raise artificial barriers and creating a vested interest in conflict. They fear that employer associations will encourage differences and issues in order to justify their continued operation.

Again, proprietors of many small business organizations frequently regard their competition with other businessmen as more significant for their success than gaining concessions from their employees. Such employers feel little need for an employer association, being convinced that they can "go it alone" without undue hazard.

Traditions of secrecy with respect to business activity also play an important part. Many employers do not wish to give competitors the information that might be divulged as a part of association membership.

The great mobility of workers in the United States — the ease with which they can change from employees to employers — unquestionably plays a large part in explaining attitudes toward employer associations. Many employers have been employers only a short time. They were formerly employees, perhaps union members. They do not feel any strong bond of fellowship with other employers. They may not be too concerned about their ability to deal with the unions of their employees.

This traditional position is giving way to the pressures of powerful unions and growing international competition. Increased public regulation of labor relations exerts a similar influence. Modern collective bargaining is becoming much more detailed and complicated.

Employers in many small businesses cannot, on their own, provide the expertness necessary to evaluate union proposals for contract clauses. They cannot, for example, calculate the costs of the complex benefit programs now being negotiated. They may feel a need for the help of association data and staff specialists in preparing for negotiations, in actual bargaining, and in day-to-day contract administration.

At the same time, employer associations offer a means of counteracting the growing political activity of unions. They can help members in expressing an employer viewpoint on many questions not directly involved in negotiation, such as minimum wage laws, unemployment insurance, and wage and hour regulations.

Attention turns, in the next chapter, to public policies, rules, and regulations with respect to relationships among employers, employer associations, and unions and their members. Major interest focuses on the development of public policy on labor relations.

ANALYTICAL REVIEW QUESTIONS

1. What are the principal reasons why unions and employers have different policies?
2. How do stockholders shape or influence company policy on manpower management?
3. (a) What were the first employer reactions to collective bargaining? (b) To what specific types of union action did they object?
4. What was the traditional employer's idea of his part or role in business or industry?
5. What is meant by personal insecurity of employer-managers?
6. Why do employers seek the loyalty of employees, and how do they visualize the effects of unions on such loyalty?
7. What are the stages in employer reactions to collective bargaining and how does each affect collective bargaining processes?
8. What is the role of a dependent union?
9. What is the role of a professional labor relations staff in a firm?
10. How do selective staffing and employee appraisal reduce and also create frictions in collective bargaining?
11. How does job evaluation affect collective bargaining?
12. What do we mean by positive bargaining?
13. How is employee development related (a) to employee participation and motivation and (b) to collective bargaining?
14. In what ways can employees be given a role in a firm's decision-making processes?
15. What have been the major reasons underlying formation of employer associations?

16. What are the principal types of employer associations?

17. Contrast the two subtypes of negotiatory employer associations in terms of decisions with which each is concerned.

18. (a) What are each of the following: (1) labor spies, (2) blacklists, (3) war chests, (4) yellow-dog contracts, (5) citizens' alliances, (6) the American plan? (b) What did these have in common?

19. (a) What is meant by the theory of countervailing power? (b) How is this theory related to employer associations and to unions?

20. Why do many employers remain outside of employer associations?

21. What forecast would you make with respect to the future of employer associations? Why?

Case 10-1

TIME FOR DECISION

Five years after graduation, you have taken on a large share of the managerial responsibility for a small family-owned factory. Your 600 employees have been members of the local of a powerful international union since 1939. Your father, who has held major managerial responsibility for 30 years, has found negotiation difficult in recent years. He has formed some strong personal dislikes for several local leaders.

Last year's negotiations ended in a stalemate and a 10-day strike, with three issues finally settled by arbitration. One demand, which was not granted, proposed that no work would be subcontracted or contracted out without the approval of the local union. The older officers of the company are convinced that the union is becoming more unreasonable in its demands. The advance "scoop" is that this year's demands will include supplementary unemployment benefits like those in the automobile industry.

In the executive committee meeting last Monday morning, one of the senior officers, the secretary of the company, proposed that the firm join a local employers' association. That association not only negotiates for its members but is also an administrative association. After the meeting your father spoke privately with you saying that he wanted you to think the proposal over carefully, for you would have to live with the decision that will be made. He suggested that you give him a brief memorandum summarizing your recommendations by Saturday night, so that he could think over your points before the next Monday meeting.

• Write out your statement, first stating what you think should be done and then listing your major reasons, as preparation for a class discussion of this case.

Case 10-2

PAY FOR PARKING

For many years the Blewett-Carter Company has provided an excellent blacktop parking lot for employees. Each employee has his numbered location. The company has charged 35 cents per week for the parking privilege, explaining to employees that this income approximates the costs of the parking lot guard and the continuing upkeep on the lot. In addition to the parking privilege, employees may ask the guard to change a tire if they have encountered trouble. Windshields are washed during the day. These services are free to employees who use the lot.

The firm belongs to an administrative employers association. That association negotiated the present contract with all production employees, a contract which includes, as one of several fringes, free parking space for employee cars.

The parking charge has for the last five years been deducted from the pay checks of employees who use the lot. Since the new contract was negotiated, the company has continued the old practice of deducting the parking charge.

Two weeks ago, an employee filed a grievance, alleging that the charge for parking is improper and that funds paid for this privilege should be repaid to employees. The grievance was submitted to the association, whose staff members represent the firm in handling all grievances. Yesterday a representative of the association informed the employee that he was justified in his complaint. He also instructed the firm to repay all employees for fees collected since the new contract became effective and further ordered the firm to discontinue the practice of charging.

• Would you advise the firm to comply? Be prepared to explain your answers.

Case 10-3

PATTERN BARGAINING

In this case, put yourself in the position of the manager of a small storage battery plant in a midwestern city. The union with which he deals also represents the employees of most of his competitors across the nation. For several years the union has insisted on pattern bargains in which local plants follow the pattern established in negotiations with one large manufacturer in the East.

The local plant has been making money, but its margin of profit has declined. Dividends have been reduced, and some local stockholders have become quite critical, calling for a change of managers.

The firm has been a member of a local employer association for many years. In an earlier period its agreements with the union were held in line with other local agreements. Since 1950, however, pattern bargaining on an industry basis has introduced many variations. Members of the local association have been critical of concessions made by the firm. They have suggested that the manager should hold the line and insist on terms comparable to those in other local contracts.

The manager is quite sure that any attempt to follow this advice will precipitate a strike. He thinks the union could take a strike better than the firm can, for local labor supplies are so tight that employees would probably find other jobs quickly. On the other hand, he suspects that one more year of pattern bargaining will result in a net loss.

• What would you do if you were the manager in this situation? List the alternatives open to him, select one of them, and be prepared with a brief justification for your choice.

LABOR RELATIONS — CHANGING PUBLIC POLICY

Employers and employees naturally get top billing in the industrial relations drama. Their organizations — unions and employer associations — are prominent in the institutional setting. Put another way, in any analysis of the behavior of modern employment relations, employers and employees play the major roles, and unions and employer associations are major institutional factors. In addition, in our society — as in all industrialized societies — the public, through its various federal, state, and local agencies, exercises an important influence.[1]

Indeed, modern labor relations policy is widely recognized as tripartite. The intentions and selected courses to be followed reflect the prominent influence of public agencies and legislation. Programs — of firms, of managements, and of unions — bear the clear imprint of public policy. In some situations the participation and influence of government overshadow and clearly dominate the decision making of management and labor.

Thus, federal courts may enforce the terms of bargained agreements. A variety of investigatory boards and commissions may intervene to prevent strikes of airline pilots or railroad employees. The

---

[1]For more detailed discussions of public policy in modern industrial relations, see Harold W. Davey, *Contemporary Collective Bargaining* (2nd ed.; Englewood Cliff, New Jersey: Prentice-Hall, Inc., 1959).

annual *Economic Report of the President* may specify "guideposts" for wage negotiations.

Today's paper may announce that a federal judge has issued an injunction ordering a union of longshoremen to end its strike and send its members back to work. In another item a threatened local strike may be called off because a state labor conciliator found a satisfactory basis for agreement between a large manufacturing concern and the union of its employees. A less prominent type of news story may report that a union has filed unfair labor practice charges against an employer with the local office of the National Labor Relations Board. A current national news magazine may feature an article about why unions object to state right-to-work laws. An employer publication editorializes against governmental efforts to force acceptance of an agency shop or to allow employees to decide that issue by election.

Public intervention is by no means limited to collective bargaining, nor is public policy unimportant in other employment relationships. While government rules and public action on strikes, racketeering, boycotts, and wage negotiations are more spectacular, public policy brings the government into many other facets of employer-employee and manager-union relationships.

Public agencies take an active part in many employment relationships without making the newspapers. Representatives of the federal Labor Standards Division check on hours of work and wage rates. State agencies inspect working conditions and the jobs held by young workers. State and local fair-employment-practice commissions seek to prevent discrimination in employment based on race, nationality, or creed. Still other agencies determine eligibility for workmen's compensation and unemployment insurance benefits and for old-age pensions or assistance.

Numerous public agencies — federal, state, and local — make and enforce public policy. Thousands of printed pages each year record their actions and rulings in which they explain and interpret federal, state, and local laws. The actions of public agencies are so important that those who represent employers and unions frequently subscribe to special loose-leaf labor services that provide up-to-date reports on these decisions and rulings.

In this chapter attention centers on public policy and government intervention in labor relations — the negotiation and administration of collective agreements. Tripartite policy on labor relations is, however, part of much broader tripartite policy on the relationships created and maintained by employment. The broad scope of public interest and concern includes at least four major areas. Public policy is thus concerned with:

1. Labor relations, union-management relationships, and dispute settlement.
2. Safety and health, factory inspection, and compensation for industrial accidents and illness.
3. Employment security, full employment, unemployment insurance, old age survivors' and disability benefits, and public employment offices.
4. Employment standards, wages and hours, minimum wages, and prevention of discrimination and of child labor.

SOCIAL GOALS AND PUBLIC POLICY

Public policy reflects public goals. It expresses the public intention to follow selected courses that are regarded as means of moving toward and possibly achieving these goals. Current public policy proposes, for example, to assist employers and unions in finding peaceful solutions for their differences. Public mediation and conciliation services are provided at both federal and state levels to implement this policy.

Policy changes with shifts in goals and in the priorities accorded these goals. Historic as well as current policy can be understood only by reference to the most important of these public goals, some of them predominantly economic, others essentially political, and many that combine economic, political, and social values. At least four general goals deserve mention as an introduction to changing public policy.

Maximum Self-Determination and Bilateral Policy

Fundamental to American public policy on labor relations has been the intention to encourage the parties to develop their own rules. Instead of starting with a detailed system of regulations, policy has generally favored bargained compromises, largely determined by the comparative economic power of the parties and limited mainly by restraints to prevent collusion. Policy has not sought to eliminate differences or argument nor to encourage a comprehensive agreement. It has, on the contrary, assumed that employers and unions should differ, dispute, and compromise.[2]

---

[2]In considerable contrast to this basic approach, major public policy in the Soviet Union is formally written by the national government. The general policy is described as "democratic centralism," combining centralized control with freedom of initiative for

Balance of Power

To protect the public interest and to facilitate compromise and self-regulation, public policy has proposed to maintain a balance of power between employers and unions. Neither can be permitted to develop power that could challenge that of the state. Each must exercise enough power to prevent unilateral policy making by the other throughout the entire employment relationship.

Public policy has recognized, from time to time, that imbalance may create serious economic hazards. Powerful employers may prevent socially desirable wage advances and greater economic security; public intervention may be necessary to establish wage minima or specify unemployment benefits. Excessive union power may push wages to levels that discourage investment, limit employment, and create inflationary pressures. Imbalance may disturb the optimum relationship among distributive shares of national income or retard the pace of economic growth.[3]

Public policy has recognized that imbalance may impose rigidities in wages and prices that handicap international competition and continuing economic growth. Employer power may restrain wages or maintain inefficient management practices. Powerful unions may force labor costs to levels that reduce sales and employment and hazard the balance of international payments.[4]

Democracy in Employment

Public policy has proposed to share the regulatory powers of government with employers and unions. Employers have, since the Industrial Revolution, exercised many rule-making privileges that affect the lives of all citizens. Unions have been granted similar privileges.

---

regional and local authorities. Workers' rights are somewhat similar to rights of American employees in the 1920's under "employee representation" plans, except that public authorities exercise the right of veto through the medium of the public prosecutor. Trade unions in Russia are neither free nor democratic, being subservient to the state. Each enterprise sets up rules of employment after consultation with the appropriate plant union committee. Increasing use is made of collective agreements; these cannot be changed during the life of the agreement (one year) except by mutual consent. Disputes go to special disputes boards or to the peoples' courts. See A. Piatakov, "Labour Administration by the State and Trade Unions in the U.S.S.R.," *International Labor Review*, Vol. 85, No. 6 (June, 1962), pp. 558–72; Jerry G. Gliksman *et. al.*, "The Control of Industrial Labor in the Soviet Union," *Research Memorandum R M 2494*, (Santa Monica, California: The Rand Corporation, February 15, 1960); "Trade Union Rights in the U.S.S.R.," *Studies and Reports, New Series, No. 49*, (Geneva, Switzerland: International Labour Office, 1959).

[3]See John Davenport, "Labor Unions in the Free Society," *Fortune* (April, 1959), pp. 132 ff.

[4]See Max Ways, "Labor Unions are Worth the Price," *Fortune* (May, 1963), pp. 108 ff.

Public policy seeks to police the exercise of these powers. It has increasingly proposed that both unions and employers be recognized and recognize themselves as semipublic agencies.

To that end public policy has noted the necessity for assuring equality of employment opportunity, with obvious implications for nondiscrimination in hiring and in subsequent employment and for the democratic control of unions.[5]

Minimizing Public Hazards and Inconvenience

Public policy has sought to encourage self-regulation but, at the same time, to minimize the hazards to public health and safety that may arise when the parties find themselves in serious disagreement. Special rules have been developed from time to time to restrict the tactics of both parties — such as strikes, lockouts, the boycott, and blacklisting — as will be noted in this chapter and that which follows. Public agencies have been assigned responsibilities for aiding the parties in finding acceptable compromises. Particular concern has arisen when the process of self-regulation breaks down in defense industries.

HISTORIC ATTITUDES

Even in the comparatively short history of this nation, attitudes toward employment relationships have undergone extensive change. The early viewpoint regarded employers as the risk-takers and job-creators. They were, therefore, deserving of public encouragement. Individual employees benefited from employers' ventures. Employee unions should not be allowed to interfere with employer efforts to create jobs.

Later, public opinion became concerned about the power exercised by employers. It was generally agreed that employees should be permitted to join unions and that employers should be required to recognize unions and bargain with employees through unions if employees preferred this arrangement. Much popular opinion continues to regard employers and managers as the residual holders of authority in employment relationships. Further changes in public policy are to be expected as the development of professional managers and the separation of ownership and management become generally

---

[5]See Kurt L. Hanslowe, "Regulation by Visible Public and Invisible Private Government," *Reprint No. 111*, New York State School of Industrial and Public Relations, 1961.

recognized and understood. More and more, public opinion has moved toward an acceptance of joint rather than unitary authority in employment relationships.

Public agencies in England and in this country have played an important part in regulating union-management relationships since the days when early union members were jailed for inviting others to join their union. The first industrial capitalists called on public agencies to ban associations of employees, to penalize would-be unionists for their alleged collusion and conspiracy, and to bar demands for higher wages. When unions first appeared, expressions of public opinion frequently described them as dangerous to society as well as to the interests of employers.

Since this early intervention in behalf of and on the side of employers, government has played a continuing though changing role in labor relations. Like a pendulum, public opinion in this country has swung from opposing unions to allowing them to exist with little regulation and from encouraging them to a more detailed regulation of their activities. This chapter provides a brief resumé of these changes and the points of view they have reflected.

In any historical review of public policy on unions and employer-union relationships, several steps or stages stand out rather clearly. Major chapters in such a review might be titled as follows:

1. Unions as conspiracies.
2. Public policy by judicial decision — symbolized by labor injunctions and yellow-dog contracts.
3. Unions as illegal restraints of trade — highlighted by the Sherman Act and the Clayton Act.
4. Unions as semipublic agencies — early expressions in the Norris-LaGuardia Act, the National Industrial Recovery Act, and the National Labor Relations Act.
5. Reaction and public regulation — evidenced by the Taft-Hartley or Labor Management Relations Act of 1947 and the Landrum-Griffin or Labor Management Reporting and Disclosure Act of 1959.

Unions as Conspiracies

Public policy on unions in the early years of our nation's history was influenced by policy in England. There, when unions first appeared, employers sought the intervention of government to prevent the organization of employees. They asked the courts to forbid these combinations on the ground that they constituted *conspiracies*. Conspiracy had been defined through the evolution of common law to mean a combination for an evil purpose, or more precisely, the combination of two or more persons to accomplish by concerted action an unlawful purpose or to accomplish a lawful purpose by unlawful means.

Early public opinion reflected the political power of employers and the popular fear that any such concerted action as that of unions might be divisive in society. Combinations whose objectives or practices appeared primarily to threaten the unity of society were regarded as *criminal conspiracies*. If they threatened to injure particular individuals or groups, they involved *civil conspiracy*. In early applications of these rules, courts held that concerted action to raise wages and to control working conditions were unlawful as criminal conspiracies because they endangered the interests of society. At the same time, unions were held liable for damages for civil conspiracies aimed at employers.

In addition to these common-law rules in England, special legislation had been enacted to control unions and employers. A series of Combination Acts, beginning in the sixteenth century and culminating in the Act of 1800, specifically prohibited concerted action by groups of employers or of employees designed to change wages or working conditions. The Act of 1800 forbade organization for the purpose of raising wages, interfering with employment and employers' hiring activities, inviting employees to join a union, or collecting funds for such purposes. In several cases employees were convicted, fined, imprisoned, or deported for violations of these rules.[6] The last of the Combination Acts was repealed in 1824. Thereafter, in a long series of laws extending to 1926, unions were also freed of the regulations imposed on their usual practices by conspiracy rules.

In the American colonies and during the early years of the new nation, no special legislation was enacted to regulate employers or employees in collective bargaining. Common-law rules carried over from English tradition were invoked from time to time, and some members of local unions were found guilty of conspiracy. However, the widespread emphasis on free land and opportunities for exploration, expansion, and changing employment status made employer-union conflict less frequent and less important in the new nation. In general, public opinion favored a hands-off attitude toward the relationships of employers and unions, modified by the general

---

[6]See James W. Kuhn, "Combination Laws of 1799 and 1800," *Labor Law Journal*, Vol. 7, No. 1 (January, 1956), pp. 19–23.

acceptance of an employer's right to operate his business as he pleased. That right could properly be protected by court orders. Public policy tended to let the parties negotiate as they pleased and agree upon whatever they could. If employers and unions failed to agree so that they became involved in strikes, lockouts, picketing, and boycotts, public policy tended to let them fight, provided, however, that employers, employer associations, and unions were expected to obey the laws that protected the peace and property of all citizens. Public policy assumed that long-established common-law rules applied to employers and union members just as to everyone else.

This early public attitude and policy tended to minimize public intervention and to allow the parties in employment relationships to make most of their own rules. If an employer refused to hire union members, these workers were expected to find a job with some other employer. If a union could not agree with an employer on working conditions, members could strike or go elsewhere. If an employer was threatened with bankruptcy because union members refused to work for him, he could make his peace with the union or find some other solution for his problem. These were problems for employers, workers, and union members rather than public problems. In this early period in our country, the criminal conspiracy rule did not achieve the prominence that was characteristic in English practice.

Public Policy by Judicial Decision

Even in these early years, however, the activities of unions were sometimes restricted by court orders designed to protect the freedom and the property of employers. The latter sought such orders to prevent what they described as the threat of irreparable damages arising out of union activities. They secured court orders instructing unions and their members not to call strikes, hold meetings, conduct parades, or engage in other concerted action. Sometimes these orders prohibited written or oral discussions of the issues. Violators could be held in contempt of court and punished by fine or imprisonment.

Labor injunctions. Injunctions were widely used after 1880, so that they became in effect a major expression of public policy. Both the extent of their prohibitions and the manner in which injunctions were issued and applied caused great concern to unionists. Wording was frequently so vague that it could be construed to include almost all union activity. Enforcement was arbitrary, with penalties for violation assessed by the court that issued the order. In effect, the opinions of judges sitting in equity became the principal expressions of public rules of the game in labor relations.[7]

In perhaps the most widely-publicized case of this type, the Pullman strike of 1894, a federal court issued an injunction that prohibited a strike by railroad employees. Because the strike was called, an early Socialist leader, Eugene V. Debs, was arrested, held to be in contempt of court, and sent to prison. His conviction was upheld by the Supreme Court.[8]

Yellow-dog contracts. Even though popular opinion was not sharply critical of unions in this period, many employers bitterly opposed and attacked employee organizations. To undermine unions some employers used *yellow-dog* or *ironclad contracts* — contracts which required employees, as a condition of employment, to declare that they were not and would not become union members. Efforts to get employees to violate these provisions and break this contract could be and were stopped by court orders.

Unions sought public intervention and legislation to declare these yellow-dog contracts contrary to public policy and illegal. Nineteen states passed such legislation. The federal government, in the Erdman Act of 1898, prohibited the use of such contracts by interstate industries. However, the United States Supreme Court, in 1908, held that this legislation violated the Fifth Amendment by interfering with the rights of employers (*Adair v. United States*, 208 U.S. 161). In 1915 the same court invalidated a state law of Kansas that prohibited such contracts in intrastate industry. In *Coppage v. Kansas* (236 U.S. 1), the Court held that the state law was unconstitutional in that it violated the Fourteenth Amendment, in which states are forbidden to deprive persons of life, liberty, or property without due process of law.

The courts thus largely created and maintained public rules on employment relationships. Their decisions on the constitutionality of laws regulating yellow-dog contracts appeared to rule out legislative interference in employment agreements or contracts. To many unionists this position showed clearly that the courts were on the employers' side. This attitude still appears in some expressions of union opinion and action.

---

[7]See Felix Frankfurter and Nathan Greene, "Labor Injunction," *Encyclopedia of the Social Sciences*, Vol. 8, pp. 653–57.

[8]*In re Debs*, 158 U.S. 564, 15 Sup. Ct., 900 (1895).

Unions as Restraints of Trade

A third stage in the development of public policy on labor relations was introduced when employers sought to bring unions under a general rule forbidding illegal combinations in restraint of trade. As unions increased in numbers, many critics of the labor movement insisted that unions, by their control of labor supplies in some markets, had become combinations in restraint of trade not unlike large-scale business combinations. This viewpoint was closely related to the earlier approach that regarded unions as conspiracies. The argument held that if business firms must be regulated to prevent combinations in restraint of trade, unionists should be restricted by the same rules.

Sherman Act (1890). In 1890 Congress enacted the Sherman Act, frequently described as an antitrust law because it outlawed what were regarded as monopolistic combinations in restraint of trade. The law provided penalties for such combinations by authorizing the assessment of triple damages for violations. Discussion at the time of its enactment centered about illegal business combinations. Almost immediately after it was passed, however, employers demanded that the law be applied to unions. In an early case the law was made the basis for an injunction against draymen and warehouse employees.[9] Other cases sought to prevent union negotiation of the closed shop, which requires employers to offer jobs only to union members, and to outlaw secondary boycotts, in which members seek to prevent third parties from buying the products of firms involved in conflict with the union.

A test of this application of the Sherman Act was provided in the Danbury Hatters' case.[10] Employees of D. E. Loewe and Company, of Danbury, Connecticut, had presented demands that the employer recognize their union and agree to a closed shop. When their demands were rejected, in 1902, the union struck and undertook a campaign in which members urged unionists and their friends to boycott the employer. A suit by the employer against the union and its members resulted in an award of triple damages amounting to $252,000 under Sherman Act provisions. The decision was sustained by the United States Supreme Court in 1908.

---

[9] *United States v. Workingmen's Amalgamated Council of New Orleans*, 54 Fed. 994 (1893).
[10] *Loewe v. Lawlor*, 208 U.S. 274, 28 Sup. Ct. 301.

Unions recognized that this decision had created a serious hazard to the entire labor movement. Since damages were assessed against both unions as organizations and against their individual members, many potential unionists might be afraid to join. Locals and internationals could be crippled if not destroyed by such assessments.

Clayton Act (1914). In 1914 unions secured a modification of Sherman Act provisions in a new antitrust law, the Clayton Act. Section 6 gave specific authorization for usual union activities and exempted unions from the coverage of antitrust rules. This section is famous for its first sentence which declares:

> Section 6. That the labor of human beings is not a commodity or an article of commerce.

Section 20 of the Clayton Act restricts the use of labor injunctions. It proposed to prevent their use against unions except in cases of irreparable injury for which there is no adequate remedy. The act declares that injunctions shall not forbid organization, assembling, or paying strike benefits. Labor leaders were much pleased by these changes, and Samuel Gompers, then president of the AFL, described the new law as "Labor's Magna Charta."

Actually, however, these changes did not prevent continued judicial regulation of union activities. Courts ruled that Clayton Act provisions did not intend to give blanket approval to all current and future union tactics and practices. In a series of decisions, the use of injunctions was approved and triple damages were assessed for practices that courts regarded as restraints of trade threatening injury to an employer's business or property. Unionists therefore continued their attacks on the use of labor injunctions and were successful in securing state laws limiting this injunctive procedure in a majority of the states. Meanwhile, public opinion and a series of liberalizing court decisions have excluded most union activities from the area regarded as illegal restraint of trade under federal laws. This process of freeing unions from charges of monopoly gained public support as popular opinion came to regard unions as essential in balancing the power of employers.

Unions as Semipublic Agencies

As noted, early years of this century were characterized by frequent conflict between unions and employers. Several powerful associations of employers undertook campaigns to eliminate or greatly restrict unions. Employers and unionists engaged in continued battles with accompanying violence in some localities. Some firms were eliminated, as were some unions. As more powerful employer associations and unions developed, they became sources of bigger, more far-reaching conflicts. Many strikes were no longer local affairs, nor were they brief encounters. Both unions and employer associations could provide benefits and support for those engaged in strikes, which could be continued for longer periods of time. Meanwhile, these conflicts affected growing numbers and proportions of citizens. Whole industries could be shut down because a few employers and unions failed to agree.

Unions gained increasing popular support. In part, this change resulted because unionists became more numerous. Meanwhile, many citizens became increasingly concerned with the rapid growth of business organizations, the numerous mergers, and the development of giant corporations. Public investigations of the activities of employer associations disclosed their frequent efforts to control the public press, public officials, and courts. Unions and their members appeared to many citizens to be underdogs in the struggle with strong, belligerent employer associations. The financial resources of unions and their members were much smaller than those of many employers and employer associations. Meanwhile, the general philosophy of business unionism achieved wide acceptance.

In the 1920's and early 1930's, the changing popular viewpoint began to crystallize. Public opinion sought:

1. To balance the power of employers and unions as a protection to employees and the public. To this end, to encourage development of strong unions and prevent employer tactics that weaken unions.

2. To safeguard the public interest and welfare by reducing the area of conflict, eliminating self-determination in the most frequent and troublesome issues. More specifically, to require employers to bargain with a union if so requested by a majority of employees and to state formal rules about appropriate bargaining units and the identification of unions to be regarded as bargaining agents in these units.

In the years of the Great Depression, following the stock market crash in 1929, changing public attitudes toward labor relations were expressed in a sharp revision of public policy. New laws in 1932, 1933, 1934, and 1935 sought to implement the objectives outlined in preceding paragraphs. On the national scene forerunners of this change could have been noted in the Railway Labor Act of 1926. In that legislation the right of employees to organize and to bargain collectively was specifically stated, and public facilities for settling employer-union disputes were established.

Norris-LaGuardia Act (1932). Formal legislative evidence that this new policy was to extend beyond the railroads and was to include all types of workers and industries appeared in the Norris-LaGuardia Act of 1932. That law specifically declared the public policy that employees should be permitted to organize and bargain collectively through unions of their own choice. In addition, the law declared yellow-dog contracts contrary to public policy and specified restrictions on the action of federal courts in issuing injunctions. Further, the Norris-LaGuardia Act limited the liability of individual union members for damages assessed against unions in cases like that of the Danbury Hatters' case. The law prescribed detailed procedure in petitions for labor injunctions. It required jury trials for unionists charged with contempt of court in such cases, except those in which the offense was directly observable by the court.

National Industrial Recovery Act (1933). In the depth of the depression of the 1930's, the National Industrial Recovery Act of 1933 was passed. It was designed to restore public confidence and to encourage reemployment and business activity. To insure the full cooperation of organized labor, the N.I.R.A. reiterated the public policy expressed in the Norris-LaGuardia Act. It declared that employees shall have the right to join unions of their choice and to bargain collectively. The new law declared that public policy could no longer tolerate employer interference in either the organization or the administration of unions. Furthermore, employers must not require employees to join a company union or an employer-dominated union. A joint resolution of Congress authorized the president to create a special National Labor Board to implement this policy.

National Labor Relations Act (1935). The N.I.R.A. was declared unconstitutional by the Supreme Court in the Schechter case on May 27, 1935, in a decision based on other provisions of the law (congressional power to delegate authority on production control and pricing).[11] Almost immediately Congress enacted the National Labor Relations Act which, without a single amendment, became the major expression of national public policy on labor relations for the next twelve years.

---

[11]*A. L. A. Schechter Corp. v. United States*, 295 U.S. 495.

The National Labor Relations Act — often described as the Wagner Act because it was sponsored by Senator Wagner of New York — made five major points in its statement of national policy on collective bargaining:

1. It explained the federal government's concern with labor relations. The preliminary statement of finding and policy in the act expressed the conviction that employer action in refusing to bargain with unions or opposing employee membership in unions creates strife and unrest and obstructs the flow of interstate commerce.

2. The act declared that inequality in the bargaining power of employers and individual employees depresses wages and aggravates tendencies toward depression so that public policy must encourage free unions of employees to achieve a balance of power.

3. The law provided special machinery to settle the two troublesome questions about (a) what shall constitute an appropriate bargaining unit (which employees shall be included) and (b) which of several contesting unions shall be recognized as the bargaining agent. A new National Labor Relations Board was authorized to determine, in disputes involving industries in interstate commerce, the boundaries of bargaining units and to certify appropriate bargaining agents.

4. To prevent employers from interfering with free collective bargaining, the Wagner Act specifically prohibited five unfair labor practices of employers. They included:
   a. Employer interference with self-organization.
   b. Employer domination of a union.
   c. Employer discrimination against an employee because of the latter's activity in a union.
   d. Employer discrimination against an employee for reporting alleged violations by employers.
   e. Employer refusal to bargain collectively in good faith.

5. The act created a new, permanent National Labor Relations Board to enforce provisions of the law. That board, generally described as the NLRB, was authorized to decide conflicts over bargaining units, certify bargaining agents, and prevent unfair labor practices of employers.[12]

State labor relations acts. Changing public policy in this period was evidenced by state as well as federal action. Federal authority covers only those industries whose major business extends into interstate commerce. Intrastate industries remain within the jurisdictions

---

[12]For more detail on these functions, see Walter L. Daykin, "NLRB Jurisdictional Standards," *Labor Law Journal*, Vol. 6, Nos. 9 and 10 (September and October, 1955), pp. 617 ff. and 696–709; also Chester A. Morgan, "Union Security-Federal or State Sphere," *Labor Law Journal*, Vol. 4, No. 12 (December, 1953), pp. 815–21.

of the states. Sixteen jurisdictions have enacted legislation that regulates relationships of intrastate employers and unions and thus supplements the National Labor Relations Act.[13]

In general, these "little Wagner Acts" express the same public policy. They require free collective bargaining, without employer interference in union affairs. Several of the state laws provide for the designation of bargaining units and the certification of bargaining agents by state agencies and outline unfair labor practices in terms similar to those of the Wagner Act. Some of them combine administration of their acts with conciliation and mediation services. Some of the more recent state laws have prohibited specified unfair practices of unions as well as of employers.

Reaction and Public Regulation

The Wagner Act and related state laws clearly evidenced a wide swing of the pendulum of public opinion, which had reacted from the earlier policies of maintaining a "hands-off" policy on the part of government, or the later tendency to restrict unions by court orders allowing a free hand for employer control. The new policy of encouraging collective bargaining and providing government intervention to assist unions was such a drastic change that many employers did not believe it would be supported by general public opinion. For two years after passage of the Wagner Act, many employers and employer associations insisted that the new law would be held unconstitutional. The Supreme Court ended these arguments by finding the law constitutional in 1937.[14]

In the years that followed, critics of the changed public policy insisted that it had gone too far. The following points were made by those who argued for modifications in public policy:

1. The rapid growth of unions after 1935 made public intervention on their side, designed to encourage unions, unnecessary and inappropriate. (Unions, it may be noted, were growing rapidly. Membership multiplied more than four times in the decade following enactment of the National Industrial Recovery Act.)

2. Public intervention on the side of unions encouraged unions to ignore the public interest and welfare in advancing their own

---

[13] Jurisdictions with labor relations acts include Colorado, Connecticut, Hawaii, Idaho, Kansas, Massachusetts, Michigan, Minnesota, New York, North Dakota, Oregon, Pennsylvania, Puerto Rico, Rhode Island, Utah, and Wisconsin. Five restrict employer practices, nine restrict both employers and unions. A few states established special boards or commissions to enforce their acts; in others the acts must be enforced by the courts.

[14] *NLRB v. Jones and Laughlin Steel Corporation*, 301 U.S. 1, 57 S. Ct., 615 (1937).

interests. Some of their practices, according to this view, interfered with trade and commerce and the rights of citizens. Most
obvious and objectionable among these practices were union re-
fusals to bargain in good faith, boycotts, jurisdictional disputes,
organizational strikes, and picketing designed to force employers
to recognize a union.

3. Public policy had given unions a semipublic status which justified and necessitated their regulation to insure that their practices were compatible with the public welfare. Their possible
   domination by Communists illustrated this need for public regulation, according to this argument.

4. Union rights and privileges, as outlined in the Wagner Act, imposed unjustified limits on the rights of citizens to jobs. By encouraging union and closed-shop agreements, public policy had
   forced many citizens to join unions to get or hold jobs.

5. Regulations imposed by the Wagner Act limited the rights of
   employers as citizens, particularly in restricting their freedom of
   speech in communications with employees.

6. If unions were to be allowed a wide area of freedom, they should
   be held responsible for their actions by permitting suits against
   them. For example, if a union broke an agreement or carried on
   a jurisdictional or organizational strike or a boycott, an injured
   employer should have the right to recover his losses by a suit
   against the union.[15]

Postwar industrial unrest. These arguments were frequently
voiced in the ten years immediately following enactment of the
Wagner Act. Employer associations were the principal spokesmen
for these criticisms. Early evidence that public opinion was shifting
in the direction proposed by these critics appeared in the provisions
of several state labor relations acts, which included some of the proposed restrictions on unions.

Immediately following World War II, union-employer conflict
attracted wide popular attention. During the war most employers
and unions had recognized their responsibility to cooperate and to
avoid strikes or lockouts. Most unions had signed a no-strike pledge.
Union officers had joined employers and public representatives as
members of national and regional War Labor Boards. They had accepted the authority of these agencies in settling disputes. By the end
of the war, a wide range of disagreements had accumulated. Both

---

[15]For interesting discussions of these changing views, see "Away with Labor Laws?"
Fortune, Vol. 47, No. 6 (June, 1953), pp. 73 ff.; Clay P. Malick, "The Confusion in Union
Status: A Proposal," *Labor Law Journal*, Vol. 2, No. 11 (November, 1951), pp. 830–45;
Nathan P. Feinsinger and Edwin E. Witte, "Labor Legislation and the Role of Govern-
ment," *Monthly Labor Review*, Vol. 71, No. 1 (July, 1950), pp. 48–61; Albion Guilford
Taylor, *Labor and the Supreme Court* (2nd ed.; Ann Arbor, Mich.: Braun-Brumfield, Inc.,
1961).

employers and unions were unhappy with some of the working conditions established during the war. Many employers and unions were anxious for an open break.

When wartime restrictions on strikes were removed, the number of work stoppages rose sharply. Both employers and unions resisted public proposals of compromise or conciliation. In several nationwide disputes federal intervention was unsuccessful in securing agreement. Many citizens were impressed with the bitterness of the conflict and the increased power and strength of unions.

Much point was also made, in public criticisms of unions, of their possible domination by Communists. Both the AFL and the CIO undertook purging campaigns to eliminate Communist leaders and unions. A dozen international unions were expelled by the CIO because of Communist domination.

Taft-Hartley Act (1947). After 12 years in which the National Labor Relations Act was, without amendment, the major declaration of federal labor policy, it was modified by the Taft-Hartley Act in 1947. The law was described as an amendment to the Wagner Act; it begins with a modified statement of public policy which explains that unions as well as employers must be regulated to protect the public interest. The law retains a declaration of the necessity for preventing employer interference with union membership and organization. It reiterates the public policy of encouraging unions as a means of equalizing the bargaining power of employers and employees. It declares that the protection of unions enforced by the Wagner Act has been effective in preventing work stoppages and encouraging the free flow of commerce. The statement adds, however, that certain practices of some unions also tend to obstruct commerce by creating strikes and unrest and that such practices should therefore be subject to public regulation.

In the sections that follow, the Taft-Hartley Act introduced a number of new rules of the game. To enforce them, the NLRB was reconstituted with five members instead of three, and the board's General Counsel was given independent status and final authority in deciding whether to prosecute complaints. Some of the rules introduced in 1947 were modified by amendments enacted in 1951.

Major changes in the rules introduced by the Taft-Hartley or Labor Management Relations Act (LMRA) may be outlined as follows:

(1) *Union security.* Under the Wagner Act the closed shop was permissible. The Taft-Hartley Act made it illegal in industries subject to the law. Also, under the Wagner Act, federal rules on union security were regarded as preempting the field so that no state could maintain policy less favorable to unions. The Taft-Hartley Act allows states and localities to make such rules on union security for intrastate industry. It thus permits states to enact laws forbidding the union shop. Further, the checkoff, formerly unrestricted, is permitted only if authorized by an employee in writing. Such authorization cannot be made irrevocable for a period of more than one year.

The union shop provision allows unions and employers to negotiate an agreement under which all employees in the unit must be or become union members. The sole test of membership, however, is the payment of initiation fees and dues. The union cannot require dismissal of an employee on any other grounds.

(2) *Union recognition.* Under the Taft-Hartley Act employers are granted the right to seek an election any time they are confronted by a union demand for recognition. The Wagner Act permitted employer petitions only when two or more unions were demanding recognition.

(3) *Foremen and supervisors.* The Taft-Hartley Act changed the rule that required employers to bargain with foremen when requested. Employers may or may not bargain with unions of supervisory employees, as they prefer.

(4) *Bargaining requirements.* Unfair labor practices specified in the Wagner Act required employers to bargain in good faith. The Taft-Hartley Act extended the same requirement to unions.

(5) *Interference in bargaining; coercion.* The Wagner Act prohibited interference by employers designed to control employees in their selection of bargaining agents but expressed no such limitation on union action. The Taft-Hartley Act forbids coercion in this selection by employers, or by unions, or by employers and unions. It also forbids coercion directed at employers by unions to require recognition of a particular bargaining agent.

(6) *Boycotts and jurisdictional disputes.* The Taft-Hartley Act introduced new restrictions on these practices. Employers are permitted to file charges alleging these practices with the NLRB, and the board is authorized to secure court orders to prevent such practices. The NLRB is instructed to give top priorities to action on such unfair union practices.

(7) *Union responsibility.* The Taft-Hartley Act specifies that unions may be sued in federal courts for breaking contracts or carrying on illegal jurisdictional disputes or boycotts.

(8) *Health and welfare funds.* Under the Taft-Hartley Act employer contributions are forbidden unless the funds are managed according to rules specified by the law.

(9) *Free speech of employers.* The Taft-Hartley Act specifically declares the right of employers to express opinions on unions and union membership, provided such statements contain no threat of reprisal or promise of benefit for employee action.

(10) *Required notice of contract changes.* Another rule introduced by the Taft-Hartley Act requires both parties to give 60-day notice of their intention to terminate or seek changes in an existing agreement.

(11) *National emergency strikes.* The Taft-Hartley Act introduced a special procedure for handling disputes that threaten the national health or safety. The Attorney General may secure an injunction to prevent or stop a strike in such cases. This court order may allow the government 80 days in which to settle the strike and to conduct an election among employees on the employer's final offer.

(12) *Structural and procedural changes.* The Taft-Hartley Act reconstituted the Federal Mediation and Conciliation Service as an independent agency. (It was formerly in the Department of Labor.) As has been noted, the act gave the NLRB five members instead of three and made the board's General Counsel independent, with much broader discretion. Under Taft-Hartley provisions, also, a statute of limitations on unfair practices is imposed so that the board does not consider charges filed more than six months after objectionable practices are alleged to have taken place. The board was given authority to secure restraining orders at once, without the delay required in earlier procedure. The board was also assigned the function of holding union-shop elections whenever the union shop was requested, but this assignment was eliminated by a 1951 amendment. In another change, the law requires that craftsmen and professional employees be given an opportunity to vote separately on their inclusion in a bargaining unit with other employees. Also, plant guards, under Taft-Hartley rules, cannot be included in the same bargaining unit as production workers.

Other requirements introduced by the Taft-Hartley Act required that unions which seek to use the law must meet certain qualifications. All such unions must file regular reports, in the detail specified, with the Secretary of Labor. They must also file affidavits certifying that their officers are not Communists. AFL-CIO officers were excluded from this requirement by 1951 amendments.

The Taft-Hartley Act also amended the Federal Corrupt Practices Act to prohibit union contributions in elections of federal officials.

Communist Control Act (1954). In 1954 the Communist Control Act added new rules designed to prevent Communist domination of employers or unions. The Subversive Activities Control Board was instructed to determine whether suspected organizations — union or firm — are Communist-infiltrated. A union found to be so infected cannot be certified as a bargaining agent under LMRA, nor can it secure consideration of an alleged unfair labor practice or use any other service or facility provided for unions by the NLRA. In addition, upon petition of 20 percent of the employees in the bargaining unit, the NLRB will hold a decertification election. An employer found to be Communist-controlled is similarly barred from use of the machinery provided by the amended NLRA.

Right-to-work laws. Perhaps the most widely discussed issue with respect to public policy in recent years concerns the requirement that employees join a union if a union shop has been negotiated. Critics argue that it is un-American to force union membership as a condition in getting employment.

The Taft-Hartley Act allowed states or localities to enforce more restrictive rules on union security than those imposed by that law. Some twenty states have enacted so-called *right-to-work laws* that limit union security by forbidding any agreement under which an employee must join a union to secure or hold a job. In 1956 Palm Springs, California, became the first city to enact a municipal right-to-work ordinance. One state repealed its law in 1956, but several other states have proposals for right-to-work laws under consideration. Under such rules the union shop is illegal, and maintenance of membership (or possibly the agency shop) is the strongest permissible type of union security.[16]

---

[16]The states with right-to-work laws are Alabama, Arizona, Arkansas, Florida, Georgia, Indiana, Iowa, Kansas, Mississippi, Nebraska, Nevada, North Carolina, North Dakota, South Carolina, South Dakota, Tennessee, Texas, Utah, Virginia, and Wyoming. In addition, Colorado and Wisconsin require that a majority of all employees must approve such a clause.

Union leaders have described these laws as "wreck" laws. As noted, they insist that unions must have security if they are to be responsible. In their opinion it is unreasonable to expect unions to discipline members and enforce the terms of collective agreements if members can quit the union and continue to hold their jobs whenever they are dissatisfied with action of the union or some of its members. Even the union shop permitted by federal law is weak in this respect, since the only grounds on which a union can demand dismissal of an employee are the nonpayment of dues or initiation fees. Union leaders point to the fact that where the union shop exists it has been approved by a majority of employees. They argue that it provides a minimum of union security for effective collective bargaining.

Critics of the union shop and supporters of the right-to-work laws insist that it is morally wrong to require any worker to join a union in order to get or hold a job, even if a majority of employees in the unit has approved such a provision. The right to earn a living by working, they argue, is much more fundamental and essential than the right to form and maintain unions. They hold that union membership should therefore be completely voluntary.

A single statement of this viewpoint may help to indicate the bitterness in attacks on closed- and union-shop provisions. Sylvester Petro declares:

> Compulsory unionism and personal freedom are incompatible. Employment in a free society is a volitional contractual arrangement between a person seeking work and a person seeking someone to work for him. But compulsory unionism is a device by means of which an outsider to the employment relationship imposes a toll upon both real parties involved. It is, therefore, indistinguishable in principle — sometimes indistinguishable in fact — from the tolls imposed by brigands and the "protection money" demanded by extortionists. If corruption prevails among the leaders of unions which practice compulsory unionism, no one should be surprised.[17]

Great heat has been generated over this issue, both because the idea of complete freedom and voluntarism in union membership has wide popular appeal and because union leaders see right-to-work laws as another step in a long series of employer attacks on unionism.

The right-to-work issue has been complicated by increasing union demands for *agency shop* clauses. They require all employees in

---

[17]Personal Freedom and Labor Policy," Institute of Economic Affairs, New York University, 1958. For more on this controversy, see *Twenty Questions about the Right to Work* (New York: National Association of Manufacturers, 1956); also Leonard Wigon and Gilbert E. Donahue, "The Right-to-Work Issue — An Annotated Bibliography," University of Illinois Institute of Labor and Industrial Relations, January, 1958, (Mimeographed).

the bargaining unit to pay dues, whether or not they are union members. They thus eliminate "free-riders" who get whatever benefits unions secure but contribute nothing to the support of the union.

Weak, young unions unquestionably benefit from union shop and agency shop provisions. It is by no means clear that they are appropriate when unions have matured.[18]

LMRDA—Landrum-Griffin Act (1959).

Big unions, big business, and big government seem persistently to challenge each other; each sees the others as dangerous rivals if not actual enemies. In recent years government has evidenced its concern about both big business and big unions. In 1957 and 1958 popular attention was directed to objectionable practices of both employers and unions by a Senate Select Committee on Improper Activities in the Labor or Management Field, chaired by Senator McClellan.

The committee brought to light numerous examples of improper conduct, including the payment of tribute and bribes by employers, other types of payoffs and shakedowns, arbitrary disciplinary actions by unions against their members, the misappropriation of union funds for the personal benefit of union officials, and careless if not criminal manipulation of union health, welfare, pension, and other trust funds. One of the most striking characteristics of the hearings was use of the Fifth Amendment — the frequent refusal of presumably responsible union officials to answer questions on the ground that their testimony might tend to incriminate them.

Largely as a result of these disclosures, the Labor-Management Reporting and Disclosure Act of 1959 imposed additional regulations on collective bargaining practice. The declaration of policy notes that "It continues to be the responsibility of the Federal government to protect employees' rights to organize, choose their own representatives, bargain collectively, and otherwise engage in concerted activities for their mutual aid or protection." The statement further notes as public policy that "it is essential that labor organizations, employers, and their officials adhere to the highest standards of responsibility and

---

[18]See Earl F. Cheit, "Union Security and the Right to Work," *Labor Law Journal*, Vol. 6, No. 6 (June, 1955), pp. 357 ff.; Maurice C. Benewitz, "Nature and Effect of State Right-to-Work Laws," *Wayne Law Review*, Vol. 1, No. 3 (Summer, 1955), pp. 165–92; Frederic Meyers, "Effects of Right-to-Work Laws: A Study of the Texas Act," *Industrial and Labor Relations Review*, Vol. 9, No. 1 (October, 1955), pp. 77–84; for an employee viewpoint, see *Trouble, U.S.A.*, a film drama available from the National Association of Manufacturers — also, that Association's *Twenty Questions about the Right to Work* (1956).

ethical conduct" in labor relations. It declares that "there have been a number of instances of breach of trust, corruption, disregard of the rights of individual employees, and other failures to observe high standards of responsibility and ethical conduct," and concludes that legislative action "is necessary to eliminate or prevent improper practices on the part of labor organizations, employers, labor relations consultants and their officers and representatives."

The 1959 act then amends several of the rules instituted by the Taft-Hartley Act, establishes a comprehensive reporting system for participants in labor relations, and creates new regulations of unions designed to protect union members and assure democratic control.

Major changes in collective bargaining rules (1) allow states to make their own rules in the area preempted by the federal jurisdiction but in which federal agencies have declined to accept responsibility, (2) permit employees engaged in an "economic" strike (see Chapter 13) to vote in NLRB-conducted elections, (3) tighten the rules on union use of the secondary boycott, and (4) restrict picketing of retail stores to prevent sales of a product involved in a dispute or as an organizing tactic. The law provides a special exception to the prohibition of the closed shop in the construction industry and the garment trades.

The LMRDA takes its title from new requirements of periodic reporting by unions, employers, and consultants. The range of required reports is very broad and provides detailed information on the activities and procedures followed in labor relations as well as all financial aspects of these activities. Particular attention is directed to union procedures in collections, disbursements and investments, calling meetings, electing officers, authorizing strikes, and conducting trusteeships.

The act not only requires that unions report their procedures; it also includes as Title I a Bill of Rights for members of labor organizations. The act specifies procedures for setting or changing dues and fees, conducting elections, and establishing trusteeships. Individual members must be permitted to challenge the actions of officers and to bring their complaints into court. Disciplinary powers of unions are limited. Gangsters, racketeers, and Communists are barred from office in unions and from practice as labor relations consultants.[19]

---

[19]For a detailed analysis of Communist tactics in infiltrating a union, see "A Case History in the Tactics of Communist Unionism," *Senate Committee Print*, 82nd Congress, 2nd Session (Washington, D.C.: Government Printing Office, 1953).

Results of this legislation are only partially discernible. But it is apparent that public policy has made a 180-degree turn from the earlier intention to avoid public regulation.

This chapter has traced the development and transition in American public policy on unions and employer-union relationships from colonial times to the present. In the United States public policy on these and other aspects of collective bargaining has not been static. While the general, long-run tendency has been to liberalize attitudes toward union membership and the practices of unions, this development has had its ups and downs, and recent years have seen an unmistakable trend in the other direction. The chapter that follows outlines current policy and notes its implications for the common and most important labor relations practices of employers and unions today.

ANALYTICAL REVIEW QUESTIONS

1. What is meant by the statement that governments set the "ground rules" for labor relations? What is public policy?
2. What features of employment are subject to government regulations?
3. (a) In what ways were unions deemed to be conspiracies?
   (b) How do you differentiate civil from criminal conspiracies?
4. What conditions in early America help account for the lack of formal governmental regulation of labor?
5. (a) How do court orders constitute a form of public regulation?
   (b) What activities did and do court orders prohibit?
   (c) What are labor injunctions?
6. On what grounds did the courts declare laws prohibiting yellow-dog contracts unconstitutional?
7. (a) Explain early employer arguments on unions as monopolies. (b) How did the Sherman Act affect the position of unions in this respect? (c) What was the outcome of the Danbury Hatters' case?
8. (a) How did the Clayton Act modify the concept of "unions in restraint of trade?" (b) Did the Clayton Act succeed in preventing labor injunctions?
9. (a) What developments suggested that special labor relations legislation was unavoidable? (b) How and why did the public come to regard unions as semipublic agencies?
10. (a) What changes were introduced by the Railway Transportation Act of 1926? (b) How did they suggest more general labor legislation at a later date?
11. What were major public objectives in collective bargaining in the early 1930's with respect to: (a) power relationships, (b) area of conflict, (c) rules of conduct?

12. Describe four major elements of public policy declared by the Norris-LaGuardia Act of 1932 with respect to: (a) right to organize and bargain, (b) yellow-dog contracts, (c) injunctions, and (d) liability of union members.

13. What were the major points made by the National Labor Relations Act in its statement of national policy on collective bargaining?

14. How did the NLRA take care of the problems of bargaining units and recognition?

15. What five unfair labor practices of employers were prohibited by the NLRA?

16. (a) Why do we have both federal and state labor relations acts? (b) Over what do the latter have jurisdiction?

17. In what sense did the NLRA and the state labor relations acts represent a reversal of the earlier "hands-off" policy on the part of government?

18. What did critics of the NLRA mean by the argument that public policy had "gone too far"?

19. How did the Taft-Hartley Act modify public policy on collective bargaining?

20. What are the major areas of regulated behavior under the LMRDA? What common activities are outside the range of regulation?

Case 11-1

CONTROL OF EMPLOYMENT

The Northern Knitting Company has five plants located in New England and the North Central States. During the past year the firm has built another plant in the South. At present the union of employees representing northern plants is negotiating a new contract with the firm. One of the union demands is for a clause guaranteeing that priorities on all work will go to the northern plants. Specifically, the union proposes that no employees in northern plants shall be laid off for lack of work unless the new southern plant is already shut down for this reason.

The employer has refused to bargain on this issue. The company simply declares that it cannot and will not consider such a demand. Negotiations are stalled, and the union says it will strike when the present contract expires, in four days.

The union has sent a delegation to meet with the City Council in your city. One of the northern plants is located there. The union wants the council to intervene, urging that the firm accept the union proposal.

• Assume that you are a member of the council, elected from a ward that includes a large number of union members in several unions. Prepare a short statement for the newspapers explaining the stand you will take on the union's proposal. Consider the possibility that the union should file charges against the employer with the National Labor Relations Board.

Case 11-2

RIGHT TO WORK

In 1963 several states were considering the possible enactment of right-to-work laws like those already in effect in some 20 states. In one state this issue was in the forefront throughout the entire campaign. Two candidates for the Senate engaged in a popular debate on the right-to-work issue. Both defined it in the same terms as a regulation that would outlaw action by an employer or a union to negotiate or enforce the union shop or in any other manner to require employees to be union members as a condition of employment.

Mr. S, one of the candidates, argued that the proposed law would be contrary to and inconsistent with existing public policy. He asked his opponent whether the latter favored unions and collective bargaining. "If we mean what we say when we declare that we favor unions and collective bargaining," he said, "and if we mean what we say about wanting responsible unions, we must give the unions security." He argued, also, that proponents of the legislation were duty bound to report on what these laws had done in other states.

Mr. T, his opponent, insisted simply that the union shop in any form was wrong in principle, in that it forced workers to pay union dues for the privilege of working. He insisted that, in such matters of principle, the facts about what may have happened in other states were unnecessary and unimportant.

• Assume you were a voter in this state. How would your vote be influenced by their positions on this issue? Be prepared to answer and to justify your decision.

CURRENT PUBLIC POLICY ON LABOR RELATIONS

The tripartite nature of policy that guides today's labor relations is clearly evident. Bargaining and administration of agreements are prescribed to an impressive degree. What firms and unions must do and what they may not do have become prominent if not dominating factors influencing what they do. Thousands of pages of rules and interpretations of rules by administrators and arbitrators appear each month. Meanwhile, political leaders — in papers, reports, and releases — issue opinions and recommendations that may not have the full force of law but require careful consideration by all the parties. They may be symptoms of legislative regulations to be expected in the future.

Indeed, regulation has become so extensive that some participants in labor relations as well as students of the field conclude that policy is essentially a matter of law, so that economic and other nonlegal values deserve little attention or consideration. Labor marketing considerations, in this viewpoint, provide few significant clues for understanding or predicting current and future behavior in labor relations.

It is clear that most modern economies simply cannot ignore the impact of collective bargaining in their social and economic programs. Collective bargaining can have significant effects on price levels, foreign competition, the balance of international payments, economic growth, and equality in economic opportunity — all representing important planks in current political programs. By continually focusing attention on the training, development, allocation, and application of manpower resources, collective bargaining can influence the quantity and quality of employment. Indeed, one major argument for public support of collective bargaining sees it as exerting a constant pressure for improving the quality of management and insuring better utilization of manpower resources. No government can ignore these relationships, and this model is so widely understood that all modern societies have recognized the necessity for tripartite policy in this area.[1]

In this country a major concern in public policy has been to allow the parties widest possible freedom and opportunity to settle their differences while, at the same time, avoiding violence or work stoppages that threaten the public health or safety. Perhaps the most obvious evidence of this policy is to be seen in federal legislation on union-management relationships on the railroads. That same example can illustrate the frustrations experienced in attempting to implement this policy.

As noted in Chapter 11, the 1926 Railway Labor Act (with amendments in 1934) established a complex procedure to assist the parties in settling their differences. Even earlier, the Arbitration Act (1888), the Erdman Act (1898), and the Transportation Act (1920) had included provisions for mediation, public investigation, and voluntary arbitration.

The 1926 law assured employees of their right to bargain collectively through undominated unions of their own choice. It provided for "adjustment boards" to be created by agreement of the parties to hear their disputes. It established a national Board of Mediation to consider grievances involving changes in wages and other working conditions and to settle issues not resolved by the adjustment boards. Special emergency boards could be appointed by the President for issues that seriously endangered public transportation services.

Despite all these detailed provisions, conflict in the first half of the 1960's created almost continuous threats of work stoppage. In the fall of 1963, Congress enacted special legislation providing compulsory arbitration of disputes involving the size of work crews. In 1964 the President personally supervised emergency conciliation growing

---

[1]See Clark Kerr, "New Opportunities for Industrial Relations," in *National Academy of Management; Proceedings of the Fourteenth Annual Meeting* (Washington, D.C.: Bureau of National Affairs, Inc., 1961), pp. 184–92.

out of the resulting arbitration award. It is clear, from this experience, that no dependable formula for effective tripartite policy and program has yet appeared.

Current public policy seeks, therefore, to prescribe rules to assure that the activities of unions and of employers, in their collective bargaining, contribute to or do not interfere with attainment of several socially-accepted, economic goals. Among the most important are: (1) an optimum of economic stability, (2) an optimum rate of economic growth, and (3) successful international competition and a favorable balance of payments. To this end public policy proposes to maintain a balance of power in union and employer power-centers and to avoid such open conflict as may threaten attainment of these goals by its adverse effects on employment and output.

In this chapter attention is directed to the principal types of current regulation. Many details are omitted, in part because they involve technicalities that are of major interest only to specialists in the field and in part because these detailed rules change from month to month.[2] For convenience these public policies are grouped about five major subjects or issues, including (1) scope of bargaining, (2) union and management security, (3) public guidelines for unions, (4) public guidelines for employers, and (5) trends in public policy.

SCOPE OF BARGAINING

As compared with earlier practice, modern collective bargaining is at once more extensive in the subjects covered in current agreements and more intensive as indicated by the detail of agreements. In much earlier practice the contract was summarized in a single page. Today's agreements are typically booklets of 15 to 50 pages.

In part, coverage has expanded as a result of negotiation; in part, the broadened scope is a result of public regulation. Both unions and employers have introduced new aspects of employment, as when unions negotiate three-month vacations or "sabbaticals" for senior employees, or employers introduce negotiated profit sharing. Meanwhile, public regulation has identified new areas as having significance for workers and hence subject to negotiation if a party proposes them.

---

[2]For details of these rules, see the special labor reporting services, including: *Labor Relations: Federal Laws* and *Labor Relations: State Laws*, Prentice-Hall, Inc.; *Labor Relations Reporter*, Bureau of National Affairs, Inc.; see also Nicholas S. Falcone, *Labor Law* (New York: John Wiley and Sons, Inc., 1962) and Sanford Cohen, *Labor Law* (Columbus, Ohio: Charles E. Merrill Books, Inc., 1964).

As defined by federal rules of the game and current policy, collective bargaining is negotiation directed toward the determination of a set of rules governing working relationships. It establishes what Professor Slichter called a system of "industrial jurisprudence." Bargaining requires that both parties meet at reasonable times and places and seek in good faith to reach agreement on the terms of a contract. Neither is required to make any specific concession or to agree on any particular terms. Intent is of utmost importance. Both have the obligation to put a resulting agreement in written form if either requests it.

Many conflicts over what must be bargained on request have been answered by the National Labor Relations Board. When a union and an employer disagree, one of the parties may file a charge of refusal to bargain. The NLRB will order the reluctant party to bargain if the issue is regarded as one properly subject to negotiation. The area of compulsory bargaining has been greatly broadened since the early days of the Wagner Act. Current policy holds that the parties can bargain on almost any issue they wish as long as they avoid collusion, in which union and employer representatives secretly conspire and connive. Each must bargain in good faith on any in a wide range of issues if requested to do so by the other party.

Perhaps the best evidence of the growing scope of bargaining is the comprehensive classification of clauses in the various labor reporting services. Wages and hours — the usual subjects in early agreements — are now only a small portion of the total. Other employment relationships, from methods of rating and appraising employees to details of promotion, layoff, recall from layoff, vacations, training programs, and retirement have become subjects of negotiation and agreement.

Job Rights

In recent years, as unemployment has remained above historic levels, unions have become increasingly concerned with the protection of jobs and job rights. They have, to that end, sought to protect their members from the impact of technological change and to insure that jobs are not lost to workers in other plants or areas. Accordingly, work rules, with full-crew provisions and production limits and protection of seniority in work assignments, have become frequent subjects in negotiation. Unions have proposed that contracts require union approval for relocations and "contracting out" or subcontracting. Employers have objected to bargaining on such issues, but NLRB decisions have ruled them to be bargainable.[3]

One of the most obvious job protection devices, negotiated in 1962 by the United Steel Workers and the can producers, grants three-month vacations, called *sabbaticals*, in each five-year period. A similar arrangement was negotiated in the basic steel agreement in 1963. The idea is said to have originated with iron workers in Australia.

Public Employees

The status of collective bargaining by public employees is somewhat confused. The general rule that employees cannot strike against the government would seem to impose a very significant limitation on bargaining practice. The fact is, however, that public school teachers, employees in public utilities, and others have struck or simply absented themselves from jobs.

The scope of public bargaining is limited by the authority of administrators, who may not have the power to change wages or salaries or the selection procedure. Unions of public employees may, however, find an avenue of more effective influence through political action. They can present the employee view before legislative committees and endorse or reject candidates for office.

Collective bargaining in the federal service was encouraged by Executive Order 10988 in 1962. That order made it clear that federal employees may join unions, including those that also include members in private industry. Their unions will be recognized by federal agencies. If an organization includes a majority of employees in a bargaining unit, it is entitled to recognition as the exclusive bargaining agent. Grievances may be carried to arbitration, but the award can only be advisory to the administrator. Employees may not strike.[4] By executive order a voluntary checkoff procedure was approved as of January 1, 1964.

---

[3]See reports and interpretations of NLRB and court decisions on "plant relocation," "contracting out," for detail and continuing reports. See especially *Town and Country Manufacturing Co.*, 136 NLRB 111, April 13, 1962.

Prior to these decisions, the general rule was that an employer need not bargain over decisions that were economically motivated and involved no discrimination against the union (*Fiberboard*, 1961). In 1962 NLRB reopened the *Fiberboard Paper Products* case and applied its ruling in the *Town and Country* case (1962) to conclude that an employer must also bargain over the effects of subcontracting on jobs.

[4]For details, see John W. Macy, Jr., "Employee-Management Cooperation in the Federal Service," *Personnel Administration*, Vol. 26, No. 1 (January-February, 1963),

UNION AND MANAGEMENT SECURITY

No question exists about the right of employees to organize and to join unions of their own choice. The federal government will intervene in interstate industry to prevent employer interference in organization or domination of employee organizations. In several states similar public intervention is provided for intrastate industries. Public agencies will assist, when requested, by designating bargaining units, certifying bargaining agents, requiring employers to bargain in good faith, and restraining employer interference in union affairs.

Unions may negotiate a union shop in employment covered by federal legislation. The closed shop is outlawed in such employment, except in the construction and the garment trades. States may make their own rules for employment not covered by the federal jurisdiction (interstate commerce) or in which federal agencies decline the opportunity to exercise jurisdiction. In some twenty states with right-to-work laws, the union shop is outlawed.

The agency shop is acceptable unless state laws forbid it; states have the right to exclude it.[5] (Election results in contests over the union shop in recent years have shown much less employee support; less than 60 percent of eligible employees voted affirmatively in 1961. At the same time, rank-and-file rejections of negotiated settlements have been growing, averaging above 10 percent in 1962 and 1963.)[6]

The growing scope of bargainable issues tends to reduce the area of management security. In current practice, however, employers frequently negotiate management security clauses that either (1) specify the areas in which management may act without restriction or (2) declare that all decisions not directly covered by contract clauses are reserved to management. Public policy interposes no objection to such negotiated security. On the other hand, public policy has shown little inclination to intervene in favor of any exclusive jurisdictional area for employers. Earlier concern about the rights and privileges of private property is less evident.

---

pp. 10–14. See also Wilson R. Hart, "The U.S. Civil Service Learns to Live with Executive Order 10988," *Industrial and Labor Relations Review*, Vol. 17, No. 2 (January, 1964), pp. 203-20.

[5]See *NLRB v. General Motors*, Sup. Ct., 1962, and *Retail Clerks Local 1625 v. Schermerhorn*, Sup. Ct., 1962. For other approaches to union security problems, see Michael Dudra, "Middle-Way Approaches to Union Security in Switzerland, Canada, and Colombia," *Proceedings of the Industrial Relations Research Association*, 1962, pp. 36–48.

[6]See *Current News*, Industrial Relations Counselors, Vol. 28, No. 26 (June 28, 1963).

Public opinion seems to have become more concerned about big unions in recent years, as indicated by an Opinion Research Corporation survey in 1963. A large majority of responses favored more rigorous regulation of unions. Possibly, if management becomes somewhat more of a profession, with recognized distinctive knowledge and skill, some area of decision making may be protected as exclusively reserved for management. In the absence of such a development, management security clauses provide only very limited protection.[7]

PUBLIC GUIDELINES FOR UNIONS

Current rules are more restrictive on unions than in any earlier period. After 1935 it could be said that public policy favored most union programs even if they created rather obvious inefficiency and waste. Current concern about manpower development, employment opportunities, international competition, and rapid economic growth has tended to temper earlier public approval.

Public policy favors the general economic objectives of unions. It accepts as desirable their proposals to control labor supplies in individual labor markets even though such control raises wage rates, but the 1962 *Economic Report of the President* suggested "guideposts" for wage increases, which were reiterated in 1963 and 1964. Industry-wide bargaining is not restricted. Rules on strikes, picketing, boycotts, and other traditional practices show evidence of tightening control, and perhaps the most obviously added intervention is that designed to insure democratic control of unions.

Strikes

As a general rule, the right to strike is not questioned. But certain types of strikes and strikes called under certain circumstances may result in severe penalties. *Sit-down strikes* are clearly illegal. They are specifically banned by several state laws. NLRB will not order reinstatement of employees who engage in such a strike. Strikes are forbidden for government employees in the federal service under provisions of the Taft-Hartley Act. Participation in a strike justifies discharge and loss of civil service status and bars reemployment in the government service for 3 years. Several states enforce similar rules.

---

[7]See *The Changing Climate of Labor Law* (New York: Industrial Relations Counselors, 1963).

Strikes in violation of an agreement can become the basis for suits against unions and can cause the loss of employment status by employees. The same penalty applies to sit-down strikes, slowdowns, and wildcat and other similar strikes. Loss of employment status means that NLRB will not order reemployment or award strikers lost-time pay.

Jurisdictional strikes are subject to a special rule that makes them an unfair labor practice under the federal law, which authorizes NLRB to secure injunctions to stop them. Employers may sue for damages occasioned by jurisdictional strikes. NLRB is authorized to settle such disputes if the parties fail to agree within 10 days.[8] *Sympathetic strikes* and *general strikes* are presumably illegal under federal law because they involve secondary boycotts. *Organizational strikes* may be regarded as illegal if they are held to involve coercion of either employer or employees. Such coercion is prohibited by the federal law.

Picketing

The rules of the game on picketing are quite complicated. The general rule, if one may be stated, is that picketing must not involve coercion, intimidation, or violence. The big question, of course, is how far picketing may go without involving these extremes. *Coercion* is involved, according to a series of court decisions, when pickets assault or threaten to assault others, when union members are threatened with expulsion or fines, when supervisors are threatened when trying to enter the plant, and when the purpose of picketing is to secure or enforce the illegal recognition of a union. Courts have been called on to rule in detail on these practices. Judges have tried to define *peaceful picketing*, although at least one court held there could be no such procedure. Rules on picketing have also been related to freedom of speech, on the ground that picketing is essentially an expression of opinion.

Picketing may be limited by court order specifying the number of pickets for each entrance. It may be regulated by the police to prevent interference with pedestrian or vehicular traffic. *Stranger picketing*, in which the pickets are not employees, is forbidden in several states. *Minority picketing*, in which pickets represent a minority of

---

[8]The relevant section is Section 10 (k) of the amended National Labor Relations Act. See Sanford Cohen, *Labor Law* (Columbus, Ohio: Charles E. Merrill Books, Inc., 1964), pp. 305–06.

employees acting without approval of a majority, may also be disapproved and prevented by injunction.

Actually, many of these restrictions may not be enforced. In many cities, unions have achieved such political power that public officials, including police, ignore and fail to enforce the rules.

Enacted in 1959, an amendment to the Taft-Hartley Act (Section 8 (b) (7)) makes it an unfair labor practice to picket or threaten to picket in situations where an object of the picketing is forcing the employer to recognize or bargain with the union (sometimes called *blackmail picketing*), or forcing employees to accept or select the union as bargaining agent. Picketing is barred if (1) the employer has lawfully recognized another union and a question of representation may not appropriately be raised, (2) a valid election under the act has been conducted within the preceding 12 months, or (3) picketing has been conducted over a reasonable period of time (not over 30 days) and no election petition has been filed.

Informational picketing to inform the public is not prohibited. *Dual-purpose picketing* (both informational and with recognition or organization as objects) is permitted; it is barred only if it stops pickups and deliveries.

Boycotts

As a general rule, a *primary boycott* — in which members of a single local union refuse to buy the product of one employer with whom they have a dispute — is regarded as legal. On the other hand, the legal status of the *secondary boycott* — in which the union seeks to enlist or compel the cooperation of neutral parties — is more complicated. In 1947 the Taft-Hartley Act instructed NLRB to secure injunctions against all such practices. Many state laws include the same rule about secondary boycotts.

Unions have sought ways to avoid these restrictions. In transportation they have negotiated *hot cargo clauses* that allow members and contracting employers to refuse to handle the products of noncooperating firms. Recent rules at the federal level are intended to prevent such evasions and proscribe secondary boycotts.

Restrictive Work Rules

The practice of some unions in requiring or trying to require the employment of more workers than are needed has also been the subject of legislation. The Taft-Hartley Act outlaws *exactions* — practices in which an employer pays for services that are not and will not be performed. However, because courts are seldom in a position to determine just how many employees are needed, attempts to prevent the hiring of additional workers not actually needed have not been successful. Unions may require employment of stand-by electricians, musicians, and stage hands. They may enforce full-crew rules on the railroads. Printers can insist on payment for setting "bogus type," which they as well as their employers know will not be used.[9]

On the other hand, public intervention in the long railroad dispute over work rules may indicate a growing popular criticism of such practices. Employer-union efforts to eliminate or reduce featherbedding by negotiation (as in American Motors and Kaiser Steel) have attracted wide attention and favorable comment. A Gallup poll in the summer of 1963 found that about half of all respondents favored legislation to restrict featherbedding.

Union Responsibility

The long trend toward greater acceptance, freedom, and security for unions has been paralleled by an increasing tendency to hold them responsible for the effects of union action. While individual union members can join unions without hazard to their private income or property, the millions of dollars accumulated by unions may be attached to compensate for damages. No question exists as to the suability of unions. Their vulnerability to fines and similar financial penalties for illegal action has been demonstrated many times.

For the most part, unions are not incorporated although incorporation is possible under most state laws, and Colorado requires it. Federal legislation permitting incorporation was passed in 1886, but it was repealed in 1932. Most unions have avoided incorporation and have opposed proposals that they be required to incorporate. Unions insist that incorporation encourages nuisance suits for damages that could force them into continued, costly litigation. Since the enactment of the Taft-Hartley Act with its specific declaration that unions may be sued for damages in federal courts and its requirement of registration, little interest has been shown in proposals to force incorporation of unions.

---

[9]See Norman J. Wood, "The Wisdom of Outlawing Featherbedding," *Labor Law Journal*, Vol. 6, No. 12 (December, 1955), pp. 4ff. For a thorough review and analysis of the legislation and court decisions on restrictive practices, see John R. Van de Water, "Industrial Productivity and the Law: A Study of Work Restrictions," *Virginia Law Review*, Vol. 43, No. 2 (February, 1957), pp. 155–96. See also *Labor Law Course* (Chicago: Commerce Clearing House and Richard D. Irwin, 1961), pp. 1637–39.

Most employers avoid suits against unions, even if they appear likely to be successful, on the theory that such suits tend to destroy employee morale, motivation, and teamwork. Members and former members may sue unions — for example, members who lose jobs on account of union disciplinary action may collect lost pay plus additional compensation for the mental distress and other intangible injuries suffered in such an experience.

Political Action

Public policy on the political activity of unions has not been clearly or sharply defined, either on the national level or by individual states. The Taft-Hartley Act forbids contributions or expenditures of corporate or union funds in national political campaigns or elections. Court interpretations indicate, however, that unions may use the editorial columns of their newspapers to endorse candidates and may pay for political advertising on the radio or television or in a newspaper. They may not, however, make direct contributions to candidates unless the funds so used have been collected from members for this purpose. The current rule that applies similar restrictions on the use of corporate and union funds in political campaigns gives only a superficial aspect of fairness since individuals in both types of organizations are not restricted.

In 1963 the United States Supreme Court contributed a new dimension to the rules on political activity. It held that union members have a right to object to union expenditures for political action and can secure a reduction in their dues proportionate to the relative allocation of union income to political action.[10]

Union Democracy

A major contribution to public policy in recent years is the intention to protect individual union members and minority groups in unions against arbitrary or discriminative action by their union or its officers. One important consideration involves the fairness with which a union bargaining agent represents individual members, and nonmembers as well, in the bargaining unit. Court decisions have defined a duty of "fair representation" in negotiations and in processing grievances.[11]

---

[10] *Railway Clerks v. Allen*, Sup. Ct., 1963.

[11] See Cyrus F. Smythe, "Individual and Group Interests in Collective Labor Relations," *Labor Law Journal* (June, 1962), pp. 439–48.

A major objective in recent legislation has been the assurance of democratic control within unions. The Landrum-Griffin Act specifies election procedures in detail. Public policy clearly intends that unions must be regarded as semipublic organizations. They must see themselves as to some degree a device for maintaining an economic balance of power. Their selection or rejection of applicants, election of officers, handling of union funds, and treatment of individual members are all matters of public concern.

Reporting and disclosure provisions of the Landrum-Griffin Act are intended to supplement requirements of democratic elections. That law also limits the use of trusteeships to centralize control by top union officials. The LMRDA specifies a limited range of conditions under which trusteeships can be imposed and restricts their operation to a maximum 18-month period unless the need for extension can be proved.

Since enactment of the law, major reasons given for imposing trusteeships include corruption (7 percent), assuring performance of an existing agreement (11 percent), financial mismanagement (12 percent), disaffiliation (10 percent), plant closings (20 percent), and internal dissension (8 percent). In 1958, before the new law was passed, internal dissension accounted for 20 percent and plant closings, for only 11 percent. Whereas there were 487 trusteeships in effect in 1959, the number was reduced to 215 in 1963.

These requirements are supplemented at the federal level by the Internal Revenue Code of 1954 and the 1954 Communist Control Act. The Internal Revenue Code of 1954 requires an annual report of income and expenditures by each national union. The 1954 Communist Control Act created a five-member Subversive Activities Control Board which is authorized to identify organizations that are "Communist infiltrated." Organizations so identified become ineligible to use the facilities of the National Labor Relations Board. Federal rules, under the Taft-Hartley Act, prohibit discriminatory dues or admission fees. Unions cannot charge long-service employees — former nonmembers — any more than new employees. Admission fees must be equal for all applicants.

Meanwhile, unions can bargain away significant seniority rights of members, when merger and dovetailing of seniority lists have this effect. (See *Dealers' Transport Company* case, 1964.)

State legislation has also been used to encourage democratic procedures. Laws generally prohibit discrimination in admission to membership or in the treatment of members and assure union members the right of judicial review in cases of union disciplinary action. However, as a general rule, courts will not intervene in behalf of a member until he has exhausted his rights to review under the union constitution. This means, in some cases, that procedure is so extended and one-sided that few members can afford to carry a grievance through it.[12]

Several attempts have been made in federal legislation to curb the racketeering activities that have long tended to appear in some segments of the labor movement. Lucrative chances for graft and corruption have greatly increased as health and welfare funds have become common. Congressional and state committees investigating administration of these funds have found many evidences of careless if not illegal practice. Such investigations have also disclosed situations in which leaders have used the power and resources of their unions for great personal gain.

The federal Hobbs Act of 1934 sought to limit shakedowns by providing penalties for any use of violence, coercion, or intimidation in interstate commerce. However, a court decision upheld a union's demand that trucking concerns put on a local driver when they entered the state or pay him a day's wages even though coercion and intimidation were involved.[13] In 1946 the law was amended to bar robbery or extortion. Under this provision demands for a payoff by union leaders can be subject to severe penalties. Much depends on the determination of public authorities. That the law has teeth is suggested by the fact that 126 persons were indicted and 39 were convicted under these provisions in 1955. Taft-Hartley provisions also prohibit exactions — enforced payments for services not performed or to be performed, including employer gifts to union officers.

Employees of Unions

Federal rules require unions to bargain collectively with their own employees on demand. In 1963, NLRB instructed the International Ladies Garment Workers Union to bargain with a union — The

---

[12]See "Union Disciplinary Powers and Procedures" (series of four articles appearing in the *Monthly Labor Review*): David A. Swankin, "Grounds for Trial of Members and Local Officers," Vol. 86, No. 2 (February, 1963), pp. 125–32; Leon E. Lunden, "Trial Powers and Procedures at the Local Union Level," Vol. 86, No. 3 (March, 1963), pp. 255–61; Leon E. Lunden and David A. Swankin, "Selected Due Process Safeguards and Appeals," Vol. 86, No. 4 (April, 1963), pp. 378–84; and David A. Swankin, "Influence of the LMDRA on Constitutional Discipline Provisions," Vol. 86, No. 5 (May, 1963), pp. 491–96. See also Alfred W. Blumrosen, "The Individual and the Union," *Monthly Labor Review*, Vol. 86, No. 6 (June, 1963), pp. 659–65.

[13]The case is *United States v. Local 807* (1942) 62 S. Ct. 642.

Federation of Union Representatives (FOUR). The ILGWU was further ordered to cease questioning employees about their membership in FOUR, to grant the pay increase requested by FOUR retroactively, and to pay interest on unpaid increases.[14]

With respect to all these rules, enforcement is far from perfect. A democratic society finds itself in difficulty in enforcing restrictive rules on large, well-organized segments of its public. Organized, powerful interest groups like unions, federations of unions, employer associations, and associations of such associations continually create difficult enforcement problems. A major reason for the increasing complexity of the rules is the fact that new ways of avoiding or evading rules are constantly being generated and tried.

PUBLIC GUIDELINES FOR EMPLOYERS

Unions have always appeared as the prime movers in collective bargaining. They have taken much of the initiative. Their role has somewhat overshadowed that of employers so that most of the public guidelines appear to be directed toward unions. At the same time, however, because of the employer's historic role, public policy imposes numerous restrictions on employer action.

Many current restrictions grew out of the belligerent tactics of early employer associations. The use of labor spies, for example, is now taboo, as are employer arsenals and private armies of guards and deputies, who frequently assumed the right to enforce their own interpretation of the law. Blacklisting of labor organizers and union members is now an unfair labor practice. Discriminatory practices directed against the employment of unionists or influencing their layoff or discharge are accepted as clear evidence of attempts to interfere with employee rights to bargain through unions of their own choice.

Interference with Unions

Several types of employer action are expressly forbidden. Employers must not interfere in the organization of unions or in employee participation in them. They must not favor any union or force employees to choose or join it. On a wide range of subjects — the range has been extended from time to time — they must not refuse to bargain when asked to do so by a certified union of their employees.

---

[14]*Labor Report Bulletin 40*, Vol. 20 (April 25, 1963), Prentice-Hall, Inc., pp. 3–4.

Neither can they refuse to supply relevant information on wages, earnings, and other employment conditions.[15] It is not clear what subjects, if any, employers can regard as definitely beyond the scope of compulsory bargaining. Wages, hours, discipline, and other working conditions including pensions, profit sharing, and welfare plans are within this scope.

One of the most interesting questions concerns the rights of employers in multi-employer bargaining. (About half of the collective agreements that involve 3,000 or more workers are of this type.) If one employer has been struck, the others may lock out their union-member employees as a bargaining tactic. They may continue to operate, using supervisory personnel or new, nonmember employees for this purpose. Such a lockout is permissible if it is *defensive*, i.e., designed to protect an existing bargaining association. It is not appropriate, however, if its purpose is to force a change in the existing pattern of bargaining.

Public Responsibility

Employers are required, as are unions, to give notice of intent to terminate or modify an agreement. If stoppages would create a serious hazard to public welfare, employers must observe the cooling-off periods provided by federal law and several states before strikes or lockouts. If an employer were found to be Communist-dominated, he would presumably be refused the use of NLRB facilities, but it is notable that no employer has been charged with such an offense.

Freedom of Speech

Employer freedom of speech is limited in that expressions of opinion on unions and union membership must not contain or be related to a threat or a promise. Employers may not, for example, say that if employees form or join a union the plant will be closed. Neither can they promise higher wages or other benefits if employees resist organization. Before a representation election, an employer may present his views, but factual information must be presented without

---

[15]See, on this point, Walter L. Daykin, "Furnishing Wage Data for Bargaining," *Labor Law Journal*, Vol. 4, No. 6 (June, 1953), pp. 417–22, and Max J. Miller, "Employer's Duty to Furnish Wage and Economic Data to Unions," *Labor Law Journal*, Vol. 6, No. 3 (March, 1955), pp. 151–64. See also *Labor Law Course* (Chicago: Commerce Clearing House and Richard D. Irwin, Inc., 1961), pp. 3025 ff.

threats or promises. The Board will consider circumstances surrounding the presentation in making its determination of fairness or unfairness.[16]

Bargainable Issues

Under federal rules, employers are required to bargain in good faith on demand by a union representing an appropriate bargaining unit of their employees. For questions about either the propriety of the unit or the union's right to represent employees, NLRB will provide answers, designating appropriate units and certifying bargaining agents.[17]

As noted, the scope of what the Board and the courts regard as "bargainable issues" has widened, with a similar narrowing of the employer's exclusive authority for decisions. At the same time, courts have been active in interpreting public policy and "labor contracts." In its 1962–63 sessions, for example, the United States Supreme Court ruled on agency shop provisions, seniority clauses, discrimination in employment practice, picketing, employee rights to sue an employer, and work rules, to mention some of the most significant decisions. Meanwhile, one recent court decision protected job rights by holding that seniority carries over to a new plant location.[18]

Employer Reporting

The LMRDA of 1959 imposes reporting requirements for employers similar to those required of unions. Employers must tell of all promises or payments to unions or their officials, expenditures designed to influence employees in collective bargaining (except the costs of employee magazines or house organs), funds used to obtain information about the internal affairs of unions in a dispute, and relationships with consultants who seek to influence or persuade employees about their bargaining activity. As a general rule, they must report all such

---

[16]See Walter L. Daykin, "Free Speech Rights of Management," *Research Series, No. 9,* Bureau of Labor and Management, University of Iowa, 1955; C. G. Bakaly, Jr. and A. C. Phillips, "An Employer's Rights in a National Labor Relations Board Representation Election, *Circular No. 28* (Pasadena, California: California Institute of Technology, Industrial Relations Center, May, 1963).

[17]Major criteria for defining appropriate bargaining units include the wishes of the parties; historic relationships in bargaining; similarities in skills, jobs, and working conditions; the range of transfers among jobs; and the industry and the organizational structure of the firm.

[18]*Zdanok v. Glidden,* 288 F (2nd) 99,

activities designed to operate in a less than open manner to affect collective bargaining.

The 1959 Labor-Management Reporting and Disclosure Act gives special attention to certain activities of "labor consultants." Normal activities of a trade or employer association are not considered as "consulting" unless association activities include getting information on union activities of employees. Normal attorney-client relationships need not be reported, but extra-counseling activities, such as efforts to prevent or undermine union organization, must be reported.

TRENDS IN PUBLIC POLICY

Despite continuing public support for collective bargaining and a relatively unshackled labor movement, current trends point toward further regulation of the parties in labor relations. High levels of unemployment and unfavorable balances in international payments create a persistent public concern about the influence and impact of collective bargaining on unit labor costs, inflationary pressures, and employment opportunities. Popular opinion is increasingly aware of the necessity for rising productivity and reduced waste in the application of manpower resources.

As Witte observed, "It is futile to talk about keeping government out of labor-management relations so long as the parties are forever turning to the government for help."[19] Both employers and unions frequently introduce and support legislation designed to develop alliances with public agencies. Witte also noted that there is something of an inherent conflict in policies that, on the one hand, allow worker-members to choose their union and, on the other, grant one union jurisdiction over a group of workers. Such conflicting policy gives great influence to the public agency that defines bargaining units and certifies bargaining agencies. As Witte notes, no Western European nation allows one and only one national union to maintain comprehensive jurisdiction within a defined field of occupations.

Maintaining a balance of employer and union power is likely to require more extensive and intensive regulation. As one aspect of this balancing act, courts may be asked to play a larger role in enforcing collective agreements, supplementing the function of such administrative agencies as national and state labor relations boards. As another

---

[19]Edwin E. Witte, "The Crisis in American Unionism," Chapter VII in *The Arbitrator and the Parties* (Washington, D.C.: Bureau of National Affairs, 1958), pp. 172–88.

expression, public policy may further encourage the organization of white-collar workers.

Unions as Monopolies

In recent years the power of individual unions and union leaders has attracted growing concern, as evidenced by congressional hearings and the prosecution of Teamster leaders. Several current proposals would "bring unions under antitrust laws." Advocates argue that although unions act as monopolies they are granted immunity from antitrust regulation; they are permitted to boycott (within limits); in most states they can require compulsory membership under union shop agreements; union leaders and members are allowed privileges not available to other, nonmember citizens.

Union leaders and spokesmen insist that unions are not monopolies in the meaning of antitrust legislation; they do not combine to restrict total output or to control product prices. They argue that compulsory membership is permitted only when supported on a democratic basis by a majority of the employees concerned and that unions enjoy specific privileges only to an extent necessary to balance the power of employers.[20]

Those who argue in favor of laws to control what they regard as labor monopoly usually assume that unions can and do affect prices, income distribution, wage rates, and employment levels. In part, the argument runs as follows: (1) unions push wage rates to levels above what they would be without collective bargaining; (2) higher wage rates mean higher labor costs; (3) wage-push pressures force higher product prices; (4) the same pressures reduce profits and make investment less attractive; and (5) the resulting impact reduces employment.

Each of these generalizations involves complex relationships on which evidence is far from conclusive. Several of them have been discussed in earlier pages. Thus, while unions may negotiate higher wages than would otherwise prevail in some situations and for limited time periods, it is doubtful that collective bargaining, in itself, has changed the relative size of distributive shares in national income.[21]

---

[20]For elaboration and evaluation, see Malcolm Cohen, "Unions and the Anti-Trust Straw Man," *Labor Law Journal*, Vol. 14, No. 2 (February, 1963), pp. 201–15; Irving Bernstein, "Labor's Power in American Society," *Reprint No. 112* (Los Angeles: University of California, Institute of Industrial Relations, 1962).

[21]See Clark Kerr, "Labor's Income Share and the Labor Movement," in George W. Taylor and Frank C. Pierson (eds.), *New Concepts in Wage Determination* (New York: McGraw-Hill Book Company, 1957), p. 287 ff. See also John Dunlop, "Discussion" in *Proceedings, Industrial Relations Research Association*, December, 1962, pp. 296–97.

Higher wage rates do not necessarily mean lower labor costs; neither do they always force higher prices.

On the other hand, it is clear that the union that does not exercise some monopolistic power is not serving its members well. It does not follow, however, that the only or best way to prevent abuses in the exercise of that power is to make unions subject to the rules of current antitrust legislation. The nature and purpose of unions do not fit the pattern contemplated in existing legislation. A different approach, tailored to the nature, function, and social assignment to unions must be found. Appropriate regulation must be directed more specifically to objectionable union policy, restrictions on work opportunities, and arrogance in the use of power.[22]

Manpower Mobility

Public intervention is likely also to induce both employers and unions to modify programs that reduce the mobility of workers. Similarly, public policy will presumably seek to encourage more extensive union and employer cooperation in apprenticeship and in negotiated retraining programs. More early vesting of pension rights and other "portability" features may be encouraged by advantageous tax shelters or similar provisions. Public guidelines in these areas may be developed to supplement current wage and price guideposts that have achieved considerable acceptance.

Policy and Social Goals

Policy and intervention may be expected to reflect the dynamics of public goals. Immediate changes will presumably seek to advance the prominent objectives of a more rapid growth rate, improved international competition, and the reduction of unemployment. Popular concern about requirements of individual conformity may encourage further intervention, with restrictions on both employers and unions to assure less interference in the personal affairs of individual employees and members.

As goals change and new priorities in problems arise, public policy and public intervention in the relationships of employers and unions can be expected to reflect these developments. New problems

---

[22]For further discussion, see George Hildebrand, "Collective Bargaining and the Antitrust Laws," Chapter 6 in Joseph Shister and others (eds)., *Public Policy and Collective Bargaining* (New York: Harper and Brothers, 1962); Simon Rottenberg, "Labor Monopoly Power Reconsidered," *Monthly Labor Review*, Vol. 86, No. 2 (February, 1963), p. 139.

will create the demand for new programs in the future as they have in the past. Disputes over bargaining units and bargaining agents brought federal and state intervention to settle such issues. Unfair labor practices were defined and restricted because such practices were regarded as having created unfair advantages. Just as public intervention sought to strengthen the power delegated to unions in the 1930's, further intervention may appear necessary to define union responsibilities in the years immediately ahead.[23]

The next chapter gives more detailed attention to one persistent problem that is closely related to collective bargaining — the problem of industrial unrest and conflict.

ANALYTICAL REVIEW QUESTIONS

1. (a) How is collective bargaining defined? (b) What are its legal connotations? (c) Does public policy make bargaining compulsory?
2. What major social and economic goals explain current public policy on collective bargaining?
3. (a) How do management security clauses affect the area of bargaining? (b) Do union security clauses have the same effects on the area of bargaining?
4. In what ways are state right-to-work laws inconsistent with national policies on collective bargaining?
5. What are the Taft-Hartley Act union security provisions? How are these related to state right-to-work laws?
6. (a) What are the major arguments for and against right-to-work laws? (b) How would you describe the proper balance between union security and individual freedom?
7. How does public policy seek to encourage democratic procedures in unions?
8. How does the NLRA protect the rights of individual union members?
9. What restrictions are provided by the Labor Management Relations Act (a) on employer action and (b) on union action?
10. (a) What are possible consequences to employees who strike in violation of an agreement? (b) What is the status of jurisdictional strikes and sympathy strikes?
11. What laws and rules apply to picketing?
12. What are the current federal rules concerning boycotts?
13. How do work rules and featherbedding affect supplies of, demands for, and prices of labor?

---

[23]See, in this connection, Clark Kerr, *Unions and Union Leaders of their Own Choosing* (Santa Barbara, Calif.: Fund for the Republic, December, 1957); *The Economic Analysis of Labor Union Power* (Washington, D.C.: American Enterprise Association, January, 1958); *Union Powers and Union Functions* (New York: Committee for Economic Development, 1964).

14. What are the current federal rules on union responsibility?

15. (a) Are unions permitted to incorporate? (b) What are arguments pro and con with respect to desirability of incorporation?

16. How does federal law seek to regulate political activities of unions?

17. If direct union political contributions are prohibited, should corporations be expected to observe similar limitations? Why or why not?

18. What laws seek to curb labor racketeering, and what practices do they forbid?

19. What influence are strong unions expected to exert on (a) employment, (b) income distribution, (c) managerial efficiency, and (d) inflation?

20. Is the economic influence of publicly encouraged collective bargaining likely to create a class struggle in this country? Explain how you arrive at a conclusion on this point.

21. What yardsticks may be applied to test the economic implications of current public policy on collective bargaining?

22. How can current public policy on labor relations be expected to affect employer objectives of maximizing profits and minimizing labor costs?

23. In what way does current public policy impose curbs on the economic objectives of unions?

24. How is current public policy on labor relations likely to affect the economic objectives of consumers?

25. Outline the major changes in public policy on labor relations that you would favor, and then explain the reasons for your suggestions.

Case 12-1

SAYBROOK CANNING COMPANY

The Saybrook Canning Company is faced with a union demand that it continue corn-packing operations. The company cans a variety of products. In recent years, however, the development of freezing processes has, in the opinion of the management, made corn-packing particularly hazardous. Investments in both farming operations and stored packs are necessarily heavy. Fluctuations in product prices have been wide. The company has been quite frank in public discussions of the probability that corn canning may be discontinued. Managers have discussed the possibility in meetings of local civic groups over a two-year period.

This spring the union representing employees has demanded a guarantee that the firm will not quit the corn-packing operation during the year ahead. Management has replied that this particular subject is not one about which it is willing to bargain. Representatives of the firm have refused to discuss the issue in bargaining sessions. Negotiations are stalemated on account of this issue, and the union has announced plans for a strike.

• Assume that you have been appointed a member of the mayor's committee which was created to get the parties to resume bargaining and to prevent a strike. Will you urge the employer to bargain with the union on this issue? Be prepared to justify your answer.

Case 12-2

WORK RULES ON CAMPUS

You have read and heard about featherbedding on the railroads, in radio and television, and in print shops, but you have had no direct personal experience until now. Now you have a featherbedding problem.

For homecoming, students have planned a Varsity Show consisting of a series of skits, dances, and musical numbers. Various groups have sent teams in for tryouts, and the winning entries have been selected. Each group provides its own scenery and props, and representatives of the groups have planned to shift the scenes as the show progresses. Assume that you are general manager of the show, with full responsibility for ticket sales, facilities, and budget. Profits, if any, are to go to the Campus Community Chest.

As an added attraction, you have contracted for a name band which will play between scenes. When their engagement was announced, you were called by the business agent for the local union of stagehands. He says you must provide a union crew or the union band cannot participate. He says it makes no difference whether you need the crew or not. You have argued with him, but he says he does not make the rules.

• You have called a meeting of your whole planning committee for four o'clock this afternoon. You are now outlining what you will say to them. What are your alternatives? Prepare a brief memorandum indicating the action you will recommend to the committee.

Case 12-3

PORTER PRODUCTS COMPANY

Porter Products is a small firm in an industry that includes many competitors, some of them larger, some smaller, than Porter Products. With 800 production employees, the firm manufactures a broad range of sheet metal products — ducts, pipe, gutters, tanks, and similar items. Gross sales in 1962 were $11,200,000; profits after taxes amounted to $642,484. Products are priced to meet the competition; however, the firm has enjoyed an excellent reputation for quality. Many customers have consistently preferred Porter materials over a long-term period.

Although employees in most competing firms — including especially the larger organizations — are members of international unions affiliated with AFL-CIO, no union represents the employees of Porter Products. Several organizing campaigns have been undertaken; the firm has not been willing to recognize any union as the bargaining agent of employees without clear evidence that it represents a majority. No union has been willing to force the issue. Executives and managers assume that some employees are union members; on the other hand, employees have made no demands for union recognition, and managers have not expressed any opposition to union membership.

During the spring and summer of 1962, new orders declined rapidly. At first, the sales manager, Cyril Smythe, assumed that this trend was a reflection of current business pessimism; the stock market suffered its most impressive decline in more than twenty years, and many business advisory services were bearish. Then he began to get disconcerting stories from salesmen to the effect that established, long-term customers were buying elsewhere, in some cases at higher prices. Somewhat later one salesman reported that a regular customer of many years, who refused to be quoted or otherwise identified, said that a union representative had advised against the continued purchase of Porter products. The representative explained that employees just did not like to install Porter material. Porter items were more difficult to handle, according to the union spokesman, and workmen found that they required more time in fitting and installation. The representative was quite firm on one point; the union was not boycotting the products. On the other hand, it would be more efficient to use some substitute.

After hearing three similar stories from salesmen, the sales manager reported this development in a Monday morning meeting of the executive committee. The firm's secretary, Mr. Hinkelbridge, an attorney by training, was pressed for opinions about the possibility of securing legal relief; he was not optimistic. The sales manager suggested that employees of Porter Products be invited to form a local of the most prominent union in the industry. He felt that the least employees could do in this situation was to pay their dues, whether or not they felt the need for a union. The president, C. E. Porter, was adamant in his rejection of this suggestion. He felt that employees should never be forced to join a union; he suspected that some hotheads in the union had fomented the campaign and would forget it in a short time. The executive vice-president pointed out, however, that if the campaign was at all effective, many employees would be out of work; he doubted that they could afford opposition to the informal boycott.

• What would be your advice to the managers of Porter Products?

CONFLICT IN LABOR RELATIONS

Much of the current public policy on labor relations described in the preceding chapter is designed to limit and restrain conflict in employment. For example, federal agencies define bargaining units and certify bargaining agents to remove these issues from the arena of open conflict. Requirements that the parties in major disputes delay strikes and permit public investigation are also illustrative. Public policy, as has been noted, does not propose that employers or unions shall or must agree perfectly on every detail of their relationship. It does not require what are sometimes called *sweetheart clauses*, expressing mutual respect if not affection. It does, however, expect the parties to work out compromises without open conflicts and violence.

Goals implied in public policy are seldom simple; goals with respect to employment relationships are no exception. Public policy obviously intends to encourage employers and employees to find bases for efficient cooperation. It seeks high-level employment and steadily increasing productivity. It proposes to encourage personal freedom in selecting jobs, with a maximum of employment opportunities for individual workers. Public policy encourages collective bargaining and bilateral policy making with respect to working relationships. It proposes public intervention when necessary to reinforce such public policy. It sees collective bargaining as a means of balancing the economic power of opponents, not of creating mutual affection or making

322

them forget their differences. It is not a marriage of employers and unions. It is not a conflict eliminator. Public policy has been developed primarily to insure a fairer contest and to facilitate a process in which the parties — employers and unions — can work out their own adjustment of differences and accommodation to each other's policies and programs. In a sense, it is a system of self-regulation and mutual adaptation that is substituted for the detailed public regulation that might otherwise be unavoidable. It usually substitutes negotiation for the crude use of economic force.

At the same time, current public policy recognizes the inevitability of — and indeed the necessity for — persistent competition and some conflict in employment. Public policy proposes accommodation and effective collaboration of unions and employers; it does not intend perfect harmony. Indeed, it proposes to prevent such comprehensive harmony as would involve collusion or conspiracy which could be costly to the public.

The goal sought in public policy on conflict is thus complex — it proposes to limit, confine, and control conflict but does not intend to eliminate it. This goal of achieving a viable but constrained conflict is widely accepted in the noncommunist industrialized societies. While many discussions of industrial conflict focus attention on its excesses, only the most authoritarian states attempt to prevent all such conflict. Students of conflict theorize that conflict is essential to insure change and prevent stagnation and decline. They note its influence in intensifying group identification and loyalty. Conflict is a classic means of resolving struggles for power among the powerful and for distributing the earnings of capital.[1]

Modern societies generally allow conflicts to express themselves in the political platforms and actions of the parties. Conflict is thus moved into the legislative area; employers and unions may take their disputes into political campaigns and propose and oppose changes in laws on union security, the use of boycotts, and other issues.[2]

---

[1]See George R. Davies, *Creative Capitalism* (Iowa City: University of Iowa, 1961), Chapter 2; see also L. Coser, *The Functions of Social Conflict* (Glencoe, Ill.: The Free Press, 1956); M. Dalton, *Men Who Manage* (New York: John Wiley and Sons, Inc., 1959); S. Krupp, *Patterns in Organization Analysis* (Philadelphia: Chilton, 1961); G. Simmel, *The Sociology of Georg Simmel*, trans. K. H. Wolff (Glencoe, Ill.: The Free Press, 1950); K. E. Boulding, *Conflict and Defense* (New York: Harper and Brothers, Inc., 1962); A. Kornhauser, R. Dubin, and A. Ross, *Industrial Conflict* (New York: McGraw-Hill Book Company, Inc., 1954); R. Dubin, *Working Union-Management Relations* (Englewood Cliffs, N.J.: Prentice-Hall, Inc., 1958).

[2]See Paul Sultan, "Right-To-Work Laws: A Study in Conflict," *Monograph Series No. 2*, University of California (Los Angeles), 1958. See also Alan K. McAdams, *Power and Politics in Labor Legislation* (New York: Columbia University Press, 1964).

Collective bargaining has been encouraged as one means of shaping and restraining conflict. It proposes that the parties negotiate away many of their differences. Just as our society has substituted legal contests or lawsuits for family feuding and personal duels, it has created collective bargaining in part to prevent the public nuisances, inconveniences, and other hazards of open conflict. We have recognized the danger that some of the issues arising out of employment may divide our citizens, create lawlessness and violence, and thus threaten the continued peace and security of our society. We assume that, with increasing experience, we can develop — within the broad framework of a system that encourages unions and collective bargaining — built-in procedures for settling most differences. Conciliation, mediation, cooling-off periods, arbitration, and formal grievance procedures are examples of these built-in safety valves. We have tried to minimize the part that government agencies play in actually deciding issues. It is our policy to discourage any tendency for either of the parties to depend on public agencies for detailed regulation of working conditions.

SOURCES OF CONFLICT

The true meaning and roots of discord and disharmony in the employment relationship deserve much more attention than they have received. Many popular explanations are rather obviously superficial. Everyone knows, for example, that employees sometimes strike for higher pay; it has been easy to generalize that employee-employer conflict is essentially a clash of economic interests. Some analyses stress an imbalance in economic power as the basic source of conflict; they see one party or the other refusing further cooperation when such a withdrawal can be expected to force concessions from the other.

Some observers see a major source of conflict in the search by employers and union leaders for added personal power. This view is frequently directed toward union leaders; it is often expressed as a conviction that the labor leader has to develop and maintain conflict in order to hold his members. In the extreme it sees racketeers as promoting conflict to further their own ends. The extent and influence of racketeering have not been measured, but it is rather clearly an exceptional — rather than the typical — pattern.[3] Some observers

---

[3] See, in this connection, Philip Taft, "Corruption and Racketeering in the Labor Movement," *Bulletin 38*, New York State School of Industrial and Labor Relations, 1958.

see industrial conflict as the calculated plan of Communist leaders, and such an explanation may be justified in a few disputes.

However realistic this type of analysis may be in some instances, it can provide only a limited and partial explanation for the persistent conflict in employment relationships.

Conflicting Values and Goals

Essentials in industrial conflict may be better understood if several levels of basic differences that exist among members of the working organization are clearly distinguished. Differences in the *systems of values* held by workers and managers represent one such level. These distinctive patterns of personal philosophy encourage the pursuit of different *goals* to be attained in the employment process.

For example, some members of the working organization may regard holding a job as essentially a necessary evil; one has to have a job to establish eligibility for unemployment benefits or for a retirement pension. For some workers, work is only a way to "make a living"; for others, however, it is a whole way of life. To some, it is a means of gaining a claim on a bit of economic power; to others, it is a ticket to citizenship in the working community, with built-in implications for status somewhat like a front-row-center ticket for the theater.

Some workers regard their work as an opportunity for adventure. Others consider employment as something like membership in a fraternity; they may be critical of new recruits who seem to them undesirable members of the brotherhood. Workers assign varying priorities to working conditions such as high wages, stable employment, or generous holidays and vacations.

Managers may see these features of employment as having quite different priorities. In their hierarchy, values of property rights and a broad sphere of management prerogatives and a full measure of employee loyalty may rank high. They may propose to minimize union intervention in managerial decisions and to maximize returns to stockholders.

Some workers and managers may put freedom to think and to act — a wide area of personal discretion and a minimum of required conformity — high in their goal priorities.[4]

---

[4]See in this connection Neil W. Chamberlain, "The Union Challenge to Management Control," *Industrial and Labor Relations Review*, Vol. 16, No. 2 (January, 1963), pp. 184–92.

Thus, although people work together, combining their ideas and energy for the purpose of accomplishing group goals or objectives, they do not form organic units. Working organizations — firms and agencies — although they are formed to facilitate collaboration — inevitably involve levels of internal conflict. Owners and employers invest their financial resources and create working organizations and provide managers or administrators and hire employees to accomplish organizational objectives and achieve their goals. But individual workers and groups of workers collaborate with other goals in mind, some of them in conflict with the goals of their organizations.

Conflicting Means

Other basic differences among cooperating parties which cause industrial conflict involve the means used to attain goals, the programs and practices of the parties. Thus, to maximize profit, an employer may provide irregular rather than steady work. A union may propose and management may oppose bargaining on farming out jobs, both positions regarded as facilitating successful competition. To encourage efficiency, some may favor centralization of authority, while others see decentralization as the best route to the same goal. Potential for conflict is evident from these illustrations.

Understanding Sources of Conflict

Comparatively little is known about the philosophies or goals of participants in employment. A few studies have sought to discover common patterns in goals. But the very complexity of individual philosophies, the persistence of conflicts within them, and the fact that they change from time to time have complicated and limited analysis. Perhaps the most promising route toward the reduction of conflict is that which proposes detailed exploration of these differences. Analysis must define goals much more sharply and then find ways of ordering them.

One approach to understanding directs attention to the overt policies of employers, managers, and employees. It seeks to compare and evaluate these specific intentions or plans — plans to maximize earnings and profits, to assure worker security, to facilitate personal development. Policies, as the guiding intentions of the parties, provide tangible clues to goals and conflicts of goals.

SYMPTOMS OF CONFLICT

It is reasonable to assume that few workers are completely satisfied with working conditions and relationships. Studies of the attitudes of employers, employees, and the self-employed toward their jobs give ample evidence of complaints and dissatisfactions. Employers and managers, for example, may feel that they are hampered by unnecessary red tape in firm policy and labor contracts. They frequently complain that neither stockholders nor employees appreciate the difficulties of managing. Even the self-employed frequently find certain working conditions unsatisfactory, frustrating, and depressing. Some of them insist that they are working too hard for hours that are too long and net income that is too meager. Studies of employee attitudes disclose a wide range of conditions in which some employees find their jobs and job-connected relationships far from satisfactory. They may be unhappy about pay or hours, dissatisfied with their foremen and supervisors, critical of promotions or employment stability. They may feel that they are mere cogs in the machine with little chance to find out what is going on or to express their opinions or suggestions.

Industrial Unrest

Behavior that seeks to express such dissatisfaction with and criticism of employment is described as *industrial unrest*. *Unrest* is generally regarded as such a degree of dissatisfaction and personal disorganization as to cause serious deviations from normal, habitual patterns of conduct. Individuals become so disturbed and frustrated that the patterns of behavior usually accepted and uncritically followed appear unsatisfying. Unrest is described as social rather than individual because it appears to be communicable from person to person. It is infectious, spreading by a sort of social contagion among members of groups.

Process in unrest. Industrial unrest is sometimes described as involving a process, with several stages. It begins with rather vaguely defined individual frustrations and dissatisfactions that may not be sharply focused even in the minds of those who feel them. This discontent may be infectious and show up in absenteeism, tardiness, disciplinary infractions, and higher levels of labor turnover. This type of unrest is frequently described as *inarticulate*, in that employees do not designate or agree upon the conditions to which they object.

If the objectionable conditions continue, unrest becomes *articulate*. Employees may complain about certain objectionable working conditions, such as heat, light, ventilation, wages, or hours of work. They may focus their complaints on one or a few particularly objectionable practices or conditions. They may discuss them in small groups at lunch in the company cafeteria or in union meetings. They may express their dissatisfaction to foremen. They may engage in something approximating *mob behavior*, with demonstrations, parades, slowdowns, and strikes. They may develop *mass movements* — for example, reformist or revolutionary unions.

Labor Turnover

In the individual firm the most frequently described indicator of unrest is *labor turnover*. The term means personnel changes in the work force. As evidence of industrial unrest, *quits* or *resignations* are the most significant type of change, but usual compilations also note *layoffs*, *discharges, total separations*, and *hires* or *accessions*. As will be evident, the most meaningful indicator is another, *replacements*; they represent rehires made necessary by separations.[5]

Other Indicators

When employee dissatisfaction builds up, it is frequently expressed in violations of shop rules. Employees become less concerned about what foremen and supervisors think of them and about their future relationships with their employer. Infractions may increase both in numbers and in the serious nature of these violations. Rising levels of unrest may also show themselves in excessive tardiness and absenteeism. Employees become less concerned about punctuality and what their employment records may show. They may be out hunting other jobs. They may simply be careless and disinterested in their work.

Employers and supervisors may detect employee frustration and disinterest and record them in the semiannual or annual personnel ratings or appraisals they give each employee. Interviews with employees or questionnaires they complete may show their increasing

---

[5]Monthly labor turnover rates on an industry basis are regularly reported by the Federal Bureau of Labor Statistics. See, for current measures, the *Monthly Labor Review* or the *Survey of Current Business*. Rates are ratios of separations (quits, layoffs, and terminations) or accessions per 100 of the average work force in the month. See also "Labour Turnover — Meaning and Measurement," *International Labour Review*, Vol. 81, No. 6 (June, 1960), pp. 513–26.

criticism and dissatisfaction. Many employers conduct *morale surveys* at regular intervals. Comparisons among departments and with earlier years and other firms provide benchmarks for identifying unusually low morale or increasing dissatisfaction.

Dissatisfied employees, as individuals or as a group, may simply slow down at their work, refusing to heed supervisors' requests or instructions to work harder or faster. They may establish more or less formal pars, quotas, or bogeys for their jobs, thus setting limits on what they will produce in an hour, a day, or a week. Such restriction of output is a frequent indication of employee dissatisfaction and frustration. Another symptom of this state of mind is a rising rate of grievances filed by employees, which allege unfair or unreasonable treatment by managers and supervisors. Employees and their unions may insist on carrying larger numbers and proportions of grievances to the terminal step in grievance procedures, that is, to arbitration by neutral third parties.

STRIKES AND LOCKOUTS

The most spectacular and widely recognized form of industrial unrest is the *work stoppage*, and the most common form of work stoppage is the *strike*. Some stoppages are *lockouts*, in which employers take the initiative and refuse employment. The distinction between strikes and lockouts, although sometimes very important in terms of possible settlement, is somewhat difficult and uncertain, since employers may create situations designed to cause employees to take the initiative and strike, and workers may find ways to force employers to take the initiative in a lockout.

The strike is often described as a union's ultimate weapon, to be used only as a last resort. It is clear that strikes can be costly to unions and their members. Their attitude toward the strike is clearly evidenced by the provisions of union constitutions. Many unions sanction a strike only after a majority vote of members in the local. They frequently specify a secret ballot and require approval by officers of the international.[6]

The fact that strikes are essentially a last resort is shown by the statistics of collective agreements and strikes. More than 100,000

---

[6]For a study of these provisions and practices, see Herbert S. Parnes, "Union Strike Votes," Princeton University Industrial Relations Section, 1956. See also, "Strike-Control Provisions in Union Constitutions," *Monthly Labor Review*, Vol. 77, No. 5 (May, 1954), pp. 497–500 and William Paschell, "Union Strike Vote Practices and Proposed Controls," *Monthly Labor Review*, Vol. 79, No. 6 (June, 1956), pp. 677–83.

collective agreements are negotiated each year, an average of almost 300 each day. More than 90 percent are signed without a work stoppage. The large majority are carried through to the end of their terms without a strike or a lockout. Time lost on account of strikes in most years amounts to only a fraction of 1 percent of total time worked. Violence is spectacular and thus attracts attention and mention in the news; it is not present in the majority of work stoppages.

On the other hand, work stoppages and violent disputes are almost as old as the system of free employment. They were used by the earliest organizations of wage earners — the ancestors of unions — to protest working conditions and to oppose new machines in the early factories and mills. They are found in every democratic, industrialized nation. And it should be clearly recognized that the threat of a work stoppage is a powerful incentive, clearly understood by both employees and employers, to settle differences and reach a satisfactory agreement.

Work stoppages are costly, although their actual costs are not readily calculated. They occasion frequent public inconvenience and may involve serious hazards to health, safety, and national defense. If employers try to carry on business as usual, their action may provoke violence and disorder. Long-continued disputes may seriously jeopardize the economic welfare of entire communities. They may create internal frictions within families if some members *scab* (accept employment while a strike is in progress) or cross picket lines.[7]

Types of Strikes

Common usage distinguishes several types of strikes, including:

(1) Economic strikes. These work stoppages are probably the most common type. They are undertaken by employees (a) to pit their economic power against employers and (b) to gain economic advantages — higher wages, shorter hours, various benefits or fringes, or others.

---

[7]The Soviet Union seeks to provide means other than work stoppages for expressing dissatisfaction and suggestions for change; few strikes are reported. The system in which unions are expected to implement public policy formally established by the party leans heavily on a complex of committees to introduce some democracy in working relationships. Principal issues, sources of criticism, include management abuses of individual employee rights, shop discipline, employee demands for higher living scales, and administration of wage and safety provisions. See Emily Clark Brown, "Interests and Rights of Soviet Industrial Worker and the Resolution of Conflicts," *Industrial and Labor Relations Review*, Vol. 16, No. 2 (January, 1963), pp. 245-55.

(2) Unfair labor practice strikes. In these stoppages employees cease work to protest alleged violations of the unfair labor practice rules imposed by federal or state legislation. They may, for example, insist that the employer has sought to dominate the union or has discriminated against certain employees on account of their union membership.

(3) Flash or quickie strikes. These are sudden stoppages undertaken by a group of employees without formal discussion and approval by their union.

(4) Outlaw or wildcat strikes. Many flash strikes are also outlaw strikes, called without authorization and in violation of the union constitution and the existing labor contract. Participation in wildcat strikes may result in severe penalties imposed on strikers by the employer, the union, or both. Such strikes may become the basis for damage suits by the employer against the union.

(5) Sit down strikes. The sit-down technique, now considered unlawful, was effective in the early expansion of industrial unions. Employees ceased work but remained in the plant at their machines.[8]

(6) Slowdown strikes. In the slowdown employees remain on their jobs but refuse to turn out the usual quantity of work. They impose rigorous restrictions on output. Employers may take disciplinary action, and they frequently retaliate with a lockout.

(7) Sympathy strikes. These are stoppages in which employees raise no issues with their employer but cease work to enforce the demands of other strikers in the same or other firms. They seek to develop indirect pressures to force compliance of the employer in another dispute.

(8) General strikes. These are widespread sympathy strikes that include all or most organized employees in a community. Thus, members of many unions might cease work to support a strike by retail clerks or bus operators. Such general strikes have been infrequent in this country.

(9) Jurisdictional strikes. Jurisdictional strikes represent conflicts over the question as to which union's members have exclusive rights

---

[8]See David B. McCalmont, "The Semi-Strike," *Industrial and Labor Relations Review*, **Vol.** 15, No. 2 (January, 1962), pp. 191–208.

to certain jobs or which union shall have the right to represent employees in a particular bargaining unit.

Right to Strike

In general, the right to strike is regarded as essential, a reassurance of personal freedom. Public policy appears to agree that to prohibit strikes would violate the Thirteenth Amendment by requiring involuntary servitude or slavery. The general right to strike is well established in American tradition.

On the other hand, all employees cannot simply strike when and where they please, or for whatever purpose. Exercise of the right may be subject to restrictions, and some types of strikes and strike behavior may occasion serious penalties. Federal government employees, as well as those in state agencies, hospitals, and public utilities in some states, are regarded as having relinquished this right as a condition of their employment. For example, federal civil service employees who strike can be discharged and cannot become eligible for any federal position for three years.

Other penalties may follow strikes in private employment under some circumstances. As noted in Chapter 12, an employer may sue a union for damages arising from a strike in breach of contract. Employees may be discharged or subjected to other penalties for participation in such a strike, or in a sit-down strike, or for violence and other illegal actions arising out of a strike. Courts may enjoin some strikes, in which case those who participate and their unions may be penalized for contempt of court. In general, courts recognize the right of an individual to strike, but they also insist that both the purpose and the manner in which a strike is conducted must be lawful. On this basis they have held sit-down strikes illegal. Similarly, a strike designed to force an employer into an illegal closed shop agreement is illegal, as is a strike to force other employer violations of the law. States are divided in their policy on the legality of sympathetic strikes and general strikes.[9]

Rights of strikers vary, also, according to the type of strike. Thus, participants in an economic strike may be replaced; in an unfair labor practice strike, they retain their status as employees and may be returned to their jobs by administrative order if the employer is found

---

[9]For an excellent outline of federal rules on this point, see Walter L. Daykin, "The Right to Strike," *Labor Law Journal*, Vol. 6, No. 6 (June, 1955), pp. 361–75. See also *Labor Law Course* (Chicago: Commerce Clearing House and Richard D. Irwin, Inc., 1960), par. 4102, p. 5026 and related footnotes.

guilty of an unfair practice. Further, an employer may not give top seniority rights to workers hired as replacements.[10] Although participants in an economic strike have no assurance of a return to their jobs, especially if the strike is of long duration and replacements have been employed, the Landrum-Griffin Act gives them the right to vote in any NLRB election held during the year following the strike.

Strike Statistics

Several quantitative reports of strikes are maintained and published by the federal Department of Labor. They indicate the numbers of strikes and lockouts, the numbers of workers involved, and the numbers of days lost on this account.

It is apparent that one strike — a stoppage by coal miners or steelworkers, for example — may involve more employees, occasion greater immediate economic losses in production and wages, and create greater inconvenience or hazard than a hundred small strikes. The length or duration of strikes creates a further complication. A few long stoppages may occasion greater losses and personal hardship than a great many *quickies* or *flash strikes*. It is evident, therefore, that even a simple measure of the seriousness of strikes must combine an evaluation of (1) their number or frequency, (2) the numbers of persons who participate, and (3) their length or duration.

Some norms or yardsticks with which to appraise current levels and trends are also needed. Several thousand strikes each year may be par for a nation whose labor force numbers 75 millions. Chances for conflict are increased as numbers of employers, employees, and unions grow. The appraisal of trends is complicated when numbers of employers and employees are increasing.

For the United States we have data on numbers of strikes over most of the years in an 80-year period. Except for some breaks in the series, available records show numbers of strikes and numbers of workers involved since 1881; days lost in strikes since 1916; and numbers of stoppages, workers involved, and days lost by months since 1916. We have some tabulations of issues in strikes and some attempted evaluations of the results of strikes for the years since 1935.

---

[10]See Morrison Handsaker, "Arbitration and Discipline for Wildcat Strikes," *Labor Law Journal* (May, 1963), pp. 395–99; David B. McCalmont, "The Semi-Strike," *Industrial and Labor Relations Review*, Vol. 15, No. 2 (January, 1962), pp. 191–208; for additional information on restrictions, see Richard S. Hammett, Joel Seidman, and Jack London, "The Slowdown as a Union Tactic," *Journal of Political Economy*, Vol. 65, No. 2 (April, 1957), pp. 126–34.

Long-Term Trends

Are we tending to have more strikes, or can we note a tendency in the other direction? What about the numbers of workers directly affected and participating in these affairs? What about the duration of strikes and the amount of time lost because of them?

Figure 13-1 shows the number of work stoppages and the number of workers involved in them since 1881. It should be noted that data are incomplete, in that figures for some years are not available. Further, it should be said that early reporting was probably not as thorough as that of more recent years, so that the data for earlier years may somewhat understate the actual situation.

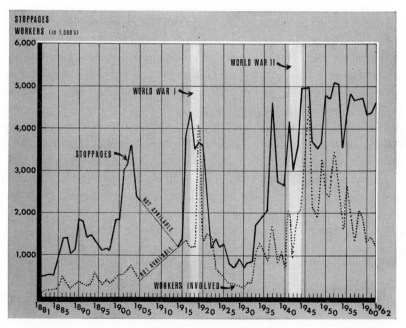

Figure 13-1
**NUMBERS OF WORK STOPPAGES
AND WORKERS INVOLVED — 1881-1962**

Source: Bureau of Labor Statistics data reported in *Monthly Labor Review*.

On the basis of this overview, it is apparent that numbers of both stoppages and of workers involved have grown. All through this period, however, the nation was growing and the labor force included more employees and more workers eligible for union membership.

Figure 13-2 shows year-to-year data adjusted for growth in numbers of employees. Workers involved in stoppages have been described as proportions of total numbers employed, and time losses occasioned by stoppages have been calculated as proportions of estimated total working time. With these adjustments, the period since World War II appears as one in which these measures show a significant downward trend.

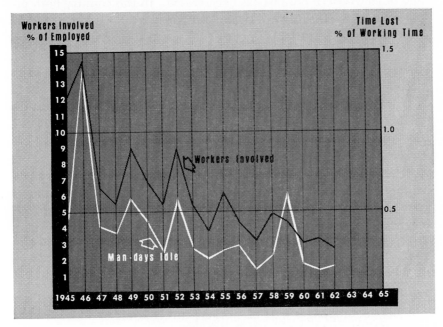

Figure 13-2
WORKERS INVOLVED AS A PERCENTAGE OF EMPLOYED AND DAYS LOST AS A PERCENTAGE OF WORKING TIME — 1945-1962

Source: Loretto R. Nolan, "A Review of Work Stoppages During 1962," *Monthly Labor Review*, Vol. 86, No. 7 (July, 1963), pp. 796–801.

Until World War II the United States appeared to be exceptional among Western industrialized nations in the upward trends in numbers of work stoppages and in workers involved. For the years 1927–1947, percentages of nonagricultural workers involved in stoppages ranged from 0.6 percent in 1930 to 11.1 percent in 1946. Ross and Irwin sought an explanation for this distinctive pattern in the extent or intensity of union organization. They concluded, however, that differences in proportions of workers involved were not closely correlated with the intensity of organization. They noted that "Workers in the United States, where the degree of organization has been low, have gone on strike more frequently than those in any other country except Australia." Also, for most of the period, the ratio of lost time to total working time in the United States was the highest of the several nations included in their study.[11]

Since World War II this distinction between the United States and other Western nations has been erased. In this country both proportions of workers involved and proportions of working time lost have declined. In recent years time losses on this account have been less than the time lost on account of coffee breaks. Perhaps the most widely expressed explanation for this reversal of trend relates it to the decline in union membership from 1955 to 1961.

Ross and Hartman, in a much more intensive and penetrating analysis, relate the change to cycles of belligerency and of strikes in *centers of conflict*.[12] They conclude that historic patterns of cycles in strikes have ended in several major centers of conflict, including apparel, automobile, coal mining, and textile industries. Similar cycles continue active only in basic steel, construction, electrical equipment, and machinery. With these terminations, even though residual levels of strikes have varied in approximate proportion to union membership, the overall, net effect is a downward trend.[13]

Patterns in Strikes

Several patterns are evident in historic data. It is apparent that numbers of stoppages and of workers involved are reduced in wartime. The duration of strikes and the time losses on this account are also restricted in such periods. On the other hand, numbers of strikes appear to rise to highest peaks in years following wars. Apparently the pressures developed during enforced wartime cooperation are accumulated and released when war ends.

Goldner has noted that numbers of strikes also seem to increase

---

[11]Arthur M. Ross and Donald Irwin, "Strike Experience in Five Countries, 1927–1947; An Interpretation," *Industrial and Labor Relations Review*, Vol. 4, No. 3 (April, 1951), pp. 323–42. See also Clark Kerr and Abraham Siegel, "The Interindustry Propensity to Strike — An International Comparison," University of California (Berkeley) Institute of Industrial Relations, *Reprint No. 69*, 1955.

[12]Arthur M. Ross and Paul T. Hartman, *Changing Patterns of Industrial Conflict* (New York: John Wiley & Sons, 1960).

[13]See also Arthur M. Ross, "The Prospects for Industrial Conflict," *Industrial Relations*, Vol. 1, No. 1 (October, 1961), pp. 57–74.

regularly in the years following presidential elections.   Apparently, political factors have an influence.[14]

The rise of new unions appears to occasion unusual numbers of stoppages.   The period immediately following organization of the CIO in 1935, when many new industrial unions were formed, illustrates this general tendency.   It is apparent whenever new unions are organized in an industry or a locality.   In such situations strikes appear as symptomatic of the dissatisfaction and bitterness that may have occasioned the organization of unions or the efforts of these unions to gain acceptance and recognition.   To some degree strikes may evidence a feeling of power on the part of newly organized union members and a desire to exercise their power and influence.   More mature unions and more secure and experienced union leaders tend to avoid strikes.   No doubt the experience of employers in collective bargaining also facilitates negotiation, compromise, and accommodation and thus avoids open breaks.

Students of strikes have sought to relate their frequency and severity to current economic conditions.   In general, high levels in strikes are more common in periods of high and rising business activity.   Periods of severe recession have relatively few strikes.   One theory of strikes explains them in terms of economic miscalculations and errors in forecasting.   According to this analysis if each party is accurately informed, balancing of economic strength can and will be accomplished by negotiation.   When essential facts are obscure, either party may misjudge his own or his opponent's strength, demand too much, and thus precipitate a stoppage.

Strikes in the United States follow a rather consistent seasonal pattern.   They appear to be influenced in part by climate and weather, with much lower levels of stoppages in winter months.   More important is the influence of contract terminations, which are concentrated in late spring and summer.   This relationship is sufficiently important to justify the hope that recent tendencies toward long-term contracts may make notable reductions in numbers of strikes, although the frequent inclusion of reopening clauses may limit or prevent this effect.

Issues and Causes

What are the principal causes of work stoppages?   Do the patterns noted in preceding paragraphs provide clues?   Some generalization

---

[14]William Goldner, *Strikes* (Berkeley: University of California, Institute of Industrial Relations, 1951).

and classification of factors appear justified, even though the exact nature of relationships between cause and effect is not clear.

For more than twenty years, the federal Department of Labor has sought to classify stoppages on the basis of the issues involved. Since 1945, this classification has noted five principal types of issues, including:

1. Wages and hours.
2. Union organization and wages and hours.
3. Union organization.
4. Other working conditions.
5. Intra-union issues.

Although the relative importance of these issues has varied from year to year, no clear upward or downward trend is apparent in any of them, except that union organization has been much less important in the years since 1947 than in the period immediately following enactment of the National Labor Relations Act. In the years before World War II, union organization accounted for about one half of all work stoppages. Since 1947, that issue has become relatively unimportant, appearing as a cause in less than 15 percent of all stoppages. It has been replaced by wages and hours (including fringe benefits) as the most frequent assigned cause of stoppages.

The number of work stoppages by government employees has been declining over the past two decades. Some 743 government strikes occurred during 1942–61, involving a total of 156,000 workers and 1,080,000 man-days of idleness. Most of them involved local governments. During 1958–61 lost time due to such strikes was only 11 out of every million days. For private industry the ratio was 2,850 for every million days of work.[15]

Strikes and lost time on account of strikes are much less prominent in European collective bargaining. In Sweden, for example, the measure of lost time is about one ninth that in this country.[16]

Future of Strikes

Forecasts and predictions of future levels of strikes lean heavily on theories that seek to explain how and why industrial conflict results in such stoppages. Several explanations have been advanced.

---

[15]Loretta R. Nolan and James T. Hall, Jr., "Strikes of Government Employees, 1942–61," *Monthly Labor Review*, Vol. 86, No. 1 (January, 1963), pp. 52–54.

[16]See "How Sweden Keeps the Labor Peace," *Business Week*, October 20, 1962, pp. 158–60.

Economic analysis of strikes has frequently sought their explanation in the material gains to be achieved by the parties. Some students have calculated and balanced the cost of time lost by strikers against their gains in long-term earnings and benefits. As noted, others have theorized that strikes occur when the parties — employers and union members or officers — err in their estimates of how much each will give or take. Some investigators conclude that a union must strike once in a while to demonstrate that its threats to do so are not pure bluffing.

Theories frequently emphasize the penetration of union membership as a major factor in both numbers and duration of strikes. Ross, as noted, relates what he calls "residual levels" of strikes to the ratio of union members to totals eligible for membership. He also notes that established cyclical patterns of strikes in several major industries appear to have terminated. As a result strike levels have shown a persistent downward trend, from 33.2 in the 1900–1929 period to 9.8 in the 1957–1960 period. Time losses declined from 296.4 days per hundred union members in the first of these periods to 181.8 days in the second. Duration shows a slight increase, from 14.6 days of idleness per hundred members in the years 1930–1947 to 18.6 days in 1957–60. The residual level of strikes may decline to about 18 million man-days per year; the average was about 32 million in the 1950's.[17]

Most current forecasts expect a decline in strike activity, in part because levels in this country have been falling in recent years and in part because levels in most Western nations are lower. Optimism is also encouraged by the increasing use of mediation, conciliation, and other "third-party" intervention — for example, "human relations" committees.

CONTROL OF INDUSTRIAL CONFLICT

Employers, unions, and public agencies have developed programs designed to avoid the hazards, losses, and waste resulting from industrial conflict. Most of these programs are inevitably directed at control of symptoms — for without clearly defined and widely accepted

---

[17]Arthur M. Ross, "The Prospects for Industrial Conflict," *Industrial Relations*, Vol. 1, No. 1 (October, 1961), pp. 57–74.

theory, no systematic, penetrating approach is possible. Rather, current programs have been built on hunches and insight; they are designed to reduce the fever of industrial unrest rather than to eliminate the basic sources of conflict.

Such an approach is inevitable at this time; current research directed at understanding organization and administration and work motivation may, however, lay the essential foundation for more effective future programs.

Employer and Negotiated Programs

Alert managers seek to discover evidences of employee irritation before they become obvious in vocal criticisms or work stoppages. Many firms undertake employee attitude or morale surveys to discover current employee opinions. Perhaps the most obvious attack on open conflict is the negotiation of no-strike clauses. Another approach, frequently negotiated, involves provision of special procedures for settling employee grievances. The terminal stage in most grievance procedures permits voluntary arbitration. Somewhat more recent is the use of neutral third parties in negotiation and prenegotiation discussions of issues.

Employee morale surveys. Many managers have undertaken studies to discover what employees regard as most important in a job and what weights or priorities they attach to these conditions. Studies of *job satisfaction* note the features of employment that workers regard as favorable and unfavorable. Managers then seek to make changes that will provide jobs and working conditions that maximize these values and thus increase the satisfaction of work.

In some cases employee *counselors* are constantly available to hear complaints. Employees may, on their own initiative, see these counselors, or the latter may ask employees to come in for a visit. Employee opinions expressed in such interviews are regarded as confidential, but complaints and dissatisfactions are noted. Thereafter, managers are advised of these comments (without identification of sources), and steps are taken to eliminate unnecessary causes of dissatisfaction.

In another procedure, employees are asked to check items in a questionnaire designed to discover their attitudes toward various current working relationships and conditions. One of the most widely used of these questionnaires directs employee attention to twenty dimensions of these relationships, including achievement, activity, ability utilization, creativity and self-expression, responsibility-dependence, variety, supervision (human relations), supervision (technical), advancement and promotion, company policies and practices, social service, social status, independence, co-workers, authority, pay, security, working conditions, moral values, and recognition. The instrument seeks to measure both the satisfaction and the importance with which employees regard these variables. Sample items from the "satisfaction" questionnaire are illustrated in Figure 13-3.

Although the evidence is not clear that high employee morale, as measured by such scales, is uniformly associated with greater effort and contribution, these surveys have encouraged programs designed to increase employee satisfaction.

Many employers now seek to eliminate sources of employee criticism and discontent by improving communication and providing opportunities for greater participation by employees in planning and decision making. Alert managers recognize that one of the most common complaints made by employees insists that they are overlooked and are not informed about what is happening or going to happen. Serious resentment also arises because many employees feel that they are not consulted about matters that concern them and in which their advice could be helpful. *Upward communications* — from rank and file through immediate supervision and into the ranks of middle management — get special attention. Current courses in management development and supervisory training stress the need for facilitating upward communications and place special emphasis on learning to listen.

In addition, *suggestion systems* have become an accepted means of facilitating upward communications and the expressions of employee opinions. Suggestions are encouraged by promises of rewards, usually scaled according to the resulting savings. Employees may also be encouraged to express criticisms through the suggestion system.

Many employers now promise maximum opportunities for employee self-development, hoping that such programs will improve employee attitudes. They provide vocational advice for employees plus a broad curriculum of training courses and guided job experience. They maintain policies of promotion from within to assure employees of maximum opportunities for advancement.

Ask yourself: How **satisfied** am I with this aspect of my job?
Very Sat. means I am very satisfied with this aspect of my job.
Sat. means I am satisfied with this aspect of my job.
N means I can't decide whether I am satisfied or not with this aspect of my job.
Dissat. means I am dissatisfied with this aspect of my job.
Very Dissat. means I am very dissatisfied with this aspect of my job.

On my present job, this is how I feel about . . .	Very Dissat.	Dissat.	N	Sat.	Very Sat.
26. The chance to tell other workers how to do things.	☐	☐	☐	☐	☐
27. The chance to do work that is well suited to my abilities.	☐	☐	☐	☐	☐
28. The chance to be "somebody" in the community.	☐	☐	☐	☐	☐
29. Company policies and the way in which they are administered.	☐	☐	☐	☐	☐
30. The way my boss handles his men.	☐	☐	☐	☐	☐
31. The way my job provides for a secure future.	☐	☐	☐	☐	☐
32. The chance to make as much money as my friends.	☐	☐	☐	☐	☐
33. The physical surroundings where I work.	☐	☐	☐	☐	☐
34. The chances of getting ahead on this job.	☐	☐	☐	☐	☐
35. The competence of my supervisor in making decisions.	☐	☐	☐	☐	☐
36. The chance to develop close friendships with my co-workers.	☐	☐	☐	☐	☐
37. The chance to make decisions on my own.	☐	☐	☐	☐	☐
38. The way I get full credit for the work I do.	☐	☐	☐	☐	☐
39. Being able to take pride in a job well done.	☐	☐	☐	☐	☐
40. Being able to do something much of the time.	☐	☐	☐	☐	☐
41. The chance to help people.	☐	☐	☐	☐	☐
42. The chance to try something different. . .	☐	☐	☐	☐	☐
43. Being able to do things that don't go against my conscience.	☐	☐	☐	☐	☐
44. The chance to be alone on the job.	☐	☐	☐	☐	☐
45. The routine in my work.	☐	☐	☐	☐	☐
46. The chance to supervise other people. . .	☐	☐	☐	☐	☐
47. The chance to make use of my best abilities.	☐	☐	☐	☐	☐
48. The chance to "rub elbows" with important people.	☐	☐	☐	☐	☐
49. The way employees are informed about company policies.	☐	☐	☐	☐	☐
50. The way my boss backs his men up (with top management).	☐	☐	☐	☐	☐

Figure 13-3
SAMPLE ITEMS FROM AN EMPLOYEE ATTITUDE QUESTIONNAIRE

Source: *Satisfaction Quetionnaire* University of Minnesota Industrial Relations Center, 1963.

No-strike clauses. Employers and unions may agree that they will not use the strike or lockout during the course or term of their joint agreement. They may provide that both shall continue working together under the existing contract until a new agreement is either negotiated or concluded by arbitration. Under usual provisions both the union and the employer may penalize employees who engage in quickie, outlaw strikes.

Many union members and leaders have become increasingly concerned about the hazards of such clauses. An employer may sue and the union may be held liable for damages thus incurred. As a result, weaker unions that cannot be sure of their ability to control members are reluctant about negotiating such a provision.

An interesting management-union innovation designed to penalize strikes and lockouts was initiated in the agreement between the Dunbar Furniture Corporation of Berne, Indiana, and the Upholsterers' International Union of North America in May, 1964. As reported by the *Wall Street Journal* (May 20, 1964), in the event of either a strike or a lockout, production continues as usual, but half of all wages plus a matching amount from the employer is deposited in trust. If the dispute is settled within the first six weeks thereafter, both parties get their contributions back. If it extends beyond six weeks, amounts returned to them are reduced to 75 percent until the end of nine weeks, to 50 percent in the following two weeks, and to 25 percent in the twelfth week. After the twelfth week, work can be stopped; but if no stoppage begins within a week, the existing contract is automatically renewed for a year. The funds on trust are given to a selected charity.

Grievance procedures. No-strike clauses may be purchased, in collective bargaining, by employer acceptance of an inclusive formal grievance procedure. Big strikes, it is often said, grow from little grievances. Within individual firms the roots of serious unrest frequently grow from the accumulation of a large number of small but frustrating irritations. To avoid this situation, almost all (approximately 95 percent) of the current labor contracts include provisions for formal grievance procedures. Similar facilities or arrangements are also provided by many employers for their employees who are not represented by unions.

Grievance procedures usually involve from three to five steps or stages. For example, in a plant in which employees are represented by a union, the first formal step involves the filing of the grievance, that is, putting it in writing. Before this step, the complaint has presumably been discussed with the shop steward and foreman.

Assume, for purposes of illustration, that a lathe operator feels that he did not get first chance at some overtime work to which he was entitled. He talks with the union representative or shop steward. They discuss the matter with his foreman who does not accept their point of view in the matter. When this employee fails to secure satisfaction from his supervisor, he may take the first step of the grievance procedure. With the help of the union steward for his shop, the employee fills out a grievance slip, describing the event that causes him to "grieve." This written grievance is presented to the foreman who notes his comments and action on the same or an accompanying form.

In the second step this written grievance may go to a grievance committee composed of union stewards and foremen or supervisors. Committee members may resolve the difficulty. If they fail or if the employee is not satisfied with the decision at this level, he may carry the grievance to the next step.

Representatives of the union may or may not be willing to carry the grievance further. They may, if they regard it as necessary, take it to another step or stage in which it may be reviewed jointly by a union officer and a designated representative of the firm, frequently the labor relations director. If these two fail to agree upon a settlement, a fourth step may take it to top officials of the firm and an international officer of the union. If it is still unsettled, a final stage may provide for arbitration by an outside, *neutral arbitrator* or *arbitration panel*.

For unorganized employees a somewhat similar procedure may be provided, except that the employee must present his own case or designate someone to represent him at each stage. In some plans the employee may select one or more other employees as his representative. In others a representative of the personnel or industrial relations department is designated to present his case.[18]

Many variations in these procedures may be noted in current practice. Some plans do not include a bipartisan grievance committee.

---

[18]See "Grievance Procedures for Unorganized Employees," Bureau of National Affairs, *Personnel Policies Forum, Survey No. 49*, October, 1958. For an interesting discussion of the use of outside mediators in settling grievances, see William H. McPherson, "Grievance Mediation Under Collective Bargaining," *Industrial and Labor Relations Review*, Vol. 9, No. 2 (January, 1956), pp. 200–12.

In some, the grievance committee is made up entirely of union representatives, and the major question they consider is whether the grievance merits their support in later stages of the procedure. Whatever the specific arrangements, these procedures seek to settle disputes and to prevent their accumulation. Many procedures set time limits on each stage to insure prompt action on such irritations.

The range of complaints regarded as appropriate for settlement through the grievance procedure or carried to the final stage of arbitration may be specifically defined in the collective agreement. Generally, although employees may "grieve" on any matter in which they feel they have been mistreated, arbitration is restricted to issues involving interpretation of the collective agreement.[19]

The realities of grievance processing are such that grievances do not always follow the contemplated route. Especially in large concerns, some grievances may be settled by a "horsetrading" process that balances one against another.[20]

Sometimes managerial complaints are also taken through the stages of the grievance procedure. Generally, however, managers take such action as seems appropriate and expect employees or the union to file grievances if they feel that employer action occasions unfairness or injustice.

Some experience indicates that white-collar workers have fewer grievances than their blue-collar associates. Most frequent subjects of grievances are discipline (including discharge), wages, hours (overtime), and promotions. An upward trend in issues involving job security — subcontracting, foremen doing production work, and conflicts in union jurisdiction — has been evident in recent years.

Voluntary arbitration. Most grievance procedures include a final stage described as final and binding arbitration. Employer and union agree to submit specified types of issues they cannot settle themselves to a neutral arbitrator or an arbitration panel of three or more members and to accept the decision of this tribunal as final and binding on both parties.

The arbitrator may be an individual selected by both parties. In another procedure arbitration is provided by a panel of three. One of them is chosen by each party and the two select a third or neutral

---

[19]For a discussion of grievance procedures in France, Germany, Norway, and Sweden, see W. H. McPherson, "Grievance Settlement Procedures in Western Europe," *Proceedings of the Industrial Relations Research Association*, December, 1962, pp. 26–35.

[20]See C. F. Smythe, "The Union as Arbitrator in Grievance Processing," *Personnel*, Vol. 40, No. 4 (July–August, 1963), pp. 49–56.

member. In still another variant some firms and unions have appointed a *permanent umpire* or *arbitrator* who hears and decides all their disputes.

The two parties submit the issue or issues to the arbitrator, whose authority is limited to these specific questions. A hearing is held in which the parties may present written and oral arguments as well as documents and other evidence supporting their positions. The arbitrator then weighs the facts and prepares a decision. He describes his findings of fact, his conclusions, and his award. The arbitrator's award answers the question submitted by the parties and thus settles the controversy.[21]

Such arbitration is *voluntary*. The parties provide for it in their labor agreement or in the employer's statement of labor policy. This procedure should be clearly distinguished from *compulsory arbitration* to be discussed in a later section of this chapter. In compulsory arbitration the parties are required by authorized public agencies to submit their differences to an impartial arbitrator or panel and to accept the resulting award as binding.

Voluntary arbitration may also be used to settle disagreements over contract terms during the process of negotiation. When the parties have settled some of their differences but find themselves in sharp and apparently irreconcilable disagreement over others, they may elect to submit the remaining issues to arbitration. Or, after prolonged negotiation, when a strike threatens from failure to reach an agreement, one of the parties may suggest arbitration as a substitute for the threatened work stoppage. Some unions and employers regularly negotiate contract clauses providing that issues not settled in bargaining, after the expiration of the existing contract, shall be submitted to arbitration.

Awards may be enforced through the courts. Courts will not ordinarily review the findings of fact; they may set aside an award on grounds of procedural errors. Some employers and managers have become concerned lest arbitration clauses be interpreted so broadly as to encourage union interference in management.[22]

---

[21]For more detail on voluntary arbitration see Spencer D. Pollard (ed.), *Arbitration and Public Policy* (Washington, D.C.: BNA Incorporated, 1961); Mark L. Kahn (ed.), *Collective Bargaining and the Arbitrator's Role* (Washington, D.C.: BNA Incorporated, 1962) and his *Labor Arbitration and Industrial Change* (Washington, D.C.: BNA Incorporated, 1963).

[22]For an excellent discussion of this question, see Benjamin Aaron, "Arbitration in the Federal Courts: Aftermath of the Trilogy," *Reprint No. 111*, University of California Institute of Industrial Relations (Los Angeles), 1962; "Symposium: Management Rights

In their settlement of disputed contract terms and, to a lesser degree, in decisions on grievances involving rates of pay, overtime, fringe benefits, and similar conditions, arbitrators may influence the price or wages of labor and other variables in labor markets. An arbitration award that sets wages for bus drivers, for example, may arrive at a different figure from that which would have been set by market forces. For this reason, and because arbitrated conditions may spread to other employment, critics frequently express concern about agreements that submit contract terms to arbitration. They charge that such arrangements may seriously disturb the normal labor marketing process.

It is doubtful, however, that arbitration has any seriously disruptive influence on labor markets. In cases involving wages, evidence on working conditions in other similar markets is usually introduced by both parties. Arbitration frequently occasions as thorough discussion of relevant wage data as could have been expected in negotiations.

Public Programs

Public policy, as noted, has sought to encourage the parties in collective bargaining to settle their issues, to find satisfactory compromises. To that end it has provided federal and state mediation and conciliation services. In addition, the courts have supported the efforts of the parties as expressed through voluntary arbitration. The right to strike has been protected.

In some disputes that are regarded as posing a serious threat to public health and safety, public policy requires the parties to delay any cessation of work until public agencies can investigate and assist the parties in coming to an agreement. In other disputes compulsory arbitration may be required. An impressive and possibly growing volume of popular opinion supports proposals for a system of labor courts modeled after those developed in several European countries.

Mediation and conciliation. Most employees have freedom to strike in the absence of no-strike clauses or when these provisions are not effective — for example, when a contract has expired. To prevent these work stoppages, public mediation and conciliation services are provided by federal and state agencies. Mediators or conciliators meet with the parties, either before a stoppage has occurred or while it is in

and Labor Arbitration," *Industrial and Labor Relations Review*, Vol. 16, No. 2 (January, 1963), pp. 183–284.

process, and try to work out a satisfactory settlement. They try to prevent strikes and to shorten those that are already in progress.

The terms "conciliation" and "mediation" are popularly used as synonymous. The federal agency in this field is known as the Federal Mediation and Conciliation Service. Some state agencies are described as mediation services while others are called conciliation services. Very strictly speaking, *mediation* implies a more positive action on the part of the agent, in which he may advance his own suggestions as a basis for settlement. *Conciliation*, on the other hand, is the process of reconciling the proposals of the parties.

In practice the conciliator or the mediator meets with the parties, encourages them to develop a clear expression of their viewpoints, eliminates misunderstandings, and tries to bring them to agreement. He may meet with the parties together or separately, seeking concessions that are mutually acceptable.[23]

No current overall measure of mediation activities is available. A summary of the issues in the more than 7,000 cases handled by the federal service in 1962 is illustrated in Figure 13-4.

Compulsory investigation and delay. For threatened work stoppages that appear likely to involve hazards to public health and safety, a variety of "cooling-off" procedures are provided, and legislation may also authorize public investigation, with or without recommendations for settlement.

Legislation requiring compulsory delay or cooling-off periods frequently specifies that no stoppage shall occur for a stated period, from 10 to 60 days after a strike or a lockout notice is filed by one of the parties. The procedure is frequently combined with an investigation by a public agency to make the issues clear to the parties and to the public. The cooling-off period has several objectives. It seeks to prevent hot-headed, impulsive action by insuring that both parties have ample time to think the matter over. At the same time, it provides an opportunity for conciliators to meet with the parties. Perhaps its greatest value grows out of the opportunity for face-saving. One or both parties may have taken arbitrary positions from which retreat would be difficult after a stoppage was in process but which can be compromised during the cooling-off period. A major task of mediators is that of finding avenues of graceful retreat for the parties.

---

[23]For more detail on mediation and conciliation, see Ann Douglas, *Industrial Peacemaking* (New York: Columbia University Press, 1964); also, annual reports of the Federal Mediation and Conciliation Service and of state services.

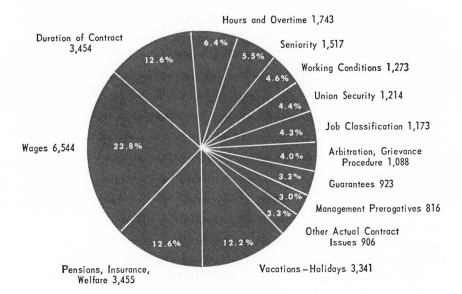

Hours and Overtime 1,743

Duration of Contract 3,454

Seniority 1,517

Working Conditions 1,273

Union Security 1,214

Job Classification 1,173

Wages 6,544

Arbitration, Grievance Procedure 1,088

Guarantees 923

Management Prerogatives 816

Other Actual Contract Issues 906

Pensions, Insurance, Welfare 3,455

Vacations – Holidays 3,341

Figure 13-4

**MAJOR ISSUES, BY FREQUENCY OF OCCURRENCE
AND PERCENTAGE OF TOTAL ISSUES INVOLVED IN
7,313 JOINT MEETING CASES CLOSED DURING FISCAL YEAR 1962**

Source: *Fifteenth Annual Report, Federal Mediation and Conciliation Service, Fiscal Year, 1962* (Washington, D.C.: Government Printing Office, 1963).

Cooling-off periods have been widely used and are prescribed by both federal and state legislation. Usual provisions are not unlike those of the pioneering law in this area — the Canadian Industrial Disputes Act of 1907. The original Canadian act applied only to public utilities and mines, but its coverage has been expanded in later provincial legislation. Although Canadian unions have criticized the act as weakening their bargaining strength, it is notable that their members joined in securing provincial laws when the Dominion legislation was voided as an improper exercise of Parliament's authority in 1925.

In this country the federal Railway Labor Act has afforded experience with similar provisions. It requires the parties to forego a threatened strike pending investigation by a special panel appointed by the President. It has probably prevented several serious strikes, but it has also had some unfortunate effects on collective bargaining. Studies of this experience note a tendency for the parties to neglect negotiation and bargaining, shifting responsibility to investigating boards during cooling-off periods and to the President if the board's recommendation is not entirely satisfactory.

The National Labor Relations Act also specifies a cooling-off period for "national emergency" disputes.[24] When, in his opinion, such a strike is threatened, the President is authorized to appoint a board of inquiry to investigate and evaluate the issues. The board reports its finding of facts — without recommendations — to the President. He may then ask for an injunction forbidding strikes or lockouts for a period not exceeding 80 days. During this cooling-off period, conciliators try to settle the dispute, and employees may be asked to vote on acceptance of the employer's final offer. State legislation in several states specifies similar cooling-off periods as well as fact-finding for disputes regarded as of great public interest.

The LMRA requires that if either a union or company wants to change, modify, or terminate a contract, it must give the other party sixty days' advance notice. If within thirty days agreement has not been reached, the party that made the initial request must notify the Federal Mediation and Conciliation Service.

Public investigation has frequently been combined with compulsory delay in a procedure described as *fact-finding*. The State of Minnesota has a typical fact-finding procedure which is applicable to all disputes that are regarded as threatening work stoppages in industries of great public interest. Parties are required to give notice to the Governor when a strike or a lockout is threatened. They must not precipitate a work stoppage during a specified period in which the Governor appoints a fact-finding board and that board has time to investigate and file its report. Boards are generally tripartite, including representatives of employers, unions, and the public, although boards in some states are composed entirely of public members. In tripartite boards the public member serves as chairman. These boards seek to evaluate the contentions of the parties, to arrive at conclusions with respect to the facts behind the dispute, and thus to provide an analysis that may be helpful in finding an equitable settlement. They have authority to require statements from the parties and to subpoena records. They seek to bring out all the facts and to marshal and weigh them. They may be authorized to publicize their findings, thus helping to develop public opinion to support a fair compromise or adjustment. In the procedure specified by the National Labor Relations Act

---

[24]For a broad view of policy and practice in handling emergency disputes, see Irving Bernstein, Harold L. Enarson, and R. W. Fleming (eds.), *Emergency Disputes and National Policy* (New York: Harper and Brothers, 1955).

for emergency disputes, fact-finders cannot make recommendations; but the logic of this provision is far from clear, for they should be in the best possible position to suggest a reasonable settlement.

There is some evidence that tripartite fact-finding is an effective supplement to collective bargaining. Experience under the Minnesota act suggests that trilateralism does generate a high percentage of peaceful settlements and that such boards in Minnesota have regularly exercised mediation functions with success.[25]

Compulsory arbitration. For local disputes in public utilities (light, power, heat) and in hospitals and similar employment, several states have experimented with compulsory arbitration. In that procedure work stoppages are prohibited, and parties are required to submit unsettled issues to final and binding arbitration. Thus, compulsory arbitration is required in nonprofit hospitals in Massachusetts, Michigan, Minnesota, New York, Wisconsin, and Oregon. A growing number of states provides similar requirements for workers in public utilities.

Both employers and unions of employees thus restrained have generally protested these provisions. Employers argue that they should not be required to assume the risks of business without freedom to manage. Employees and their unions insist that they should be free to accept or reject employment on such terms as they can negotiate. Some change in employer attitudes is suggested by the fact that some employers in ocean transportation appeared in support of a proposal for compulsory arbitration in 1963.

Meanwhile, in 1963, the United States Supreme Court held that the Missouri law on strikes in public utilities was not enforceable because it was in conflict with federal legislation. The legal status of compulsory arbitration is far from clear.[26]

The provisions of several state laws appear somewhat unfair to employees. They forbid stoppages but limit the range of issues subject to arbitration — usually only issues relating to wages and hours of work can be arbitrated. While the prevention of work stoppages in such industries may justify restrictions on the right of employees to strike, fairness demands that all issues in dispute between the parties

---

[25]See Joseph Lazar, "Tripartitism in Minnesota," *Industrial Relations*, Vol. 2, No. 2 (January–February, 1963), pp. 119–26. See also Joseph Lazar, Vincent Lombardi, and George Seltzer, "The Tripartite Commission in Public Interest Labor Disputes in Minnesota, 1940–1960," *Labor Law Journal* (May, 1963), pp. 419–33.

[26]See *Division 1287, Street, Electric Railway, and Motor Coach Employees* v. *Missouri*, US Sup. Ct., 1963, 53 LRRM 2394.

should be subject to full investigation and arbitration with compulsory acceptance of resulting awards. For example, if employers and employees cannot agree upon the terms of a pension or retirement plan, it seems quite unreasonable to require employees to forego the use of the strike weapon and, at the same time, to limit compulsory arbitration to wages and hours.

New Approaches to Industrial Conflict

There is frequent criticism of present levels of industrial conflict in the United States and of current private and public programs for reducing unrest and settling disputes. Many comments compare American experience with that of foreign industrialized nations, suggesting that we should be able to learn from their experience. Frequent proposals suggest supplementary federal controls in national emergency disputes. Others see the need for a formal system of labor courts.

Emergency disputes. Questions may reasonably be raised about the tendency to apply procedures that are designed to prevent serious hazards to health and safety to disputes that involve no such jeopardy. In some states a large proportion of all strikes have sometimes been subjected to these controls. For a variety of reasons — pressure from one of the parties, the desire to avoid public inconvenience, or because an administration seeks favorable publicity from its intervention — almost all threatened disputes may be regarded as falling under the rules for emergency cases.

Somewhat the same questions have been raised about so-called "national emergency strikes." Analysis of the economic impact of many such disputes justifies serious doubt about the propriety of designating them as involving emergencies. One investigation of several strikes that were regarded as involving great public interest and concern gave special attention to their possible implications for consumers. In these cases, findings indicate that from the consumer viewpoint, "the national emergency problem is limited to the railroads."[27] As Hildebrand notes, most consumers' essentials involve

---

[27]See George H. Hildebrand, "An Economic Definition of the National Emergency Dispute," in Irving Bernstein *et. al.* (eds.), *Emergency Disputes and National Policy* (New York: Harper and Brothers, 1955). See also Frank C. Pierson, "An Evaluation of the National Emergency Provisions," Chapter VIII, pp. 129–46 of the same volume and Charles M. Rehmus, "Taft-Hartley Title II: An Emergency at Sea," *Labor Law Journal*, Vol. 14, No. 10 (October, 1963), pp. 865–73 (*Reprint Series No. 26*, University of Michigan–Wayne State University Institute of Industrial Relations).

local goods and services. For industrial users the emergency label may be justified on coal and basic steel industries. In addition, international tensions can, of course, create special concern about the production of goods having military and national defense significance. All in all, however, the range of industries having what may be described as "emergency potential" appears to be narrowly limited.

Questions are also raised about the fairness of controls that force employees to stay on the job against their will while employers continue business essentially as usual. In some cases, of course, government has invoked the right to seize the plant — as in railroad strikes — so that employees are required to work for the government. But profits continue to accrue to owners.[28]

Frequent suggestions would limit profits accruing to employers during whatever period employees may be required to accept and work under conditions imposed as an emergency measure. It is assumed by those who advance this proposal that the parties would thus be encouraged to bargain and to find a satisfactory basis for agreement.

Another frequent suggestion sees the need for a "choice of procedures" approach, rather than the specific program outlined by the Taft-Hartley Act. Thus, the President might use the injunction, compulsory investigation, fact-finding (with or without recommendations for settlement), seizure, compulsory arbitration, appointment of a special commission (as in the railroad dispute over featherbedding in 1960), or a recommendation for Congressional investigation and legislation. Or the President might choose not to act. Such an approach has been tried in the "Slichter Law" in Massachusetts.[29]

Labor courts. Various proposals have suggested that special labor courts be made available to the parties and be required in disputes regarded as creating emergencies. Perhaps the most frequently suggested pattern is that developed in Sweden.

---

[28]For the record of cases in which this device of govenment seizure has been used, see Bernard Yabroff and Daniel P. Willis, Jr., "Federal Seizures in Labor Management Disputes, 1917–1952," *Monthly Labor Review*, Vol. 76, No. 6 (June, 1953), pp. 611–16; See also Herbert R. Northrup and Gordon F. Bloom, *Government and Labor* (Homewood, Illinois: Richard D. Irwin, Inc., 1963), pp. 354–57. A significant proposal has been made for two classes of emergency disputes. For critical disputes compulsory arbitration would be required; in less critical cases partial compulsory operation would supply goods and services needed for the public welfare. See C. F. Smythe, "Public Policy and Emergency Disputes," *Labor Law Journal* (October, 1963), pp. 827–33.

[29]For a brief analysis of experience in the 23 Taft-Hartley Act applications since 1948, see Northrup and Bloom, *op. cit.*, pp. 358–62.

The Swedish Labour Court was established in 1929 to hear and judge disputes arising out of collective agreements. It has no jurisdiction over wages or other economic issues during negotiations. It is exclusively competent in matters falling within its jurisdiction — other courts cannot entertain such cases.[30] Its decisions are final and not subject to appeal except in cases of gross miscarriage of justice. The court has three public, three labor, and two employer members; two labor and two management members preside in each case. From 1929 to 1953 the court made 2,860 decisions; 90 percent of the cases were initiated by employees or their organizations. In its decisions the court does not seek compromise (the English Industrial Court does). Nor does the Swedish Labour Court try to encourage the parties to settle, a practice followed by the similar Danish agency. As a result, the Swedish court has created a body of labor law; many rulings have become statute law. In recent years, however, both parties have shifted away from using the Labour Court and have veered toward arbitration and other means of settlement.

In this country the nature of proposals for a special court is well illustrated by a current suggestion for creation of a Critical Disputes Board. The CDB would be tripartite, appointed by the President, and would be authorized to make wage and price recommendations and to publicize them in an attempt to exert public pressure. The ad hoc CDB would be created when public labor-management advisers certified to the President that a dispute was critical, i.e., likely to lead to a strike or lockout.

Third-party intervention. In the immediate future increased third-party participation in all stages of collective bargaining appears likely. Popular concern over wage pressures that generate inflation can be expected to grow as international competition becomes more obvious. Wage negotiations become increasingly difficult in the face of internationally determined prices and reduced profit margins.

Meanwhile, the same market condition encourages speeded technological change, which in turn creates an added feeling of insecurity on the part of workers. Well-established union practice in such circumstances involves the negotiation and defense of work-rules that provide at least temporary job protection. Employers can bargain for the elimination of these restrictions, but the issues thus created are

---

[30]Folke Schmidt, *The Law of Labour Relations in Sweden* (Cambridge, Massachusetts: Harvard University Press, 1962), pp. 39–53. See also B. Olsson," Employment Policy in Sweden," *International Labour Review*, Vol. 37, No. 5 (May, 1963), pp. 1–22 (Reprint).

among the most difficult, and conflict may be protracted and violent. Work-rule issues in two-party bargaining evoke an emotional response, with obvious hazards to peaceful settlement.

Two clearly distinguished types of third-party participation can be used. One type involves an invitation from one or both parties. It is *voluntary* on their part. The invitees may represent a public agency or may be neutral third parties. Thus, the parties in collective bargaining may ask the help of federal or state mediation or conciliation services. Or they may agree to submit unsettled issues to arbitration.

In the second type of third-party participation, the parties are to some degree required to accept assistance. Participation is *compulsory*. Most obvious in this type is compulsory arbitration. Somewhat similar is the requirement that the parties accept the services of mediators and fact-finding boards. In somewhat milder intervention, parties may be called together by special investigating committees, which seek to develop guiding principles and policies away from the emotional strains of negotiating sessions.

What is new about third-party participation is the practice of inviting outsiders to play a part before issues arrive at a critical, decisive stage. It encourages third-party assistance in early stages and in preparation for bargaining instead of at the end of that procedure. In both Kaiser Steel and Armour Packing plans, these neutrals help to define difficult issues. They may contribute special expertise and knowledge in analyzing such problems. Third parties do not settle issues by fiat; like mediation, they supplement but do not replace collective determination.[31]

What is old about third-party participation is the fact that third parties have been assisting in negotiation and dispute settlement without being legally required or authorized for many years. Thus, the Atomic Labor Management Relations Panel has served since 1949 in fact-finding and making recommendations. The building trades have long maintained a panel, including a neutral chairman, to resolve jurisdictional differences. Since 1961 a tripartite missile sites commission has sought to develop rules for resolving conflict in this relatively new field.

Meanwhile, courts have been active third parties in collective bargaining, particularly in the settlement of disputes. They have been

---

[31]In the basic steel industry many of the same functions have been performed by a continuing committee that includes no outsiders but confers and studies issues in the periods between negotiatory sessions.

drawn into controversies to interpret statutory and common law rules and, more recently, to enforce labor relations board orders and arbitration awards. As a general rule, they have been concerned with procedural rather than substantive questions in this enforcement. As the scope of arbitration and administrative regulation has expanded, however, they have been under pressure from some employer groups to review substantive issues as well.

It should be noted that the practice of *continuous bargaining* or *year-round bargaining* has been encouraged by third-party participation. In this practice company and union hold frequent scheduled conferences to compare notes on practice under the existing agreement and to discuss what one or both parties may regard as desirable future changes. They may agree upon interpretations and clarify unanswered questions and issues. They gather and compare relevant information and thus narrow and define their differences as preparation for subsequent formal negotiation.

Third-party participation is likely to become more common. If it is widely developed on a voluntary basis, third-party participation may reduce pressures for some compulsory form. It seems reasonable in view of our experience to expect that both types will increase.[32]

Creativity in employment relationships. Conflict is and has been and presumably will be one of the most obvious characteristics of working relationships in a democratic society. Modern theories of work recognize that it is the elusive, not-yet-attained personal goals that provide principal motivations for work. Struggles to attain these goals are to be expected; conflict arises over the means to be used in their attainment. In part, such conflict expresses differences in opinion as to how the products of work shall be shared. In part, conflict develops from the tactics, the programs, and practices of the parties.

Wise social policy must seek to constrain these conflicts so that they do not rupture the fabric of political unity. At the same time, it must preserve the right to protest and fight and the necessity for doing so. It is by no means the social goal of perfect industrial peace that assures greatest values and continuing progress in democratic societies. Rather, it is the goal of persistent but restrained conflict.

---

[32]For an excellent overview, see George H. Hildebrand, "The Use of Tripartite Bodies to Supplement Collective Bargaining," *Labor Law Journal*, July, 1961, pp. 655 ff. See also, J. J. Bambrick, Jr. and A. A. Blum, "Labor Relations in the Atomic Energy Field," NICB, *Studies in Personnel Policy*, No. 158, 1957; and The Missile Sites Labor Commission, *Report to the President* (Washington, D.C.: Government Printing Office, 1962).

John W. Gardner has stated this goal and associated institutional provisions effectively in his description of the ever-renewing society:

> Perhaps the most important characteristic of an ever-renewing system is that it has built-in provisions for vigorous criticism. It protects the dissenter and the non-conformist. It knows that from the ranks of the critics come not only cranks and troublemakers but saviors and innovators . . . It must have some capacity to resolve conflicts, both internal and external. Without such capacity, it either will be destroyed or will dissipate its energies in the maintenance of fiercely entrenched feuds. . . . It devises institutional arrangements that provide a harmless outlet for minor tensions and resolve some of the worst tensions before they reach the point of explosion.[33]

At the same time, both the conflict and the socially-imposed restraints create pressures for innovations in management and in collective bargaining. Creativity in work is by no means restricted to the development of new products and productive processes. New approaches — the use of third-party, prenegotiation committees, union-management cooperation, and many others — are to be expected. Their benefits can be more rapidly multiplied when expanded management and industrial relations research provide prompt assessments of contributions and limitations.

The next chapter introduces another major area of employment problems which represent our failure to attain the goal of full employment — the goal of providing enough employment opportunities for our growing labor force.

ANALYTICAL REVIEW QUESTIONS

1. Why is industrial conflict a matter for public concern?
2. (a) How many work stoppages do we have during a year on the average? (b) How many million man-days of idleness?
3. (a) How many collective agreements are negotiated each year? (b) What percent of these do *not* involve work stoppages? (c) What percent of total time worked is lost on account of strikes?
4. (a) What social and economic purposes are served by conflict? (b) How do our collective bargaining theories and practices both regulate and facilitate conflict?
5. How and why may collective bargaining processes be regarded as self-regulating?
6. What current theories seek to explain conflict in work?
7. How and why have we sought to reduce the area of conflict in labor-management relations?

---

[33]John W. Gardner, "Renewal in Societies and Men," *Looking Ahead* (National Planning Association), Vol. 11, No. 3 (April, 1963).

8. What are some "safety valves" in our collective bargaining arrangements?

9. What are some of the major dissatisfactions with employment relationships and working conditions?

10. (a) Is some dissatisfaction with work desirable? (b) What is meant by pathological dissatisfaction?

11. Why are strikes less prominent in Communist nations?

12. What are the most common overt evidences of unrest in employment?

13. Are strikes generally popular with union members? Why or why not?

14. What three measures of strikes must be considered in assessing their importance?

15. What strike statistics are currently available and where may they be obtained?

16. (a) Have proportions of workers involved in strikes in the United States tended to increase? (b) What adjustments need to be made in interpreting the raw data of strikes? (c) What factors account, in part, for the trend in strike statistics?

17. (a) What are the trends with respect to numbers of strikes and days lost per year per worker? (b) What patterns are discernible? (c) What economic and social factors appear to have an effect?

18. How can strikes be explained in terms of economic miscalculations?

19. What is the seasonal pattern of strikes in the United States?

20. (a) How does the United States Department of Labor classify issues in work stoppages? (b) What has been the principal cause of strikes?

21. How do strikes involve balancing long-run and short-run economic consequences? Give an illustration.

22. (a) What are economic strikes? (b) What can happen, under LMRA, to the employment status of strikers?

23. (a) What is an unfair labor practice strike? (b) What rules apply, under LMRA, to the employment status of strikers?

24. (a) List the principal types of strikes. (b) In general, what can be said about the legality of each?

25. How are flash and outlaw strikes differentiated?

26. Do all of the types of strikes tend to have the same economic consequences? Why or why not?

27. (a) How is job satisfaction related to unrest? (b) What policies do alert employers follow in attempting to prevent unrest?

28. What role do employee attitude surveys play in reduction of conflict?

29. (a) What are grievance systems? (b) How are they related to resolution of industrial unrest?

30. What are the principal stages or steps in grievance systems?

31. (a) What do we mean by voluntary arbitration? (b) Why is it voluntary? (c) How is it differentiated (1) from compulsory arbitration and (2) from mediation and conciliation?

32. How is arbitration used in negotiation?

33. How may permanent arbitrators facilitate the settlement of industrial disputes?

34. Explain the frequent concern about economic effects of voluntary arbitration.

35. How do no-strike clauses help in the prevention and settlement of labor disputes?

36. What economic losses are occasioned by strikes?

37. (a) Do all employees have a right to strike? (b) In what respects is this right to strike limited? (c) What penalties may be invoked?

38. (a) Describe mediation or conciliation processes. (b) How are they different?

39. (a) What do we mean by cooling-off periods? (b) Give some typical provisions.

40. (a) Describe fact-finding policies and procedures. (b) How do they differ (1) from arbitration and (2) from mediation and conciliation?

41. What are the principal arguments for and against compulsory arbitration?

42. What special problems are associated with public control of emergency disputes?

43. (a) What is a national emergency dispute? (b) What economic criteria can be used to identify emergency disputes?

44. (a) Should we pass laws forbidding all labor-management conflict? Why or why not? (b) Suggest some possible economic consequences of such laws.

Case 13-1

A STRIKE IN STEEL

Assume that you are the manager of a small manufacturing firm. You are much concerned about a threatened strike in the basic steel industry. You are well aware of the old adage: "There is no such thing as a short steel strike." If a strike comes, your plant can operate only as long as its raw steel lasts. On the other hand, an inventory large enough to keep your plant going a month costs about $800,000, which you would have to borrow.

• You need to make an accurate forecast of the probabilities that the strike will be called. Make a list of the conditions that you will look into as a basis for your prediction and action.

Case 13-2

REPORTING ON A MORALE SURVEY

Dick Brown is the vice-president for industrial relations in the Consolidated Vasol Company. The firm manufactures a wide range of small metal parts and fittings that are sold to manufacturers. More than a year ago he became convinced that many employees were less than happy with their jobs. He suggested that the firm undertake a formal attitude survey, cooperating with the industrial relations center of a large university in the development and the administration of a questionnaire for that purpose. The proposal was debated by members of the board of directors for several months, for some of the directors were sure this procedure would suggest criticisms to employees who would not otherwise have thought of them. Finally, however, the board approved the survey.

Results have just been made available to Mr. Brown. They show that employees have many objections to current working conditions. Most of the objections appear to be of the type that can be reduced or eliminated by cleaning up portions of the plant, installing somewhat better ventilating equipment, and improving facilities for employee parking. However, a very common complaint insists that no one ever tells employees about prospects for the future, either for themselves as individuals or for the business as a whole. Most serious, Brown feels, are the frequent highly critical comments on supervisors. Many employees have written in such comments as "Fire my foreman" or "Get some competent supervisors."

Mr. Brown is quite disturbed about the report on the attitude survey. He wonders whether he should report in full and with complete candor to the board. Does the report justify the prediction that attitude surveys inevitably suggest sources of employee dissatisfaction? What shall he do about the common criticism of foremen and supervisors?

• Be prepared with a list of specific suggestions you could make to Mr. Brown in this situation.

Case 13-3

TO STRIKE OR NOT TO STRIKE

Try to put yourself, for this case, in the position of a local union president. Your union represents all the production employees — 650 of them — in a small factory. You have been negotiating for 60 days. You feel certain that for several years the firm — which is a family-owned corporation — has cleverly manipulated negotiations to give employees much less than they should have received in both wage rates and fringes as measured by agreements in other similar plants.

This time your negotiating committee has expressed determination to gain a 25-cent across-the-board hourly increase. The employer stands firm on his offer of 10 cents. On benefits you have come to an agreement that adds about 3 cents per hour. You are seriously considering a strike. It will be the first since formation of the union in 1947. Union members are looking to you for leadership in this decision. The employer has publicly stated that he (1) will not be "pressured" into any added concessions by a strike, (2) will continue to operate the plant if employees strike, and (3) will not allow any contract clause to be determined by an outside arbitrator.

• Make a list of the factors you will consider in making a decision. Put the items down with a one-sentence statement of their implications, to help you decide, like this:

Factor	*Importance*
(1) Local labor market	If tight, strikers can get temporary jobs elsewhere
(2)................	....
(3)................	....
(4)................	....

EMPLOYMENT: GOALS AND REALITY

This chapter introduces Part IV, which is concerned with employment and with labor problems representing failure to attain employment goals. To some degree, of course, all of the problems discussed in earlier chapters are associated with employment; much of the unrest and conflict to which attention was directed in the preceding chapter reflects unsatisfactory employment or the threat of unemployment. Other problems to be discussed in later chapters involving wages, fringe benefits, hours of work, retirement, and other working conditions are also directly and obviously associated with employment.

Employment may reasonably be regarded as the central and essential setting for all of labor economics and labor problems. The employment process — which brings human resources into combination with capital and management to provide products and services — is the central interest of labor economics. Employment is the means through which manpower resources are utilized and, to a large degree, developed and conserved. Employment creates the working relationships that are widely described as "industrial relations."

For this reason, it is inevitable that many of the personal and social goals that have been described in some detail in earlier chapters involve objectives and ends that can only be attained through the employment process. These goals can be achieved only to the extent that employers find enough qualified workers at the right time and place and that members of the labor force find enough jobs for which they are suited. Analysis of employment problems begins, therefore, with a review of the major goals that are to be attained through employment.

Employment is the means by which human resources are applied and made useful and valuable through their combination with other factors in providing goods and services that people want and will buy. For the individual, employment is the process of delivering services to those who will pay for them — the process of finding and holding a satisfactory job or a series of jobs during his working lifetime. In our society the process begins with a choice of jobs — a decision as to where, when, and in what kind of job we will try to find satisfactory work. It continues as we practice our trade or profession, or work at one or more jobs. The process is complicated because universal, satisfactory employment — with people working at jobs that are acceptable both to the individual worker and to society — is not at all automatic or certain. Some jobs may be distinctly unsatisfactory to some workers. Other work, as in the case of child labor, may be objectionable from a social viewpoint. Many workers may at any given time be unable to find the kinds of jobs they regard as satisfactory. They may be unemployed, or they may be working at jobs they regard as unsuited to their interests and talents. One man, employed as a hod carrier, may be talented as a musician. He may want to work in an orchestra but may be unable to find such work or enough of it to pay his bills. Another may not find the kind of work he prefers in the area in which he wants to live. Some workers who want full-time jobs find only part-time work and are thus *underemployed*.

Underemployment means working under conditions that preclude use or application of the workers' full potential of skills and ability. This condition may not be obvious; American agriculture, for example, involves extensive *disguised underemployment*. Several million agricultural workers are needed only part of the time and may not be using their top abilities most of the time. Disguised underemployment is characteristic of many if not most industries, however, for both managers and rank-and-file employees may spend impressive portions of their time performing tasks that could be delegated to less skilled workers.

We have widely recognized social goals or objectives to be achieved in and through employment. Because employment does not

always achieve these objectives, we have serious employment problems. The first *Manpower Report of the President,* in 1963, clearly recognized this relationship in its preface:

> This first Manpower Report to the Congress is couched in
> terms of immediate problems and specific proposals to meet them.
> But however separate these problems may seem, collectively they
> represent the gap between our manpower performance and our
> objective of the full use of our human resources: . . .
> Nothing more exactly identifies the totalitarian or closed
> society than the rigid and, more often than not, brutish direction
> of labor at all levels. Typically, this is done in a quest for efficiency
> that is never attained. By contrast, it is our contention that public
> and private policies which facilitate free and prudent choices by
> individuals as to where and at what they shall work will, in the
> end, produce by far the most efficient, as well as the only morally
> acceptable, distribution of manpower.[1]

EMPLOYMENT GOALS OR OBJECTIVES

It is not surprising that our social goals, so far as employment is
concerned, are complicated rather than simple. Our expectations for
work are inseparable from the whole complex of our social, political,
and economic objectives. We expect employment to provide economic
support for us and our families; to satisfy many of our personal needs
for expression and recognition; and to complement and facilitate
political democracy, participation in self-government, and attainment
of other political, social, and ethical ideals.

We expect to achieve many of our most highly regarded personal
and social goals through employment. We work in order that we may
live according to our personal and family standards and may travel
or study or support our charities, churches, and what we regard as
other worthy causes. We recognize the fact that most of our dreams
can come true only through employment.

Personal Goals — Income

Most of us work at least eight hours each day and five days almost
every week throughout the year. Our earnings constitute what is
called the *compensation of employees* in the accounting system we apply to
national income. The significance of that segment as a part of total
national income is clearly evidenced by the data in Figure 14-1 which

---

[1] *Manpower Report of the President* (Washington 25, D.C.: United States Government
Printing Office, March, 1963), p. xii.

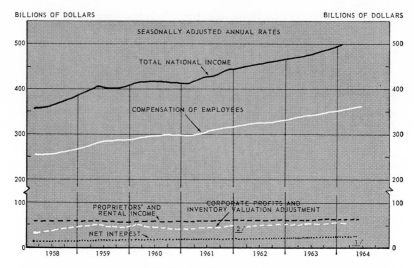

¹Preliminary estimates by Council of Economic Advisers.

²Data beginning 1962 have been adjusted for effects of new depreciation guidelines ($2½ billion for 1962) and therefore are not comparable with previous data. Data for Alaska and Hawaii included beginning in 1960.

Figure 14-1
NATIONAL INCOME BY TYPE

Source: *Economic Indicators*, June, 1964, p. 3.

shows how the national income is divided among employees, proprietors and rental property owners, capital suppliers, and business corporations. Over a long period of years the compensation of employees has amounted to about two thirds of the total national income.

In another, related method of accounting, wage and salary disbursements are calculated as one major source of personal income. Wage and salary disbursements exclude employer contributions for social insurance. Another category, called "Other Labor Income," includes employer contributions to private pension and health and welfare funds; this category also includes compensation for injuries, directors' fees, military reserve pay, and a few other minor items. As may be noted from Figure 14–2, wage and salary disbursements have been maintained as a rather steady proportion averaging about two thirds of total personal income. When the second category is added to provide a combined measure sometimes described as "Labor Income," the proportion is about 70 percent, considerably higher than that prevailing in years before World War II.

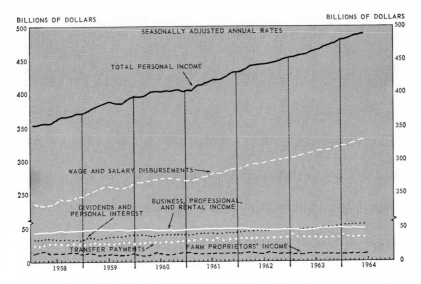

Figure 14-2
SOURCES OF PERSONAL INCOME

Source: *Economic Indicators*, June, 1964, p. 4.

This personal worker income is so important to each of us that "employment security" — i.e., the assurance of an opportunity to work regularly and steadily — must be recognized as a major individual and social goal. As has been widely noted, such "job security" has become a major union goal. Many of the work-spreading work rules negotiated by unions represent their efforts to assure continuing work opportunities for members. For example, the "sabbatical" plan negotiated by the Steel Workers sought, as a part of the total agreement, to assure some 25,000 jobs.

Social Goals

Many of our most important social goals or objectives lean heavily on employment for their attainment. Better housing, public health and education, as well as political stability and national security are adversely affected if human resources are not effectively applied or if we permit extensive waste of workers' potential services.

Viewed from a purely economic angle, any interference with employment — or employment that elicits less than the top long-term contribution of each worker — results in waste.

Full employment. In our society public policy seeks as a general objective to reduce the waste of human resources to a minimum. While some earlier societies regarded manpower as cheap since it was available in supplies exceeding demands and, hence, freely expendable, we recognize that our present and prospective supplies of competent workers are in limited supply.

One of our major social goals is an increasing supply of goods and services, a higher standard of living — not only jobs for all who want them, but cars for all who want them, and second cars, too. In the quest for more goods and services, we also seek to avoid waste of resources that reduces our standard of living. We propose to prevent the personal and family hardships arising out of unemployment and underemployment. Our public policy proposes that each person who wants to work and is capable should have an opportunity to make his maximum contribution. We are firmly committed to this policy which we call *full employment*. In most casual thinking it is regarded as meaning that every worker will be able to get a job. W. H. Beveridge, one of the most ardent English proponents of this full employment goal, described full employment as always providing more vacant jobs than unemployed applicants for jobs. Full employment, in his use of the term, proposes such a continual excess of jobs that sellers of services always have a choice.[2]

The *Economic Report of the President* for 1962 describes three major reasons for national concern about high levels of unemployment. As a nation we are concerned about minimizing economic distress. Unemployment, although not a perfect measure of distress, is accompanied by difficulties that range in seriousness from inconvenience to catastrophe. We are concerned, also, because unemployment is in direct conflict with — and prevents attainment of — our goal of a choice of jobs for all who are able to work and want to do so. Third, we are concerned about unemployment because it occasions a waste of productive resources, both human and material; the goods and services that could have filled the needs of citizens are lost.[3]

---

[2]W. H. Beveridge, *Full Employment in a Free Society* (New York: W. H. Norton and Co., 1945), pp. 18 ff.

Full employment is a concept that has several possible meanings. As Miernyk has noted, our full employment policy seeks to maximize demands for labor, while the British policy attempts to minimize unemployment. Our concept leans heavily on effective labor marketing processes to insure that demands are translated into actual employment. See William H. Miernyk, "British and American Approaches to Structural Unemployment," *Industrial and Labor Relations Review*, Vol. 12, No. 1 (October, 1958), pp. 3–19.

[3]See *Economic Report of the President*, 1962, pp. 40–42.

Full employment as a goal in our thinking means more than merely the prevention of unemployment, however. It includes the prevention of underemployment. We are critical of jobs that fail to use all available skills and abilities of employees. Meanwhile, in our emphasis on full employment, we cannot overlook the possibility of *overemployment*; for individual and social goals may vary so that what an individual may regard as appropriate employment may appear from society's standpoint as overemployment. For example, several million workers in the United States are *moonlighters* — multiple job-holders. Some of them hold one full-time job plus one or more part-time jobs. (See Chapter 17) When they work fifty or sixty hours per week, their work may create a serious social problem if it interferes with their participation in family and community activities. It may contribute to problems of juvenile delinquency if it means that they neglect their responsibilities as parents. It may not permit the informed political participation expected of citizens in a democratic society.

We have no widely accepted standards of overemployment. In general, however, we object to work that interferes with the greatest possible development of highest talents — like child labor — or work that prevents what we regard as normal participation in family and community affairs. Furthermore, we seek to avoid and generally regard as overemployment such strenuous or protracted work as may injure the health and continued productivity of workers.

Employment and growth. One of our major objectives is relatively rapid economic and cultural development. Its economic phase is symbolized by a growing national product and rising national and per capita real income. Employment, as the major source of product and income, must continue to expand if economic growth meets our expectations and goals. The waste occasioned by unemployment and underemployment must, for this reason, be minimized. Wide current interest in the Manpower Training and Development Program reflects the assumption that rapid growth requires continuing retraining to provide qualified workers for changing jobs.

Agreement on goals. Because our personal value systems or preferences vary widely, we find disagreements about what are the most desirable employment conditions. Some of us prefer to work 50, 60, or 70 hours per week. Some workers want to and do hold two full-time jobs. We have, however, wide agreement on several basic objectives in employment, which have been outlined in Chapter 1.

REALITIES IN EMPLOYMENT

How well do the facts of current employment measure up to these goals? Do we have as many jobs as job-seekers? Is the choice of jobs free and unrestricted? Are our jobs stable? Do they provide a maximum of economic security compatible with adequate opportunities for personal development and growth? Do they offer greatest possible protection against work-connected health hazards? Do they balance a fair day's work with fair and reasonable compensation? Does our employment minimize the waste of human resources through unemployment, underemployment, or overemployment?

Current Reports

For the current facts of employment and unemployment on a nationwide basis, major reliance is placed on the *Monthly Report on the Labor Force* (widely described as the MRLF) compiled and released by the Federal Bureau of Labor Statistics. As noted in Chapter 2, a second source, the Department of Labor's monthly report of employment, hours, and earnings in nonagricultural employment, is based on voluntary reports from about 150,000 employers who hire more than 20 million workers. A third source of overall, national facts is the Bureau of Employment Security in the Department of Labor. The Bureau's monthly report of the numbers of initial claims for unemployment insurance and the volume of insured unemployment provides a useful check on the other series.

Economic Indicators publishes national aggregate data on employment and unemployment each month in tabular and graphic form. This regular feature facilitates a ready grasp of the current situation at the same time that it provides six years of earlier monthly data for quick comparison and perspective. For longer comparisons the *Economic Report of the President* summarizes annual data since 1929. The annual *Manpower Report of the President*, released in March of each year, provides much more detailed analyses of both employment and unemployment.

We know more about these gross figures of employment and unemployment for the nation as a whole than we know about employment conditions in many localities. However, for major cities the federal-state system of employment offices now provides local estimates based on employer requisitions and on employee applications for jobs or unemployment insurance. Local employment offices provide data by which the localities they represent are classified by the Bureau of

Employment Security according to the balance of jobs and job-seekers in both current and prospective periods.

The data released in these sources are seasonally adjusted to emphasize significant time-to-time changes. Monthly survey estimates are supplemented at less frequent intervals by a variety of special studies of part-time employment, personal characteristics of the unemployed, family status, multiple job holders, and other refinements in the basic data of the series.

In 1962 the United States Bureau of Labor Statistics began calculating a measure of time lost on account of unemployment. Data have since been extended back to 1955 (see Figure 14-3). The index is based on the total number of hours of possible full-time employment for the civilian labor force. Unemployment is assumed to represent 37.5 hours per week per unemployed worker, and losses for part-time workers whose unemployment is for economic reasons are calculated as the difference between 37.5 hours and hours actually worked. (Those on part-time for noneconomic reasons are not included in these calculations.) This rate has varied from 4.8 to 8.8 in the period since 1956. This measure — time lost — is more sensitive than the data of unemployment; it marks changes that may be obscured or

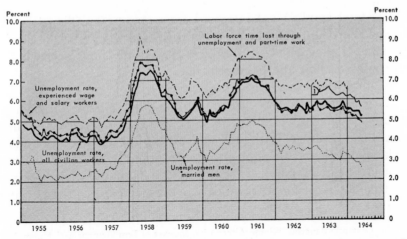

[1]Series revised beginning January 1963 to reflect whether unemployed persons sought full- or part-time jobs.

Figure 14-3
TIME LOST AND UNEMPLOYMENT

Source: *Monthly Report on the Labor Force*, May, 1964, p. 10.

delayed in unemployment data. On the other hand, the time lost measure does not reflect the contrary impact of overtime.[4]

The same figure notes the different rates of unemployment for married men and for experienced wage and salary workers, as compared with all civilian workers. It is worth noting that the rate for experienced workers with established attachments to the labor force is not unlike the pattern of all civilian workers. On the other hand, the rate for married men is significantly lower.

Historic and Current Levels of Unemployment

The general pattern of employment and unemployment is one of increases in both, highlighted, however, by the dramatic expansion of unemployment during the Great Depression of the 1930's. (See Figure 14-4.) As was indicated in the earlier discussion of participation rates, the labor force has grown — from approximately 50 million in 1929 to some 75 million in 1963. Early data on employment and unemployment are no more than estimates, for they were calculated from decennial census figures for "gainful workers." On the basis of reports from individual employers, a current total of employment was calculated and subtracted from the total of "gainful workers" to estimate unemployment.

As total employment increased from about 50 million in 1929 to more than 70 million in 1963 (69 million civilians plus the armed forces), unemployment has varied from practically none (according to early estimates) to approximately one fourth of the labor force in the depth of the depression of the 1930's.

A seasonal pattern is apparent in the data of both employment and unemployment. As noted, the labor force expands during summer months and contracts in the fall and winter. Employment follows a similar pattern, and unemployment also generally increases in total as the labor force expands. The unemployment pattern is more complicated, however, for it includes a seasonal increase in the winter months.[5]

---

[4]See Gertrude Bancroft, "Some Alternative Indexes of Employment and Unemployment," *Monthly Labor Review*, Vol. 85, No. 2 (February, 1962), pp. 167–74.

[5]Since 1955 labor force component estimates (for unemployment and employment) have been available with an adjustment that attempts to eliminate the portion of the variation due to seasonal influences in order to try to show the influence of trends. In effect this adjustment is an approximation based on the average of past experience.

For a discussion of procedures used to adjust for seasonality, see M. S. Raff and Robert L. Stein, "New Seasonal Adjustment Factors for Labor Force Components," *Monthly Labor Review* (August, 1960), pp. 822–27; see also United States Department of Labor, *Reprint No. 2349, 1960*.

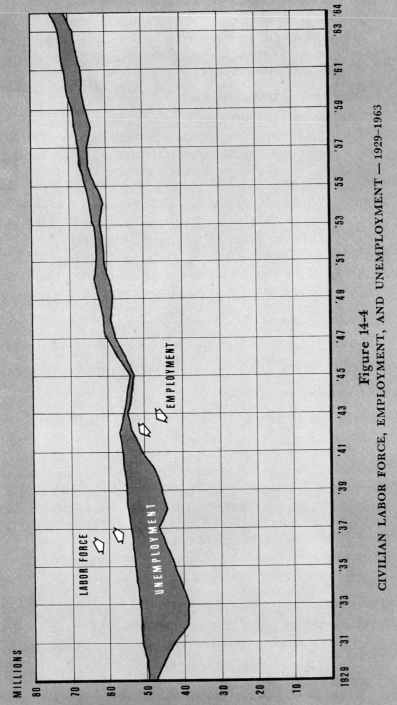

Figure 14-4

CIVILIAN LABOR FORCE, EMPLOYMENT, AND UNEMPLOYMENT — 1929–1963

Sources: *1956 Historical and Descriptive Supplement to Economic Indicators; Economic Report of the President, 1964,* Table C-19, p. 230.

The cyclical pattern of employment is evident from Figure 14-3. Employment declines in recession and increases in recovery. Unemployment follows an opposing pattern. The cyclical pattern shows a very wide amplitude in the 1930's and comparatively minor deviations from the trend since World War II.

Rising Levels of Unemployment

One major shift has attracted wide attention and created great concern. That is the apparent tendency for the percentage of unemployment to move and remain higher in recent years than in earlier postwar periods. In 1929 the level was about 3.2 percent. It increased to 24.9 percent in 1933 and held at levels above 10 percent through 1940. In the World War II period it was reduced to 1.9 percent in 1943, 1.2 percent in 1944, and 1.9 percent in 1945. In immediate postwar years it ranged from 3.9 percent in 1947 to 5.9 percent in 1949. Levels were low in the early 1950's — 3.3 percent in 1951, 3.1 percent in 1952, and 2.9 percent in 1953. Since that time the lowest level was 4.2 percent in 1956. The rates for recent years are:

1957	4.3 percent
1958	6.8 percent
1959	5.5 percent
1960	5.6 percent
1961	6.7 percent
1962	5.6 percent
1963	5.7 percent
1964	5.0 percent Est.

The persistence of relatively high levels in periods of recovery and prosperity has been described as "prosperity unemployment." Annual levels of 5.5 to 6.0 mean that some monthly rates have exceeded the 6 percent mark, frequently described as the "danger line" and a signal for pushing the panic button. Popular concern about this rising volume of unemployment has been heightened by the fact that each recent recovery phase in business has been characterized by a higher level of unemployment than the preceding recovery.

The significance attached to this development was emphasized in the 1962 report of the President's Council of Economic Advisers, which calculated that a 4 percent maximum level of unemployment should be established as an objective. If it had been attained in 1961, according to the CEA, the gross national product would have been 40 billion dollars higher than it was. The Council argued that:

1. The trend rate of growth of GNP, adjusted for changes in unemployment levels, has averaged about 3½ percent in the period following the Korean War.
2. Potential GNP for any year since 1955 is computed by extrapolation of the trend line at a 3½ percent rate for each year since 1955.
3. Actual GNP is less than this trend-line potential GNP — in 1961 it was $40 billion less.[6]

The Council concluded that each percentage point of progress toward 4 percent in the unemployment rate has meant a gain of roughly 3 percent in total output in postwar periods of expansion. Improved employment conditions not only put more people back to work but have other employment effects as well (e.g., increased labor force participation, longer hours of work, and better use of plant and equipment and nonproduction workers). The CEA summary of these changes is reproduced as Table 14-1, which shows how the $40 billion gap would have been closed if unemployment had been reduced to 4 percent.

Table 14-1

ALLOCATION OF ESTIMATED $40 BILLION GAP BETWEEN POTENTIAL AND ACTUAL GROSS NATIONAL PRODUCT — 1961

Source	Associated Increment of Output (billions of $)
Total	40
Lower unemployment	15
Larger labor force in response to greater demand	4
Longer hours of work per man associated with higher utilization	5
Greater productivity per man-hour associated with higher utilization	16

Source: Council of Economic Advisers, *Economic Report of the President*, January, 1962, p. 50.

In essence, this view holds that the waste arising out of unemployment levels in excess of 4 percent is intolerable. Finding ways of maintaining employment and restraining unemployment can increase labor force participation, expand weekly hours of work, provide full-time for many part-time jobs, and improve the output of those who are employed but are underemployed in their jobs.

[6]*Economic Report of the President*, January, 1962, pp. 51.

INTERNATIONAL COMPARISONS

Because national goals are somewhat similar, levels of employment and unemployment are a matter of great concern in nations
around the world. For the less-developed economies reliable measures
are infrequent or unavailable; many of them do not have dependable
data on population or labor force. Comparisons can be made, however, among most European nations and with Canada and Japan.
The United States Bureau of Labor Statistics has provided the graphic
comparison of rates of unemployment shown as Figure 14-5.

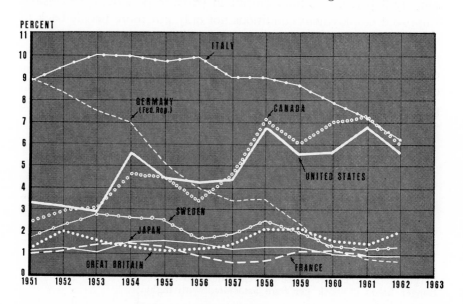

Figure 14-5
INTERNATIONAL COMPARISON OF UNEMPLOYMENT

Source: United States Bureau of Labor Statistics, Robert J. Myers, "The Unemployment Problem: What We Can Learn from European Experience," April 20, 1963. Mimeographed.

The general impression created by the figure is one of rising levels
of unemployment in Canada and the United States and of declining
or approximately level rates in the other nations. It may be noted,
also, that the rates of unemployment for Canada and the United
States are consistently higher than those of other nations, except for
Italy and Germany. In the German Republic rates since 1956 have
been well below those in this country.

Reliability of Indexes

A common criticism of international comparisons of employment and unemployment, heard in the United States, charges that methods of counting vary so widely that no conclusions are justified. In the United States major reliance is placed on sampling and personal interviews. As a result, the numbers reported as unemployed represent a statistical expansion of numbers of those who have reported themselves as out of work during the week of the sample. Some of these workers are available only on a part-time basis; others are high school or college students looking for vacation jobs. Still others may be willing to work if and when the right job comes along.

Some limitations on the implications of international comparisons are imposed by different methods of counting; others arise out of different definitions of the employed and unemployed. Some foreign practice gives more attention and weight to what is usually described as *attachment to the labor force*, that is, experience in working. Also, foreign practice often bases estimates on registrations for work in employment offices rather than on household interviews.

On the other hand, Canada and Japan both use sampling surveys similar to the MRLF in the United States — the Canadian data are quite comparable to the MRLF and require no adjustment. While Italy uses registrations at employment offices for its one major series, the Central Institute of Statistics (ISTAT) makes quarterly surveys comparable to the MRLF. Germany, too, relies heavily upon employment exchange registrations but also has an annual household sample survey called a microcensus.

The French use two major systems, one a count of those receiving unemployment relief and the other a report of registrants seeking jobs. They also make sample household surveys, but at irregular intervals. Sweden relied for many years on unemployment statistics collected by the trade unions. Since 1956 registrations of unemployed at local employment offices have been used; and beginning in 1959, national sample surveys have been made. The Swedish samples are based on individuals, rather than households, and most of the interviews are conducted by telephone.

It is somewhat ironic that Great Britain, the birthplace of the household sample survey, does not use this technique but relies on registrations at public employment exchanges. Studies of their concepts and methods suggest a substantial underenumeration of the unemployed, as determined by definitions used in the United States.[7]

Myers and Chandler undertook a comparison of unemployment rates in eight nations in 1960 and adjusted their reported rates to make them comparable. Their conclusions are summarized as follows:[8]

NATIONAL UNEMPLOYMENT RATES — 1960

	Civilian Labor Force	Unemployment Rate
	(Millions)	(%)
Canada	6.4	7.0
United States	70.6	5.6
Italy	20.9	4.3
Great Britain	23.9	2.4
France	19.1	1.9
Sweden	3.7	1.5
Japan	43.5	1.1
West Germany	25.2	1.0

It may be noted that their careful adjustments make only a few changes in relative positions, as compared with Figure 14-5. It is also notable that, contrary to common belief, household labor force surveys do not always give the highest estimates of unemployment. In only France and Sweden (and the United States) do the household surveys yield higher unemployment rates.[9]

Such comparisons make it clear that in both Canada and the United States rates of unemployment are usually higher than in other industrialized nations. The same conclusion is suggested by comparisons of minimum levels. Perhaps because their economies are smaller and possibly less complicated, European nations regard our assumption that 2 to 3 percent is a minimum rate as unrealistic.

---

[7]For details see Robert J. Myers and John H. Chandler, "International Comparisons of Unemployment," *Monthly Labor Review*, Vol. 85, No. 8 (August, 1962), pp. 857–64; Robert J. Myers and John H. Chandler, "Toward Explaining International Unemployment Rates," *Monthly Labor Review*, Vol. 85, No. 9 (September, 1962), pp. 969–74; and Joseph S. Zeisel, "Comparison of British and U.S. Unemployment Rates," *Monthly Labor Review*, Vol. 85, No. 5 (May, 1962), pp. 489–501. See also the *Manpower Report of the President* (Washington 25, D.C.: United States Government Printing Office, March, 1963), p. 49.

[8]Robert J. Myers and John H. Chandler, "International Comparisons of Unemployment," *Monthly Labor Review*, Vol. 85, No. 8 (August, 1962), p. 863.

[9]Other countries with regular sample surveys of the labor force include the Philippines, Puerto Rico, Israel, Egypt, and Finland. Denmark and a number of other countries have made experimental and ad hoc surveys. Russia, as noted, does not officially recognize any unemployment. No realistic data on unemployment or underemployment (the Russian substitute or alternative) are available.

Explanations and Excuses

As noted, many critics of international comparisons argue that the figures are not comparable and that the differences do not actually exist. Also, some comfort is found in studies that show our unemployed as including many who are not "breadwinners" and others whose efforts to find jobs are only temporary or casual.[10]

Some of the difference in national rates may reflect different traditions with respect to working careers. American workers presumably feel less attachment to a single employer. Similarly, employers feel less responsibility for the total careers of employees. The degree of job attachment is stronger in countries other than the United States and Canada. Once a worker is established in a regular or permanent position, he is quite unlikely to experience layoff or separation. In Italy presidential decrees to this effect have the status of law; in Germany, France, Great Britain, and Japan, social custom and tradition play an important role. Labor mobility is low as is short-term transitional unemployment in these countries.

Differences in national rates are real and may represent serious difficulties in bringing job opportunities and willing workers together. Workers may face unusual difficulties in learning of job opportunities for which they are qualified. Our combination of public and private employment offices in the United States may be less adequate and effective than similar services in smaller nations. We may do a less efficient job of providing employment information and balancing existing supplies and demands.

Changing Supplies and Demands

Comparatively high levels of unemployment in the United States may be in part occasioned by recent and current rapid growth of labor supplies. War babies have come into the labor force in large numbers in recent years. The rate of growth of the labor force has been high as compared with that of the 1930's. So, however, have the rates of growth in European nations and in Japan. Both Germany and Japan had even faster rates of growth during this period with generally lower unemployment levels. Sweden had a labor force growth about the same as ours but kept unemployment at low rates.

---

[10]For example, a study of 3,000 unemployed, out of work for five weeks or longer in 1961, found that less than half had a regular attachment to the labor force and had been persistently seeking work. More than one third were "secondary" workers. Another third was composed of workers without family responsibilities. See Industrial Relations Counselors, *Current News*, Vol. 28, No. 25 (June 21, 1963), pp. 125–26.

It has been suggested that perhaps our problems are complicated by the increasing participation of women, many of whom enter the labor force in middle age and without work experience or training. Their lack of preparation for employment may be a significant consideration. It is notable, however, as Myers and Chandler have reported,[11] that our participation rates for women are about the same as those of France and Great Britain; in Germany and Japan women make up 40 percent of the work force. In Canada, Sweden, and Italy women's participation rates are between 26 and 31 percent. Age variations in the various national labor forces are equally inconclusive as a source of explanation in unemployment rates.

It appears, therefore, that explanations emphasizing differences in labor supplies are scarcely adequate in justifying our poor showing in international comparisons. Some of our comparatively high unemployment may be attributable to difficulties in marketing and some may reflect the quality or qualifications of our supplies. In the aggregate, however, our experience with increasing supplies is not distinctive.

Since differences in labor supplies and in geographic and other types of mobility provide rather limited explanations for our comparatively high rates of unemployment, current opinion tends to emphasize the inadequacy of demands for labor. On the one hand, expressions of this view point the finger at displacements of workers by automatic machinery. On the other, the major clue is seen in an inadequate rate of economic growth.

In the years since World War II, much popular analysis of our comparatively high rates has pointed to rapid technological change — popularly described as automation — as the principal explanation. The argument holds that we have eliminated jobs more rapidly than we have created new ones. No doubt changing job requirements thus established, compounded by the immobilities imposed by our geographic size and the failure to provide continuing retraining for many workers, represent one significant clue to our distinction. We have significant new demands for labor, but we do not have qualified workers available at the time and place where they are needed.

Technological change can explain the displacement of workers formerly employed in the jobs later performed by machines. It leaves unanswered the question as to why new jobs were not created in numbers adequate to balance labor supplies. The answer to that

---

[11]Robert J. Myers and John H. Chandler, "Toward Explaining International Unemployment Rates," *Monthly Labor Review*, Vol. 85, No. 9 (September, 1962), pp. 969–74.

question must be found in the rate of economic growth. An international comparison of growth rates by Myers and Chandler shows the close correlation between these rates and levels of unemployment. Economic growth in the United States — as measured by real GNP — averaged 2.9 percent in the 1951–1960 decade. Only England experienced a lower rate, 2.7 percent. Canada averaged 3.6 percent; Sweden, 3.7 percent; France, 4.2 percent; Italy, 5.8 percent; West Germany, 7.2 percent; and Japan, 8.7 percent.[12]

Full employment is a goal of every industrialized economy, for any failure to attain that goal occasions serious waste and handicaps the attainment of other social as well as individual objectives. In recent years the United States has experienced levels of unemployment higher than those in most industrialized economies. Moreover, the rates seem to show a persistent trend toward higher levels. The problem thus posed is complex. Explanations of experience in this country require careful consideration of factors affecting both supplies of and demands for labor. The development of effective programs designed to move toward the goal of full employment requires a careful evaluation of employment theory and of the major factors affecting employment levels. The chapter that follows pursues this analysis.

ANALYTICAL REVIEW QUESTIONS

1. Why is employment described as "central" to the study of labor economics?
2. What is underemployment? Is it limited to part-time workers?
3. Why can we not all agree on a pattern or system of employment goals?
4. How is "compensation of employees" different from wages or earnings?
5. How are "sabbaticals" related to job security?
6. Show how waste may arise out of employment.
7. How would you define the concept of full employment?
8. Show that manpower can be in short supply in the midst of high level unemployment.
9. Among the reasons for concern about unemployment, which seems to you most important? Why?
10. What are the hazards of overemployment?
11. What is your appraisal of moonlighting as a factor in unemployment?
12. How is employment related to economic growth?
13. Revise the list of employment goals to rank them in the order of their importance, as you see them.
14. Show that our employment goals are both like and unlike those in other industrialized nations.

---

[12]*Ibid.*, pp. 971–72.

15. To discover current levels of employment and unemployment, what sources would you consult?
16. In what ways is the measure of time lost more useful than that of numbers drawing unemployment benefits?
17. Why are current data on employment and unemployment seasonally adjusted?
18. What is prosperity unemployment?
19. What is the rationale behind the goal of no more than 4 percent unemployment?
20. What is the basis for criticizing international comparisons of unemployment figures?
21. Why are the unemployment rates in the United States and Canada comparatively high?
22. Should the employment of married women be controlled to facilitate their replacement by heads of families in periods of high unemployment? Why or why not?

Case 14-1

MOONLIGHTING TEACHER

Mr. Zebediah McQuarry teaches mathematics in Central High School. He handles a full schedule of classes plus his home-room and related responsibilities. In addition, he assists in coaching baseball. He has been teaching 15 years and receives the highest salary paid at Central.

At 8:00, two nights each week, he teaches shop mathematics in an evening class designed for employed and unemployed workers who are preparing for different jobs than they hold or have held. The program is sponsored by the State Departments of Education and Employment Security. Classes are held in the Labor Temple. Mr. McQuarry receives a fee of $35 for each evening's work.

The community has been concerned by reports that some 5.7 percent of the national labor force is moonlighting while almost 6 percent are unemployed. Everyone knows someone who is holding a second job. Several employers and a couple of local unions have come out against the practice, however, and members of the school board are concerned about the activities of several teachers, including Mr. McQuarry. About 10 percent of the teachers in grade school and high school regularly work at second jobs.

• Prepare a short "position paper" on this question, one which you would be willing to have published in the local paper or elsewhere.

Case 14-2

WORKING WIVES

The editor of the local weekly has editorialized on the employment of married women. He concludes that fully 90 percent of the unemployed in Gopher Prairie County could be put to work if married women with employed husbands gave up their jobs. He suggests that every firm in the county make a case-by-case study and release all such married women unless there are "significant" special reasons for their employment.

His editorial has been reprinted in several other papers in the valley.

• Take a position on his proposal and prepare a letter of not more than 250 words which would be suitable for publication in a local newspaper.

UNEMPLOYMENT: TYPES AND THEORIES

Unemployment is our number one economic problem. It wastes the lives of men and women, depriving both them and the Nation. Our continued underuse of human and physical capacity is costing us some $30 to $40 billion of additional goods and services annually. This means a considerably lower standard of living than we would otherwise enjoy.[1]

The unemployed, like the poor, are always with us. Chapter 14 has indicated that (1) we have seldom if ever even temporarily attained our goal of full employment, (2) we seem to have been losing ground since the mid-1950's, and (3) we have not fared as well in this respect as have many of our international competitors. The survey presented in Chapter 14 is necessarily impressionistic. The problem deserves more detailed attention and analysis.

This chapter proposes such a closer, more critical analysis. First, it describes the several statistically most important types of unemployment, classified in terms of their immediate sources or causes. Then, attention is directed to differential rates of unemployment among groups of workers. Finally, the chapter outlines employment theories, the plausible relationships that are generally described as explanations of changing levels of employment.

---

[1] *Manpower Report of the President* (Washington 25, D.C.: United States Government Printing Office, March, 1963), p. xi.

TYPES OF UNEMPLOYMENT

Unemployment is clearly not a simple phenomenon. Some of it represents only a temporary idleness between jobs. Some of the unemployed, on the other hand, have been out of work and seeking work for months or years; some have not found a job since they entered the labor force as threshold workers. Thus, during 1961, a total of about 82 million different people worked at one time or another. A little more than half that number, some 43 million, held full-time jobs throughout the year. About 15 million were unemployed at one time or another in the year; five million had two or more "spells" of unemployment. About two million did not work at all during the year. Almost 32 million reported part-time work.[2] The average employment in 1961 was 66,800,000, and the average unemployment was 4,800,000 or 6.5 percent of the 74,175,000 average labor force.

It is evident that national averages present a blurred and somewhat obscure picture of both employment and unemployment and of the changes that take place within totals and averages. For convenience in a more detailed consideration of the problem and its roots and sources, several types of unemployment may be distinguished.

Since employment involves a balancing of labor supplies and labor demands, it is convenient to use such a model to identify types of unemployment. One major type of unemployment can be described as immediately attributable to demands for labor that total less than available supplies. Total effective demand for goods and services (by consumers, businesses, and governments) may be insufficient to employ all persons seeking work under existing technologies, hours of work, and wage rates. Such a category of *demand unemployment* can express seasonal or cyclical fluctuations or a long-term, persistent trend in demands. Demand unemployment can be characteristic of an industry, an area or region, or a total national economy.

A second major type of unemployment is directly related to the mechanisms by which demands are filled and supplies employed. In such *marketing* or *frictional* or *structural unemployment*, demands remain unfilled at the same time that supplies are not fully utilized because the two are not perfectly meshed or linked. Workers are idle while

---

[2]Cal Rosenfeld, "Work Experience of the Population in 1961," *Monthly Labor Review*, Vol. 85, No. 12 (December, 1962), pp. 1347–58.

job vacancies are unfilled. Such structural factors concentrate unemployment among workers in particular areas, industries, and occupations, while jobs are seeking workers elsewhere or with different qualifications. For the most part, this result follows from changes in jobs to be filled without parallel changes in the qualifications of workers, so that *technological unemployment* is an important factor in structural unemployment.

In another sense structural unemployment can be described as personal, for some of it is traceable to the distinctive personal and group characteristics of the unemployed.

In outline, these types of unemployment may be related somewhat as follows (note that types are not mutually exclusive):

Types of Unemployment by Immediate Source or Cause

  I. *Demand* (local, regional, national)
     Seasonal fluctuations
     Cyclical fluctuations
     Growth
       Technological displacement
       Persistent unemployment

  II. *Structural* — marketing
     Frictional — transitional
     Technological
     Spot
     Personal

  III. *Supply*
     Personal — qualitative

Such a classification, although useful, has limitations that should be clearly recognized, for the categories thus defined are interrelated. For example, when the total of demands for labor is relatively high, as in periods of recovery from depression or recession, marketing frictions are reduced. Employees in one locality need not move to another to find a suitable job. Market knowledge is improved, for employers advertise their needs. Time losses between jobs are reduced. Even those who have minor personality problems or limitations are tolerated when the criterion for selection is a "warm body." Employer job specifications become less rigorous.

It is equally clear that the impacts of several types of unemployment may be simultaneous and mutually reinforcing. Cyclical may be supplemented by seasonal and technological, for example. Technological may be augmented by personal and structural. Further, as the outline indicates, what appear to be the proximate or immediate "sources-causes" of unemployment vary in terms of perceptions and viewpoints. To some observers, most unemployment may appear to be personal, i.e., occasioned by the shortcomings and lack of qualifications of available labor supplies. The same situation may be viewed also as arising out of imperfect marketing in which demands for and supplies of workers — as they are — are not balanced because of immobilities or pricing policies or ignorance. Thus, high unemployment among unskilled workers may be interpreted as the immediate result of geographic immobility or ignorance of opportunities or public interference in the form of legally prescribed minimum wages.

Demand Unemployment

The outline of immediate sources of unemployment indicates three major types of demand unemployment. Most obvious in every tabulation or chart is the pattern of seasonal fluctuations. Most spectacular in such tabulations is cyclical unemployment. Probably most complex and possibly most important in terms of the total of unemployed workers is growth unemployment.

Seasonal unemployment. In terms of numbers of workers affected and numbers of days lost, a major type of unemployment is that described as seasonal. It results from reductions in demands for labor attributable either to the seasonal pattern of consumers' habits and customs or to variations in production associated with climatic change. Demands for coal, fuel oil, and heavy clothing necessarily vary with climatic change. The Christmas holiday season, June as the month of brides, and Easter as the time for new styles all have effects on time-to-time demands for labor. Similar variations in employment opportunities result from seasonal patterns of production, particularly those in agriculture. Spring, summer, and fall create special demands for farm labor, which may be required for only a few weeks or months. Planting and harvesting can be undertaken only when climate, soil, and crops are ready. Construction activities are also influenced by climatic changes.

Employment reaches its peak in July and is lowest in January. Unemployment is at a maximum in June, because of the influx of students, with January the second highest month; unemployment reaches a minimum in October.[3] Seasonal unemployment is heaviest

---

[3]See "Seasonal Variations in the Labor Force, Employment and Unemployment," United States Bureau of the Census, *Current Population Reports, Series P-50, No. 82*, April, 1958.

in the production and distribution of nondurable consumption goods. Capital goods industries and those producing consumers' durables provide more stable employment throughout the year.

Major effort to control seasonal unemployment has sought to stabilize employment within firms. This result may be attained by a variety of managerial practices, of which the most common are stockpiling and building up inventories during slack seasons; regularizing distribution and sales; diversification of products and *dovetailing* (for example, producing furnaces and garden tools, lawn mowers and snow removers); and finding complementary markets, in North and South America, for example.

Attempts to reduce seasonal unemployment are generally called *employment stabilization*. The burden of stabilizing seasonal employment in the United States is placed upon individual employers. Public policy seeks to induce employers to stabilize by offering reduced unemployment compensation tax rates (*merit rating*) for employment stability. In general, it is to the enlightened self-interest of employers to stabilize employment and output, although this may in some cases reduce the impetus to expand which would create additional jobs. Stabilization permits the employer to operate at a point approximating lowest total unit costs of production; it is more expensive to maintain a plant that has substantial variation in levels of output. The employer saves not only on costs of capital but on labor costs as well because of savings in overtime when not running at over- or extra-capacity; he saves on unemployment taxes and labor turnover costs when not running at undercapacity. Under variable levels of output, work scheduling and staff services can be more costly; it is difficult to expand and contract the management team. Conversely, under stabilization, workers are less likely to hold back on production through fear of layoff. Furthermore, protracted layoffs may result in the worker's skills getting "rusty" and in the employer's loss of a significant portion of his trained labor force.[4] Programs to reduce seasonal unemployment vary from firm to firm and from industry to industry.

Cyclical unemployment. Cyclical unemployment is essentially depression unemployment. This type of unemployment causes widespread concern because prolonged depression and idleness create personal disorganization and desperation in which citizens may accept

---

[4] As is well known, public policy in the United States does not encourage arrangements for output and employment stabilization between and among firms in an industry, that is, cartels. Such arrangements are not uncommon, however, in European and other countries. In socialist countries the state can stabilize employment by industries.

or welcome radical social and political change. The movements led by Hitler and Mussolini gained wide acceptance in part because they promised jobs to vast armies of unemployed. Communism has recruited its supporters most effectively in situations characterized by widespread frustration growing out of unemployment.

Cyclical unemployment appears as an accompaniment of the recession and depression phases of business cycles. These periods of reduced activity are followed by stages of recovery and prosperity in which cyclical unemployment is reduced. Students of business cycles have traced them back into the ages described by Old Testament writers. There is general agreement, however, that the amplitude of these fluctuations was magnified by industrialization and capitalism. Cycles have been attributed to many sources; theories relate them to the weather, variations in agricultural production, sunspots, and — in modern experience — to wars, excesses in saving over investment, unwise investment and expansion, overextension of personal credit, and changes in the distribution of national income. A pattern composed of long (50-year), intermediate (10-year), and short (4-year) cycles has been frequently described.

Depressions can occasion vast unemployment, which is most serious in the capital goods industries and those producing consumers' durables. For example, in the 1929–1931 depression period, employment declined more than 30 percent in lumbering and millwork, metal working, and mining and about 28 percent in building and construction, according to one local study. In contrast, it declined 23 percent in retailing and only 8.5 percent in food, drink, and tobacco manufacturing. In a major depression, however, all industries and occupations are affected.

The pattern of unemployment in this country for the last quarter century is apparent in Figure 15-1 which shows annual averages of unemployment as a percentage of the labor force since 1929. The figures includes annual indexes of industrial production (based on 1957–1959 = 100) as a measure of cyclical changes in business activity. The seriousness of unemployment in the 1930 depression is clearly evident, as are the peaks in 1933 and 1938. In 1933 almost 25 percent of the entire labor force was out of work; in 1938 almost 20 percent of all workers were unemployed.

Concern about the seriousness of cyclical unemployment has been growing for several reasons. Three recessions — in 1954, 1958, and 1961 — have been marked by high levels of unemployment (see

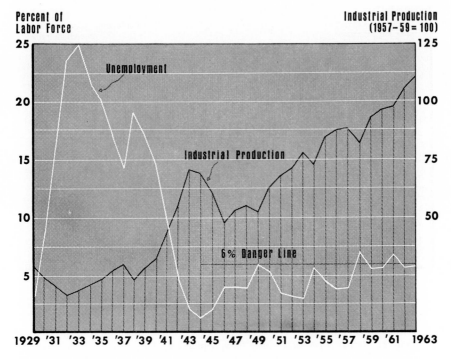

Figure 15-1

UNEMPLOYMENT AND INDUSTRIAL PRODUCTION — 1929–1963

Sources: Current issues of *Economic Indicators* and *Supplements*.

Figure 15-2). In each of these recessions, the decline in employment is more precipitous than the recovery. Peaks of prerecession employment appeared in July, 1953; July, 1957; and May, 1960. The span or interval from one high to the next has been 48 months in 1953–1957 and 34 months in 1957–1960. Low points in employment appeared after 13 months, in August, 1954; after 9 months in April, 1958; and after 9 months in February, 1961. Recovery takes longer. Even more serious is the fact that unemployment in the years following each of these recessions has remained at successively higher levels; it has not fallen to the levels of preceding periods of prosperity. Thus, in 1949, the peak of unemployment began to subside and by 1953 had fallen below 3 percent. In 1956 the level fell to 4 percent. In 1959 the low was about 5 percent, and in 1962 and 1963 the lowest level was about 5.5 percent. Further, each of these recovery periods was featured by larger numbers of long-term unemployed. It is clear that cyclical unemployment is indeed a continuing problem.

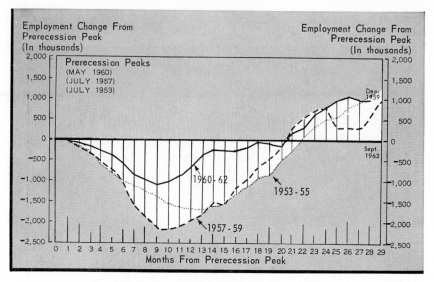

Figure 15-2
UNEMPLOYMENT AND BUSINESS CYCLES
(Seasonally adjusted data)

Source: *Monthly Report on the Labor Force*, September, 1962, p. 5.

Growth factor. The demand side of the employment equation seems to be closely related to the rate of economic growth. To provide full employment, demands must increase to balance the continuing increase in job-seekers. In aggregative analysis, total numbers of jobs must be measured against total numbers of workers.

Frequent reference has been made in earlier chapters to the continuing expansion of the labor force. Figure 14-4 (page 371) indicates the long-term pattern of growth since 1929. Over the thirty-year period shown there, annual growth in the labor force has averaged about 675,000. Persistently high levels of unemployment in recent years suggest that demands for workers have not kept pace with labor force growth in this period. Major concern arises out of prospects in years ahead when the rate of growth of the labor force will be much higher.

Estimates of the labor force make the problem clear. The number of new entrants in the 1960's will be about 13 million, some 50 percent more than in the decade of the 1950's. (Such estimates are based on the age distribution of the population.) In 1965 about 3,800,000 citizens will become 18 years of age, as compared with 2,600,000 in

1960. The 1963 *Manpower Report of the President* notes that "If in the next five years we provide new employment at the pace of the last five, by 1967 unemployment will come to over 5½ million, or more than 7 percent of the 1967 labor force."[5]

The same report compares past experience with current and prospective developments and argues that the recent 5½ percent rate of unemployment "has resulted largely from a slowing down of the rate of economic growth."[6] In support of this conclusion, the report points to the 1947–1957 period in which nonfarm employment increased at a rate of 1.9 percent per year — about 900,000 jobs. Since 1957, increases in employment have averaged about 0.9 percent annually — less than 500,000 jobs.

Wilcock and Franke argue that the major cause of high unemployment levels in recent years has been inadequate growth.[7] They suggest that the gap between what we can and what we do produce is increasing and that lack of growth in the economy is thus responsible for unemployed human resources. They note that declines in total unemployment have been closely related to increases in output (GNP). When unemployment increases, however, long-term joblessness increases at a more rapid rate; and when unemployment declines, long-term unemployment declines more rapidly. They take this as evidence that employers do not hesitate to hire long-term unemployed in upswings and, hence, that structural unemployment is sensitive to economic growth.

Technological change. In current popular thinking, reduced or slowly-growing demands for labor are intimately and directly related to automation and other forms of technological change. Men are displaced by machines. Jobs are eliminated by automatic controls that utilize the process of feedback to replace human control.

The reality of such changes is apparent; in analyzing their contribution to problems of unemployment, the major question is their impact — the extent or measure of their influence on employment. Although most popular interest is directed to the influence of technological change on total demands (the quantities of jobs to be filled), it must be clear that changes also affect kinds of jobs, in terms of required workers' qualifications.

---

[5] *Manpower Report of the President* (Washington 25, D.C.: United States Government Printing Office, March, 1963), p. xv.
[6] *Ibid.*, p. xi.
[7] R. C. Wilcock and W. H. Franke, "Will Economic Growth Solve the Problem of Long-term Unemployment?" *IRRA Proceedings* (December 28–29, 1961), p. 47.

Technological unemployment is that which can be attributed directly to changes in productive technology — the processes in which resources are combined. It reduces or eliminates work opportunities. Technological changes vary the "mix" of human and other resources in specific processes so that jobs disappear. Some changes substitute machines for men and result in "work-saving," which means that one man, with new equipment, facilities, or procedures, creates as much product or provides as much service as 2, 10, or 50 men before the change.

Technological change is as old as men and societies and has been a major force in the long-term expansion of employment and the rise of wages and scales of living. At the same time, it has been a subject of constant concern and frequent conflict, especially since the Industrial Revolution, which greatly speeded its tempo. Philosophers have worried about its concentration of economic and political power and its tendency to foster autocracy in employment. Observers have questioned the desirability of accompanying *job breakdown* in which simplification of jobs may increase the routine and drudgery of jobs.

By definition, technological change modifies techniques of production. It provides ways of creating equally good or superior products and services, frequently using fewer people in these processes. Three types of technological change may be distinguished. One improves the method of applying human effort; it finds more effective ways of raising or lowering, carrying, turning, adjusting, and otherwise using the physical and mental energy of workers. A second substitutes other types of power — water, steam, electricity, or atomic power — for the energy of people. A third increases the effectiveness of human effort by supplying improved tools and equipment. Evidence of the first type of change is usually less spectacular than the others and less widely reported. The facts on increased horsepower per worker and on growing capital investments are more readily noted, measured, and described.

The first type of technological change, although generally not startling or alarming, has attracted growing attention since it has been formalized and advertised as *work simplification*. In earlier periods workers and supervisors presumably made improvements in the way they worked largely on a trial-and-error basis. In modern industry alert management studies jobs to discover how they may be performed more efficiently. Careful analysis of just exactly what a worker does becomes the basis for simplifying job performance.

Changes in sources of power and the substitution of horsepower for human energy are widely recognized. The federal Census of Manufacturers indicates that horsepower available for use of the average employee increased from 1.14 in 1869 to 2.1 in 1899 and to 6.5 in 1939. Work energy supplied by mineral fuels and water power has increased, since 1850, from less than one billion horsepower hours to almost 400 billion.

The third subtype of technological change — the expansion of capital facilities — has been the subject of numerous studies. In the United States the average capital-worker ratio has increased from about $500 per employee in 1850, to $2,000 at the turn of the century, to $12,000 in 1952, and to about $20,000 in 1962.

Results of these changes, as measured by output per worker, have been described in Chapter 3. There, attention was called to the difficulties involved in imputing cause to each of the contributing changes that have influenced productivity. We do not know precisely how many jobs have been eliminated by changes in technology in any given period, for we cannot be sure how much of the growing productivity results from greater skill, higher motivation, better management, and other coincident changes. We do know that the changes are uneven, with varying impacts on different industries, and that the speed of technological change varies from time to time.

Automation is both a new name given to a long-established process and a new form of technological change. Strictly speaking, it refers to changes that involve *automatic feedback* to manipulate controls. In the automated drilling process, for example, the machine corrects itself. Feedback provides an almost instantaneous check on the operation, which is translated into a simultaneous correction or adjustment, as needed. The principle, it should be clear, is not new. Household thermostats have illustrated its effectiveness for at least two generations. Through feedback and resultant control, automation tends to replace supervision as well as production workers.

The model for relating automation to employment is far from simple. For an industry-wide model, major independent variables include the state of the art, the pace of innovative suggestions, availability of capital and of qualified personnel, and elasticity of product demand.[8] Only the most obvious and superficial effects of the impact of technological change can be stated with assurance. It is evident

---

[8] J. R. Gass, "Research into the Social Effects of Automation," and P. Naville, "The Structure of Employment and Automation," *International Social Science Bulletin*, Vol. 10, No. 1 (January, 1958), pp. 16 ff. and 70–81.

that such change influences job opportunities, worker satisfaction, and long-term unemployment.

Professor Yale Brozen[9] lists several variables that modify the effects of technological change on employment. Among the most important is the elasticity of product demand. Another is the proportion of labor costs to total costs. Several others exert lesser influence but may be important in some situations.

In many short-term technological-change situations, serious unemployment frequently appears. It tends to strike those least able to make quick changes — older employees, the semiskilled, and the unskilled.

The fact that these changes tend, in the long run, to expand employment opportunities and to increase the value of each hour of work does not prevent occasional serious hardship. Neither does it eliminate the fear that men will be displaced or actually outmoded by machines. As Brozen has said, "If we were to trace a history of fear of technological change, we could go back a century to the Luddites' fear of power machinery, half a millenium to the hostlers' and inn-keepers' fears of the stage coach, a millenium to the fullers' fears of mechanical fulling." He concludes that "If any fear of technical progress is justified, however, it seems that automation is the least to be feared among the many episodes of change human society has endured."[10]

What about the aggregative long-term effect of such changes? Here, the answer seems as clear as any based on historic evidence can be. Over the years, in spite of all the changes that have reduced demands for manpower in particular jobs and industries, our economy has provided jobs for a continually growing labor force. While the net effect of such changes is to provide fewer jobs in many industries and occupations, these same changes have spurred the expansion of employment in other jobs and industries. They have facilitated a continuing growth in the economy as a whole, both in the United States and in other industrialized nations, that has overcome much of the destructive influence exerted by these changes.[11]

---

[9]For his discussion of factors that cause more rapid change in some industries than others, see his "Invention, Innovation, and Imitation," *American Economic Review*, Vol. 41, No. 2 (May, 1951), pp. 239–57. For a summary of short-term effects, see his "Studies of Technological Change," *Southern Economic Journal*, Vol. 17, No. 4 (April, 1951), pp. 438–50. See also William Haber and H. M. Levinson, *Labor Relations and Productivity in the Building Trades* (University of Michigan Publications Distribution Service, 1956).

[10]Yale Brozen, "Economics and the Changing Technology: the Economics of Automation," *American Economic Review*, Vol. 47, No. 2 (May, 1957), p. 339; see also "Automatic Technology and Its Implications," *Bulletin No. 1198*, Bureau of Labor Statistics, 1956.

[11]*Forbes*, June 1, 1963, pp. 27–29.

Arnold Weber concludes that technological change has not caused a reduction in aggregate employment, although it has resulted in a structural shift in employment opportunities. Thus, for example, in 1956 for the first time there were more white-collar than blue-collar people in the labor force; by 1955 more were employed in service-producing than goods-producing industries. While the average skill level, following automation, may increase, the skill levels of many new jobs under automation may not increase, and indeed may decrease. Automation has discouraged the use of incentive wages; the concept of wage is being replaced by the concept of salary, and many blue-collar workers are being shifted from an hourly to a salary compensation base.

Weber also finds that automation changes the traditional boundaries of the firm. Thus, for example, maintenance work is subcontracted to other firms. Automation changes the nature of work from machine operation to machine tending and machine watching.[12]

On the other hand, it is not clear that technological change in the 1960's has displaced workers more rapidly than in the preceding decade. Further, the Council of Economic Advisers reported in 1963 that a comparison of the years from 1948 to 1957 with those since 1957 contradicts the usual conclusion that unemployment has become more severe among unskilled and semiskilled workers. There is no assurance that automation has changed levels of *job satisfaction*, although it seems to have increased the proportions of jobs requiring higher skills. Following automation, larger proportions of employees are included in higher labor grades.[13]

It is sometimes argued that technological advances concentrate judgment, decision making, and ownership of property in the hands of the few, so that they destroy morale and motivation. Some philosophers suggest that these changes exert a powerful influence against spiritual development.[14]

---

[12]Arnold Weber, "Adaptation to Technological Change Under Collective Bargaining," *Proceedings of the 12th Annual Labor-Management Conference*, West Virginia University, April 12–13, 1962, pp. 8–15.

[13]See Louis E. Davis, "The Effects of Automation on Job Design," *Industrial Relations*, Vol. 2, No. 1 (October, 1962), pp. 70–71; "Adjustments to the Introduction of Office Automation," *Bulletin No. 1276* (Washington, D.C.: Department of Labor, 1960); Barry M. Ginsberg, "The Impact of Automation on Wage and Salary Administration," *I.L.R. Research*, Vol. 9, No. 1 (1963), pp. 3–9.

[14]See, for details and discussions of these points, Brozen, "The Value of Technological Change," in *Ethics*, Vol. 42, No. 4 (July, 1952), pp. 249–65; "The Social Impact of Technological Change," *Journal of Engineering Education*, Vol. 41, No. 3 (November, 1950), pp. 148–54; and "Technological Change, Ideology, and Productivity," *Political Science Quarterly*, Vol. 70, No. 4 (December, 1955), pp. 522–42. See also L. Reed Tripp (ed.),

Although some applications of automation may encourage job-enlargement and increase variety in work, the more common impact is likely to reduce job interest and challenge. Managers will face continuing problems in seeking to maintain interest, and worker demands for reduced working hours will be encouraged.[15]

Technological changes have eliminated many jobs and caused worker concern and worry and resistance to change. Further, concern is greater in this country than in many other industrialized nations. In many older nations, employees with extensive seniority cannot be readily released, and somewhat the same employment rules have achieved acceptance in many recently-developed economies. At the same time, in the older nations, public relief programs with special, long-term benefits for those who are replaced by machines have long, traditional acceptance. (Canada provides financial aid for such workers.) Other common public programs provide travel expenses for relocation when acceptable replacement jobs are available.

In many industries — but in some much more than in others — technological change precipitates serious hardships for displaced workers. Managements and unions have tried to find ways to cushion these effects. In railroads, meatpacking, on the airlines, in the auto-mobile industry, and elsewhere, these efforts persist. In some cases the problem is a serious one for managers as well as for employees, for one common union approach involves the insistence on work rules that restrict flexibility in work assignments and in output. Many of the "solutions" negotiated in such situations create new security systems to reduce work-rule restrictions.[16]

Unions cannot ignore the concern of their members about job security as involved in this type of unemployment. They have frequently sought to negotiate terms designed to soften its impact. While unions cannot stop the change, create new jobs, or simply

Industrial Productivity: A Social and Economic Analysis (Madison: Industrial Relations Research Association, 1951).

[15]William A. Faunce, Einar Hardin, and Eugene H. Jacobson, "Automation and the Employee," *Annals of the American Academy of Political and Social Science*, Vol. 340 (March, 1962), pp. 60–68.

[16]See Charles C. Killingsworth, "Cooperative Approaches to Problems of Technological Change," Chapter 4 in Gerald G. Somers *et. al.* (eds.), *Adjusting to Technological Change* (New York: Harper and Row, 1963). For an excellent case study of the automation impact in an Indian metal products plant, see Julius Rezler, "Automation: The Nut and Bolt Division of Company X," (available from the author in the Graduate School of Loyola University, Chicago). For an analysis of the impact of technological change on the railroads, see Edward B. Jakubauskas, "Technological Change and Recent Trends in the Composition of Railroad Employment," *Quarterly Review of Economics and Business*, Vol. 2, No. 4 (University of Wisconsin, Industrial Relations Research Center, 1963).

balance reduced demands for labor by reductions in working hours, they can ease transitions, negotiate special benefits for affected workers, and encourage added public assistance in arranging shifts to new jobs. They can and do negotiate a variety of job security rules. If managers find that these rules seriously handicap efficient operations, unions bargain for early retirement and other special benefits for workers who are displaced, as they have in automobile, rubber, steel, and railroad industries and in longshoring.[17]

The President's Advisory Committee summarized the problem of technological unemployment neatly, as follows:

> Three central propositions have emerged in the Committee's consideration of the significance and impact of automation and other technological advances.
>
> First, automation and technological progress are essential to the general welfare, the economic strength, and the defense of the Nation.
>
> Second, this progress can and must be achieved without the sacrifice of human values and without inequitable cost in terms of individual interests.
>
> Third, the achievement of maximum technological development with adequate safeguards against economic injury to individuals depends upon a combination of private and governmental action, consonant with the principles of the free society.[18]

Structural Unemployment

Structural unemployment — including frictional or transitional — is that which is directly and immediately attributable to difficulties and delays in matching available jobs and people. It is closely related to labor mobility discussed in Chapter 6. In part it is transitional, representing time lost in transfers from one job to another. In part it is frictional, representing difficulties and delays encountered in the job-worker matching process.

The unemployed in transitional unemployment are those who are "between" jobs. They have quit or have been released. They are looking for new jobs which they have not yet found or in which they

---

[17]See Charles Killingsworth, "Cooperative Approaches to Problems of Technological Change," *Reprint Series No. 59* (Michigan State University, School of Labor and Industrial Relations, 1963); Jack Barbash, "The Union Response to Technological Change," *Annual Conference Proceedings* (Montreal: McGill University, Industrial Relations Centre, 1961), p. 93; for other viewpoints, see "Impact of Automation and Technological Change on Employment and Unemployment," *BES No. R-206* (Washington, D.C.: United States Department of Labor, September, 1961).

[18]*The Benefits and Problems Incident to Automation and Other Technological Advances*, Report of the President's Advisory Committee on Labor-Management Policy, January 11, 1962, Washington, D.C., p. 1.

have not begun to work. The length of time during which they are unemployed varies greatly among members of the group and is affected by current labor market conditions. Many thousands of the unemployed, seeking work, fail to connect with employers looking for the same type of workers. The measure of such frictional losses is not known; no nationwide accounting provides comprehensive data on unfilled openings.[19] Some indirect indicators are available in such measures as the National Industrial Conference Board's index of help-wanted advertisements and the reports of federal-state employment services.

It is clear that a considerable volume of transitional unemployment is unavoidable. It is the price we pay for freedom in choosing and changing jobs and for our versatility, adaptability, and progress. It is also clear that, while society gains from this flexibility, resulting unemployment may create serious personal and family distress. Periods of transitional idleness may be extended for some groups of workers, particularly those who are older or those whose skills have not been updated.

Frictional unemployment always includes many workers who are temporarily out of work, on layoff, or awaiting new assignments within 30 days. In August, 1963, for example, 410,000 of the 3,857,000 unemployed were in this category. Voluntary job changes have accounted for about 10 percent of our unemployment in recent years of prosperity, and as much as 20 percent of current unemployment may be attributable to frictions involving recent entries into the labor force. Thus, transitional unemployment is quantitatively important in a society that emphasizes a process of free labor marketing.

Structural unemployment arises out of the changing nature rather than the aggregate quantity of demands; it expresses the inability of available manpower to meet job specifications for newer types of work opportunities. Over longer periods these structural changes in demands may be drastic, as illustrated by the declining demands for farm labor, for horseshoers, or for telephone operators and the growing demands for engineers, scientists, and data processing technicians. Structural changes are by no means a recent development; they have featured every advance in the tools and techniques used to make human effort more effective. They were a prominent feature of the Industrial Revolution in the 17th and 18th centuries.

---

[19]See, however, "Special Groups of Unemployed Persons," in Table C-21, *Economic Report of the President*, 1963, p. 197.

In 1963 the *Manpower Report of the President* took special notice of this type of change. In his message to Congress, the President noted that:

> The changing structure of employment, from manufacturing production to private and public services, may be seen from the singular fact that nearly two thirds of the new jobs added to the economy in the past five years have been in State and local government, for the most part in teaching.[20]

Structural unemployment is a major type. It is neither a new development nor, apparently, one that has attained growing importance or impact.[21]

Although structural unemployment, as a prominent part of the total, has attracted wide attention and comment, several rather careful studies indicate that it has not become more important in recent years. Solow notes, for example, that no unusual concentration of unemployment among industrial and blue-collar workers is evident. Further, there has been a substantial decline in the volume of unfilled job opportunities.[22]

Persistent and spot unemployment. Rising levels of "prosperity unemployment" have been accompanied by its concentration in areas of persistent unemployment. Some labor market areas have not moved out of the criticial surplus classification for many years. In these "depressed" areas, demands for labor do not provide jobs for local suppliers even in the peaks of business cycles.

Analysis of these local market areas discloses a complex of types of unemployment. Seasonal and cyclical unemployment are involved. Technological and cultural changes may have reduced demands, as in West Virginia coal production. Some areas have rapidly expanded supplies as a result of recent migration, as in automobile manufacturing centers. Local supplies may include unusually high proportions of the "difficult-to-employ" groups, the inexperienced, untrained, minorities, and others.[23]

---

[20]*Manpower Report of the President* (Washington 25, D.C.: United States Government Printing Office, March, 1963), p. xi.

[21]See *Higher Unemployment Rates, 1957–1960; Structural Transformation or Inadequate Demand*, Subcommittee on Economic Statistics, Joint Economic Committee, 87th Congress, 1st Session, Washington, D.C., 1961, pp. 55–58. For more on job dislocation, see Louis A. Ferman, "Some Conceptual and Methodological Considerations in the Study of Job Dislocation," *Proceedings, Industrial Relations Research Association* (December, 1962), pp. 315–24; see also the discussion by Richard C. Wilcock in the same volume, pp. 341–43.

[22]Robert M. Solow, "A Policy for Full Employment," *Industrial Relations*, Vol. 2, No. 1 (October, 1962), pp. 5–6.

[23]Eva Mueller and Joy Schweidskamp, *Persistent Unemployment, 1957–1961* (Kalamazoo, Mich.: The W. E. Upjohn Institute for Employment Research, November, 1962).

Spot unemployment: distressed areas. In some areas demands for labor have declined far below those in earlier periods. Former employees have been out of work over long periods of time. The Bureau of Employment Security identifies them as "areas of substantial and persistent labor surplus" and describes two major criteria for inclusion in this group: (1) at least 6 percent unemployment and (2) average annual rates of unemployment at least 50 percent above the national average for 3 of the most recent 4 years, or 75 percent above the national average for 2 of the most recent 3 years, or 100 percent above the national average for one of the last 2 years.

Spot unemployment in distressed areas has received increasing attention in recent years, although the problem is not a new one. Most large cities and especially the older ones have experienced the decline of certain sections. In the United States, in the words of the Committee for Economic Development, "Quite a number of our local economies have not only failed to keep pace with the growth of the nation, but have actually moved backward while the nation was moving forward."[24] In these centers the CED notes that "High and persisting unemployment has caused prolonged human suffering and extended economic waste."

The number of such areas varies from time to time; in May, 1964, there were 17 major areas, 96 "smaller" areas and 449 "very small" areas of substantial and persistent unemployment. All areas so designated are eligible to become "redevelopment areas" under the Area Redevelopment Act.

Causes of the decline of a major local industry, as identified by the CED, include competition from other firms or other products, changes in production technology, changes in locational advantages, competition from abroad, and exhaustion of local natural resources.[25] Galloway, in an analysis of distressed areas, concludes that because these cities have relatively low productivity industries, they provide less attractive opportunities for investment and employment. There are two possible sources of low productivity: (1) lagging technology in these industries or (2) low market value of the product they produce. Both of these possibilities are national rather than local in origin.[26]

---

[24] *Distressed Areas in A Growing Economy*, Committee for Economic Development, June, 1961, p. 5. For current classifications of areas, see *Area Labor Market Trends* (monthly), Bureau of Employment Security, United States Department of Labor, Washington, D.C.

[25] C.E.D., *op. cit.*, p. 24.

[26] Lowell E. Galloway, "An Economic Analysis of Public Policy for the Depressed Area," *Industrial and Labor Relations Review*, Vol. 5, No. 4 (July, 1961), pp. 500–509.

Spot unemployment may be chronic or acute. It is likely to be chronic in areas built around declining industries and may be acute in areas experiencing temporary declines in demand for their specialized production.

Personal Unemployment

Analysis of the overall "number one" problem of unemployment cannot probe deeply without noting the possibility that the unemployed may be a distinctive type of people. Popular discussions frequently suggest such conclusions in describing those out of work as largely unemployable or in allegations that many of them do not really want to work or work only long enough to establish eligibility for unemployment benefits.

Perhaps the most common popular assumption about unemployment tends to explain it in terms of a large "hard core of chronic unemployables." Experience following the Great Depression and each recession in the postwar period indicates that the "hard core" idea is generally exaggerated. Most of the alleged unemployables get jobs when business activity improves.

On the other hand, unemployment may have a tendency to create chronic unemployables. Many may become personally disorganized by their failure to find jobs. Forced to live in slum areas, many of the unemployed feel isolated and forgotten. They may lose touch with reality. (In Detroit former Packard employees, out of work for ten years, still expressed their expectation that the old plant would call them back.)[27]

DIFFERENTIAL RATES OF UNEMPLOYMENT

It is clear that the impact of unemployment is not evenly distributed over all types of workers or industries or occupations. Past practice seems to have reserved jobs for preferred people, members of the majority groups. The *Manpower Report of the President* notes several types of workers who are subject to "the most serious, persistent and intractable unemployment problems."[28] Among these groups are

---

[27]See "Who are the Unemployables?", *Business Week*, February 9, 1963, pp. 68–70. See also Robert L. Stein, "Work History, Attitudes and Income of the Unemployed," *B.L.S. Special Labor Force Report*, No. 37, December, 1963.

[28]*Manpower Report of the President* (Washington 25, D.C., United States Government Printing Office, March, 1963), p. 40. See also Seymour L. Wolfbein, *Employment and Unemployment in the United States* (Chicago: Science Research Associates, 1964).

young people, workers in the older age groups, nonwhites, the relatively unskilled, and workers in industries that are presently declining. In addition, unemployment strikes hardest among secondary workers, the uneducated, the handicapped, and those who work part time.

Thus, in 1962, when workers under 25 represented less than a fifth of the total labor force, they made up a third of the unemployed. In the same year, male workers, 55 to 69 years of age, had an unemployment rate of 4.7 percent as compared with a rate of 3.8 percent for men 30 to 54 years old. Negro workers, who made up 11 percent of the civilian labor force, were 22 percent of the total of unemployed. Unskilled workers have consistently shown the highest level of unemployment, and second place has gone to semiskilled production workers in manufacturing.

The President's Committee on Youth Employment has noted the dimensions of unemployment among those in the 16 to 21 year age group and the unusual current and prospective levels.[29] The Committee notes that during school months in 1962 from 600,000 to 800,000 members of this group were out of school, out of work, and seeking jobs. About one sixth of the total of unemployed are represented by this younger age group. In the 1960–1970 decade 26 million new job seekers will enter the labor force.

The special problem of nonwhite workers has been extensively explored. Figure 15-3 illustrates some of the details.

Educational attainment is a factor of great importance in unemployment. Over the years since 1950, unemployment rates are consistently higher for those with lesser educational attainment. Professor Charles Killingsworth made the comparisons shown in Table 15-1 on page 402. They indicate that this relationship has become increasingly significant.

Forecasts are inevitably pessimistic. In the decade of the sixties, the demand for professionals is expected to grow 40 percent, but for common labor no growth is expected. For the 26 million new workers expected to enter the labor force in the 1960's, 7½ million will not have a high school education, and 2½ million will not have a grade school education. Hence the prospect is for rising unemployment rates among these new entries.

Secondary workers contribute a disproportionate share of total unemployment. One study of claimants for extended benefits found

---

[29]See *The Challenge of Jobless Youth* (Washington, D.C.: United States Government Printing Office, 1963).

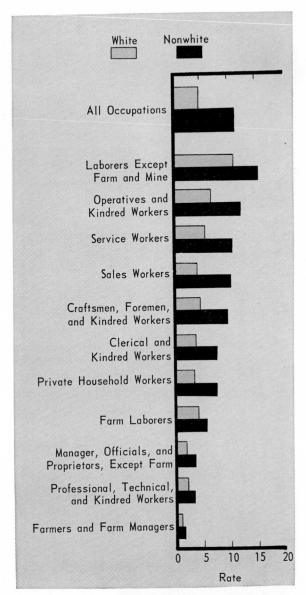

Figure 15-3
UNEMPLOYMENT RATES BY COLOR AND OCCUPATION — 1962

Source: *Employment Security Review*, United States Department of Labor, June, 1963.

that 36 percent of claimants are secondary wage earners (not principal breadwinners). Since about 30 percent of married couples have both husband and wife in the labor force (compared with 11 percent

Table 15-1
EDUCATIONAL ATTAINMENT, LABOR FORCE AND UNEMPLOYMENT—
APRIL, 1950, AND MARCH 1957, 1959, AND 1962
(Civilian Labor Force 18 Years Old and Over)

Years of School Completed	Percent of Group Unemployed					Percentage Distribution of Total Labor Force				
	1950[1]	1957	1959	1962	Percentage Change 1950–1962	1950	1957	1959	1962	Percentage Change 1950–1962
Elementary:										
Less than 5[2]	7.8	7.7	10.0	9.7	+24	8.5	6.2	5.3	4.6	−46
5 to 7	7.6	6.0	9.8	8.3	+ 9	14.4	11.1	10.2	9.1	−37
8	6.1	4.7	7.0	7.2	+18	18.6	16.1	14.9	13.3	−28
High School:										
1 to 3	6.5	5.1	8.5	8.3	+28	19.0	19.3	19.8	19.3	+ 2
4	4.2	3.0	4.8	5.1	+21	24.1	29.5	30.7	32.1	+33
College:										
1 to 3	3.6	2.9	3.5	3.7	+ 3	8.1	8.6	9.3	10.7	+32
4 or more	1.9	0.7	1.4	1.4	−26	7.3	9.2	9.7	11.0	+51
Total	5.7	4.1	6.2	6.0	+ 5	100.0	100.0	100.0	100.0	

[1] All unemployment rates in 1950 adjusted upward: (1) for census undercount of labor force and unemployment compared with the Current Population Survey and (2) for persons with a job but on temporary layoff or waiting to be called to a new job, excluded from the unemployment classification in 1950 but included in 1957 and later.

[2] Includes those reporting no school years completed.

two decades ago), many of the extended claimants (long-term unemployed) apparently had additional sources of family income to help tide them over.[30]

Unemployment strikes harder at part-time workers, who may thus combine unemployment with underemployment.

The unemployed frequently combine several of these characteristics. Many Negroes, for example, are likely to be qualified only for occupations that are especially subject to unemployment. Although they are improving their educational attainment, they are still seriously handicapped in this respect. Unemployment rates for Negroes increase twice as rapidly in recessions as for white workers. Only about one third as high proportions of Negroes are in professional and managerial occupations as is true of whites. Negro employment tends to center in industries that are declining; agriculture is the outstanding example.[31]

UNDEREMPLOYMENT

Unemployment involves obvious waste. Underemployment is usually less obvious, but the waste thus occasioned is nonetheless real, and the two forms of waste are closely related. Unemployment strikes the underemployed with a disproportionately heavy impact. The fact that many of them are already performing at less than their top skills or potential contribution makes them particularly vulnerable.

No one has estimated the total waste involved in all forms of underemployment, nor is anything more than a crude "horseback" guess possible. The most obvious and measurable form of underemployment is that of part-time workers who are available for full-time employment. If the designation is applied to those who are employed less than 35 hours per week, their numbers have averaged from less than five to almost nine million in the years since 1956.

Numbers of part-time workers can, however, be misleading if they are regarded as an accurate measure of underutilization, for a major portion of the total is composed of workers who are not available on a full-time basis. Thus, in September, 1962, for example, when 8,690,000 workers were employed on part-time (less than 35-hour)

---

[30]"Secondary Wage Earners and the Unemployed," *Associated Industries of Cleveland Newsletter*, No. 420 (August 1, 1962), pp. 1–2.

[31]See Marian Hayes, "A Century of Change: Negroes in the U.S. Economy, 1860–1960," *Monthly Labor Review*, Vol. 85, No. 12 (December, 1962), pp. 1359–65. See also the *Manpower Report of the President* (Washington, D.C.: United States Government Printing Office, March, 1964), pp. 95–121.

schedules, 6,445,000 reported noneconomic reasons for their reduced work-time. (They were, for example, housewives or workers who were ill or who were prevented from working by bad weather or holidays.)

For the same month, however, 2,245,000 worked short weeks for economic reasons. They are more likely to be adult males, predominantly in blue-collar occupations, young workers, and adult women in service occupations. Among those working part-time, but seeking full-time employment, nonwhites are disproportionately represented. For the 1956–1964 period, the Department of Labor summarizes the extent of part-time employment as shown in Figure 15-4.

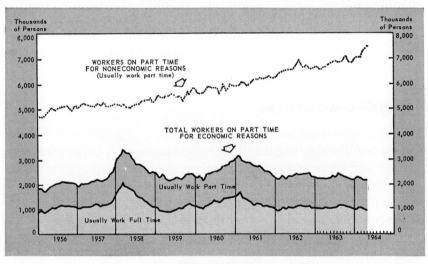

Figure 15-4
PART-TIME WORKERS — 1956–1964
(Seasonally Adjusted Data)

Source: *Monthly Report on the Labor Force*, May, 1964, p. 13.

Part-time employment has been growing at a faster rate than full-time employment, and this trend is expected to continue in the coming decade. In the decade of the 1950's, total employment increased 8 million, about 13 percent. During the same period, part-time employment increased by 3.4 million, up nearly 40 percent; full-time employment was up only 8 percent.[32]

---

[32]See Robert L. Stein and Jane L. Meredith, "Growth and Characteristics of the Part-Time Work Force," *Monthly Labor Review*, Vol. 83, No. 11 (November, 1960), pp. 1166–75. See also Thomas A. Mahoney, "Factors Determining the Labor Force Participation of Married Women," *Industrial and Labor Relations Review*, Vol. 14, No. 4 (July, 1961), pp. 563–77. See also Samuel Saber, "Work Experience of the Population in 1962," *B.L.S. Special Labor Force Report*, No. 38, January, 1964.

THEORIES OF EMPLOYMENT AND UNEMPLOYMENT

Preceding sections of this chapter have noted the immediate or proximate sources of unemployment and underemployment and the types of unemployment thus identified. As a basis for sound public policy, analysis should look further to discover why and how unemployment is generated. What are the principal forces behind time-to-time variations in demands for and supplies of labor and their balance or imbalance?

Such a question, it should be noted, focuses attention on the volume or amount of employment rather than its nature or content. Our theories of employment — tentative explanations of how employment is created and maintained — have long been focused on the balancing of numbers of workers and jobs. We have been much more concerned about unemployment than about underemployment — about our failure to find jobs for people than about the manner in which their talents, skills, and experience are utilized in the jobs they may secure or hold. We have emphasized quantitative rather than qualitative employment.

Theories of employment are plausible explanations of variations in the volume of total employment and unemployment. They represent tentative assumptions or opinions about which variables are believed to exert major influence in the relationships of the job-creating and job-maintaining process.

Theory Bridges

Such theories of employment deserve the careful scrutiny of all students of labor economics, for they exert a dominant, controlling influence in our selection of employment programs. For example, for those who hold that the major factor behind unemployment is excessive wage rates, proposed programs are designed to reduce and constrain wage rates. Similarly, a theory that recognizes labor immobility as an important factor in unemployment would presumably support a nationwide program of public aid in recruitment and job-finding. Such theories thus represent theory bridges between policy and programs. Citizens, businessmen, and public officials — all accepting the same general policy — may propose and support quite different programs because they hold different theories of employment.

Changing Employment Theory

Modern employment theory differs sharply from that of earlier periods; it suggests quite different factors as exerting major impact on levels of employment and unemployment. As a result, new programs for achieving social goals are suggested.

The fact that employment theory has changed and is changing is readily understandable; the employment process in today's industrialized economies shows little resemblance to the simpler process of historic societies. In a very simple economy both numbers and types of jobs may be largely dictated by one or more leaders. Robinson Crusoe, for example, made such decisions within the constraints imposed by his labor supply. Members of a tribe of American Indians might be assigned tasks and duties by the chief, with such counsel as he sought from senior braves. In medieval periods employment opportunities were narrowly defined by tradition and manorial authority. Many workers were "born to their jobs." They were given little choice, jobs were assigned, and hours of work defined by manorial lords.

Jobs in modern totalitarian nations may be created and assigned by similar authority and fiat. Political leaders can solve the problem of providing full employment by edict; they can and do frequently assert that there is no problem of unemployment.

In free societies employment theory changed as economies shifted from an agricultural to an industrial basis. Theory has continued to change as industrialized economies become more complex.

Current theory follows the pattern already established in this chapter in distinguishing two major sources of unemployment, i.e., (1) structural imbalance and friction in the labor marketing process and (2) inadequate demands or, in the aggregate, an inadequate total demand for labor.

Structural Factors

As noted, structural factors are complex. They may be regarded as involving all the labor market frictions described in the preceding sections of this chapter. In some popular usage the term is frequently given a more restrictive meaning; it refers to the more persistent structural dislocations, that is, failures to match worker knowledge of opportunities and worker qualifications to employer offers and job specifications.

In the words of the Council of Economic Advisers:

> Structural unemployment may be regarded as an extreme form of frictional unemployment. It occurs when inability or failure to make the necessary adjustments concentrates unemployment of long duration or displaced workers in particular areas and occupations, while elsewhere jobs are seeking workers of quite different qualifications.[33]

Major questions about structural unemployment concern (1) its proportion of total unemployment and (2) the trends, if any, in its level.

Guesses and opinions put the average of those whose unemployment is attributable to structural maladjustment at from one fifth to one fourth of the total unemployed in recent years. At the same time, the opinion has been frequently expressed that structural unemployment is increasing in the aggregate and as a proportion of total unemployment. Exponents of this view see a rising rate of technological change and argue that growing numbers of threshold workers add to the volume of job-finding and extend the time lost in matching people with suitable jobs.

Several studies that have sought to evaluate these contentions have failed to substantiate them. The 1962 *Economic Report of the President* reports that "careful analysis at the Council and elsewhere — notably in a recent report by the staff of the Joint Economic Committee of the Congress — lend no support to the view that frictional and structural unemployment is a rising proportion of the labor force."[34] Similarly, in the 1963 *Economic Report of the President*, the Council of Economic Advisers notes that "these problems of adaptation have not constituted a greater cause of unemployment in recent years than in earlier periods."[35]

Labor Pricing

An obviously potential barrier to balance in individual labor markets is the price of labor. If large numbers of workers make their services available only at prices above those which employers regard as reasonable, that condition can create unemployment. Labor's pricing can be uninformed or inaccurately informed. Workers can

---

[33] *Economic Report of the President*, January, 1962, p. 45.

[34] *Ibid.*, p. 48.

[35] *Economic Report of the President*, 1963, p. 25. Similarly, Gordon concludes that structural unemployment has shown no relative increase since the mid-1950's. See R. A. Gordon, "Has Structural Unemployment Worsened?" *Industrial Relations*, Vol. 3, No. 3 (May, 1964), pp. 53–77.

be as unaware of employer wage offers as of related job offers. Within a single market the total of employment can be adversely affected at a particular time by monopolistic labor pricing, in which organizations of workers set prices too high to clear the market.

Classical employment theory, developed during the period when the factory system was emerging, emphasized rates of wages as a principal influence in levels of employment. Earliest classical wage theory accepted short-term supplies of labor as fixed and assumed full employment. Wage rates became the resultant; they were determined in the short-run by the wages fund and in the long-run by costs of subsistence, i.e., of reproducing labor supplies (see Chapter 20).

Later, as unions of workers appeared in labor markets, they advanced a *lump of labor theory* which held that the total volume of employment was, in the short run, a constant determined in advance by employers on the basis of their estimates of labor requirements. Labor supplies were also fixed. The controllable variable was the amount employers would pay—the wage rate.

Classical and neoclassical theory emphasized employment in the individual market; general levels of employment were aggregates of these individual labor markets. In each such market, at any particular time, labor supplies consist of various quantities — usually regarded as numbers of workers — available for hire at a range of prices. They create the supply schedules already familiar to students of economics. At a comparatively low price smaller quantities of labor are available. At higher prices more labor is offered. Similarly, demands for labor in each market at a given time are schedules of total employer offers to purchase various quantities of labor at a range of possible prices.

Levels of employment in such a market are directly affected by the elasticities of demand and supply, that is, their responsiveness to price changes. Either or both may be inelastic in that changes in price have little effect on quantities offered or purchased. Either or both may be relatively elastic so that a change in the market price results in wide variations in the quantities made available for hire or for which offers are made.

In such a market the level of employment is established by the balancing of these supply and demand schedules, and the marginal productivity theory of wages is, at the same time, a theory of employment. For competitive firms the theory is essentially an employment theory, since wage rates are fixed or already determined for the individual employer and employment levels are the dependent variable.

The competitive employer's decision is "How many units of labor shall I hire?" at the given (by the market) wage rate. The marginal productivity theory is discussed in more detail in Chapter 21.

Unemployment, according to this traditional model, may arise from several conditions that create imbalance or frictions in these marketing processes. Market ignorance — meaning a lack of accurate market information — is a major factor. It may create a situation in which both job-seekers and jobs are available but potential employers and employees do not find each other. Ignorance may cause employees to place too high a price on their services or employers to bid too low. It may cause more workers to enter a particular market than will be hired at the price established by the market.

A second major source of possible imbalance in such a market is the immobility of the factors. All of the factors are characterized by some degree of immobility. This is apparent in the physical facilities, including buildings, machines, and equipment. Potential workers are subject to several important types of immobility.

A third source of imbalance in which supplies and demands fail to clear the market is the imposition of market controls by employers or employees. Employers may agree among themselves upon their maximum price, or a union of employees may set a minimum figure. Monopolistic and monopsonistic practices in labor markets may affect supplies, demands, price, and sales as they do in other markets.

Students of this process have long pointed to another immediate source of friction — the inflexibility or *stickiness* of prices, including those of labor. From the viewpoint of traditional employment theory, this characteristic of wages frequently appears as a major source of unemployment. In periods of falling commodity prices, wage rates frequently resist similar reduction and decline more slowly.

This traditional view has many current advocates who see high levels of aggregate unemployment as resulting principally from inter-ference with normal pressures toward equilibrium in individual mar-kets. They generally emphasize, as major sources of imbalance, sticky prices and private and public programs of intervention and control. Markets would clear, in this view, if left to themselves. Although what Brozen describes as "exogenous factors" — monetary policy, tech-nological and consumer changes, the tax structure, and the weather — may cause reduced employment, flexible prices can counteract if not overcome these adverse influences. As Brozen puts it, "We can plausibly argue that the unemployment we suffer, and have suffered, is a consequence of administered prices and wage rates, given the monetary circumstances described above."[36] Employment could be maintained at high levels if upward wage movements were restrained after employment has turned downward. On this point Brozen suggests escape clauses facilitating flexibility in long-term collective agreements and regulation of "labor monopoly" under antitrust rules. He concludes that "Perhaps the community and employees must be taught that an employer who cuts wage rates, or fails to give a wage increase in times of declining business, is performing a social service and maintaining employment by doing so."[37]

Price must be clearly recognized as a factor in the imbalance of labor demands and supplies and thus a source of structural — that is, marketing — frictions. Major differences in theory are concerned with its weight and influence. In the traditional view pricing of labor holds top priority as an explanation. In more recent theory it is regarded as important but not dominant.

National Income and Demands for Labor

Criticism of the traditional competitive theory gained wide acceptance after unemployment reached unprecedented high levels in the depression following 1929. The traditional prescription with its emphasis on individual labor markets appeared particularly inappropriate and ineffective when practically all markets were characterized by oversupplies of labor and vast unemployment. In its place, the national income theory was advanced as a more appropriate and promising approach. This more recent theory differs in that its viewpoint is aggregative.

Several circumstances explain the emergence and wide acceptance of this macro point of view. Perhaps the most immediate or proximate was the worldwide depression of the 1930's. That depression was characterized by drastic, almost catastrophic, unemployment in many nations. The efforts of political, business, and union leaders to restrict the impact of recession on employment and to hasten recovery were ineffective over a period of several years.

---

[36]Yale Brozen, "Means for Maintaining Economic Stability," *Journal of Farm Economics*, Vol. 40, No. 5 (December, 1958), pp. 1069–78, quote on page 1072.

[37]*Ibid.*, p. 1078.

The greatest individual contribution to the new theory was that of John Maynard Keynes, who published his *General Theory of Employment, Interest and Money*[38] in 1936. His statement challenged the usefulness of traditional economic analysis and of public policies and programs that accepted its assumed implications. It attracted immediate and widespread attention, for it was a direct attack on the most commonly and widely accepted point of view. In most western nations leaders had assumed that labor markets, like all other markets, were essentially self-correcting if given time. Many leaders and citizens assumed that price and wage readjustments from time to time were, as they always had appeared, inevitable.

Keynes and his followers argued that the classical, orthodox, and traditional theory was not a "general" or "universal" theory. Rather, it was a "special" theory which explained market behavior only under very distinctive and generally unrealistic conditions, particularly those of expanding economies. They advanced what they described as a "general" theory, which they insisted had much wider applicability. That theory, in essence, holds that aggregate employment is largely explainable as a function of national income. Levels of employment, in the aggregate, are strongly influenced by the level of and the distribution of a nation's income. Employment levels rise and fall as does this aggregate national income, being further influenced by the manner in which that income is distributed among various levels and types of income receivers. The volume of employment at any time is regarded as largely determined by the level of total spending, and spending is a function of income — more specifically, disposable income (DI). For the most part, as has been indicated, the demand for labor is derived. Consumers seek the products of work rather than the work in and of itself. Hence, as total disposable income rises, it puts pressures on both quantities of consumer goods and services and on the prices of these items. Pressures for goods create demands for added workers.

Disposable personal income. A crude indicator of levels of spending is provided by the *gross national product*. A much more useful measure is that of *disposable personal income*, which sets approximate limits on consumption and saving.[39] Even these limits are somewhat flexible,

---

[38]New York: Harcourt, Brace and Company.

[39]The process of refinement involves several steps: (1) *gross national product* is reduced by the amount of *capital consumption allowances* to measure *net national product;* (2) *public subsidies* (less the current surplus of government enterprises) are added to the *net national*

being modified by the actions of credit-creating facilities — banks, small loan agencies, consumer credit, and partial-payment plans.

At any one time the level of disposable income provides a significant clue to total employment. Effects of changes in the level of disposable income also vary, however, in terms of current levels of economic activity, together with consumer and manager forecasts of future activity. Thus, a rise in DI may force higher prices rather than a higher level of employment if employers are unwilling to undertake the risks of expanded production. If the economy has been operating at a level of low employment, however, an increase in spending is likely to create substantial improvement in employment without forcing price increases. The more intensive and efficient utilization of capital equipment in these circumstances can expand employment and output without raising prices. When, on the other hand, increased spending takes place in a period of high level economic activity, the major impact is likely to fall on prices rather than on employment.

Public spending. Analysis to this point leads to a frequent popular conclusion that the major clue to full employment is regulated spending, particularly enforced spending. If spending is the source of employment, in this view, then public policies should discourage saving and encourage spending at whatever levels are necessary for full employment. If private citizens do not, on their own initiative, spend enough, government can spend it for them. Government is a major consumer; the volume of its spending can be of such magnitude as to exert great influence both in the total of spending and on attitudes of private spenders and investors.

Government spending can intend to be either pump priming or compensatory. In *pump priming*, the major intent is short term — to provide a "shot in the arm" and thus to generate private confidence and stimulate private spending. In *compensatory public spending*, the program controls levels of government spending to balance changes in private spending. The influence of usual and emergency government spending are graphically suggested in Figure 15-5, where three levels of spending are shown.

---

product, and *indirect business taxes* and *business transfer payments* are subtracted to calculate *national income;* (3) to discover *total personal income, national income* is reduced by the amounts of *corporate property and inventory valuation adjustments* and *contributions for social insurance* and is increased by the total of *government transfer payments to persons,* the *net interest paid by government,* and *business transfer payments;* and (4) *disposable income* is *personal income* less *personal taxes.* For detailed data of these adjustments, see *Economic Report of the President,* 1964, pp. 222, 223, and 226.

Opponents of such government intervention refer sarcastically to "spending ourselves into prosperity" and advocate balancing the government budget as a surer method of improving business confidence and creating adequate employment. Supporters, on the contrary, argue that if government maintains a consistent policy of compensatory spending, the knowledge of this intention will, on its own, create confidence and encourage equilibrium at a high level.

It is clear that although government is a major consumer and investor in our

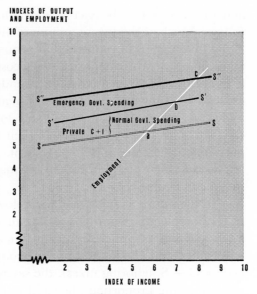

Figure 15-5
EMERGENCY PUBLIC SPENDING AND EMPLOYMENT

economy, the influence of government expenditures is offset in part by the fact that private income has been reduced by taxation to provide government income. Some of what government buys or invests would have been spent by private consumers, using the same income. On the other hand, government can buy or invest when private consumers will not. The impact of public spending depends on its timing and a variety of concurrent conditions. Among the most important are:

1. Consumer stocks of durable goods. If they are low, pressures for expansion and private activity are more easily generated.
2. Public confidence in the government's competence and intentions. If the public assumes that bureaucrats know enough about the controls to manage them effectively, these conclusions give greater influence to the public spending policy.
3. The method of financing such spending is an important conditioner. If public spending is to be balanced by current taxes, its influence is thereby reduced. If government proposes to spend first and tax later, regaining its balance by taxes based on higher levels of activity and employment, the influence of compensatory spending is likely to be increased.

Some popular confusion as to what and how much government spending can do is created by a strong trend toward *social investment* and the prospect of heavier proportions of social investment in the future. Much of the future growth of all economies will involve ever-larger investments in ventures that cannot or are unlikely to be undertaken directly by private firms. Very costly interplanetary exploration is an illustration. Expensive military and defense programs are already evident. Meanwhile, heavy investments have become essential for highways, for sanitary systems, and for subsidized research in the physical and social sciences and their applications in engineering, medicine, education, and management. Meanwhile, also, our society has become increasingly aware of the major significance of investment in education and training.

In the future, it appears, full employment is likely to be supported in considerable measure by growing increments of social investment. Such a forecast implies significant changes, not only in the role of government but also in the entire economy. In the equation of income ($DI = C + S$, ignoring taxes), the savings proportion must probably grow, and the proportion allocated to consumption must reflect this shift. While this change may be small in the aggregate, it may involve important changes in the role of workers. If social investment is to expand, workers' incomes may become a more important source of savings than in the past. Government may, for example, sell national *growth bonds* or interplanetary exploration bonds to sophisticated workers whose saving is increased in part by their understanding that full employment requires such investment or taxation to permit public, i.e., government, investment.

Spokesmen for unions have frequently translated the emphasis on spending into a *purchasing power theory* of prosperity. The key to high level employment, in this view, is purchasing power in the hands of consumers. On this basis the union view supports government spending when unemployment rises, even if that means an unbalanced government budget. Further government action may well take the form of borrowing rather than taxing, since this does not reduce purchasing power in the hands of consumers. Government action may also reduce taxes as a step in the same direction, but such tax reductions should be directed mainly at consumer incomes so that more purchasing can create more jobs. [40]

---

[40]For a detailed explanation of this position, see "What Everyone Should Know About Government Spending and Full Employment," *Publication No. 53* (Washington: Industrial Union Department, AFL-CIO, 1963). For further discussion of the purchasing power theory of wages, see Chapter 22, pp. 624–25.

Some articulate spokesmen for various groups conclude that there is no necessity for carrying this analysis any further. The clue to perpetual full employment is adequate spending; if individuals do not spend enough, let government supplement their spending. They advocate public policy that will insure spending for persistent prosperity and employment. It should, however, be clear that such an interpretation is inadequate. It is evident that:

1. Public spending must be carefully monitored or it will be ineffective in stimulating private spending and may spur inflation.
2. The volume of significant spending is that of total spending in the economy.

The 64-dollar question, therefore, concerns the factors other than government spending that influence private spending and, in turn, levels of employment.

Consumption and saving. Spending is, in itself, a complex process involving both consumption and investment. Although both C and I can and do create demands for labor, their impact is distinctive. Consumption creates short-term demands; investment operates through a more elaborate process involving saving and subsequent decisions to spend. Consequently, the impact of consumption and investment are not the same; the pressures toward full employment they generate are different. So also are their consequences in terms of economic growth.

Modern employment theory cannot, therefore, neglect the question: What factors explain the distribution of disposable income between consumption and investment? One rather evident answer points to the level of disposable income. It is clear that income receivers make different dispositions of their incomes at different levels. Such variations reflect what are described as the *average propensity to consume* (APC) and the *average propensity to save* (APS). Both are conveniently stated as proportions or percentages of DI. As DI = S + C, then:

$$APC + APS = 1$$
$$APC = 1 - APS$$
$$APS = 1 - APC$$

These average propensities are useful in indicating what happens to totals of savings and consumption at various levels of income.

As a guide to public policy and programs designed to maintain full employment, however, we also need a clue to the probable effect of changes in DI on these average propensities. We need to consider *marginal propensities*. The question becomes: What happens to MPC (marginal propensity to consume) and to MPS (marginal propensity to save) as NI grows or declines?

These marginal propensities are of great significance in employment theory.[41] The answer to questions about changes in MPC and MPS occasioned by variations in DI is by no means certain. Perhaps the most common opinion holds that as income increases, MPS also grows and MPC declines. However, some opinion regards the marginal propensities as relatively unchanging. These differences in theory result from analysis of the circumstances that appear to influence these propensities.

The most important of these conditioning forces or factors — influential in determining propensities to consume and to save — may be described as follows:

1. When consumer debt is relatively high, the propensity to save is likely to be high and the propensity to consume consequently reduced.
2. When liquid assets in the hands of consumers are high, this condition tends to increase propensities to consume.
3. Propensities to consume are likely to be lower when consumers have relatively large stocks of consumers' durable goods.
4. Forecasts of changes in consumer prices influence propensities to consume and to save. If prices are expected to fall in the immediate future, propensities to consume are thereby reduced. Similarly, predictions of rising prices may increase propensities to consume.

Multiplier and accelerator. Consideration of marginal propensities must also note the highly significant influence of related *multiplier and accelerator effects* on pressures toward equilibrium. In terms of jobs, a billion dollar increase in disposable income may not simply generate a billion dollars in additional wages. Only a part (although a major portion) of the increase becomes available for wages. But this increase is multiplied as it circulates through the economic system.

---

[41]MPC is a ratio of vertical to horizontal change and thus a measure of slope in the consumption schedule. In the linear equation $Y_c = a_c + b_cX$ (where $X = DI$), MPC is the b_c or the increase in height for each added increment of disposable income. The a_c is the level of the schedule at $X = O$. Similarly, MPS is the ratio of vertical to horizontal change in the savings schedule; $Y_s = a_s + b_sX$ (where X is DI).

The *multiplier* is the reciprocal of the marginal propensity to save.[42] In effect, the multiplier exerts a compounded pressure. Thus, if investment is increased by one billion dollars and MPS = 0.25, the multiplier will tend to generate savings to match a four billion dollar expansion. This illustration should not be interpreted as suggesting that the multiplier is effective only on changes in saving nor that the multiplier operates only in terms of expansion. Programs may propose increases in other components of income, and the multiplier may reduce as well as magnify.

The significance of both consumption and saving for employment is further emphasized because of the *accelerator effect*, which notes that increased consumption tends to induce increased investment, or more exactly, that new investment is proportional to consumption. Attention is directed to changes in investment rather than the total. The accelerator exerts little influence in a period of serious depression; it aggravates pressures on prices in periods of high employment. The accelerator effect is evident in added or "induced" investment in capital goods and inventories.

Thus, increased spending does not simply create employment to the extent that it provides jobs directly. Its influence is magnified by the multiplier and supplemented by the accelerator. These are, however, roundabout results. They move toward a new and higher level of employment by overlapping steps. They involve delayed as well as immediate action. No small part of this cumulation of impacts comes through the investment process, and the amount of the total impact is directly conditioned by changing propensities to consume and to save.

Investment and employment. Employment is generated by spending. Increased consumption involves direct spending and hence an obvious immediate fillip to employment. Savings follow a less direct route. Some savings may not be immediately invested, and some funds for investment may be created by banking or other credit institutions. That decisions to save and decisions to invest may not be made by the same individuals nor for the same reasons is most important.

Savings result from decisions, for various reasons, to defer consumption. Some saving is apparently a matter of tradition, habit, and perhaps morality. Thrift, which includes saving, is a prominent plank in the platform of the *protestant ethic*. Some savers seek to

---

[42]Multiplier $= \dfrac{1}{\text{MPS}}$

create a "nest egg" to buy a home or to purchase other property when "the price is right." For many, saving is for protection in old age or illness or to ensure children's education. To only a limited extent is saving sensitive to and determined by current levels of interest rates, as suggested by classical economic theory.

Investment, on the other hand, is for profit and is principally influenced by opportunities for profit and interest.

Levels of both savings and investment are in part a function of disposable income, but this relationship is more direct with respect to savings than with respect to investment. As a result, variations in levels of disposable income, as modified by propensities to consume and to save, are correlated with levels of employment; but their impact is further influenced by the rapidity with which savings are invested. Investment is subject to multiplier and accelerator effects; uninvested savings are not.

Higher levels of income permit greater saving; lower levels may cause *dissaving*, in which consumption exceeds disposable income, as indicated in Figure 15-6. Thus, in 1932 personal consumption expenditures exceeded disposable personal income by 0.6 billion dollars. In 1933 this excess was also 0.6 billion. In 1963, in contrast, 29.4 billions — 7.3 percent of disposable personal income — were saved.[43]

Savings decisions and investment decisions, as noted, are distinctive. Investors are concerned about interest rates and possibilities of appreciation and gain. The rate of interest exerts an obvious influence, as does the comparative advantage of reinvestment and the promise of continuing or increasing returns from investment. Investors also look to the state of the arts and prospective inventions

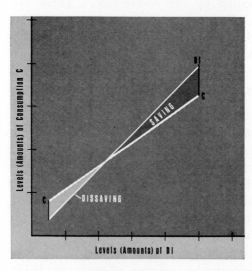

Figure 15-6

VARIATIONS IN SAVING BY CHANGING LEVELS OF DISPOSABLE INCOME

[43]See *Economic Report of the President*, 1963, Table C-15, p. 190.

and technological changes. They see a variety of conditions affecting the climate for investment, including probable taxes, prospective costs of doing business, estimates of future consumption, and, perhaps most important, the vague condition generally described as "business confidence" — a composite of expectations of economic expansion or contraction, fears of or hopes for government intervention, predictions about international relations, and many others. The popular barometer of the complex of business confidence is the stock market.

Planned investment may, at any particular time, be less or greater than planned savings. When PI exceeds S, pressure toward a higher level of economic activity is created. Similarly, when S exceeds PI, pressure is thereby created for a lower than current level.

Levels of saving and investment may be the most critical factors affecting levels of economic activity and employment. If savings and investment plans are balanced, no pressures for change are thereby created. If, however, planned savings amount to 20 billion dollars in a total income of 100 billion while planned investment is at a 30 billion dollar level, the 10 billion dollar excess tends to force business activity to higher levels, with resulting pressures on employment and the price level. A market will be created for 110 billion dollars worth of product; the flow of income will generate added consumption and saving. As noted, the marginal propensity to save will probably rise as a result of the increase in income. Economic expansion will continue toward a new balance of saving and investment.

Potential and actual output. Modern employment theory directs major attention to conditions affecting aggregate demands for labor in the national economy. In tracing the threads of relationships, it identifies levels of national income as the major factor in such demands. National income and prospective changes in it influence consumption, savings, and investment, which, in turn, create demands for labor. This relationship is by no means simple; it is modified by the interrelationships of consumption and investment and by such external considerations as public confidence and changing international relationships. Modern theory is by no means a simple spending theory.

Rather, the crux of full employment can be related to the balance of actual and potential gross national product as the source of national income and disposable personal income. The Council of Economic Advisers, the most articulate spokesman for this view, emphasizes the

GNP gap and pictures the relationship as shown in Figure 15-7. The Council, noting that no "precise and invarying connection exists between higher output and reduced unemployment," finds that:

> . . . postwar experience indicates that a reduction of 1 percentage point in the global unemployment rate at any moment of time is associated, on the average, with an increase in real GNP of slightly more than 3 percent.[44]

The Council further notes that each recent expansion or recovery period has failed to bring actual GNP up to potential, with resultant blunting of incentives for investment and innovations. Council estimates of desirable job-creation in 1963, not including additions necessitated by technological change, are summarized as follows:[45]

	Millions of Jobs
To reduce unemployment of present labor force from 5.6 percent to 4 percent	1.1
To provide for added workers drawn back into the labor force	.8
To employ normal annual increase	1.2
Total	3.1

The Council calculates that to provide these added jobs in one year would require "an 8 to 9 percent increase in GNP at constant prices."[46] As a practical objective, the Council concludes that an interim annual goal of 4 percent or more throughout the decade is essential, as compared with a potential of 3½ percent and an actual growth of 2.7 percent in the 1955–62 period. For the future the clue to economic stability and satisfactory employment is a balance in growing demands and growing capacity. Governmental programs to expand demand must be provided whenever the rate of growth of demand is less than that of capacity.[47]

The major complication in such estimates and programs is their effect on price levels. CEA calculations refer to stable prices and constant dollars. Experience in European nations and in Japan suggests, however, that whenever comparable rates of unemployment have fallen below 4 percent, the cost of living has risen. That hazard not only complicates but could defeat the movement toward full employment.

---

[44]*Economic Report of the President*, 1963, pp. 26–28.
[45]*Ibid.*, pp. 38–39.
[46]*Ibid.*, p. 41.
[47]See "Kennedy's Formula for Full Employment," *Business Week*, January 26, 1963, pp. 110–13.

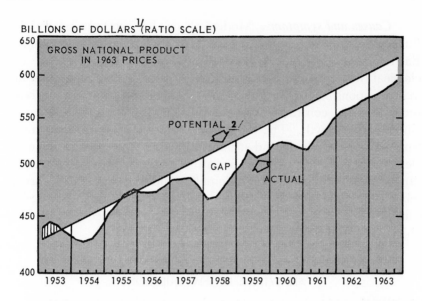

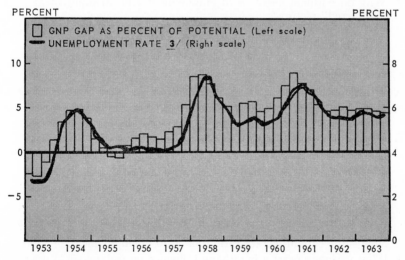

[1]Seasonally adjusted annual rates.
[2]3½% trend line through middle of 1955.
[3]Unemployment as percent of civilian labor force; seasonally adjusted.

Figure 15-7

GROSS NATIONAL PRODUCT, ACTUAL AND POTENTIAL, AND UNEMPLOYMENT RATE

Source: *Economic Report of the President,* 1964, p. 38.

Causes and symptoms. Modern theory has exerted a powerful influence on public programs designed to encourage full employment. Earlier analysis — especially the individual-market-oriented, neoclassical theory — had suggested that the private firm and union held major responsibilities for balancing supplies and demands. Modern theory, on the contrary, places the principal emphasis on economic climate and growth. The trend of business activity, as distinguished from seasonal, cyclical, and structural factors, becomes the subject of elementary concern. This aggregative view places principal responsibility on government and public policy and programs only indirectly related to employment. Today's public policy and programs deserve careful attention and evaluation in terms of current theory. That is the objective of the following chapter, Chapter 16.

ANALYTICAL REVIEW QUESTIONS

1. Why do national averages of employment and unemployment present a "blurred" picture?
2. Try to express the major types of unemployment in the form of a diagram, indicating variables as factors in demands and supplies.
3. Why can structural unemployment also be described as personal?
4. Why does employment peak in July?
5. What are the principal means of controlling seasonal unemployment?
6. How was unemployment related to the movements led by Hitler and Mussolini?
7. When is the next recession in employment to be expected? Explain.
8. Do you conclude that we may or may not have a repetition of the unemployment of the 1930's? Why?
9. In what way is unemployment related to economic growth?
10. Why have numbers of new jobs not equalled numbers of new threshold workers since 1957?
11. Is technological change different from automation and, if so, how?
12. How is the capital-worker ratio related to unemployment?
13. What variables exert a modifying influence on technological unemployment?
14. How does technological change affect the "boundaries" of firms?
15. What steps would you propose to reduce worker resistance to change?
16. What are job security rules?
17. Show that structural unemployment is related to worker mobility.
18. Is transitional unemployment unavoidable, even in totalitarian nations?
19. What is meant by prosperity unemployment?
20. Identify the ten distressed areas nearest to you.
21. Show that spot unemployment may be chronic or acute.

22. Who are the chronic unemployables and what other terms are used to describe them?
23. Show that the impact of unemployment varies by types of workers.
24. Why does unemployment strike hard at part-time workers?
25. Do you conclude that underemployment is growing or declining?
26. Distinguish the classical analysis of unemployment from that of the national income approach.
27. In the classical view what were major variables affecting employment and unemployment?
28. How does the national income theory identify major variables?
29. How is disposable income related to unemployment?
30. What is your position on pump priming and compensatory spending as means of reducing unemployment?
31. Why is social investment likely to grow in the future?
32. What is the rationale of the purchasing power theory of prosperity?
33. Why do C and S and MPC and MPS vary for income receivers in different income brackets?
34. What conditioning factors are most important in influencing levels of investment?
35. How do the multiplier and accelerator get into the act?
36. What conditions occasion dissaving?
37. How does the "GNP gap" influence employment and unemployment.

Case 15-1

UNION DEMANDS AND EMPLOYMENT

In 1964 federal tax rates on both corporate and individual incomes were reduced. The change increased disposable income for most citizens. Meanwhile, unemployment at the beginning of the year averaged more than 5 percent.

In negotiations early in the year, several unions proposed that premium rates of pay for overtime be changed from time and a half to double time. They argued that the higher rates would tend to spread employment, while any added costs would be counterbalanced by increased sales and reduced taxes on corporate profits.

At the same time, the usual union demand for wage adjustments proposed an increase of at least 3 percent. On this point the union argument held that such an increase would be noninflationary and was necessary to maintain consumer demand for the constantly growing total output of the economy.

• How would you, if you were an employer, react to these demands?

• Prepare a memorandum summarizing your conclusions about the implications of these demands for employment and unemployment.

Case 15-2

SEASONAL LABOR TURNOVER

You work for a firm that has great seasonal fluctuations in output. Substantial layoffs and recalls of employees are almost a weekly occurrence. The boss reprimands the sales manager because orders come in bunches and then "peter out." Inventories pile up and the production manager never seems to know when to increase production or when to stop. Overtime and labor turnover costs are excessive. The comptroller is always complaining about too little working capital. The advertising man says he does not get a decent budget. The foremen complain about the green help they get. Unemployment insurance taxes are at the maximum rate.

• What would you do to straighten out the situation?

Case 15-3

MACHINES AND JOB SECURITY

You are the business agent of Local 605. One firm with which you bargain proposes to install new machines that will cut labor requirements for your union members by 20 percent. They propose to cut the price of the product 10 percent, and you suspect that this will increase demand for the product by at least 400 percent. Several key members of the union policy committee suggest resisting introduction of the new machinery by having the members restrict output on the new machines.

• What advice would you give these committee members? What plan of action would you lay out for your union, and how would you attempt to "sell" it to the members? What arguments would you use?

Case 15-4

PROGRAM FOR SPOT UNEMPLOYMENT

Assume that your community has a serious chronic spot unemployment problem. The principal industry, aside from retail stores and services, has long been the railroad shops. Technological change in railroading has forced a decision to shut them down. Several hundred workers will be released within the next few months.

You are the assistant office manager for a small insurance company that has grown up in this community. You have been active in the Junior Chamber of Commerce which is much concerned about the impending "disaster." You have been appointed chairman of a committee to work on the problem. Committee members are not agreed about what should be done. Some suggest raising local capital and offering to build a plant for some manufacturer who is willing to move to your community. Others want the city and the county to entice a new factory into the city by promising tax-free operations for ten years. Perhaps the largest group wants you to go to Washington to seek aid from the federal government.

• Prepare a statement of your own suggestions that you can present at the next meeting of your committee. Can you get help under the A.R.A.?

FULL EMPLOYMENT POLICY AND PROGRAMS

Programs designed to achieve or move toward the goal of full employment involve attacks on all the types of unemployment described in preceding chapters. Programs are presumably a product of policies and theories; they seek to implement policies by means or action which appears appropriate in terms of generally accepted theories. Several programs, for example, involve measures designed to stimulate economic growth on the theory that an inadequate rate of growth results in the creation of too few jobs.

Other programs are designed to reduce structural unemployment by improving the quality of labor supplies and facilitating the labor-marketing process. Some programs are multipurpose; they are intended as double- or triple-threat attacks on demands, marketing, and the qualifications of job-seekers. Area redevelopment is an example. In addition, several programs seek to reduce the hardship and distress occasioned by unemployment at the same time that they facilitate reemployment.

It is frequently said that some programs propose to treat the symptoms rather than the basic maladjustment. A short answer to this argument would note that unemployment exerts a cumulative impact; it feeds on itself. Thus, symptoms can become causes. Unemployment of every type reduces demands and creates concern about the health of the economy.

Programs involve all levels of government and public agencies as well as private firms and their managements and unions. Countries and cities have, at times, provided "made-work" programs. States have a major share of responsibility for the public employment offices and the administration of unemployment insurance. Individual firms and unions have developed supplementary unemployment benefits, dismissal pay plans, guaranteed annual wages, automation funds, and other programs designed to stabilize employment or earnings.

Major responsibility for leadership in public programs, since 1946, has been assigned to the federal government. This development began when the federal government was given emergency responsibilities during the Great Depression of the 1930's, in which it supplied matching funds for public construction by state and local agencies (Public Works Administration, PWA) and used federal resources to offer employment in numerous projects, including those in education and the arts (Works Progress Administration, WPA).

THE EMPLOYMENT ACT OF 1946

The role of the federal government was formally defined as the long-term development and maintainance of employment opportunities by the Employment Act of 1946. That legislation, frequently described as the "full employment act," charges the federal government with responsibility for maintaining economic health. *Economic health* is in effect defined as a condition that assures adequate employment opportunities. The intent of the act is thus described:

> Sec. 2. The Congress declares that it is the continuing policy and responsibility of the Federal Government to use all practicable means consistent with its needs and obligations and other essential considerations of national policy, with the assistance and cooperation of industry, agriculture, labor, and State and local governments, to coordinate and utilize all its plans, functions, and resources for the purpose of creating and maintaining, in a manner calculated to foster and promote free competitive enterprise and the general welfare, conditions under which there will be afforded useful employment opportunities, including self-employment, for those able, willing, and seeking to work, and to promote maximum employment, production, and purchasing power.

The background of this legislative statement was a growing popular recognition that both individual and social welfare requires adequate employment opportunities for all who want to work. The widely accepted protestant ethic teaches the virtues of work and thrift; its dicta are meaningless without job opportunities. Public policies expressed the social intention to give everyone who wants to work a chance to work. The Employment Act of 1946 goes a step further; it declares our intention to use the resources of the federal government to create and maintain such opportunities. The act is a statement of general, broad intent. In preliminary versions of the bill (called the Full Employment Act of 1945) it was stated that "All Americans able to work and desiring to work are entitled to an opportunity for useful, remunerative, regular and full-time employment." The preliminary versions outlined specific means whereby the government would act to stimulate employment through federal investments and expenditures and through other public programs. Both the specific definition of the purpose (jobs for all) and the specific means the federal government should use to attain the purpose contained in the original proposals were deleted and do not appear in the 1946 act.

The effect of the 1946 act has been to focus attention of top government officials, the Congress, and the public upon the economic health of the nation. It provides for a periodic economic examination for the nation similar to periodic physical examinations for individuals. Although the act does not provide specific programs, the process of pointing up the problems has resulted in numerous suggestions for their solution.

The act is implemented in part by a public forecasting service to improve the knowledge and predictions of both employers and employees. The Federal Council of Economic Advisers prepares an *Annual Economic Review* for the President, who transmits his *Economic Report* to Congress. Somewhat later each year, the Senate and the House Joint Committee on the Economic Report of the President submits its evaluation of the President's report. Each month the Joint Committee releases *Economic Indicators*, with current data on national production, income, employment, earnings, business activity, prices, currency and credit, and finance. The Federal Reserve Board conducts an annual survey of consumer finances and releases forecasts of capital investment. In addition, local employment offices release monthly reports of supplies of and demands for labor in their individual localities. The Federal Bureau of Employment Security compiles, classifies, and publicizes these local reports.

A variety of federal, state, local, and private or collectively bar-gained programs have been developed to improve and maintain employment opportunities. The federal government has undertaken the most inclusive programs, including those designed to minimize cyclical fluctuations and stimulate economic growth. Through the Bureau of Employment Security in the Department of Labor, it coordinates the nationwide system of public employment offices or exchanges to which workers may apply for help in finding jobs and receiving unemployment benefits. Other programs may include *made-work*, in which public funds are used to create such jobs as leaf-raking or tree-trimming or gardening. Programs may involve vast public works projects — highways, public buildings, sanitary sewer systems, flood control, and many others. Nationwide programs also include the subsidization of worker retraining and the advancement of capital for redevelopment in distressed areas and those of chronic or persistent unemployment. Programs may erect tariff barriers to protect jobs from the competition of foreign products. They may offer public guarantees of loans for construction or grant tax advantages for exploration (as in petroleum and mining industries). Other programs have been proposed: comprehensive tax reforms, further reductions in hours of work, and many others.

Federal government leadership is supplemented, as noted, by state and local public programs and by a variety of private and collectively-bargained arrangements. For convenience, attention in this chapter turns first to federal programs designed to increase and maintain demands for labor. Thereafter, sections of the chapter note programs intended to improve labor supplies and to facilitate the labor marketing process. A final section notes some major private and union-employer negotiated programs.

MAINTAINING DEMANDS FOR GROWING SUPPLIES

To increase demands, the obvious prescription is to speed the pace of job-creation. Some individuals and groups regard this goal as dubious; they propose to cut the cloth of existing employment to fit numbers of job applicants, to spread existing demands among existing supplies. They advocate *work-spreading*, with *full-crew rules* that stabilize *technical coefficients;* for example, two men for each locomotive or a crew of three pilots and an engineer for each airliner.

To increase demands, the usual prescription involves measures designed to speed the rate of economic growth. New jobs are to be created by continuing expansion. Some programs contemplate a "perpetual recovery," in which new jobs balance the net growth in labor force plus the displacements occasioned by structural changes.

Advocates of this type of program base their diagnosis and therapy on what has been described, in Chapter 15, as the national income theory of employment. They may and generally do recognize the importance of marketing and structural maladjustments, and they favor supplementary programs to facilitate more rapid readjustments. They see the basic problem, however, as explained by the shortage of new job opportunities.

President Kennedy attracted wide attention to the growth problem by his 1961 declaration that an annual growth rate of 4.5 percent is well within our national capability. Attention was also attracted to the possibility and desirability of a speeded growth rate by the action of the 20 member nations in the Organization for Economic Cooperation and Development in setting 4.1 percent per year and 50 percent for the 1960–1970 decade as a combined target rate of growth.

As noted in the preceding chapter, the major factors in growth are levels of national income, saving, and investment — all in turn are subject to the persistent influence of the business climate and public confidence. Current public programs are designed to influence these variables. The Kennedy administration emphasized this approach. Federal government efforts to speed the rate of growth have been the highlighted features of annual *Economic Reports* since 1963.

Federal Program for Growth

The general aim of the federal government program has been to minimize the gap between potential GNP and actual GNP and thus to maintain a relatively high level of growth in income. The President, in his 1963 *Economic Report*, described the program and its rationale as follows:

> An economy that fails to use its productive potential fully feels no need to increase it rapidly. The incentive to invest is bent beneath the weight of excess capacity. Lack of employment opportunities slows the growth of the labor force. Defensive restrictive practices — from featherbedding to market sharing — flourish when limited markets, jobs, and incentives shrink the scope for effort and ingenuity. But when the economy breaks out of the lethargy of the past 5 or 6 years, the end to economic slack will by itself mean faster growth. Full employment will relax the grip of

restrictive practices and open the gates wider to innovation and change.[1]

The Council of Economic Advisers, in the same report, describes what it views as the "determinants of growth" and the essentials in a program for growth as follows:

> Starting from our present position of underutilization, it has been estimated that we can achieve an increase of about six-tenths of a percentage point in our average annual growth rate for the 1960's by reducing our unemployment rate to 4 percent with the concomitant increase in utilization of capital facilities. This rise in the growth rate comes as a bonus to successful employment policy. Once underutilization of productive capacity has been eliminated, our rate of growth will depend upon the pace at which productive capacity itself expands. Growth of productive capacity in turn is the sum of (a) the percentage rate of growth of the labor force adjusted for changes in the average workweek, and (b) the percentage rate of increase in productivity per man-hour. Public policy can accelerate growth of productivity mainly by stepping up the pace of our efforts to:
>
> — improve the education, health, occupational skills, motivations, and attitudes of the labor force;
> — build up the stock of private producers' plant and equipment, and improve its composition by age, type, and location;
> — increase the stock of public physical capital, including roads, water systems, school buildings, and hospitals;
> — improve the terms on which the economy has access to natural resources, whether through domestic production or imports;
> — advance the level of technology, covering the range from managerial and organizational competence to scientific and engineering understanding;
> — raise the efficiency with which capital, resources, technology, and labor are used;
> — improve communications systems so as to accelerate the dissemination of information on technological, commercial, and employment opportunities.[2]

It is notable that the first item in the list of steps to be taken involves improvement in the qualifications and motivation of the labor force. Programs for that purpose are noted in a subsequent section of this chapter. It is also notable that the Cabinet Committee on Economic Growth, appointed in 1962, emphasized full employment as a

---

[1]*Economic Report of the President*, 1963, p. xxiv. See also Sar A. Levitan, *Federal Manpower Policies and Programs to Combat Unemployment* (Kalamazoo, Michigan: The W. E. Upjohn Institute for Employment Research, February, 1964).

[2]*Ibid.*, pp. 60–61.

prerequisite to such growth. Rapid growth and full employment are thus interrelated in current goals and policies.

The general policy of balancing real and potential GNP must be achieved primarily through subordinate financial policies, especially those in the areas of taxation, monetary policy, and debt management. In each area, policy must seek to facilitate more rapid growth with, however, persistent attention to the balance of international payments and price stability.

Hazard of Inflation

All programs for more rapid expansion thus face delicate problems; they must avoid sudden upsurges, followed by recessions. When expansion assumes the aspects of a "boom," it generates price increases and thus creates the setting for a subsequent "bust." Programs must hold the line against inflation. The optimum rate of new-job creation must be one that represents a pace that can be sustained without rapid advances in prices. That may mean something less than the ideal of full employment. The Council of Economic Advisers, in 1962, concluded that the *optimum rate of unemployment* for the immediate future was about 4 percent, which would permit an optimum annual growth rate of 4 to $4\frac{1}{2}$ percent.[3] In effect, the average 4 percent level of unemployment is thus defined as the immediate "full employment" goal.

To avoid inflation, advocates of the growth program conclude, requires that wage increases be held within the range of average productivity gains, $2\frac{1}{2}$–3 percent. Only by such constraint can the upward pressure on prices be kept in check. At the same time, this objective also requires a careful balance in the extension of credit since lending institutions could upset the applecart if their actions facilitated a rise in prices.

Critical Views

The position thus described — with balance in rising GNP, national income, wages, and prices — represents the public approach and view, as currently expressed by economic advisers at the federal level. Employer, union, and other groups question its logic and soundness. Spokesmen for the Chamber of Commerce of the United States question the logic of economic security through growth. Since rapid growth features rapid technological change, slower growth can reduce

---

[3]*Economic Report of the President*, 1962, p. 9.

numbers of displacements. Indeed, "For maximum security we must turn to a static economy and a status society."[4]

The Chamber suggests that union and government policies may be more important and neglected sources than limited growth and points to three types of recent unemployment: (1) legislated unemployment (labor laws), (2) administrative unemployment (rulings of administrative agencies), and (3) union-generated unemployment (principally pressures for wage increases). E. P. Schmidt, the Chamber's spokesman, concludes: "Government deeds and misdeeds are at the heart of all three types of needless hardship."[5]

Meanwhile, union spokesmen see the clue to more jobs in balanced spending rather than growth. They argue that if spending in the private sector is not sufficient, the federal government should "go against the tide" and increase spending. Unbalanced budgets should not be avoided when unemployment is high; they are not inflationary in a time when we have idle resources.[6]

The union position thus goes part of the way in accepting the national income theory. But it equates wages and income and ignores the hazard of rising price levels as well as the role of saving and investment. It assumes propensities that guarantee appropriate consumer spending, saving, and investment. It overlooks the facts of life with respect to inflation and unemployment — for example, the 20 percent rise in consumers' prices in the 1950's when unemployment averaged about 5 percent.

In essence, the most articulate critics of the growth rate approach object to the implied controls or regulations and their impact on such special groups as investors and union members. In addition, some economic analysis raises pertinent questions about assumed relationships. Many objections see the price of growth — in terms of regulation — as too high.

To walk the tightrope between desirable expansion and undesirable inflation must almost certainly necessitate increasing government control. Employers, financiers, and citizens must be required to pattern plans and actions to be consistent with the total program. Opportunities for individuals and groups to profit from nonconformance

---

[4]"The Promise of Economic Growth," *Report of the Committee on Economic Policy, 1959,* p. 20.

[5]See *Unemployment — Some Neglected Causes* (Washington, D.C.: Chamber of Commerce of the United States, 1962), p. 17.

[6]See *What Everyone Should Know About Government Spending and Full Employment,* Industrial Union Department, AFL-CIO, 815 16th Street, N.W., Washington 6, D.C.

are inevitably a hazard to such a delicate balance as must be maintained.

Individual and group objections are understandable. Some union spokesmen, for example, have criticized the government formula for wage gains — the "guideposts" for noninflationary wages. This formula was described in 1962 as follows:

> The general guide for noninflationary wage behavior is that the rate of increase in wage rates (including fringe benefits) in each industry be equal to the trend rate of overall productivity increase.[7]

Similarly, industrialists have questioned the establishment of a public policy guide for prices — price reduction if the industry's rate of productivity increase exceeds the overall rate and price increase if the opposite is true.

The Chamber of Commerce has explained its view of the growth approach. Recognizing that unemployment "is a waste of resources," it is nevertheless true that in some cases putting the unemployed to work costs more than it saves. It requires the diversion of other resources that are in short supply to less than their most effective use. As the Chamber puts it:

> It is possible, in other words, that maximizing production is not the same as maximizing employment. If we must choose between the two, it seems logical to choose to maximize production. The problem, of course, lies in devising acceptable means to avoid hardship for those who, through no fault of their own, are unemployed.[8]

Public regulation, in the opinion of some economists, may in itself handicap growth more than it helps. Exponents of this view suggest that unrestricted competition is a better guide to the efficient allocation and utilization of resources than public leadership and constraint. Competitive market forces have been effective in the past; why is there need for a shift in policy now?[9] In this view, the way to reduce discrimination against certain groups is "to offer a class of workers at bargain rates." Similarly, the way to insure training or retraining is to remove minimum wage requirements and allow employment of trainees at reduced rates. Such a practice is presently permitted in the needle trades.

---

[7]*Economic Report of the President*, 1962, p. 189.

[8]*Washington Report*, Vol. 2, No. 45 (November 1, 1963).

[9]See, for example, George J. Stigler, "Policies for Growth," in *Proceedings of a Symposium on Economic Growth* (Washington, D.C.: The American Bankers Association, February 25, 1963), p. 106.

Such criticism points to another big question mark in any such program — can its advocates gain enough public agreement and acceptance to make it work? The theory on which it is based is highly plausible. However, its implications involve restraints, if not formal controls, that may be unacceptable to citizens whose acceptance and conformity are essential to the success of the venture.[10]

Taxation and Tariffs

Advocates of further public intervention conclude that growth requires carefully coordinated monetary and fiscal programs, for disposable income, saving, and investment are obviously important variables affecting employment. Closing the gap between potential and actual GNP cannot be left simply to chance and market factors. Tax changes assume importance, in part, because they can influence levels of spending.

The argument for such changes has been widely discussed since the Kennedy administration presented its first *Economic Report*. It may be summarized as follows:

The national budget can be in balance at a time when the economy is out of balance (e.g., with unemployment too high). Total spending of consumers, businesses, government, and foreigners for United States goods in 1962, for example, fell about $35 billion short of potential output at 4 percent unemployment. With taxes cut, consumers would spend more. Firms would expand production to meet this added consumer demand and would increase investment in plant and equipment. A cut in business taxes would increase this tendency, as would added anticipated profits from the increased volume of business.[11]

This emphasis on taxation as a factor was emphasized by President Kennedy in his first manpower report in March, 1963:

> In order to succeed, a manpower policy requires above all the creation of an adequate number of job opportunities. I have urged the Congress to enact *tax changes* which will provide enlarged consumer markets and encourage increased investment, thereby setting

[10]This difficulty is evidenced by the trend toward increased government vigilance in oligopolistic pricing in steel, petroleum products, and similar situations.

For a convenient summary of views on inflation, see Martin Bronfenbrenner and F. D. Holzman, "Survey of Inflation Theory," *American Economic Review*, Vol. LIII, No. 4 (September, 1963), pp. 593–661.

[11]See the address of Walter W. Heller in *Fiscal and Monetary Policy*, Proceedings of a conference of the President's Advisory Committee on Labor Management Policy, Washington, D.C., November 14–15, 1962, pp. 10–11.

in motion demand for additional work and workers — which in the spiral of economic progress will generate larger markets, additional investment, and more job opportunities. Tax reduction will provide the single strongest push possible to move the economy toward achievable full employment.

The tax program also includes several proposed changes which are important to the development of a sound labor market policy: Deductions for child care for certain workers would be liberalized; treatment of moving expenses of employees would be broadened, fostering greater mobility; and inequities in tax treatment of older people who continue to work would be corrected.[12]

The argument was expanded in the 1963 *Economic Report*, as follows:

Economic policies for 1963 couple pursuit of employment objectives with stimulation of more rapid economic growth. U.S. growth has been lagging. From 1955 to 1962, the economy's potential grew at an estimated annual rate of $3\frac{1}{2}$ percent, nearly a percentage point lower than its growth rate from 1947 to 1955. Actual output grew even more slowly, averaging 2.7 percent a year in the 1955–1962 period. This performance falls short of our aspirations, both as stated by the President and as translated into our share of the Organization for Economic Cooperation and Development commitment to a 50-percent growth target for the 1960's (for the 20 member nations as a group). These aspirations can be realized only by stepping up our growth rate to 4 percent and beyond as we move through the decade. . . .

Fuller utilization of existing resources provides the primary spur to growth; indeed, it is a virtual prerequisite to speedier growth. A tax program aimed at high employment simultaneously stimulates growth by (1) pushing production increasingly toward higher use of plant capacity and thereby stimulating new investment to expand that capacity, (2) drawing more workers into the labor force and upgrading others from inferior to superior uses, (3) decreasing the resistance of labor and management to the risks of technological change, and correspondingly relaxing the grip of restrictive practices, (4) providing a business climate which tests ingenuity and invigorates a spirit of boldness and innovation, and (5) increasing the profitability of business investment, and generating an enlarged flow of funds to finance such investment.[13]

Opponents of this approach aim most of their attacks on its inevitable effect in unbalancing the federal budget, with a consequent increase in the national debt. They argue that (1) such deficit financing is inherently inflationary and (2) it involves committing the future income of workers, who must repay the obligations thus incurred. The inflationary pressure in deficit financing is real, but its impact is dulled

---

[12]*Manpower Report of the President* (Washington 25, D.C.: United States Government Printing Office, March, 1963), p. xviii.

[13]*Economic Report of the President*, 1963, pp. 42–43.

when resources are unused and unemployment is high. How much inflation is induced will depend, also, on the effectiveness of such guideposts as have been described.

Over a longer time period, advocates of tax reduction insist, the expansion thus induced will tend toward balanced budgets based on the higher income level. Higher GNP will mean greater government income. Multiplier and accelerator effects will lift the economy toward higher levels of balance in which debt can be repaid out of enhanced income. Meanwhile, they note, the public debt has not increased in proportion to the growth of GNP, nor is it high compared to that of other nations. Indeed, public debt as a percentage of GNP has been declining since 1945.[14]

Tariff readjustments may also exert an influence on employment. They may increase job opportunities if they facilitate exchanges in which larger quantities of American products are sold abroad. They may reduce such opportunities if foreign products replace those of domestic industry at home. The magnitude of these changes can be estimated, but only with caution and a wide margin of possible error.

Such estimates indicate that tariff reductions designed to effect close cooperation with the Common Market nations might displace from 32 to 68 thousand American workers each year. Reciprocal gains in job opportunities could equal or exceed these totals.

The Trade Expansion Act of 1962 gave the President authority to decrease all tariffs by 50 percent, to modify other import restrictions, and to negotiate reductions as high as 100 percent with the European Economic Community. The act includes authority to readjust rates or impose quotas when concessions cause serious injury. It also grants technical, financial, and tax aid to firms adversely affected. Further, it provides special "readjustment allowances" for workers who may receive these benefits for as long as 52 weeks.

Area Redevelopment

It is generally agreed that increased demands for labor in the aggregate will not automatically remove the special problem of distressed areas. While growing total demands can be expected to improve the situation, the distressed areas require special attention. Programs can seek (1) to increase local demands, (2) facilitate the movement of workers to other areas in which appropriate opportunities exist, and (3) improve the quality of local supplies so that workers

---

[14]*Ibid.*, p. 80.

can qualify for new types of work that may be created in a redevelopment process or are available elsewhere.

The CED study, mentioned in Chapter 15, developed a complex of programs tailored to individual localities and including studies of local experience, union-management cooperation, federal leadership, improved educational preparation for work with added vocational training, use of unemployment benefits to encourage retraining, expanded employment service activities, urban renewal and other land-use programs, and special rapid amortization and other tax advantages.[15]

The Chamber of Commerce of the United States suggests many of the same changes, adding a special emphasis on improving labor mobility, greater flexibility in costs (including wage costs), and the moderation of union work rules.[16]

The Area Redevelopment Act of 1961 provides several types of federal aid for distressed areas. While workers are not encouraged to move elsewhere by direct travel or resettlement allowances, they are advised of employment opportunities in other localities. Federal aid takes the form of loans to private firms, grants for public improvements that will increase private employment, and technical assistance in developing new products and markets. Federal funds are also provided for retraining unemployed workers. In addition, the Public Works Acceleration Act of 1962 provides funds for expanded public projects in distressed areas.[17]

The problem of distressed areas in this country will require continued and probably expanded attention. The whole national economy suffers from the serious waste of unused resources, especially human resources. Some unemployment in such areas reflects forces generated outside the area; it is an inevitable result of progress, i.e., changes otherwise beneficial to the total economy. It is thus a social cost of such advances and hence properly chargeable to the total economy.

Attacks on the problem must probably include both redevelopment and the relocation of many workers. They must almost certainly include expanded retraining programs to prepare workers for new jobs in new industries, both in the area and in other localities

---

[15]*Distressed Areas in a Growing Economy*, pp. 39–71.

[16]See *Automation and Unemployment* (Washington, D.C.: Chamber of Commerce of the United States, 1961), pp. 30–31.

[17]*Manpower Report of the President* (Washington 25, D.C.: United States Government Printing Office, March, 1963), p. xvii.

where employment is expanding. Public works expansion and acceleration appear likely to do little more than simply provide temporary relief. The record of local community development programs is inconclusive.[18]

Foreign Programs

Foreign experience may provide some guidance for American programs. Several nations have experience in providing public assistance to labor-surplus areas. Great Britain, for example, has authorized aid to transferring workers since 1909. In 1962 the six European Coal and Steel Community countries (Netherlands, Belgium, Luxembourg, Germany, France, and Italy) undertook a joint program to rehabilitate regions suffering from persistent unemployment. Almost all noncommunist European countries now have programs for national government assistance to labor-surplus areas.

England, for example, has provided aid in resettlement for several hundred thousand workers, with payments for transportation and other moving costs. Emphasis has shifted, in recent years, from mobilizing workers to developing industries where workers live. Under the Local Employment Act of 1960, the Board of Trade makes grants and loans to private firms for building or builds and leases facilities if firms locate new plants in areas designated by the Board.

Belgium passed a Regional Development Act in 1959 under which areas are designated for public construction, low interest loans, guaranteed loans, and tax incentives. While little emphasis is placed upon worker relocation, workers who cannot be locally employed may receive full traveling and moving expenses. Unemployed coal and steel workers receive *readaption assistance* in the form of generous unemployment insurance or readaption training at full salary for 12 months plus training costs.

Since 1951 West Germany's assistance to labor-surplus areas has included public loans to industrial, handicraft, and tourist industries and to redevelopment associations, as well as both loans and grants to improve public facilities and vocational training. Resettlement aid is available if the need is proved. The unemployed can be given travel expenses and a daily allowance until receipt of the first paycheck if

---

[18]See J. R. Fernstrom, "A Community Attack upon Chronic Unemployment — Hazelton, Pa.: A Case Study," *Studies in Unemployment* (United States Senate Special Committee on Unemployment Problems, 86th Congress, 2nd Session: United States Government Printing Office, 1960), p. 398. See also Sar A. Levitan, "Area Redevelopment; An Analysis of the Program," *Industrial Relations*, Vol. 3, No. 3 (May, 1964), pp. 79–95.

no suitable job is locally available and if a nontemporary, similar job is assured in the new location.

Sweden provides worker assistance in relocation as well as public assistance in redevelopment.[19]

IMPROVING MARKETING AND SUPPLIES

Structural unemployment is traceable to the mismatching of workers and available work. Some structural unemployment is distinctly frictional; the two essentials to work are separated principally by the fact that workers do not know the facts or are otherwise prevented from coming together with available work at the necessary time and place.[20]

Marketing Facilities and Mobility

Programs designed to overcome labor marketing frictions and to mobilize workers have been described in some detail in earlier chapters. Chapter 6 has indicated the usual informational bases for job choice and the limits of existing forecasts of future job opportunities. The problem of *lead time*, of long-time advance planning for many occupations, deserves special attention; it gives great significance to the extent and accuracy of occupational forecasts and to details of job requirements.

The structure and operation of the public employment service and the work of private job-finding services has also been described in Chapter 6, as have fair employment rules and related efforts to reduce the impact of discrimination in hiring.[21]

Reducing frictions in the marketing process is a major avenue of attack on structural unemployment. Improving information, reducing discrimination in hiring practices, and facilitating the meeting of employers with jobs to be filled and potential employees with skills to be

---

[19]For details see "Aid to Labor Surplus Areas in Great Britain, Belgium, the Federal Republic of Germany and Sweden," *Foreign Labor Information* (United States Department of Labor, May, 1960).

[20]See G. G. Somers, E. L. Cushman, and Nat Weinberg, *Adjusting to Technological Change* (New York: Harper and Row, 1963); also William H. Miernyk, "British and American Approaches to Structural Unemployment," *Industrial and Labor Relations Review*, Vol. 12, No. 1 (October, 1958), pp. 3–19.

[21]For a concise summary of European (France, Great Britain, Netherlands, and Sweden) public policy on labor marketing and the responsibilities of the public employment service, see Alfred L. Green, *A Study and Appraisal of Manpower Programs* (Division of Employment, New York State Department of Labor, September, 1963).

used are important steps toward full employment.   Providing transportation aids and moving assistance are other programs that can be helpful.

Severance Pay

Severance or dismissal pay plans grant immediate cash benefits to released workers and may facilitate the search for other jobs and provide a degree of economic security during the transitional period. Some recent plans provide for training benefits, including tuition and fees, as well as subsistence. Other recent modifications relate benefits to opportunities for transfer — waiving benefits if the employee refuses such an offer — while other modifications provide travel expenses to facilitate movement to new jobs.

Improved Worker Qualifications

It is widely recognized, however, that no small portion of total unemployment in recent years is directly attributable to the fact that job-seekers are not qualified for such jobs as are available. The problem is structural. While sex and race play some part in disqualification, and while age is also a significant factor, education and skill level are major sources of mismatching. The simple facts are that unemployed workers do not have the essential educational backgrounds and skills required for many of the newer jobs that have replaced earlier and now outmoded assignments.[22]

The realities of this deficiency or inadequacy are widely recognized. The Secretary of Labor described this situation, in April, 1963, as follows:

> My testimony, as Secretary of Labor, in support of the National Education Improvement Act of 1963, S. 580, reflects the realization that full employment in this country depends on full education.
>
> These are actually comparative terms, and there has always been something of this relationship between learning and making a living. I refer, however, to the effect of what we loosely call "automation" upon the interdependence of education and employment.
>
> Unless and until the educational system in this country is significantly strengthened, the danger spots that have already shown

---

[22]For details, see William Haber, Louis A. Terman, and James R. Hudson, *The Impact of Technology and Change* (Kalamazoo, Michigan: The W. E. Upjohn Institute for Employment Research, September, 1963).

up in our manpower situation are going to continue to get worse. One is the concentration of unemployment among unskilled workers. The other is the imminent shortage of personnel in a good many skilled, professional, semiprofessional, and technical occupations. . . .

Today, unskilled workers make up 5 percent of the work force. But almost 15 percent of all the unemployed are in this group. Unemployment is over twice as high among the younger worker group and among nonwhite workers — the two groups in which there are the largest percentages of unskilled workers — than it is in the work force as a whole.

What this means in terms of educational needs is obvious. We simply cannot any longer afford to let boys and girls leave the educational system unprepared to use their minds as well as their muscles. We must, in one way or another, see to it that they have what today's — and tomorrow's — labor market requires. The margin for educational error or failure, which is what the unskilled jobs in the old work force constituted, has been taken up by machines.[23]

Worker obsolescence. The realities of rapid worker (and manager) obsolescence are becoming clearer to all. The necessity for broad basic education and frequent retraining and refresher training is equally evident, but where the responsibility rests for such education and training is not so clear. It is apparent that workers, managements, unions, and the public all share in the benefits of adequate programs. All have taken some responsibility for experimental programs.[24]

It is widely recognized that there is very limited work for untrained, raw labor. Further, the *lead time* in preparing most workers for work is a long one. To make adequate supplies of qualified workers available for job X in 1970 may easily require that educational preparation must be planned several years in advance. With a speeded rate of technological advance — to be expected in years ahead — one rather obvious requirement is careful long-term scheduling of training and retraining. Public plans, and most private plans, to date are distinctly short term and fall far from meeting this basic requirement.[25]

The educational payoff. At the same time, the dollar values of education are widely appreciated, and the concept of "investing in people" has achieved wide acceptance. Becker, for example, found

---

[23]Statement of W. Willard Wirtz, Secretary of Labor, before the Subcommittee on Education, Senate Committee on Labor and Public Welfare, on S. 580, National Education Improvement Act of 1963, April 30, 1963.

[24]See Clarence D. Long, "Prosperity Unemployment and Its Relations to Economic Growth and Inflation," *American Economic Review*, Vol. L, No. 2 (May, 1960), pp. 145–61.

[25]See, for example, Phyllis Groom, "Retraining the Unemployed: IV. The Bridgeport Program," *Monthly Labor Review*, Vol. 85, No. 1 (January, 1962), pp. 24–29.

that education pays an 11 percent return on investment. While this rate of return might not apply under different economic conditions, the general implications are supported by other studies.[26]

Denison found that economic progress is closely related to investment in education. He concludes that if the 1960 labor force had been only as well educated as the 1950 labor force, our national production in 1960 would have been 10 percent lower than it was. He suggests that among possible means of increasing the growth rate to 4 percent per year, one is to add one and one-half years of school for everyone completing school between now and 1980 or "make equivalent improvement in the quality of education."[27]

Programs designed to remedy educational and skill shortcomings and to provide "full education" for American workers take several forms. Among the oldest are restrictions on child labor and encouragement of vocational training programs. More recently developed approaches involve expanded vocational guidance and public retraining programs.

Child labor. A long-established public policy in the United States has proposed that children be required to complete stated levels of educational attainment and that they be prevented from working pending that achievement. In essence, this policy assumes that child labor involves *overemployment*. Allowing children to accept employment can interfere with their training and development and can reduce their subsequent adult contribution. It can preclude the development of highest skills and talents.

Both federal and state regulations restrict the employment of children, and state laws require school attendance. For many years federal legislation regulating the employment of children was regarded as unconstitutional. Federal laws of 1911 and 1919 were so regarded by the Supreme Court. In 1924 Congress approved a constitutional amendment which did not receive approval by the necessary two thirds of the states. Meanwhile, in a somewhat different attack, the federal Fair Labor Standards Act of 1938 prohibits "oppressive child labor" in interstate commerce or the production of goods for such commerce. *Oppressive child labor* is that involving (1) any

[26]See, for example, Gary S. Becker, "Underinvestment in College Education," *American Economic Review*, Vol. L, No. 2 (May, 1960), pp. 346–54; also, H. S. Houthakker, "Education and Income," *Review of Economics and Statistics*, Vol. 41, No. 1 (February, 1959), p. 24.

[27]Edward F. Denison, "The Sources of Economic Growth in the United States and the Alternatives Before Us," *Supplementary Paper #13* (Committee for Economic Development, New York, 1962).

employment under 14 years of age, (2) employment under 16 except during nonschool hours and in accordance with working conditions specified by the Secretary of Labor, and (3) employment under 18 in a hazardous occupation.

Every state has a child labor law. These laws follow similar patterns but vary widely in their standards for employment of children. Wherever state standards for employment of children are higher than federal standards, the state standards prevail. Major provisions in the various state laws may be summarized as follows:

1. *Minimum age.* Twenty states and Puerto Rico have a 16-year minimum for employment in manufacturing. Nineteen states and Puerto Rico set a 16-year minimum for all employment (except domestic and agriculture) during school hours. The remaining states set a 14- or 15-year minimum age for work during school hours in most gainful occupations.

2. *Employment certificates.* All but 5 states require employment certificates or work permits for children under 16. About half of the states require such certificates for those 16 and 17 years old. Certificates are usually issued by local public school officials, or by state departments of labor or education. Proof of age, physical fitness, and educational attainment is usually required.

3. *Hours of work.* Most states limit work to 8 hours a day and 48 hours a week for minors under 16 or, in some states, under 18. For children under 16 attending school, 21 states and Puerto Rico limit working time to 3 or 4 hours a day, or count the time at school as part of the maximum work day. Twenty-three states, the District of Columbia, and Puerto Rico prohibit more than 12 hours of night work for children of both sexes under 16 in all or most occupations.

4. *Hazardous occupations.* Almost all states provide a higher minimum age, 16 or 18 years, for employment in hazardous occupations.

5. *Compulsory school attendance.* All but three states require children between certain ages to attend school full time. The upper age limit is usually 16, 17, or 18. In about two thirds of the states, children may be released earlier or upon completion of the eighth grade to take a job.[28]

Job forecasting and vocational counseling. It follows directly that the higher the required level of education in a job, the longer the lead time for preparation. Basic data for educational programs must, therefore, include realistic forecasts of occupational requirements. Satisfactory vocational guidance requires advance information on both

[28]See Ora Mitchell and Sylvia R. Weisebrodt, "State Child Labor Standards," United States Department of Labor, *Bulletin 158*, Revised 1960.

numbers of opportunities and job requirements of future jobs. Long-term plans to improve the qualifications of the labor force can only be as good as these predictions of long-term job requirements.

The Bureau of Employment Security is charged with major responsibility for providing current and future information on available jobs and job requirements. It currently surveys and classifies about 800 areas with respect to relationships of labor supplies and demands. The Bureau, in cooperation with state agencies, conducts "skill surveys" in local areas, covering both present and prospective (2- to 5-year) requirements. More than 125 such surveys have been undertaken in 43 states. The Bureau prepares *Occupational Guides* and the *Occupational Handbook* which describe job requirements in terms of education and experience. In 1964 the Chairman of the Council of Economic Advisers proposed addition of a national *job vacancies index* to provide reliable information on current and prospective labor needs by occupation and locality.

The Bureau and local state employment services work with and supplement vocational guidance and counseling services provided by high schools. The Bureau has developed aptitude tests for more than 400 occupations, including the *General Aptitude Test Battery* (GATB) and an *Interest Check List*. In 1962, employment service offices conducted more than 2 million counseling interviews.[29]

All vocational guidance is handicapped by the limitation of occupation forecasts. At the same time, studies of training channels are needed, for formal education is only a part of the process of preparation for work.[30]

Vocational education. Specific training for a vocation other than the professions is uncommon rather than common in the United States. Historic public policy generally opposed vocational training at the high school level on the ground that it is incompatible with an open-class social system. Such training, in this view, restricts the later choice of work; the vocationally trained youngster faces narrower opportunities than other high school graduates. This, it should be noted, is a frequently expressed opinion; the evidence is not so clear.

Some pressure against vocational education has come, also, from organized workers who fear that vocational graduates may weaken

---

[29]See *Manpower Research Bulletin No. 1* (Washington, D.C.: Office of Manpower, Automation and Training, July, 1963), Chapter 4.

[30]"Educational Attainment of Workers, March, 1962," *Special Labor Force Report No. 30* (Washington, D.C.: Bureau of Labor Statistics, May, 1963), Reprint from *Monthly Labor Review* (May, 1963), pp. 504 ff.

the bargaining power of those presently employed. As a result, less than one third of current high school students receive vocational training in high school or in college. As a further result, vocational training has been diluted; many students get only a brief contact with existing programs.

Despite these restrictions, many localities maintain vocational high schools, and federal subsidies for vocational education have been provided for almost fifty years. In 1917 the federal Smith-Hughes Act provided for an annual grant of $7.2 million, to be matched by the states — $3 million was to be used for training in agriculture; $3 million for trade, industrial, and home economics education; and $1 million for teacher training. In 1946 the George-Barden Act provided an additional annual appropriation of $29 million for these programs, plus a fourth — distributive education. In 1958 the National Defense Education Act (Title VIII) appropriated $15 million annually to train highly skilled workers needed in defense industries.

In 1961, 3.9 million youths and adults were enrolled in federally supported vocational education classes. Slightly more than 40 percent of these were in home economics, about 25 percent in trade and industry, and about 20 percent in agriculture; no other occupational category included as much as 10 percent of the students.

In another type of vocational training, both federal and state governments have cooperated with employers and unions to provide opportunities for *apprenticeship*. Such programs represent traditional preparation for several types of craftsmen. They date from the handicraft system, which preceded industrialization. In these historic programs learners develop trade knowledge and skills by working with and under direction of senior craftsmen or journeymen. In the United States at least fifty crafts maintain established apprenticeship requirements. Many of the modern programs combine classroom and on-the-job experience. Federal leadership and aid in apprentice training has been provided since 1937 through the Department of Labor.

Current programs are far from adequate to meet present or future needs. In many crafts numbers of graduates from apprenticeship programs do not equal the numbers who leave the craft each year. Some programs cannot be regarded as educationally efficient; the same or superior training could be provided in a shorter time and with other accompanying advantages. In some crafts ratios of apprentices to journeymen are intentionally restricted to limit supplies of fully-qualified workers. Employers are frequently reluctant about participating in such programs because they impose additional, time-consuming responsibilities on senior workers.[31]

Retraining. Worker obsolescence refers, of course, to current workers — those already in the labor force. The rather obvious prescription for worker obsolescence is retraining. What such workers need is an opportunity to gain new skills, to supplement their present and perhaps inapplicable knowledge and know-how. As the term "retraining" is now used, however, it may also include preliminary job training for young workers who have gained little or no work experience.

Retraining is by no means a new or novel type of job preparation. Some retraining takes place in most jobs. Workers learn to perform many new tasks as a part of their day-to-day work experience. Many firms and agencies have well-established training programs to facilitate continuing personal development for various types of employees, from semiskilled to managers.

Many other firms, however, maintain no such programs. Their employees may seek to retrain themselves, but comparatively few of them have either the guidance or the motivation to maintain this effort. Their skills face the constant hazard of becoming obsolete. They may lose their jobs. If they do, they are likely to face long periods of unemployment.

Meanwhile, estimates suggest that many millions of workers are "functional illiterates"; they know so little about the three R's that they cannot be readily trained for even semiskilled jobs.

This problem has received growing public attention as union leaders and others have pointed to the impact of automation and the threat of even more drastic displacements to be anticipated as computers are combined with machines. As one expression of this view, the 1963 *Economic Report* suggests that "education must not stop in the classroom." The same report goes on to note that "the individual and the private firm have shouldered the primary responsibility for the retraining required to keep pace with technical advance." It observes further that the government must supplement these private efforts,[32] for most workers must plan on *multiple careers* in the future.

---

[31]See Phyllis Groom, "An Assessment of Apprenticeship," *Monthly Labor Review*, Vol. 87, No. 4 (April, 1964), pp. 391–95; Felician F. Foltman, "An Assessment of Apprenticeship," *Monthly Labor Review*, Vol. 87, Nos. 1 and 2 (January and February, 1964), pp. 28–35 and 143–48: Sar A. Levitan, *Vocational Education and Federal Policy* (Kalamazoo, Michigan: The W. E. Upjohn Institute for Employment Research, 1963).

[32]*Economic Report of the President*, 1963, p. xxvii.

Public programs in this area include those provided by the Area Redevelopment Act (1961), the Trade Expansion Act (1962), and the Manpower Development and Training Act (1962). An additional federal program has been proposed in the President's recommendation of the Youth Employment Act.

Training under ARA programs. The Area Redevelopment Act provides funds for retraining selected workers for periods up to 16 weeks. Trainees receive subsistence or support equal to the average unemployment compensation benefit in the state. Opportunities to enroll are limited to adult unemployed workers, and courses must be geared to existing job openings. About one third of the three thousand counties in the United States qualify for assistance under the act. These counties include about 20 percent of the population and 30 percent of the unemployed.

From October, 1961 (when funds first became available under this act) through June, 1962, 144 training projects were approved for 114 areas, with training opportunities for 9,074 workers in 286 areas. Pennsylvania, West Virginia, Kentucky, and Michigan had the largest numbers of projects. Training was designed for 89 occupations, of which the most common were in manufacturing (48.5 percent), metal working (29.4 percent), and clerical and sales (21.9 percent). Almost one third of all trainees were in metal working, with 22 percent of the trainees in clerical and sales courses.

Of all trainees, 64 percent were men. Almost 45 percent had been out of work for more than 26 weeks. One third were 35 or more years of age, while about half were 20–34 years old. Some 78 percent had attended or finished high school.

Of those admitted to courses, 14 percent had left without finishing the training. Approximately 50 percent (3,302) were enrolled on June 30. Some 36 percent (2,304) had completed their courses, and 60 percent of that number had taken jobs. Fifty-six percent took training-related jobs.[33]

The MDTA program. The Manpower Development and Training Act of 1962 (Public Law 87-415) requires that the Secretary of Labor take steps to determine the skill requirements of the economy and to promote diversified training programs designed to provide needed new skills. The Secretary is instructed to conduct appropriate research, to study technological changes and the mobility of workers, to evaluate

---

[33]See "Eight Months' Training Experience Under the Area Redevelopment Act," *Monthly Labor Review*, Vol. 85, No. 12 (December, 1962), pp. 1375–78.

developmental practices, and to disseminate information on manpower needs. The Labor Department is to select candidates for occupational training and to pay allowances to participants in training programs. Under the 1962 provisions training could be given to those who (1) were unemployed, (2) were working below their skill capacities, (3) were working less than full time, (4) had skills which were becoming obsolete, or (5) were between 16 and 22 and needed further training. However, regular training allowances were available only to the unemployed with at least three years' work experience who were heads of families. Allowances could compensate for transportation and for living away from home, if such arrangements were necessary. Lesser allowances — not over $20 per week — were available to those 19-22 years old. Allowances were reduced if trainees were also working.[34] The Department of Health, Education and Welfare has responsibility, under the act, for providing training instructors and facilities. Training could continue for as long as 52 weeks.

MDTA training programs began in September, 1962. By July 1, 1963, 1,504 projects and 57,693 trainees had been approved and 1,057 projects with 29,800 trainees were under way. Total allowances and training costs for approved projects amounted to $70 million. The largest numbers of trainees were in New York, California, and Illinois. Principal occupations were machine operators, stenographers, auto mechanics, clerk typists, nursing aids, and sewing machine operators, with many others involving fewer trainees.

Some 62 percent of the trainees were heads of families. More than one fourth had been unemployed for 5 to 14 weeks. The largest age group — 22–34 years — included 43.9 percent of the trainees. Fifty percent were high school graduates.[35]

On the basis of limited experience, evaluation of these public programs cannot be conclusive. The Secretary of Labor has noted that costs average from $1,000 to $1,250 per trainee. He suggests that

---

[34]For details, see An Explanation of the Manpower Development and Training Act (Washington: Department of Labor, December, 1962); see also Lester Velie, "A Second Chance for George," Reprint from The Reader's Digest, June, 1963.

[35]Press release, Bureau of Employment Security, July 1, 1963; see also "Manpower Development and Training Act," Report of the Secretary of Labor, Transmitted to Congress, February, 1963 (Washington 25, D.C.: United States Government Printing Office, 1963).

One special approach to training initiated under MDTA is the Demonstration Manpower Program. It seeks to show that unemployed with unusual problems can be trained for employment. It directs attention to the undereducated, unskilled, handicapped, members of minority groups, and those with language or cultural barriers. Some 26,000 trainees were included in programs approved in the first six months of 1963. See Bridge to Employment (Washington, D.C.: Department of Labor, 1963).

if the program reemploys the trainee at one step higher on the occupational ladder, it will increase the individual's annual income by more than the training costs and that government would recoup one third of total costs through increased taxes and reduced unemployment compensation during the next year.[36]

Similarly, in Massachusetts a study compared 204 workers who undertook the retraining program in 1960 with a control group that did not. In terms of comparative costs of unemployment insurance benefits, the state saved almost one fifth of the costs of training in one year.[37]

On the other hand, serious limitations of these programs are clear from this short experience. Numbers of trainees represent little more than a drop in the bucket of the unemployed.

Basic to the success of these programs are dependable forecasts of future manpower requirements. In-firm programs have some advantage in this respect. Broader community retraining requires much more information regarding prospective demands than has been available. Area redevelopment programs must include careful studies of economic opportunities likely to attract investment and provide employment for retrained workers. Selection of those to be retrained and counseling retrainees represent problems about which much more needs to be known. For unemployed workers the decision to try out for retraining may be difficult. Many older workers who have the requisite intelligence may be fearful of going back to school. The limitation of a maximum of 16 weeks under ARA, and similar but longer (52-week) limitations in MDTA, may be unrealistic for many occupations. Unemployment programs in 27 states require unemployed to be seeking and available for work if they are to be eligible for benefits; they are thus discouraged from undertaking training. Many workers simply do not have the basic general education on which to build occupational training. Courses in the three R's may be more appropriate than occupationally oriented courses.[38]

---

[36]Testimony before Senate subcommittee as reported in *IRC Current News*, Vol. 28, No. 22 (May 30, 1963), p. 112.

[37]*Business Week*, May 11, 1963, p. 48.

[38]See, for an excellent analysis, Arnold R. Weber, "Retraining the Unemployed," *Selected Papers, No. 4* (Chicago: University of Chicago Graduate School of Business, 1963). See also, "The Fort Worth Project of the Armour Automation Committee," *Monthly Labor Review*, Vol. 87, No. 1 (January, 1964), pp. 53–57; also, Sar A. Levitan, *Vocational Education and Federal Policy* (Kalamazoo, Michigan: The W. E. Upjohn Institute for Employment Research, May, 1963). For a comprehensive review of the retraining program as of the end of 1963, see *Manpower Research and Training Under the Manpower Development and Training Act* (Washington, D.C.: United States Department of Labor, 1964).

These and other limitations are clear from several case studies of retraining programs. In the Armour and Co. Oklahoma City plant, of 433 employees idled when the plant closed, 170 applied for retraining. After tests and interviews, 58 were qualified for some type of retraining. Of these, 52 completed their training programs. Two years later, only 15 were on jobs for which they had received training, 13 were making some use of it, and 24 were not using their training. In Omaha, of 600 packing house workers displaced, 64 accepted retraining, and 6 got jobs for which they had received training. In one packing plant 53 percent of the workers remained unemployed two years after the plant closed.[39]

In Bridgeport, Connecticut, the public employment service selected 2,143 persons for possible retraining, interviewed 1,550, rejected 560 as unsuitable and 401 as not interested. Only 598 were recommended for testing. Of these, 201 did not appear, 248 failed, and 140 were selected for training. Only 84 completed the training.[40]

The whole picture may not be as discouraging as these experiences indicate. We may learn how to do better. If retraining becomes common, workers' reluctance to enter programs may be greatly reduced. Improvements in courses and methods of instruction, including teaching machines, may make courses more effective and less costly.

In December, 1963, Congress amended the 1962 MDTA Act to extend it for another year — to June 30, 1964 — and to incorporate a number of improvements. Matching of funds by states was delayed for one year. A major change authorizes training for the "functional illiterates" for a 20-week period. The age of eligibility to receive training allowances was reduced from 18 to 17. One distinctive new provision involves a pilot program in relocating the unemployed. It provides a combination of grants and loans to pay up to 100 percent of the cost of relocating those who cannot be expected to find full-time employment in their home communities and who have bona fide offers of employment.

On the other hand, current programs only scratch the surface of the problem. Retraining needs and worker obsolescence extend all across the occupational ladder. One study of engineers, for example,

---

[39]Reported in *John Herling's Labor Letter*, November 17, 1962, p. 4.

[40]Fred A. Ammon, "Retraining — How Much of an Answer to Technological Unemployment?" *Personnel Journal*, Vol. 41, No. 10 (November, 1962), p. 507.

found 17 percent unemployed, with many needing similar retraining.[41]

Youth Employment Act. In 1962, and again in 1964, federal legislation proposed a Youth Employment Act, under which special attention would be given to jobs for those 18 and 19 years old. The bills placed major emphasis on reducing dropouts from school and developing skills that can be useful in subsequent working careers.[42]

Several reasons explain why this group requires special consideration. Unemployment strikes hard among threshold workers. They offer the longest-term investment opportunities, and they are not likely to enter the usual ARA and MDTA retraining programs because they may not be in redevelopment areas or have not become family heads or established eligibility for unemployment benefits. Further, they need a different type of long-view counseling and training.[43]

STABILIZING WAGES AND INCOME

Several public and private programs represent action designed to maintain and stabilize employment. They propose to attack unemployment by introducing a stabilizing influence on employment and worker income. Their major objective is to counter cyclical unemployment, but they also propose to cushion the impact of seasonal and transitional idleness. Many are not single-purpose programs; they involve elements of relief and the reduction of hardship from unemployment as well as its reduction.

Some plans contemplate reserves of preplanned public construction which can be expanded when unemployment reaches critical levels. "Made work" programs are among the most common proposals for immediate relief; extensive public works programs were undertaken during the Great Depression of the 1930's.

More recently, Canada has experimented with a public incentive for private construction as a counterseasonal device. Beginning in 1963, this counterpeak-load program gives a $500 tax-free bonus to home construction begun before December and concluded by March 31st.[44]

---

[41]William A. Douglass, "The 'Engineer Shortage' — What Is Its Nature?" *Personnel Administration*, Vol. 26, No. 2 (March-April, 1963), pp. 20–24.

[42]See Sar A. Levitan, *Youth Employment Act* (Kalamazoo, Michigan: The W. E. Upjohn Institute for Employment Research, 1963).

[43]See "Young Workers: Their Special Training Needs," *Manpower Research Bulletin No. 3* (Washington, D.C.: Department of Labor, May, 1963).

[44]"Thawing Ice-bound Jobs," *Business Week*, November 23, 1963, p. 112.

Unemployment Insurance

No discussion of policy and programs for attaining full employment can omit unemployment insurance, despite the fact that it is popularly regarded as more of a relief measure than as a means of attaining higher levels of employment. Several less extensive but similar or related programs must also be recognized as having significant economic implications in this connection, including temporary extensions of unemployment insurance, supplementary unemployment benefits, guaranteed annual wage plans, and automation funds.

Since details of benefits, coverage, and eligibility for unemployment insurance are to be discussed in some detail in Chapter 23, only the broad purposes and outlines of the program require attention here. At this point major interest concerns its impact on employment. For that purpose the essentials of the unemployment insurance program can be outlined as follows:

1. The system was established by the Social Security Act of 1935. Benefits became generally available in 1938. The system involves cooperation of the federal government and state governments. Taxes for support of the program are collected by both federal and state governments. The federal Bureau of Employment Security administers the federal portion of the total program. Employment security departments provide administration at the state level. Benefits are paid through the local offices of state employment security agencies.

2. The system presently covers more than 47 million wage and salary jobs, constituting slightly more than three fourths of the total of such "employee" positions. Workers excluded vary from state to state, but major groups include state and local employees, domestics, agricultural workers, and those in small firms — a total of about 14 million.

3. Benefits are paid, after waiting periods of varying length, to unemployed workers who meet specified and varying state requirements for eligibility. Levels of benefits vary both in terms of previous earnings and because states follow different formulas for their calculation and specify different maxima. In some states they include additional allowances for dependents. Although benefits are based on earnings and are chargeable against employer funds, they can be paid to workers who move. Benefits are available as a matter of rights, not of demonstrated need, but eligibility generally requires that recipients must be seeking work.

4. Benefits are payable on a weekly basis with varying state rules as to the maximum number of weeks, generally 26. As a result of this maximum, many unemployed exhaust their benefits.

5. Benefits are financed by payroll taxes paid by employers. The federal government taxes all employers of two or more but allows employers to avoid about 90 percent of federal taxes if they have met state tax requirements. Federal taxes are based on the first $3,000 of earnings. States tax payrolls at rates adjusted for experience rating, i.e., employers pay more if they or their industry have lower ratios of reserves to benefits paid.

A program of such magnitude has many potential effects on employment and unemployment. What its actual total effects are or have been is not readily measured; hence, some of these impacts have become the subject of controversy.

Lower levels of employment. It may be argued, for example, that the availability of benefits increases unemployment and discourages employment. Thus, some workers who would take jobs may not do so because they can draw benefits. This is possible if opportunities do not offer "suitable work," essentially like the usual job in which the worker has been employed. Although this result is frequently charged, no dependable evidence of its extent or significance is available. To a considerable extent, this effect can be charged to coverage of seasonal workers, particularly married women and part-time workers; some proposals have suggested their elimination from coverage.[45]

As noted earlier in this chapter, benefit requirements may, in most states, prevent retraining and thus handicap reemployment and future levels of employment. If an unemployed worker must take a job whenever it becomes available, he may hesitate to start in a retraining course. Similarly, administrators of such courses may not select him for training. Several current proposals seek to eliminate this condition by encouraging states to consider attendance in an approved retraining course as the equivalent of the "actively seeking work" requirement.

In early experience the payment of benefits sometimes appeared to interfere with movement to other localities where work was available. Although states have always cooperated in an interstate benefit payment plan, claimants from outside the state have sometimes encountered more critical evaluation of their claims. Recently, some states have set lower maximum benefits for workers who move outside, apparently to discourage such departures. If this type of regulation becomes common, it could exert a significant influence on worker mobility and thus on employment levels.

---

[45]See James O'Connor, "Seasonal Unemployment and Unemployment Insurance," *American Economic Review*, Vol. 52, No. 3 (June, 1962), pp. 469–70.

On the other hand, the availability of benefits may make workers more mobile by providing resources for travel. Unemployment insurance can, therefore, facilitate the search for jobs. It presumably does exert such an influence in the requirement that benefit receivers must be actively seeking work.

A major objective of the system, frequently described by its early supporters, is employment stabilization. Merit rating provisions, by which employer tax rates are adjusted according to the level of reserves held in employer accounts, are designed to encourage employers to stabilize employment. This economic payoff is worthwhile for many employers. The same provision may, of course, encourage employers to stabilize at relatively low levels and thus adversely affect the level of total employment.

Increased stability. Some stabilizing effect is to be expected as a result of the penalty imposed on employees who quit their jobs. They may be ineligible for benefits or may have to observe a longer waiting period. This requirement, it should be noted, may also restrict worker mobility. Employees may hesitate to move lest they lose the protection available to them in present jobs.

One major impact on employment is likely to follow from the support provided for employee incomes by unemployment insurance. The unemployed worker finds his income reduced but not eliminated. His level of purchasing and consumption are presumably lower. For the duration of his idleness or until benefits are exhausted, however, he is assured of a stable if much reduced weekly income.

The magnitude of this influence is determined primarily by the level of benefits and their duration. There have been few studies of benefit adequacy, probably because the question of what is adequate is controversial. Father J. M. Becker found that, by and large, benefits are sufficient to keep workers off relief rolls.[46]

Benefits v. wage loss. It is clear that benefits thus paid do not, by any means, balance the total wage loss. The 3 billion paid out in 1962, for example, has been estimated as about 20 percent of the wage loss. In part, this small fraction results from the fact that benefits rarely exceed 50 percent of wages. As Figure 16-1 indicates, average benefits in 1962 exceeded 40 percent of average weekly wages in covered employment in only 4 states. In 6 states, average benefits fell below 30 percent of average wages.

---

[46] Joseph M. Becker, S.J., *The Adequacy of the Benefit Amount in Unemployment Insurance* (Kalamazoo, Michigan: The W. E. Upjohn Institute for Employment Research, 1961), p. 51.

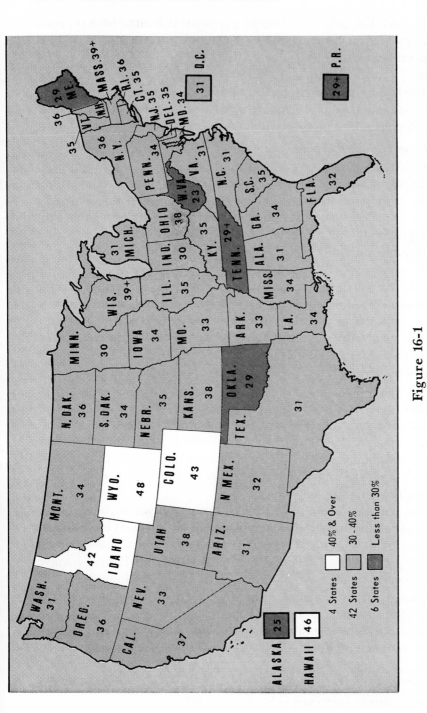

Figure 16-1

AVERAGE WEEKLY BENEFITS AS A PERCENT OF AVERAGE WEEKLY WAGES IN COVERED EMPLOYMENT, 1962[1]

[1]Weekly benefits include dependents' allowances.

Source: "Handbook of Unemployment Insurance Financial Data, 1946–1963," *BES No. U-73* (Washington, D.C.: Department of Labor, Revised May, 1964), p. 55.

In part, the volume of benefit payments is limited by state rules on the maximum benefit period which stop payments to many unemployed before they find jobs. In 1962 the exhaustion rate was 27.4 percent. It was highest in 1940 (50.6 percent), 1958 (31 percent), and 1950 (30.5 percent). Exhaustion tends to reduce the counter-recessional influence of unemployment insurance in second and later years of reduced business activity.

Countercyclical impact. Stabilized employment and supported worker income almost certainly cushion the impact of recessions. It may be significant, in this connection, that no postwar recession has become a major depression, as was true in earlier periods. In the 1938-1963 period, some $34 billion was distributed to the unemployed. Their propensity to spend, under these circumstances, means that benefit funds probably added many times this amount to GNP.

To some extent this stabilizing effect of added income for the unemployed is countered by a depressing effect on total employment. The program reduces income, part of which would otherwise have been distributed to the same or other recipients at an earlier time. Amounts paid out in benefits have been collected as payroll taxes, paid by employers. At the same time, these taxes may have encouraged price increases and thus lowered demands for labor. Lester estimates that not more than one third of the tax load is shifted to consumers in the form of higher prices.[47] This conclusion follows from the fact that tax rates vary widely, depending in part on experience in stabilizing employment. High rate employers would hesitate to shift because lower-rated competitors would feel no similar need for price increases. Further, the tax is in part a cost that can be shared with government through the corporate income tax.

On balance, unemployment insurance appears to be a major means of countering cyclical unemployment and to exert a stabilizing influence on that which is essentially seasonal. It may have exerted some depressive effect in periods of expansion, and it may involve some hazards to labor mobility and hence to continuing adjustment and change. It is significant that while many critics would change details of the system, no one has proposed trying to do without it. On the other hand, its favorable influence is probably restricted by tendencies to make it both a stabilization and a relief program.

---

[47]Richard A. Lester, "Unemployment Insurance Financing: Problems and Prospects," *Employment Security Review*, Vol. 29, No. 8 (August, 1962), pp. 18–21. See also his "The Economics of Unemployment Compensation," *Research Report Series, No. 101* (Princeton University Industrial Relations Section, 1962).

Temporary extensions. In recent recessions, in 1958 and again in 1961, the federal Congress has enacted special legislation to supplement the basic unemployment insurance program. The prime cause for such action has been the levels of exhaustions. Legislation has provided federal funds for additional benefit periods to the long-term unemployed. In recent years, also, most states have lengthened the maximum duration of benefits to 26 weeks. Several states have sought to meet the "duration" problem in recessions with emergency extensions to be triggered by indicators of unusual distress. Proposed legislation at the federal level would grant federal funds to supplement benefits for workers whose unemployment persists.

The Temporary Unemployment Compensation Act of 1958 and the Temporary Emergency Unemployment Compensation Act of 1961 also provided loan funds to states whose reserves were inadequate to meet liabilities. The impact of the whole unemployment insurance program, so far as its countercyclical effects on employment are concerned, could be seriously jeopardized if insolvency prevented payment of benefits. Experience to date raises serious question about the ability of some states to regain balance and maintain solvency. A reasonable question concerns the appropriateness of states as the unit for reserves and benefits.

As a result of experience in 1958 and 1961, many critics of the system conclude that a sound insurance program must be a federalized program. Others propose regional units or a heavy federal subsidy to insure solvency as well as greater uniformity in benefit amounts, duration, and eligibility requirements. (See Chapter 23.)

Supplementary Unemployment Benefits

The countercyclical impact of unemployment insurance is compounded by negotiated supplementary unemployment benefit plans (See Chapter 23). These programs, initiated in 1955 in the automobile industry, establish special reserve funds built up by employer contributions from which unemployed workers, eligible for unemployment compensation, are paid a supplement to assure a higher proportion of wages. In addition, some plans provide separation payments in amounts based on length of service. They are available to workers who are not eligible for pensions.

These programs make the impact of unemployment benefits much greater and may also encourage employers to avoid layoffs.

They provide, in current plans, supplements to bring total benefits to more than 60 percent of wages for periods up to 52 weeks. Employer contributions vary with the changing level of reserve funds.

Automation Funds

A direct attack on worker displacement as a result of technological change is the purpose of several types of automation funds. In several industries, among them coal mining, long-shoring, and meat-packing, the way to technological change has been smoothed by these provisions. In negotiated arrangements, employers have agreed to contribute stipulated proportions of payrolls to funds which are used to provide dismisssal pay and retraining.[48]

Plans are in no sense standardized. In a variety of specific provisions, they share the gains to be made by technological advances and provide compensation coupled with opportunities for retraining for displaced workers. Experience with such arrangements is limited, but they seem to have facilitated more rapid change. They have eased the burden of unemployment and possibly have encouraged workers to move to other jobs.

In meat-packing, for example, Armour and Company and the United Packinghouse Workers created the Armour Automation Fund. When the work force is reduced, the fund helps workers find other jobs, offers early retirement to older employees and severance pay or retraining to others, and facilitates transfers to other Armour plants where operations continue. The fund works closely with the Federal Bureau of Employment Security and state employment agencies.[49] It grants TAP — technological adjustment pay — for between-job support to workers who elect to take new jobs in other plants. Funds may be used to pay for retraining.

Experience with such plans is limited; their potential contribution has not been established. Reports indicate serious difficulties in retraining and in relocating displaced workers. Such programs must be recognized as experimental; the Armour plan set aside a substantial fund for study of these problems. It is doubtful that such plans can become a major factor in meeting unemployment problems, and public expectations of their contributions may be unreal. On the other hand, they are a step in the right direction; the experience they provide can

---

[48]For details, see Thomas Kennedy, *Automation Funds and Displaced Workers* (Boston: Harvard Graduate School of Business Administration, Division of Research, 1962).

[49]See "Packing up an Armour Packing Plant," *Business Week*, July 20, 1963, pp. 80–82.

help to develop more effective approaches to the persistent impact of essential change.[50]

Reduced Resistance to Change

Such plans deserve special mention because they propose not only to reduce the waste inherent in unemployment but also that occasioned by fear of unemployment. It seems clear that such fear is a source of conflict and work rules that reduce productivity. It is basic to much of the featherbedding discussed in Chapter 12. Its influence on employment has a spiral pattern. Fear generates inefficiency which, in turn, increases costs and reduces effective demands for workers.

In steel, the Kaiser Steel Company and the United Steel Workers negotiated a plan to overcome such fears in 1963. The plan proposes to share savings in production costs with workers. The four-year contract outlaws strikes, guarantees levels of fringes and benefits comparable to those negotiated elsewhere, protects workers against layoffs from technological and work-rule changes, and offers employees a chance to share in cost savings if they wish to discontinue the wages provided under existing incentive plans.

Employees get 32.5 percent of cost savings, regardless of the source of savings or the profits of the firm. Workers displaced by change continue to receive wages until a new job is found for them. If reduced sales forces layoffs, employees receive unemployment benefits plus SUB.

Early experience has been favorable. Employees have received substantial supplements to wages as a result of cost savings.

Work-Spreading

For a century at least, another favored attack on unemployment involves reduced hours of work. The argument is not complicated: if 10 men want to work and only 8 are employed, why not divide the work among the 10? If the 8 work 40 hours per week, why not cut the week to 32 hours and put all the men to work? Chapter 17 examines the significance of hours and such related considerations as the place of leisure in modern society.

---

[50]See Edwin Young, "The Armour Experience: A Case Study in Plant Shutdown," Chapter 6, in Gerald G. Somers, *et al.* (eds.), *Adjusting to Technological Change* (New York: Harper and Row, 1963).

ANALYTICAL REVIEW QUESTIONS

1. How does unemployment "feed on itself"?
2. What are "made-work" and "work spreading" programs?
3. Why is the Employment Act sometimes described as the "Full Employment Act"?
4. Distinguish public policy from public programs.
5. List at least five types of programs designed to reduce unemployment.
6. Explain the current federal policy and its rationale.
7. Why is inflation a persistent hazard to the federal policy and programs?
8. Evaluate the position taken by the Chamber of Commerce regarding the federal program.
9. Why do critics see hazards of increased regulation in the growth program?
10. How are taxation and tariffs related to employment and unemployment?
11. What do fiscal policies and budget balances have to do with employment?
12. Explain the objectives in area redevelopment programs.
13. Cite and evaluate foreign experience in similar programs.
14. What are the arguments for and against the relocation of workers?
15. Is dismissal or severance pay a useful device for reducing unemployment? Why or why not?
16. Explain the growing concern about worker obsolescence, and suggest means of reducing it.
17. How does child labor become a matter of concern in programs for full employment?
18. Who provides job forecasting and vocational counseling services?
19. What are your predictions with respect to vocational education?
20. Who should assume major responsibility for providing retraining — employers, unions, the federal government, state or local governments, or the individual worker?
21. How does MDTA differ from ARA?
22. What seem to be the most serious problems in retraining programs?
23. What are the arguments for a special Youth Employment Act?
24. How does unemployment insurance fit into the total program, including ARA and MDTA?
25. In what ways does unemployment insurance stabilize employment?
26. Who really pays the unemployment insurance taxes; where does their impact fall?
27. How do exhaustions of benefits defeat basic objectives of the Unemployment Insurance program?
28. Explain the purpose and function of supplementary unemployment benefits.
29. What are TAP plans and automation funds?
30. How does the Kaiser Steel-USW plan tend to reduce resistance to change?

Case 16-1

NEGOTIATING FOR "SUB"

Assume that you are a member of a local union which is negotiating a renewal of its labor contract with a manufacturing firm in which you are employed. You have 15 years of service with the firm and have purchased 40 shares of its stock through the employee stock purchase plan. Business has been good; profits are higher than in any earlier year. Employment has been stable for most employees, but about 30 percent more are hired during the peak months than in the rest of the year. All production employees belong to the union.

In the preliminary discussion of union proposals, several members of the local have suggested that major emphasis should be placed on getting supplementary unemployment benefits patterned after those in the automobile industry. More specifically, they suggest that the union propose a package increase in pay to include a cash, across-the-board increase of 6¢ per hour; increased hospitalization and medical care, costing about 3¢ per hour; liberalization of the private pension plan, costing another 3¢; and SUB, to be provided by 5¢ per hour contributed by the employer to a reserve fund for that purpose.

• What position will you take on the SUB proposal? Prepare a short outline of the arguments you will advance in the next meeting of the local. Be sure to cover the questions of (1) alternative uses of the 5¢ contribution and (2) values of SUB to members of the union.

Case 16-2

A GUARANTEED ANNUAL WAGE

You are one of three proprietors of a very successful electronics manufacturing company. Your firm employs approximately 400 production workers. They have not, so far as you know, joined a union, although several attempts have been made to organize them.

You belong to a local association of employers. As a member participating in an association study, you have recently completed a careful analysis of your employment stability over the 10 years since you started. While the most impressive characteristic of this record is the rapid growth of the firm, you have also noted the fact that each year more than 70 percent of all production employees have had no layoff or loss of working time except for their own personal reasons. Since you have heard a good deal about union demands for a guaranteed annual wage, you are wondering if some such plan would help in recruiting and in maintaining a spirit of teamwork among your employees.

• Prepare a proposal for such a program of guaranteed employment that you can present to your partners. Comment on the following points and any others you regard as important: (1) Which employees are to be included? (2) How much will it cost? (3) Is it likely to destroy individual incentive? (4) How will it affect morale? (5) How would SUB affect it?

Case 16-3

STATE UNEMPLOYMENT

You are a member of the Governor's Advisory Council on Employment Security in your state. National unemployment rates on a seasonally adjusted base are running about 6 percent. In your state unemployment is averaging almost 10 percent, although this varies greatly from area to area within the state. You know the industrial situation in your state and what industries and occupations are "sick." The Governor has asked you to draft a program of (1) steps the federal government can take to help your employment situation, (2) steps the state can take, and (3) steps local communities can take.

• Outline these three programs and analyze their expected economic effects. Be sure to consider interrelationships between and among the three programs.

EMPLOYMENT, WORKING HOURS, AND LEISURE

"Overtime in Midst of Job Failure" is the title of a recent report on current union demands for more jobs and fewer working hours per week. That news story recounts the testimony of Joseph A. Beirne who told a Congressional committee that 30 percent of the workers in the telephone industry averaged 44.1 hours per week in 1962. He calculated that without overtime 17,250 additional workers would have had jobs.[1]

PRESSURE FOR SHORTER WORKING PERIODS

The situation revealed by the statistics relating to the telephone industry, when combined with unemployment statistics, is a major stimulant for the pressure to obtain shorter working periods. The persistent demand for more leisure is the second major aspect of efforts to secure shorter working periods.

Unemployment and Hours of Work

To many workers, employed as well as unemployed, and to many citizens, the most obvious attack on prosperity unemployment is one that would spread the work. If jobseekers exceed jobs, why not divide existing demands among the seekers, reducing the individual

---

[1] *Business Week*, November 2, 1963, pp. 54–56.

share of work by whatever proportion is necessary to achieve full employment? If 10 qualified workers are available and only 8 are hired, and if the 8 work 40 hours per week, why not hire the 10 for 32 hours each? This question is even more widely asked if the 8 who are working average 44 or 48 hours per week.

The question has been more frequently and persistently raised in the 1960's because no small portion of the work force is working more than 40 hours and is being paid premium wage rates, generally time and a half for the hours beyond 40.

Leisure and Hours of Work

The persistent demand for more free time is perhaps a pressure that is as old as man. Certainly, it has been apparent since earliest industrialization.

While no means exists for measuring this pressure, it may well grow at an accelerating rate. Psychological work theory has long stressed a hierarchy of human needs and hypothesized that, as lower level subsistence and material needs are satisfied, desires for satisfaction turn to such needs as those for social acceptance, recognition, self-expression, and self-actualization. While these "higher-level" needs can be satisfied to some extent on the job, many if not most workers must find satisfactions in their homes, families, social groups, and communities, and in travel, sports, and recreation. For that purpose they must get away from their jobs.

To the extent that work cannot in itself provide these higher levels of satisfaction, *leisure* (defined as voluntary freedom from work) seems likely to become a major goal in our society. A society in which subsistence and material needs can be readily satisfied seems likely to move its goals ahead toward the nonmaterial satisfactions that now fascinate its citizens. Current hours of work must inevitably become less and less attractive unless work itself offers these satisfactions.

A good deal of evidence suggests that work cannot or seems unlikely to provide the satisfactions demanded by citizens of a truly affluent society. Indeed, as has been frequently noted, work has come to be regarded as something that must be done. Hence, many workers seek to minimize it and to escape from it through recreation, including sports, movies, and television.[2]

---

[2]See Marcia L. Greenbaum, "The Shorter Workweek," *Bulletin 50* (New York State School of Industrial and Labor Relations, June, 1963). She quotes (p. 44) Walter Buckingham who suggests that such current escapes are replacing drink as the "curse of the nineteenth century worker."

On the other hand, the virtue of working is deeply imbedded in some of our strongest and most persistent traditions. The protestant ethic has exerted and continues to exert a powerful influence in our thought; it places a high value on work and thrift. While a case can be made for wide acceptance of leisure as a more important goal than work, such a shift can be contemplated as only a slow, gradual development. It may come, but it can only emerge slowly. Meanwhile, society and its citizens face difficult ideological conflicts in reconciling pressures for less work with the determination to regard work as the natural activity and idleness as a problem.[3]

The problem is less difficult for professionals, who may find great personal satisfactions in their work. Many professionals and managers presently work longer hours than do production workers. Perhaps this differential will grow.

In any case, ideas about what the term "leisure" means and how it should be regarded are likely to get a good deal of airing in the immediate future. Several recent proposals suggest that workers be given more leisure, which is to be used, for example, in retraining and preparing for changing work assignments. On the other hand, leisure has its critics, as is evident from the declaration (generally credited to a prominent steel executive) that "leisure should be abolished"; and the values of leisure have often been questioned by those who feel that "idle hands" encourage undesirable behavior.

Leisure has long been regarded as an important element in the good life toward which citizens should and do aspire. Aristotle described leisure as "freedom from the necessity of labor." Greek and Latin words for "work" define it as "un-leisure." In historic societies leisure was regarded as representing an opportunity to think broadly, to cultivate the mind, and was thus a goal to be regarded as having top priority or value.

Modern notions of leisure tend to relate it to relaxation and recreation, rather than to this historic concept. Moreover, we can anticipate many questions about the concept of leisure as a part of our social search for policies with respect to employment. What meaning of leisure is appropriate for a wealthy, democratic society? Is all "un-work" time leisure? Is time spent in educational activities leisure? Are students in college enjoying leisure in the classroom or only outside

---

[3]Father Purcell argues for such a reconciliation. He concludes that "People need to see that work and leisure need not be polarities. They can be fused. . . . Work need not be a frustration for a Christian. Work *can* be a rich fulfillment." Theodore V. Purcell, "The Meaning of Work," *New City*, Vol. 1, No. 9 (September, 1962), pp. 8–9.

these sessions? Or must leisure involve time used to think and to contemplate, with no restraints on the scope of such mental excursions?[4]

CHANGING HOURS OF WORK

The long-term trend of daily and weekly hours of work has been downward. The workday extended from sunrise to sunset in the American colonies, with a 6-day week. Earliest agitation on working hours in this country sought a limit of 12 to 14 hours per day. In 1840, when federal employees were granted a 10-hour day, work weeks of 70 to 84 hours were the rule. The 8-hour day for federal employees was instituted in 1868. Campaigns for a 10-hour day in private employment were common in the early 1900's. Average weekly hours of full-time workers amounted to about 72 in agriculture and about 66 in industry in 1850. By the end of the century, these were reduced to about 67 and 56. In 1948 average weekly hours in agriculture were about 55 and, in nonagricultural industries, about 43. By 1956 these workweeks had declined to about 47 and 41.

The Bureau of Labor Statistics has collected and published annual data on average weekly hours in manufacturing since 1919. Several other industries were added later. The Census Bureau began collecting household data on hours of work in 1941. BLS data are provided by employers in a large sample of establishments. The Department of Labor now provides regular monthly reports in its *Monthly Report on the Labor Force*. They include: (1) household data collected and tabulated by the Bureau of the Census for the Bureau of Labor Statistics; (2) data on insured unemployment provided by the Bureau of Employment Security; and (3) establishment data on employment, hours, and earnings that are reported directly to the Bureau of Labor Statistics.

The Data

As the Bureau of Labor Statistics puts it, "Not much comprehensive, reliable information on hours of work is available for the period before World War II."[5] Only rough estimates can be made for earlier periods. Estimates were made, however, for a special Congressional

---

[4]See Sebastian de Grazia, *Of Time, Work and Leisure* (New York: The Twentieth Century Fund, 1962).

[5]Joseph S. Zeisel, "The Workweek in American Industry, 1850–1956," *Monthly Labor Review*, Vol. 81, No. 1 (January, 1958), pp. 23–29.

Report in 1893. Later studies sought to combine sample data from various sources to provide a long-term view of changes.[6] In 1955 a series describing average weekly hours worked was developed by J. Frederick Dewhurst and Associates.[7] Early estimates and approximations have been combined with data from more recent BLS studies to provide the series shown in Figure 17-1.

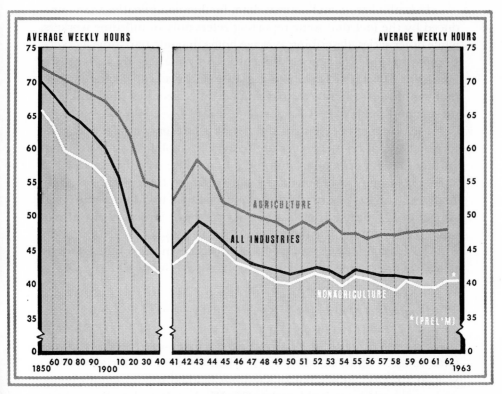

Figure 17-1
ESTIMATED AVERAGE WEEKLY HOURS IN AGRICULTURAL AND NONAGRICULTURAL INDUSTRIES — 1850–1963[1]

[1]Annual averages. All employed persons, including self-employed and unpaid family workers.

Source: *Monthly Labor Review*, Vol. 81, No. 1 (January, 1958), p. 24; Dewhurst and Associates; and Bureau of Labor Statistics.

While it is quite clear that, over the years, numbers of hours spent on the job each week have declined, precise measurement of that decline is difficult. Such measurement is complicated by the fact that

[6]For example, Paul H. Douglas reviewed these earlier data in his *Real Wages in the United States* (Boston: Houghton Mifflin Co., 1930).

[7]*America's Needs and Resources — A New Survey* (New York: The Twentieth Century Fund, 1955).

reporting is not uniform; some data are derived from the payroll reports of employers, which describe actual hours worked or paid for. Other series reflect actual hours as reported from household surveys in the *Monthly Report on the Labor Force*. Still other reports refer to *standard* or *scheduled hours*, and others refer to *straight-time hours*, thus excluding overtime.

In both historic and current data, further complications are introduced by the fact that some reporting refers only to full-time workers, while other series, describing average hours, include part-time workers. Comparisons are made more difficult also by the fact that changes in hours are associated with both seasonal and cyclical fluctuations, so that significant differences may appear as a result of the timing of surveys and samples.

Measurement of changes and trends is further complicated by the fact that actual hours at work are reduced by holidays and vacations. In the opposite direction, multiple job-holding, usually described as *moonlighting*, may occasion hours much longer than those reported. As a result, all long-term comparisons are subject to considerable error. Amounts of time paid for but not worked have increased because of more paid holidays, vacations, and other fringes.[8]

To evaluate trends, each of these variables in the total of working hours requires some attention, as do comparative working hours in modern industrialized nations.

Limitations of averages. Reports of average hours must be regarded as crude measures of change, in part because they combine so many divergent patterns. The average includes and represents a very wide range. Thus, in May, 1963, when the average for all workers was 40.7 hours, 20 percent of the total worked more than 49 hours, and another fifth worked less than 35. Workers in railroading, wholesale trade, mining, and forestry and fisheries averaged between 42 and 45 hours. Industries with an average of less than 35 hours included retail trade, education, entertainment, and recreation.

Overtime. Actual hours include overtime; scheduled hours do not. Overtime is by no means an insignificant part of the total. Thus, in 1963, the Department of Labor reported that actual hours in manufacturing were approximately at the same level as in 1946 (40.3). The average workweek for men in the 25–64 year age group was reported

---

[8]Since 1947, the Manufacturing Census and Annual Survey data are for hours worked. See John W. Kendrick, "Productivity, Costs and Prices," Chapter 2 in *Wages, Prices, Profits* (New York: American Assembly and Columbia University, 1959).

as 45 hours. More than 15 million workers regularly worked overtime. Eighteen percent of the labor force worked more than 48 hours per week. Overtime accounted for 7 percent of all manufacturing activity, and premium pay for overtime accounted for approximately 10 percent of the average worker's total earnings.

To avoid the complications introduced by overtime and as one means of providing a closer check on trends, another measure notes proportions of all workers who actually worked for various numbers of hours in the workweek.

Full time and part time workers. The distinction between all workers and full-time workers is important. From 1948 to 1960, for example, hours of all workers in nonagricultural industries declined from 41.9 to 40.1; those for full-time workers declined from 45.2 to 44.6, according to one study.[9] About one fifth of all nonagricultural workers are part time, with a heavy concentration in the less skilled occupations.

As noted in Chapter 15, current information on the extent of part-time work comes from two principal sources — the reports of employers to the Department of Labor and the sample survey of households. The most inclusive appraisal is that provided by frequent MRLF special surveys of part-time employment. They distinguish those who normally work full time from the usual part-time workers, and they list the reasons for part-time work.

Annual average numbers of part-time workers increased from 6.9 million in 1949 to almost 9 million in 1962. Numbers of part-time nonagricultural workers in recent years may be summarized as follows:[10]

	Voluntary Part-time	Part-time for Economic Reasons	
		Usually Full-time	Usually Part-time
(thousands of persons 14 years of age and over)			
1957......	5,181	1,183	986
1958......	5,215	1,638	1,315
1959......	5,569	1,032	1,304
1960......	5,815	1,243	1,317
1961......	6,148	1,297	1,516
1962......	6,597	1,049	1,287
1963......	6,808	1,069	1,219

[9]Peter Henle, "Recent Growth of Paid Leisure for U.S. Workers," *Monthly Labor Review*, Vol. 85, No. 3 (March, 1962), p. 250.

[10]Data from *Manpower Report of the President* (Washington 25, D.C.: United States Government Printing Office, March, 1964), pp. 205, 207.

It should be noted that more than two thirds of these part-time workers are voluntarily on short shifts. They include many housewives, students, and older workers who cannot undertake full-time assignments. At the same time, however, it is notable that more than two million workers, in each recent year, were on part time for economic reasons.

Part time for economic reasons varies with the business cycle. For nonagricultural workers, this segment made up from 4.5 to 5.7 percent of total employment in the recession years of 1949, 1954, 1958, and 1961 as compared with from 3 to 3.7 percent in 1951, 1952, and 1962.

Part-time employment is characteristic of semiskilled and unskilled workers in trade, service, and construction and of very young workers and those over 65. It is more common among nonwhite than among white workers, so that the total pattern is closely comparable to and a part of the general employment of unskilled, minority groups (see Figure 17-2).

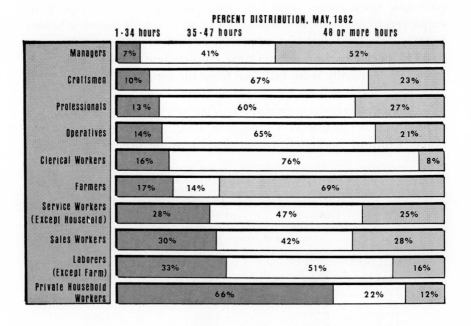

PERCENT DISTRIBUTION, MAY, 1962

1 - 34 hours   35 - 47 hours   48 or more hours

Managers — 7%, 41%, 52%
Craftsmen — 10%, 67%, 23%
Professionals — 13%, 60%, 27%
Operatives — 14%, 65%, 21%
Clerical Workers — 16%, 76%, 8%
Farmers — 17%, 14%, 69%
Service Workers (Except Household) — 28%, 47%, 25%
Sales Workers — 30%, 42%, 28%
Laborers (Except Farm) — 33%, 51%, 16%
Private Household Workers — 66%, 22%, 12%

Figure 17-2

OCCUPATIONAL DIFFERENCES IN PART-TIME WORK — 1962

Source: Bureau of Labor Statistics data.

This large segment of part-time workers contributes a significant portion of total hours worked. The *Manpower Report of the President* notes that "in the private, nonfarm economy most of the increase in wage and salary employment since 1957 is accounted for by a rise in part-time employment, chiefly in the trade and service industries."[11]

Holidays and vacations. Comparisons of changes in hours are further complicated by changes in annual work time occasioned by the trend toward more holidays and longer vacations. Such changes have influenced the total working time as well as that available for leisure activities. Each holiday reduces the average workweek by about nine minutes and each week of vacation may be regarded as a reduction of about 46 minutes per working week.

Numbers of paid holidays have been growing. They increased during World War II because payment for holidays was permitted as noninflationary under wage and salary controls, on the theory that actual production increased proportionately. BLS surveys indicate that about three fifths of all workers now enjoy 7 or more paid holidays.

Numbers of paid holidays vary from one locality to another. Some holidays are legal; most states specify Christmas, New Year's, Washington's Birthday, Memorial Day, Independence Day, Labor Day, and Thanksgiving. Some add Columbus Day and Veterans' Day. Other holidays have been negotiated; recently many agreements specify a half day before Christmas and New Year's and the Friday following Thanksgiving. In some industries agreements now allow each employee to celebrate his birthday as a holiday. Practice may substitute another day for paid holidays that fall on a weekend. Banking and finance typically provide the most liberal holiday policies; they provide from 9 to 11, or more, paid holidays per year. For production workers, the public utilities lead. For both office and plant employees, fewest holidays are provided in retail trade.[12]

The extension of paid vacations to salaried workers dates roughly from World War I. For most production workers, paid vacations became common during or immediately following World War II. In 1940 about one fourth of all union members received paid vacations, generally for one week. In 1957, 91 percent of workers covered in similar agreements received paid vacations, and 84 percent included a

---

[11]*Manpower Report of the President* (Washington 25, D.C.: United States Government Printing Office, March, 1963), p. 51.

[12]Peter Henle, *op. cit.*, pp. 249–57.

maximum of three weeks for long-service employees. Almost all metropolitan workers are now eligible for paid vacations, and MRLF surveys indicate that by 1961 workers averaged 1.3 weeks of actual vacation.[13]

The length of the individual vacation is generally related or "graduated" to years of service; for example, the general rule in the printing and publishing industry in 1960 made the maximum three-week vacation available after five years of service. In petroleum and chemicals the full three weeks required 10 years of service. BLS has reported some 400 formulas for calculating vacation pay.[14]

The trend in paid vacations is upward, according to a BLS survey in 1961.[15] The two-week maximum period dominant in 1949 was found in less than 10 percent of labor agreements in 1961. In 1961, 43 percent of all graduated plans provided for maximums of four weeks or longer. The extension of maximum vacation periods has been accompanied by reduction in length-of-service requirements. Whereas 19 percent of white-collar workers and 6 percent of production workers were employed under plans providing as much as 4 weeks of paid vacation in 1952–53, by 1961–62 these proportions were 47 and 38 percent.

The significance of vacations, so far as leisure is concerned, took a sharp jump in 1962 when the Steelworkers initiated a special extended vacation or "sabbatical" plan in aluminum and steel contracts. These plans, justified by the Union as workspreading, extend the paid vacations for long-service employees. As subsequently modified, such employees became eligible for extended vacations or sabbaticals of as much as 10 to 13 weeks in each five-year period.

The exact influence of increased numbers of paid holidays and longer paid vacations on actual hours worked is not easily measured. For both holidays and vacations some part of this trend is mainly influential on earnings; workers may elect to receive the extra pay and to continue working. In the "sabbatical" plans this option is restricted; the employee may, for example, elect to work not more than 3 of the 13 weeks.

---

[13]*Ibid.*, p. 254.

[14]See "The Expanding Vacation," *Fortune* (September, 1961), pp. 195 ff.

[15]Frank W. Merritt, "Paid Vacation Provisions in Major Union Contracts, 1961," *Monthly Labor Review*, Vol. 85, No. 8 (August, 1962), pp. 875–81. For a 1964 report in detail, see *Union Contracts and Collective Bargaining, Report Bulletin 22* (Englewood Cliffs, New Jersey: Prentice-Hall, Inc., April 20, 1964).

Moonlighting. The data of weekly hours are also complicated by moonlighting, the practice in which full-time workers hold second and third jobs. They may report only on their full-time job. They may seek to avoid reports on second jobs by using another name. Such evasive practices make the reliability of survey information somewhat questionable.

The best available data are those developed in the MRLF surveys. They indicate that some 3.9 million persons were multiple job holders in May, 1963 — about 5.7 percent of all those employed. If agricultural workers are excluded, moonlighters made up from 6 to 10 percent of nonagricultural employment. Men are more likely to hold second jobs than women — about 6 percent for men and 2 percent for women. Men in the 25-44 year age range have the highest rates. While it is sometimes argued that "moonlighters" take jobs that could go to unemployed, the facts do not appear to justify this conclusion. Some 500,000 persons had second jobs as managers and professionals in 1962; only 200,000 unemployed were seeking work in this broad category of jobs, and many did not have the specific skills needed.

One million persons had dual jobs operating their own farms or businesses. Of the remaining 2 million jobs, almost all of which were part-time and seasonal, factors such as mismatching of location of supply and demand, and jobs usually held only by men or women, reduce the availability of these jobs to the unemployed. Further, were dual job holding forbidden, many employers might prefer overtime to hiring extra help.[16]

Recent surveys suggest that the numbers and proportions of moonlighters may be increasing. The 1963 study found that about 5.7 percent of the total labor force were moonlighters. As compared with a similar count in December, 1960, this represented a 13 percent increase. The trend is not at all certain, however. Earlier studies that compared annual averages found little change from 1957 through 1959.[17] In 1963 moonlighters reported a median workweek of 52 hours, composed of a normal, first job of 40 hours and 12 additional hours on second or third jobs.

---

[16]See Jacob Shiffman, "Multiple Job Holders in May, 1962," *Monthly Labor Review*, Vol. 86, No. 5 (May, 1963), pp. 516–23; see also Gertrude Bancroft, "Multiple Job Holders in December, 1959," *Monthly Labor Review*, Vol. 83, No. 10 (October, 1960), pp. 1045–51. See Forrest A. Bogan and Harvey R. Hamel, "Multiple Jobholders in May 1963," *Monthly Labor Review*, Vol. 87, No. 3 (March, 1964), pp. 249–57.

[17]Gertrude Bancroft, "Multiple Job Holders in December, 1959," *Monthly Labor Review*, Vol. 83, No. 10 (October, 1960), pp. 1045–51.

Annual work time. A realistic comparison of time-to-time changes in hours would require a concept something like actual annual working hours which would include straight time and overtime and which would eliminate unworked vacations and holidays. It might compare only the experience of full-time workers. It has been suggested that such a work-year figure might also exclude paid coffee breaks, lunch periods, and wash-up or clean-up time, which are established features of about one fifth of all negotiated agreements.[18]

Attempts have been made to take some of these influences into account in comparisons for the years since 1940. It has been calculated, for example, that workers gained 1½ hours from shorter work weeks, a total of 75 hours per year. From 6 days of added paid vacations, they gained 48 hours. From 4 days of added holidays, they gained 32 hours. Thus calculated, the total reduction is 155 hours per year in this 20-year period.[19]

International Comparisons

Although the labor movements in many foreign nations have sought to achieve a 40-hour week, actual hours are generally longer than those in this country. Several nations have had a legal 40-hour week for many years. France, for example, made such a provision in 1930. Data for Tables 17-1 and 17-2 are available from a 1963 report by the Commissioner of Labor Statistics.[20] They indicate wide observance of a 6-day or 5½-day workweek. The move toward a shorter period has been slowed by tight labor markets in many nations and by programs designed to speed economic development.

In most European nations overtime rates include a premium of 25 percent. Holidays are more numerous.

The Pace of Reduction

The reality of a long-term downward trend in hours of work in this century is reasonably clear, as is the trend toward added leisure. But the precise measurement of these trends is not simple. As preceding paragraphs indicate, available data are essentially crude. There

---

[18]See Dena G. Weiss and Ernestine M. Moore, "Paid Rest Periods in Major Contracts, 1959," *Monthly Labor Review*, Vol. 83, No. 9 (September, 1960), p. 958; and Dena G. Weiss and Theresa L. Ellis, "Paid Time for Washup, Cleanup, and Clothes Change in 1959," *Monthly Labor Review*, Vol. 83, No. 9 (September, 1960), p. 964.

[19]Peter Henle, *op. cit.*, p. 256.

[20]"Hours of Work in the United States and Abroad," *Monthly Labor Review*, Vol. 86, No. 8 (August, 1963), pp. 925–34.

Table 17-1

NORMAL WEEKLY MAXIMUM HOURS IN SELECTED NATIONS

Country	Fixed by —		Country	Fixed by —	
	Law	Collective Contract		Law	Collective Contract
Australia[1]........	40	——	Israel.........	47	47
Austria..........	48	45	Italy...........	48	[6]44–48
Belgium.........	48	45	Japan..........	40	——
Canada[2].........	44–48	40–44	Netherlands.....	48	45
Denmark........	—	43	Norway........	45	37–42
France..........	40	([3])	Sweden........	45	40–42
Federal Republic.			Switzerland.....	48	45–46
of Germany....	[4]48	[5]40–47	United Kingdom	—	42–44

[1]The hours of work are determined by an arbitration system established under a constitutional provision.

[2]The hours of work are determined by provincial legislation.

[3]In the steel industry, 42 hours.

[4]The general standard fixed by law is 8 hours a day, with special regulations governing Sunday work. Indirectly, this means a regular 48-hour workweek.

[5]Average 44.

[6]Average 46.

Source: "Hours of Work in the United States and Abroad," *Monthly Labor Review*, Vol. 86, No. 8 (August, 1963), p. 933.

Table 17-2

HOURS WORKED PER WEEK
IN MANUFACTURING IN SELECTED NATIONS[1]

Country	Date	Average Hours Worked[1]
Australia........................	December 1962	39.99
Austria.........................	December 1962	43.0
Canada.........................	September 1962	41.4
France..........................	September 1962	45.9
Federal Republic of Germany.......	September 1962	44.5
Italy............................	February 1962	[2]168.3
Japan...........................	September 1962	49.3
Netherlands.....................	1961 ————	46.7
Norway.........................	December 1961	{ [3]41.6 [4]37.7
Switzerland......................	September 1962	45.7
United Kingdom..................	October 1962	46.2

[1]The data for Austria, Canada, Germany, and Switzerland represent hours actually worked; those for the remaining countries show hours paid for.

[2]Average monthly hours for period of January–April 1962.

[3]Male.

[4]Female.

Source: "Hours of Work in the United States and Abroad," *Monthly Labor Review*, Vol. 86, No. 8 (August, 1963), p. 933.

is difficulty in discovering actual time spent in working, and the reciprocal time available for leisure cannot be readily evaluated. It is
possible, for example, that modern workers spend more time getting to
and from work. One study calculates this loss as 8½ hours per week.[21]
In addition, the fact that many workers now own their home may
require 5 to 7 hours of home maintainance per week, which may not be
regarded as leisure.

Wilensky notes, also, that some of the added free time is a sort of
required idleness to "make jobs go around." He concludes that "increasing millions are reluctant victims of too much leisure."[22]

In general, the facts indicate that hours have been reduced. They
also suggest that the pace of such reduction has declined; the data
suggest little or no change in average weekly hours since 1948.

Figure 17-3 provides an overview of the data of hours and man-
hour output for the years since 1909. The hours shown are for production workers in manufacturing, including hours worked or paid for —
not scheduled hours. Indexes of output per man-hour are those
developed by the Bureau of Labor Statistics for nonagricultural industries. They are of major interest in attempting to understand past
change and forecast future changes.

From the data on which the figure is based, it seems quite clear
that no simple straight-line trend for changes in hours is appropriate.
The pattern indicates a more rapid downward slope in years before
World War II and a much slower rate of decline since the war.

GOALS AND POLICIES WITH RESPECT TO WORKING HOURS

Although the pressure for shorter hours comes from all or almost
all workers, spokesmen for hourly-rated employees have been most
articulate. This follows, in part, from the fact that they suffer the
major share of unemployment. At the same time, these occupational
groups feel more need for nonworking, free time because their work
is less satisfying.

The goals of individuals rather obviously differ so far as their
interest in shorter hours are concerned. In part, these differences
reflect varying on-the-job satisfactions, as suggested in the preceding
paragraph. In part, they may well be influenced by different needs:

---

[21]Sebastian de Grazia, *Of Time, Work and Leisure* (New York: The Twentieth Century Fund, 1962).

[22]Harold L. Wilensky, "The Uneven Distribution of Leisure: The Impact of Economic Growth on 'Free Time'," *Social Problems*, Vol. 9, No. 1 (Summer, 1961), pp. 32–56.

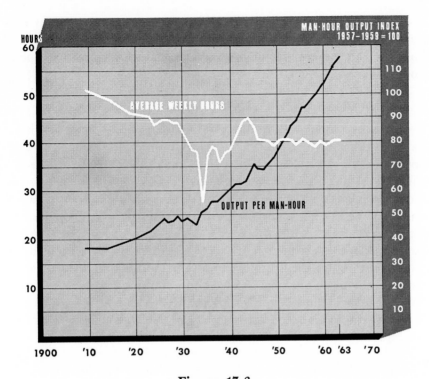

Figure 17-3

AVERAGE WEEKLY HOURS AND OUTPUT PER MAN-HOUR
IN THE UNITED STATES — 1909–1963

Sources: Bureau of Labor Statistics data on hours represent the average of hours worked or paid for in manufacturing industries as reported in annual *Economic Reports* and BLS releases; see, for example, *American Workers Fact Book* (Washington, D.C.: Department of Labor, 1960), pp. 88–89. Data on output are BLS indexes that adjust the value of the national product in fixed prices to numbers of man-hours and are reported as output indexes for the nonagricultural industries on a labor-force basis. The earlier indexes were based on 1947–49 = 100 and have been transposed to the 1957–59 base used in current reporting. See *Economic Report of the President*, 1963, p. 209, and *American Workers Fact Book*, pp. 90–91.

the part-time worker who wants to be full-time may favor longer hours for himself and shorter hours for other, competing workers. In part, they express philosophical views of work which may reach a stage approaching an "occupational phobia."[23]

No simple generalization about individual goals and policies is possible. It is appropriate, however, to consider the positions — with

---

[23]See John Chamberlain, "Role of the Individual in the Modern World," *Wall Street Journal*, November 16, 1962, p. 12.

respect to working hours — of union members and leaders, of employers and their associations, and of public policy. It is particularly important that the economic assumptions and rationale of each position be clearly recognized.

Union Views

The union viewpoint has probably attracted more attention than the other two. Unions have quite consistently proposed shorter hours. While they have, from time to time, noted the desirable advantages of more time away from work, they have pinned most of their arguments on the values of reduced hours as a means of reducing unemployment. Since the 40-hour week has achieved popular acceptance as a sort of standard, they have frequently selected the 35-hour week and the reduction of overtime as their preferred policies — that is, the routes they propose to attain the full-employment goal. Unions may also recognize shorter hours as a means of maintaining union size and influence, providing jobs that will hold present members in the union, and perhaps increasing numbers eligible for membership.

The union position has been widely publicized both by AFL-CIO and by many member and nonmember unions. The most common statement proposes a 35-hour week of five 7-hour days, with no reduction in weekly earnings and premium rates (double time) for overtime.[24] The basic premise of this position was stated by Samuel Gompers in 1887. He said, "So long as there is one man who seeks employment and cannot find it, the hours of labor are too long."

Shorter hours and wages. The union position sees a relationship between reduced hours and increased pay; it was put in rhyme in the 1860's in a couplet attributed to the wife of a union leader:

> Whether you work by the piece or the day,
> Decreasing the hours increases the pay.

Current union demands still lean heavily on the *lump of labor theory* which holds that demands for labor are inelastic; there is just so much work to be done in any specific period, and it can be spread among existing workers without much concern about effects on labor costs. On this basis union proposals for reduced hours consistently propose no reduction in take-home pay.

---

[24]Perhaps the best published expression is "Shorter Hours: A Tool to Combat Unemployment," *Publication No. 129* (Washington, D.C.: AFL-CIO, 1963).

Purchasing power. Today's unions frequently substitute a "purchasing power" argument for the somewhat simpler "lump of labor" position. They bolster this increased spending view with the further assumption that shorter hours would result in higher levels of productivity, thus reducing the pressure toward higher unit labor costs. The AFL-CIO position on these relationships has been stated as follows:

> But under the most typical and likely circumstances, a company reducing its workweek by several hours ordinarily will have to immediately hire additional workers to provide those hours of work if it wants to maintain approximately the same output or service as before.
>
> The longer-run effects then hinge on productivity movements and whether demand for its products increases sufficiently to enable savings from economies of increased production to finance continued payment to workers. In principle, the combination of the new hiring by this and other companies will build aggregate worker income, and, in turn, demand for the products.
>
> The pivotal question, of course, is to what extent, by serving to maintain and often to increase employment, shorter hours will be the dynamic new ingredient needed to bolster demand and increase it to the point where more and more companies have to expand employment further and thereby carry along an accelerating rate of economic and employment growth.[25]

Effects on productivity. The union rationale sees the rate of productivity advance, the industry's cost structure, the effect of hour reductions on equipment and technology, the trends and levels in demands for products, the rate of use of plant and equipment, and the effect on labor costs as major variables deserving consideration in achieving reductions in hours. In support of their proposals, unions note that shorter hours may permit a faster pace, both on machine-paced jobs and when pace is set by the individual. They point to experience indicating that shorter hours have reduced waste time and absenteeism and have increased productivity. Further, if leisure is used for education or for other self-development, it can be regarded as a worthwhile investment that will yield future returns in increased productivity.

Negotiation or legislation. Unions propose to carry out their policies through negotiation and by encouraging legislation to reduce straight-time hours and increase overtime premium rates. They have negotiated 36-, 35-, and 30-hour weeks. (A 25-hour week for Local 3

---

[25]*Ibid.*, pp. 24–25.

of the International Brotherhood of Electrical Workers was negotiated in 1962.) They have suggested higher penalty wage rates for overtime, as noted. In addition, they have negotiated *short workweek benefits* requiring employers to pay for a portion of the wage loss occasioned by less than full-time work. In the 1961 automobile contracts, the benefit for scheduled short weeks is 65 percent of the difference between wages for 40 hours and hours actually worked. For unscheduled short workweeks beyond the control of the employer, the benefit is 50 percent of lost wages. The 1962 steel contracts provide that workers called in for a week's work will get at least 32 hours of pay, even if a layoff results from a cut in production schedules.

Flexible workweek. Meanwhile, Walter Reuther has proposed an amendment to the Fair Labor Standards Act that would encourage a flexible workweek — hours of work would be adjusted upward or downward according to the level of unemployment. At times the workweek would be cut to 30 or 35 hours, with no reduction in pay for workers whose weekly employment was thus reduced. Funds to pay for the unworked time would be provided from a national adjustment fund. In the beginning this fund would be created by a federal loan, but the loan would be repaid and the fund would become self-supporting through revenue from a payroll tax, probably of 1 percent. Employers who refused to participate in the program would be required to pay for overtime at double-time rates for hours in excess of the reduced workweek.[26]

Employee opinions. Unions insist that they represent the prevailing opinions of workers. They conclude that shorter hours have not exerted a significant influence on moonlighting. They conclude also that the way to limit moonlighting is to increase income since "the critical element in whether moonlighting is stimulated (by reducing hours) . . . has not been the number of hours on the primary job, but the need or desire to maintain an accustomed income level."[27] They note that recent public opinion polls show that proportions favoring shorter hours have been growing.[28] They argue that a union strong enough to force reductions in hours beyond the general pattern of

---

[26]See the Resolution of the AFL-CIO Convention of 1961 reported in "Shorter Hours: A Tool to Combat Unemployment," *Publication No. 129* (Washington, D.C.: AFL-CIO, 1963), pp. 51–52; also, "Plan for a Flexible Work Week," *Business Week*, March 2, 1963, p. 27; and Otto Pragau, "Adaptation to Technological Change Under Collective Bargaining," *Proceedings of the 12th Annual Labor-Management Conference* (West Virginia University, April 12–13, 1962), p. 7.

[27]"Shorter Hours: A Tool to Combat Unemployment," *op. cit.*, p. 37.

[28]*Ibid.*, pp. 30–31.

these changes provides greater job security for its members. This demonstration of power holds members and strengthens the bonds of their organization.

Further, unions answer the argument that demands for fewer hours simply seek more pay by noting that, for employers who pay overtime rates, higher wage rates would be easier for unions to negotiate in most cases than the roundabout route of hour reduction.

Employer Policies

Spokesmen for employers have historically opposed most reductions in weekly hours. Many of their early arguments are no longer advanced; few employer statements today argue against reductions in hours on moral grounds or suggest that employees will misuse their added hours to engage in socially undesirable orgies or debauchery.

Almost all managers expect reductions in working hours, as evidenced by a several-year study of their forecasts. They argue that shorter hours are a proper long-term goal. Their present objections are directed against (1) what they regard as too rapid a pace in these reductions, (2) legislation that imposes a set pattern of reductions on all or a large part of industry, and (3) negotiated or legally required reductions in numbers of straight-time hours that are intended principally to insure higher earnings through more hours at premium rates of pay, rather than fewer hours of work.

Major arguments in current employer policy can be outlined as follows:

1. Reducing numbers of hours per week almost inevitably raises unit labor costs and reduces employment.
2. Reducing hours tends to reduce national income; it is thus a retrogressive step rather than an influence toward economic growth.
3. Reducing hours, through its influence on labor costs, handicaps American employers in international competition.
4. Employees as a whole do not favor the hour reductions proposed by union spokesmen.
5. Legislation is not a desirable means of regulating hours.

Labor costs and employment. Employer and union attitudes are similar in their assumption that decreasing hours increases pay. For the employer, however, the meaning is somewhat different; he means that unit labor costs are almost certain to be increased by reductions in hours, particularly if they are accompanied by higher premium rates for overtime.

Reduced hours mean higher labor costs, in the usual employer view, in part because they consistently require a shorter workweek without reductions in weekly earnings. On this basis, the Chamber of Commerce describes the frequent union proposals as a disguised wage increase, a "deceptive maneuver to raise wages."[29] Thus, a reduction from 40 to 38 hours would require an approximate 5 percent increase in rates; the 35-hour week, about a 14 percent rise; and a 32-hour week, about 25 percent.

In 1962, when AFL-CIO President Meany advocated a standard workweek of 35 hours with overtime at the premium rate of double the hourly rate, employers saw his proposal as involving an increase of from 14 to 29 percent in direct labor costs.

Under such circumstances the increased cost of labor would reduce demands for labor, which are by no means inelastic. Management would take steps to reduce its use of labor. Employers might try to raise product prices, which would presumably also reduce the quantities sold. The change would be inherently inflationary. Employer spokesmen recognize the union answer that increased worker purchasing power would offset the higher costs. Employers counter with the assertion that this argument confuses wage rates with total payrolls and worker income. Insofar as total work income remained the same or was reduced, there would be no total increase in purchasing power. The same result follows if reduction in hours causes inflation.

In the employer view shortening hours can only spread employment and conceal unemployment. If the work is evenly distributed among more workers and if productivity per hour is unchanged, then the total product remains the same and workers who reduced their hours must simply produce less.

If hourly productivity were increased under shorter hours, in the employer view, this effect might in itself displace workers and defeat the employment goals of hour-reduction. Further, the evidence that reduced hours cause increased hourly productivity is not convincing to employer spokesmen. They recognize the historic parallel in shorter hours and rising productivity, but they question the assumption of

---

[29]"Shorter Work Week — A Disguise for Wage Raise," Chamber of Commerce of the United States, Vol. 1, No. 51, Special Supplement, December 21, 1962.

causality. They conclude that shorter hours may tend to reduce productivity because workers with whom work is shared may not be as well qualified for jobs as those whose hours are reduced. Further, if employers try to advance the pace of work to balance shorter hours, employees often regard this change as an unreasonable *speedup*. Unrest and conflict may be generated by such employer action.

Also, if hours of primary workers are reduced, additional secondary workers may feel the necessity to seek work. If they are unable to find jobs, they will increase the numbers of unemployed.

In summary, employers conclude that reducing hours cannot be regarded as an effective therapy for unemployment. It may, to some degree, spread existing jobs among more workers, but in doing so it inevitably sets the stage for additional unemployment. By its effect on labor costs, it is likely to reduce employment rather than increase it.

Reduced national income. In the common employer view reducing hours appears as a reduction in the total quantity of employed labor resources. Such a reduction would exert a strong influence toward reduced national income and would be a step backward so far as economic growth is concerned. At the same time, spreading employment through shorter hours would reduce the efficiency of utilization for labor resources, thus introducing a further pressure toward decline, rather than growth, in total production.

International competition. Higher unit labor costs and less efficient utilization of labor resources, in this view, must inevitably handicap employers who seek to enter foreign markets. Since workweeks are already much longer in foreign nations and since many of them are rapidly improving their efficiency in employment, less efficient utilization of resources could well result in more unemployment in this country. In any case, our policy should be one seeking more rather than less efficient utilization of all our resources. It must also generate lower prices if we are to hold our own in international markets.

Employee preferences. Employer representatives see most of the pressure for shorter hours as essentially a union-inspired means of increasing weekly wages. Employees, in this view, are not demanding less time at work. Indeed, many of them want to work longer hours. The evidence on that point is clear in the widespread practice of moonlighting or multiple job holding. The *Washington Report* of the Chamber of Commerce quotes George Brooks, former research director for the Pulp, Sulphite and Paper Mill Workers in support of this employer argument, as follows:

> Aside from a worker's desire for their paid holidays and paid vacations there is no evidence in recent experience that workers want shorter daily or weekly hours. The evidence is all on the other side. Hundreds of local and international officials have testified that the most numerous and persistent grievances are disputes over the sharing of overtime work.[30]

Legislated hours. The employer view has generally opposed legislative measures requiring greater penalties for overtime or lower trigger points for such premium rates. Employers argue that legislation imposes an unreasonable uniformity that may be inappropriate for many industries. Among the significant differences among industries are the rate of productivity gain, the industry's cost structure, and fringe benefits.[31] Further, legal rules may prevent many workers from making their own choice as to how to take the fruits of their increasing productivity.

Why overtime? Why do employers apparently prefer overtime to hiring more workers? There are several reasons:

1. Overtime may be cheaper if the workers involved are more efficient than those available as possible additions.
2. Overtime takes care of temporary needs without creating an added liability for unemployment insurance which may, in turn, be reflected in higher payroll taxes.
3. Costs of other fringe benefits, including pensions, holidays, vacations, hospitalization, and others, for added workers may be greater than the usual premium rates paid for overtime.
4. Hiring added workers may require capital investments and supervision that are more costly than overtime. (This consideration follows only if added workers cannot be accommodated with existing facilities and shifts.)
5. As individual workers, many employees want the overtime and have become accustomed to counting on it. Substituting added workers may encounter employee and union opposition.

Public Policy

Public policy can reasonably be assumed to accept the long-term goal of continual reductions in working hours and increased time for nonworking activities. No formal statement of that acceptance can

---

[30] *Washington Report*, Chamber of Commerce of the United States, Special Supplement, December 21, 1962.

[31] See "What a 35-hour Work Week Would Mean," *Business Week*, October 20, 1962, pp. 132 ff.

be cited, but a long history of federal and state legislation has moved toward that goal. On the other hand, the government has, at times, indicated its opposition to sharp reductions and proposed longer hours.

Objectives in public policy on hours have been complicated rather than simple. Restrictions on hours in some legislation have been justified by such considerations as the health of workers, protection against work accidents, the proper parental care of children, and protection of the public health and welfare (as in transportation). Some early federal legislation set weekly hours for federal employees as a guide or example for other employers. Public concern in earlier periods related to "wearing out workers before their time" and causing work accidents that added to the public burden of caring for disabled workers and their families.

Legislation. Many early proposals for mandatory shorter hours were aimed at overemployment rather than unemployment. Reducing hours was to be the means of keeping workers from doing too much — women for whom shop and home responsibilities were assumed to be combined, the overambitious or greedy, and workers whose exhaustion might endanger the health of fellow workers or the public.

For many years, courts held that federal regulation of hours for persons other than federal employees was unconstitutional. This position was modified, and federal legislation is now accepted as governing employment in industries that involve interstate commerce. In a parallel pattern early state regulation was upset by court decisions, but subsequent interpretations permit such legislation. In later years of the 19th century, state laws affecting hours of women and children came to be accepted as constitutional, but those affecting men were frequently questioned. After the Supreme Court upheld Utah legislation limiting hours in mining and smelting in 1898, however, many states enacted laws dealing with what is regarded as hazardous employment. In 1913 Oregon passed a general 10-hour law, which was upheld. Thereafter, state legislation in this area became common.

The long-term policy of the federal government is presumably expressed in such legislation as the Fair Labor Standards Act of 1938 (as amended), the Walsh-Healey Act of 1936, and the Davis-Bacon Act of 1931. The Walsh-Healey Act is a "public contracts" law; it requires that contractors supplying material for the federal government meet specified standards in working conditions, including hours and wages.

The Davis-Bacon Act is a "prevailing wage" law and imposes similar restrictions on contractors engaged in public construction paid for with federal funds. Also, some evidence of public policy can be inferred from the establishment of the 40-hour week by several codes created as a part of the national recovery program in the 1930's.

Wage and hour law. The most inclusive federal legislation is the Fair Labor Standards Act of 1938. Section 7 of the act established a "standard" workweek of 40 hours and required premium pay for overtime at not less than one and one half times the regular hourly rate. Exemptions were provided for special groups and circumstances.

The 40-hour week became a sort of national standard as a result of the 1938 legislation. During World War II the government released industry from this limitation and established a "minimum wartime workweek" of 48 hours by executive order. Except for this wartime relaxation, however, the federal government and state governments have accepted 40 hours as an appropriate current objective.

Inflation and growth. Recently, public policy has opposed further reductions, despite union proposals for a 35-hour week and a higher, double-time premium on overtime. In part, this opposition is based on conclusions that such a change would be inflationary. Spokesmen for the federal administration also argue that it would interfere with progress toward a more rapid rate of growth and that it is not needed nor likely to be effective as a means of reducing unemployment. Further, as a pressure toward higher prices, it could adversely affect the international balance of payments.

This opposition to immediate reduction was evidenced by the President's Advisory Committee on Labor Management Policy in 1962. With union members dissenting, the Committee expressed the view that "the development of programs directed at the achievement of full employment" was more significant "than the consideration of a general reduction in the hours of work."[32]

The *Economic Report of the President* for 1962 provides further evidence; it assumes that averages of hours worked will continue to decline as in the past. It does not encourage sharp reductions.[33] The Secretary of Labor, in 1962, clearly stated the administration's position that reducing hours would not be helpful in reducing unemployment.[34]

---

[32]"Report to the President on Automation," January, 1962, pp. 13–14.
[33]*Economic Report of the President*, 1962, p. 116.
[34]*New York Times*, May 16, 1962, p. 31.

In 1963 similar views were expressed by numerous witnesses before the House Select Committee on Labor. They generally opposed a bill to amend the Fair Labor Standards Act by lowering the number of hours to be paid for at straight-time rates.

Public policy, in summary, favors continuation of the long-term trend toward shorter hours, but it does not join with union proposals for a sharp reduction to be achieved either by legislation or negotiation.

PROSPECTIVE CHANGE IN HOURS OF WORK

In the face of a good deal of uncertainty as to precisely what has happened to working hours and to leisure, predictions about what will happen must carry at least as great a possible error. Just as we know that working hours have declined in the past, most of us are reasonably certain they will continue this trend in the foreseeable future. Vacations and holidays seem likely to involve more paid free time. Agitation for 35-hour workweeks seems to have gained additional momentum in recent years, and public determination to restrict inflation seems likely to favor additional leisure in lieu of higher wage rates.

The $64 question is, of course: how much? To what extent and at what pace are these influences likely to reduce hours of work? A closely related question concerns the part changing hours of work can play in achieving other economic and social goals of our society.

Trend Projections

Many, perhaps most, forecasters have contented themselves with projecting linear trends of past reductions. Thus, it has been suggested that weekly hours have declined by about a quarter of an hour each year, on the average, since 1909 (from about 51 hours per week to about 40). One forecast notes that if this pace is unchanged, the 35-hour week could be established by 1979.[35]

Other forecasters are by no means so sure of this trend, nor of its persistence. They feel the need for a rationale or explanation that can provide more dependable bases for estimates of the future. Analysis generally relates hour reductions to changes in productivity. It concludes that reductions in hours are essentially substitutes for potential increases in earnings. Workers, as the value of each hour's work grows, choose between added wage income and additional free

---

[35] *U.S. News and World Report*, October 28, 1963, p. 84.

time. Legislative regulations, in this view, may encourage the choice of added nonworking time and may provide penalty wage rates for that purpose. But the ultimate choice is the workers'.

Hours and Productivity

Analysis turns, therefore, to a consideration of past experience in relationships of changes in working hours and changing productivity.[36]

Paul Douglas found, in an analysis undertaken in the 1930's, that employees in earlier years had divided their increased productivity between shorter hours and added earnings in a 1 to 3 or 1 to 4 ratio, taking most of the gains in higher wages.[37] It seems quite clear, from the data of Figure 17-3 that this ratio has changed significantly; workers have chosen to accept a larger share of productivity gains as added income in recent years. Following the pattern, for example, Einar Hardin has estimated that the most likely reduction of the workweek in the 1960's will represent an 80-20 split between higher income and shorter hours.[38]

All comparisons of productivity changes that have accompanied the long-term reduction in hours are handicapped by the complexities in measuring working hours already noted. For example, real product per worked man-hour increased about 3.4 percent per year in the 1948–1957 period; but it increased only 3.1 percent per paid man-hour.[39]

It is clear from Figure 17-3 that the pattern of productivity gains over the past 50 years is not one of constant, uniform year-to-year growth. Although the general upward trend is clear, a simple linear trend is not appropriate. Increases prior to 1933 were not as rapid as those since that time. For the 1909-1933 period, the average annual rate of increase was about 1.8 percent. For the later 1933-1962 period, it was almost 3 percent.

---

[36]Average rates of change in hours and in output or productivity for specific periods may be calculated, although their aggregative and possibly nonrepresentative nature should be evident. Thus, for the entire period from 1909 through 1963, the average annual rate of growth in output is about 1.8 percent.

[37]Paul H. Douglas, *Real Wages in the United States* (Boston: Houghton Mifflin Co., 1930), Chapter XII.

[38]See his "Automation, Education and the Shorter Workweek," in Luther H. Evans and George E. Arnstein, *Automation and the Challenge to Education* (Washington, D.C.: National Education Association, 1962).

[39]See John W. Kendrick, *Wages, Prices, Profits* (New York: American Assembly and Columbia University, 1959), p. 43.

The slower rate of hour reduction and the more rapid increase in output in the second period seem to indicate that workers' preferences have changed. They have sought to take their gains in earnings. The period of most rapid increase in productivity is also that of least reduction in hours.

In part, of course, this change may be a reflection of the influence of increased vacations, holidays, and similar fringe benefits, which are not adequately reflected in average hours. Workers may well have preferred these paid releases from the job instead of formal reductions in hours. On the other hand, it is clear that average hours have changed little since the immediate postwar period (although the "paid for" data of the series probably understates the change.) Some rather impressive reduction in hours, like that of earlier years in this century, may be in the offing. Perhaps we are almost ready for a general 37- or 36-hour week.

Worker Preferences

It seems more likely, however, that the big change is in workers' preferences, and the major question in forecasting concerns the persistence of this shift in choices. Perhaps most workers will prefer higher wages to further reductions. Several forecasters assume that this is likely. They point to the fact that public polls have indicated little interest in shorter hours. They interpret moonlighting as carrying that same implication. Some evidence points the other way, however; members of the Oil, Chemical, and Atomic Workers International Union were polled on this point in 1957 and indicated little interest in a shorter workday but favorable attitudes toward fewer workdays per week, longer vacations, and more frequent three-day weekends, in that order.[40] It seems likely that most employees want changed work schedules rather than shorter hours per se. They are not so much interested in shorter workdays; what they seek is longer weekends and vacations. As rank-and-file employees become more secure and sophisticated, with automobiles, campers, boats, and trailers, their objective is likely to become more free time in units that permit travel and formal recreation.

---

[40]Marcia L. Greenbaum, "The Shorter Workweek," *Bulletin 50* (New York State School of Industrial and Labor Relations, June, 1963), p. 38.

Hours and Efficiency

One major stumbling block in all forecasting is the general lack of knowledge about possible relationships between working hours and efficiency. While it seems clear that very long hours in many or most occupations result in fatigue that handicaps output per hour, the effect of reducing hours from 40 to 36 or 35 or 32 are largely conjectural. Such evidence as is available indicates that reductions to 40 hours have generally been accompanied by increased hourly output. Some wartime studies concluded that the 40-hour week was most efficient, but the setting for these studies was distinctly not normal. Other studies have tended to support this conclusion, but some others have raised questions about it.[41] It seems likely that the relationship between hours and efficiency varies among industries and occupations so that any generalization is unjustified. It is probable, also, that any reduction in hours, particularly if weekly earnings are not cut, would encourage management to seek improvement in its utilization of labor and thus generate strong pressures toward greater hourly productivity. The same tendency may be inherent in automation; as it reduces drudgery and fatigue, higher hourly output may be encouraged.

It is possible, also, that further extensive reductions in hours can come only as large numbers of low-income families move into more adequate or comfortable income brackets. Perhaps the major key to more leisure is a broader prosperity, with further leveling of incomes, rather than average wage increases.[42]

General Conclusion

It is likely that, in the public interest, any sharp, drastic changes in hours should be avoided. Such precipitate change does not provide ample time for difficult personal and social adjustments. Thus, if legislation specifies reduced straight-time hours, its impact should probably be delayed for two or more years after its enactment.

Considering all these possible variables, it seems reasonable to expect a slowdown of the long-term trend and a continuation of the shorter-term trend. Hours will continue to decline, but the rate is likely to be low. Much depends on experiment and research with respect to various lengths of workdays and workweeks. The trend

---

[41]*Ibid.*, p. 29, for references to these studies.

[42]For a convenient bibliography, see "Hours of Work," *Selected References, No. 109* (Princeton University, Industrial Relations Section, January, 1963).

toward longer vacations, more holidays, and longer weekends seems likely to slow further reduction in formal hours of work.

On this basis a reasonable expectation would suggest an average of about 1 to 1½ hours per week per decade for the next twenty years — perhaps a formal 4½-day, 36-hour workweek, with many more weekend holidays and much longer vacations by 1985.

ANALYTICAL REVIEW QUESTIONS

1. Why are programs for reduced hours sometimes regarded as tactics for raising wages?
2. Is there enough work for all if it were divided equitably?
3. How do you forecast the future of leisure in our society?
4. Why may the demand for leisure grow at an accelerated pace?
5. What is meant by the protestant ethic?
6. How have concepts of leisure changed?
7. (a) Describe the long-term trend in working hours in the United States. (b) How have employees divided their increased productivity between leisure and added earnings?
8. Is the 40-hour week optimal from the standpoint of efficient utilization of labor resources? Why?
9. (a) What do we mean by the demand for leisure? (b) How is this related to optimal usage of labor resources? (c) Is this an efficiency concept or a value concept?
10. What laws regulate hours of work? Contrast state and federal provisions.
11. How do actual hours differ from scheduled hours and straight-time hours?
12. What trend is evident in holidays and vacations?
13. How are sabbaticals a factor in balancing work and leisure?
14. How do part-time workers and moonlighters affect averages of working hours?
15. Compare hours in the United States with those of other industrialized nations.
16. What changes are evident in the pace of change in hours?
17. Why have unions consistently proposed shorter workweeks?
18. How do they relate hours to purchasing power and productivity?
19. Explain the union proposal for a shorter workweek.
20. Explain the historic employer position regarding hours of work.
21. Do reduced hours per week mean higher labor costs? Always? Never?
22. How can shorter workweeks conceal unemployment?
23. Is there a serious hazard in a uniform legislative standard for hours of work? Why or why not?
24. Why have federal government spokesmen frequently opposed reductions in the workweek?
25. Explain the argument that a shorter workweek can be inflationary.

26. What would be your forecast of average weekly hours for 1975? 1990? Explain the basis for your projections.
27. How is it likely that workers' preferences have changed?
28. Should employers experiment with variations in the length of the work-week?

Case 17-1

IMPOSING HIGHER OVERTIME RATES

In early 1964 President Johnson indicated his intention to suggest or require by legislation that some industries be required to pay double-time rates of wages for overtime. His plan would establish tripartite committees to review experience in each industry where overtime is high, and these committees would report their recommendations to the Secretary of Labor. The Secretary would be given authority to impose the higher rates.

• If you were appointed a member of such a committee, what questions would you raise and what facts would you seek as a basis for your recommendation?

WAGES: GOALS, LEVELS, AND STRUCTURES

Part IV considered the importance of full, satisfying, and developmental employment to all employees and to the economic and political stability of our industrialized society. Closely related to employment in its personal, social, and economic importance is the payoff for working — economic compensation for the contribution of labor. This chapter and the four that follow shift our attention to another important subsystem in our industrial relations system. They turn to the economic payoff for workers — to wages, to our society's wage goals and objectives, to our theories about the factors that explain wage levels and differentials, and to our unsolved wage problems, of which there are many.

In its broadest economic meaning the term "wages" is used to describe all types and forms of compensation for human resources. In this meaning, wages include the hourly pay of production workers, the weekly or monthly salary of clerical workers or supervisors, and the salary plus bonus of managers and executives. The term is also frequently expanded to include an allocation of some part of business profit as the compensation of proprietors and to include the fees charged by self-employed professional workers.

In somewhat more restricted economic usage *wages* are regarded as the accepted method of paying those who work for and under the direction of others as production, shop, or hourly rated workers. In this sense wages are distinguished from the fees of self-employed professional workers and from the salaries of supervisors, managers, and clerical and office workers. Wages in this sense are, to define the term by repetition, the compensation of wage earners, the numerous employees who use the tools and equipment of their employers to produce goods and services that are sold by their employers.

In all of these meanings, wages are of great importance in a free-enterprise economy. They are prices on human services. Prices perform important functions in any economy built around free markets. The first section of this chapter explains this special role of wages in our economic system.

The second section of this chapter is concerned with definitional matters, essentially types and forms of compensation. These definitions are needed to facilitate understanding of the sections and chapters that follow.

Wages influence employment decisions, which in turn affect commitment, development, allocation, utilization, and conservation of our manpower resources. Both absolute and relative wage comparisons are significant. Wage levels, differentials, and structures — the subject of the third section of this chapter — are the foundation of wage policies, programs, and theories.

The next chapter takes up wage problems, including wage criteria, real wages, public wage controls, and international wage comparisons. The concluding chapters in Part V deal with historical and modern wage theories and their suggestions for prevention and amelioration of wage problems — and more important, implications for attainment of personal and social wage objectives.

THE ROLE OF WAGES

In a society that maintains free markets, with private property and freedom of exchange, purchasers of labor's services must pay a price for them much as those who buy property must compensate its owners. That price is the wage. In slavery, or in a totalitarian state, workers may be supported — provided with means of subsistence — in lieu of wages. The appearance of free artisans — independent craftsmen — was one of the first signs of transition from slavery and serfdom to the enterprise system. Expansion of the general practice of paying wages for work has been a distinctive characteristic of this entire evolution or industrial revolution.

Wages — as we use the term — were far less important in other and earlier types of economies. In slavery, compensation took the form of a gift or a gratuity from the master — usually a place to live and a "handout" of food and other necessities. In the agricultural system that preceded the age of handicraft production, many workers were compensated by being allowed to farm a bit of land for themselves. In some early communistic societies members were compensated for working by allowing them to share — usually according to family needs — in the common pool of products and services. In handicraft production journeymen received wages, but apprentices were given only their keep while they learned their trade.

As free economies have developed, the wage-paying system has come to affect growing proportions of all citizens. Larger sections of the population have become wage earners. Older manorial estates with their serfs and slaves were broken up, and capitalistic industry — replacing the interim handicraft system — has required vast numbers and concentrations of employees.

These changes have made wages the principal source of income for very large portions of our society. Those of us who sell our services have to depend primarily on our earnings to buy what we and our families need. While all of us depend in part on various public services, most of us regard our pay — our wage or salary — as our major source of income. We use the public services — schools, fire departments, highways, defense facilities, libraries, and many others. We know, however, that we pay some share of the cost of these services and that they can provide only limited assistance and support. From our point of view, the principal source of our material welfare is our earnings. Therefore, in our type of economy, wages and earnings assume great personal importance. They are *the* accepted payment for participating and contributing one's services. They are *the* payoff, *the* reward for working.

At the same time, these payments have a great importance in the operation of our economy as a whole. In the aggregate they make up the largest single type of income. Compensation of workers is consistently larger, in its total, than all the other types of income combined. For this reason, the stability and continuity of workers' income is a matter of concern to all modern industrial societies. Any reduction in aggregate wage income may have immediate effects on demands for the services and the products of the entire economy. This is particularly true because wage earners have a comparatively high *propensity to consume*. In other words, most wage income is quickly spent to buy the goods and the services required by wage earners and their families. This quick spending of workers' income is quite different from what may be done with some other forms of income — interest or dividends, for example — which may at times be temporarily withdrawn from the markets of the economy.

Major Economic Functions

In our system, wages are important not only because they are the principal payment for work and the largest source of income but also because wage rates or labor prices are expected to play a major part in creating both an efficient *allocation* or *disposition* of human resources and their careful *utilization* or *application*. At the same time, wages as a whole play a vital role in maintaining a satisfactory level of purchasing power or disposable personal income. This purchasing power should be balanced with our total output of goods and services to insure the smooth functioning and stability of the whole economy. These social assignments to the wage system in a free, industrial economy should be clearly understood, for they help to explain our continued concern about amounts and levels of wages.

Allocating human resources. We expect the wage system to attract people to the jobs in which they can make the greatest contribution. This means that wages or the promise of future wages is, in our society, depended on to exert the principal influence in moving our human resources out of less productive and into more productive jobs. For example, relatively high wages for engineers in electronics industries are expected to be the principal incentive to stimulate their transfers to this industry. Offers of higher wages should, we expect, move them from jobs in which their contribution is less and, at the same time, encourage young workers into this field. Higher wages are expected to move agricultural workers into industrial jobs in expanding industries. The prospect of relatively high wages is relied on to encourage men and women to serve apprenticeships for the skilled trades or to undertake lengthy college and university training for the professions, i.e., manpower development.

Wages are the principal means we use to stimulate occupational and industrial as well as geographic mobility. We do not expect our human resources to shift from job to job, from industry to industry, and from place to place because they are so directed by some executive order or government edict. Rather, they tend to make these shifts in response to the push and pull of wage differentials, the differences between lower and higher rates.

Utilization of human resources.   At the same time, wages are expected to force employers to make the best possible use of labor, to develop workers' talents, and to apply their services efficiently. The prices paid for labor permit its profitable employment only if it is efficiently applied. If one employer is not using the highest capabilities of his employees, another employer in another industry — perhaps in another area — may make these workers a better offer based on better use of their abilities and skills.

Wages are expected to provide a powerful and major incentive for individual employees to apply their best efforts in the best jobs they can find. Wage rates are, in this situation, major motivators for workers. If an employee does not seek and find a job in which he can and does exert his best effort and talent, he will tend to earn less than his maximum. If he is not zealous in his search for the best possible job, the result is similar. If he fails to transfer when a better job becomes available or if he is unwilling to work hard, these failures to maximize his contribution tend to reduce his potential wage income.

Thus, the labor-pricing wage system motivates both employers and wage earners toward the best possible allocation and application of human resources. Such use of labor tends to maximize both the labor contribution to the total output of our economy and the compensation of our human resources.

Economic stabilization and growth.   At the same time that it thus encourages the most efficient allocation and utilization of our human resources, the wage system is expected to maintain stability and to encourage continued growth in our economy. On the one hand, we seek to balance income with production, thus providing markets for our products and services and preventing runaway inflation or disastrous deflation. In addition, we seek this objective in a developing, expanding economy. Our population and labor force are growing and will presumably continue to do so. We expect wages or earnings to provide support for added numbers and, at the same time, to permit rising scales of living for all our people.

Neither of these assignments to the wage system is simple, and they are somewhat opposed to each other. Preserving balance and stability means that rates and levels of pay must be closely related to both the volume and the pricing of final products. The aggregate or total of wages must maintain a parity with the total value of products and services. Since wages are a major share of disposable income, if their aggregate should decline without a corresponding reduction of output, the result may well be deflationary. On the other hand, a relatively rapid increase in total wages — faster than that in total product — can create a powerful pressure toward inflation. At the same time, a rise in wage payments that was not justified by increased output could reduce the share of income going to suppliers of capital and discourage investment. Meanwhile, we expect both wage income and total production to grow more than the increase in population, thus permitting rising real wages and living scales. We propose stability combined with growth. This is obviously a big and at the same time a difficult and delicate assignment to the wage system.

Consideration of these economic assignments to the wage system should suggest the reasons for our continuing social interest and concern about wages. To meet these responsibilities, labor pricing processes must follow a narrow line, avoiding excessive deflation on the one side and excessive inflation on the other. Every wage adjustment and negotiated increase tends to influence the disposition of our labor resources and the efficiency with which they are applied. The aggregate of these changes may exert a definitive influence on our political stability and economic prosperity.

Labor pricing must accept major responsibility for preserving balance in the entire economy while at the same time facilitating its continued growth and expansion, because labor income is the dominant segment of total income and purchasing power. In these complex relationships, changes in wages always hold the threat of plunging the whole economy into disastrous depression or inflation or blocking the path to steady growth.

Personal Function of Wages

These social assignments to the wage system in a free economy are paralleled by the individual and personal dependence on wages, which is as obvious if not as complicated. Each individual worker expects his wage or compensation to make many of his dreams come true. Except as he may have other forms of income — from land, savings, or other property — his earnings largely determine his material scale of living. Pay for working influences most of his activities and attitudes, as well as those of all members of his family.

Personal and familial expectations from the wage system make heavy demands on it. Family members expect earnings to make possible what they regard as a fair livelihood and scale of living. Many wage earners and their families demand that wages permit continuing improvement in their living scales. Our society encourages this expectation. The wage an individual receives is expected to show the comparative worth and contribution of his skill, training, or experience as compared with other earners. The wage or salary thus tends to indicate the social status of the earner and that of his family.

This current relationship of earnings and status is in sharp contrast to some older social systems, in which caste and family determine status. In our society what all members of the family do and think and feel is directly influenced by the family's income. For the majority of our families, the principal item of income is the earnings of the head of the household. That income determines our scales of living and may readily influence our whole philosophy of life.[1]

Wage Share of National Income

We are determined, as a nation, that the aggregate wage share in national income shall be maintained at a level that insures adequate demands for goods and services and thus stabilizes the economy. This objective assumes that wage earners must receive such a continuing share in the total income of the economy as will preserve an ideal combination of balance and growth. Wages must provide adequate purchasing power in the hands of those who will use it to maintain a market for our growing output. National wage policy and the monetary and fiscal policy of the federal government are designed to approximate this ideal distribution. (See Chapter 22.)

Maintaining such a stable distribution of income as will balance inflationary and deflationary forces from year to year is by no means a simple operation. The problem is complicated by the fact that some delay is unavoidable between the time actual payments are made and the time when these facts become known. We have, however, made rapid progress in recent years, both in reporting the distribution of national income and in forecasting and estimating future payments.

Maintaining the desirable balance is made somewhat more difficult by the fact that efforts to control the distribution process must be based largely on data describing gross labor income and total compensation of employees. These data are further complicated by

---

[1]See, for example, Mason Haire, Edwin E. Ghiselli, and Lyman W. Porter *et. al.*, "Psychological Research on Pay," *Reprint No. 220* (Berkeley: University of California Institute of Industrial Relations, 1964); available also in *Industrial Relations*, Vol. 3, No. 1 (October, 1963), pp. 3–49.

the fact that some labor income takes the form of employer contributions to the deferred benefits of social insurance (unemployment and old age). At the same time, some of the income credited to workers must be paid by them as their contribution for such insurance. Neither of these deductions is immediately available for personal expenditures. On the other hand, payments of social insurance benefits now constitute an important addition to wages and salaries in the total of current purchasing power.

For evidence on what is taking place in the aggregate income-distributing process, our national accounting system provides two continuing monthly indexes. Both have been extended back to 1929 to provide perspective. One describes distribution of the total national income in terms of the amounts going to the compensation of employees, profits, business and professional income, farm income, interest, and rental income. The other describes personal income in terms of its sources, including the income from labor, proprietorship, rent, dividends, and interest.

Table 18-1 shows the importance of workers' income as evidenced by each of these series. The table also indicates the range of variation in labor's share in the years since 1929. Further, the table provides an index of industrial production as a measure of cyclical changes in business activity. Figure 18-1 on page 502 supplements the table by showing how other shares in national income have changed since 1929.

The table and the figure provide data for several relevant observations, which may be outlined as follows:

1. In this period as a whole, the absence of economic stability is apparent. The most recent half of the period, however, has shown only minor recessions, with a fairly steady upward trend in business activity. These same years of comparative stability are characterized by a consistently steady distribution of national income to the compensation of employees.

2. Compensation of employees has averaged approximately two thirds of total national income for the period as a whole. It has ranged from 58.2 percent in 1929 to 71.2 in 1962. On the other hand, steady allocations at about the 70 percent level are notable during recent years of prosperity.

3. Wages and salaries have averaged about two thirds of total personal income, ranging from 58.7 percent in 1929 to 68.5 percent in 1964.

4. The sharp increase in personal contributions for social insurance from $0.1 billions in 1929 to 12.5 billions in 1964 is especially noteworthy.

Table 18-1
NATIONAL INCOME, PERSONAL INCOME, AND INDUSTRIAL PRODUCTION — 1929–1964

(All money amounts in billions of dollars)

Year	Industrial Production Index (1957–59 = 100)	National Income			Sources of Personal Income			
		Total National Income	Compensation of Employees[1]		Total Personal Income	Wages and Salaries[2]		Personal Contributions for Social Insurance
		Dollars	Dollars	Per Cent	Dollars	Dollars	Per Cent	Dollars
1929	38	$ 87.8	$ 51.1	58.2	$ 85.8	$ 50.4	58.7	$ 0.1
1934	27	49.0	34.3	70.0	53.6	33.7	62.9	0.2
1939	38	72.8	48.1	66.1	72.9	45.9	63.0	0.6
1945	71	181.2	123.2	68.0	171.2	117.6	68.6	2.3
1950	75	241.9	154.2	63.3	228.5	146.4	64.1	2.9
1955	97	330.2	223.9	67.8	310.2	210.9	68.0	5.2
1960	109	414.5	293.6	70.8	401.3	271.3	67.6	9.2
1961	110	426.1	302.1	70.9	417.4	278.8	66.8	9.5
1962	118	453.7	322.9	71.2	442.1	297.1	67.2	10.2
1963	124	478.4	340.4	71.1	463.0	312.3	67.4	11.8
1964[3]	132	497.1	352.5	70.8	479.1	328.0	68.5	12.5

[1]Compensation of employees include employers' contributions for social insurance.

[2]Wages and salaries are the compensation of employees excluding employers' contributions for social insurance.

[3]Preliminary.

Sources: *Historical Supplement to Economic Indicators* and current issues of *Survey of Current Business.*

The changing relative shares in national income are shown in Figure 18-1. Compensation of employees has been increasing at the expense of business, rental, and interest income. While gross profits have stabilized in recent years at about 10 percent of national income, it should be emphasized that this is before taxes.[2]

[2]In 1960 for example, gross profits in durable goods manufacturing were $14 billion before taxes and $7 billion after. Profits as a percent of national income should not be confused with profits as a percent of sales, or investment. In durable goods, in 1960, profits as a percent of sales were 8 percent before taxes and 4 percent after taxes. In 1960 corporate income and profits taxes made up $22 billion of total tax collections of $92 billion. An additional $12 billion was collected in excise taxes.

In 1929 business income accounted for 28.3 percent of national income. Interest amounted to 7.3 percent and rental income to 6.2 percent. In the depth of the great depression, in 1932, interest was 12.7 percent and rent 6.4 percent. In 1942 business income amounted to 31.7 percent of the total; in 1948, to 31.8 percent. By 1959, when the compensation of employees accounted for 69.6 percent, business received 22.7 percent, interest 3.9 percent, and rental income was 3.0 percent. For details, see Reuben E.

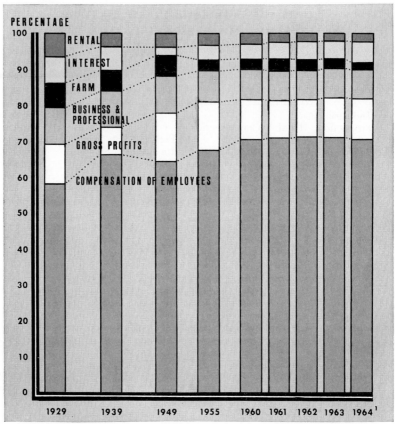

¹Preliminary

Figure 18-1

CHANGING PERCENTAGE DISTRIBUTION
OF NATIONAL INCOME —1929–1964

Sources: United States Department of Commerce and current issues of *Survey of Current Business.*

A shift in status from self-employed to employment offers a partial explanation of the increased compensation of employees over the long period. Employees of private firms and government constituted 78 percent of the persons engaged in production in 1929 and 85 percent in the early 1960's. Private employees' compensation

Slesinger, "Factor Payments in the Distribution of National Income," *Western Business Review*, Vol. 6, No. 4 (November, 1962), especially pp. 43 and 51.

When considering labor's share of total product, it is important to note carefully the basis for comparison. Thus, for example, labor's share of business gross product in the United States has fluctuated from a low of 46 percent to a high of 54 percent during the period 1929–1960. See John E. Hotsun, "The Constancy of the Wage Share: The Canadian Experience," *The Review of Economics and Statistics*, Vol. XLV, No. 1 (February, 1963), p. 84.

increased from 52 percent in 1929 to 57 percent in the 1960's; government employees' compensation increased from 6 percent to 13 percent of the national income in the same period.

The decline of agricultural proprietorships sharply reduced the number of self-employed; farm operators made up 13 percent of all persons engaged in production in 1929 and only 4 percent in the early 1960's. Increasing home ownership helps explain the decline in the rental component of national income, as do government efforts to provide low-cost housing.[3]

FORMS OF WAGE PAYMENTS

It is important to note and distinguish some of the most important forms or types of workers' compensation and some more precise definitions of these various forms. More careful usage is essential to the full understanding of both our public wage policy and our major wage problems. Loose usage may introduce unnecessary errors in the analysis of labor pricing processes and of the impact of labor income on the economy. We could be misled, for example, if we confused trends in wage rates with those in earnings or in the labor costs of products. We could arrive at unjustified conclusions and accept dubious public programs if we failed to distinguish changes in money or dollar wages from those in *real wages*, that is, wages measured in purchasing power. Wage rates, salaries, earnings, and labor costs should be carefully distinguished in any analysis involving labor income. In addition, several special types of compensation, including fringe payments, profit sharing, and cost of living and productivity adjustments should be clearly defined and understood.

Wages and Salaries

For about 59 million of the approximately 75 million in our labor force, compensation for working takes the form of wages or salaries. Thus, wage earners in this broad sense of that term represent about 80 percent of the total labor force. The remainder are (1) business proprietors, property owners, and employers, who take their principal compensation from profits, rent, and interest and (2) the self-employed, who combine profits and fees in their proprietory income.

---

[3]W. S. Measday, "Labor's Share in the National Income," *The Quarterly Review of Economics and Business*, Vol. 2, No. 3 (August, 1962), pp. 25–33.

In much of our thinking about wage earners, however, we distinguish those who receive hourly, daily, or piece-rate wages from salaried personnel. In this distinction *wages* are payments for work calculated on a short-term basis. They are usually based on hours of work or the number of units produced. Amounts paid may vary from day to day or from week to week, depending on the stability of employment or on the worker's output. They include payments to the largest group of workers, those described as *hourly rated employees*, and are the usual method of compensation for rank-and-file, manual, or production workers.

The amount paid these wage earners is based in part on their *wage rates*. Two types of rates are commonly used. One is an *hourly* or time rate, which bases payments on the amount of time spent at work by the employee. The second is the *piece* rate, which pays workers on the basis of their output, at so much per unit — per piece, pound, yard, or bushel, for example. For many employees the systems are combined. Workers are paid a *guaranteed hourly rate* plus extra pay for output above a stipulated par or standard. Some *incentive wage plans* (the best known are standard hour plans, the Taylor differential piece rate, the Halsey, the Rowan, and the Bedaux plans) provide more complicated wages, calculated according to formulas that vary the rate paid per piece with changes in the levels of individual output. Workers may thus earn premiums and bonuses. In some practice, *group incentive payments* to individual workers vary according to the production or output of the whole work group.

Expanding automation will force a continuing decline in the use of individual piece rates and other forms of wage incentive plans. When machines control both the rate or pace of production and the reduction of errors and maintenance of standards, individual worker incentives are obviously inappropriate. To some extent individual incentives may be replaced by group plans, in which both direct and indirect workers are included. Some form of group bonus may be appropriate for managers and executives on the assumption that efficiency is a result of management effort and judgment.

Salaries are payments calculated and paid on a longer-term basis than wages, usually a month or a year. They are uniform from month to month, without reference to fluctuations in employment or output. They are the established method of compensation for supervisors, foremen, managers, and most staff and clerical employees such as engineers, accountants, industrial relations or personnel directors, secretaries, typists, and many others.

Earnings. Some confusion is frequently created by the fact that the term "wages" is also widely used to refer to the end-product of wage rates and employment, that is to *earnings*. It should be clear that weekly or monthly *earnings* of hourly rated employees may be changed by variations in the rate or in the number of hours worked. Sometimes, reference is made to *take-home pay*, which is the amount of earnings for a specified pay period less deductions for withholding (for federal and state income) taxes, union dues, contributions, private insurance, pensions, and other such purposes. To avoid confusion, earnings should be sharply differentiated from both wage rates and take-home pay. The hourly or piece rate of wages means little, either to an individual worker or as a factor in aggregate worker income, if the wage earner is not working or is employed only a few hours per day or week.

Wage scales. Reference is frequently made to the *wage scale* in an industry or to the scale for an individual occupation. Strictly speaking, a wage scale is a series of rates. In popular usage, however, the term "scale" is used to refer either to a single negotiated rate for one job or to a whole system or "structure" of rates fixed by a labor agreement. Thus, the scale for carpenters in Chicago is the rate agreed upon by the union and the association of contractors. When labor contracts are negotiated on an industry rather than a trade or a craft basis, the term "scale" may be used to describe the whole structure of occupational rates thus determined.

Fringes

In addition to wages and salaries, employees may receive a wide range of additional benefits and services, generally described as *fringes*. Most common among them are life insurance, pension systems, and hospitalization paid for by employers. They were first called fringes during World War II, when economic controls imposed rigorous restrictions on wage increases. Additions of these extra, nonmonetary, noncashable benefits and services were frequently allowed by wage stabilization agencies on the ground that they did not exert an unstabilizing, inflationary effect on the economy.

The number and the variety of these fringes have grown rapidly. This development has been speeded because unions have recognized a chance to get "bargains" in these benefits and have made them a favorite subject for collective bargaining. Employees can get more for their money by purchasing life insurance or hospitalization or other such benefits on a group basis. Their interests may be better served by having a 5-cent increase expended for a medical care plan than by taking the same increase in cash.

Many employers have favored these fringes both as a means of recruiting and holding employees and also because expenditures for such benefits are regarded as business expenses for tax purposes. The excess profits tax on business earnings has encouraged these fringes, making it possible to pay a large share of their costs with funds that would otherwise be paid as taxes. Employees gain because benefits thus provided are usually nontaxable income for the benefit receivers. Hence, a 5-cent per hour increase paid in the form of fringes may be worth considerably more than 5 cents added to the wage rate.

Fringes are no longer a rare or unusual or wartime phenomenon. Some of them were, of course, provided by some firms and for limited groups of employees long before the war accelerated their provision. They were and are widely described as "employee benefits" and "employee services." In some cases they were established by paternalistic employers who sought to gain the favor of employees or who regarded the provision of security for workers as an employer's responsibility. They have become a part of wages because employers, employees, and public policy favor them. They provide a type of compensation for work that neither hourly rates nor piecework payments have included. Pensions and other welfare provisions, for example, meet public and individual demands for "insured" economic security. Paid vacations and holidays encourage leisure that has long been prized by workers and regarded as socially desirable and that might not be accepted if costs were simply added to the usual pay check.[4]

In current practice in the United States, the number of such benefits has grown rapidly, and new fringes are constantly appearing. Table 18-2 lists more than 100 fringes that have achieved wide acceptance. A complete list, if one were available, would probably include at least 200 types.

---

[4]Some economists hold that fringe benefits act as barriers to employment because employers would rather work present employees overtime rather than hire additional employees, in order to avoid long-term fringe and benefit commitments. For a critique of the rationality of this position, see Joseph W. Garbarino, "Fringe Benefits and Overtime as Barriers to Expanding Employment," *Industrial and Labor Relations Review*, Vol. 17, No. 3 (April, 1964), pp. 426–42.

Table 18-2

TYPES OF FRINGE BENEFITS

1.

Extra payment for time worked
Cost-of-living bonus
Holiday premium
Overtime premium
Shift premium
Weekend premium

2.

Payments for time not worked
Call-back pay
Call-in pay
Cleanup time
Clothes-changing time
Dental care time
Down time
Enforced absences
Family allowance
Holidays paid for but not
  worked
Jury duty pay
Layoff pay
Machine setup time
Medical time
Military induction bonuses
Military service allowance
National Guard duty
Paid death-in-family leave
Paid lunch periods
Paid sick leave
Portal-to-portal pay
Religious holidays
Reporting pay
Reserve military pay
Rest periods
Room and board allowance
Severance pay
Supper money
Time spent on contract
  negotiation
Time spent on grievances
Travel allowances or
  expenses
Vacation pay
Voting time
Witness time

3.

Payments for employee security
Contributions to:
  Accident insurance
  Disability insurance
  Employees' thrift plans

Employees' stock purchase
  plans
Group hospitalization
  insurance
Group surgical insurance
Individual hospitalization
  insurance
Individual surgical
  insurance
Life insurance
Medical insurance
Old-age and survivor's
  insurance
State disability insurance
Unemployment compen-
  sation
Workmen's compensation
Credit unions
Death benefits
Employees' loan associations
Health and welfare fund
Home financing
Mutual benefit associations
Payment of optical expenses
Pensions
Railroad retirement tax
Railroad unemployment
  insurance
Savings bond administration
Sickness benefits insurance
Supplements to unemploy-
  ment compensation
Supplements to workmen's
  compensation

4.

*Nonproduction awards and
  bonuses*
Anniversary awards
Attendance bonuses
Christmas bonuses
Quality bonuses
Safety awards
Service bonuses
Suggestions awards
Waste elimination bonuses
Year-end bonuses

5.

Payments for employee services
Annual report to employees
Beauty parlors
Cafeterias
Canteen service

Charm courses
Company athletic teams
Company housing
Company orchestra
Company stores
Cooking schools
Dietetic advice
Educational assistance
Employee counseling
Employee discounts on pur-
  chases
Employee parties
Employee pleasure trips
Employee publications
Financial advice
Flowers for ill and deceased
  employees and families
Free laundry
Functions for retired
  employees
Free meals
Golf instruction
Hospital facilities
Health education
Income tax services
Information racks
Legal aid
Libraries
Lunch period entertainment
Medical exams (voluntary)
Moving expenses
Music at work
Music lessons
Nursery
Paid club memberships
Paid magazine subscriptions
Parking space operation
Purchasing service
Reading room facilities
Recreational facilities
Restroom facilities
Safety clothes at company
  expense
Safety programs
Scholarships
Showers and locker rooms
Transportation
Vacation facilities
Visiting nurse
Vitamins and salt tablets
Wedding gifts
Work clothes at company
  expense

Numerous studies have calculated the cost of these supplements to wages and salaries. Their costs have increased as the number and variety of fringes has grown. In the United States, in 1963, fringe benefits cost an average of 25.6 percent of business payrolls, or $1,431 annually per worker. Variations in individual companies ranged from 7 to over 70 percent of payroll, according to the Chamber of Commerce of the United States. Annual fringe payments per employee increased by $177 from 1961 to 1963.[5]

Fringe costs are generally higher in foreign nations. For example, in 1960, they were slightly higher — as a percentage of wages — in Great Britain, twice as great in Belgium and West Germany, almost three times the American level in France, and 3 1/2 times in Italy.[6]

Profit Sharing

Profit-sharing plans have had a spectacular growth since 1939. In that year there were only several hundred programs in the United States. Today over 90,000 companies have employee profit sharing. One of every 6 companies with 20 or more employees shares profits, and a majority of employees participate in 70 percent of the plans. From 1955 to 1961 the increase was threefold. Most plans today are deferred plans, i.e., with profit shares paid into a trust fund and distributed at retirement, death, disability, or severance.[7]

Several hundred firms that maintain systems of profit sharing are members of the Council of Profit-Sharing Industries. The Council has published frequent reports on the experience of member firms and encourages a continuing research program.[8] The Council reports that profit-sharing plans have increased output, reduced waste, and increased employee teamwork and enthusiasm. Where they have these effects and where they are related to employee efforts and contributions, they may represent a desirable method of employee motivation.

However, not all profit-sharing plans meet the above conditions. In some cases profit sharing with wage earners may not be in the

---

[5]*U.S. News and World Report*, October 5, 1964, p. 94.

[6]*Business Week*, December 31, 1960, pp. 95–97.

[7]See B. L. Metzger, "Will Profit Sharing Help Your Firm?," *Management Aids, No. 157* (Washington, D.C.: Small Business Administration, October, 1963), p. 1.

[8]See Edwin B. Flippo, *Profit Sharing in American Business* (Columbus, Ohio: Ohio State University Bureau of Business Research, 1954). For highly interesting reports on profit sharing, see the frequent publications of the Profit-Sharing Research Foundation, Evanston, Illinois, including B. L. Metzger, *Profit Sharing in Perspective — In American Medium-Sized and Small Business*, 1964.

best interests of either the participating workers or the public. In spite of the fact that employers may act with the most generous and idealistic intentions, the practice may have undesirable effects. Wages are presumably a compensation for effort and energy in the productive process, which wage earners can and do supply. Profits, however, as payments for risk taking, are due to many factors other than employee efforts, and are expected to fluctuate from time to time, if not to alternate with losses. It is doubtful whether wage earners should be paid for or be expected to take risks arising from factors and conditions lying beyond their efforts and control. Most of them do not have the personal reserves that this type of risk-taking implies.

If a firm's business is such that profits are steady and if the profit portion of employee compensation is relatively small, the practice may be useful to the employer and satisfying to employees. If profits fluctuate widely from year to year, profit sharing is of doubtful value to either party. Moreover, any general extension to a large part of all industry could have several undesirable results: (1) the wide adoption of profit sharing might create a persistent pressure toward inflation to provide the fillip or stimulus to continued high dollar profits; (2) it could occasion sharp year-to-year fluctuations in employee income and thus generate an unstabilizing effect throughout the entire economy, a result that is directly opposed to current public policy, which seeks to maintain stability in purchasing power; (3) in a period of recession, a sharp reduction in worker income might act as a multiplier in speeding a downward, deflationary spiral.

Employee Stock Ownership

Since the earliest plans for profit sharing appeared, some firms have preferred arrangements that encourage employees to own stock in the employing firm. Some distribute stock to employees in lieu of a cash distribution of profits. Others use the employee's share of profits to purchase stock to be held in a trust fund. More common practice offers stock to employees at a discount and facilitates its purchase on a time-payment basis.

Sale of stock to employees is not new, having been undertaken as early as 1829 in England. Several hundred plans have been advanced in this country, beginning with that of the Pillsbury Flour Mills in 1882. More than a thousand such plans were reported in the 1920's.

Stock purchase plans suffered a severe setback in the depression following 1929, and many of them were discontinued at that time. A study reported by the National Industrial Conference Board in 1953 could find only 69 formal plans still in operation.[9] In current practice they are frequently combined with deferred profit sharing and the investment of employee savings in other securities, including government bonds.[10]

Escalator Clauses

Many employees now receive what are called automatic adjustments in their salaries and wage rates. Automatic or "formula" wage adjustments in long-term contracts are of two principal types, contingent and scheduled. *Contingent adjustments* are dependent on an event that may or may not occur (e.g., increase in cost of living). *Scheduled adjustments* are those that definitely will occur with the passage of time (e.g., 8¢ an hour in each of the next three years) or an increase based on a predetermined historic productivity increase.

Automatic adjustments now characterize most major labor contracts. The most common pattern is a combination of escalator and scheduled adjustments; scheduled increases alone are next most common, while comparatively few contracts call for cost-of-living adjustments alone.[11]

Garbarino concludes that such automatic wage adjustments as productivity increases and cost-of-living escalator provisions probably add to the "inflationary potential" of wage policy.[12]

Cost of living adjustments. In an attempt to equate wages with price changes, adjustments may be made to changes in cost of living as measured by a specified index. In some earlier practice these automatic changes were tied to variations in product prices.[13] Today, these escalator provisions generally involve a procedure in which wage rates are checked at regular periods and adjusted if the cost of living has changed in a specified degree.

---

[9]"Stock Ownership Plans for Workers," *Studies in Personnel Policy, No. 132*, 1953.

[10]Stock purchase plans appeal more to supervisory and clerical (white-collar) employees than to rank and file employees. In the General Motors plan, for example, 88 percent of the 100,000 eligible salaried employees joined in the first year.

[11]Joseph W. Garbarino, "Bargaining Strategy and the Form of Contracts," *Industrial Relations*, Vol. 1, No. 2 (February, 1962), pp. 73–88. See also "Deferred Wage Increases and Escalator Clauses, 1952–1963," United States BLS, *Report No. 235*, February, 1963.

[12]Joseph W. Garbarino, "The Economic Significance of Automatic Wage Adjustments," Chapter 8, in *New Dimensions in Collective Bargaining* (New York: Harper and Brothers, 1959).

[13]For details of these earlier plans, see "Escalator Wage Adjustments Based on Price of Product," *Monthly Labor Review*, Vol. 73, No. 1 (July, 1951), pp. 48–49.

As of January, 1957, the Bureau of Labor Statistics estimated that some 3.8 million employees were covered by these escalator provisions. By 1963 only 1.8 millions were so covered. The most common arrangement requires either a quarterly or a semiannual adjustment in rates of pay amounting to 1 cent per hour for each 1/2-point change in the cost-of-living index.

The index most frequently used for this purpose (in 90 percent of negotiated plans) is that known as the Consumer Price Index, prepared by the federal Bureau of Labor Statistics. It is widely known as the CPI. The CPI is described and discussed in Chapter 19.

When these escalator clauses became most popular, in the years following World War II, serious questions were raised about their probable effects on the economy. Some observers feared that their wide use would introduce continuing instability. In periods of prosperity, it was argued, they would almost certainly create continuous inflation. A price rise would automatically occasion a wage increase. Rising wages would in turn force even higher prices. On the other hand, even a slight recession abetted by escalator provisions would involve a special hazard of increased deflationary spirals. Whenever business activity showed signs of easing, a slight fall in consumers' prices would touch off a round of downward wage adjustments, reducing purchasing power and speeding deflation and recession. How real or serious these hazards may be is not known. Escalator clauses have not spread to any large proportion of all employment. In many plans the increases resulting from a long series of upward adjustments have been incorporated in base rates, which are not subject to automatic reduction.

Improvement factors.   Improvement factors or productivity increases are a comparatively recent development. They are a means of assuring employees that their money wages will not remain fixed but will rise from year to year. They provide a means by which employees share directly in the growing productivity of industry. For that purpose they specify an annual increment to be added to wage rates. The practice achieved national recognition when it was written into the UAW-General Motors contract in 1948. Several million employees are now covered by agreements that include such clauses.[14]

---

[14]For a critical evaluation of these provisions, see Jules Backman, "The Economics of Annual Improvement Factor Wage Increases," *Business Series*, No. 10, New York University School of Commerce, 1952; also Dale D. McConkey, "Productivity and the Annual Improvement Factor," *Personnel*, Vol. 35, No. 1 (July–August, 1958), pp 61–66.

Plans do not attempt to relate wage adjustments to each employee's personal or individual increase in output or productivity. Most of them do not even relate the additional wages to increased productivity in the employing firm but base adjustments on the long-term average annual gain for all manufacturing industries; this latter increase has averaged some 2½ to 3 percent per year. Plans provide for the sharing of this increase with employees through a specified "across-the-board" annual advance in wage rates.

The basic idea of the improvement factor represents a sharp change from earlier policy with respect to the manner in which increased efficiency is expected to benefit employees. In the past we have generally assumed that increased productivity would result in lowered costs that would, in turn, become the basis for lower product prices. Thus, all consumers — including the employees who produced more — would benefit. The newer improvement factor seeks to insure direct participation by employees in the increased value they help to create. These productivity increases share the growing output directly with production workers, rather than with consumers as a whole.

As in all such innovations, some possible hazards are involved in any wide application of the practice. It may limit the extent to which nonemployee consumers can share in the growing output of industry. How much these other consumers may lose under this arrangement depends in part on the effects of improvement factor provisions, if any, on employee motivation and output. To date no evidence of a significant change in income distribution or in employee productivity has been noted.

Since this type of wage increase assumes that productivity is growing, an individual firm in which no such growth occurs may encounter difficulties if forced by negotiation to provide the standard 2 or 3 percent annual increase. Some critics of the practice note that since increases in efficiency frequently result from the contribution of greater investment and improved management, arbitrary allocations to wages may destroy the incentive to invest and to improve management. On the other hand, the practice might raise labor costs enough to force management into more efficient use of labor. It could act as a force toward continuing advances in methods of employing and applying manpower as well as all other resources.

Labor Costs

Employees tend to view wages as income, but employers are more concerned with wages in their role of costs.

To think clearly about economic processes involving labor costs and wage rates, we must understand that these two measures are identical to wages only when wage rates are paid on the basis of units of output. It follows from this distinction that increases in wage rates and in earnings may not increase unit labor costs or the aggregate proportion of costs attributable to labor. If output per worker is increased, higher wage rates may be paid while unit labor costs are falling. If other costs are rising, higher wage rates and earnings may become a smaller proportion of total costs.

WAGE STRUCTURES

Wage structures have two major characteristics: (1) wage levels and (2) wage differentials. *Wage levels* (or, more properly, wage and salary levels) are averages of rates paid in a particular labor market. *Wage differentials* describe the dispersion or range of wage rates in a market.

To illustrate, by examples: Workers in Country A have an average wage rate of $2.50 per hour; in Country B they average $1.00 per hour. Country A obviously has a higher wage level, and the use of an average helps provide understanding of this facet of comparative wage structures. Now for another example: Wages in Country A range from $2 to $3 an hour; in Country B, from 50¢ to $2.50. Obviously, there are wider differentials in wage rates in Country B, both absolutely and relatively. In this discussion of wage structures, attention will first be given to wage levels, then to wage differentials, and next to their interrelationships.

Wage Levels

There are as many kinds of wage levels as there are labor markets. We can conceive of wage levels for an economy, a firm, an industry, a department within a firm, a union, an occupation, a geographical area, and many others. All of these wage levels are related, in varying degree, to the extent that there is competition between and among labor markets. If the wage level for teachers goes up sharply, presumably more people will enter teaching and fewer will be available for other occupations.

To stress a point made earlier, wage rates are prices for labor of varying kinds; wage levels are average prices for labor. This means that wage levels are related to price levels and structures and are not isolated phenomena. Thus, for example, labor competes with capital for a share of the national income. Entrepreneurs compare labor substitutes through cost comparisons. If wage rates get out of line with other prices, inflation may result. Distortions in wage levels (out of line with other prices) may be accompanied by unemployment. Wage levels have an important effect upon international trade, although, as was noted above and in Chapter 3, labor productivity and labor costs must also be considered in reasoning about effects of wage levels.

All of the various kinds and types of wage levels are interrelated, as was noted above. What happens to wage levels in the steel industry is not unrelated to our national wage level, and vice versa. In some cases relationships among various kinds of wage levels are direct and powerful; in other cases relationships are remote and weak; and there is a vast array of relationships between these extremes.

Simple wage-level models. The correlates of wage levels, or independent variables that affect wage levels, may be shown in the form of simple hypothetical models. It is hypothesized that different independent variables affect the various kinds of wage levels in different ways, i.e., that a separate model is needed for each kind of wage level. Illustrative models are shown for the economy in general, a firm, and a local union. In each of the three models (Figures 18-2, 18-3, and 18-4) the wage level is the dependent variable; there are two sets of independent variables and a set of intervening variables. Each model shows the direction of the hypothesized relationships. In the column of plus (+) independent variables are those which will (it is hypothesized) raise the wage level; in the minus (−) column, those that will lower it. At the bottom of each model is a group of intervening variables — i.e., those which may tend to raise or lower the wage level, depending upon further refinement in definition and observation.

To "read" Figure 18-2 (General Wage Level), note that immobility of labor supplies, pool of unemployed labor, and family working units tend to lower (−) the wage level. These are shown on the left side of the chart. Note that full employment, high educational levels, and high profits (on the right side of the chart) tend to raise (+) the wage level. At the bottom of the chart, it is noted that such variables as government policies, climate, and customs and institutions may modify the effects of the independent variables — i.e., intervene or moderate their effects.

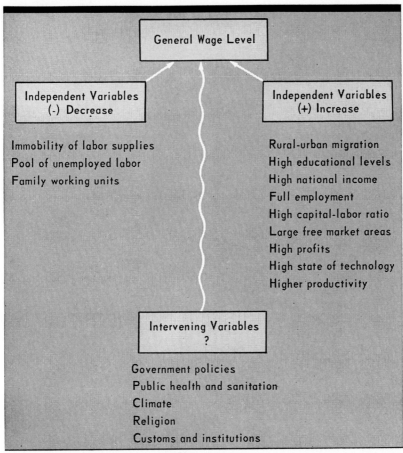

Figure 18-2
GENERAL WAGE LEVEL: A SIMPLE MODEL

Figures 18-3 and 18-4 can be "read" in similar fashion.

Figures 18-2 through 18-4 are models only in the crudest sense. They specify variables and their direction and thus have the raw material for theories and hypotheses. It should be apparent, however, that such models, while a worthwhile first step, have major limitations. Even if the semantic difficulties of adequately defining the variables are ignored, these models are very elementary. Their usefulness is further limited because they do not assign priorities or weights to the various independent variables.

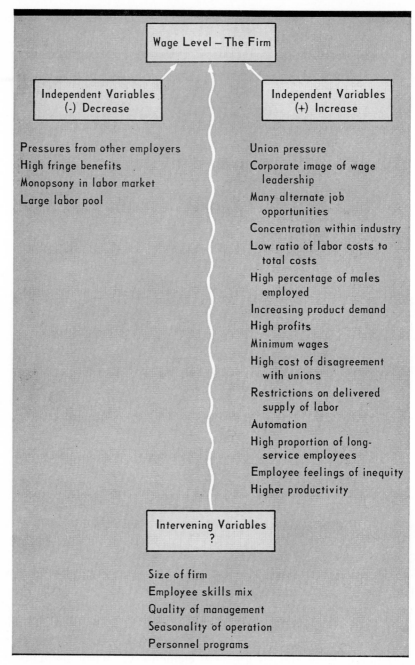

Figure 18-3
FIRM WAGE LEVEL: A SIMPLE MODEL

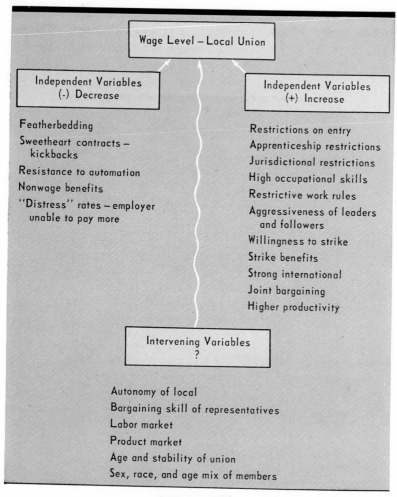

Figure 18-4
LOCAL UNION WAGE LEVEL: A SIMPLE MODEL

"Tighter" wage-level models. An example of a more refined or "tighter" model of the general wage level is provided by Melvin W. Reder.[15] His theory is: If the amount of involuntary unemployment is sufficiently large, the money wage level will fall; and if it falls sufficiently, this will increase the quantity of labor hired.

First, he states his given conditions: (1) stock of capital equipment and plant; (2) labor supply (a constant); (3) state of production

[15]Melvin W. Reder, "The General Level of Money Wages," *Reprint No. 31* (Berkeley: University of California Institute of Industrial Relations, 1951).

technique; (4) consumption, investment, and liquidity preference functions; and (5) stock of money and other liquid assets. The model which results from this defined and specified framework is shown in Figure 18-5.

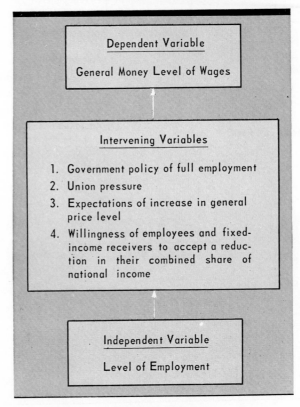

Figure 18-5
**A MODEL OF GENERAL WAGE LEVEL
AND LEVEL OF EMPLOYMENT**

Models can be improved in their efficiency by stating them in mathematical form. Footnote 16, for example, contains a hypothetical model by John Dunlop which is concerned with the general level of money wage rates.[16]

---

[16]John Dunlop, "The Task of Contemporary Wage Theory," in John Dunlop (ed.), *The Theory of Wage Determination* (London: Macmillan & Co., Ltd, 1957), pp. 22–25. It is recommended that students who desire a more detailed explanation of this and the following mathematical model (by Goldner) refer to the sources cited in this and the

Professor Goldner is one of those who have sought to develop an empirical model of wage determination for specific labor markets. He has used data provided by Bureau of Labor Statistics community wage surveys for standard metropolitan areas (SMA) to provide the regression equation model shown in footnote 17.[17]

Some of the problems associated with wage levels are discussed in this and the following chapter. A principal focus of many wage

following footnote.

$$W = \text{wage rate}$$
$$E = \text{employment}$$
$$P = \text{product price}$$
$$O = \text{output}$$
$$N = \text{nonwage income}$$
$$\text{(equivalent to profits, } \pi)$$
$$WE/PO + N/PO = 1 \text{ (national income can be divided into wage income and nonwage income)}$$
$$W = PO/E - N/E$$
$$O = \overline{O} \text{ (given)}$$
$$WE + N = PO \text{ (by definition)}$$
$$O/E = (E) \text{ (production function)}$$
$$W = F(E,N) \text{ or } W = F(E, \pi)$$
$$P = f(O/E, W_t)$$

The general level of wages is a function of employment levels (E) and profits (π), and the price level is another function of past wages and productivity.

[17]William Goldner, "Labor Market Factors and Skill Differentials in Wage Rates," *Reprint No. 108* (Berkeley: University of California Institute of Industrial Relations, 1958), p. 6; also available in the *Proceedings of the Industrial Relations Research Association*, 1957, pp. 207–16.

1. $W = 49.36 + 0.54Z_1 + 1.00Z_2 + 0.28Z_3 + 0.21Z_4$ where W is the wage level in cents per hour; Z_1 is the percentage of wage workers covered by union contracts; Z_2 is the log of population; Z_3 is the percent of total employment in durable goods manufacturing; and Z_4 is the ratio of per capita rural income to per capita urban income in the metropolitan region.

He further concludes that:

2. $S = 114.57 + .46Z_1 + 1.16Z_2 + .04Z_3 + .00Z_4$
3. $U = 37.15 + .47Z_1 + .72Z_2 + .40Z_3 + .30Z_4$
4. $S-U = 77.42 - .01Z_1 + .44Z_2 - .36Z_3 - .30Z_4$
where S = the SMA skilled wage level in cents per hour; U = the SMA unskilled wage level in cents per hour; and Z_1, Z_2, Z_3, and Z_4, are defined as above.

theories is the prediction of wage levels, as will be found in Chapters 20 through 22. Appropriate policies concerning wage levels depend, at least in part, upon understanding of wage theories. Generally, we rely upon market forces to effectuate what we regard as appropriate wage levels; sometimes we handle wage level problems through public regulation (e.g., minimum wage laws and equal pay laws). Appropriate wage levels for economic growth and full employment are widely debated. These debates reflect, in part, our inadequate understanding of forces that affect wage levels. Thus, for example, union effectiveness in raising wage levels for their members is a great and continuing controversy among labor economists, as discussed in Chapter 22. The need for a more formalized public policy in matters affecting wage levels is widely debated, as is a bewildering variety of prescriptions. This will be apparent in the next chapter and in Chapters 25 and 26.

Wage Differentials

Should a painter be paid $2 or $5 per hour? What is a fair rate of pay for a lathe operator or a truck driver? One would certainly answer, "That depends," and perhaps one would add that it depends primarily on what other comparable workers are paid. We recognize that pay for each job is related to the pay for other jobs.

Wage and salary differentials are characteristic of all economies in which demands for and supplies of workers are allowed to exert a major influence in labor pricing. Apparently both employers and employees use the wages paid for other jobs as benchmarks in creating their demand and supply schedules for each occupation. Certainly we tend to judge the fairness of our pay by reference to the wages or salaries paid for other jobs. If our job requires more skill, training, or experience, we expect to be paid more than someone who works in a job having less stringent requirements. We expect our rate to have a *differential* over the other job rate. Similarly, the employer or manager offers higher rates of pay to those who are expected to contribute greater skill, or who accept heavier responsibilities, or who are willing and able to take jobs that most other workers avoid.

Wage and salary differentials and their resulting structures are readily observed at the local and plant level. The building trades structure in one city, for example, provides top rates for electricians, with lower rates for plasterers, bricklayers, plumbers, carpenters and painters, in that order. A local intraindustry or intraplant structure is composed of a series of job rates, ranging upward from that paid the least skilled common laborer to that of the most skilled and responsible employee. Here is an illustration representing the wage structure of a metalworking plant.[18]

Job	Wage Rate	Differentials
Pattern maker	$2.16	
		) − .23
Screw machine operator	1.93	
		) − .28
Millwright	1.65	
		) − .13
Power shear operator	1.52	
		) − .01
Crane operator	1.51	
		) − .14
Plater	1.37	
		) − .05
Riveter	1.32	
		) − .02
Electric truck operator	1.30	
		) − .11
Tool crib attendant	1.19	
		) − .03
Punch press operator	1.16	
		) − .06
Watchman	1.10	
		) − .02
Common labor	1.08	

Development of differentials. What explains the emergence of rates and differentials among jobs, industries, and localities? As already noted, they develop in the labor marketing processes, which tend to price labor according to estimates of the value or worth of each job and the availability of adequate supplies.[19]

Differentials express valuations of what we pay for in work. Perhaps the most obvious consideration is skill — the knowledge and the

---

[18]From David Belcher, *Wage and Salary Administration* (New York: Prentice-Hall, Inc., 1955), p. 245. In plant wage structures, a 1962 survey by the National Industrial Conference Board found from 5 to 90 labor grades, with 19 as the median number. A "labor grade" is a group of jobs with a common rate or a common rate range. In the most common practice, the differentials between minima in adjacent ranges varied from 5 to 10 percent of the lower minimum. Variations within ranges are normally from 30 to 40 percent of the minimum. See Michael E. Edmonds and George W. Torrence, "Erecting the Salary Structure," *Management Record*, Vol. 24, No. 10 (October, 1962), pp 26–28.

[19]For an interesting analysis of such differentials, see Sumner H. Slichter, "Notes on the Structure of Wages," *Review of Economics and Statistics*, Vol. 32, No. 1 (February, 1950), pp. 80–91. For an example of a model designed to explain interindustry variations in wage structures see Joseph W. Garbarino, "A Theory of Inter-industry Wage Structure Variation," *Reprint No. 26* (Berkeley: University of California Institute of Industrial Relations, 1950); for another example of a wage level model see David G. Brown, "Expected Ability to Pay and Inter-industry Wage Structure in Manufacturing," *Industrial and Labor Relations Review*, Vol. 16, No. 1 (October, 1962), pp. 45–62.

ability required by various jobs. The assumption of responsibility is another important ingredient. In many intraplant and some intraindustry structures, the relative levels of job rates are set by a process that combines from five to fifteen factors in each job as the basis for compensation. This process of *job evaluation* compares jobs in terms of these factors, totals the contribution of each job or group of jobs, and thus creates point values that can be translated into wage rates. The most commonly considered factors are skill, experience, responsibility, and working conditions.[20]

The appearance and development of wage differentials is an important feature of the process of industrialization. When an agrarian society feels the first impact, very wide wage differentials appear. Supplies of industrially trained labor are relatively small and inelastic. Qualified workers may have to be imported from older industrial economies. Their wage is likely to be much higher than that of native agricultural workers. Interarea differentials may be greatly increased if the industrialization is confined to a limited section of a nation. As the process of industrialization proceeds, differentials tend to narrow. Surpluses of relatively unskilled agricultural labor are reduced as more workers are drawn into industrial employment. More widespread education and special training for jobs in industry tend to reduce the differentials favoring industrial workers. Public policy may specify a variety of wage supplements as means of controlling the inequities created by industrialization and thus reduce the range of interindustry wage differentials. Continued industrialization produces fringes that make differentials in wage rates less important.

Wage structures continue to change in mature economies. Intraindustry differentials are lowered when decision making is centralized. Inflation appears to narrow all differentials, as do periods of high level employment. Industries with comparatively low labor costs (as a proportion of total costs) show more rapid changes in structures than high-labor-cost industries.[21]

---

[20]For details of this procedure, see David W. Belcher, *Wage and Salary Administration* (Englewood Cliffs, New Jersey: Prentice-Hall, Inc., 1962); E. Lanham, *Administration of Wages and Salaries* (New York, Harper and Row, 1963), pp. 107–206; Adolph Langsner and Herbert G. Zollitsch, *Wage and Salary Administration* (Cincinnati: South-Western Publishing Company, 1961), pp. 125–308.

[21]For details and illustrations see John T. Dunlop and Melvin Rothbaum "International Comparisons of Wage Structures," *International Labor Review*, Vol. 71, No. 4 (April, 1955), pp. 3–19. For a detailed analysis of changing wage structures in Western nations during the period since the 1930 depression, see Lloyd G. Reynolds and Cynthia H. Taft, *The Evolution of Wage Structures* (New Haven: Yale University Press, 1956). See also John E. Maher, "The Wage Pattern in the United States, 1946–1957," *Industrial and*

Shrinking differentials and contracting or narrowing wage structures create serious current wage problems. Reduced differentials cause concern among workers who have long gauged the fairness of their rates by such yardsticks. These changes affect their status in working relationships as well as their incomes. Similarly, reduced wage rate advantages for skilled workers may destroy the incentive to undergo lengthy apprenticeships or special training and thus reduce future supplies.

Relating Wage Levels to Differentials

As stated previously, wage structures have two major components — i.e., level (or height) and differential (spread or dispersion). It has also been noted that there are as many wage structures as there are labor markets. All of these levels, differentials, and structures are related, in varying degree. The basic question here is: How are these relationships determined?

John T. Dunlop has provided the best answer to this question to date by showing interrelationships of internal (plant) and external (market) wage structures.[22] Dunlop posits wage structures as balanced systems whose elements are: (1) job clusters, (2) plant wage structures, and (3) wage contours. Throughout, "key jobs" provide essential linkages (the basis for relating) between jobs and structures.

Key jobs are those used as "bench-marks" for purposes of job and wage comparison. Generally, they are important because of their position in a job structure. Key jobs are jobs well known to employees, unions, and management; are important in the production process; are relatively stable in content; and exist in other firms and labor markets, thereby making comparisons possible.

A *job cluster* (or job structure) consists of one or more key jobs and jobs related to it. For example, a machinist job may be the key job in a cluster; various other jobs such as helpers and sweepers may be related to machinists not only in terms of the production function but also in terms of wages. Job clusters, according to Dunlop, are a stable group of jobs within a company, linked together by technology, administrative arrangements (or organization), and social custom.

Labor Relations Review, Vol. 15, No. 1 (October, 1961), pp. 3–20; for a criticism and reply, see Maurice C. Benewitz and Alan Spero in *Industrial and Labor Relations Review*, Vol. 16, No. 1 (October, 1962), pp. 122–25, and Maher's reply, pp. 125–33.

[22] John T. Dunlop, "The Task of Contemporary Wage Theory," in George W. Taylor and Frank C. Pierson (eds.), *New Concepts in Wage Determination* (New York: McGraw-Hill Book Co., Inc., 1957), pp. 127–34.

The *wage structure of a plant* is made up of all its job clusters, linked through their key jobs.

A *wage contour* is the wage structure of a group of companies, linked together by a common product market, labor market, or both. A wage contour has common: (1) job clusters (or occupations), (2) industry sectors, and (3) geographical location. Contours may thus be national, regional, or industrial.

Wage structures are dynamic and changing. *Wage forces* (or factors that cause change) usually are concentrated on key jobs in job clusters. These forces spread internally through the plant wage structure and externally through wage contours. Any time a key job rate is changed it will have some impact upon other jobs within and beyond companies.

COMPARATIVE WAGE SYSTEMS

To provide a basis for improved understanding, the present chapter is concluded with a brief discussion of the Soviet wage system and comparative wage rates in some European countries. Note that the Soviets, too, are concerned with structures, levels, and differentials. Their forms of wage payments are similar to ours in some respects and dissimilar in others. Above all, note that market forces in Russia do not have the same role or influence that they have in the United States.

Russian Wage System

A massive program of wage reform was begun in Soviet Russia in 1956. It sought to rationalize or structure the nation's entire system of wages and salaries, except in agriculture. In part this action was caused by the freeing of the labor market in the 1950's, after fifteen years of job freeze and direct controls. There was almost no interindustry labor mobility. Other causes were centered in troubles with their wage and salary system. Thus, for example, basic wage scales constituted less than half of total earnings in basic industries. Production standards were loose, and "production bonuses" that had little relation to effort or efficiency were given.[23]

---

[23]See Walter Galenson, "The Soviet Wage Reform," in *Proceedings of the Industrial Relations Research Association*, 1961, pp. 249–65. See also his "Wage Structure and Administration in Soviet Industry," *Reprint No. 221* (Berkeley: University of California Institute of Industrial Relations, 1964). For an interesting comparison see Charles Hoffman, "Work Incentives in Communist China," *Industrial Relations*, Vol. 3, No. 3 (February, 1964), pp. 81–97.

The new wage policy was designed with three major objectives:

1. To provide motivation and incentive for work of desired quantity and quality.
2. To act as a mechanism for allocating labor supply.
3. To serve as a means of distributing income.

According to Galenson, the Soviet wage structure is built on the basic wage scale, consisting of six or seven labor grades with successive grades expressed as a ratio of the first (lowest) grade. All jobs get slotted in a labor grade. The number of wage scales (which are different for different industries) was reduced from 213 to 10 by April, 1960. The basic scales are like a job structure obtained from job evaluation. When the job structure is priced, the price is set for grade one, and then other prices fall into place automatically (by use of ratios). Variations in pricing are permitted for heavy and light work, unpleasant working conditions, and other factors similar to American job evaluation plans. While differentials in the basic plans provide for a ratio of 2:1 for jobs at the top of the scale over jobs at the bottom of the scale, these "extra factors" may result in ratios ranging as high as 5:1. Although the official Soviet policy is to narrow differentials, Galenson's studies show that, in fact, they have been widened in recent years.[24]

The Russians use incentive wages more than any other nation. In March, 1963, 63 percent of Soviet wage earners were paid on a piece-rate basis.

Hours of work have been reduced to seven hours per day with an average 41-hour workweek. In 1964 plans were announced to reduce hours gradually to 35 hours per week although no starting date was set and hours were not reduced. It should be noted that when hours are decreased in Russia, production quotas remain the same as they were when the longer hours were in effect.

The external wage structure is set by relating the first labor grade in the basic wage scale for each industry. These are pegged, not by market forces, but by the importance of that industry to national objectives. In general, the highest base wage scales are set for critical (heavy) industries, with low scales for consumer goods industries.

Salary structures are related to wage structures through a process resembling salary evaluation. Salaries for foremen are used as the base for the entire salary structure; foremen receive a 10 to 15 percent

---

[24]It should be noted that data on earnings of Soviet workers are frequently unavailable; data on rates are much more common.

higher differential. Clerical salary workers receive 80 percent of industrial workers' wages, while engineering and technical workers get 160 percent of the wage earners' rate. Rate ranges are used for salary workers. Thirty-five basic salary schedules take care of most industries; two basic clerical salary plans cut across industries. Executive bonuses are now limited to 60 percent of salaries in coal, oil, steel, and chemical industries, and 40 percent elsewhere.

Thus, in summary, these revisions are designed to provide better motivation and productivity, to allocate labor more efficiently, and to reduce inequities.

Purchasing power of Soviet workers has been rising steadily in recent years, mainly as a result of rising wages. But, by 1958 real earnings in the Soviet Union, although higher than in the 1930's and 1940's, were still 8 percent below 1928. In part this is due to emphasis upon capital goods production rather than consumer goods production. By 1958 capital goods production was up 570 percent and consumer goods production was up 270 percent over 1940 levels.

Food costs in Russia remain high. In 1959 a Soviet worker would have had to work 28½ hours per week (of the then legal 46-hour workweek) to purchase basic foods for his family. The high cost of food may help explain the higher female labor force participation rate (47 percent in Russia, compared with 35 percent in the United States).

Average money earnings per month in Russian cities in 1959 were about 800 rubles, or $80 U.S. This was up sharply from 600 rubles in 1953. A minimum wage of 270 rubles a month in nonurban areas was decreed in 1957.

There is no income tax in Russia, but the costs of consumer goods include a heavy tax; about one half of consumer prices is represented by this disguised tax. This tax pays for such consumer services as "free" medical care.

The average worker in Moscow has to work longer than his counterpart in New York City to buy basic consumer goods: in 1959, for beef and milk, 4 times longer; for butter, 9 times longer; for clothing, 8 to 16 times longer. However, this differential is being reduced; thus, for example, in 1953 a Moscow worker had to work 10 to 20 times longer for clothing.[25]

---

[25]Edmund Nash, "Purchasing Power of Workers in the U.S.S.R.," *Monthly Labor Review* (April, 1960), pp. 359–64. See also A. Nove, "A Study of Soviet Wages," *British Journal of Industrial Relations*, Vol. 1, No. 1 (February, 1963), pp. 62–72. A valuable source on all Soviet labor legislation is contained in the United States Bureau of Labor Statistics, *Report No. 210*, "Principal Current Soviet Labor Legislation," January, 1962. The BLS Division of Foreign Labor Conditions has issued more than a score of reports on labor

Wage Rates in Europe

Average hourly wage rates in manufacturing in the United States are higher than in Europe, but from 1958 to 1962 they increased at a faster rate in European countries. Thus, while the United States wage rate increased 16 percent, rates were up 16 percent in Great Britain, 19 percent in Italy, 30 percent in Sweden and France, and 39 percent in West Germany.[26]

The nature of wage forces, or why wage rates change, is discussed in the next four chapters. The present chapter has been largely one of description and definition — of preparation for the entire section on wages in this book. In the next chapter we will use these basic definitions and concepts as a basis for discussing wage policies and problems. The three chapters after that are concerned with wage theories — i.e., tentative explanations of wage levels and differentials.

ANALYTICAL REVIEW QUESTIONS

1. How is the wage system related to industrialization?
2. What are the major economic functions of wages?
3. Why do wages have an impact upon utilization of human resources? How and in what ways do wage payments motivate employers?
4. Why is labor pricing so important in growth and stability of the total economy?
5. Why is the wage share of national income a matter of concern to economists?
6. What percent of national income in the United States goes to compensation of employees? How does the share going to employees compare with other distributive shares?
7. What accounts for the increased share of national income going to labor? Are unions and collective bargaining prime forces in this redistribution?
8. Why is it important to define wage terms carefully?
9. How are "fringes" related to "take-home-pay"? How do income tax laws make fringes a "bargain" for employees?
10. In what countries are fringe benefits higher than in the United States?
11. Do fringes reflect mostly "needs" or "productivity" of workers?
12. What has happened to the number of profit sharing plans in the United States? When are "deferred" plans paid off to employees?
13. How are cost-of-living wage adjustments and improvement factors alike? How do they differ?
14. How do real wages differ from money wages?
15. What are the two most important characteristics of wage structures? How is each of these defined?

---

conditions and legislation in foreign countries — for a good example, see BLS *Report No. 188*, "Labor in India," April, 1961.

[26]*U.S. News and World Report*, November 5, 1962, p. 19.

16. What may happen when there are distortions in wage levels?

17. What are some of the variables that tend to lower wage levels in a labor market? To raise them?

18. How does Reder relate involuntary unemployment to money wage level?

19. What factors underlie wage differentials? What economic roles do differentials play?

20. What is meant by job evaluation?

21. How are job clusters, plant wage structures, and wage contours related? What provides the linkage?

22. What are the common elements in a wage contour?

23. What are the three major objectives of Soviet wage policy?

24. How is the Soviet internal wage structure constructed? Is it similar to the United States wage structure? Why or why not?

25. How is the basic wage scale for each industry determined in Russia?

26. How do real wages in Russia compare with real wages in the United States?

Case 18-1

SWEDGER DIFFERENTIAL

Consider the problem of Dr. Smythe, an arbitrator. The case is an unresolved issue involving a possible wage rate increase on a single job, that of swedger. The employer and the union settled all other issues in negotiating a new contract and agreed to submit this one to him.

The union argues that the swedger rate should be increased 10 cents per hour. The employer opposes any increase. The argument advanced by the union is based on historic rate relationships and wage structures in the industry. The union points to the fact that the rate on this job was, for 30 years, 10 cents above that of assembler. The differential fell to only 5 cents as a result of negotiations last year. This year, the union seeks to restore the traditional differential. The employer does not dispute the union's contention as to these facts.

The employer argues that the job of the swedger has been somewhat simplified by a new machine, and this point is not disputed by the union. The employer further insists that the present job requirements are such that an assembler with one week of experience in the swedger job can perform the latter in an entirely satisfactory manner.

• These are the facts. Consider this statement as Dr. Smythe's "finding of facts." Make his award, with stated reasons.

Case 18-2

COMMON FRONT ON WAGE OFFER

You have recently become the general manager of a small agricultural processing plant in a city of about 25,000 people. The plant employs some 200 local residents. The employees are not members of any union.

The firm has maintained what it regards as a fairly liberal policy with respect to wages. The absence of a union among employees, in spite of several attempts to organize them, is regarded by officials of the firm as evidence that wages must have been satisfactory. On the other hand, you have faced increasing difficulty in getting and holding employees. During the preceding fall, your operations were severely handicapped by vacancies. You know that at least one other local factory has hired away several of your employees.

A week ago you attended a luncheon to which you were invited by the manager of one of the other local plants. The group included managers of the five local manufacturing firms. Your host suggested that you all get together on wage offers this year. He argued that your past practice is simply increasing turnover and encouraging shopping for jobs. All the other managers who were present seemed to agree with him. It is your impression that they will conclude an informal and highly confidential agreement on the wage rates to be offered on the most common jobs.

• You intend to present the question of joining in this move to your firm's executive committee, with your recommendations. First decide what you will recommend. Then, in a single page that can be placed before each member of the committee, justify these recommendations by citing reasons.

Case 18-3

SEMISKILLED WAGE LEVEL

Assume that you have in your community a manufacturing plant which is a subsidiary of a major producer with headquarters in a distant city. Employees have recently formed a union. At a meeting a week ago, the union members agreed on minimum wage rates they will accept and a deadline for negotiation of a contract. For semiskilled workers the minimum rate asked is $2.10 per hour. The local manager has publicly stated that he has been instructed to pay no more than $1.85 per hour. He needs 450 semiskilled employees.

• Assume that you have been appointed a member of a local citizens' committee to prevent a strike while maintaining fairness and equity in the dispute. Outline on one page the points you will stress in a statement to the committee. Be sure to state your replies to issues of labor market monopoly, monopsony, and possible effects on the local economy, all of which have been raised by newspaper editorials.

WAGE POLICIES AND PROBLEMS

In every modern industrialized society, wages are, in popular language, the lifeblood of the economy. To individual citizens and their families, wages are almost life or death matters. To society as a whole, the continuing, adequate flow of expendable income is a "must" or essential of the highest priority. The always precarious economic balance of the society can be maintained only by preserving appropriate relationships among wages, production, and price levels. Wages, because they represent such a dominating segment of expendable income, must be regarded as of primary importance in economic stability. Interference with their continuing provision of an adequate aggregate of immediately expendable income invites economic recession and threatens economic collapse.

Wages exert a similarly important influence in the economies of most households. Any interference with the flow of wages into the family treasury threatens disaster. The persistent adequacy and fairness of wages is therefore of continuing concern to most of the men and women who work and to every member of their families.

Wage problems — i.e., failures to attain personal and social wage goals — lead to a constantly changing complex of programs designed to adjust and control compensation for work. Wage policies set objectives of compensation programs and seek to prevent or ameliorate wage problems. Wage objectives and policies of employers, unions, and the public may and do differ, as will be noted below. Increasingly, however, public policy plays a dominant role.

The present chapter has four major sections. First, there is a discussion of public policy on wages, together with union and employer policy. Resultant conflict and disagreement in wage programs are traced to their origins in the absence of uniform wage criteria and disagreements on wage theory. The next section is concerned with some of the common wage yardsticks and criteria, with special emphasis upon needs, real wages, and living costs. Problems of determining equity or fairness in wages are given special attention. Public wage controls, including wage payment laws, equal pay laws, wage-hour laws, and minimum wage laws, are the subject matter of the third section of this chapter; their economic implications are examined. The chapter concludes by directing attention to problems of wages, inflation, and unemployment. As was true of Chapter 18, the present chapter seeks to provide a background of facts, viewpoints, and problems to facilitate understanding of the next three chapters on wage theories.

PUBLIC POLICY ON WAGES

Our public policy — our stated social intention with respect to salaries and wages — is closely related to the role of wages outlined in the previous chapter. In part, our public policy supports individual wage objectives; we propose to help individuals make progress toward the scales of living to which they aspire. In part, public wage policy seeks to advance other social and economic purposes and objectives, including political democracy and economic stability and freedom.

What are our major intentions with respect to wages? What tests must wages and salaries meet to be socially satisfactory? At least five "planks" in our accepted wage "platform" may be noted. They include:

1. *Certainty and assurance of payment.* A comparatively simple but important public policy holds that wages shall be paid when due. It recognizes the fact that individual wage earners may have limited resources and reserves so that employers might gain unreasonable concessions or create serious hardship by delaying payments. Our policy therefore proposes such public intervention as may be necessary to protect wage earners and insure prompt payment.

2. *Fairness and comparative equity of rates.* Our public policy assumes that wages should be fair, without specifically defining that

term. Our thinking on this point combines several obvious measures or marks of fairness, including output, contribution, and need. Wages should provide an incentive for a full "fair day's work." Differentials should be justifiable in terms of relative contributions. Wage structures should provide incentives for finding good jobs and preparing for maximum personal contributions. Hence, we seek to preserve what we regard as proper structures and differentials.

We cannot ignore the fact that the fairness of wages is not easily appraised. What appears a fair wage to one of us may seem quite unfair to others. It is, for this reason, often said that no one can prove that any particular wage rate is fair or just. The fairness of a rate depends on what yardsticks are applied. Several wage theories discussed in following chapters provide clues useful in this connection.

3. *Adequacy and decency of earnings.* In another accepted wage policy, we propose that wages should make possible a comfortable and decent standard and scale of living for workers and their families. Here again, we have some trouble in defining what we mean by "comfort" and "decency," but the broad objective of our policy is evident. We are determined to eliminate what we regard as *substandard* rates of pay — those that do not measure up to this criterion.

4. *Progress and rising real wages.* We are firm believers in progress and improvement in wages. We want no fixed or permanent level of real wages for any class of wage earners. Rather, we propose continued advances from year to year so that the prospect of ongoing improvement may avoid frustration on the part of workers and provide greater incentives for working.

5. *Balance and economic stability.* We recognize that wages and salaries represent the largest share of income and purchasing power; hence, we regard the aggregate of these payments as a keystone in the arch of continuing economic stability, growth, and prosperity. Wage income as a whole is to be maintained at a level that will assure a market for our output. We propose to discover and maintain an optimum relationship between wage income and total national income.

Union Policy and Public Policy

These general objectives for wages cannot be divorced from our other labor policies. Our stated intention to encourage unions, for example, must be related to and appropriate for wage policy. Does our endorsement of the idea of unions mean that we also accept all union wage goals as public objectives? Or are our policies with respect to unions on the one hand and wages on the other inconsistent and conflicting?

Such questions require consideration of union wage policy and the effects of unions on wages. It has been frequently said that union wage policy merely proposes "more," that unions seek simply to force greater and greater concessions from employers. This, however, is a serious oversimplification. While the general wage policy of unions is presumably to advance the real earnings of their members, many union leaders and bargaining representatives show a keen understanding of the "facts of life" in labor markets. They have no intention either of seeking such increases as may force large numbers out of work or of pricing employers out of business. In such balanced policy the objectives of unions are not directly inconsistent with public policy.[1]

On the other hand, if strong unions can and do change the basic distribution of the national income, that action might interfere with public policy designed to stabilize the economy. It is possible, therefore, that union policy could directly conflict with public policy so that our policy favoring unions and collective bargaining would be inconsistent with accepted public wage policy.

This possibility suggests that the actual effects of union wage policies and programs deserve careful consideration. How have they affected levels of wages, total amounts paid their members, and distributive shares in national income?

Studies find different, conflicting answers to these questions. Professor Arthur Ross concludes that unions in the markets he examined have raised wage rates.[2] On the other hand, Professor John E. Maher, in a careful study of differentials between bargained wages and those in similar plants without unions, found no significant differences. He notes, however, the possibility that the effects of unionism may be significant beyond the bargained industry or plant.[3]

Under these circumstances we cannot be sure that public policy on unions and on wages is entirely consistent. We need more

---

[1]For a detailed story of union wage policies since 1900, see James S. Youtsler, *Labor's Wage Policies in the Twentieth Century* (New York: Twayne Publishers, 1956).

[2]See his "The Influence of Unionism Upon Earnings," *Reprint No. 5*, University of California Institute of Industrial Relations, Berkeley, 1948; his "Trade Unions as Wage-fixing Institutions," *American Economic Review*, Vol. 37, No. 4 (September, 1947), pp. 588 ff.; and "Productivity and Wage Control," *Industrial and Labor Relations Review*, Vol. 7, No. 2 (January, 1954), pp. 177–91. Several investigators have studied the experience of specific industries to evaluate the part played by unions in advancing wages. See, for example, Stephen P. Sobotka, "Union Influence on Wages: The Construction Industry," *Journal of Political Economy*, Vol. 41, No. 2 (April, 1953), pp. 127–43. He concludes that it is probable that unions in this industry have raised wages. See also the discussion of the bargaining theory of wages in Chapter 22.

[3]See his "Union, Non-union Wage Differentials," *American Economic Review*, Vol. 44, No. 3 (June, 1956), pp. 336–52. See also J. W. Garbarino, "Unionism and the General Wage Level," *American Economic Review*, Vol. II, No. 5, Part 1 (December, 1950), pp. 893–95. Questions of union impact on wages are discussed in more detail in Chapter 22.

extensive studies to provide added understanding of the relationship of unions and wages.

Employer Wage Policy and Public Policy

If union wage policy may be described as "more," employer wage policy may be described as "less." Both are obvious overgeneralizations and yet each contains some reasonable approximation of reality. Historically, employers frequently found themselves with a relatively free hand in wage determination. Many wage laws may be traced to employer wage policies of the past. Substandard wages were in part responsible for minimum wage laws, for example. Some of the problems of inequity in wages occasioned equal pay laws. Lack of provision for employees' economic security when jeopardized by accidents, unemployment, and old age resulted in laws providing for such security, as is discussed in Chapters 23 and 24. Most public policy on wages represents attempts to correct what were widely regarded as deficiencies in employer wage policies. There is little question that employers in the past found their policies in conflict with public policy on many of these issues.

In recent years, however, employers have been much more alert to employee and public reaction to wage policies. They have learned to deal with unions instead of following policies of negativism and resistance, as noted in Chapter 10. They have gone beyond and ahead of union and public policy in their attempts to meet some of our social goals. Job evaluation and employee ratings, measurement of productivity and incentive payments, wage surveys and formal wage policy statements — these are examples of recent employer wage practices that tend to advance the major public wage goals given at the beginning of this chapter.

But even as "there are unions and unions," "there are employers and employers." A small but significant percentage are caught each year in violation of minimum wage laws and overtime pay laws, for example. Other violations and actions inconsistent with public policy could be cited. Such employers could gain an unfair competitive advantage over employers who conform with public policy. Cases of this type are unfair not only to other employers, but to employees as well.

As in the case of union wage policies, we do not know the full impact of employer wage policies. More research in this area is needed. Joint union-employer wage policies reached through collective bargaining call for similar study.

Disagreement on Wage Programs

Differences in wage policies result in disagreements on wage programs. Several reasons exist for sharp differences in our attitudes toward wage goals and objectives, on the one hand, and programs of action designed to influence wages, on the other. Among the most important are the facts that (1) we have no universal, objective yardsticks of wage fairness or adequacy, so that opinions differ as to the seriousness of various problems; and (2) we have inadequate knowledge of the factors affecting wages, so that we disagree about ways and means of achieving accepted goals. Each of these conditions deserves brief explanation.

Absence of objective yardsticks of wage fairness. We have no simple, widely accepted objective yardsticks for evaluating the seriousness of various wage problems. As a result, opinions differ as to which problems are most serious and hence deserving of priorities in wage programs. To some the existence of unfairness and various types of inequities is most objectionable. They may place "equal pay for equal work" at the top of the list, so far as action is concerned. Others may regard the continued payment of substandard rates as the most immediate and pressing problem. Still others are more concerned with stability and adequacy of labor income in the aggregate. Such differences in personal impressions, opinions, and values create disagreement on priorities in public programs. It is well to remember in this connection that, with our present knowledge, no one can prove beyond the possibility of contradiction that any particular job rate is right or wrong or can demonstrate conclusively what that rate should be.

This absence of an "absolute" or "Bureau of Standards" criterion or yardstick with which to measure the rightness of individual rates creates confusion and disagreement with respect to social action. It permits each individual to apply his own standards of rightness and thus to establish personal priorities on wage problems. As noted below, the most common subscales or values in these personal yardsticks are the worker's need, his contribution, the employer's ability to pay, and relationships among going rates in appropriate labor markets.

Each of these elements in wage criteria is in itself something of a rubber yardstick. It includes no standard scale or measure. Need may be regarded as involving almost any amount from that providing subsistence for a single worker with no dependents to what is required to maintain a family of five on a comfort-and-decency level. Contribution may be a matter of pure impression or the result of job evaluation that involves rating a dozen job elements or factors, each estimate to the third decimal point. Ability to pay may be completely ignored, appraised in terms of the employer's statement of profits or losses, or judged by opinions and impressions of the effects of wage rates on sales. Going rates may be those in what are regarded as similar markets in the locality or those in the industry in what are believed to be similar localities. The range of resulting personal conclusions as to what rates are fair, adequate, and justifiable is obviously broad.[4]

Disagreement on wage theory. A second major reason why we have general agreement on wage goals combined with disagreement on wage programs is the fact that we have only partial understanding of the factors that influence or determine wages. We have no settled, demonstrated scientific principles. Rather, we have a number of theories about wages. We have no single, universally used road map indicating the shortest highways toward the destinations identified as our wage goals. As a result, our citizens propose a variety of tours and short cuts, some of which take off in opposite directions.

At one extreme, for example, some citizens have concluded that poverty and wage inadequacy are entirely explainable in terms of the perversity of human nature. They conclude that these conditions persist primarily because some workers have low personal ideals, ambitions, and aspirations. To put the situation briefly, they are lazy and shiftless. Such observers may conclude that no social action or wage programs are appropriate and that only the slow process of a long-term educational program can effect the desired changes.

A somewhat similar conclusion as to appropriate social action or inaction is implied in the opinion that wage rates and earnings are the result of inexorable laws of demand and supply. Exponents of this viewpoint may conclude that nothing can be done about wages or that the situation will take care of itself and is naturally self-correcting.

If we knew with mathematical precision just what conditions or factors determine wage rates and labor income, agreement on public

---

[4] Jules Backman, *Wage Determination: An Analysis of Wage Criteria* (Princeton, N.J.: D. Van Nostrand Co., Inc., 1959).

programs might be more readily attained. Such understanding would indicate the possibilities of successful action and the social costs or sacrifices in each course. In the absence of such knowledge, public action has had to depend on a variety of wage theories, plausible explanations advanced as indicating probable relationships among wages and factors affecting wages. Wage theories are the subject matter of the next three chapters.

FAIRNESS IN WAGE RATES

Although most of us are agreed that wages should be fair and equitable, we have widely different ideas as to what these terms mean. As was noted above there are no absolute, objective, universally accepted yardsticks of fairness.

Most wage decisions involve use and comparison of several yardsticks rather than a single yardstick. Those most commonly considered include productivity or contribution, employee needs, ability to pay, and going rates. Misunderstandings may and do occur frequently because of confusion over money wages versus real wages. Also, there are substantial differences in values and opinions about appropriate occupational differentials. The concept of fair or equitable wages means different things to different people. Such differences transcend customary employer or employee viewpoints. Even within employer and employee groups, there is less than consistency of agreement with respect to whether or not wages are fair and equitable.

Why do we not or can we not agree on a simple yardstick? The major reason is that fact that we do not agree entirely on two essential considerations. The first of these is what we pay for in wages. Here, we use several measures or criteria. Second, we do not agree on which of these considerations deserves greatest weight. As a result, we may arrive at quite different conclusions about what is a fair rate of pay for any individual worker. Consider, for example, how one would arrive at a fair wage for the garage mechanic who maintains a home and has seven dependents or the typist who is living with her parents, is receiving alimony, and has no dependents.

Common Yardsticks of Wage Fairness

What are the most common yardsticks we apply in these and thousands of other similar situations? Which of them is most important? We can list several of these yardsticks, as follows:

(1) Contribution. In much of our thinking, we assume that we want to pay each worker according to what he contributes. If he is unskilled, we conclude that he can and will probably contribute less than if he were skilled. If he is new and inexperienced, his contribution in most jobs is likely to be less than that of long-term, experienced workers. If he works more zealously, we think he should earn more.

One will notice at once that this yardstick is in itself a combination of several others. Moreover, few of the component measures are entirely objective. For example, what is the measure of skill? Is it years of formal training or apprenticeship, or is it some test of the worker's actual performance? How can the influence or value of experience in a worker's contribution be appraised? What measure is appropriate for zeal, application, and effort? Insofar as each standard appraises intangibles, each is likely to result in varying appraisals.

(2) Need. At the same time, many of us want to consider an employee's need in evaluating his wage. Does it permit him to live respectably? Can he maintain his family and support his dependents on his earnings? In some earlier societies this yardstick was regarded as most important. When the influence of church leaders was dominant in such matters, a just-price doctrine prescribed wages that met wage earners' needs and permitted them to raise families and maintain their status. In some countries today wages are formally adjusted to need through the specific provision of *family allowances.* These supplementary wages, added to regular wages and adjusted to the number of each worker's dependents, are common in several European and South American nations and in Canada. For many supporters of Marxian economic philosophy, the doctrine of "to each according to his need" is accepted as the ultimate principle of workers' compensation. Russia and the satellite nations, however, have concluded that such wages do not provide an adequate incentive for strenuous effort in what they regard as the present transitional stage.

(3) Ability to pay. Many of our citizens are also concerned about the employer's ability to pay various wage rates. They do not want too-high wage rates to handicap an employer in his product market. They want him to maintain employment, stay in business, and perhaps expand. At the other extreme, they want him to share some of his success and profit with the members of his work team.

In the application of this yardstick, few would make it the major or dominant consideration. They would not propose that wage rates be closely or tightly bound to profits, for in any such arrangement many wage rates would fluctuate sharply from time to time. In many firms they might fall precipitately or remain low for extensive periods. Similarly, wage rates tied closely to ability to pay might result in a rapidly shifting, quite different, and less satisfactory distribution and application of our human resources.

Serious consideration of the yardstick of ability to pay generally appears as a limiting factor rather than a prescriptive or determining factor. We are forced to consider ability to pay when application of other yardsticks indicates a wage rate that may force some employers out of business. Establishments whose profits are small — at the margin — may find that a rate suggested by contribution or need would make continued operations unprofitable. In such cases, especially when unemployment is extensive, we have modified our application of the other yardsticks to take account of ability to pay, as in setting minimum wage rates under federal and state laws. A major question in most of these wage determinations is their possible effect on employment.

(4) Going rates. Unquestionably, the most commonly applied criterion is a composite of the three already described, plus some others. It is what is widely described as the *going rate*, sometimes lampooned because "nobody knows where it's going or where it came from." It is the generally current rate for the same or similar jobs in the community. Sometimes it is readily determined, as, for example, when it is specified by law or by widely observed collective agreements. Sometimes it is obscure, as when several rates can be found on what appear to be similar jobs.

This yardstick is frequently applied, principally because it is widely accepted. Many of us conclude that a rate must be about right if it has such acceptance. Moreover, it is quantitative and objective. It gives us something tangible and fairly definite, as compared with the impressionistic character of most other yardsticks.

Each yardstick of fairness, equity, and adequacy of wages has special appeals to certain segments of the population. In addition, priorities among yardsticks change through time. Perhaps the two most commonly accepted yardsticks, and these contain obvious elements of conflict, are contribution or productivity and need—personal and family. We discussed productivity in detail in Chapter 3. Now let us turn to concepts of need, including real wages.

Criteria of Need

Basic to ideas of adequacy and fairness is agreement that wage rates should be related to the amounts that workers and their dependents need. To pay less is frequently described as *exploitation*, a term that carries the connotation of taking unfair advantage of workers. It suggests that employers are making an inefficient use of human resources. Very low wage rates create conditions approaching those of slavery or peonage, which are objectionable in our type of political and social organization. Historic literature in this field makes frequent reference to a *living wage* — a wage that permits wage earners and their dependents to maintain what were regarded as minimal scales of living. We have long objected to *subsistence wages* — those that only permit workers to continue their existence.

What levels of wages should be regarded as essential to meet workers' needs? Studies of wage earners' budgets and detailed living costs have sought to define the wage income necessary to provide minimum standards of comfort and decency. Such calculations are complicated by the facts that: (1) we do not agree on what constitutes a minimum of comfort and decency; (2) standards of comfort and decency are constantly changing; (3) price levels and the costs of goods and services purchased by wage earners are also changing; and (4) wage earners do not have uniform responsibilities in terms of families or dependents. As a result of these complications, our estimates of necessary minimum wage rates and earnings have to be approximations, applicable to some theoretical average wage earner. This situation is not likely to change, since each of the four conditions noted is persistent. Conceptions of necessities and luxuries are subject to wide variations. Bitter arguments can develop over whether a need or decency budget should include tobacco, beer, television, and an automobile.

Living costs and family size. Some facts are available with respect to what workers actually spend. The Bureau of Labor Statistics now reports on living costs for wage earners' families in major cities. Data represent actual expenditures as evidenced by studies of city workers' family budgets.[5] A recent comparison of these costs is shown in Table 19-1. Incidentally, the range of these varying costs — from the lowest in Houston to the highest in Chicago — has declined as regional wage differentials have narrowed. The Bureau of Labor Statistics also maintains its Consumer Price Index which measures time-to-time changes in the aggregate cost of items in the wage earners' budget.

Table 19-1
COSTS OF CITY WORKERS' FAMILY BUDGETS — 1951 AND 1959[1]

Cities	1951 Annual	1959 Annual
All cities surveyed	$4,162	$6,124
Atlanta	4,315	5,642
Baltimore	4,217	5,718
Boston	4,217	6,317
Chicago	4,185	6,567
Cincinnati	4,208	6,100
Cleveland	4,103	6,199
Detroit	4,195	6,072
Houston	4,304	5,370
Kansas City	3,960	5,964
Los Angeles	4,311	6,285
Minneapolis	4,161	6,181
New York	4,083	5,970
Philadelphia	4,078	5,898
Pittsburgh	4,203	6,199
Portland, Oregon	4,153	6,222
St. Louis	4,112	6,266
San Francisco	4,263	6,304
Scranton	4,002	5,693
Seattle	4,280	6,562
Washington, D.C.	4,454	6,147

[1]For city worker with wife and two children. City worker's family budget calculated by Bureau of Labor Statistics of U.S. Department of Labor.

Family income. In 1961 there were 57.5 million households in the United States. Of these 46.3 million (80 percent) were family units, and 11.2 million (20 percent) were single and unrelated individual

[5]The estimate provides a "modest but adequate" standard, not "minimum maintenance" or a "luxury" level. It does not show how an average family does spend or should spend its money. Instead, it is an estimate of the total cost of a representative list of goods and services considered necessary by four-person city families to maintain a level of adequate living. A similar budget for a retired couple has also been developed. See M. S. Stotz, "The Interim City Worker's Family Budget," *Monthly Labor Review* (August, 1960), pp. 785–808; see also, M. S. Stotz, "The BLS Interim Budget for a Retired Couple," *Monthly Labor Review* (November, 1960), pp. 1141–57.

units. The median family size in 1961 was 3.3 individuals. Those families which did not have any wage or salary earners numbered 3.6 million.

Average family income has more than doubled in the post-World War II period (from $3,000 in 1947 to $6,200 in 1963), but because of rising prices, this represents only slightly more than a 50 percent increase in terms of constant dollars. In 1947 one half of the families in the United States had incomes below $3,000; by 1963 less than one fifth had annual incomes below $3,000.[6] It is predicted that this percentage will decline to 12 percent by 1980.

In United States metropolitan areas in 1960, income after taxes of all families and consumers averaged $6,090, 52 percent higher than in 1950. In terms of constant dollars, this was a 23 percent gain in purchasing power.[7]

The richest 1 percent of United States adults holds 28 percent of the United States' total personal wealth.[8]

Two thirds of all United States families with an income of $10,000 or more a year have two or more working members, according to a survey by the National Industrial Conference Board. There are 6.5 million families in this upper income bracket; in 40 percent of these the wife is the supplemental earner. One fourth of such families have three or more earners. Three of five heads of these families are over 45 years of age, one in four is a college graduate, and one in four works as a laborer or clerk.[9]

Low-income families are concentrated among nonwhite families and in certain sections of the nation. In 1961 nonfarm families had median incomes of $5,924, and farm families averaged $3,241. White family heads earned $5,981; nonwhite heads earned $3,191.

War on poverty. In 1964 the administration of President Johnson "declared war" on poverty. The standards used to define poverty were families with incomes below $3,000 and unrelated individuals

[6]See "Income of Families and Persons in the United States: 1963," United States Bureau of the Census, *Series P-60, No. 42,* June 12, 1964; for current data see subsequent issues of *Series P-60.* The most complete study and analysis of family income will be found in James N. Morgan *et al., Income and Welfare in the United States* (New York: McGraw-Hill Book Company, Inc., 1962).

It should be noted that even the concept of poverty appears to be changing. For example, Harlan County, Kentucky, is officially a depressed area, but 67 percent of its residents have television sets, 59 percent have cars, and 88 percent have washing machines.

[7]See H. H. Lamale, "Workers' Wealth and Family Living Standards," *Monthly Labor Review,* Vol. 86, No. 6 (June, 1963), pp. 666–86.

[8]"Income Revolution Slows Up," *Business Week,* September 28, 1963, p. 144.

[9]*St. Paul Dispatch,* October 15, 1963, p. 27.

with incomes below $1,500. Some 9 million families and 5 million individuals with a total combined membership of 33 to 35 million people were living at or below the "boundaries of poverty" in 1962. Families with incomes below $3,000 are more likely to be headed by a female, or a person 65 years or older, or one with an education of 8 years or less. They are more likely to be nonwhite, from rural farm areas, and more of these families have no wage earners.[10]

Average family incomes show wide variation from one region to another, as is indicated in Figure 19-1. The occupation of the head of the family also creates significant differences.[11]

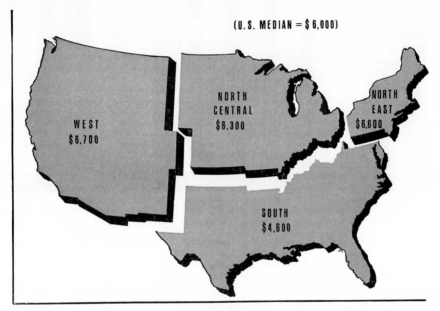

(U. S. MEDIAN = $ 6,000)

WEST $6,700

NORTH CENTRAL $6,300

NORTH EAST $6,600

SOUTH $4,600

Figure 19-1
MEDIAN FAMILY INCOME BY REGION — 1962

Source: Bureau of the Census, *Series P-60, No. 41* (October, 1963), p. 1.

Sex differentials in income. There are substantial differences in earnings of men and women, as shown in Figure 19-2. In part this condition arises out of differences in occupations, but sex differentials in wage rates on similar jobs are also persistent. These income data

---

[10]*Economic Report of the President*, January, 1964, pp. 59–73.

[11]For an informative analysis of individual and family incomes, see Herman P. Miller, *Income of the American People* (New York: John Wiley and Sons, 1955).

are also influenced by the stability of employment and the persistence of part-time jobs.

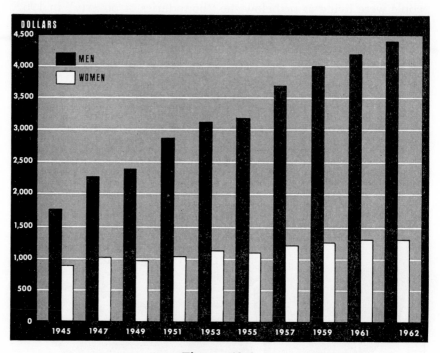

Figure 19-2
MEDIAN INCOME OF MEN AND WOMEN
FOR THE UNITED STATES — 1945–1962

Source: Bureau of the Census, *Series P-60, No. 30* (December, 1958), p. 3; *No. 39* (February, 1963), p. 26; *No. 41* (October 21, 1963), p. 2.

Cost of living: CPI. Money income varies in value, i.e., purchasing power. Real wages represent the buying power of money wages. The common practice adjusts measures of money income by reference to a "consumer price" or "cost-of-living index."

The CPI, the *consumer price index* provided by the Federal Bureau of Labor Statistics, measures the cost of a fixed "market basket" of items assumed to represent the purchases of moderate income urban families and single individuals in each of 50 cities and metropolitan areas. The content of the market basket represents buying patterns (to replace "what families bought") in the period 1960–1961. The "contents" or items are held constant so that changes in cost of the market basket represents changes in prices, not changes in living standards. The index is based on the changing costs of some 300 items in the major classes of food, rent, clothing, and sundries. Individual items to be included are determined by analyzing annual budgets of urban wage earners. The index is based on average prices in 1957, 1958, and 1959. For this reason it is said to have a 1957–1959 base, and the index number for that period is set at 100. Individual series are maintained for major metropolitan areas. They are combined to provide a nationwide index. For the United States as a whole, an index is also available for families only.[12]

Figure 19-3 shows changes in the general index for the nation as a whole since 1913. That figure clearly indicates how increases in

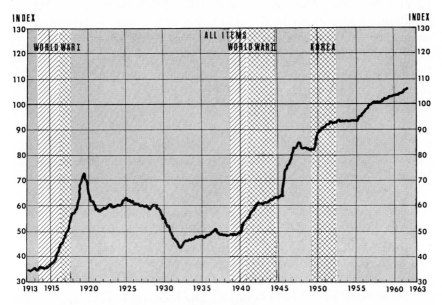

Figure 19-3
CONSUMER PRICE INDEX FOR WAGE-EARNER AND
CLERICAL-WORKER FAMILIES IN U.S. CITIES
(1957–1959 = 100)

Source: Bureau of Labor Statisticschart and current issues of *Monthly Labor Review.*

---

[12]See Phyllis Groom, "New Features of the Revised CPI," *Monthly Labor Review*, Vol. 87, No. 4 (April, 1964), pp. 385–90.

Measuring the purchasing power of the wage dollar is complicated by continuing changes in buying habits. The wage earner of a century past spent 94 percent of his earnings on essentials, as compared with 57 percent in 1950. In 1901, 43 percent was spent for food; the current ratio is 31 percent. Recreation and education took 2.7 percent in 1901, as compared with 5.8 percent in 1959. See *How Buying Habits Change* (Washington, D.C.: Department of Labor, 1959).

consumer prices, particularly in the years during or directly following wars, reduce the purchasing power of wage dollars (real wages). It is notable that interest in *escalator provisions* (see p. 510) has been greatest in periods of rapidly rising living costs.

Purchasing power; real wages.   Wage rates and earnings are usually stated in terms of dollars and cents. Gains or increases in these measures of worker income are also usually described in terms of money. For example, a common rate of pay for bricklayers in one locality in 1940 was $1 per hour. The comparable rate in 1963 was $3.50 per hour. This means that the later rate was $3\frac{1}{2}$ times as great as that of 1940. Does it mean that the bricklayer has gained an additional 250 percent in the real value or purchasing power of his wage rate? As almost everyone knows, the answer to this question is negative. The money wage rate was $3\frac{1}{2}$ times as great, but the brick-layer could not purchase $3\frac{1}{2}$ times as much as he could in 1940. His real wage, the buying power of his dollar wage, was affected by changes in the prices he must pay for what he buys. Each dollar lost same of its buying power.

Real wages can be described in dollars by relating rates to prices in a selected base period, using the Consumer Price Index described in earlier paragraphs. Suppose we want to express the 1940 or the 1963 wage rate in terms of 1957–59 dollars. The Consumer Price Index averaged 48.8 in 1940. Each 1940 dollar would buy 100/48.8 of what a 1957–59 dollar would purchase. Hence in 1940 the $1 wage rate was worth $2.05 in 1957–59 dollars. In 1963 the same index was 106.7. Each 1963 dollar was worth 100/106.7 in 1957–59 dollars, or $0.94. This means that the $3.50 wage rate in 1963 was worth $3.28 ($3.50 × $0.94) in 1957–59 dollars. The increase in real wages from 1940 to 1963 was from $2.05 to $3.28 in 1957–59 dollars, or 60 percent. While the bricklayer's wage rate rose to $3\frac{1}{2}$ times its earlier level, prices rose to 2.18 times their 1940 level. His hourly rate would buy more, but only about 60 percent more, for the wage rate increased only 1.60 times as much as prices.

In the United States, money wages have increased more rapidly than costs of living, so that real wages have also risen. It is notable that the years since 1900 have been characterized by much more rapid increases in both wages and prices than was typical during the preceding century. This has been, by comparison, a half-century of inflation. However, although increases in wage rates have frequently lagged behind similar rises in consumers' prices, real wages have made marked gains throughout these years.

Table 19-2 has been prepared to provide a view of major wage and price changes since the early years of the present century. The measure of wages is hourly earnings in manufacturing. Column II lists these dollar earnings. Column III shows the Consumer Price Index, based on 1957–59. In Column IV dollar earnings have been "deflated" to provide a measure of earnings in constant 1957–59 dollars by dividing dollar earnings for each year by the CPI for the same year. These measures of real wages for each year have then been described in Column V as index numbers, based on 1957–59 as 100. Such data make the long-run upward trend in real wages quite clear.

Table 19-2

**WAGE AND PRICE CHANGES
IN MANUFACTURING — 1919–1963**

I	II	III	IV	V
			Real Wages	
Year	Average Hourly Earnings (in Mfg.)	Consumer Price Index 1957–59 = 100	Dollars 1957–59 = 100	Index 1957–59 = 100
1919	$0.47	60.3	$0.78	37.6
1924	0.54	59.6	0.91	43.3
1929	0.56	59.7	0.94	45.5
1934	0.53	46.6	1.14	57.0
1939	0.63	48.4	1.30	62.6
1944	1.01	61.3	1.64	79.2
1949	1.38	83.0	1.67	80.5
1954	1.78	93.6	1.90	91.5
1959	2.19	101.5	2.16	103.9
1960	2.26	103.1	2.19	105.5
1961	2.32	104.2	2.23	107.2
1962	2.39	105.4	2.27	109.4
1963	2.46	106.7	2.31	111.2

Sources: *Economic Indicators* and *Historical Supplements to Economic Indicators*. (Wage data are for employees in manufacturing.) See also *Economic Report of the President*, 1964, Tables C-29 and C-43.

Figure 19-4 has been prepared to suggest what has happened to both money wages and real wages since 1820.[13] Although such historical data with respect to both wage rates and costs of living must be

---

[13]Recent data on money wages and real wages are shown in Table 19-2.

regarded with caution, particularly during the century before 1920, the long, rising trend in both series is clear.

The change in scale in this figure to show recent changes in more detail tends to obscure the sharp rise since 1930. While generalizations based on the earlier indexes are somewhat hazardous, the evidence indicates a new and steeper upward trend in the years since the great depression of the 1930's.

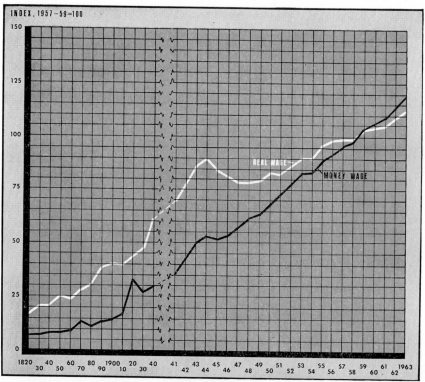

Figure 19-4
CHANGES IN MONEY WAGES AND REAL WAGES — 1820–1963

Source: Data from Paul H. Douglas, *Real Wages in the United States* (Boston: Houghton Mifflin Co., 1930), pp. 392–93; A. H. Hansen, "Some Factors Affecting the Trend of Real Wages," *American Economic Review* (March, 1925), pp. 27–48; and recent Bureau of Labor Statistics series.

The long view is useful, but it cannot be more than an approximation. Precision in such long comparisons is not to be expected. The data from which early indexes have been created are samples. The linking of indexes and frequent changes in base periods introduce errors so that the reliability of comparisons is reduced the further they reach into historic measures. Consumers' purchases change; as a result, the meaning of earlier cost-of-living indexes is not identical with that of more recent measures.

The long view does suggest a trend of 2 to 3 percent improvement in real wages per year. The pace of that improvement seems to have speeded since the depression of the 1930's. Real wages have in the past doubled in 35- to 40-year periods.

Depression and wages. All these time-to-time comparisons of wages clearly indicate the disastrous economic effects of business recessions. Depressions tend to reverse the trends that move toward accepted social goals. They reduce per capita and family incomes. They destroy employment and cut wages and earnings. Depressions quite literally make the rich relatively richer and the poor poorer. Proportions or shares of income going to relatively high-income groups tend to increase in recession and depression and to decline in periods of prosperity. Lower income receivers get less income and a lesser share of the total when business recedes.

Criteria of Equity and Fairness

As long as there are differentials in wages, and as long as there are different value systems concerning what are "fair" rates, then questions of equity in wage policies, programs, and structures will be raised. Indeed, there is much reason to believe that many workers are more interested in differentials than in wage levels.

Inequity or unfairness. Current rates may be regarded as unfair because they seem to undervalue workers' contributions or to fail in meeting individual or family needs. They may seem inequitable if they discriminate against an employer — appearing too high — or against an employee — being lower than the going rate.

Much of our thinking about inequities in wage rates retains elements of wartime wage policy. During World War II wages were closely controlled as part of the general economic stabilization program. A few adjustments, however, were permitted to remove inequities, so that public agencies had to develop criteria to be applied to such cases.

Several types of unfairness were noted. The rules accepted as *intraplant inequities* those situations in which (1) an employer paid different rates for the same or similar work and (2) differences in rates failed to reflect differences in contribution and worth of the services. *Interplant inequities* were evidenced by rates lower than those paid for the same jobs by other employers in the same locality or industry. The application of such yardsticks, however, involves difficult judgments and decisions. Even the equal-pay-for-equal-work rule encounters complications. Jobs that have the same title may not involve identical tasks. Part of the pay rate for some jobs may be regarded as payment for training that will be useful to the employer when the workers are promoted. If some workers do not intend to remain in employment — housewives, for example — or are not promotable, perhaps a lower rate for them is justified.

Comparisons of the contributions of various jobs are always complicated. In many firms major dependence is placed on a system of *job evaluation*, in which each job is rated on required skill, training, experience, responsibility, and other job factors. Each is compared with other jobs in terms of this standard job-rating scale. Even with such systems, controversies frequently arise over the fairness of rates.

Interplant comparisons are also difficult. The duties and responsibilities of each job may not be specifically described. The same job may carry a different designation in various plants. Further difficulty arises from variations in methods of payment. Some firms use a single flat rate for each job; others have rate ranges that permit different rates on the same job to pay for seniority, merit, or experience. Still others combine these provisions with bonus or profit-sharing provisions. Wide variations in fringes — pensions, retirement funds, overtime, and others — are common. *Shift differentials* may readily confuse the picture by providing premium rates (generally 5 to 15 cents higher) for the same job on unpopular shifts. Further complications arise out of differences in the continuity of employment. Maintenance craftsmen in a large plant — painters, steam fitters, plasterers, and others — may receive an hourly rate lower than that of other similar craftsmen in the community because they are assured year-round employment.

Skill differentials. Another clear pattern shows an obvious leveling tendency, reducing skill differentials and narrowing the range of industry wage structures. This trend was accelerated by wartime wage stabilization in World War II, which raised substandard rates and encouraged "across the board," equal dollar and cent increases to all employees.[14] Expansion of industrial unionism since 1935 has exerted a similar pressure, augmented by pattern bargaining, minimum wage laws, and inflation. Low rates have moved closer to top rates. In the traditional pattern during the first quarter of this century, top skilled rates in a plant wage structure were usually about 180 percent of the lowest, common labor rate. That spread has now declined to about 140 percent. One study found that the range of skill differentials in industry as a whole was reduced from 105 percent of base rates in 1907 to about 55 percent in 1947. An index, based on 100 for unskilled rates, stood at 205 for top skills in 1907, 180 in 1931–32, and 155 in 1947.[15]

White collar differentials. Another major shift has reversed the relative positions of white-collar and hourly-rated production workers. Whereas the white-collar group long enjoyed a differential over some craftsmen and most semiskilled operatives and common labor, this situation has been changed.

At the turn of the century, average annual earnings of clerical workers were about double those of production workers. Thus, for example, in 1890 annual salaries of clerical workers were $848 and production workers earned $439. In 1910 the salaries were: clerical, $1156 and production, $558. This ratio continued into the 1920's — although by 1926 clericals earned $2310 and production workers $1309.[16] Since World War II the differential in favor of white-collar workers has largely disappeared. In 1964 production workers averaged over $100 a week, with most clerical salaries somewhat below that. A part of the change in the white-collar, blue-collar differential may be attributed to the larger proportions of women in clerical work in recent years, while annual earnings of males reflect the relatively larger percentage increases going to blue-collar workers in the same period. Dollar earnings and percentage increases may be summarized as follows:[17]

---

[14]For the story of wartime regulation and its effects on wage structures, see John B. Parrish, "Impact of World War II on Internal Wage Rate Structures," *Southern Economic Journal*, Vol. 15, No. 2 (October, 1948), pp. 134–51.

[15]See Harry Ober, "Occupational Wage Differentials," *Monthly Labor Review*, Vol. 67, No. 2 (August, 1948), pp. 127–34. Dunlop and Rothbaum calculated the range of differentials in such structures as 165 percent in 1937–40 and 137 percent in 1952–53. This trend in the United States is compared with that in Italy (154 percent in 1937–40 and 125 percent in 1952–53) and France (130 percent in 1937–40 and 123 percent in 1952–53). See John T. Dunlop and Melvin Rothbaum, "International Comparisons of Wage Structures," *International Labour Review*, Vol. 31, No. 4 (April, 1955), pp. 1–19.

[16]United States Bureau of the Census, *Historical Statistics of the United States*, 1960, pp. 91–92.

[17]Data from "Income of Families and Persons in the United States: 1962," Bureau of the Census, *Series P-60, No. 41*, October, 1963, p. 51. Data are for male workers only.

	1939	1962	% Increase
Blue-Collar Workers:			
Craftsmen and foremen	$1,309	$5,737	338%
Operatives..................	1,007	4,601	357%
Laborers...................	673	2,895	330%
White-Collar Workers:			
Professional and technical...	1,809	6,870	279%
Clerical...................	1,421	5,187	265%
Sales......................	1,277	5,267	312%
Managers..................	2,136	7,099	232%

Note the fact that annual earnings of male craftsmen and foremen, lower than those of clerical workers in 1939, were higher in 1962; all of the blue-collar groups had higher percentage increases than the white-collar groups during this same period.[18]

One major influence toward this leveling process is inflation. Dunlop and Rothbaum conclude that periods of high-level employment also tend to reduce differentials, while unemployment is associated with the widening of wage structures. They conclude that other influences tending to narrow differentials are centralization of decision making and the economic development or industrialization of a nation.[19]

PUBLIC WAGE CONTROLS

Not all matters of wage determination are left to be resolved by employers, employees, and unions. Increasingly a "third party" — the public — has intervened. Wage laws prescribe limits, floors (and at times ceilings) on wages. Regulatory mechanisms to enforce such standards are provided by federal, state, and local governments. Thus, we have assurance of payment laws, equal pay laws, and minimum wage laws.

[18]For a discussion of these changes, see Herman P. Miller, *Income of the American People* (New York: John Wiley and Sons, 1955), p. 105 ff.; Kenneth M. McCaffree, "The Earnings Differential Between White Collar and Manual Occupations," *Review of Economics and Statistics*, Vol. 35, No. 1 (February, 1953), pp. 20–30; Jean A. Flexner and Anna-Stina Ericson, "White-Collar Employment and Income," *Monthly Labor Review*, Vol. 79, No. 4 (April, 1956), pp. 401–09. See also, Clarence D. Long, *Wages and Earnings in the United States, 1860–1890* (Princeton, N.J.: Princeton University Press, 1960); Robert Ozanne, "A Century of Occupational Differentials in Manufacturing," *Review of Economics and Statistics*, XLIV (August, 1962), pp. 292–99; Jack Stieber, *The Steel Industry Wage Structure* (Cambridge: Harvard University Press, 1959).

[19]For an interesting study of wage changes in 210 firms, see Mitchell O. Locks, "The Influence of Pattern-bargaining on Manufacturing Wages in the Cleveland, Ohio, Labor Market, 1945–1950," *Review of Economics and Statistics*, Vol. 37, No. 1 (February, 1955), pp. 70–76. For a further discussion of the factors influencing wage differentials see M. W. Reder, "The Theory of Occupational Wage Differentials," *American Economic Review*, Vol. 45, No. 5 (December, 1955), pp. 833–52; also Lloyd G. Reynolds and Cynthia Taft, *The Evolution of Wage Structure* (New Haven: Yale University Press, 1956).

Assurance of Wage Payment

Wage earners sometimes have difficulty in collecting the wages they have earned. Employers sometimes fail to pay at regular intervals, allowing wage obligations to accumulate. A few employers have failed to pay wages already earned and due their employees, claiming that available funds and resources were inadequate. In other situations some employees have been paid in scrip, the private "money" of an employer, cashable only in his company store. Employees frequently involve themselves in debt, incur heavy obligations, and spend their wages before they get them. In such situations they may face attachments or garnishments that slow up if they do not stop the family income. Sometimes employees have had to "kickback" a portion of their earnings to employers, foremen, or others for the privilege of working.

Guaranteed payment. Most states now have legislation designed to insure that employees get paid. Such laws specify regular pay periods, usually once each week or two weeks. They require payment at once if an employee is discharged. They bar payment in scrip. They frequently forbid payment in bars and taverns.

Other laws are designed to prevent the complete cessation of wage payments to employees who have incurred debts by limiting the amount or proportion of wages that can be taken by creditors. They limit the proportion of wages that can be collected by *garnishments*, which are court orders that collect earnings from an employer before the worker gets them. They prescribe procedures and limitations on *wage assignments* in which employees authorize creditors to collect from employers in payment of employee debts. They also prohibit the seizure of workers' tools as payments of debts.

Other laws also insure the payment of earnings by giving them preference over other types of claims against the assets of employers. If an employer is forced into bankruptcy or goes out of business, wage claims have a top priority as charges against whatever assets are available. For building tradesmen, *mechanics' lien laws* make wages a first claim on the employers' and owners' assets so that they must be paid before other obligations for goods and materials. In addition, federal and state laws frequently specify that employers on public works provide *payment bonds* to assure the regular compensation of those who work on these projects. Further, many states now maintain special agencies to give free assistance to employees in collecting the wages they have earned.

Antikickback laws. To protect workers against *kickbacks*, in which they are required to return a portion of their earnings to employers or others as payment for the privilege of working, the federal Copeland Act of 1934 makes any such practice illegal on federal projects and contracts. It provides severe penalties for employers, foremen, or others who try to collect such assessments from workers in interstate employment. Questions have been raised in this connection about the frequent requirement that employees join a union and pay union dues or fees as a condition of employment in such situations. The courts have held, however, that the law does not apply to payments to union officials who collect dues for union membership as a condition of employment.[20] Several states have similar legislation applying to employment in intrastate industries.

Equal Pay Laws

One common type of intraplant inequity has resulted in legislation. That is the payment of lower rates to women than to men on the same job. Twenty-three states now have equal-pay-for-equal-work laws that apply to specified industries. The rule of equal pay is enforced on government contracts, and the federal government has long followed this practice for its employees. In addition to the state legislation, many collective agreements contain equal pay clauses.

In 1963 the federal government passed equal pay legislation. Women must receive pay equal to men if their jobs have substantially similar job requirements and working conditions. Although coverage is somewhat broader than the Wage-Hour Law, only about 6 to 7 million women will be "protected"; 18 million women workers are not covered. It should be remembered that executives and professional workers are exempt from the Wage-Hour Law and also the Equal Pay Law. Women paid on incentive rates or piece work will get equal rates, not equal pay. Employers are not allowed to equalize by cutting rates of men. Enforcement is by the courts, not by an administrative agency. Some critics of this legislation raise the familiar

---

[20]See the Supreme Court decision in *U.S. v. Carbone*, (1946), 327 U.S. 633; 66 S. Ct., 734.

argument that this law will reduce employment opportunities for women because of higher costs of employing women.[21]

The federal act became effective on June 11, 1964. However, it should be noted that 23 states were already enforcing similar laws at the time the federal legislation was added. It should also be noted that coverage of this provision of the Wage-Hour Law is broader than that enforcing minimum wages. The equal pay rule affects all nonexempt employees of employers with two or more employees, without reference to the annual volume of sales (as in the case of minimum wage requirements).[22]

Minimum Wages

We have used the power of public regulation to insure at least minimal payments to millions of wage earners. In some legislation the minima thus specified are based on concepts of need. In other legislation we have aimed at the maintenance of established wage rates and the prevention of wage cuts below these prevailing rates. Much of the thinking behind current public programs has sought to assure a socially acceptable minimum wage, or, as it is frequently described, to put a "floor" under wage rates. The purpose is clear; we intend to require payment of rates at least as high as these minima, which represent our estimates of the lowest acceptable rates of pay. To put it another way, we intend to set labor standards, one of which is a minimum standard for wages. In this same language any lesser rate is substandard.

Wage-Hour Law. National policy on such minimum wages is clearly indicated in the federal Fair Labor Standards Act of 1938 The declaration of public policy in Section 20 of the act states that working conditions in interstate commerce that are "detrimental to the maintenance of the minimum standard of living necessary for health, efficiency and the general well-being of workers" have objectionable economic effects. Very low wages are regarded as constituting unfair competition, leading to labor disputes and interfering

---

[21]*U. S. News and World Report*, June 3, 1963, pp. 97–98.

[22]Nonprofit educational, religious, and charitable organizations are exempt from equal pay provisions. The states with such laws are: Alaska, Arizona, Arkansas, California, Colorado, Connecticut, Hawaii, Illinois, Maine, Massachusetts, Michigan, Montana, Missouri, New Hampshire, New Jersey, New York, Ohio, Oregon, Pennsylvania, Rhode Island, Washington, Wisconsin, and Wyoming. For details, see "Economic Indicators Relating to Equal Pay, 1963," *Pamphlet 9*, Women's Bureau, United States Department of Labor, 1963.

with the "orderly and fair marketing" of goods. On that basis the act established a single minimum wage for interstate industry with special procedures for setting higher minimum rates in individual industries. The nationwide minimum was originally 25 cents per hour, effective on October 24, 1938. Numerous amendments since that time raised the minimum rate (to $1.25 in 1963) for most workers covered by the act, with time and one-half regular rates for hours worked over 40 in one week. There are numerous exemptions for selected industries such as hotels, motels, restaurants, amusement places, hospitals and rest homes, government employees, and small retail and service establishments (under $250,000 retail sales annually). Child labor provisions prohibit employment of children under 16 in most occupations, and under 18 in hazardous jobs.

In 1961 coverage was extended to cover employees in: (1) large retail and service establishments ($1 million or more annual sales), (2) construction firms ($350,000 volume), and (3) gasoline service stations ($250,000 annual sales). For these employees the following hourly minima apply: $1.00 on September 3, 1961; $1.15 on September 3, 1964; $1.25 on September 3, 1965. Overtime premiums for these employees are as follows: after 44 hours, September 3, 1963; after 42 hours, September 3, 1964; after 40 hours, September 5, 1965.

Failure to pay the statutory minimum wage and overtime compensation results in cumulative back wage liabilities. Unpaid wages may be restored by government enforcement. Serious violations of the law may result in civil or criminal action.

Federal minimum wages and overtime rules are largely self-policing; employers, unions, and many employees are alert to possible violations in most industrialized localities. Nevertheless, the federal wage and hour division conducted 44,000 investigations involving 23,000 firms and 1.5 million employees during 1961 and 1962. These activities resulted in wage adjustments that added 34 million dollars to the earnings of 200,000 employees.[23]

State minimum wage laws. In addition to this federal legislation, 32 states have minimum wage laws that apply to specified employees in intrastate industries. In some states legislation establishes a flat or single minimum rate. A more common provision creates boards or commissions that hold hearings and determine minimum rates

---

[23]*Business Week,* January 5, 1963.

from time to time for each of the covered industries. Most laws apply only to women and children.[24]

Prevailing wage laws. The federal government and all states also have prevailing wage laws that require payment of "going" wage rates on public construction. The federal law is the Davis-Bacon Act of 1931. This federal law requires the Secretary of Labor to determine prevailing rates in the locality in which such work is to be done. Contractors must agree to pay at least these minimum rates.

Public contracts laws. Another type of wage legislation requires minimum standards in all work performed on public contracts. For the federal government, the Walsh-Healey Act of 1936 requires contractors to meet specified labor standards in working conditions, including wage rates, on all contracts in excess of $10,000. One of the most rigorous standards involves minimum rates of pay to be determined by the Secretary of Labor as prevailing in similar industries in the locality.

The Walsh-Healey Act requires overtime pay at a rate of not less than 1 ½ times the basic rate for work over 8 hours per day or 40 hours per week. Thus, premium pay requirements are more stringent than under the Fair Labor Standards Act (which requires overtime over 40 hours per week with no daily requirement). No male under 16 years of age, or female under 18, may be employed on these public contracts. (The FLSA sets a minimum age of employment as 16 for both sexes, with 18 the minimum in hazardous occupations.) Prevailing wages under Walsh-Healey go beyond minimum wages in the usual sense. Generally, they are determined by the Secretary of Labor to be the union rate or scale with related fringes.

Economic effects of minimum wages. What are the economic effects of minimum wages? The answers to this question are far from simple, and the evidence is not conclusive. As usual in economic analysis, most or some of the answers are definitely related to the specific assumptions made about labor markets. Also typical is the

---

[24]New York City became the first city to create its own minimum wage legislation in 1962. The minimum rate, covering all employees except executives, administrators, professionals, outside salesmen, baby-sitters, volunteers, student or handicapped workers for nonprofit institutions, members of religious orders, counselors in children's camps, public employees, and similar groups began at $1.25 per hour and advanced to $1.50 per hour in September, 1964. The 1962 law was unconstitutional; constitutionality of the 1964 law is being tested. See M. Benewitz and R. E. Weintraub, "Employment Effects of a Local Minimum Wage," *Industrial and Labor Relations Review*, Vol. 17, No. 2 (January, 1964), pp. 276–88.

fact that empirical verification of effects is difficult because of the contaminating effects of uncontrolled variables in the real-life situation. Finally, effects should be judged in terms of goals or objectives, and here it is difficult to provide a clearcut classification of economic and other types of goals — for example, social — that would be acceptable generally.[25]

The following are rather generally looked upon as being among the goals of minimum wage legislation:

1. Raise wage rates.
2. Increase income of wage earners.
3. Eliminate substandard working conditions or poverty.
4. Prevent exploitation of wage earners.
5. Redistribute income.

In a sense goals (1) and (2) are the positive side of the coin and goals (3) and (4) are the negative side. Goal (5) may be regarded as more of a social value or goal than an economic goal.

It should be noted that these goals do not include the goal of *more* employment. Instead the emphasis in minimum wage legislation is upon *better* employment for those who have jobs. Indeed, proponents of minimum wage legislation probably would argue that the values of better jobs are more important than the values of having more jobs, and that the possible loss of substandard jobs is a price they are willing to pay for better jobs. They would argue that substandard jobs are undesirable per se for those holding such jobs. They would argue that substandard jobholders represent a threat to those with better or standard jobs because low-wage workers can produce goods that may sell for less than similar goods made by higher-paid wage earners.

Let us review briefly four economic factors related to the effects of minimum wages. These are: (1) labor cost effects, (2) effects of varying elasticities of demand for product (and hence labor), (3) substitution effects, and (4) labor productivity effects.

First, there is no simple and direct relationship between wage rate levels and labor costs (see Chapter 18). Lower wage rates do not

---

[25]For convenient references on the economic effects of minimum wages see: George T. Stigler, "The Economics of Minimum Wage Legislation," *American Economic Review*, Vol. 36, No. 3 (June. 1946), pp. 358–65; John G. Turnbull, C. Arthur Williams and Earl F. Cheit, *Economics and Social Security* (New York: The Ronald Press Company, 1957), pp. 482–500; Joseph Shister, *The Economics of the Labor Market* (2nd ed., New York: J. B. Lippincott Company, 1956), pp. 283–95; Lloyd Reynolds, *Labor Economics and Labor Relations* (2nd ed., New York: Prentice-Hall, Inc., 1954), pp. 660–66; and Richard A. Lester, *Labor and Industrial Relations* (New York: The MacMillan Company, 1951), pp. 362–69.

necessarily mean lower labor costs; higher wage rates do not necessarily result in higher labor costs.

The wage paid divided by the number of physical units produced in a given time period gives the labor cost per unit. Such cost items are presumably used by employers in their marginal comparisons of employee contribution and in their employment decisions. It is frequently assumed that minimum wages will raise labor costs as well as wage rates. It should be noted that not all employers come under the same minimum wage legislation and hence differential competitive effects can result, that is, those not covered may have an advantage from the standpoint of labor costs. This can shift production from covered to noncovered firms, industries, and regions. Hence, equalization of wage standards may often be regarded as desirable, although firms with a differential advantage offer stirring arguments to the contrary.

Second, the elasticity of demand for the product is very important in determining how much of an increase in labor costs employers can pass on to their customers.[26] This becomes important in the minimum wage case because, as noted above, it is customary to assume that minimum wage rates increase labor costs — and further, that employers will try to pass these costs on to their customers. Their ability to pass on the increase depends upon the elasticity of the demand for the product. In general, the greater the elasticity of demand for the product, the greater the employment effect of a minimum wage, for presumably it would be more difficult for the employer to raise prices (to pass on his increased labor costs) and hence more workers would have to be laid off.

Third, the effects of substitution should be considered. One form of substitution involves consumers' relative preferences for an alternate final product or service. This would be reflected in the elasticity of demand for the product, and hence the effects are included in the discussion in the paragraph above. Another possibility of substitution involves using other factors of production than the (presumably) less efficient factor represented by marginal workers who are to receive the new, higher minimum wage. These other factors can be capital (in the form of improved machines), more efficient labor of another

---

[26]It will be recalled that the demand for a good is elastic when the relative change in the price is accompanied by a *larger* relative change in the quantity taken; if the proportion of change in demand for the good is smaller than the relative price change, then the demand is said to be inelastic.

type, improved methods, and combinations of these. Such substitutions might also lower labor costs through changes in technical coefficients.

This brings us to the *fourth* factor, productivity. If for some reason the increased minimum wages brought forth proportionately greater or equal productivity, labor costs would not increase. If productivity did not change, then labor costs would be increased.

Some advocates of minimum wage legislation argue that an increase in labor costs would spur employers to develop more efficient production methods. Others hold that perhaps employees would and could work harder and thus increase their productivity.

Unfortunately, empirical evidence is limited.[27] As explained earlier, it is difficult to isolate the effects of minimum wage legislation. Most minimum wage laws (particularly those of national coverage) have become effective in periods of inflation and rising wages, accompanied by shortages of labor supplies and brisk employer demand for labor. Often legal minimums are so far below average wages that the effects are practically meaningless. Further, the degree of labor force attachment of so-called marginal workers may not be very strong, and unlike "regular" workers they may enter and leave the labor market without much regard to wage rates. Studies of labor mobilities (see Chapter 6) show such lack of attachment.

United States Department of Labor studies of the effects of the $1.00 (March, 1956) minimum wage are inconclusive. Effects in six cities studied were quite varied. The immediate effect was to raise average wages in subject industries and to widen relative wage differentials between subject and nonsubject industries. Two years later no clear-cut pattern of differentials was found. Employment effects were obscured in a maze of other forces and were not isolated in these studies.[28]

In summary, in a competitive situation, if minimum wages are not accompanied by proportionate or higher productivity, labor costs

---

[27]For reports of experience with minimum wages, see Isador Lubin and Charles A. Pearce, "New York's Minimum Wage Law: the First Twenty Years," *Industrial and Labor Relations Review*, Vol. 11, No. 2 (January, 1958), pp. 203–19; John M. Peterson, "Employment Effects of Minimum Wages, 1938–1950," *Journal of Political Economy*, Vol. 65, No. 5 (October, 1957), pp. 412–30. See also, John M. Peterson, "Research Needs in Minimum Wage Theory," *Southern Economic Journal*, Vol. 29 (July, 1962), pp. 1–9; Richard A. Lester, *Economics of Labor* (2nd ed.; New York: The Macmillan Co., 1964), pp. 503–27, and Lloyd G. Reynolds, *Labor Economics and Labor Relations* (4th ed.; Englewood Cliffs, N.J.: Prentice-Hall, Inc., 1964), pp. 525–28.

[28]See "Effects of the $1 Minimum Wage in Six Areas, 1956–1959," *Monthly Labor Review*, Vol. 83, No. 5 (May, 1960), pp. 472–78.

will increase. This tends to have the effect of raising the supply curve, since the employer must consider his intrafirm wage structure and seek to retain traditional relationships among jobs (that is, he must raise rates not only at the lower end of his wage structure where the minimum wage has direct effects, but also at all levels of the structure to preserve the relative rates of compensation for all types of jobs). If the employer cannot change the demand schedule (and under competitive conditions it is assumed that this is impossible), then there may be (1) fewer workers employed and (2) a lesser amount of goods and services produced.

However, this is only the first effect. The displaced members might find jobs in other industries, presumably those not covered by minimum wage legislation. While this might involve a misallocation of resources (in the economic sense), total employment in the aggregate might not decrease. Presumably total output of goods and services would diminish unless the workers who received wage increases as a result of the minimum wage increased their productivity sufficiently.

In the noncompetitive situation the expected effects also depend upon the assumptions made. In the case of monopsony, a minimum wage could actually increase employment.[29] In quasi-monopsonistic situations, the effects would be more difficult to predict and assess. It has been suggested that a series of administered prices (minimum wages) could conceivably be set for each such firm (varying of course with the cost and demand situation) that would result in increased employment. The difficulties of doing this in a dynamic real-life situation are so complex that even the staunchest advocates of this position seem to regard this concept as little more than a possibility.

Displaced workers who cannot obtain other jobs and whose productivity is so low that they cannot obtain work of any kind may be forced to withdraw from the labor market — unemployables in the economic sense. They still have economic needs, and two means of assistance for them have been suggested. First, some argue that the displaced should be continued in employment, receiving the

---

[29]In general, the monopsonist sets production at the point where his marginal cost curve intersects the marginal revenue or demand curve. The wage paid is below this point (where a line drawn perpendicular to the base intersects the average cost curve). As long as the minimum wage exceeded this wage rate, up to but not including intersection of the marginal cost and demand curves, employment would be increased by the minimum wage. Maximum employment would result from a wage at the point where the average cost and demand curves intersect. (See Figure B-6 in Appendix B.)

difference between their productivity and the minimum wage as a sort of disguised benefit. Second, others argue that payment on a needs basis would be handled better through some sort of public or private benefit program. They contend that an admixture of needs and efficiency concepts in wage payments would dull incentive. They argue that family size and income (and related variables) rather than industry and occupation (the basic unit for minimum wage laws) is a more appropriate base for determination of needs.

Progress in removing low wage rates is not to be accomplished through legislation alone. There must be sufficient demand for labor to provide employment at higher wage rates. Increased job opportunities and increased labor mobilities in times of high labor demand enable workers to move from low paying jobs (e.g., agriculture) into higher paying jobs. At the same time, workers must be sufficiently productive to be worthy of their hire (in the economic sense). A policy of economic growth, with attendant increased demands for labor, can do more to reduce low wage rates than a series of minimum wage laws during a recession. Indeed, as a sort of "proof of the pudding," when times are good (in the sense of a high demand for labor), there is little pressure for minimum wage laws or for increased minimum rates.

Wage Guideposts

In January of 1962, the Council of Economic Advisers advanced "guideposts" for noninflationary wage and price behavior. Productivity increases were the basic yardstick. The basic guide for wages: increases in wage rates (including fringes) in each industry should be equal to the trend rate of overall productivity increase. (From 1947 to 1960 productivity in the private sector of the economy was up 3 percent annually).

Modifications in the basic guide permitted higher increases in industries: (1) unable to attract sufficient labor or (2) where present rates are inequitable, i.e., lower than earned elsewhere for similar work. Lower (than guide rate) increases were recommended in industries: (1) suffering from continuous unemployment or (2) where wage rates have been exceptionally high.

Concerning prices, they should fall in high productivity industries and rise in low productivity industries, with average prices remaining stable.[30]

---

[30]*Economic Report of the President, 1962*, pp. 185–90.

These guidelines lack official means of enforcement, although the power of the President and other executive agencies, plus public opinion, might be of some influence. The famous 1962 steel settlement is a case in point.

The guidelines face other practical difficulties. Productivity measures are poor or nonexistent in many industries, as noted in Chapter 3. Unions respond to the guidelines as a "floor" from which to raise their demands. Many groups, including the federal government, apparently ignored the guidelines in their wage settlements and adjustments. The suggested modifications are so loose that employers and unions derive opposite conclusions using the same general rules in a single dispute. Lack of an enforcement policy and a detailed rules-making agency do not help matters.

Some critics argue that while the guideposts might be appropriate for a full employment economy (4 percent unemployment), they are obviously inappropriate for a less-than-full-level employment economy. They suggest that wage rate advances lower than productivity advances would reduce labor costs, raise profit levels, and thereby encourage more investment and employment. They object further to a national wage policy geared primarily to the objective of preventing inflation, and argue that labor demand and supply situations must be considered also. Finally, some of the critics argue that the competitive labor market is still the best wage regulator and that monopoly powers of both unions and employers should be curbed by law.

Joseph W. Garbarino holds that attempts to apply general wage formulas to specific contract situations will tend to be inflationary. He points out that:

1. Productivity changes are specific and variable — not general.
2. Labor supply and demand factors are different in specific markets.
3. Market prices for various firms fluctuate differently.

Hence, in an economy with free enterprise and free collective bargaining, any national wage formula becomes unworkable if it uses only general or average wage, price, and productivity increases.[31]

WAGES, INFLATION, AND UNEMPLOYMENT

Wages represent buying power for workers. If prices remain stable, an increase in wages means that workers can buy more goods

---

[31] Joseph W. Garbarino, *Wage Policy and Long-Term Contracts* (Washington, D.C.: Brookings Institution, 1962), Chapter 4.

and services. If, on the other hand, prices increase more than wages, the worker's buying power is reduced, as we have noted in our discussion of real wages above. In general, when money supplies increase at a faster rate than supplies of goods and services, prices rise.

Two types of inflation are sometimes distinguished: "demand-pull" and "cost-push." *Demand-pull inflation* comes about when the supply of goods and services is less than the consumer demand. Thus, for example, immediately following World War II, stocks of non-military consumer goods were low, consumer demands were high, and they had the money to make their demands effective. *Cost-push inflation* results from efforts of various income groups to increase their share of goods and services, money supplies, or both. Businessmen may seek to increase profits, or workers may force up money wage rates; if the net effect is to increase prices beyond productivity increases, then inflation results.[32]

In practice it is difficult to determine the cause or source of inflation, i.e., whether it is demand-pull or cost-push, for there are too many uncontrolled variables and forces involved. This difficulty, however, has not stopped attempts to specify the cause of inflation. That supposed causes of inflation are typically "viewed with alarm" stems from the differential consequences of inflation to diverse income groups — e.g., fixed income groups lose buying power, inflation may affect investment, and inflation may distort balance of payments in foreign trade.[33]

Inflation may and does have effects upon employment levels. Deflation may result in unemployment. Inflation may increase employment, or it may increase incomes of those with jobs, holding employment levels about the same as they were originally.

Unions, through their wage demands, are alleged to be responsible for much cost-push inflation through the use of so-called monopoly powers. This concept is examined in more detail in Chapter 22. In the meantime, however, it should be noted that public policy may seek to prevent wage-induced inflation through direct wage (and

---

[32]See Thomas Wilson, *Inflation* (Cambridge, Massachusetts: Harvard University Press, 1961). For a convenient and extensive summary of inflation theory, see Martin Bronfenbrenner and F. D. Holzman, "Survey of Inflation Theory," *American Economic Review*, Vol. LIII, No. 4 (September, 1963), pp. 593–661.

[33]The problem of inflation is worldwide. From 1958 to 1963 living costs in the United States and Canada rose 6 percent. In the same period prices rose in: Argentina, 289 percent; Brazil, 515 percent; Indonesia, 944 percent; Australia, 8 percent; United Kingdom, 11 percent; West Germany, 12 percent; India, 14 percent; Italy, 15 percent; Sweden, 15 percent; Japan, 27 percent; and Israel, 30 percent. *U.S. News and World Report*, October 28, 1963, pp. 58–60.

price) controls, as in World War II and the Korean Conflict, or through guideposts and public opinion.

Wage Rates and Unemployment

Although criteria of wage payments reflect both need and contribution considerations, ultimately profit and productivity limit wage payments. When wage rates get too high competitively, the following sequence may occur: labor costs get out of line, profits decline, and employment opportunities decrease. Hence, "ability to pay" is an important restraining force on wage rates.

Pay cuts are not unheard of in modern times. In October, 1963, for example, at the Erie (Pennsylvania) Forge and Steel Corporation, the United Steelworkers accepted a cut of 17¢ an hour in basic wages plus 7½¢ in fringes, based on the company's declining "ability to pay."[34]

Professor A. W. Phillips advanced the theory that the percentage rate of change in money wages in the United Kingdom is largely explained by the level of unemployment and its rate of change. This "Phillips curve" explanation has not stood up under tests made in the United States, whether aggregate or local labor market data were used. Philip Ross suggests that the response of wages may be a function of the duration and periodicity of unemployment as well as its level and rate of change.[35]

This chapter has been concerned with wage problems and policies. Like the previous chapter on definitions, wage systems, wage levels, differentials, and structures, the present chapter has sought to provide additional background about the nature of wages — policies and problems, concepts of fairness in wages, public wage controls, and so-called wage inflation. Such background about the "what" and "how" of wages is essential in considering the "why" of wages, the subject of the following three chapters. In the next chapter we turn to a discussion of historical wage theories. As will become apparent, most wage theories are also theories of employment, i.e. wage levels affect employment levels and vice versa.

---

[34]*U. S. News and World Report*, October 28, 1963, p. 87.

[35]Philip Ross, "Labor Market Behavior and the Relationship Between Unemployment and Wages," *IRRA Proceedings*, December 28–29, 1961, pp. 275–88.

ANALYTICAL REVIEW QUESTIONS

1. How are wage problems defined? How are wage policies related to wage problems?
2. What are 5 major goals of our public wage policy?
3. How could union wage policy conflict with public wage policy?
4. What employer programs have as their aim increasing equity in wage payments?
5. Why are wages of primary importance in economic stability?
6. Why do we have trouble in deciding what is a "fair" wage rate?
7. What are the most important wage criteria?
8. Why is "ability to pay" not the most commonly accepted wage criterion?
9. Why have our wage criteria been described as "rubber" yardsticks?
10. Why is wage theory related to solutions of wage problems?
11. Why is a minimum wage, based on need, difficult to determine?
12. What has happened to average family income in the United States since World War II? In money terms? In real income?
13. How is high family income related to the number employed in such families?
14. What is the CPI? What does it measure? How is the CPI used in wage escalation?
15. How are real wages defined? In the long run, in the United States how much have real wages increased each year, on the average?
16. What are some of the major types of wage differentials?
17. What factors tend to narrow wage differentials? Widen them?
18. What do mechanics' lien laws and payment bonds have in common?
19. Under the federal equal pay law, under what conditions do women qualify for equal pay?
20. Under the FLSA in what way are very low wages regarded as constituting unfair competition?
21. What are the goals of minimum wage legislation?
22. How does elasticity of product demand relate to employment effects of minimum wage legislation? What is the role of substitution in this relationship?
23. How do economic growth and full employment affect low wage rates? How are labor mobilities involved?
24. Differentiate "demand-pull" from "cost-push" inflation.
25. How are wage guideposts supposed to work? What modifications have been suggested?
26. Why may attempts to apply general wage formulas to specific contract situations be inflationary?

Case 19-1

MINIMUM WAGES IN LAUNDRIES

George Porter has just been appointed to a state minimum wage board. He finds that the board has before it a proposal to raise the minimum rates of pay for laundry workers. The current minimum is 80 cents per hour. Although most workers in local laundries are organized, the scale under existing labor contracts provides the same base rate as the legal minimum. In some outlying areas many employees are being paid as little as 60 cents per hour.

In the first hearing, advocates of a higher minimum, including representatives of the union, expressed the opinion that the rate to be established should provide "a living wage for the worker's family." They insist that $40 per week or $1 per hour is the least that should be considered. In answer to one board member's question as to the basis for this opinion, a union spokesman outlined a minimum budget for a family of four. It includes food, clothing, furnishings, fuel, items for car expense, cigarettes, and movies.

Employers in the industry are opposed to any increase. They cite their loss of business to home laundering and insist that higher costs will simply encourage more laundering at home, thus eliminating many laundries and much of the present employment in the industry.

• What additional facts and factors would you wish to consider if you were George Porter? How would you go about deciding this case? How would you weigh the various contentions of employers and union? What decision would you reach? Why?

Case 19-2

IMPROVEMENT FACTOR INCREASE

At a recent meeting of the board of directors of the Whole Wheat Milling Company, the president told members that he understood the firm's employees plan to ask for an improvement factor clause in their new contract. The contract must be negotiated soon, for the present agreement expires in 60 days.

Directors have discussed the new contract in broad detail and plan to insist on at least a three-year agreement. They are prepared to negotiate an increase each year based on increasing costs of living. No increase in output per employee has appeared during the present decade. On the contrary, man-hour productivity has declined. The firm's physical plant and equipment had required only minor repairs, and no changes have been made in technology. The president sees no basis for productivity increases. He says they are nothing more than an excuse for unjustified wage increases. They are, in his words, "just another fringe, a gift to employees, for which they have given and plan to give nothing in return."

• Several members of the board have asked your opinion and recommendation. They fear a bitter struggle over this improvement factor increase. Prepare a confidential memorandum for them indicating your conclusion as to what position they should take on the proposed improvement factor.

Case 19-3

LOCAL 144 AND NISSWA DEVELOPMENT COMPANY

Harold Jacobs is the business agent for Local 144, which is negotiating a contract with the Nisswa Development Company, a small manufacturing firm. Practically all issues had been settled, but company and union could not agree on the rate of pay for the most common job in the plant. Members of the union insisted that the job should pay $2.15 per hour. Their conclusion was based on analysis of rates being paid on similar jobs in several other plants. Each time Jacobs advanced this argument, however, the labor relations director of NDCO read the following statement taken from a report prepared by the firm's job analysis section:

> Our time studies show that this job should be paid at the rate of $1.95 per hour because that is the value contributed by an average employee working at an average pace.

Jacobs felt that there were errors in this conclusion. He could not, however, prepare what he regarded as a convincing attack on it. Finally, the firm proposed arbitration of this single issue. The union agreed.

• Assume that you are acting as arbitrator and have found that the union is correct with respect to the going rate. The statement quoted by the labor relations director is also accurately quoted. How will you rule and how will you explain your decision?

Case 19-4

REAL WAGES — '62 AND '64

The Swillager Manufacturing Company of Cougar, Arizona, was negotiating a renewal of its collective bargaining agreement with production workers in September, 1964. The average hourly rate under the terminating agreement was $2.20, negotiated in September, 1962. The union proposed an average increase of 16¢; the company offered 11¢.

The company argued that $2\frac{1}{2}$ percent per year (or 5 percent for 2 years) was the maximum consistent with public policy designed to prevent inflation. The union replied that 11¢ was scarcely enough to permit employees to keep even with rising living costs.

The local cost-of-living index (based on 1957–59 = 100) was 105.5 in September, 1962, and 107.5 in September, 1964.

• What percent increase in real wages (for the two-year period) is represented by each of the proposals? What increase in cents per hour would be necessary to provide a $2\frac{1}{2}$ percent annual increase in real wages?

HISTORICAL WAGE THEORIES

Disagreement over wage policies and programs, problems, and solutions — as noted in the previous chapter — is in part attributable to the absence of objective yardsticks and to disagreement on wage theory. Variables that influence wage levels and differentials are inadequately defined and understood because our knowledge of these relationships is incomplete. In Chapter 4, on industrial relations systems, hypotheses, theories, models, and systems were discussed; also, variables and relationships. Wage theories involve many of these concepts, with wage rates, differentials, and levels being the most common dependent variables. Numerous independent variables, as will be noted, change through time. Most wage theories also seek to predict levels or quantities of employment, as noted previously. Historical wage theories have limitations, it is true, but these very limitations often provide clues for more adequate and realistic explanations that improve later wage theories. Thus, for example, the five theories discussed in the present chapter are essentially explanations based on labor supplies — a defect that is remedied, at least in part, in the following chapter on marginal productivity wage theory, where demands for labor receive more emphasis.

THE NATURE OF WAGE THEORY

Theories of wages are tentative, plausible explanations of wage rates and structures. They are attempts to describe the "why" of wage rates and salaries, and sometimes of earnings, and to relate these conditions as well as wage structures and differentials to other factors that influence or condition them. They note that wages and salaries change from time to time and vary from one market to another. They seek to identify and describe sequential and functional relationships between wage rates and salaries, on the one hand, and causes or factors, on the other. The range of what may be regarded as conditioning or causal factors is very broad. In one theory, for example, the magnitude of wage funds in the hands of employers may be regarded as most important. Another may stress the costs of reproducing labor. Among other factors considered important are the productivity of workers, the levels of business activity, the assumed schedules of labor demands and supplies, and the size and distribution of the national income. Wage theories explain wages as being influenced or determined by these relationships.

Wage theories are not new. For almost as long as wages (and salaries) have been paid for workers' services, attempts have been made to explain the amounts, levels, differences, and changes in wages. Some earlier theories, influential for a time, have been largely discarded, having few if any advocates today. Others have been discredited, but some of the programs they seemed to justify still have popular acceptance. In general, wage theory has grown and developed, incorporating additions here and modifications there, as our economic system has changed and knowledge and impressions of wage relationships have increased.

One's understanding of wage theories will be facilitated if one notices significant differences in the *setting* in which each appears and the particular wages it seeks to explain. The setting is highly important because all theories have developed to fit existing facts and situations as they appeared at the time. A theory designed to explain wages in a predominantly agricultural society might be expected to emphasize factors quite different from a theory that was developed in a fully industrialized economy. Important facts change from one setting to another — from place to place and time to time.

Wage theories differ also in their *focus*, the particular characteristic or type of wages in which they are interested. Some theories focus on a mythical average of all wages. Some explain wage rates, wage structures, and differentials in individual labor markets. Other theories consider the aggregate of wages in a society or nation as the dependent variable. Some theories emphasize a static focus and an explanation of rates at a given time. Others seek to explain dynamic changes in rates from time to time.

A third and most important distinction among the several wage theories involves the *types of factors* or independent variables that are regarded as influencing wages. One theory might, for example, place greatest emphasis on population as a factor, while another might suggest that employer hiring practices exercise the definitive influence.

Finally, interest in wage theories centers on their *implications* for individual and social action — what they imply can or should be done. Theories have exerted and continue to exert great influence on wage programs.

SIGNIFICANT FEATURES OF HISTORICAL WAGE THEORIES

In the descriptions of wage theories that follow, these significant features of each theory are emphasized. Each theory is considered in terms of:

1. Its setting — the times, places, and circumstances in which it was advanced.
2. Its focus — the wage facts and the types of wages with which it is concerned.
3. The nature of the theory, that is, the factors regarded as most influential.
4. Its implications for action.

The Just Price Theory

Perhaps the earliest wage theory to have continuing influence was also the simplest, so simple that it can only be regarded as a wage theory by adopting a very broad definition of "theory." Those who advanced it knew how the price of labor was determined, for it was set by the order of public authorities. The question raised in the theory is not what factors determine wages, but rather, what should be considered in determining the price to be set.

Setting. The just price viewpoint had wide acceptance in the Middle Ages, before the emergence of industrialized economies. Wages at the time were gradually becoming more important as numbers of free artisans or craftsmen increased. Most workers were serfs or slaves, supported by their masters. Governments of the principalities and embryo nations of Europe were autocratic. Church and state were closely related. Markets and prices were generally regulated. Prices were regarded as involving important ethical questions, and church authorities advanced guiding principles for their control. A general theory of "just price" was widely accepted in the pricing of commodities. The same rule was applied, in modified form, to the setting of wages for the small but growing numbers of free artisans.

Focus. An increasing proportion of workers had achieved the right to sell their services for wages. These artisans or craftsmen were somewhat mobile, offering their skills for sale to potential employers and thus creating a labor marketing process that appeared likely to assume increasing prominence. This development forced attention to a relatively new problem for societies accustomed to slavery and serfdom where labor was compensated and supported on manorial estates. That problem concerned the proper, ethical price of free labor.

Factors. What considerations held top priority in determining the prices to be paid for artisans? In the philosophy of the period, this question became: What are the principles of justice and equity that must be considered by wage-setting authorities? What considerations should determine the price of labor? What yardsticks can be used to measure the adequacy of wages? Answers to these questions held that the principle of "just price," already accepted in other markets, was also applicable to the wages of workers. A just price must be adequate to assure the continued availability of goods. A just wage must assure the continued availability of the services of independent craftsmen. Hence, wages should be set at a level that would permit craftsmen to live and to support their families on a scale that would maintain these supplies. Workers would not, with such wages, be able to improve their economic position. Neither would they have to lower their scales of living. The theory evidences acceptance of the relatively static social system of the period.

Action. The appropriate action is apparent and requires little elaboration. Authorities were charged with the responsibility of seeing that wages were just. They had to develop and apply measures of fairness based on the criterion expressed in the theory. They found some wages so low as to justify arbitrary increases. They did not hesitate, on the other hand, to restrict wage increases that appeared unjustified by the doctrine. These guiding principles were applied over a long period of time. They were used to justify parliamentary restrictions on wage increases in 1351 when the "black death" reduced labor supplies in England. Available workers were required to accept wage rates prevailing before the plague. The viewpoint has some continuing influence in present policy and practice. It is not unrelated to demands for a living wage and yardsticks of need that may be used to set legal minimum wages. Further, present-day wage disputes are frequently settled by decisions that relate rates to the customary or established status of wage earners. The argument may be made, for example, that building craftsmen have always maintained higher living scales than factory employees, or that public employees should not have to lower their living scales to work for government agencies.

The Subsistence Theory

In the period dominated by the Industrial Revolution, when labor marketing became common and wages the usual method of compensating workers, economists became much concerned about wages and the conditions that influenced wage levels. They recognized payments for the services of labor as a major cost of production. They saw the wage-fixing process as one of the important elements in the new industrialized economy. They speculated about what forces determined the prices paid for human services. They developed tentative explanations, which are now generally described as *classical wage theories*. Adam Smith, Thomas Malthus, David Ricardo, and John Stuart Mill are among the most prominent names associated with this analysis. Smith published his *The Wealth of Nations* in 1776. Malthus released the first edition of his *Essay on Population* anonymously in 1789. Ricardo's *Principles of Political Economy and Taxation* appeared in 1817. John Stuart Mill's *Principles of Political Economy* was published in 1848. These and other economists of the classical school developed and advanced two tentative explanations of the wage-setting process. They were and are generally described as the *subsistence theory* and the *wages fund theory*. The subsistence theory is an explanation of long-term trends in prices of labor, while the wages fund theory seeks to explain current wage rates and short-term changes in labor prices.

Setting. As noted, this explanation was advanced during the period of early industrialization. The handicraft system was declining in importance as a source of employment, giving way to early factories.

Wage earners — formerly limited to master craftsmen, journeymen, and apprentices — now included many unskilled men, women, and children. Urbanization was creating additional social problems as workers moved to factory sites and tried to find homes in these small communities.

Dating the period may be facilitated by reference to a few highlights of this development. It was a period of rapid colonization and expansion in foreign trade. Power sources were being developed and used in production. What is widely described as the first factory in England was a silk mill, established in 1718. The Watt steam engine was first used in a cotton mill in 1785. Adam Smith's *Wealth of Nations* carries the same date as our American Revolution.

Current political thinking at this time was influenced by a sharp shift away from *mercantilism* and toward the *laissez-faire*, physiocratic viewpoint. Whereas mercantilists had regarded rigorous and meticulous public control of economic activity as essential, physiocrats favored much greater economic freedom. Mercantilism proposed to regulate all imports and exports and to maintain a controlled balance of trade that would increase national supplies of gold and other precious materials. Mercantilists favored an enforced expansion of foreign trade. In contrast, the physiocratic viewpoint saw little need for public intervention or regulation. Rather, what was desirable was a maximum of freedom from all public interference. If left alone, according to this view, the economy would automatically operate in the best interest of the nation as a whole. Physiocrats spoke of the importance of *natural laws* in economic activity and progress. They proposed to identify and understand such laws, including those that explained the distribution of income to land, labor, capital, and the entrepreneur or risk taker.

Focus. Earlier economic thinking had generally emphasized the welfare of the state. The classical approach reflected changes in political philosophy in showing much greater concern for the rights of individuals. The period was one in which theories of political democracy and the equality of citizens became popular. Classical wage theories were advanced as an economic accompaniment to the political views that erupted in American and French revolutions.

The subsistence theory is primarily concerned with the general level of wages. Numbers of wage earners were increasing as factories replaced the home workshops of handicraft production. Many women and children, formerly regarded as dependents, were joining the labor force. Wages — usually paid by the day or the week — became the principal source of family income and support, replacing the earlier support of agricultural workers, who were paid "in kind," or in shares, or were allowed to live in homes and to maintain themselves on the estates of landlords. One of the most important changes involved the loss of economic independence by nonagricultural workers. Many former independent craftsmen had become factory employees. Adam Smith reports that the ratio of dependent employees to independent artisans by 1775 was 20 to 1. Urbanization of the population was an impressive movement. Population was growing rapidly, largely as a result of a falling death rate.

Craftsmen had lost status in the change to factory production. Real wages were gaining slowly, and living scales were advancing, but serious unemployment and depression had become more frequent. Business fluctuations were more violent. For example, in one such recession in 1680, half the population of England was supported in part by charity. In spite of rising living scales, problems of personal and family hardship and poverty were evident.

Population trends suggested tremendous possibilities for increase. Means of subsistence, particularly foodstuffs, were also increasing, but at a slower rate than population. Agricultural production was suffering from failure to rebuild the soil.

Factors. Adam Smith set the stage for the subsistence theory by advancing a *labor theory of value.* He concluded that the full value of any commodity is the amount of labor it will buy. Real prices of all commodities, by which Smith meant relative prices, according to this analysis are the amounts of toil required to secure them. One commodity costs twice as much as another because it requires twice as much toil. However, the measure of toil and labor value is not simply the man-hour or the man-day. Smith noted that it also involves modifications to take account of different types and conditions of work. Smith listed five such differentials, including (1) hardship or unpleasantness, (2) difficulty of learning the job, (3) stability of employment, (4) responsibility or trust inherent in the job, and (5) the chances of success or failure involved in the work. (Incidentally, this Smithian analysis is not greatly different from modern systems of job evaluation used to establish individual job rates.)

Smith's analysis thus provided a plausible explanation of wage structures and differentials and the general rule with respect to demands for labor. Demands were related to the value of products. This analysis created a framework for understanding the basic forces behind demands for labor and the range of wage rates at any time. There remained, however, the question as to what factors set the general level of labor prices.

The Malthusian analysis contributed an explanation of long-term changes in aggregate supplies of labor. Malthus made his contribution to the subsistence theory of wages by advancing a *theory of population growth*. He described what he regarded as a general theory of population. Ricardo and others used this population theory as the basis for the long-term, subsistence theory of wages. Malthus concluded on the basis of historic evidence that populations have an inherent tendency to multiply, to double each 25 years. Means of subsistence, on the other hand, as illustrated by grain production in several nations, appeared to be increasing much more slowly by a consistent periodic addition, an arithmetic rate of increase. Hence, Malthus concluded, the pressure of population always pushes against subsistence as numbers of people increase toward these limits of subsistence. Malthus then described several types of checks on population growth that held it or cut it to dimensions prescribed by this alleged relationship.

Ricardo translated these ideas into a *long-term wage theory*. Wages, he concluded, tended to equal the cost of reproducing labor.[1] They could be no more, for any temporary wage above subsistence costs would be followed by an increased labor supply. This larger supply would be cut back by the positive checks described by Malthus, including famine, war, and pestilence. The cost of maintaining a labor supply equal to existing means of subsistence was, in Ricardo's terms, the *natural price* of labor.

Under the subsistence theory, workers, with alleged practically limitless reproduction instincts, would tend to have as many children as they could support and feed. Any increase in real wages would mean that more of their children would live, that is, they would be able to feed a larger family. On the other hand, the supply of land was limited, agricultural techniques were regarded as fixed, and diminishing returns were held to be especially true for agriculture;

---

[1]Stigler contends that Ricardo emphasized an *empirical* rather than analytical theory of labor value, and notes that, except in the case of constant costs, no adequate theory of relative values can ignore demand. G. J. Stigler, "Ricardo and the 93% Labor Theory of Value," *The American Economic Review*, Vol. XLVIII, No. 3 (June, 1958), pp. 357–67.

hence the supply of food limited the effective result of the alleged tendency to procreate without limit.

The subsistence theory held that there was a relatively fixed stock of food. If population increased more than available food supplies, people would die off until there was enough food for those remaining. If there was surplus food, numbers would increase until food supplies and population were in balance. This was a natural, if cruel, "law of nature."

Action. This subsistence theory suggested inaction rather than action. It indicated that little could be done by employers, employees, or society to improve the lot of wage earners. Kindhearted attempts to raise their living scales by raising wages could only lead to increased misery as numbers of workers increased beyond means of subsistence. This theory thus became a justification for avoiding all attempts to interfere in labor marketing processes.

It should be noted that the subsistence theory involved at least two major errors, both much more obvious today than when the theory was advanced. First, the theory erred in its observation and forecasts with respect to means of subsistence. Subsequent discoveries opened up new land, much of which still remains to be developed. New means of reclamation and soil building, more intensive cultivation, new varieties of grain, irrigation, and other advances in agricultural technology (including possible gains from manipulated radiation) indicate no such narrow limits on subsistence as were observed by Malthus.

Second, it is apparent that cultural factors, living standards, and ideals of family life play a more dominant role in population growth than the theory assumes. Whatever the biological potential of population growth, its influence is modified by the material comforts and nonmaterial values people want for themselves and their families. Population in modern societies has not increased up to the limits of subsistence, in the Malthusian-Ricardian sense. However, it is worth noting that world population is expected to double in the next 40 years, according to a report by the United Nations Department of Economics and Social Affairs, and that Asia's population will triple. Perhaps there will be substantial reason to reexamine the subsistence theory.[2]

---

[2]See "An Overcrowded World," *U.S. News and World Report*, Vol. XLV, No. 5 (August 29, 1958), pp. 48–50.

The Wages Fund Theory

Setting. The wages fund theory — the short-term classical explanation of wages — was developed in much the same setting as the subsistence or long-term half of classical wage theory. It was described by Ricardo, by N. W. Senior, and by John Stuart Mill, to name only the most influential proponents of this viewpoint.

Focus. The facts on which attention focuses in the wages fund theory are different from those considered in the subsistence theory. This companion theory asked different questions. It was concerned with the short-term, year-to-year variations in the general level of wages. It was apparent that while available supplies of workers and means of subsistence might change somewhat from year to year, wages varied much more widely. Many short-term increases and decreases in the level of wages could not be adequately explained by variations in supplies of grain and other foods. They could not be attributed to changing supplies of labor, for population changes were much slower. What factors could explain the frequent year-to-year shifts in labor prices? The wages fund theory sought to supplement the Malthusian analysis and to explain these short-term variations.

Factors. The theory advanced a concept of the market price of labor, rather than its long-term *natural price*, which was regarded as amply explained by the subsistence theory. The *market price* of labor was explained as resulting principally from two variables, the number of available workers and the size of the wages fund. The *wages fund* was described as a portion of what Mill called "circulating capital," held by entrepreneurs who had accumulated these resources from their operations in earlier years. They used part of this circulating capital to purchase facilities and materials, paying rent and interest; they allocated another portion — the wages fund — to buy labor. The amount of their allocation to wages, together with the supply to be employed, established the market price for labor in each working period.

The wages fund was held to be relatively fixed in the short run, and represented an "advance" to labor in the new "roundabout" system of production, industrial capitalism.

It is apparent today that there is no fixed sum of wages (Mill and others were primarily discussing a state of competition with minimum normal profits) and that wages can come at the expense of profits or from expansion of credit. (There is more than a superficial resemblance, however, between today's guaranteed annual wage plans and a wages fund concept.) With respect to the concept that wages are an advance to support labor until their product is finished and sold, Francis A. Walker, one of the first great American economists, noted that workers in effect made an advance to employers since they did not get paid until at least the end of the week; coupled with the fact that production is a continuous process, a case can be made that labor makes the advance. William Thomas Thornton, British economist and a close friend of Mill, also attacked the wages fund concept as being an inadequate concept of value because it seemed to regard demand for labor as fixed. It did not explain the amount of labor demanded by the employer and hence the size of the fund he would need.

Action. Implications of the wages fund theory for the social control of wages were about as negative as those of the subsistence analysis. There appeared little that could be done by public action, either to change the volume of the wages fund or to vary the amount of available labor. Moreover, labor as a whole or as represented by certain organized groups of workers could only make matters worse by intervention in the process. Whatever one group of workers received in excess of the market price must be subtracted from what was distributed to other wage earners. Employer action or public intervention or even employee efforts to advance wages, if they were effective, would mean that other employees received less. The theory was regarded as expressing an unchanging and unchangeable law of supply and demand. The Irish economist, J. E. Cairnes, is generally credited with the most effective short summary of these implications. He concluded that, so far as workers are concerned, "The margin for the possible improvement of their lot is confined within narrow barriers which cannot be passed, and the problem of their elevation is hopeless."[3]

Both of the classical theories, by their gospel of hopelessness and inevitable poverty, exerted a far-reaching influence on popular attitudes toward the developing science of economics. When the classical theories were described as stating an "iron law of wages," this characterization did much to justify Carlyle's conclusion that economics was indeed a "dismal" science.

---

[3]J. E. Cairnes, *Political Economy* (New York: Harper and Brothers, 1874), p. 291.

Residual Claimant Theory

It remained for an American, Francis A. Walker, to add insult to injury in the classical analysis, so far as labor is concerned. Walker, writing in 1888, sought to explain the distributive process, the relative size of the wages fund, and allocations to rent, interest, and profit. He put his conclusion bluntly: "Wages equal the product of industry minus the three parts already determined in their nature and amount." According to Walker, labor gets what is left. His viewpoint was described as the *residual claimant theory*, for obvious reasons.[4]

The residual claimant theory, like the wages fund theory, was not a complete theory in the analytical sense. It was incomplete because it did not explain why labor rather than land or capital got the residual, nor did it explain how much would be left over for labor. All it said was that given the sum of A, B, C, and D, if you know A, B, and C, D is the amount remaining. The theory could as easily have been a residual profit theory.

The residual claimant wage theory contained little if any implications for action, either private or public. In a sense, however, Walker may be regarded as a precursor of the marginal productivity theory, discussed in the next chapter. He held that if labor was more efficient and did not use more land or capital in increasing output, the added production would increase the residual going to labor. It would not be necessary to increase the price of land and capital (rent, interest, profit) because by definition no more was needed. Or if the increase in labor productivity exceeded costs of necessary additions to the stock of land and capital, the remainder of the increase (after paying land and capital) could go to increase the residual. Hence, labor could improve its lot by improving its efficiency or productivity. Thus, although the basic residual claimant theory is essentially a tautology, Walker did offer a clue for action to improve labor's income, namely, increased efficiency of labor — produce more and you will earn more.

Karl Marx: Surplus Value and Exploitation

In the smoggy atmosphere of these dismal and dismaying forecasts by which leading political economists had philosophized the masses of workers into eternal misery and poverty, Karl Marx gave

---

[4]See his *Political Economy* (New York: Henry Holt and Company, Inc., 1888), pp. 248–50.

strident voice to a different interpretation of wages and the future fortunes of workers. Its implications appeared to justify drastic action by wage earners everywhere. His theory and interpretation stimulated the development of labor organizations among wage earners in the principal industrial nations and their combination in the *first international*, the International Working Men's Association, formed in London in 1864. The Marxian viewpoint continues to exert influence today and is implicit in the current program of international communism.

Setting. Marx lived from 1818 to 1883. The Marxian statement gained popular attention in the last half of the nineteenth century. As a whole, the period was dominated by growing industrialization, with more factories, more factory workers, larger populations, long hours of work, and frequent and extensive unemployment. Large numbers of workers were often forced to live on meager public relief. Depressions were frequent. Public opinion generally held that these misfortunes, casualties, and disasters were inevitable.

In industrial nations the "haves" and the "have nots" appeared more prominently identified and distinguished than before. In part, this was true because proportions of those who had wealth were larger than in earlier societies. In part, the difference was more obvious because the "have nots" were concentrated in urban areas where their poverty was readily observed.

Focus. Marx, in effect, asked the questions: Why are wage earners as a class paid so little? Who gets the obviously growing wealth created by industrialization and why? Why doesn't this wealth make wage earners rich?

Marx was impressed by the accomplishments of another class that gained prominence as a result of this process of industrialization — the *bourgeoisie*, private property owners or capitalists. He noted that in a hundred years of industrial development, productivity had grown rapidly, development of natural resources had exceeded all earlier history, invention had been speeded, new products and new demands had been created, and international trade had been expanded. On the other hand, Marx pointed to the recurring epidemics of overproduction and depression. He was impressed by what he regarded as a tendency toward the elimination of small tradespeople and shopkeepers, in which they were forced to become members of the masses of employees — the *industrial proletariat*. Further, according to Marx, workers had failed to benefit from these changes. The wage earner could only look forward to a future as a pauper. The questions he raised and answered were focused on the process in which production grew but wages remained low. The rich got richer, but the poor failed to gain. Why?

Factors. Marx made no serious criticism of subsistence and wages fund theories in societies dominated by the enterprise motive, although he saw somewhat more importance in cultural and traditional standards of living as explaining wage differences from time to time and place to place. He accepted much of Smith's analysis of wage differentials, placing special emphasis on the cost of learning skills. He accepted the conclusion that the masses had little prospect of improvement in the then-current social and political system.

From Smith and Ricardo, Marx took the labor theory of value, agreeing that the true value of all commodities is their labor cost. His contribution lies largely in his explanation of the wage-setting process. He concluded that in this process the bourgeoisie entrepreneurs collect the value created by labor, but they pay labor only its cost of subsistence. This procedure creates what he called *surplus value*, which was divided among the shares going to rent, interest, and profit. Surplus value is the excess of value created by labor over labor's cost of subsistence. Since all value is created by labor, this skimming the cream by employers was, in Marxian terminology, *exploitation*. The Marxian theory is an explanation of the distribution of income and the exploitation of wage earners.

Action. The Marxian theory was full of implications for action, as Marx indicated. These conclusions were summarized by Marx and Friedrich Engels in the *Communist Manifesto* in 1848. The statement holds that since capitalists exploit the masses, the thing to do is to abolish capitalists and to substitute public or social ownership of capital. The industrial proletariat must assert its power, organize, revolt, and seize the means of production and establish the "classless society," according to Marx. Distribution of the products of labor should, he insisted, grant individual income according to need. Such distribution would abolish poverty and depression. Marx and Engels concluded the *Manifesto* with the classic socialist call to action: "The proletarians have nothing to lose but their chains. They have a world to win. Working men of all countries, unite!"

It is not surprising that the Marxian theory held wide appeal, in view of the dismal prospect that was expressed by classical theorists and that had achieved popular acceptance. Marx suggested a way out. In somewhat modified form, the novelty of the analysis — the theory of surplus value — has plausibility. Marx criticized the wage-fixing process as the imposition of a private tax or deduction from wages for the use of land, capital, and entrepreneurship. What he suggested was the elimination of private ownership of land and capital and the substitution of public control for that of capitalists. He proposed revolutionary action by workers to effect this change.

Marxian philosophy. The concept of *historical materialism* and *economic determinism* advanced by Marx and Engels held that history consists of a series of class struggles between the exploiters and the exploited, the rulers and the ruled. Social institutions are modified by economic developments in the realms of production and distribution. Thus, for example, the capitalist bourgeoisie with their machines were revolutionary and helped bring about the downfall of nobility. In turn the economic system of capitalism contains the seeds of its own destruction through the medium of the economic class struggle between owners (bourgeoisie) and workers (proletariat). Machines create a permanent wage-earning class consisting of semiskilled and unskilled workers. Machines make possible employment of women and children, hence driving men's wages down through competition for jobs. Wages fall as low as possible, that is, to the subsistence level. The middle class will be wiped out and skilled workers will be reduced to homogeneous, interchangeable units with their skills only those of machine tenders. Wealth will be concentrated increasingly in the hands of the bourgeoisie. Overproduction of goods will tend to cause serious depressions. Workers should unite into trade unions as a means of banding together for *political* strength, although Marx and Engels held that unions would not alleviate the economic or material problems of workers because all workers would become homogeneous, unskilled, interchangeable units and because chronic overproduction would lead to increasing chronic unemployment. The bourgeoisie finally have to support the proletariat and thus "produce their own grave diggers." The more technical progress there is, the greater the poverty of the masses. Finally and inevitably (economic determinism), the proletariat will violently overthrow the bourgeoisie and control their own classless society.

"Proof" of the downfall of capitalism.   Marx and Engels held that the underlying causes of historical change are to be found in the development of new modes of production and distribution.   The rise of machines and of the bourgeoisie were parallel. Marx forecast the fall of capitalism by citing six economic changes that would make this inevitable.   These were:

1. The concentration of production into larger-scale units.
2. The concentration of control and management.
3. The concentration of wealth among fewer and fewer persons.
4. The wiping out of the middle class.
5. The reduction of all labor to common unskilled labor.
6. The decline of wages to a subsistence level.
   (The last three propositions account for the proletariat and their reasons for unrest leading inevitably to revolution.)

Were Marx and Engels right?   Over a hundred years have passed since the above forecasts were made. To date Marx and Engels were partly correct on propositions 1 and 2, but wrong on propositions 3 through 6.

There has been a concentration of production in large-scale plants, although not without limit because apparently plants can be too large for most efficient production.   There has been a concentration of control and management — in the United States the top 500 firms produce about 20 percent of our national income. But there has been a counter tendency toward diversification rather than concentration of ownership.   The largest United States corporation has more stockholders than employees, for example. And with the rise of professional management, direction of production and distribution is much less intimately related to ownership of the means of production.   So Marx and Engels were partly right on their forecasts of concentration of production and on concentration of control and management.

They were wrong on their forecasts of concentration of wealth, wiping out of the middle class, reduction of labor to the common unskilled level, and the falling of wages to a subsistence level.   As shown in detail in Chapters 18 and 19, just the opposite has occurred with respect to each of these propositions.   Hence, it is apparent that Marx and Engels were wrong in their premises and also in their conclusion. This is not the same as saying that the concept of historical materialism is completely wrong and that economic developments do not shape history or social events.

In the years since Marx wrote, political reforms have accomplished many of the changes he suggested. Noncommunist societies today still prefer the institution of private property for most land and capital, holding that this provides an essential incentive. But modern societies combine some public ownership with income, inheritance, and other taxes that redistribute income and wealth to increase the share going to wage earners. They have substituted public taxes for what he regarded as a private levy. Labor organization is now encouraged. Current economies have thus accomplished some degree of the Marxian objectives without revolution. The whole of his program still represents the ideological ultimate if not the practical and immediate objective of modern communist nations.

ANALYTICAL REVIEW QUESTIONS

1. Why are wages, wage rates, and earnings matters of continuing controversy and dispute?
2. (a) What differences of opinion exist with respect to appropriate yardsticks for wages? (b) Do employees and employers arrange yardsticks in different orders of priority? (c) What do you think they rate at the top of their respective lists?
3. (a) Why and how do differences in wage theories affect our knowledge and understanding of wage relationships? (b) How are "theories" related to "reality"?
4. How are improved measurements of wages related to wage theories?
5. What is a wage theory and what does it seek to explain?
6. (a) In what terms are theories usually stated? (b) What purposes are served by having theories? (c) What determines a theory's usefulness?
7. (a) What are the differences between dependent and independent variables. (b) What are functional and sequential relationships?
8. How are focus and setting related to (a) development of theories and (b) their implications for individual and social action?
9. Describe the just price wage theory in terms of: (a) setting, (b) focus, (c) major considerations involved, and (d) appropriate action suggested by the theory.
10. What were just prices and just wages assumed to provide in terms of economic resources and living standards?
11. (a) Why is the subsistence theory of wages a long-run theory? (b) What was a counterpart short-run theory?
12. (a) How were mercantilism and laissez-faire concepts related to the subsistence theory? (b) Do present world population trends suggest that this theory is still adequate?
13. According to Adam Smith the man-hour or the man-day is not the sole measure of labor value. What other factors are involved according to Smith?

14. (a) Under the subsistence theory, what happened when wages (1) rose above subsistence levels and (2) fell below? (b) Why did the subsistence theory suggest social and public *inaction* rather than action?

15. Describe two major errors in the subsistence theory.

16. (a) Briefly explain the wages fund theory. (b) Under this theory what factors determine the market price of labor?

17. How are wages determined under the residual claimant theory?

18. Why is the surplus value and exploitation theory more indicative of social action than other wage theories?

19. (a) According to Marx, why were the rich getting richer and the poor getting poorer? (b) Where did the surplus value come from? (c) What did bourgeoisie entrepreneurs collect for labor's services? (d) What determined what they paid labor for their work?

20. (a) What social action did Marx and Engels call for? (b) How should income be distributed?

21. What were some of the principal errors in the Marxian analysis in terms of the economic facts and predictions upon which the analysis was based?

22. What changes in the direction suggested by Marxian analysis have been made in the United States?

MARGINAL PRODUCTIVITY THEORY

Skepticism about wage theories is desirable because it encourages further study, investigation, and analysis. It has stimulated the search for demonstrable relationships and led to the development of modern wage theories, which are the subject for consideration in this and the next chapter. Attention is directed in the present chapter to the marginal productivity theory. Note must also be taken of the modifications introduced by studies of imperfect competition, which occasioned what are described as *marginal value-revenue amendments*.[1]

SIGNIFICANT FEATURES

The marginal productivity theory is the early 20th century model, continually expanded and modified throughout the past

---

[1]For a comprehensive discussion of wage theories, see George W. Taylor and Frank C. Pierson (eds.), *New Concepts of Wage Determination* (New York: McGraw-Hill, 1957). See also John T. Dunlop (ed.), *The Theory of Wage Determination*, Proceedings of a Conference held by the International Economic Association (New York: St. Martin's Press, 103 Park Avenue, 1957); K. W. Rothschild, *The Theory of Wages* (Oxford: Basil Blackwell, 1956); Sidney Weintraub, *An Approach to the Theory of Income Distribution* (Philadelphia: Chilton Company, 1958); Lloyd G. Reynolds, "The State of Wage Theory," pp. 234–40, and Charles A. Myers, "Empirical Research on Wages," pp. 241–51, in *Proceedings* of the Industrial Relations Research Association, Dec. 28–30, 1953; Melvin C. Reder, "Wage Determination in Theory and Practice," in Neil W. Chamberlain *et al.* (eds.), *A Decade of Industrial Relations Research, 1946–1956* (New York: Harper and Brothers, 1958), pp. 64–97; see also Allen M. Cartter *Theory of Wages and Employment* (Homewood, Ill.: Richard D. Irwin, 1959) and N. Arnold Tolles, *Origins of Modern Wage Theories* (Englewood Cliffs, N.J.: Prentice-Hall, 1964).

60 years.   The early 1900 model had a continental motif, for it expressed the subjective, almost introspective, viewpoint of the Austrian School of economic theorists.   An American, John Bates Clark, is usually credited with the most penetrating early statement of the theory in his *Distribution of Wealth*, published in 1899.[2]   The theory has been widely accepted and used as a key to the behavior in individual labor markets by most of the economists who have presented an explanation of wages since that time.   It is still widely described as the "orthodox" theory, although labor economists do not regard even the most refined statement of the theory as an entirely adequate explanation of wage rates.

Setting

The marginal productivity theory was developed in a period of continuing economic expansion and progress.   Populations were increasing, as were the real wages and the living scales of workers. New resources were being discovered and exploited.   Technological change was rapid and impressive in many industries.   Boom and bust were prominent in the broad fluctuations of business activity both in this country and abroad.   In these sharp changes, readjustments became matters of great concern, focusing attention on what appeared to be an essential in these periods — the flexibility of prices.

Rapid changes in combinations of resources spotlighted the role of marketing and prices in local as well as national economies.   Recessions appeared to be characterized if not caused by market frictions and out-of-line and "sticky" prices.   Recovery from depression appeared to be dependent on readjustments in prices and the clearing of markets.   Expansion and economic development emphasized the necessity for flexibility in the allocation of all resources, including labor.

The same expansion called attention to the importance of the risk-taking, entrepreneurial function.   Industrial empires were created by venturesome empire-builders in railroads, petroleum, and other industries.   They opened up new sections of this continent, developed its natural resources, and employed the rapidly growing labor force.

The labor-marketing process attracted attention in this period, in part because the scarcity of labor in some markets encouraged private recruiting in foreign nations and in part because labor surpluses and wide unemployment created serious social problems in

---

[2]New York: The Macmillan Company.

recession periods. While some popular attention turned to arguments about whether immigration should be encouraged or limited, problems of unemployment and poverty among wage earners also created wide concern. To some it appeared that the huge profits and private fortunes of the empire-builders were made possible by the exploitation of wage earners. Wages, according to this viewpoint, were consistently low and inadequate. Others, however, saw the frequent depressions and mass unemployment of the period as the result of wage rates that were too high and too inflexible.

Both popular viewpoints focused attention on labor allocation and marketing processes. Such an emphasis was encouraged also by the viewpoint of most economists. They too were impressed with the importance of the marketing function in the economy. Economics appeared to be principally a science of marketing, and labor economics (which first established itself as a distinctive field in this period) became that portion of the discipline which analyzed the processes of labor markets.

Focus or Emphasis

The marginal productivity analysis of wages raises and seeks answers to two major questions. One of them notes historic, *long-term* advances in real earnings and asks what factors explain this continuing increase. Generally, the question refers to long-term changes in *specific* labor markets, although some analysts have added confusion by assuming a hypothetical *national* labor market and talking about factors causing long-term changes in *the* labor market.

The other question relates to the obvious *short-term* variations in prices paid for labor in specific markets. While the long-term upward trend in wages has been evident, sharp short-term reductions have been apparent and frequently more spectacular. Particularly in earlier years of the present century, most depressions and wide unemployment seemed to end only after wages (and prices) were readjusted downward. While the general upward trend in business could explain price and wage increases, wage reductions appeared as a contradiction of this trend. Further, it was apparent that short-term wage changes did not follow a uniform pattern in all industries or all labor markets. Notable differences distinguished markets for labor used to produce capital equipment and consumers' durables, on one hand, and consumers' nondurable goods — such as foods and clothing — on the other. These differences focused attention on short-term wage changes and individual labor markets. They thus defined the second major question, which asked why these short-term fluctuations occur and what factors explain their pattern.

The marginal productivity theory provides tentative answers to both the long-run and the short-run questions. In these answers the focus of attention is on the labor marketing process, including the actions of individual employers and firms and individual workers and their unions.

At the (micro) level of the firm (in competition), the marginal productivity theory is essentially an *employment* theory; the predicted outcome is the level of employment, since the wage rate is given for the firm. At the macro level, however, the marginal productivity theory is more properly a *wage* theory.

Demands and Supplies

Up to this point, we have been discussing wage theories that tend to emphasize explanations of the *supply* side of labor rather than demand; they assume demands for labor as given. The wages fund and residual claimant theories push toward an explanation of employer *demand*, but again they do not tell us much about the forces behind these demands. The marginal productivity theory is important because it gives us an answer to the question: "What determines how much labor an employer (or employers) will demand?"

The principal answer given to the question of long-term advances in the price of labor may be summarized in the concept of the *capital-worker ratio*. Long-term wage rates are, according to the marginal analysis, the result of interaction between two variables in labor markets — supplies of labor and supplies of capital. Although each is a substitute for the other, each is also complementary. Employers must have both, and their decisions as to bids or prices are greatly influenced by the comparative availability of the two. In the period in which the marginal productivity theory was advanced, discoveries of new natural resources and supplies of capital had increased and were increasing more rapidly than supplies of labor. The capital-worker ratio was growing. Added capital available to the average worker made his efforts more effective and productive and, at the same time, created a favorable relationship for labor that could result in the rising trend in wages. Productivity began to move to the fore in the explanation of wages.

Answers to the question regarding short-run fluctuations in labor market prices emphasize a similar balancing of demands and supplies. Rates result from the combination of employers' estimates of worker productivity or contribution and employees' offers to sell their services. The first factor creates market demands. The second provides labor supplies — the amount available for hire at various prices. These are the two major variables: employers' demands for labor and potential employees' supplies of labor.

Basic Assumptions

To understand the marginal productivity theory requires a knowledge of its underlying assumptions. The theory represents a generalized explanation of (1) why an employer hires labor and (2) how much labor he hires. In general, there is a tendency for employers (1) to hire labor as long as it makes a greater proportionate contribution to net revenue than does any other factor of production and (2) to hire units of labor up to the point where the marginal revenue product of labor equals its price — where the value of what labor produces equals the wage paid. These conclusions result from certain logical assumptions and their interrelationships rather than from empirical observation and measurement.

This discussion begins with certain simple assumptions that probably do not accurately portray most, if any, real life situations.[3] This is done because it is easier to illustrate and see effects of the factors or variables that account for answers to the questions: (1) how much labor will employers hire (instead of some other factor) and (2) how much will employers pay labor? In general, the key factor in answering these questions is the value of the productivity of an added unit of labor — that is, its marginal productivity. Four major principles, or assumptions, provide the basic framework for the marginal productivity theory. These are the principles of: (1) maximization, (2) substitution, (3) diminishing returns, and (4) marginal comparison.

Principle of maximization. The *principle of maximization* holds that employers seek to maximize their profits. To do this they combine

---

[3]This discussion makes the traditional assumptions of economic competition. These are probably familiar to most students and are stated more explicitly in Appendix B. They are referred to as needed in the discussion that follows; and modifications (for example, in cases of imperfect competition) are noted in the text. This approach represents a value judgment on the part of the authors that simplicity in presentation is preferable at this stage of explanation.

factors of production in such a way that the value of output is at a maximum in comparison with the costs of producing that output. Thus, if one man and a shovel can dig a ditch, or two men can dig a ditch with their bare hands, the employer will select the combination that gives him the highest profit. He compares the efficiency of various factors of production, always tending to substitute a more efficient for a less efficient factor.

The cost of using an additional unit of the factor is known as the *marginal outlay*. The added revenue or income the employer gets by using the added factor to increase his output is known as the *marginal revenue product*. In general, an employer will use factors until their marginal outlays and revenue products are equal. If he can gain $25 in income by hiring a man for $20 a day, he will do so. He will not hire an additional man for $25 a day if his gain in revenue is only $20 and (1) either the cost of more men is higher or (2) the contribution of more men is less.

Principle of substitution. To realize the principle of maximization, employers are assumed to utilize the *principle of substitution*, that is, using the most efficient combination of the *factors of production*. Thus, labor competes with and may be substituted for capital, and vice versa. If automatic telephone exchange equipment is more efficient than manual or hand switchboard operators, the machines will be substituted for labor. The decision depends upon the relative cost of each in comparison with relative revenues, or more simply, the comparative value of the marginal productivity of each factor. In general, the employer will substitute factors of production for each other until the value of their marginal products are all equally proportional to their prices. Thus, if the cost of added labor is $10 and its added product is valued at $20 and if the cost of added capital is $40 and its added product is valued at $80, their proportionate marginal contributions are equal, and there is no incentive for the employer to prefer use of one factor rather than the other.

Note that in making this comparison the employer is really comparing two sets of variables: (1) the price of the factor and (2) the value of the added output or the marginal revenue product of the factor. If either variable changes, he must reconsider his recipe or combination of factors. In the simplest explanations of marginal productivity, both price of the product and productivity of labor are *assumed*. Price may be held constant while productivity varies, for example. This is the case for the individual firm in a competitive situation, wherein it is assumed that its output is such a small proportion of the total market that the firm has no direct effect on prices or costs of its factors of production.

Principle of diminishing returns. The *principle of diminishing returns* is a major assumption in the marginal productivity analysis. This principle holds that, after a certain combination of factors, marginal revenue product will decline or diminish as increasing units of *variable* factors (for example, labor) are used in combination with a constant amount of *fixed* factors (for example, capital). Again it is stressed that this is an *assumption*, not an empirical expression of the technical laws of production. This assumption says, in effect, that if the employer knows the price of labor (or wage) and knows the value of the product of various sized work teams, he can then decide on the optimal or most efficient size of work team to use with a fixed amount of capital. If he is in a competitive situation, the price of labor is determined by the market and does not vary with the number of units he hires, that is, the wage rate is fixed to him. Hence the key to his decision making is the marginal productivity of his labor — how much more revenue can he obtain by hiring an additional (marginal) laborer? The price of the product for this competitive employer is also determined by the market and hence is fixed to him. Therefore, if he knows how much more product can be obtained by adding extra men to his work team (their marginal productivity), he can make his decision with respect to the most profitable number of men to have on his work team. This also determines the wage paid to the marginal employee (that is, the value of his marginal product) and to all other employees, because by *assumption* all employees are regarded as equally efficient and interchangeable production units.

Principle of marginal comparison. It should be noted also that the employer *must* pay this wage rate or go out of business. If he tried to pay less, other employers would hire his help away from him and could do so at a profit because the value of labor's marginal productivity exceeds the lower wage rate offered by the initial employer. If the employer paid a higher wage rate, he would operate at a loss, since the marginal worker or workers would be costing more than they were adding to revenue.

Briefly summarizing the four principles above:
1. Employers seek to *maximize* profits.
2. In the process of production, they tend to *substitute* more efficient for less efficient factors of production.

3. Production functions are assumed, that is, relationship of input of factors to their output. For purposes of our analysis, we assume *diminishing returns*.
4. The employer tends to calculate his labor needs by comparing the output of various sized work teams — the principle of *marginalism* or marginal comparison.

As a general theory, the marginal productivity doctrine holds that under conditions of perfect competition employers tend to hire employees up to the point where the value of the marginal productivity of that factor is equal to the wage rate — where the contribution of the last employee hired equals his wage — where labor cost and return are equated. So stated, this is a theory of employment. Marginal analysis goes further, however, and explains that wage rates will tend to equal the marginal contribution of labor units in each labor market.

Amplification of the Theory's Basic Concepts

The above discussion contains the gist of the marginal productivity theory in its simplest form. The pages that follow make these basic concepts clearer by means of more detailed explanations of both the variables and the processes involved. Attention is given first to expanding the concept of the basic variable, marginal product.

Marginal product. The employer's demand for labor is based on his estimates of the return or product he will get from work teams of various sizes. Under the principle of diminishing returns, total product will increase as more men are added; but beyond a certain point, average product will decline and so will marginal product. This marginal product is crucial to the employer in his short-run hiring decisions. The *marginal product* is the added output of a work team obtained by adding one more man to the work team. Since all of the men are assumed to be of equal efficiency, the marginal product must be ascribed to the new work team arrangement and not to the last man hired.[4]

In a price system economy such as ours, an employer must price the value of the output of each of the several size work teams so that he can compare costs and income in dollar, rather than physical, terms. He knows the price of the goods his labor produces, which is fixed by the market. This price is constant as far as the employer is

[4]An example of marginal physical product calculation is given in Table 1 of Appendix B.

concerned and does not vary with his output.[5] All he has to do is multiply the various marginal physical outputs by the price to obtain the value of the marginal product. This process is illustrated in Table 21-1. Assume a wage rate of $8 per day, a price of $1 per unit of product, and the marginal product schedule for a firm which is shown in Table 21-1.

Table 21-1
CALCULATING MARGINAL PHYSICAL PRODUCT

Size of Work Team	Physical Product		Price	Marginal Revenue Product
	Total	Marginal		
1	10	0	$1	—
2	22	12	$1	$12
3	36	14	$1	$14
4	44	8	$1	$ 8
5	50	6	$1	$ 6
6	54	4	$1	$ 4

The last column of the table, headed "Marginal Revenue Product," represents the added value to an employer of work teams of various sizes. He can obtain the revenue shown in that column for each increment added to his work team. Thus, if he increases his team from 4 to 5 men, the addition of the fifth man brings him added revenue, or marginal revenue product, of $6. In the competitive situation he will offer a price or wage of $6 for labor, which is said to be his *demand price* for labor when he employs 5 men. When he employs 4 men, his demand price is $8, and when he employs 6 men, his demand price is $4.

The employer's *demand for labor* (in a firm) is thus seen to be the marginal revenue product for work teams of varying sizes. The *demand schedule* for the employer is the series of prices shown in the last column of the above table. This can also be shown in the form of a demand curve by plotting the same data. We have illustrated this in

---

[5]In the competitive situation. In the noncompetitive situation he must consider price variations; presumably the price decreases as more units are offered on the market.

Figure 21-1 by plotting work teams on the horizontal or X axis and plotting marginal revenue product (or employer's demand price) on the vertical or Y axis. The data used to construct the demand curve are taken from the table above where we presented the demand schedule, that is, the marginal revenue product for work teams of various sizes. Figure 21-1 also shows the supply price of labor, as will be noted. We will show also how an employer relates his demand and supply curves so that he can select the most profitable size for the work team.

In this Figure 21-1 the demand curve is labeled *MRP*, which is the marginal revenue product for varying size work teams. A team of 3 adds a value of $14, whereas a team of 4 adds a value of $8 as shown in Table 21-1 on page 595. The employer is faced with the question of what size team he should use.

Obviously he needs to know his costs, or the wages he must pay. Since he is in a competitive situation, he has to pay the market rate of $8 for each employee he uses regardless of the number he employs. Hence the supply curve and the marginal outlay curve coincide as shown on the line MO. His principle of maximization will show him that he should use a team of 4 men because at that point his marginal revenue product (MRP) and his marginal outlay coincide.

If he uses a team of 3 men, this is not his best combination because all combinations of labor units less than 4 men will produce more additional revenue than their cost of employment. He will not use 5 units, because the added man yields a marginal revenue product of only $6, whereas the employer has to pay out an added $8 in wages; hence, he would lose $2 on this combination.

From the foregoing example, the importance of marginal productivity considerations to the individual employer or the firm should be apparent. Whereas most previously dis-

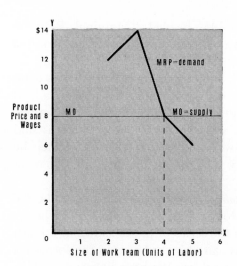

Figure 21-1

LABOR DEMAND AND SUPPLY FOR A COMPETITIVE FIRM

cussed wage theories emphasized supply factors, the marginal productivity theory emphasizes demand, with marginal productivity being the key to understanding employer demand.

Demand for labor in a market. The next step is to show how the price of labor for a market is determined in the competitive situation.[6] Let us begin with a discussion of the market demand curve. Let us assume that we merely add up the individual demand schedules of all firms in the market to obtain a composite demand schedule of total demand for labor.[7] This in effect gives the marginal productivity for all labor employed in the market and shows what employers would bid for various quantities of labor. They would increase their total work teams *in toto* in increments as they did before.

A basic assumption behind the down-sloping demand curve is that added output can be sold only by reducing the price. Thus, as employment expands to include added increments of labor, marginal revenue product declines. Employers will offer each additional increment of labor (demand for the factor) the value of its added production, namely, its marginal revenue product. This is illustrated in Figure 21-2 on page 598.

Supply of labor in a market. In the competitive firm situation the individual firm will buy all of the labor it needs at a uniform price because it uses an insignificant portion of the total labor available. For the market, however, it is assumed that additional supplies would be forthcoming only at higher prices. Hence, the supply curve slopes up and to the right. This will be illustrated below.

Market wage rate. The significance of labor supply and demand curves for a market is twofold. The intersection of the two curves determines (1) the market wage rate and (2) volume of employment.

---

[6]As noted in Chapter 5, there are many labor markets, including occupational, geographical, industrial, and combinations of these. The principles discussed in this section apply to any of these markets. Thus, for example, this section and that which follows could have been called "Demand for, and supply of, labor in an *industry*," thereby representing application of these principles to a more specialized market.

[7]This simple assumption can be modified in more complicated analysis to take account of changes in price of product and declining marginal productivity as more of the factor is employed. See John F. Due, *Intermediate Economic Analysis* (Chicago: Richard D. Irwin, Inc., 1950), pp. 169–70; Neil W. Chamberlain, *Labor* (New York: McGraw-Hill Book Company, 1958), pp. 331–32. In general, marginal productivity is lower for the industry because of diminishing returns and the fact that product price is not constant as it is for the firm; instead it declines, as in monopoly, because additional output can be sold only at a lower price.

It will be recalled that in the example of the firm (shown in Figure 21-1) it was stated that the wage rate is determined by the market, and hence given for the firm. Now it should be shown how this process occurs. Figure 21-2 illustrates this in graphic form. The exact shape of the supply and demand curves is not as important at this stage of the discussion as the fact that they intersect — and that the point of intersection determines the wage rate and the volume of employment.

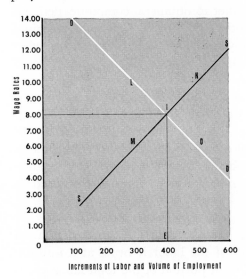

Figure 21-2
**LABOR DEMAND AND SUPPLY
IN A COMPETITIVE MARKET —
THE PRICING PROCESS**

Figure 21-2 depicts the upward sloping supply curve for the market as S-S. At a wage rate of $6.00, 300 units of labor would be supplied. At a rate of $10.00, 500 units would be supplied. The downward sloping demand curve is D-D. At a rate of $14.00, employers would demand only 100 units of labor. At a rate of $8.00, their demand would be 400 units. The point of intersection is at I. On the vertical or Y axis we can read the market wage rate which is $8.00. On the horizontal or X axis we can read the volume of employment (E) at this wage rate, 400 workers.

The wage rate of $8.00 is the market rate because any other rate would not maximize returns. If entrepreneurs used 300 units of labor, they would have to pay $6.00 per unit of labor supplied (M), and would receive a return of $10.00 on each unit (L). Until they reached 400 units, each unit of labor added would return more than it cost.

If, however, entrepreneurs add labor beyond point I, each unit of labor added would cost more than it would add to the value of the product. Thus, for example, if 500 labor units were used, the supply price would be N or $10.00, while the value added by each unit would be O, or $6.00. The loss with the 500th increment of labor would be $4.00.

Each unit of labor added beyond point I would yield a loss. Each unit of labor added before point I would fail to maximize profits. Hence, the point of equilibrium would be at point I, where costs and returns yield the maximum net return.

Relating the market wage rate to the firm wage rate. In Figure 21-1 the supply curve for the competitive firm is MO-MO, a line parallel to the base. This supply curve is at a rate of $8.00. This is the market rate, and the firm must pay at least this rate or it will not be able to get employees; if it pays more than this rate, it will lose money because each employee will cost more than the value of his product (i.e., MRP will be less than MO).

To clarify the relationship between the market rate and the firm's wage rate, note Figure 21-3. This illustration is a composite of Figure 21-1 (left portion of Figure 21-3) and of Figure 21-2 (right portion of Figure 21-3). The wage rate of $8.00 is determined by the market and is described as WR. The wage rate of $8.00 is also the rate the firm must pay for all units of labor it uses. Its supply curve, MO, is parallel to the base.

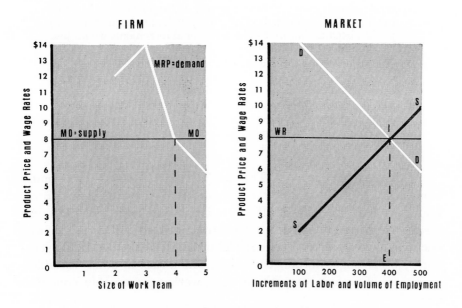

FIRM   MARKET

Figure 21-3

**LABOR DEMAND AND SUPPLY
IN THE MARKET AND FOR A COMPETITIVE FIRM**

Nature of labor demand. Perhaps the nature of labor demand in a competitive market will be made clearer by the following eight general assumptions and principles:

1. As more units of input are employed (for example, labor) more units of output are produced.
2. As output is expanded, additional units of output can be sold only at a lower price than the previous price for a smaller output.
3. Each unit of output is identical and interchangeable; hence, the price of each unit must be identical in the competitive situation.
4. The principle of diminishing returns means that output per increment declines as more employees are employed with a fixed stock of capital.[8]
5. The worth or value of any employee to an employer is represented by the market value of his additional output over and above what the team output would have been without his employment.
6. Employers seek to maximize profits, that is, to have income exceed outlay by as much as possible. If they act in accordance with this objective, they will not pay an additional increment of labor *more* than the value its output would add to total revenue (that is, its marginal revenue product) because this would tend toward loss rather than a profit. If employers pay *less* than the marginal revenue product, they will not be maximizing profits, because failure to hire additional increments would lose revenue in excess of their cost.
7. It is assumed that labor is mobile, has perfect knowledge of market conditions, and will move about from job to job until it receives the market value of its services.
8. Finally, a condition of equilibrium is reached where neither employers nor employees can gain any more from additional movement, and then wages paid equal the marginal value of goods produced by labor.

Nature of labor supply. The *supply of labor* depends upon many variables, including size of the population, size of the labor force, hours worked, intensity of effort, and skill and ability of the labor force. As previously noted, workers are influenced in their labor force decisions by wage rates, desire for leisure, living costs and living standards, job prestige, working conditions, and a host of other variables. In a state of perfect competition, each worker presumably competes

---

[8]Added increments of employees produce proportionately less additional output than did a previous smaller number of employees; but because total output increases, the output can be marketed only at a lower price. With added inputs of labor in an industry, therefore, marginal revenue product declines, that is, the marginal return to employers declines as more men are added.

with other workers and will offer his services at a slightly lower price than other workers if necessary to get the job he wants.

In general, an increase in labor supply tends to move the supply curve downward and to the right. This tends to increase employment, but at lower wage rates. A decrease in labor supply raises the supply curve up and to the left, and it has the dual tendencies of reducing employment and raising wage rates.

Sometimes the supply curve is assumed to have an "S" shape, i.e., it is assumed to be upward sloping and to the right at lower wage rates (as shown in Figures 21-2 and 21-3), but then it is assumed to take a different slope, upward and to the left. This is the so-called *backward sloping supply curve.* It is held by many economists that this provides a more realistic picture of real-life labor market behavior. A backward sloping supply curve is illustrated in Figure 21-4. A supply curve of this shape can be substituted for the supply curve that slopes only upward and to the right, and the same principles of determining wage rates and employment levels will hold. The intersection of the demand and supply curves will still determine the wage rate and the volume of employment.

In Figure 21-4, S-U is an example of an upward sloping supply curve, of the type we have used in our previous examples. The backward sloping supply curve is S-S, sloping upward and to the left from point Z. Finally, the curve slopes upward and to the right again at still higher wage rates, thus completing an appearance similar to the capital letter "S."

The bottom half of Figure 21-4 depicts the so-called *income effect.* This is based on the assumption that workers wish to exchange or sacrifice leisure to obtain income. In our example they will do this up to point Z. Beyond this point, where the supply curve SS

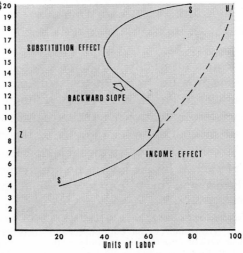

Figure 21-4
BACKWARD SLOPING
SUPPLY CURVE FOR LABOR

slopes upward and to the left, the *substitution effect* is in evidence, i.e., workers wish to substitute more leisure for added income. In this portion of the supply curve, note that fewer units of labor are offered at higher rates. Finally, the income effect takes over as the curve again slopes upward and to the right, in the upper right hand portion of Figure 21-4.

Whether or not the regular upward sloping supply curve is based on less realistic assumptions than the backward sloping supply curve is a moot question. There are those who argue that moonlighting and overtime work are examples of the unreality of the assumptions underlying the backward sloping supply curve.[9] In any event, as noted previously, either supply curve may be used in marginal productivity analysis.

Changes in the shape of supply and demand curves.   All of these relationships assume a perfectly competitive labor market, an oversimplified model of real-life behavior designed to explain the influence of productivity upon wage rate and employment levels.[10] The competitive situation is very short run and assumes no major changes in variables affecting supply and demand curves.

In the real-life world the competition among individuals postulated by the theories of perfect competition does not exist generally. Concerted action by employers and/or employees may interfere with competitive processes. Thus, for example, a union of employees might secure control over certain jobs and (as is fairly typical) offer employee services only at a single rate, regardless of the quantity taken. This would change the shape of the supply curve. Instead of rising upward from left to right, the curve would become a line parallel to the X axis. If the group-determined rate were equal to the old competitive market rate, there would be no change in wage rate or quantity of employment. If the rate were raised above the old competitive rate, then employment would decline to a point determined by the intersection of the new parallel supply curve and the demand curve. Employers would not hire more than this because

---

[9] See Harold G. Vatter, "On the Folklore of the Backward-Sloping Supply Curve," *Industrial and Labor Relations Review*, Vol. 14, No. 4 (July, 1961), pp. 578–86.

[10] We assume (1) that both buyers and sellers possess full knowledge of the market and their various opportunities to improve their position, (2) that they will and are able to change their actions to take advantage of opportunities to improve their economic position, (3) that no single buyer or seller can affect market price by his actions, (4) that there is no collusion on the part of either buyers or sellers, (5) that units of labor are homogeneous, interchangeable, and of identical value, (6) that only one price can exist for the entire process, and (7) that the situation described is only for a short period of time so that new forces outside of the market cannot affect the current situation.

the market value of labor output (marginal productivity) beyond this level of employment would be less than the cost of securing labor, and hence they would cease hiring at this point.

We can contemplate a continuing series of marginal productivity calculations and equilibrium adjustments as changes occur in the variables that affect supply and demand for products and for labor. The demand for labor depends upon the marginal productivity of labor, which in turn depends upon (1) its efficiency, (2) the supplies of other factors with which labor can be combined, and (3) the state of production techniques. Basically, of course, the demand for labor is traceable to the product demand curve. If labor works harder and turns out more product in a given time period, this tends to increase its marginal productivity and employers are willing to bid more for workers' services. Similarly, new machinery and new techniques can make labor more efficient and hence increase the value of its marginal product. Such events tend to move the demand curve up and to the right of its former position. If labor becomes more efficient, that is, increases its marginal productivity, wage rates will rise and so will employment. It should be emphasized, however, that the marginal productivity of labor can increase also if output remains the same but the price of the product goes up. This increases the value of the marginal product, that is, increases marginal revenue product.

On the other hand, a large increase in numbers employed might lower marginal productivity because of the influence of diminishing returns. Collusion on the part of employers or a monopsonistic situation may result in labor receiving less than its marginal revenue product. *Monopsony* means one buyer; *oligopsony* means very few buyers, who can therefore affect price. Increase in labor supplies, collusion of employers, and employer monopsony tend to lower the demand curve and move it down and to the left of its former position. Monopsony tends to reduce wage rates and employment levels. It is important to realize that factors other than labor effort influence marginal productivity of labor, as just noted.

Marginal productivity in the economy. As noted earlier in this chapter, employers in any market have to decide how much labor and how much of other resources represent the most efficient combination. They do this by equating the relative marginal contributions of all of the factors of production. However, many factors, including labor, are used in more than one market, and employers must also decide which market offers the most likely place to obtain maximum rewards for the various factors. For example, marginal productivity of labor in market A is compared with marginal productivity in markets B and C. Here again factors of production are shifted until their relative marginal contributions are approximately equal in all markets. This point of equilibrium will occur when labor in each of its uses is being paid the value of its marginal product. Where labor is paid less than its marginal productivity in a market, employers in another market will tend to bid more than those workers are currently receiving. Where labor is paid more than the value of its marginal product, employers will tend to lay workers off, and hence such labor will tend to shift to alternate employments. In essence, this is the basic process of labor marketing, discussed in Chapter 5. The importance of marginal productivity in employer calculations should be apparent. Also, the crucial roles of labor market information, labor mobility, and other factors discussed in Chapter 6, should be noted again. Labor marketing processes center about equilibration, with emphasis upon maximization and substitution.

Units of labor. The whole labor marketing process is complicated by the difficulty of defining a unit of labor, already noted in Chapter 5. Although the unit most commonly used in current practice is the man-hour, that unit is obviously far from uniform. In relatively few markets this difficulty is reduced by bidding for measurable output or product.

Elasticities of demands and supplies. Careful, detailed statements of the theory must also call particular attention to the importance of varying elasticities in demands and supplies — their responsiveness to changes in price. The whole marketing process, including levels of both wages and employment, is directly conditioned by this characteristic of market schedules.[11]

Elasticities may vary considerably from one market to another and from time to time in the same markets. The demand for electric service linemen in Lester Prairie, Minnesota, for example, may be

---

[11]Elasticities are measured as the relative degree of change in quantities for which bids are made or which are offered for hire as compared with a relative change in price. For example, if a 5 percent increase in price is accompanied by a similar 5 percent increase in the amount of labor available for hire, the elasticity of supply is unitary, that is 1:1. Elasticity is pictured, in the usual graphic model of a market, by the slope of lines representing supply and demand schedules. Technically it is better to draw supply and demand curves using logarithmic scales on both price and quantity axes, because logarithmic scales show proportionate change.

quite inelastic at this particular time. Approximately the same number of linemen will be offered employment by the local power and light company at all rates within a broad wage band. Such a situation may be pictured by an almost perpendicular demand curve with only a slight trend toward the right as prices are reduced.[12]

In another market in the same locality — the market for huskers in the local sweet-corn cannery — demand may be relatively elastic. At lower wage rates the employer may be willing to hire large numbers of huskers. If the firm must pay much higher rates, it can better afford to rent or lease mechanical husking machines for the season. In such a market the demand curve shows much greater responsiveness to price changes.

Elasticities of supplies may show similar variation and have equally important effects on wages and employment in particular markets. For example, supplies of competent professors of physics are distinctly limited in all markets. Offers of higher rates of pay by particular institutions may cause transfers from one to another, but the total supply in a market that is at least nationwide is so limited that only a few additional applicants can be supplied at higher rates. The supply curve in such a market is sharply inclined, ranging over a small segment of the base line (that is, inelastic). In the corn-husker market already mentioned, however, the supply may be quite elastic. At higher wage rates many housewives may accept jobs, and men and women already working at one job may also become available in their "off" hours. Here the supply curve is more nearly horizontal and extends over a broader segment of the quantity scale (that is, elastic).

Elasticities may change sharply from time to time. In periods of expansion, for example, elasticities of demand and supplies may be quite different from those in recession or depression in the same markets. Since any change in these schedules has obvious implications for both wage rates and employment, elasticities are factors of major significance in both prediction and control. For an example of the effects of elasticities, see the section on economic effects of technological change in Chapter 3.[13]

---

[12]Demand and supply curves are assumed to last for a very short instant of time. In the case of demand, this assumption requires holding of consumers' preferences and incomes as fixed.

[13]For a more detailed discussion of factors affecting elasticities of labor demands, see Appendix B, pages 796–97.

Action

The marginal productivity theory provides many suggestions for prediction and control in labor markets. Control of long-run trends in wages and employment may be effected through control of the capital-worker ratio. The growth of either capital or the volume of labor supplies may be manipulated. To raise real wages, for example, encouragement may be given to the accumulation of capital by measures designed to raise interest rates and encourage saving or by special tax advantages given to venture capital. Labor supplies may be controlled by restricting or facilitating immigration or by limitations on child labor or opportunities for training.

In the short-run situation the amount of labor demanded and the amount supplied may be varied by manipulating wages. Perhaps the most obvious suggestion from the simple model of labor marketing points to this importance of wage rates as a control. It has been widely interpreted as emphasizing the importance of wage flexibility as an essential to stable employment. The theory has frequently been used to justify sharp wage-rate reductions as means of clearing markets in which there is serious unemployment and to argue against minimum wage legislation or fixed union scales that may prevent the unrestricted balancing of supplies and demands. In a sentence, the basic theory suggests that markets *will clear themselves* if they are not fixed by government or by monopolistic employers or unionized employees. If allowed to operate freely, they will allocate labor's services to jobs in which they are most valuable because they can contribute most.

Major actions suggested by the classical marginal productivity theory are several. First, and most important, is the crucial role of productivity in explaining allocation and use of resources and their rewards. Higher wages can come only from higher production. Second, improper allocation of resources (for example, unemployment) can be handled by price adjustments, that is, all available resources can be used if prices (in this case, wage rates) are right, and higher prices will call forth additional supplies of resources as needed. Resources will shift in response to price changes. Third, the market system is largely self-regulatory. It can get out of balance if monopolists and others use collusion, politics, and brute strength to cause interferences with self-regulating market forces. Hence, the government should not interfere with markets except to prevent abuses of market power. The government can set rules of the game that make market participation fair and equal but leave the basic market forces undisturbed so that they can be self-correcting. Although classical marginal analysis permits solutions of general equilibrium (for an entire economy), more emphasis is placed upon partial equilibriums (for parts of the economy). There is little concern with aggregative or macro economic problems and major concern with micro aspects.

CRITICISMS AND AMENDMENTS

For most of the sixty years in which the marginal productivity theory has been widely known, economists have tried to explain that it describes a basic tendency in economic market behavior rather than the overt, observable actions that frequently appear in labor markets. This distinction is highly important. The theory describes a hypothetical model. What actually happens is rarely, if ever, as simple as the model suggests. Nevertheless, the underlying tendency to balance demands and supplies is present, and knowledge of the tendency helps one to understand market behavior.

Numerous assumptions are essential in the statement of any simple, generalized rule of human behavior. We could not, for example, state the general principle that people will come inside to get out of the rain without recognizing that we are making many assumptions. We must assume that a shelter is available and that they can come in and are not required by their work or other circumstances to stay out. We also assume that they do not want to get wet.

The conceptual statement of the simple marginal productivity theory necessarily involves similar assumptions, and these limit the operational usefulness of the theory. Thus, for example, the theory is concerned with real wages and assumes constant aggregate real demands for goods and services.[14] Further, the assumptions of pure competition, perfect markets, and the static state provide a highly abstract model removed from the realities of this changing and dynamic world. However, the theory, with its assumptions, provides a preliminary analytical step toward insight and understanding. That understanding can be extended by further analyses designed to discover the added effects of conditions that do not fit these simpler assumptions.

The limitations of general theories about the way people behave is widely misunderstood. Those who do not understand are likely to

---

[14]In effect, Say's law of markets is assumed to hold, and hence there is no real problem in connection with an adequate demand for goods and services. Say's law holds that there cannot be overproduction since every item produced can be exchanged for some other item, given completely flexible wages and prices.

be impatient with and critical of the generalization or theory. Such misunderstandings and criticisms of the marginal productivity theory have been common. The meaning of the theory and its usefulness, however limited, may be clarified by giving some attention to the most frequent criticisms.

Criticisms of the Theory

Perhaps the most common criticism asks why the theory is not demonstrated in each specific market. For example, can the theory provide a complete explanation of current wages of bricklayers in Nisswa, Minnesota, and if not, why not? The answer to the first question is negative, so far as the simple model is concerned. That model explains the tendency toward a market price in a competitive market, making several assumptions that are not realistic for this particular market. It assumes full market knowledge by buyers and sellers and competition among them. It assumes the mobility of labor as well as other factors. The market in Nisswa is not such a market. Only one contractor employes bricklayers. The bricklayers are members of a union. They have agreed not to cut prices. Realistically, also, there are only three bricklayers in Nisswa, and each lives with his own or his wife's parents. They will not move under any ordinary circumstances.

Other criticisms question the ability of employers to appraise the productivity of additional increments, the assumption that workers know how to value their services, and the usefulness of a model or theory that makes unrealistic assumptions and cannot be demonstrated. Here again, the answer is that the theory describes general tendencies, recognizing that there are many exceptions to each of them. Some employers may be unable to place accurate values on added increments. However, some such process is clearly evident in their bids for workers. Some employees may not actually set an offering price on their services. Here again, however, it is clear that most employees follow some such practice, since some of them accept employment while others reject employment at whatever rates are established.[15]

---

[15]Critics of the marginal productivity theory (MPT) of wages have attacked the reality of both its assumptions and conclusions. Among the assumptions attacked are:
1. The assumed dominance of profit maximization in business firms.
2. Businessmen's knowledge of marginal net production curves.
3. The existence of a free competitive economy.
4. Perfect mobility of labor.
5. Full employment of labor and capital.

The model is a useful tool in spite of its limitations. Even if the productive factors are not fully mobile, if perfect market knowledge is never achieved, and if both employees and employers make only crude guesses about the value and the contribution of labor, the model helps to understand the pricing of labor and its hiring. With continued study the effects of these and many other limitations can be discovered and appraised.

In short, the model gives a clue to basic trends in the processes of resource pricing and allocation. It describes an underlying tendency in market pricing. Even though unrealistic, such a model can provide insight into underlying factors and relationships. If the conditions that distinguish the model from the actual can be noted, analyzed, and evaluated, more complex but more realistic models can be developed.

Amendments to the Theory

A modification in the simple model is well illustrated by what may be called the *marginal value-revenue amendment*. Perhaps the most serious shortcomings of the simple model arise out of its assumptions of free competition. To reconcile the theory with the frequent monopolies of buyers and sellers in individual labor markets, economists have developed several amendments to the marginal productivity analysis. For example, recognition of the reality of monopsony — a single buyer — and of monopolistic offers of labor's services in many labor markets has encouraged analysis in terms of monopolistic competition.

The major difference in a model revised to take account of monopsony is evident in changes in demands. A single buyer is

---

6. Equality of bargaining power.
The following are some of the major arguments against the conclusions of the MPT:
1. The determining role of the marginal product overemphasizes demand and underemphasizes supply factor schedules.
2. Economic facts do not support the alleged relationship between wage rates and volume of employment.
Those theorists who defend the MPT argue that:
1. The theory may have weakness in the short run and for individual firms, but it is valid for the long run and the economy as a whole.
2. A theory should not be tested by the real-world validity of its assumptions or its conclusions.
As a result of such arguments there is a belief among American economists that we urgently need a new wage theory. (See for example, Julius Rezler, "Current Issues of Labour Economics in The United States of America," *International Social Science Journal*, Vol. XIII, No. 1 (1961), pp. 1–20.) For a critique of traditional marginal productivity theory and labor market concepts, with insistence upon needs for more emphasis upon real-life, empirical findings in formulating wage theories, see Richard A. Lester, *Economics of Labor* (2nd ed.; New York: The Macmillan Co., 1964), pp. 255–89.

assumed to create the entire schedule of demand. If this buyer is not only a monopsonist in this market but also a monopolist in the product market (for example, the sole producer of a patented product), he may set quite different values on the increments of labor from those of a competing buyer. The latter may be assumed to have little concern about the effects of increased output on product price. He sees the price of products as determined in a product market that is beyond his control. The monopolist, however, must regard the possibility of declines in his product price as his output increases. He must consider the marginal *value* or marginal *revenue* product produced by each added increment of labor, rather than an addition of physical product with fixed unit values. As a result, his estimates of value added by various increments may be lower than those of the competitive bidder for these services. His demand schedule may look different from that pictured in Figure 21-1, indicating the reduced value he places on larger quantities of labor. As a result, both the market price and the volume of employment may be affected by this absence of competition. Additional discussion and examples of marginal revenue product and marginal outlay situations will be found in Appendix B.

A whole series of revised models may be developed to illustrate variations in the basic pricing process occasioned by the absence of free competition.[16] For example, monopoly in labor supplies requires such modifications. If a market is dominated by a union, all the services of employees may become available at a single price. All increments described in the simple model pictured in Figure 21-2 may be priced at $3.50, for example. In such a situation this fixed price becomes the dominating factor, and employment becomes the dependent variable. This revised model receives further attention in the discussion of bargaining theory in the next chapter.

In some labor markets supplies may decline with higher price tags on labor. If the husband can make $3 an hour for his unskilled work, his wife and her brother may both remain out of the labor supply in the same market.[17] If the best the husband can get is $1.50

---

[16]For an excellent discussion of the modifications introduced by monopoly, monopsony, and oligopsony, see Mary Jean Bowman and George Leland Bach, *Economic Analysis and Public Policy* (2nd ed.; New York: Prentice-Hall, Inc., 1949), pp. 464–80 and 506–21.

[17]Such changes create a negatively inclined, backward-sloping supply curve that may tend to parallel the demand curve. If the curves do not intersect, no simple marketing determination of wages or employment is possible. Such a situation has appeared in some single-industry communities. Even if the curves intersect, equilibrium is likely to be unstable. Intersection at low levels encourages continually falling wage rates as added supplies of workers seek jobs they now find necessary. Intersection at high rates is likely to leave a large number of unfilled jobs.

an hour, his wife, her brother, and their two high school children may try to get similar unskilled work. As has been evident in numerous local labor markets in recent years, labor supplies may be expanded if moonlighters — employees who hold two or more jobs — regard earnings on one job as inadequate.

Two occurrences in the 1930's helped climax a series of developments which pushed wage theory closer to reality. One was the persistent and serious unemployment problem of the 1930's. The other was the emergence of a strong labor movement and widespread free collective bargaining in the United States in the same decade.

These "operational" developments (in the sense that this term is used in Chapter 4) were paralleled by "conceptual" developments, including Keynes's *General Theory of Employment* (discussed in more detail in the next chapter) and the writings of the economists (e.g., Chamberlain at Harvard) on monopolistic competition. These developments led to the so-called *national income* (or *full employment*) *theory* and the *bargaining theories* of wages discussed in the next chapter. Both have roots in classical marginal productivity theory; neither fully rejects it. Instead, both of these theories may be viewed as amendments to the more severely abstract marginal productivity theory — amendments that bring the original model closer to the real world.

ANALYTICAL REVIEW QUESTIONS

1. Why is skepticism about wage theories desirable?
2. Briefly describe the setting of the marginal productivity theory.
3. What two major questions does the marginal productivity theory seek to answer?
4. Why is the marginal productivity theory essentially an employment theory for the firm?
5. What two variables interact to determine long-term advances in the price of labor?
6. Are capital and labor complementary? Supplementary? Both complementary and supplementary?
7. Under the marginal productivity theory, why does an employer hire labor? What determines how much labor he will hire?
8. What do employers compare in making their decisions concerning production?
9. How is marginal outlay different from marginal revenue product?
10. What is meant by the term "diminishing returns"?
11. How is an employer's marginal revenue product related to his demand curve for labor?

12. What determines the supply price of labor to a competitive employer? What is the shape of this curve?
13. Why does an employer not always use a work team that maximizes his marginal revenue product?
14. Why is a market demand curve down-sloping?
15. What two values are determined by the intersection of supply and demand curves in a competitive labor market? Why does this intersection lead to equilibrium?
16. What assumptions are made about variability of output of individual employees in the marginal productivity theory?
17. What happens to the labor supply curve when the supply of labor is increased?
18. What happens to the demand curve when the demand for labor is decreased?
19. Differentiate the income effect from the substitution effect in the backward-sloping supply curve.
20. Can marginal revenue product increase without an increase in physical productivity? Why or why not?
21. How is elasticity defined?
22. Is a sharply inclined supply curve elastic or inelastic? Is a nearly horizontal supply curve elastic?
23. How do product demand elasticities affect labor demand elasticities?
24. Are unions more effective in altering labor demand or labor supply schedules? Why?
25. What action is suggested by the marginal productivity theory? What should be the role of government according to this theory?
26. What are some of the major arguments against the conclusions of the marginal productivity theory?
27. What is the marginal value-revenue amendment to the marginal productivity theory? Why is it important?
28. Under what conditions might one find a negatively inclined (downward-sloping) supply curve of labor?
29. Is the marginal productivity theory concerned with money wages? Real wages? Both?

FULL EMPLOYMENT AND BARGAINING WAGE THEORIES

FULL EMPLOYMENT WAGE THEORY

While each wage theory previously discussed focuses attention on wage-determining variables, each implicitly involves something of a corollary theory of employment. In contrast, the full employment or national income theory of wages begins with concern about factors affecting levels of employment throughout the entire economy. Its primary questions concern aggregate wage-employment relationships. Answers to these questions involve an explanation of wages, for wages appear inseparably related to levels of employment. In Chapter 15 we discussed many of the major variables and relationships in employment; these will be given only summary discussion below.

Setting

The full employment theory first achieved wide acceptance in the years following the worldwide depression of the 1930's. It is essentially a business cycle theory of employment and wages and could also be described as a theory of business cycles. It was advanced during and following the most devastating depression of this century.

In the 1930 depression popular concern in democratic nations centered on unemployment. Citizens were critical of political inaction that waited for readjustments in prices, including wages, to reverse the cycle and stimulate renewed economic activity. Workers were unwilling to contemplate further wage cuts when their earnings were already sliced by unemployment and part-time work. Popular demands called for governmental intervention in international trade as well as in many domestic markets.

The worldwide impact of the depression encouraged both a national and an international viewpoint in appraising its problems. They were clearly not attributable simply to local market frictions. Attention was attracted to the importance of fiscal, monetary, and banking policies and programs of central governments. In efforts to discover the roots of cyclical fluctuations, questions were raised about the whole process of economic growth and development.

Numerous theories were advanced to answer these questions. In this country a *theory of economic stagnation* received wide attention and acceptance. It suggested that invention and the discovery and the development of new resources introduced irregular "shots in the arm" in industrial economies. They occasioned periods of rapid expansion. In the intervals between these impacts, business opportunities were restricted, savings tended to accumulate as investments were reduced, and economic stagnation appeared. This stagnation was the cause of recessions, which tended to set off spirals of depression. The process was so complex and inclusive that individual firms could do little or nothing to stem the tide. Such a viewpoint focused attention on the national economy and the world wide economy rather than on individual firms and markets.

Focus

An explanation of wages and wage changes in such a setting inevitably directed attention to general wage levels rather than to wage rates in local labor markets. Explanations sought to relate levels of aggregate wages in a whole national economy and changes in these levels to other aggregative variables.

The explanations developed in this period are a part of the national income theory of employment. Keynes is the recognized spokesman for those who advanced this full-employment viewpoint. His *General Theory of Employment* (1936) provides the basic analysis on which the theory is based. Keynes directed his attention to the question: What factors or conditions explain the levels on which all types of resources are employed? His objective, as indicated by the title of his book, was the exposition of a *general* theory of employment to replace what he regarded as earlier *special* theories applicable only to the employment of individual factors or periods of economic expansion or to limited markets characterized by competition, monopoly, or modified competition. The question of wages thus becomes an inquiry as to the part they play in affecting the employment of people and other resources and, more specifically, the factors in this aggregative employment process that affect wages.

Factors

The resulting wage theory is in part a theory of manipulated allocations of income to labor and in part a psychological theory as that term is popularly used. Aggregate wages are regarded as directly affected by central government policy and practice with respect to public services provided for workers and paid for from public funds. They are also influenced by public benefit programs that distribute unemployment, old-age, and other such grants to workers and their dependents. The theory is mainly concerned with insufficient aggregate demand for labor; it has little concern for structural transformations and distortions.

As a psychological theory, major determinants of aggregate wages are the *anticipations* of consumers and business leaders. These anticipations are conditioned by their attitudes and morale — the optimism or pessimism, the assurance or insecurity, with which they view the future. Anticipations create *propensities* to consume, to save, to invest, to expand or contract, to venture, or to "pass." These propensities provide the clue to what happens in all markets and thus to the pricing as well as to employment or unemployment of resources.

Several economic factors are interrelated with these psychological considerations in influencing long-run levels of wages. They include the productivity of labor and the general price level. Productivity is directly affected by the capital-worker ratio, improvements in techniques and equipment, and hence the propensity to invest. Changes in the general price level affect aggregate wages both by their tendency to increase or decrease the real wage — the purchasing power of money wages — and by their influence on propensities to buy, save, invest, and expand. Because of this relationship, Keynes notes that public policy may choose between the alternatives of a fixed price level and higher wages or a falling price level and stable wages.[1] Other alternative choices are also possible, of course. Workers and the public could seek to equate wage increases with labor productivity increases and thus to maintain a stable price level, for example. Generally speaking, however, unionized workers in framing their demands seek the highest wage rate they can negotiate and are not limited by actual labor productivity increases. Such demands tend to be inflationary, that is, to raise prices. If prices rise as much as wages are increased, there is no gain in real wages. These and other alternative policy considerations are discussed more fully later in this chapter under the heading "Collective Bargaining, Inflation, and Employment."

Labor markets are not self-correcting. National income theorists argue that the national or aggregate of labor markets is not self-correcting for at least two major reasons: (1) the forces causing and maintaining full employment lie largely outside of labor markets and (2) the self-correcting mechanism (equating of value of marginal product of all factors of production under laissez-faire conditions) has not proved effective — free markets do not seem to reach an equilibrium position at the point of full employment. Instead, they may equilibrate at a position of less than full employment and stay that way, unless forces outside the labor market come into play; hence, they are not self-regulating. National income theorists argue that full employment is a function of national income. Few, if any, economists would contend that the basic roots of national income lie in labor markets. Full employment, therefore, is the resultant of forces largely outside of the labor market.

The classical and neoclassical economists placed emphasis upon obtaining a maximum output of goods and services desired by consumers through proper (marginal) balancing of resources. National income economists, on the other hand, place primary emphasis upon attaining and maintaining full employment, with relatively little emphasis upon the maximization of productivity of labor through optimal allocation and utilization. Hence, it might be said that there is a difference in emphasis between the classicals and the national income theorists, with the former emphasizing productivity and the latter emphasizing jobs for all.

---

[1]J. M. Keynes, *The General Theory of Employment*, pp. 270–71. For a more recent explanation of the Keynesian analysis, see Barbara Wooton, *The Social Foundation of Wage Policy* (London: George Allen and Unwin, Ltd., 1956).

Labor supply is a function of money wages.[2] The classical marginal productivity theory was based upon real, not money scales. Money was regarded as a "neutral" factor, and demand was assumed to be constant. To the Keynesians, money is not "neutral," and demand does vary. Further, the Keynesians assumed that workers preferred to "think" or make their decisions in money wage terms. They assume, with some good evidence to support them, that labor supplies are a function of money wages rather than real wages. Further, they assume that money wages are apt to be "sticky" or rigid, i.e., workers will strongly resist cuts in money wage rates — indeed, that they will prefer unemployment to cuts in money wage rates, i.e., their "hard won labor standards."[3]

A proposed solution to unemployment by cutting wage rates, and hence bringing labor supply and demand into balance or equilibrium, would result in a new equilibrium *at less than full employment.* This follows from assumptions which the Keynesians made about the shape of the labor supply curve. Because of worker preferences for money wages, with resultant stickiness of money wage rates, and because of unions which enabled workers to resist wage cuts, the lower end of the supply curve of labor should be depicted as approximately parallel to the base (almost perfectly elastic). The classical supply curve was more inelastic and intersected the demand curve to the right of the Keynesian supply curve. Hence the intersection of the Keynesian supply curve with a lower demand curve (e.g., during a depression)

---

[2]For an excellent, penetrating analysis, see Allan M. Cartter, *Theory of Wages and Employment* (Homewood, Ill.: Richard D. Irwin, Inc., 1959), pp. 136–41.

[3]The concept of wage rigidity has been attacked by Clarence D. Long. He notes that various reasons are advanced for absence of contractions including union resistance; minimum wages; insistence of unorganized workers on maintaining their living standards; reluctance of employers to invite public disapproval, to provoke union organizing efforts, or to risk loss of key employees; and bureaucratic wage policies of big firms and big unions.

As noted later in this chapter, some economists hold that unions are responsible for initiating and aggravating inflation; others hold that wage increases lag price increases, and that, if anything, unions and collective bargaining have lengthened the lag.

Long offers evidence to show that wages in the United States were far from rigid in the period 1860–1958 and that the steep trend of wages has concealed wide fluctuations rather closely associated with the business cycle. It should be noted that Long is talking about hourly earnings, not hourly wage rates. Real wages have not been as sensitive, with their fluctuations having an amplitude of one third that for money wages.

The sensitivity of wages to economic downturns stems from the effect unemployment has in dampening union bargaining power, a reduction in overtime premiums when business and employment fall off, and employee downgrading (e.g., shifts from durable goods to service occupations).

Long concludes by noting that money wages have not tended to lead productivity, employment, or wholesale prices in expansion. Instead, they have tended to lag. Wages have also tended to lag rather than lead prices in expansions of long cycles. See Clarence D. Long, "The Illusion of Wage Rigidity: Long and Short Cycles in Wages and Labor," *Review of Economics and Statistics,* Vol. XLII, No. 2, Part 1 (May, 1960), pp. 140–51.

occurred to the left of the older classical supply curve, i.e., *at a lesser volume of employment.*

Under these circumstances consumption was curtailed with the proposed solution being to increase aggregate demand — not to modify the supply curve (by wage cuts, for example).

The differences between the classical and Keynesian labor supply curves may be observed in Figure 22-1, a formulation from Allan Cartter.[4] The classical supply curve is ABC; the Keynesian curve is ABE. In the classical theory supply and demand intersect at B, with employment at N, and a wage rate of W. When the demand for labor declines (e.g., to D'D'), under the classical theory, supply and demand intersect at g, with employment at N' and wage rate at W'.

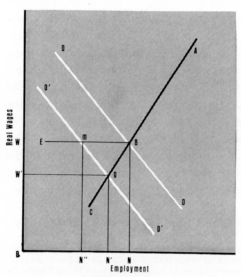

Figure 22-1

THE CLASSICAL AND KEYNESIAN LABOR SUPPLY CURVES

Source: Reproduced by permission from Allan M. Cartter, *Theory of Wages and Employment* (Homewood, Ill.: Richard D. Irwin, Inc., 1959), p. 140.

But the Keynesian supply curve is ABE, reflecting labor resistance to wage cuts. Hence under the Keynesian formulation, when demand is reduced (D' — D'), supply and demand would intersect at m, with employment at N″, and a wage rate at W. The amount of unemployment would be NN″, and this is described as *involuntary unemployment.* A new short-run labor market equilibrium with substantial unemployment may be said to exist at point N″. Here the point that Keynes sought to stress was the proposition that unemployment could not be cured by wage rate reductions.[5]

Employment falls when national income declines. To the national income economists, underspending is the major cause of less than full

---

[4]Cartter, *op. cit.*, p. 140, reproduced by permission of Richard D. Irwin, Inc.

[5]*Ibid.*, p. 143. The supply curve ABE in Figure 22-1 is a fairly good approximation of the labor supply curve in a labor market with a powerful union.

employment. In brief, the national income, full employment process consists of deciding (1) how many people need jobs and (2) what level of national income is necessary to provide this many jobs. To eliminate unemployment, national income is increased until everybody who wants a job has a job.

National income equals the total of consumption plus private and public investment. Consumption expenditures seem to vary much less than investment. Most wage and salary earners can save little and, therefore, have little money, if any, to invest. Higher-income earners usually save and invest more than do those with lower incomes. Since there are so many more low-income than high-income people, the average propensity to consume (the percent of income spent) is relatively stable.

The propensity to invest seems much more variable. The propensity to private investment is dependent upon the marginal efficiency of capital, that is, the expectations of profits to be made from additional investment.[6] These expectations may and do vary from time to time. They may be high as a result of inventions, wars, new natural resource discoveries, or pent-up consumer demand following wartime rationing. Expectations may be low following a period of heavy sustained investment, with entrepreneurs feeling that the early investors have taken the cream off future profit possibilities and that available investment opportunities leave them only "skim milk." In such circumstances they may not invest, awaiting more profitable opportunities.

Now recall that national income equals consumption plus investment. If investment declines and consumption remains fairly constant, then national income declines. And, the theory goes on, when national income declines, employment falls and unemployment increases.

Even in prosperity, as well as in depression, the roots of unemployment are ever-present. Good times are those when general income is high. More people have higher incomes and tend to save more; hence, relative consumption tends to decline.

But consumption is only part of national income. If investment takes up the slack in consumption, then national income will not decline. With savings increased, will not investment increase by the amount of increased savings?

---

[6]Few entrepreneurs would be naive enough to believe that past earnings alone would provide a sufficient guide to determine such marginal efficiency.

National income theorists argue that it might not and probably will not. Remember that in many cases savings are made by one group of people (wage and salary earners and property owners) and investments by another group (entrepreneurs). Even though the supply of savings increases, investment might not increase as much because of a lowered marginal efficiency of capital — that is, investors might have expectations that they could not invest the added savings profitably. Thus, private investment would decline, and national income (and employment) would decline.

What could be done to correct this? One solution would be to try to induce consumers to spend more and save less, that is, to increase consumption. (The 1964 income tax cut in the United States was an attempt in this direction.) But consumers have minds of their own. They might not want to buy more and save less, even though interest rates on their savings were lowered. A second solution might be to induce more private investment, for example through lower taxes on business or through accelerated depreciation — anything to increase the anticipation of profits and hence additional investment. That, too, might be inadequate to maintain national income.

A third solution remains. There are two major types of investment, private and public. A decline in private investment can be offset by an expansion of public spending — for anything from leaf raking to new roads and interplanetary exploration.

The essence of national income theory thus is apparent. Through economic planning, with appropriate governmental action and control over spending, it is possible to maintain a level of national income sufficient to provide full employment.

Government stabilization of national income and employment. In times of war, acts of God, and other major noneconomic events, usual market processes are modified. The government can act to avoid inflation during wartime through direct wage and price controls, rationing, increased taxes, and compulsory savings plans. It can channel production through loans, purchases, priorities, allocation of resources, and similar measures.

Fortunately we do not live in a world of continual wars and other holocausts. Most of us are most concerned with peacetime economies. But even peacetime economies in modern capitalist nations are not stable. We have business fluctuations ranging from prosperity to depression and in between. Both inflationary and deflationary effects are likely to be cumulative — people feel more like spending (consuming and investing) when times are good, and they tend to grow more and more hesitant about spending when times are rough. National income theorists point out that the government can do much to reduce cyclical swings, that is, to stabilize national income and thus employment. Three major approaches include monetary policies, fiscal policies, and direct controls.

Monetary policies. Monetary policies seek to control supplies of money and credit. They may manipulate interest rates through open-market operations expanding and contracting bank reserves, thus tightening or loosening credit. If credit is easy to get, investment is encouraged. When credit is hard to get, investment is discouraged. Experience seems to indicate that monetary policies are rather limited in their real-life effects; that is, lowering of interest rates by itself produces an expansion, but only a slight expansion, in investment. Other factors seem to have more effect upon investment and employment, especially during severe depressions. Monetary policies are useful in keeping an adequate money supply in times of prosperity and may facilitate other government policies.

Fiscal policies. Fiscal policies have received increasing attention as a stabilizing device in recent years. Fiscal policy is the adjustment in levels and forms of governmental income and expenditures, usually with the intention of thereby adjusting levels of national income. Fiscal policy is more direct than monetary policy in its effects upon government income and expenditures. Taxes play a major role both in inflation and deflation. Taxes can reduce or alter consumer spending and investment, thereby changing the national income. Government expenditures increase total consumption and investment, hence increasing national income (and employment). Government expenditures are likely to raise national income by more than the amount of the actual government expenditure because of the multiplier effect in which they stimulate added private investment and consumption.

Direct controls. Direct controls are surer means of affecting national income levels and structures, but they reduce personal economic freedom. The government (as in wartime) may control prices, wages, investment, production, and consumption. Allocation and rationing are generally required; wage and salary controls are used, as are price controls. Use of partial controls, rather than full controls, may seriously interfere with the remaining portions of the free-enterprise price system.

Action

Keynes described the national income theory in terms of alternative actions. His statement does not consider inaction and a freely competitive price for labor as acceptable in modern industrial societies. The question therefore becomes one of what sort of controls over wages should be exerted in order to meet the basic goal of full employment. In the short run, in his opinion, and with exceptions for declining industries and necessary transfers to other employment, societies should seek to maintain stable money wage levels. In the long run, money wages should be increased slowly, while the price level is controlled to insure stability. Such controlled wages appear essential to insure full employment. Short-run controls maintaining the stability of wages will maintain business, individual confidence, and the propensity to consume. In neither short nor long run should money wages be reduced, since such reductions would reduce the propensity to consume, create expectations of business recession, encourage disputes and work stoppages, increase the burden of debts and taxation, and occasion price instability.

The most obvious action implications are those prescribing public planning and policy with respect to price and wage levels as a condition essential to full employment. Wages as a whole cannot be permitted to adjust themselves, freely rising or falling with changing demands or supplies or shifts in the bargaining power of the parties. Some exponents have suggested development of a national wage policy to be accepted by unions and employers as a basic guide in their wage negotiations. (See the discussion of "Wage Guideposts" in Chapter 19.)

The theory's action implications for wages are inextricably interwoven with public programs designed to maintain full employment. The full-employment program proposes that the fiscal and monetary policies of central governments be planned and adapted to maintain national income, savings, investment, and consumption at appropriate levels. Rationing and rigorous control of all prices may be necessary as emergency measures to restrain inflationary tendencies.

Not everybody is delighted with the prospect of additional spending, for such spending can be inflationary unless accompanied by a corresponding increase in the supply of goods and services. While this danger is generally recognized by economists, it is contended that such stimulation need not be inflationary at a time when the nation has idle economic resources, including plant and equipment operating below full capacity. However, in addition to the inflationary potential posed by national income, full employment wage policies, there is another, concurrent development that could be inflationary — namely, the wage pushes of unions and collective bargaining. This latter set of variables is the subject matter of the so-called collective bargaining wage theory, to be discussed in the next part of this chapter.

Shortcomings of National Income Analysis

The national income theory is macro, or aggregative in focus. It deals with *general* productivity, *general* wage increases, *general* price increases. This is in keeping with the current state of the national income theory, which has developed few concepts concerning employment, cost, price, and wage structures and differentials for firms, local and regional markets, and industries.[7] Further, the national income theory is essentially short-run. It places heavy emphasis upon demand aspects and offers little explanation about supplies of factors other than money — for example, the theory basically treats labor supplies as fixed. The national income theory can operate in money terms or real terms, but it lacks an adequate means of relating these two systems,[8] yet this is essentially the heart of the wage problem.

Public policy suggested by the theory and the emphasis on full employment and controlled wages requires a sharp break from traditional viewpoints. Some critics have charged that the Keynesian analysis is merely a rationale for economic revolution. Without such name-calling, it is apparent that this analysis suggests more public intervention and regulation than appeared appropriate from earlier theories. To maintain full employment in all markets at stable or rising wage rates could lead directly to controls on consumption. Regulation of wage levels could readily lead to restrictions on union demands and on negotiated increases. The implication of a balanced wage structure, meaning the preservation of existing differentials, involves some conflicts with the framework of progress and improvement in employment, wages, and living scales.[9]

---

[7]See Melvin W. Reder, "Wage Determination in Theory and Practice," in the IRRA Volume edited by Neil W. Chamberlain *et al.*, *A Decade of Industrial Relations Research: 1946–1956* (New York: Harper and Brothers, 1958), pp. 64–97. This is an excellent summary of many research papers over a decade.

[8]On all these points see Frank C. Pierson's excellent discussion in George W. Taylor and Frank C. Pierson, *New Concepts in Wage Determination* (New York: McGraw-Hill Book Co., Inc., 1958), p. 29.

[9]See Alvin H. Hansen, *Economic Policy and Full Employment* (New York: McGraw-Hill Book Co., Inc., 1947), pp. 157–58. See also Sidney Weintraub, *Some Aspects of Wage*

The Keynesian opinion that money wages should be controlled to promise and insure continued increases involves inflationary possibilities, but probably no more than our accepted objective of improved living scales for workers. Some economists who accept the theory would avoid objectionable inflation by direct control of price levels. A reasonable question, in this process of building one economic control over another, concerns our ability to plan and execute such comprehensive management and the possibly catastrophic consequences of small errors or mismanagement. Whether these dangers are greater in a managed economy than in one that reflects the independent decisions of business and labor leaders is a fair question. An even more interesting question, however, is whether we can gain the major advantages of some controls and still retain some of the most important values of freedom.[10]

PURCHASING POWER THEORY OF WAGES

Julius Rezler identifies a *purchasing power theory of wages* held by union economists and some manufacturers. In brief, it holds that total wages should be sufficient to enable recipients to consume all goods and services produced. Otherwise lesser consumption would curtail production and cause unemployment.[11] This theory, widely held but not fully developed, has as antecedents the underconsumption theory of the business cycle, the Keynesian theory, and wage concepts of American trade unionists.[12]

The AFL-CIO has ardently advocated a purchasing power theory of full employment. Spokesmen contend that the federal government has full responsibility for full employment and that if spending is not sufficient in other sectors of the economy, the federal government should "go against the tide" and increase spending. Unbalanced budgets should not be avoided when unemployment is high and are not inflationary in a time when we have idle resources.[13]

Theory and Policy (Philadelphia: Chilton Books, 1963); Edmund S. Phelps (ed.), *Private Wants and Public Needs* (New York: W. W. Norton and Co., Inc., 1962).

[10]Students who can enjoy a highly technical analysis of macro theory should see Sidney Weintraub, "A Macro-economic Approach to the Theory of Wages," *American Economic Review*, Vol. 46, No. 5 (December, 1956), pp. 835–56.

[11]Julius Rezler, "Current Issues of Labour Economics in the United States of America," *International Social Science Journal*, Vol. XIII, No. 1 (1961), p. 10.

[12]See *Poverty and Deprivation in the United States*, Conference on Economic Progress, 1001 Connecticut Ave. N.W., Washington 6, D.C., 1963, for a "liberal" union and farmer expression of a purchasing power argument based on deficit public spending and a call for income redistribution.

[13]See, *What Everyone Should Know About Government Spending and Full Employment*, Industrial Union Department, AFL-CIO, 815 16th St. N.W., Washington 6, D.C.

The purchasing power argument has the advantage of simplicity — indeed, it is too simple. Note that wages are not synonymous with income. If wages increase at the expense of other segments of income, there will not be an increase in total income. Even if total income increases, it does not follow that purchasing power will automatically increase. Not all wage earners are in low-income brackets and thus have to "spend it as fast as they get it." Propensities to save, invest, consume — productivity and prices — are all related to purchasing power. Employment levels are also important. Thus, for example, raising wage rates will not increase purchasing power unless employment remains constant or expands. Pumping more money into the economy will not raise purchasing power per se. Inflation can actually decrease purchasing power in real terms, i.e., amount of goods and services obtained. To argue that inflation is impossible or unlikely when there is substantial unemployment is to ignore the facts of life. Unemployment in the United States averaged about 5 percent in the decade of the 1950's. The Consumer's Price Index increased about 20 percent during that same time period.

COLLECTIVE BARGAINING WAGE THEORY

In the previous chapter, concerned largely with simple abstract models of the marginal productivity theory, brief reference was made to modifications, such as the marginal revenue amendments, that would bring the theory closer to reality.

Many writers on monopolistic competition, while not concerned wholly or even mostly with labor problems, noted that workers did not have to compete with each other in a world of strong unions. They could alter the shape of the supply curve they offered. They could and did withhold labor supplies in a monopolistic rather than competitive manner. The bargaining theorists, like the Keynesians, seek to modify the classical marginal productivity theory to fit reality more closely, as they see it. And as with the Keynesians, empirical evidence seemed to support their description of the real life world. In unionized labor markets one does not find an infinite variety of wage rates, or the conventional upward-sloping supply curve of the classical competitive marginal productivity theory. The existence of a "union scale" does not correspond with the competitive assumptions.

Setting

The setting for both the Keynesian theory and the bargaining theory was the depression of the 1930's. We need not detail that setting here, because this has been discussed in Chapters 7 and 8, and in Part III of the present volume. It will be sufficient to recall that public policy encouraged growth and activities of unions and collective bargaining and that unions grew in power and strength — they could make their demands effective, and did.

Focus

The focus of the bargaining theory may be stated simply: Can unions, through collective bargaining, raise wages for union members above those that would prevail in unorganized competitive markets? Or, stated in other terms, can unions raise wages for their members above those of nonunion members? What impacts do unions have upon wage levels and differentials? And what impact do unions have upon employment levels?

Factors

The bargaining theory of wages, in essence and without qualifications, holds that wage rates in each market are fixed by the comparative economic strength of the bargainers. Strength in this sense means the ability to withhold supplies and to refuse employment. (It should be noted that both unions and employers may and do utilize noncompetitive strategies, powers, and programs, as discussed in operational and descriptive terms in Chapter 9.)

This theory does not discard marginal productivity assumptions, but it places emphasis upon marginal cost and marginal revenue amendments, representing varying degrees of monopoly and monopsony in labor markets. (See Figure B-9 in Appendix B.) The theory suggests that the price of labor is largely determined by the relative ability of employers and employees to get along without each other. Advocates and proponents of the bargaining theory regard it as a powerful argument for unions.

The marginal productivity theory has provided a background for those who view economic strength as a major factor. By definition, such strength exerts a direct effect on marketing. If unions can facilitate the withholding of labor, they can thus create an upward pressure on wage rates. The bargaining theory can be regarded as an amendment to, rather than a contradiction of, the marginal productivity theory.

On the other hand, collective bargaining appeared as the introduction of monopoly and therefore as improper to those who thought the simple marginal analysis described natural laws of what should happen rather than what happens. Their reaction was further confused, if somewhat modified, by some advocates of unions who argued that unions would achieve higher wages by increasing worker productivity. Ignoring the concept of marginality, they argued that unions could thus actually justify and insure higher wages. Unions can and do raise productivity, they insisted, by screening admissions to their ranks, requiring competence of their members, and providing special training in apprenticeships. They select members who are productive, thus increasing the average output of workers. They aid members to improve themselves. If productivity determines wages, unions could justify increases. On this basis spokesmen for the American Federation of Labor frequently indicated their acceptance of the productivity theory of wages. The substitution of average productivity for marginal productivity in such an analysis is frequently ignored.

Wage levels result from the comparative strength of the bargainers in labor markets, according to the bargaining theory. If labor supplies are represented by individual employees, wages are likely to be low because such workers have little bargaining strength as compared with that of an employer. On the other hand, if all employees are organized, they may have greater bargaining strength than any single employer. High wages are to be expected in this situation. Employers also can bargain as single monopsonists or as a group. This is the simple, popular statement of the theory.

Economists have generally expressed some reservations about any such simplified statement. Rather, the bargaining theory is regarded as an appropriate adaptation of the marginal productivity analysis. It may be compared, in this respect, to the marginal revenue amendment required by employer domination in a monopsonistic situation. The bargaining theory can be regarded as a part of the marginal analysis if supply and demand curves in labor markets are regarded as bands having some width, instead of lines, as shown in Figure 22-2. This assumes that both employers and employees create their schedules with a range of discretion and flexibility. Intersections

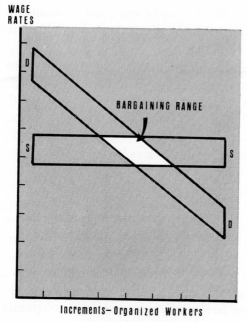

WAGE RATES

BARGAINING RANGE

Increments—Organized Workers

Figure 22-2
SIMPLE BARGAINING MODEL

then represent a range of wage rates. Employers have in mind a range of rates within which they will hire various numbers of increments. Employees have in mind somewhat similar ranges. Bargaining power exerts its major influence within the range thus defined.

Stated as an amendment to the marginal productivity analysis, the bargaining theory appears consistent with experience in periods of high-level business activity, although analysis is necessarily complicated. How well the theory fits realities in a period of falling prices remains to be seen.[14]

Bargaining by strong unions may have long-term as well as short-term effects. It may tend to hold wage rates in the high section of the band over a long period of time. On the other hand, strong union bargaining might influence employers to plan on a shift toward a thinner mix of labor. An employer who finds himself consistently weaker than the union with which he must negotiate may decide to substitute other factors in the future. In individual markets this effect could encourage more rapid technological change and thus restrict future employment at the same time that it increased the capital-worker ratio.

The simple bargaining theory discussed above suffers from a lack of specificity in prediction. It notes that wages will be indeterminate within the white area (intersection of the bands) in Figure 22-2, and it holds that if unions are stronger than employers, wage rates will tend

---

[14]For attempts to compare the theory's implications with experience, see Arthur M. Ross, "The Influence of Unionism Upon Earnings," *Reprint No. 5* (Berkeley: University of California Institute of Industrial Relations, 1948); R. A. Lester and E. A. Robie, "Wages Under National and Regional Collective Bargaining," Industrial Relations Section, Princeton University, 1946; and R. A. Lester, "Influence of Unionism Upon Earnings," *Quarterly Journal of Economics*, Vol. 62, No. 5 (November, 1948), pp. 785–87.

to be higher, toward the upper end of the white area. If employers are stronger, wage rates will tend toward the bottom of the white area. Likewise, if unions are stronger and succeed in raising wage rates, employment will tend toward the left side of the white area in Figure 22-2, i.e., will be less. If employers are stronger and wage rates are lower, employment will tend to the right side of the white area, i.e., will be greater.

But beyond this area of indeterminacy, set by the intersection of the supply and demand bands, the simple bargaining theory lacks precision. The question may be raised, for example, about whether unions try to maximize wage rates, employment, or labor income. The simple theory does not give an answer. Consideration of union and employer preference functions, and costs of agreement and disagreement, provide more precision in the bargaining theory.

Union preference functions. One of the knottiest questions about union wage policy has to do with what unions are trying to maximize. One possibility is *maximization of wages per member.* This can be accomplished at the expense of driving out members through unemployment or of not taking in new members. In the long run this would tend to destroy the union. Even maximizing the average income of all members of the union would lead to the same eventual result. Loss of employment and membership would be strong deterrents to pursuit of such policy.

Another goal might be *to increase the size of the membership.* This could be done, but increasing supplies might lower wages or result in much part-time work and unemployment. Hence, this makes an unlikely objective.

Another objective might be to attempt *to maximize the wage-bill-aggregate of wages* received by the entire membership. But this, too, is an unlikely objective, because in cases where demand is elastic, although a wage reduction would result in more employment and hence enlarge the wage-bill, it would leave each member not as well off as before.

In light of these difficulties, Albert Rees has suggested that unions are interested in both: (1) raising wages and (2) having a large membership — but the relative emphasis given to each of these twin objectives will vary from union to union and from time to time. In general, Rees holds, unions will fight harder to prevent wage cuts than to raise wages; they will be more concerned about preserving employment of present members than increasing membership. And in pursuing each goal, they must consider costs (e.g., of strikes) as well as gains.[15]

There is no single objective of union wage policy that typifies all unions in all circumstances — nothing, for example, which compares to the assumed common objective of profit maximization held by employers. Union objectives of maximizing wage rates and of maximizing employment may be regarded as substitutes (even though imperfect ones) for each other. Thus, in moving from any established wage-employment position, it would take a big increase in wage rates to compensate for a decrease in employment and a big increase in employment to compensate for a decrease in wages. In essence, this variant of bargaining theory assumes that unions prefer wage increases to employment increases in good times (when demand increases) and prefer employment reductions to wage reductions in poor times (when demand decreases).[16]

Unions operate with economic and social restraints in mind and must modify policy to accommodate these constraints. Thus, for example, a union faced with sharply falling employment opportunities for members will probably emphasize employment and job protection rather than wage increases. Or, if public policy is fostering strong antiunion legislation, unions may be less vigorous in their demands. Conversely, when employment, prices, and volume of sales are rising, unions can increase wage pressure. Employers are less likely to offer resistance under such circumstances. Indeed, they may pay considerably above union scale — the so-called *wage drift* (wage drift is much more common in other industrial nations than it is in the United States).

Even as employers compare wage rates with other employers (largely for cost purposes), unions compare wage rates with other unions (for political and prestige reasons). In general, where economic constraints collide with political pressures for raising wages, the former are more powerful and controlling.[17]

---

[15]Albert Rees, *The Economics of Trade Unions* (Chicago: University of Chicago Press, 1962), pp. 52–54.

[16]For a discussion of preferences based on indifference analysis, see Allan M. Cartter, *Theory of Wages and Employment* (Homewood, Ill.: Richard D. Irwin, Inc., 1959), pp. 86–115. Another excellent discussion of monopsonistic supply curves will be found in Frederic Meyers, "Price Theory and Union Monopoly," *Industrial and Labor Relations Review*, Vol. 12, No. 3 (April, 1959), pp. 434–45.

[17]Rees, *op. cit.*, p. 55. As noted in Part II of this book, union wage policy toward individual firms strongly seeks standardization, or to "take labor out of competition;"

Employer preference functions. The employer's preference is to stick to employment and wage combinations that intersect the marginal revenue product curve, since that maximizes his profit. Thus, his preference path is similar to that described in Figure 21-1, page 618. The modification to the marginal productivity theory from the preference assumptions results from the postulation of a different supply curve — one that is more "L" shaped, i.e., closely parallels the "Y" axis (wage rates) in the upper portion of the supply curve and then suddenly parallels the "X" axis (employment) in the lower half of the supply curve. The area of settlement is restricted to the range of areas where the union and employer have coincident preferences. In essence, these simple preference path amendments to the marginal productivity theory still leave a band of indeterminacy as in Figure 22-2, although the range of indetermination is reduced.[18]

Comparative costs of agreement with costs of disagreement. More sophisticated analysis of collective bargaining strategy uses the concepts of "preference paths" for employer and union and reduces the range of indetermination by comparing estimated costs of agreement with costs of disagreement in the particular bargaining situation.[19] Even more complicated models are available based on formal game theory, which include estimates of risks involved, satisfactions, and the effects of the power of one party to inflict loss upon the other.[20]

The details of these more sophisticated analyses are beyond the scope of the present introductory volume. In a general and basic sense, however, more formal bargaining theory may be described as follows:[21]

1. Free collective bargaining involves the risk of work stoppages.
2. Work stoppages mean that the parties can lose as well as gain from their disagreement.
3. Therefore, each party must always consider two sets of costs involved in collective bargaining:
   a. The cost of disagreeing with the opponent.
   b. The cost of agreeing with the opponent.
4. The cost of disagreement to the union is the loss of wages to its members during the work stoppage.

hence, union wage policy seeks to reduce differentials for similar work. The union policy-maker is very much interested in reducing geographic differentials. That unions have not been completely successful in attaining geographical equality may be due, at least in part, to geographical variations in both quantity and quality of available labor supplies.

[18]For a brief discussion, see David W. Belcher, *Wage and Salary Administration* (2nd ed.; Englewood Cliffs, N.J.: Prentice Hall, Inc., 1962), pp. 43–49.

[19]See Allan M. Cartter, *Theory of Wages and Employment* (Homewood, Ill.: Richard D. Irwin, Inc., 1959), pp. 77–133.

[20]See J. Pen, "A General Theory of Bargaining," *American Economic Review*, Vol. 42, No. 1 (March, 1952), pp. 24–42.

[21]See Allan Cartter, *Theory of Wages and Employment, op. cit.*, pp. 116–20.

5. The cost of disagreement to the employer comes from the loss of profit resulting from a decline in production and sales during the stoppage.
6. The cost of agreement for each party is the difference between:
   a. The income flow obtained if the opponent's terms are accepted.
   b. The income flow obtained if one's own best terms are accepted.[22]

These newer bargaining theories are stronger analytical tools because they take account of: (1) the power of one party to inflict a loss upon the other and (2) the ability to influence a shift in the opponent's position by a shift in one's own position. In brief, skillful bargainers can directly and specifically influence the opponent's will to resist or concede.

Allan Cartter pictures the decision process as follows:

1. Each party has a "bargaining attitude."
2. This may be represented by the following formula:

$$\text{X's bargaining attitude} = \frac{\text{cost of disagreeing with Y}}{\text{cost of agreeing on Y's terms}}$$

3. Bargaining attitudes are unfavorable to settlement when the above formula yields a value of less than one.
4. Bargaining attitudes are favorable to settlement when the above formula is equal to or greater than one.

If neither party's bargaining attitude is favorable, presumably a work stoppage will result. As the stoppage continues, their bargaining attitudes will become more favorable to settlement, and a compromise, or settlement, will be reached. Compromise solutions or "offers" reduce the opponent's costs of agreeing and, therefore, his propensity to continue the conflict.[23]

Action

Action prescribed by the bargaining theory is clear. To raise rates, stronger union organizations would be encouraged. To hold wage rates down or to lower them, stronger employer associations

---

[22]These income flows are through time and must be capitalized, even as the possible costs of disagreement are long-run and, hence, must be capitalized.

[23]Allan M. Cartter, *Theory of Wages and Employment* (Homewood, Ill.: Richard D. Irwin, Inc., 1959), pp. 116–22. An earlier statement of a bargaining theory based upon employer's *concession curves* and union's *resistance curves* will be found in J. R. Hicks, *The Theory of Wages* (New York: The MacMillan Co.), p. 144. Hicks's model is less useful in that it does not take account of how subsequent offers affect propensities to concede or continue the conflict. For an account of laboratory bargaining experiments using models, see Carl M. Stevens, *Strategy and Collective Bargaining Negotiation* (New York: McGraw-Hill Book Co., Inc., 1963).

would be prescribed or union power would be reduced. Much of the immediate postdepression public policy and the economic program of the New Deal was obviously dictated by this theory. At the same time, the short-term theory suggests that unions, if they are to hit the top of the possible wage range, must know the facts of business experience, profits, costs, and prospects. Knowledge of each market is an important element in bargaining strength. The theory suggests, therefore, continued union study and improved market knowledge. At the same time, it explains some employer reluctance to release such detailed information.

The theory explains wage rates in specific labor markets. When regarded as a modification or adaptation of the marginal productivity analysis, the theory suggests nothing additional with respect to levels of employment. If bargained wages fall within the discretionary band, employment may not be affected much if at all. If they are higher or lower, the general marginal analysis is relevant. The theory is only indirectly concerned with the broader political, social, and economic implications of bargaining strength. Stronger unions or employers may create many other problems — political influence, long work stoppages, and more bitter employer-union conflict, for example.

Many employers and conservative political groups seek ways of regulating union power, including "right to work" laws and placing of unions under business monopoly statutes. So-called economic guideposts, discussed in Chapter 19, represent a public attempt to make voluntary wage restraint more effective.

Union Power Constrained by Elasticity and Substitution

Even though unions can influence, shape, and control labor supply curves, union influence on relative earnings is largely dependent upon the elasticity of demand for union labor. The more inelastic the derived demand for labor, the smaller the effect of a wage increase on employment, and hence the greater the influence of unions on relative wages.

The union effect on demand for labor is limited largely by availability of substitutes for labor. These substitutes are considered in both technical (or engineering) terms and economic terms. Substitutes are powerful constraints upon union wage demands. They have important bearing upon relative wages, because if wages get too high, employers will substitute other factors of production.

Further, while some forms of labor may be noncompeting, other forms of labor may be competing (e.g., white- vs. blue-collar, semi-skilled vs. skilled), and employers have opportunities to substitute one type of labor for another. They can also substitute nonunion for union labor, and thus the profitability of substitution places decided constraints on the abilities of unions to obtain higher relative wages. (Remember that substitution is concerned with *relative* costs and returns.)

As noted below, there is little research evidence on the employment impact of labor's relative wage gains, i.e., higher wage rates. In theory union pressures could cause employment to be less than it otherwise would, and such pressures could cause employers to try harder to substitute other factors for labor.

Note also the role of consumers in resisting what they regard as excessive prices. John Dunlop provides an example of truck-driver rates for roughly comparable jobs in Boston, in July of 1953. Magazine drivers received a rate of $2.49; beer drivers, $1.90; and laundry drivers, $1.28; this shows how differences in the product market are reflected back into the labor market.[24] Presumably the demand for commercial laundering service is very elastic; if wage rates and related prices go up too much, housewives will do their washing at home — i.e., there is a limit beyond which unions cannot push wage rates.

COLLECTIVE BARGAINING, INFLATION, AND EMPLOYMENT

Union pressures to raise wage rates have encountered strong resistance from employers and increased concern on the part of the general public. Are union demands inflationary? Do union members get a disproportionate share of income? Do unions, through their wage policies, reduce employment opportunities? These are questions that are widely debated, generally in heated, emotional, and partisan terms. They are significant questions related to collective bargaining wage theory.

Union Wage-Push Inflation

As noted in Chapter 19, union "wage-push" or "cost-push" inflation works as follows. If workers, through their unions, push up

---

[24]John T. Dunlop, "The Task of Contemporary Wage Theory," in G. W. Taylor and Frank C. Pierson, *New Concepts in Wage Determination* (New York: McGraw-Hill Book Company, Inc., 1957), p. 135.

wages faster than their productivity gains, labor costs go up. Employers tend to raise prices to cover these added costs (although they are limited in this if they have elastic product demand curves). When prices go up, real wages decline, and hence labor may not really gain in terms of living standards. Unions try to raise wages again, and the whole process starts over. One can visualize wages chasing prices up a spiral staircase and never quite catching up, or passing. When money supplies increase faster than the increase in goods and services, inflation results. (An alternative response to higher wage costs is lowered employment, of course.)

The basic question underlying the "wage-push" thesis is: What caused wages to go up? Was it the union, or was it something else?

If a union has asked for and received 15¢ an hour more through negotiations, it is obvious that the union is responsible for the gain. Or is it? Sometimes the "obvious" overlooks other factors. If the demand for labor is sufficiently strong, wages might have gone up without the union effort. Thus, for example, while clerical workers are not generally organized, they have been in tight supply, and their rates have risen sharply in recent years. Hence, it can be argued, as Rees does, that unions might be said to be responsible for the timing, but not the amount, of wage increases.[25]

Here we have a real dilemma in that we cannot be sure it was the union per se that caused wages to rise. Difficulties in isolating variables make this a difficult question to research. And most economists agree that we have both cost-push and classic excess-demand or "demand-pull" inflation. It should be recalled that demand-pull inflation occurs when the money people have to spend grows more rapidly than the amount of goods and serivces, and hence people bid higher prices to be sure to "get their share" of the goods.

Union responsibility for higher prices is more than an economic concern — it is also a political concern. Some employers and some sections of the public attempt to assess the "blame" for higher prices on unions. Higher prices are regarded as undesirable in an economy that seeks to avoid inflation. Hence, if it can be shown (or if it is contended) that unions through their demands for "exorbitant" wages cause prices to rise unduly, then the remedy is simple — unions should be restrained. But, as we have just seen, unions may not be responsible, or responsible alone, for higher prices. The truth of the

---

[25]Albert Rees, *The Economics of Trade Unionism* (Chicago: University of Chicago Press, 1962), p. 105.

matter is that in the long run, unless there is sufficient consumer demand, unions cannot push prices up indefinitely. They have their best chance to do so in situations where product demand is inelastic. But, one must ask where that inelasticity came from. Did it come from union efforts?

In general, anybody who tries to explain American consumer buying behavior on the grounds that consumers make their demands largely because of union influences would be laughed off the soap box. This is obviously too simple an explanation of the complexities of consumer motivation. Further, the existence of substitute products and services enables consumers to purchase nonunion or other union products.

On the other hand, those who argue in favor of special laws to control "labor monopolies" (i.e., unions) assume that labor unions can and do affect wages, wage rates, and employment levels. Evidence concerning union impact on wage rates is inconclusive. It is difficult to separate the influence of group participation from that of the many factors that influence wage decisions.

Unions and Relative Wage Shares

There have been a number of studies of the influence of unions on relative wages. Two major types of study may be differentiated: One compares wages in an industry before unionization with wages after unionization (longitudinal), and the other compares union with non-union wages in the same industry at the same time (cross-sectional). While the various studies are not alike in concept and method, in general, according to Albert Rees, they conclude that, on the average, unions have been able to obtain wages about 10 to 15 percent higher than for similar nonunion groups.[26]

Sumner Slichter also concluded that collective bargaining does create inflationary pressure. He noted the relative inelasticity of short-term demands in various labor markets. In the short run, wage variations exert limited influence on employment. Unions are thus encouraged to make wage demands that encourage, if they do not absolutely require, an upward adjustment in prices.[27] H. Gregg Lewis holds that unions had higher average wages for members by 25 percent or more in the mid-1930's, by 5 percent in the late 1940's, and by

---

[26]Rees, *op. cit.*, p. 79.

[27]Sumner H. Slichter, "Do the Wage-Fixing Arrangements in the American Labor Market Have an Inflationary Bias?" *American Economic Review*, Vol. 44, No. 2 (May, 1954), pp. 322–46.

10–15 percent in the late 1950's; however, union wage effects differ substantially among industries.[28]

Sultan, on the other hand, has reported a very broad study comparing the wage experience of organized industries with that of unorganized or partially organized industries. He concludes that union pressure "has not served to increase the distributive share going to labor in those industries which are highly unionized, relative to those industries which are not."[29] Clark Kerr takes a similar stand. He holds that with minor exceptions, "trade unionism in the United States has had no important effect on labor's share of the national income."[30]

Unions as economic institutions do not have a controlling impact on income redistribution. Instead government fiscal policy (e.g., graduated income tax and welfare policy) has been the major force in this direction. It is not collective bargaining but political activity (including that of unions) that appears to be most effective in income redistribution.

Unions and Employment Levels

Lowell E. Galloway argues that the labor market is a reasonably efficient geographical allocator of labor resources but that it is less effective in allocating resources on an occupational and industrial basis. Labor unions, according to Galloway, interfere with opportunity-cost mobility; union restrictions to protect their wage gains have the effect of lowering employment levels in union sectors, shifting employment to nonunion sectors with a resultant depression of nonunion wage rates.[31]

John Dunlop has analyzed employment effects of collective bargaining, starting with the usual arguments: (1) Unions push wages up higher than they would be without unions; (2) Since the demand for

---

[28]H. Gregg Lewis, *Unionism and Relative Wages in the United States* (Chicago: University of Chicago Press, 1964).

[29]Paul E. Sultan, "Unionism and Wage-Income Ratios: 1929–1951," *Review of Economics and Statistics*, Vol. 37, No. 1 (February, 1954), pp. 67–73. He includes an excellent list of references (in footnotes) to other attempts to find answers in empirical data. See also Edward S. Mason, "Labor Monopoly and All That," in *Proceedings of Industrial Relations Research Association*, December 28–30, 1955, pp. 188–208, and the ensuing controversial discussion by Peter O. Steiner, Jules Backman, Peter Henle, Charles C. Killingsworth, and Matthew A. Kelley, pp. 209–32; George H. Hildebrand, "The Economic Effects of Unionism," in Neil C. Chamberlain *et al.* (eds.), *A Decade of Industrial Relations Research: 1946–1956* (New York: Harper and Brothers, 1958), pp. 98–145.

[30]Clark Kerr, "Labor's Income Share and the Labor Movement," in George W. Taylor and Frank C. Pierson (eds.), *New Concepts in Wage Determination* (New York: McGraw-Hill Book Company, 1957), p. 287.

[31]Lowell E. Galloway, "Labor Mobility, Resource Allocation and Structural Unemployment," *American Economic Review*, Vol. LIII, No. 4 (September, 1963), pp. 694–716.

labor is elastic, the volume of employment will be less. Dunlop argues that since the first portion of this argument has not been verified, the conclusion is not appropriate. Critics of unions usually present lists of adverse effects, without mentioning their beneficial effects in terms of increased productivity and output. These benefits, according to Dunlop, include:

1. More skilled labor force.
2. Improved job information and mobilities.
3. Higher morale.
4. Improved safety, health, and accident programs.
5. Larger span of years in the labor force.
6. Product standardization in highly competitive industries.
7. Pressure on management to be more efficient.[32]

PUBLIC POLICY ON WAGES: CHOICE AND DILEMMA

Appropriate public policy on wages involves many considerations including alternative objectives, theories, and programs. It is not a simple task to select from among several wage theories or to decide which is most appropriate or which portions of one theory should be blended with portions of another theory as an integrated basis for explanation, prediction, and control. Nor is it a simple task to integrate wage theories with employment theories and theories of labor movements. And yet unless these interrelationships are recognized, public policy can lead to undesired consequences and side effects.

Theories of labor movements, of employment, and of wages represent significant partial industrial relations subsystems. But, for any total system, it is essential that the parts integrate and mesh properly. Hence, the importance of the concept of a total or general industrial relations system, as discussed in Chapter 4. In very simple terms, it is not sufficient to consider public policy on wages without reference to other partial industrial relations systems. Take, as an example, four conflicting employment goals, one of which is higher wages.

Four Conflicting Employment Goals

We have four conflicting employment goals — conflicting in the sense that they cannot all be realized simultaneously. These are: (1) full employment, (2) free collective bargaining, (3) higher wages, and (4) stable prices.

---

[32]See John Dunlop, "Discussion," *Proceedings of the Industrial Relations Research Association*, December, 1962, pp. 296–97.

If we seek the goal of highest possible wage rates regardless of productivity, for example, we imperil the goal of stable prices. If we compel unions to exercise restraint in their demands (e.g., limit their wage askings to the same increase as productivity increases) we circumscribe a major purpose of free collective bargaining, i.e., competition among unions to see who can get the biggest increase. And if one union fails to exercise restraint, others can scarcely be expected to keep restrained voluntarily.

One means of forcing wages and productivity to increase proportionately is direct wage and salary controls. In addition, profit and price controls probably would be needed, since labor would not be likely to agree to a wage freeze if prices and profits continued to rise. But then we would not attain the goal of free collective bargaining as it is now institutionalized, since unions would no longer be free to push for wages beyond the maximum set by the government.

Another way to keep wages and productivity in alignment might be the threat of unemployment. In a full-employment economy this is not much of a threat. But even a full-employment economy gets out of order occasionally, and instead of increased government spending to reduce employment, a surplus pool of unemployed could be left unemployed. This could possibly cause union members to urge their leaders to take it a bit easy on the size of any requested wage hike. This solution is sometimes suggested by certain employers who argue that "there's nothing wrong with labor that a good shot of unemployment won't cure." This treatment allegedly increases employee productivity as well as restraining requests for higher wages. The "shot of unemployment" cure obviously defeats the goal of full employment.

Returning again to the central problem of four conflicting employment goals, it appears possible to attain several of the four but not all four simultaneously. Hence, something has to give. Which of the goals shall it be? This is a crucial question of public policy. It is a question to which we shall return again in Chapters 25 and 26.

Secular Inflation

The public usually sets public policy and to date has provided a fairly consistent answer to the question of which goal is least important. It has chosen to sacrifice price stability. The price of full employment appears to be inflation plus more of a managed rather than a free economy. By and large the public seems to agree that a little inflation is desirable.

How much is a little inflation? Some economists conclude that 1 percent a year is not bad. Others say 2 percent or more. They say that this is not too high a price to pay for the three goals of full employment, higher wages, and free collective bargaining. Is not this really better than the mass unemployment of the 1930's? It encourages investment and provides an impetus to expand our economy with an increasing stream of goods and services.[33] Of course, those on fixed incomes might suffer, but we will take care of that by giving them a "cost of living adjustment." This, of course, has an additional inflationary effect.

There remains the question of how a little inflation can be contained to prevent a big inflation. It has been wisely said that inflation feeds on its own flames. Other economies have been burned out by the flames of inflation. We can probably control inflation through monetary and fiscal policies and controls, but in so doing we may have to give up some of our freedoms. Whether we will be willing to pay the price is up to the public — it is a question of policy, not entirely a question of economics.

The Role of Profits

It is important to recall the role of profits in a free-enterprise economy. Profits are the compass that guides a free-enterprise economy. Higher profits in a relatively competitive society tell us that consumers want more of a certain type of goods and services. Lower profits generally mean that consumers want fewer of a certain type of goods and services. This means that higher profits indicate the need for added investment and allocation of additional resources (including labor) to meet new or additional consumer demands. In short, profits act like a servomechanism to alter the flow of resources.

In a full-employment economy the problem of attracting resources is difficult because there are few if any idle resources, especially labor. It is usually necessary to raise wage levels in more profitable industries to accomplish reallocation of labor supplies.

---

[33]See, however, Melvin W. Reder, "The General Level of Money Wages," Industrial Relations Research Association, *Proceedings*, December 28–29, 1950, pp. 198–202. Reder argues that a "little" inflation may *not* be so harmless because, with secular inflation, parties to economic processes will anticipate the *continued* raise, attempt to beat anticipated price rises, and thus cause the price level to rise faster.

This can be, and usually is, inflationary. The alternatives are misdirection of resources or finding additional labor supplies of the type needed. If wages and employment would decline sufficiently in low-profit industries, the effects of reallocation of labor resources in a relatively competitive full-employment economy would be less inflationary. But wage rates are sticky or inflexible, and wage-rate reductions are the exception rather than the rule; hence, labor reallocation in full employment usually involves inflationary wage increases. Confiscation of extra profits through excess profit taxes could seriously impair the direction of resources in a dynamic economy. One alternative would be government planning and controls — for example, manpower allocation. To many citizens this seems to be too high a price, and a little inflation seems to be the preferable alternative, as previously noted.

Market Forces Versus Institutional Forces

Employers who wish to expand their output in a full-employment economy usually have to raise wages to hire employees away from other firms. They are willing to do this because they predict that they can pass the added costs on to consumers (their product and labor demand curves have shifted upward and to the right). Thus, if product demand increases, wholly aside from increases in productivity, wages can rise. And the increased demand for labor need not have originated with unions at all.[34]

But the point remains that unions as institutions do seek to raise wage rates each year for the most part. In fact, unions compete and vie with each other in the amount of increases they can obtain. They are not particularly concerned in most instances with the demand schedules for products made by their employers and often ask for wage increases even though the employer faces a declining demand for his output.[35]

---

[34]See Neil W. Chamberlain, *Labor* (New York: McGraw-Hill Book Co., Inc., 1958), Chapter 21. Shortages of white-collar workers during the past decade (typically unorganized) plus employers' policies of raising wages for nonunion employees at the time of a union increase (perhaps to prevent office unionization) have brought substantial wage and salary increases to nonunion employees. See also the excellent summary of many studies on this problem by George Hildebrand, "The Economic Effects of Unionism," in the IRRA Volume edited by Neil W. Chamberlain *et al.*, *A Decade of Industrial Relations Research: 1946–1956* (New York: Harper and Brothers, 1958), pp. 98–145.

[35]It has been argued by union leaders that such wage increases are a spur to managerial efficiency and that this encourages management to undertake reductions in costs through improved methods, better machines, etc. Unions point out that all costs are not *labor* costs, and that higher labor costs — if they lead to reduction in other costs — can actually result in lower *total* costs per unit of output.

Employers are generally more responsive than unions to shifts in demand for their products and labor surpluses. When product demand falls off, they tend to resist wage increases; when available labor supplies are large (many unemployed), they also resist wage increases.

The institution of free, competitive collective bargaining is a constant potential inflationary force, whereas employers are generally inflationary with respect to wages in good times and deflationary in bad times.[36]

Motivation in Secular Inflation and Full Employment

With jobs for all and steadily rising wage rates regardless of productivity, it is possible that worker motivation to give a full days' work for a full day's pay might diminish. Fear and reward are two prime instruments for changing behavior. Remove fear (of unemployment and low wages) and perhaps you remove an important portion of employee incentive. Incentive pay plans, profit sharing, and nonfinancial devices may offset employee tendencies toward "goofing off" in production. Reduced motivation may also affect employers if they believe that the government will bail them out through additional spending. The sense of balance between productivity and income may be dulled for all under full employment with secular inflation.

The crucial role of productivity in real wage determination cannot be emphasized too strongly. Neither the full employment theory nor the collective bargaining theory alone offers complete explanations of wage levels and differentials or of employment levels. As Allan Cartter says in the conclusion of his classic work on wage theory, ". . . whether we view the firm, an industry, or the economy as a whole, the principles of marginal productivity remain the cornerstone on which the theory of wages and employment rests."[37]

---

[36]The combination of long-term collective agreements and provisions for deferred wage increases complicates the problem of relating wage advances to productivity. Each year several million employees become entitled to increases ranging, in recent years, from less than 5 to more than 14 cents per hour. For 1964 the most common rate of increase was 7–8 cents per hour. Numbers of workers eligible to receive such increases vary widely from year to year because of the varying lengths of agreements and the dates when they become effective. In 1964, 2.3 million workers were scheduled for such increases; in 1963, the number was 3.3 million. See George Ruben, "Deferred Increases Due in 1964 and Wage Escalation," *Monthly Labor Review*, Vol. 86, No. 12 (December, 1963), pp. 1394–97.

[37]Allan M. Cartter, *Theory of Wages and Employment* (Homewood, Ill.: Richard D. Irwin, Inc., 1959), p. 179.

ANALYTICAL REVIEW QUESTIONS

1. What is meant by "economic stagnation"? What effect does this have upon employment levels?
2. How are anticipations related to expectations in economic behavior?
3. What alternatives for public policy on wages and prices did Keynes suggest?
4. Why are labor markets not self-correcting?
5. Do the variables that determine full employment lie inside or outside of labor markets?
6. What was the role of money as a variable in the classical theory of marginal productivity?
7. Did Keynes use real or money wages in his explanation?
8. What is meant by "sticky wages"? What effects do these have upon employment?
9. How does the Keynesian supply curve of labor differ from the classical supply curve? What is the effect on employment levels of using the Keynesian assumption?
10. Under the Keynesian theory is the proposed solution to unemployment to alter the supply curve or the demand curve? Why?
11. What is meant by the term "involuntary unemployment" under the Keynesian analysis?
12. Why did Keynes argue that wage rate reductions would not cure unemployment?
13. Which of the propensities (to consume or to invest) is most variable? Why?
14. How is national income defined?
15. Of what is full employment a function?
16. How can the government control national income?
17. Is national income theory most concerned with seasonal, technological, structural, or cyclical unemployment?
18. What does monetary policy seek with respect to employment? How?
19. How do taxes affect inflation? Deflation?
20. Why did Keynes argue that stable wages (in the short run) were essential to full employment?
21. What are the disadvantages of public works programs created to cure unemployment?
22. How does the full employment theory explain wage structures and differentials?
23. Do costs determine prices?
24. What operational questions arise in trying to carry out the full employment theory?
25. What are the principal shortcomings of the purchasing power theory of wages? What is the role of underconsumption in causing unemployment?
26. What is the principal question raised by the bargaining theory of wages?
27. How does the relative strength of labor and management affect supply and demand curves?

28. Why does the simple bargaining theory suffer from a lack of specificity in prediction?
29. Which of the union preference functions is most likely to be encountered in real life? Why?
30. How would one expect union preference functions to vary in prosperity and depression?
31. What is meant by "wage drift"?
32. In general, are economic or political constraints most important in union wage policy?
33. What is the most common employer's preference function on wages? Where does he always want supply and demand to intersect?
34. What two sets of costs must bargainers consider?
35. How is the cost of agreement defined in collective bargaining theory? How is bargaining attitude defined? Why is bargaining attitude important?
36. What are the principal restraints with respect to union influence on wage differentials?
37. Describe the processes of "wage-push" inflation.
38. What are the two major types of inquiry with respect to the impact of unions on relative wages?
39. How effective has collective bargaining been on income redistribution?
40. According to Galloway, how do unions affect opportunity-cost mobility?
41. What would happen to employment if wage rates were increased during a depression?
42. Why can we not attain our four conflicting employment goals simultaneously? Which one have we apparently chosen to sacrifice? Why?
43. With the full employment and collective bargaining wage theories, can we abandon the marginal productivity theory? Why or why not?

Case 22-1

SNOW PAINT COMPANY

"The bargaining theory of wages proves that workers can get whatever wage they want provided they are willing to organize and strike." This quotation appeared in a mimeographed flyer distributed by the union in the Snow Paint Company plant in a midwest city. The article went on to say that workers in the plant could blame no one but themselves for the fact that their wages were only slightly above the minimum specified under the Fair Labor Standards Act. Reference was made to the fact that the firm had paid $3 per share dividends for each of the past 10 years. (The stock is not listed; but over-the-counter it is presently bid $22 and asked $24.)

The author of the statement urges union members to authorize a strike to strengthen the hands of the negotiating committee, which is presently bargaining a new agreement. He argues that wages should be at least 50 percent higher than they now are.

• Would a strike insure higher rates than will be secured without it? Will the strike authorization be enough or must members of the union actually go out on strike? Be prepared to discuss these questions during the class period.

JOB AND WAGE SECURITY: INCOME MAINTENANCE

This chapter, and the one that follows, constitute Part VI of this book. They are concerned with still another partial industrial relations system — income maintenance through job and wage security programs. Actually, as noted in the pages that follow, operational economic security systems are both private and public with numerous gaps, overlaps, and inconsistencies. In part this reflects the lag in conceptual systems and theory in this increasingly important area of labor economics. Conceptual orderliness and balance are lacking in the components of our economic security system as well as in the whole. This will be evident throughout Part VI.

The present chapter provides background on employee welfare and social insurance and discusses unemployment insurance, guaranteed annual wages, workmen's compensation and work-connected illness, nonwork-connected disability, and employee benefit plans. The problems of old age, retirement, and death, including old-age assistance and health insurance, private and public pension plans, and retirement programs, are discussed in Chapter 24.

BACKGROUND: WELFARE AND SOCIAL INSURANCE

When the average employee loses his job, he loses his right to participate in many activities formerly provided by the "open-sesame" of a paycheck. Without job rights the value of other rights are reduced sharply. He still has the right to buy anything he wants, to move his home and family, to send his daughter to college — but the exercise of these rights frequently must be backed up by cash or by credit. And cash or credit comes from a job. With a job he is secure in most phases of his life. Without a job he faces insecurity.

Employees and the public (and they are largely synonymous in our society) feel strongly about job security and maintenance of income, which constitute two of our major economic goals. We have much social policy and legislation dealing with job rights and job protection. We are still experimenting and groping with solutions to problems of job protection; our experience in this regard is very brief and limited. About the only major conclusions we seem to have reached is that the average employee cannot be expected to deal with job loss alone and that it is better to prevent job loss if possible than to try to compensate for it.

Loss of income through loss of a job may result from unemployment, accidents and illness (both on and off the job), old age, and death. We may seek to prevent such circumstances or to ameliorate their economic consequences through forms of income maintenance. Increasingly we seek to relate income maintenance to former job rights (before we lost the job). Increasingly we seek to extend these post job rights to our dependents. While employees seek to build up insurance, savings, and other means so that they will have personal resources for such contingencies, historically such personal private resources have been inadequate. Employer, union, and joint programs have been tried, but with distinctly limited success. Today public programs bear the brunt of income maintenance. Some of these public programs are *welfare programs*, based on needs — generally such programs are not related to prior job rights and employment experience. Increasingly, however, these programs may be conceived as being of an insurance nature; for they are based on job rights, with contributions made while employees are working which accumulate benefit rights (income) to be used when jobs and their wage rights are lost. When such insurance is provided by governments, it is called *social insurance*.

Growth of Welfare and Benefit Programs

Within one generation, from 1935 on, there has been a phenomenal growth in welfare and benefit programs in the United States.

Not all of these are necessarily job related. Major emphasis in these programs is upon amelioration (e.g., unemployment compensation; workmen's compensation; and old-age, survivors, and disability insurance). There are also programs based upon concepts of prevention (e.g., guaranteed annual wages and selective retirement plans). The extent and costs of income maintenance are impressive. Thus, for example, the amount expended on social welfare and benefit programs reached some $66 billion in 1963. Social welfare expenditures increased from 9.5 percent of GNP in 1935 to 11.6 percent in 1963. (Note that as we are using the term, "social welfare" includes public welfare programs, social security, and public health and education programs.)

SOCIAL WELFARE EXPENDITURES IN THE UNITED STATES — 1963[1]

Social Insurance and Related Programs.............	$25.7 billion
Public Aid.......................................	5.5
Veterans' Programs...............................	5.4
Other Welfare Programs..........................	1.5
Health and Medical..............................	5.7
Education.......................................	22.2
Total...	$66.0 billion

Private employee benefit plans have increased sharply in recent years, up from almost $1 billion in 1950 to over $4.5 billion in 1963.

PRIVATE EMPLOYEE BENEFIT PLANS[2]

	1950	1963
Retirement......................	$335 million	$2,200 million
Temporary Disability.............	330	860
SUB.............................	——	110
Life Insurance...................	300	1,350
Total.........................	$965 million	$4,520 million

Social Security

A term related to social welfare is *social security*, which includes a wide variety of programs — not just "the old-age pension" as used in laymen's discussions. Social security in the United States may be classified under three major groupings:

---

[1]Ida C. Merriam, "Social Expenditures and Worker Welfare," *Monthly Labor Review*, Vol. 86, No. 6 (June, 1963), pp. 687–94.

[2]*Ibid.*

1. Social Insurance
    a. Old-Age, Survivors, and Disability Insurance (OASDI)
    b. Unemployment Insurance (UI)
    c. Workmen's Compensation (WC)
    d. Temporary Disability Insurance (TDI)
2. Public Assistance Programs
    a. Old-Age Assistance (OAA)
    b. Aid to Dependent Children (ADC)
    c. Aid to the blind
    d. Aid to the permanently and totally disabled
    e. General assistance (relief)
3. Social Services
    a. Public health services
    b. Special services for children
    c. Veterans' pensions and services
    d. Services for the blind and handicapped
    e. Public employment services
    f. Civilian vocational rehabilitation[3]

It will be noted that all subgroupings under "Social Insurance" and the last two groupings under "Social Services" are directly related to employment; the other categories are not. Only those categories related to employment are discussed in this volume.

The basic objective in social security is to assure the economic essentials to all people on the occurrence of the personal contingencies of life which, in the absence of such protection, result in want and suffering, possibly even starvation and death. Witte stressed the point that this does not mean the government assumes full responsibility for full support of all people — this would be true in a communist, not a free enterprise society. Instead, in the United States we seek to provide only the essentials of life to those who do not have means, in circumstances beyond the control of the individual. Responsibility for support still rests upon the individual — and should, according to Witte.[4]

Public benefits involving insurance have generally followed a pluralistic pattern; they are decentralized, with responsibility divided among the federal government, state and local governments, and employers. As one result, eligibility differs from one region or locality to another. As still another, amounts of benefits have generally increased more slowly than wages.[5]

---

[3]Edwin E. Witte, "Social Security in the United States" (Mimeographed, University of Wisconsin, September, 1959), pp. 4–5.

[4]See Edwin E. Witte, "The Objective of Social Security," *Review of Social Economy*, Vol. XVII, No. 1 (March, 1959), pp. 23–33.

[5]For details, see Herman M. and Anne R. Somers, "Unemployment Insurance and

Some programs date back to the early 1900's (e.g., workmen's compensation). Most social security programs in the United States had roots in the Social Security Act of 1935. Some programs are essentially federal in character (e.g., OASDI), while others are operated by the 50 states (e.g., UC and WC). These differences in federal versus state-run programs arise from differences in powers accorded the various governments by the United States Constitution. In very general terms the federal government has powers to regulate interstate commerce and some forms of taxation. The states have the so-called "police" powers to protect health and welfare, some powers of taxation, and the right to regulate local or intrastate matters.

In the discussion of the various laws and programs below, the specific government(s) involved will be noted. Public and private security programs in the United States have had a piece-meal development and are based on differing objectives and principles.

Compensation principle. In theory, occupations with greater risk of accident, unemployment, or income loss might be expected to have a higher wage to compensate for such risks, thereby balancing out net advantages and disadvantages. In general, this does not happen in most occupations. Hence, we have adopted the social insurance or *compensation principle*, whereby the cost of production bears a compulsory charge to distribute costs of these risks over a wider base and to ensure that specific benefits will be available for those who are the victims of such risks. The utility of having income following a job-income reduction is generally greater than the disutility of the loss of the contribution to a fund for such benefits.[6] So-called social insurance reflects both welfare (or need) and insurance principles, although the latter generally predominate.[7] Social insurance differs somewhat from private insurance in that the former is compulsory and may reflect additional social objectives (e.g., redistribution of income through putting a floor under protection).

Service and income benefits. The form of protection afforded by social insurance may be service (e.g., hospital care), income, or both.

Workmen's Compensation," *Proceedings, Industrial Relations Research Association* (December, 1956), pp. 120–44.

[6] See J. G. Turnbull, C. A. Williams, Jr., and E. F. Cheit, *Economic and Social Security* (2nd ed.; New York: The Ronald Press Co., 1962), pp. 197–98 and 263–65. This is probably the best single source on the economics of job-related income maintenance, insecurity, and security.

[7] See Harry Malisoff, *The Insurance Character of Unemployment Insurance* (Kalamazoo, Michigan: The W. E. Upjohn Institute for Employment Research, 1961), pp. 9–10.

While *service benefits* ensure that funds are spent in their socially intended manner, they result in loss of economic freedom to the recipient. *Income benefits* provide such freedom of choice, and increasingly
in the United States recipients are receiving a higher proportion of
income benefits.[8] Unemployment insurance is an example of income
benefit protection.

UNEMPLOYMENT INSURANCE

Since 1935 our federal-state cooperative system of unemployment
insurance has been given three major assignments: (1) to provide
income to those whose customary earnings are stopped by involuntary
unemployment; (2) to provide, through a system of merit or experience rating affecting the tax liabilities of employers, a financial incentive for stabilizing employment; and (3) to maintain purchasing
power and employment by replacing wage losses.[9]

Background

Unemployment insurance in this country followed and benefited
from the experience of several European nations, which had experimented with it for many years. Earliest local programs appeared in a
number of European cities. Belgium and Denmark provided public
subsidies for such benefits in the first decade of the present century.
England inaugurated a nationwide program in 1909. Although many
bills providing for similar arrangements were introduced in Congress
and in various state legislatures, none was approved until 1932 when
Wisconsin established the first state system. While funds were being
accumulated under that law, and before any benefits were paid, our
present system was created by the federal Social Security Act of
1935.[10]

---

[8]See Turnbull, Williams, and Cheit, *op. cit.*, Chapter 1; for an excellent summary of
yardsticks for evaluating economic security programs, see p. 33.

[9]For current information on unemployment insurance programs, see the United
States Department of Labor, Bureau of Employment Security monthly publication *Unemployment Insurance Statistics.* The first issue is January-February, 1964; this new publication
replaces the publications, *The Labor Market and Employment Security* and *The Insured Unemployed,* which were discontinued with their December, 1963, issues.

[10]See Arthur Larson, *Know Your Social Security* (New York: Harper and Brothers,
1955); "Twenty Years of Unemployment Insurance in the U.S.A.," *Employment Security
Review*, Vol. 22, No. 8, August, 1955 (entire issue); Arthur Larson and Merrill G. Murray,
"The Development of Unemployment Insurance in the United States," *Vanderbilt Law
Review*, Vol. 8, No. 2 (February, 1955), pp. 182–217. See also Eveline M. Burns, *Social
Security and Public Policy* (New York: McGraw-Hill Book Co., Inc., 1956); Margaret S.
Gordon and Ralph W. Amerson, *Unemployment Insurance*, University of California (Berkeley)
Institute of Industrial Relations, 1957.

Both the federal government and the state governments play important parts in our unemployment insurance program. The Social Security Act provided a powerful incentive for states to create their individual systems of unemployment benefits. That act assesses a federal tax of 3.1 percent on the payrolls of all covered employers. States are permitted, however, to collect and retain almost 90 percent of that tax — 2.7 percent of payrolls — by setting up a system of benefits that meets federal standards and imposes a state tax on payrolls for that purpose. All states have done so.

Under the resulting arrangements, states operate their "benefit" or "compensation" or "insurance" programs and assess payroll taxes for that purpose. The average state tax was 2.3 percent of covered payrolls in 1963. States set the conditions of eligibility for and level of benefits. They receive, appraise, and pay approved claims. The Federal Bureau of Employment Security establishes procedural standards, supervises state programs, and checks state compliance with federal standards. If state procedures are acceptable, federal funds are allocated to the states to pay administrative costs. The funds collected by each state are held in individual state accounts by the federal government. The unemployment insurance system is thus sharply differentiated from another major Social Security Act program, that providing old-age and survivors insurance, which is entirely federal. On the other hand, old-age assistance, which is also provided for under the Social Security Act, combines state and federal administration and funds.

Coverage

If by coverage we mean what employers are taxed for unemployment insurance, we must note that at least two answers can be given. Federal taxation extends to all employers who employ 4 or more employees for at least 20 weeks, with specified exemptions. State laws, on the other hand, vary as to tax coverage of employers, with a majority taxing employers of 4 or more. Four states include employers of 3 or more. Twenty states now provide coverage of all employers of 1 or more, except for specified exemptions.

If by coverage we mean the numbers of employees eligible for benefits, we can say that coverage throughout the nation now extends to some 47 million. (It has more than doubled since 1935 when about 20 million were covered.)

Figure 23-1 shows unemployment insurance coverage and several types of noncovered employment.

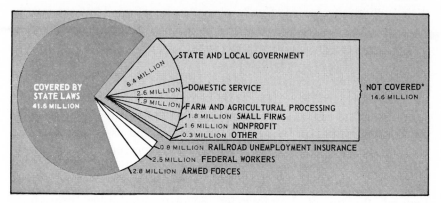

*Excludes clergymen and members of religious orders, student nurses, internes, and students employed in schools where enrolled.

Figure 23-1
UNEMPLOYMENT INSURANCE COVERAGE OF WAGE AND SALARY WORKERS
(1962 Calendar Year)

Source: *Unemployment Insurance Review*, Vol. 1, No. 4 (April, 1964), p. 26.

Eligibility

The eligibility of individual employees to receive unemployment insurance benefits depends upon the provisions of state laws and hence varies widely from state to state. The resulting "employment or wage qualifications" are quite complicated, being stated in terms of a number of tests. Most important are the weeks of earlier employment, or dollar earnings in one or more quarters, or both. No generalization is possible, for there is no simple, common pattern. Further, these qualifications are continually being changed. The common provision, however, specifies a minimum of employment or of earnings without which no employee can be paid weekly benefits.[11]

---

[11]Readers interested in such details can secure on request recent releases from the Bureau of Employment Security that describe "Significant Provisions of Unemployment Insurance Laws," including the detailed state-by-state requirements for eligibility. Current developments are available in *Unemployment Insurance Review* and *Unemployment Insurance Statistics*, both published monthly by the Bureau of Employment Security, United States Department of Labor.

Benefits

Weekly benefit amounts are determined by somewhat complicated calculations in most states. All states specify minimums and maximums. Benefits may be determined as a certain fraction of wages in the quarter of highest earnings during the preceding year, generally one twentieth or one twenty-fifth. The weekly benefit calculations weight benefits in favor of those with lowest earnings. They may include supplements for each dependent (from $1 to $8). They may be measured as a fraction of the average weekly wage (50 percent is common) or of annual wages. There is no uniformity and little in the way of a pattern in these provisions. In February, 1964, the average weekly benefit check was $36.24, with wide variations among the states. Total benefits of almost $3 billion were paid in 1963.

When the first state legislation was enacted, maximum weekly benefits were generally set to approximate one half of earnings, with a specified dollar maximum. Over the period since that time, limitations on maximum benefits have tended to reduce the proportion of wages represented by benefit payments. Some studies have found that total benefits, in some cases, amount to less than one third of wage losses because of stipulated maximum benefits. All such comparisons must be regarded with caution, however, because measures of wages include important elements beyond take-home pay. They include, for example, prepayments of income taxes on earnings. In 1961, 46 percent of all claimants drew maximum benefits.

Benefits are not paid when an employee first loses his job in most states. Unemployed workers must wait for a specified period before they become eligible for benefits, with a one-week waiting period the most common requirement.

Duration of benefits. The most common state provisions allow a maximum of 26 weeks of benefits in one year. Minimum benefit periods vary among the states. During the 1958 and 1961 recessions over 2½ million claimants in each year exhausted their state benefit entitlement before finding work. In 1958 the federal government passed the Temporary Unemployment Compensation Program (TUC) which in effect provided up to a 50 percent increase in benefit duration for those who exhausted regular benefits; states could elect to come under this act, enact their own laws, or not extend benefits. Employers in states participating in TUC were assessed additional taxes to provide for such benefits. In 1961 the federal Congress passed the Temporary Extended Unemployment Compensation Program (TEUC) in which the additional and temporary costs of extended benefits were shared by all the states without regard to specific benefits.

Labor unions, employees, and other groups are seeking to extend the length of the benefit period. Conversely, many employers argue that this would defeat what they regard as the basic purpose of unemployment insurance — i.e., to tide workers over for short periods between jobs, not to provide a "dole" or a form of relief.[12]

Adequacy of benefits. Richard A. Lester estimates that benefits for total joblessness under regular state and railroad programs[13] of unemployment compensation seem to compensate for no more than 20 percent of the wage loss from total unemployment. If wage loss from partial unemployment is included, the compensation rate shrinks to about 15 percent, on the average.[14]

In another study Father J. M. Becker found that by and large benefits produce sufficient income to keep workers off relief rolls. For primary workers, benefits were not sufficient to replace 50 percent of the wage loss. He concludes that benefits for the average primary beneficiary should certainly equal at least 50% of net wages and perhaps should equal a higher percentage.[15]

Experience Rating

All states include tax provisions that are intended to encourage employers to stabilize employment and avoid unemployment. These

---

[12]A survey of the personal characteristics of those who exhaust benefits showed that 61 percent were males, approximately 40 percent were between 25 and 44 years old, and 62 percent were primary or sole wage earners in the households they represent. Secondary workers — generally wives — made up about one fourth of the total, and an additional 11 percent were unmarried secondary workers. See "Family Characteristics of the Long-Term Unemployed," *TEUC Report Series No. 4*, United States Department of Labor, January, 1963.

[13]Railway employees are covered under the Railroad Unemployment Insurance Act of 1938. This law provides unemployment benefits, cash sickness benefits, and extended unemployment benefits. Benefit rates are 60 percent of pay, with a maximum of $51 per week. Unlike "regular" UC, there are no disqualifications for quits or discharges.

[14]Richard A. Lester, "The Economic Significance of Unemployment Compensation, 1948–1959," *The Review of Economics and Statistics*, Vol. XLII, No. 4 (November, 1960), pp. 349–72.

[15]Joseph M. Becker, S. J., *The Adequacy of the Benefit Amount in Unemployment Insurance* (Kalamazoo, Michigan: The W. E. Upjohn Institute for Employment Research, 1961), p. 51.

experience or *merit rating* provisions permit the employer to make important savings in his state unemployment insurance tax rate by avoiding claims for benefits from his employees. State payroll tax rates can be reduced to levels as low as zero percent by avoiding the release of workers or their successful claims for benefits.

These provisions are by no means universally approved. Union spokesmen have charged that the possibility of employer tax savings through limited benefit payments causes many employers to oppose the liberalization of benefits and to contest claims without respect to their merit. These and other critics of merit rating argue that this attitude frequently restricts the granting of unemployment benefits, which they regard as the major purpose of this legislation. They argue, also, that ratings are not really earned; they result from conditions over which employers have little control. Employer experience and resulting tax rates are unquestionably influenced by many conditions other than employer efforts to stabilize employment. The general level of business and the tightness or the looseness of labor markets have obvious effects on employment in individual firms and on the speed with which released employees are reemployed.

On the other hand, public opinion seems to feel that the system will be more effectively administered if employers are motivated to police its operations. With somewhat the same viewpoint as that in which unions are encouraged as a check on the economic power of employers, employer policing of unemployment insurance is encouraged by these merit rating provisions. It is notable that public support for them has grown as experience has accumulated.[16]

In the decade of the 1950's the average employer tax rate was 1.5 percent; in 1963 the average rate was 2.3 percent. (In 3 states employees also pay taxes for UC.) The tax rate is computed on the basis of covered payrolls. Under the federal law only the first $3000 of wages and salaries earned in a year are included in the tax base. Six states have a state tax base of $3600 or more.[17]

---

[16]See Richard A. Lester, "Financing of Unemployment Compensation," *Industrial and Labor Relations Review*, Vol. 14, No. 1 (October, 1960), pp. 24–34; also his *The Economics of Unemployment Compensation* (Princeton, N.J.: Industrial Relations Section, Princeton University, 1962).

[17]However, the federal credit for state taxes applies only to the first $3,000. Amounts above this are not eligible for the federal offset. Hence, the federal standard tends to discourage enlargement of the taxable wage base in the individual states.

Another way to compute the tax burden is the "effective tax rate," defined as the percent of dollar UC taxes as a share of total covered wages, not total taxable wages. Because of the low tax base, taxable payrolls have less cyclical variation than total payrolls. In recessions the tax burden rises as a percent of total payroll and, hence, has a countercyclical effect.

Disqualifications

States vary widely in their practice in disqualifying the unemployed. The usual bases are voluntary quits without adequate cause, discharge for cause (misconduct), refusal to accept suitable work, and idleness occasioned by a labor dispute. Disqualification may be temporary, for a stated period, or it may cancel all rights to benefits. At the heart of differences in rules and practice is a conflict in theory. Most disqualifications are imposed as punishment. Temporary disqualifications, however, add the theory that persistent failure to find a job reflects labor market conditions over which the worker has no control.

Reserves

As a minimum, each state's reserve funds should be equal to benefit costs experienced in the worst recession period in the last decade. Usually a reserve of $1\frac{1}{2}$ to 2 times the worst experience is considered more appropriate. It has been suggested that "trigger points" be established so that when reserves are low in relation to benefits, increased tax rate schedules would go into effect; conversely, when reserves are high, tax rate decreases would be made. Such flexible financing might be paralleled by flexible benefits, with maximums as a percentage of average weekly wages. (Seven states now use such formulas.)

The Philosophy of Unemployment Insurance

The philosophical basis for unemployment insurance requires thoughtful consideration by all citizens. Is it intended to be simply a relief measure designed to introduce system in granting temporary aid to those who need it? Is it primarily a pump-priming device whose major purpose is to stabilize the economy? Is it an insurance program designed to spread the risk and cost of involuntary idleness? Is it, or can it be, a combination of all three?[18]

Can states be expected to measure up to their responsibilities by providing adequate taxes? Is the present system of compartmentalized reserves, held in state-identified funds, appropriate for our economy?

---

[18]See in this connection, Harry Malisoff, "The Challenge of Unemployment Insurance," *Industrial and Labor Relations Review*, Vol. 14, No. 1 (October, 1960), pp. 50–51; see also his *The Financing of Extended Unemployment Insurance Benefits in the United States* (Kalamazoo, Michigan: The W. E. Upjohn Institute for Employment Research, April, 1963).

Are federal standards of eligibility, benefit amounts, duration, and disqualification necessary to make the program effective?

The evidence is clear that many states have not levied taxes adequate to meet recession needs. Temporary federal loans have been necessary to keep funds solvent. The availability of such loans probably encourages these states to avoid increasing tax rates. However, recession difficulties have been encountered by less than half the states. Studies by the Bureau of Employment Security indicate that the average cost ratio of benefits to taxable wages in 1951–1960 was 3.22 percent. Aggregate reserves in 1960 amounted to 1.8 times this ratio in the highest cost year, 1958. In 1961 half the states had reserves twice as great as their cost ratios, despite persistence of an outdated tax base of $3,000 in earnings. It appears that the problem in other states arises largely out of their determination to keep taxes low to gain an advantage in interstate economic competition.

One solution would pool a portion of state reserves, thus sharing risks and costs. Another would impose higher tax requirements by federal law, a more obvious step toward federalization of the system.[19]

It is apparent that most of us now accept unemployment insurance as here to stay. The original opposition to the whole program as a matter of principle has largely disappeared. Our primary purpose appears clearly to be the provision of assistance for those who become unemployed and who want to resume working. We intend that the program shall ease the burden of transitional unemployment, that which takes place between jobs. Our two major problems are (1) how to insure adequate benefits to ease and facilitate this transition and (2) how to protect the program from distributing its funds to unworthy recipients — those who are not seriously looking for work.

In the immediate future, therefore, we can expect to see public attention focused on these two problems. In popular terms the issue will be whether anyone who has worked long enough to become eligible has a "right" to benefits for the maximum period or whether this assistance in larger, more effective amounts shall be limited to those who will use it only while they are changing jobs.

Incidentally, also, future attention may be attracted to the possibility that voluntary quits or resignations should not automatically disqualify employees. Our economic system gains much of its

---

[19]See Fred Slavick, "Ability of the Federal-State Unemployment Insurance System to Provide Benefits in Time of Recession," *Proceedings, Industrial Relations Research Association*, 1961, pp. 178–93.

dynamic quality and strength from the mobility of our labor force. Quitting to search for a better, more promising job is one expression of this mobility. Provisions that penalize such venturesomeness tend to destroy this highly important quality.[20]

Recommended Changes

The following recommendations to improve our unemployment insurance system were made in 1962 by President Kennedy:

1. Extension of the benefit period by as much as 13 weeks for workers with at least 3 years of experience in covered employment.

2. Extension of benefit periods for those with less than 3 years of covered employment. Such extension could be "triggered" when insured unemployment reaches 5 percent and the number of benefit exhaustions over a 3-month period reaches 1 percent of covered employment.

3. Incentives for the states to increase benefits so that the great majority of covered workers would be eligible for weekly benefits equal to at least half their weekly wage.

4. Extension of coverage to at least 3 million additional workers.

5. Improved financing by raising the payroll base from $3,000 to $4,800.

6. Reinsurance grants to states experiencing high unemployment insurance costs.

7. Provisions which permit claimants to receive benefits while attending approved training or retraining courses.[21]

Economic Effects of Unemployment Insurance

What are the economic effects of unemployment insurance, including taxes and benefits? Do these programs cause unemployment? prevent unemployment? reduce unemployment? How do they affect wages, purchasing power, and allocation of resources?

To answer these questions, we may first recall that unemployment insurance has a variety of purposes, as noted. It seeks to: (1) prevent unemployment, (2) minimize the adverse effects of unemployment to

---

[20]The current system has probably encouraged some married women and part-time workers to seek seasonal jobs. This effect could be minimized by reducing benefits for intermittent workers and making duration dependent on length of prior employment, thus tending to distinguish these "temporary" workers. That move would, however, tend to handicap the countercyclical effect of the program. See James O'Conner, "Seasonal Unemployment and Unemployment Insurance," *American Economic Review*, Vol. 52, No. 3 (June, 1962), pp. 469–70.

[21]*Economic Report of the President*, January, 1962, pp. 20–21.

the individual by "tiding him over" between jobs, and (3) benefit society by providing a supplement for reduced purchasing power. Second, unemployment insurance is designed primarily for prevention and amelioration of frictional, seasonal, and other short-run types of unemployment rather than longer-run cyclical or secular types. Third, unemployment insurance is something different from an insurance program in the usual sense. It is difficult to predict or forecast unemployment, and hence the risk factor is uncertain. In addition, unemployment may be cumulative and reinforcing. This makes it more difficult to spread risks, a basic insurance principle.[22] Inability to use the usual actuarial concepts makes prediction of results more difficult. We are handicapped also by lack of empirical research studies of these problems.

Two major phases of the unemployment insurance program, taxes and benefits, deserve consideration. The payroll tax represents a potential or actual added cost to the employer. Presumably he will try to shift this tax to consumers or employees or both. The strength of his desire to shift probably will be affected by the importance of his labor costs to total costs. The higher the proportion of labor costs to total costs, the greater is his incentive to shift. The rate of the tax also may affect his desire to shift the burden. The higher his tax rate, the more likelihood of attempts at shifting. In many cases UI taxes are a small proportion of business expense, and hence there is little incentive to shift. Further, in effect the federal government absorbs part of the tax for many firms because of the corporate net income tax, which takes a substantial proportion of net profits (almost half) in many firms.

The employer's ability to shift the tax to consumers depends upon the elasticity of demand for the product. The greater the inelasticity, the easier it is to shift. His ability to shift the burden to employees depends upon the labor supply curve. In general, if labor is in excess supply and if the employees are not unionized, it is easier to shift the burden. If he cannot shift the burden either way and has to bear it

[22]Some convenient references on the economic effects of unemployment compensation are: (1) Joseph Shister, *Economics of the Labor Market* (2nd ed., New York: J. B. Lippincott Co., 1956), pp. 301–09; C. R. Daugherty and John B. Parrish, *The Labor Problems of American Society* (Boston: Houghton Mifflin Co., 1952), pp. 668–73; M. J. Bowman and G. L. Bach, *Economic Analysis and Public Policy* (New York: Prentice-Hall, Inc., 1943), pp. 815–18. See also Arthur Larson, "The Economic Function of Unemployment Insurance," in *Proceedings, Industrial Relations Research Association*, December 28–30, 1954, pp. 152–63.

himself (and does not have a sufficient profit margin to absorb the added cost), he may reduce his level of output and employment; the economic effect is similar to increasing wage rates, thereby raising the supply curve of labor.

Richard A. Lester has estimated that no more than one third of unemployment taxes is shifted to consumers in the form of higher prices.[23] The tax rate varies greatly among industries and within a single industry, reflecting differentials in unemployment experience. The fact that there is great variation within an industry would tend to make high-rate employers hesitant to try to shift, because low-rate employers would not feel as strong a need for a shift. Hence, the only portions likely to be shifted would be taxes borne in common (e.g., the 0.4 percent federal tax and the state minimum).

Effects of unemployment insurance on employment.

In competitive markets the unemployment compensation tax would tend to reduce employment and output unless there was a compensating increase in employee productivity. It has been argued, for example, that employees might feel more secure in their jobs under unemployment insurance and less responsive to the "lump of labor" doctrine, and hence they would produce more. On the other hand, it has been argued that union seniority provisions provide sufficient job security for the more productive members of a firm's labor force and hence that unemployment insurance would have relatively little incentive effect except on low-seniority employees. Here again it is apparent that armchair speculation is not enough and that we need empirical studies to get at the realities in specific labor markets.

If employees' productivity is unchanged by provision of unemployment insurance, the effects of the tax probably would be reduced employment and output. If the tax were shifted to employees, their wages would be (in effect) lower than they otherwise would be, and hence their purchasing power and demand would presumably decline. If the tax were borne by the employer, his profits would decline and he might not be able to make the same level of reinvestment.

However, the other "half of the scissors," benefits, must be considered. Presumably the unemployed would have a high propensity to spend rather than to save. Would not their spending offset the reduced spending of employers who bear the major burden of the taxes?

---

[23]Richard A. Lester, "Unemployment Insurance Financing: Problems and Prospects," *Employment Security Review*, Vol. 29, No. 8 (August, 1962), pp. 18–21.

The spending of benefits by the unemployed would tend to increase the demand for goods and services. Employers would respond by expanding output. By expanding output they could reduce unit costs of their fixed overhead items. In order to expand they would need to increase their demands for raw materials and labor. Assuming that they hired back the unemployed, the slump in output and employment would be reduced since those reemployed would again have wages to spend, and hence (unless they saved a significant portion) demand for goods and services would be restored to former levels. From an economic standpoint idle resources would be employed again, thereby improving the efficiency of the economy.

The incidence of the tax is important in attempting to assess its economic effects. Employees are the major consumer group and hence may be expected to be affected by whatever shift of taxes the employer is able to make, that is, whether to consumer or to employees or to both. The economic effects of unemployment insurance on individual employees may represent a form of wage transfer. The tax is assessed on wages of all covered employees, but those with most seniority are least likely to get benefits. If the employer can shift the tax to employees, presumably it is shifted to all of them. Those with low seniority are most likely to get unemployment insurance benefits, and part of their benefits will come from higher seniority employees who presumably could have received higher wages (by the amount of the tax) had not the tax been in effect.

Unemployment insurance as a stabilizing device. Unemployment insurance compensation is expected to act as a stabilizing device. In good times we accumulate reserves for bad times, thereby having an anti-inflationary effect. In bad times we reduce unemployment insurance reserves by paying out more in benefits than we receive in taxes, thereby counteracting deflationary effects. Thus, in good times unemployment insurance taxes tend to provide employment levels that are lower than they otherwise would be; in bad times unemployment insurance benefits tend to maintain employment at levels higher than they otherwise would be. This is the general ameliorating effect.[24] However, the preventive goal of unemployment insurance may offset the ameliorating effect because of the experience rating provisions of the various state laws.

---

[24] The *individual* ameliorating effect applies to the individual employee who may have his "good times" income reduced if he bears all or part of the tax and may have his "poor times" income increased by the amount of the benefits he receives. If he has borne none of the tax and gets benefits, he has increased his income (at somebody else's expense).

It will be recalled that experience rating seeks to provide an incentive to employers to prevent unemployment, or at least to stabilize employment.[25] Taxes on employers are lower when employment is stable or rising (usually in good times). As a result of this employment stabilization incentive effect, payments made to the benefit fund tend to have the opposite of an anticyclical effect. Lower rate tax payments come into the fund in good times, and higher rate tax payments come into the fund during bad times (because employment stabilization experience is worse). Thus, experience rating, through raising tax rates in bad times, may increase the employer's costs at a time when he is already in trouble.

This tendency may be less obvious in a period of good times and inflation such as we have had since World War II. Employment and payrolls have increased substantially, and hence reserve funds have continued growing even at comparatively low tax rates. But, and this is very important, the potential liability has increased greatly. The adequacy of existing reserve levels may be more illusory than real as demonstrated by experience during the relatively minor (in comparison to the 1930's) increase in unemployment in 1958. In a period of heavy unemployment, for example, 10–15 percent or more, taxes would have to be increased sharply, thus intensifying rather than mitigating deflation.

A further setback to the countercyclical concept results from uses made of the reserve fund. If, during prosperity, the government uses the funds as part of its general revenues and increases government spending in the same amount as the payroll taxes, this obviously represents merely a transfer of spending and does not dampen inflation. During an ensuing depression it would then probably have to increase general (as well as payroll) taxes to meet accrued liabilities, thereby adding to the deflationary effect.

GUARANTEED EMPLOYMENT AND SUPPLEMENTARY BENEFITS

At about the same time that the unemployment insurance system was getting under way, other forms of employment and wage protection were being tried. These include plans for guaranteed annual wages, supplementary unemployment benefits, and dismissal pay.

---

[25]The employer may stabilize by reducing his work force to the extent of eliminating marginal employees who became submarginal by virtue of the payroll tax.

Guaranteed Annual Wage

Guaranteed employment plans, instead of ameliorating the effects of job loss, seek to prevent job loss. In their approach these plans go beyond employment stabilization by providing employees with guarantees of wages and/or employment. Various guarantee plans have been tried and many are still in operation, but their total number is probably less than one hundred.

In one approach to the assurance of stable employment, some employers have guaranteed a full year's work or pay each year to all employees who meet stipulated minimum length of service requirements. In some cases these arrangements have been established on the initiative of the employer. In others, unions have negotiated contracts calling for such a *guaranteed annual wage* (GAW). In recent years the GAW has become a common union proposal in contract negotiations. The United Automobile Workers union has spearheaded this drive.

Some firms have had long experience with such provisions. Among the best-known plans are those of Procter and Gamble (since 1923), the Hormel Company, and the Nunn-Bush Shoe Company.[26] Usual provisions assure at least 48 weeks of work or pay during each year for employees who qualify. Qualification is based primarily on employment for a stated period. Programs usually require extensive planning of both sales and production and careful internal controls of these activities to smooth peaks and valleys in operations. Frequently, the plans permit ready transfers of workers from one job to another.

Guaranteed employment programs are designed primarily to overcome seasonal fluctuations rather than other types of unemployment, although they are also helpful in technological changes and readjustments. In effect, they put those who are regarded as "established" or "permanent" wage-earning employees on an annual minimum salary basis. In addition to the guarantee of an annual minimum salary, they also permit added earnings if product demands require extensive overtime. On the other hand, the guarantees apply, in most plans, only to the central core of long-service employees.

---

[26]For details of these plans, see Henry C. Thole and Charles C. Gibbons, "The Guaranteed Annual Wage and Business Stabilization," (a bibliography), The W. E. Upjohn Institute for Community Research, Kalamazoo, Michigan, June, 1955; E. J. McCarthy, "Wage Guarantees and Annual Earnings: A Case Study of George A. Hormel and Company," *Journal of Business*, Vol. 29, No. 1 (January, 1956), pp. 41–51.

How widely can this type of arrangement be developed? Is the guaranteed annual wage likely to become a generally accepted form of compensation for wage earners? Is it feasible for any large segment of the labor force? What economic considerations affect its acceptance, and how would general adoption of these plans affect our economy?

These questions have been widely debated. Advocates of annual guarantees of work or wages argue that employers would and do expect to support farm animals — mules are the favorite example — on an annual basis. Why should they do less for men? These proponents insist that the annual support of essential workers in an industry is a proper cost of production, and any added expense occasioned by this guarantee should be incorporated in the cost and price of the product. They argue that stabilization can be accomplished and employment guaranteed by better management and that employers should be required to do a better job of planning and scheduling work. They point to our general acceptance of the principle of steady jobs and urge employment guarantees as a means of achieving this goal. Those who favor some form of guaranteed employment also argue that the effects would be cumulative: guaranteed wages would tend to stabilize purchasing power and thus maintain demands for the services of these and other workers. Further, they say that such guarantees would be more economical in that necessary leveling of production would obviate the need for importing short-term employees in peak periods.

Critics of these guarantees generally insist that they are possible only in a limited range of consumer goods industries for which retailers can be encouraged to order on a periodic quota basis. They point to the historic, wide cyclical swings in employment in capital goods industries as evidence that stabilization in such industries with the costs of guaranteed annual wages would price their products out of their markets. They also insist that such guarantees, if widely applied, would seriously handicap the economy by their effects on labor mobility.

Studies of the long-term employment experience of many firms suggest that guarantees could be extended to rather large portions of their employees without additional cost. These workers have been steadily employed, with stable earnings, in the absence of formal guarantees. In such cases, of course, questions may be raised as to what GAW would add. In the case of some other firms, guarantees appear feasible if managements are granted flexibility in the assignment of work. Costs are directly related to the proportion of all employees covered and the flexibility in work assignments.

Supplementary Unemployment Benefits

In 1955 a variation of the earlier employment or wage guarantees attracted wide attention when the provision was negotiated by the United Automobile Workers (CIO) with both Ford and General Motors. As noted, this union has long campaigned for a guaranteed annual wage. Employers in the automobile industry have argued that, although they have been quite successful in reducing seasonal peaks and valleys, other fluctuations in demand are so great as to make wage guarantees impossible. The 1955 contract established a somewhat different type of wage security, commonly described as *supplemental unemployment benefits* (SUB). As specified by these contracts in the automobile industry and several others, each employer contributes to a special reserve fund, which then provides supplements to unemployment insurance benefits for employees of the firm who are laid off. Together with the usual unemployment insurance benefits, these supplements allow payments to the unemployed that approximate two thirds of weekly take-home pay. Over 2 million workers now are covered by SUB in its various forms.

Typical provisions of these original SUB plans may be outlined as follows. Special benefit payments are made to unemployed workers as a supplement to their unemployment insurance benefits. In the Ford and General Motors plans these payments are drawn from reserve funds created by the employers' contributions. Such contributions continue until the individual firm's reserve reaches a specified total, which is calculated by reference to the number of covered employees. Contributions are resumed whenever the reserve falls below this "floating" maximum. Benefits are paid, after a one-week waiting period, whenever an employee is laid off "without cause." For the first four-week period, benefits provide a total (with unemployment insurance) equal to 65 percent of regular earnings. Thereafter, for a longer period (up to 26 weeks) supplements maintain a level of 60 percent of usual earnings. In renegotiation of contracts there is a continuing tendency to liberalize benefits and increase contributions.[27]

---

[27]Less than 4 percent of all wage and salary workers are covered by SUB. Declines in employment in steel and autos have just about offset new coverage. In 1962 steel changed its benefit formula so that the weekly payment including UC is 24 times the

The glass industry plan is different from the auto and steel plans (which are alike) in that it is a deferred savings plan with vested rights. Each employee has his own account or security fund, which is his if he quits, or retires, or is dismissed. Obviously, the glass industry plan facilitates labor mobility to a much greater degree than the auto or steel plans.

Many questions have been raised about these private unemployment insurance plans. To some critics they are primarily a device developed by unions to force more generous payments under the public unemployment insurance system. Some critics insist that they will become unpopular with long-service employees, whose seniority protects them against layoff and thus prevents them from receiving benefits. Others hold that they are inevitably divisive in the unions that secure them, arraigning the interests of older, long-service employees against those of newer members.

Questions are also raised as to the effects of these arrangements on labor mobility and the allocation of human resources. Are they likely to keep unemployed workers from making desirable shifts to other industries and localities? Will they so increase labor costs as to restrict profits and sales?

These plans may be expected to modify manpower management practice in the industries in which they are accepted. They add another, and an expensive, type of fringe payment. They may justify more careful checking on employee effort and output, perhaps through improved personnel or performance ratings. They may justify more careful recruitment and hiring, together with increased attention to employment stabilization, since the plans permit impressive employer savings if reserve funds remain at specified levels.

Little evidence indicates how union members may react to these new arrangements. Perhaps the failure of many unions to propose that similar plans be provided for their members indicates some skepticism. No impressive movement of potential employees into labor markets with SUB plans has been reported.[28]

---

average hourly wage plus $1.50 for each dependent up to four. While the worker is drawing UC, maximum SUB benefit is $37.50 plus $1.50 per dependent; after UC expires, the maximum is $60 plus $1.50 per dependent. The company obligation is up from a maximum of 5¢ an hour to 9½¢ per hour.

Auto plans in 1961 changed the benefit plan to 62 percent of straight time before tax pay, plus $1.50 per dependent up to four, less UC benefits. Weekly maximum SUB benefits are $40, in some cases payable for as much as 52 weeks a year.

[28]For observations and forecasts about these plans, see John W. McConnell, "Private Unemployment Pay Plans — Economic Effects," *Monthly Labor Review*, Vol. 79, No. 3

Economic Effects of GAW and SUB Plans

In general, GAW tends to make labor a fixed cost, whereas SUB is more of a variable cost.[29] We can begin our analysis by reference to two major social objectives: (1) to maintain a flexible, dynamic economy with mobility of resources responsive to the price system and (2) within this framework to provide optimal income and employment stability — optimal in the sense that it will not interfere with flexibility and growth. Actually there is much income and employment stability within our economy, although very little of this is guaranteed by law. Instead such stability is due to satisfactory economic performance of employers. They have many reasons for desiring economic stability without the added impetus of GAW. While firms may be successful in meeting relatively minor seasonal and other short-run output and employment fluctuations, few firms could singlehandedly overcome cyclical fluctuations.

Most GAW plans guarantee either income or employment, or both. The liability of the guarantee depends upon: (1) the proportion of employees covered, (2) the length of time the guarantee is good for, (3) the extent of the wages or employment guaranteed to covered employees (for example, number of weeks or amount per week), and (4) the "escape clause" that would nullify the guarantees (for example, act of God, disqualifications, etc.). The company can offset this liability to some extent by attempting to regularize production and

---

(March, 1956), pp. 300–03; Jack Chernick, "The Guaranteed Annual Wage, Employment and Economic Progress," *Industrial and Labor Relations Review*, Vol. 9, No. 3 (April, 1956), pp. 469–73. For greater detail, see Earl F. Cheit, "Appraising the New G.A.W. Bargains," *Current Economic Comment* (University of Illinois, Bureau of Business Research), Vol. 18, No. 1 (February, 1956), pp. 3–11; Michael T. Wermel and Geraldine M. Beideman, "Supplemental Unemployment Benefit Plans — Their Economic and Industrial Relations Implications," Industrial Relations Section, California Institute of Technology, January, 1957. See also "In Labor," *Business Week* (August 8, 1961), p. 62; and "Digest of Nine Supplemental Unemployment Benefit Plans: Early 1963," United States Bureau of Labor Statistics, *Bulletin No. 1365*, May, 1963.

[29]For references on economic effects of GAW, see: Murray W. Latimer, *Guaranteed Wages*, Report to the President by the Advisory Board, Office of War Mobilization and Reconversion (Washington, D.C.: U.S. Government Printing Office, 1947); A. H. Hansen and P. A. Samuelson, "Economic Analysis of Guaranteed Wages," *U.S. Bureau of Labor Statistics Bulletin 907*, 1947; A. D. H. Kaplan, *The Guarantee of Annual Wages* (Washington, D.C.: The Brookings Institution, 1947); Jack Chernick, "A Guide to the Guaranteed Wage," *Bulletin No. 4*,(New Brunswick, New Jersey: Rutgers University, Institute of Management and Labor Relations, 1955).

See also W. A. Berridge and C. Wolfe, "Guaranteed Employment and Wage Plans," *National Economic Problems Bulletin No. 428* (Washington, D.C.: American Enterprise Association, Inc., 1948); "Supplementation of Unemployment Benefits," (Washington, D.C.: AFL-CIO Industrial Union Department, 1956); "The Economics of the Guaranteed Wage," (Washington, D.C.: Chamber of Commerce of the United States, 1953); Seymour E. Harris, "Economics of the Guaranteed Wage," *Proceedings, Industrial Relations Research Association*, December 28–30, 1954, pp. 164–85.

stabilize employment through dovetailing, diversification, production for stock, and other devices previously mentioned (see Chapter 15).

The long-run economic implications of an extended application of GAW plans is far from clear. They might have some tendency to deter ventures into new businesses or new products. They could exert an influence toward mergers and combinations. At the other extreme, they appear in some instances to have caused employers to "farm out" work and to contract for outside services.[30]

As noted, the initial effect of the guarantee is to make a portion of the firm's labor costs fixed rather than variable. The greater the guarantee, the higher the proportion of fixed obligations assumed by the firm and the less the firm's ability to reduce costs in time of adverse business conditions. Several potential consequences are related to this fact: (1) Firms may limit guarantees to the point where they contribute little to economic stability, that is, give the guarantee only to the hard core of their basic employment. (2) Firms may hesitate to put in such plans if other firms do not for fear it would put them at a competitive disadvantage. It has been suggested that if all the firms in an industry would install similar plans simultaneously, this objection might be overcome. It is likely, however, that the degree of cooperation needed to do this might result in anticompetitive arrangements that would be opposed to the public welfare. A similar suggestion that firms in a community jointly undertake such plans seems to overlook the fact that many firms compete industry-wide rather than community-wide. (3) Firms with guaranteed employment plans may hesitate to expand, since their potential fixed obligation would increase. Thus, desirable economic growth might be lost. (4) In adverse circumstances firms might curtail their investment in new plant and equipment. The combination of these latter two effects (nonexpansion and reduced investment) might result in stabilized levels of output and employment that would be lower than if no guarantees were in effect. (5) Many firms have wide fluctuations in the demand for their products and services. GAW per se probably

---

[30]See Campbell R. McConnell, "Pros and Cons of the Guaranteed Annual Wage," *Labor Law Journal*, Vol. 7, No. 7 (July, 1956), pp. 414 ff.; John W. McConnell, "The Guaranteed Annual Wage," *Industrial and Labor Relations Review*, Vol. 1, No. 2 (March, 1955), pp. 2–4; also his "The Guaranteed Annual Wage," *ILR Research*, Vol. 1, No. 2 (March, 1955), pp. 2–4; Otis Brubaker, "Guaranteed Annual Wage," *Labor Law Journal*, Vol. 4, No. 6 (June, 1953), pp. 387 ff.; Morris A. Horowitz, "Wage Guarantees of Road Service Employees of American Railroads," *American Economic Review*, Vol. 45, No. 5 (December, 1955), pp. 853–66; *Economics of the Guaranteed Wage* (Washington: Chamber of Commerce of the United States, 1953).

would have little effect on stabilizing consumer demand for products unless these plans were very widespread (almost universal). Widespread compulsory GAW plans probably would require extensive and intensive federal controls over production, wages, and prices inconsistent with our concepts of free enterprise economy.

Employers can attempt to meet their guarantees through one of two basic methods — *reserve financing* or *pay-as-you-go*. Employment and wage levels could be higher in good times under a pay-as-you-go system, but in poor times firms might not be able to meet their guarantees. Thus, total employment and wages might be lower over a time span including both good and bad times. Reserve financing probably would result in relatively lower employment and wage levels in good times but would show more favorable results in poor times. On balance, reserve financing might be expected to do a better job over the entire employment cycle.

The intended effects of the reserve plan are to take some of the top off the boom and to use this to fill in the trough so it will not go so low. The actual effects require fine forecasting, for if a firm takes too much "off the top" in good times, it may curtail investment and growth too much. If the reserve is too small, the company will find it inadequate to meet obligations in bad times when this is very costly; further, this could drain working and potential investment capital in such a way as to accelerate deflationary effects.

Probably more important than the method of financing is the amount of flexibility the employer has over his work-force assignments. If he can recoup his guarantee costs through increased employee production, his labor costs are not increased. But if through rigid seniority or jurisdictional requirements he is unable to shift employees from an idle department to one that needs extra help, he is increasing his labor costs by paying added wages for no return. As one union leader remarked, "The price unions must pay for employment stabilization is increased employer authority over work assignments," that is, increased flexibility of the work force.

Of course employers may and probably will try to shift the costs of their guarantees, just as in the case of unemployment compensation payments and minimum wages. They may attempt to shift the costs to consumers through higher prices or to employees through relatively lower wages. Failing these alternatives, they may take the costs out of reserves (but only in the short run) or in the form of lower profits.

Again we find ourselves discussing the relative saving-spending-purchasing-power arguments. Under reserve plans, if the incidence is on consumers and/or wage earners, effects would tend to be anti-inflationary and would tend to level consumption and output by reducing spending in good times and increasing spending in poor times. In essence this merely transfers consumption through time and does not raise the total level of consumption, output, and employment. It smooths things over and may change the patterns of buying. Of course, in times of full employment, inflation, and labor shortages, the wage earner and/or consumer might gain by having some of his money purchasing power saved for him rather than to experience the effects of price inflation.

If the costs were to come out of profits, this might increase consumption expenditures to the extent that stockholders save more and spend less than other consumers. Effects on investment could be serious. Firms might hesitate to invest, especially in bad times, because of the need to keep liquid assets to meet their guarantees.

The net effects of GAW-SUB plans would seem to be: (1) a shifting of purchasing power (rather than creation of purchasing power) from those with jobs to those without jobs for limited time periods; (2) a very limited anticyclical effect — other measures of public policy probably would be more effective; (3) a less flexible economy — there would probably be less labor and other resource mobility; (4) possibilities of the creation of two classes of employees — those covered by guarantees, who have it good, and those not covered, who take more risks (probably the younger, less-skilled employees who may have greater need for stability); (5) possibility of reduced incentive to investment; (6) higher labor costs per unit to the extent that the employer might have to pay for some labor he cannot utilize.

For these and other reasons, the older type GAW plans were never very extensive. At the time of the famous Latimer report (1947), fewer than 200 firms had such plans covering about 61,000 employees with guarantees usually limited to one year.

Hence, as noted above, some of the major CIO unions introduced the SUB concept as an alternative approach. As previously observed, this was in effect a limited guarantee designed to supplement unemployment compensation benefits. This overcame a major employer objection to the older GAW plans by limiting their risk. It also shifted emphasis away from employment stabilization to unemployment compensation supplementation. Under SUB plans, contributions are made to private rather than public funds. SUB administrative arrangements are different from unemployment compensation, although SUB and UC private and public administrative arrangements are geared to each other in various ways in the several states. Economic effects of SUB are more like UC than like GAW.

Several likely additional consequences of the newer plans may be: (1) compression of wage structures — lower seniority and lower wage rate employees would gain at the expense of higher seniority and higher wage rate employees; (2) reduction of interemployer labor mobility (unless we get more "income security" or vested plans like the glass plans); (3) lower employment levels if employers hesitate to hire additional temporary employees; (4) probably an increased tempo of automation as labor becomes more of a fixed cost (although this may be slight since the big impetus to automation comes from the vastly superior efficiency of new machines and methods and not from minor GAW-SUB effects); (5) lower labor turnover, although "turnover-prone" employees are probably not so likely to be included in the plan, and hence this effect should be slight; (6) slight effect on investment unless reserves get much larger.

In brief, the employment stabilization effects of SUB plans in their present form are likely to be quite limited. Other market forces will probably have much more influence. When Russia puts up a lunar vehicle, our government buys more hardware; consumers tend to buy cars when they want them regardless of GAW-SUB. There is probably little inherent in GAW-SUB to cause increased labor productivity; hence the most likely effects are shifts of purchasing power from good times to bad and from secure employees to those less secure. Other than these effects, GAW-SUB does not produce economic miracles. As one of a battery of stabilization devices, GAW-SUB may make a contribution to employment stability. But the effects will probably differ from one situation to another for firms with different proportions of labor costs, for firms with expanding or declining demand, and for firms with different proportions of high- and low-seniority employees.

Dismissal Pay

Another widely used device designed to ease the impact of unemployment and to facilitate finding another job is dismissal pay or severance compensation. Plans provide that employees who are permanently separated from the payroll without cause receive a special benefit to "tide them over" until they can find another suitable job. Some employers have established severance pay on their own initiative; in other situations this provision has been negotiated. In several foreign nations specified amounts of dismissal pay are required by law in the absence of advance notice that an employee will be released.

In the United States severance pay plans are found in about one fourth of union contracts. The most common provision is one week's pay for each year of service. Two thirds of the plans place a ceiling on benefits with the typical limitations between 8 and 15 weeks of pay. The most common service requirement is 1 year; one fourth of plans require 2 years of service. One fourth of the plans deny benefits to those who resign; some plans deny benefits to those discharged or when release is caused by merger or sale of the business.[31]

In some firms severance pay is granted to encourage the early retirement of employees who have become ill or disabled. In some, severance pay is used to pay benefits to surviving dependents of deceased employees.

Two distinct methods of calculating benefits are common. One provides a *uniform* or flat allowance, stated in terms of a specified number of weeks' pay. This is less frequent than the *graduated* plans which take into account the length of service and the rate of earnings, together with several other possible factors. Another frequent arrangement pays off in terms of a percentage (for example, 2 percent) of total earnings during the period of employment. Some plans pay off in a single lump sum. Others provide weekly payments. They are intended to facilitate the job-hunting activities of those who have been released. Weekly payments, it should be noted, make recipients ineligible for unemployment insurance in some states.

Severance compensation is a firmly established benefit. It provides obvious assistance in transitional unemployment. By financing at least a short period of idleness, severance pay may facilitate careful selection of a new job, resulting in a desirable mobility and more satisfactory employment. Major questions about the practice concern: (1) the desirable amount of such payments; (2) what

---

[31]See *Basic Patterns in Union Contracts* (5th ed.; Washington, D.C.: Bureau of National Affairs, Inc., April, 1961), pp. 40:6–40:7.

principles should guide the relationship of benefits to prior employment and earnings; (3) whether benefits should be paid in installments or as lump sums; and (4) whether these should be a bar to eligibility for unemployment insurance benefits.

ACCIDENTS AND ILLNESS

The preceding section of this chapter discussed problems of economic insecurity resulting from loss of income due to unemployment. Other major sources of income loss and insecurity are accidents and illness.

There are more accidents away from work than in the workplace. In 1963, for example, there were 101,000 accidental deaths in the United States; there were 9,300,000 disabling injuries. Most deaths (43,600) were due to motor vehicle accidents; there were 14,500 who died from work accidents. Most disabling injuries (over 4 million) occurred in homes; there were some 2 million disabling injuries at work. Accidents were the leading cause of death among all young persons 1–36 of age.

Total accident costs in the United States in 1963 (for all types of accidents, at work and away from work) were $16.1 billion, including $4.7 billion in wage losses; accidents cost employers in excess of $65 per employee per year (including all workers, not just those killed or injured). Accidents cost 230 million man-days of time loss each year— 40 million man-days by injured workers and 190 million more days by other workers. There is a "carryover" of 130 million lost man-days from one year to the next.[32]

Industrial (Work-Connected) Accidents

An appreciation of the problem of industrial accidents is handicapped by difficulties of measuring the hardship they create. Some types of accidents, involving sprains, cuts, and scratches, happen frequently, but most of them create no permanent handicap. Other types are much less frequent, but they may cause the death of workers or permanent disabilities. Some of these disabilities are partial; they cause the loss of an eye or one arm, for example. Other disabilities are total; they completely prevent any return to employment.

---

[32]See *Accident Facts: 1964 Edition*, National Safety Council, 425 N. Michigan, Chicago 11, Illinois.

Because these effects of work-connected accidents are so different, no simple measure of their seriousness and importance is possible. For even the simplest appraisal, it is necessary to measure both the frequency and the severity of work-connected accidents. To measure accident *frequency*, we count the number of accidents that occasion lost time extending beyond the shift in which the accident occurs. We calculate a *frequency rate* as the number of disabling injuries per million man-hours of work. The *severity* of industrial accidents is generally measured in terms of the amount of lost time they occasion. *Severity rates* are calculated for a firm or industry as the numbers of days lost per million man-hours of work.[33]

Industry differences. Industries show wide differences in their accident experience. Some industries, like coal mining and lumbering, have many severe accidents resulting in permanent disability or death. Other industries, notably communications and electrical equipment, have few accidents, and those that happen generally occasion only minor scratches, cuts, and bruises. Some industries, like cement and steel, have few accidents, but those that occur are likely to be severe. Others, for example meat packing, have many accidents, but they are generally minor in terms of long-term disabilities.

This comparison is evident in the graphic summary of frequency and severity rates for various industries prepared by the National Safety Council and shown in Figure 23-2.

Trends in frequency and severity. Some progress in reducing these accident hazards in employment is apparent. Employers, unions, and public agencies have joined in safety programs to prevent accidents. These programs usually include five major steps, including (1) the maintenance of careful records of all accidents, (2) identification of unsafe machines and practices, (3) regular safety inspections, (4) use of machine guards and safety devices, and (5) enforcement of safety rules and regulations. These safety programs have "paid off" by continued reductions in both frequency and severity rates.[34] These changes can be clearly seen in the thirty-seven-year records of the National Safety Council, graphically shown in Figure 23-3.

---

[33]To permit plant-to-plant and time-to-time comparisons, we have standard time charges for various types of permanent disabilities. For example, loss of one finger is counted as 300 days lost, loss of an arm as 4,500 days, and death as 6,000 days.

[34]From 1940 to 1960, employment increased 42 percent, while total disabling work injuries were up only 7 percent.

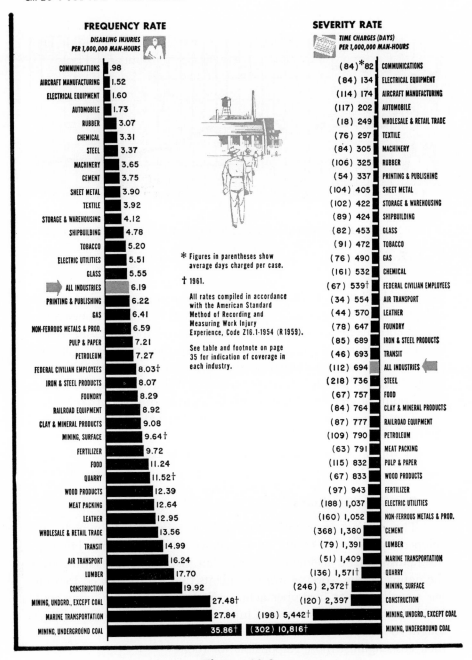

FREQUENCY RATE

DISABLING INJURIES
PER 1,000,000 MAN-HOURS

COMMUNICATIONS	.98
AIRCRAFT MANUFACTURING	1.52
ELECTRICAL EQUIPMENT	1.60
AUTOMOBILE	1.73
RUBBER	3.07
CHEMICAL	3.31
STEEL	3.37
MACHINERY	3.65
CEMENT	3.75
SHEET METAL	3.90
TEXTILE	3.92
STORAGE & WAREHOUSING	4.12
SHIPBUILBING	4.78
TOBACCO	5.20
ELECTRIC UTILITIES	5.51
GLASS	5.55
ALL INDUSTRIES	6.19
PRINTING & PUBLISHING	6.22
GAS	6.41
NON-FERROUS METALS & PROD.	6.59
PULP & PAPER	7.21
PETROLEUM	7.27
FEDERAL CIVILIAN EMPLOYEES	8.03†
IRON & STEEL PRODUCTS	8.07
FOUNDRY	8.29
RAILROAD EQUIPMENT	8.92
CLAY & MINERAL PRODUCTS	9.08
MINING, SURFACE	9.64†
FERTILIZER	9.72
FOOD	11.24
QUARRY	11.52†
WOOD PRODUCTS	12.39
MEAT PACKING	12.64
LEATHER	12.95
WHOLESALE & RETAIL TRADE	13.56
TRANSIT	14.99
AIR TRANSPORT	16.24
LUMBER	17.70
CONSTRUCTION	19.92
MINING, UNDGRD., EXCEPT COAL	27.48†
MARINE TRANSPORTATION	27.84
MINING, UNDERGROUND COAL	35.86†

* Figures in parentheses show average days charged per case.

† 1961.

All rates compiled in accordance with the American Standard Method of Recording and Measuring Work Injury Experience, Code Z16.1-1954 (R 1959).

See table and footnote on page 35 for indication of coverage in each industry.

SEVERITY RATE

TIME CHARGES (DAYS)
PER 1,000,000 MAN-HOURS

(84)*82	COMMUNICATIONS
(84) 134	ELECTRICAL EQUIPMENT
(114) 174	AIRCRAFT MANUFACTURING
(117) 202	AUTOMOBILE
(18) 249	WHOLESALE & RETAIL TRADE
(76) 297	TEXTILE
(84) 305	MACHINERY
(106) 325	RUBBER
(54) 337	PRINTING & PUBLISHING
(104) 405	SHEET METAL
(102) 422	STORAGE & WAREHOUSING
(89) 424	SHIPBUILDING
(82) 453	GLASS
(91) 472	TOBACCO
(76) 490	GAS
(161) 532	CHEMICAL
(67) 539†	FEDERAL CIVILIAN EMPLOYEES
(34) 554	AIR TRANSPORT
(44) 570	LEATHER
(78) 647	FOUNDRY
(85) 689	IRON & STEEL PRODUCTS
(46) 693	TRANSIT
(112) 694	ALL INDUSTRIES
(218) 736	STEEL
(67) 757	FOOD
(84) 764	CLAY & MINERAL PRODUCTS
(87) 777	RAILROAD EQUIPMENT
(109) 790	PETROLEUM
(63) 791	MEAT PACKING
(115) 832	PULP & PAPER
(67) 833	WOOD PRODUCTS
(97) 943	FERTILIZER
(188) 1,037	ELECTRIC UTILITIES
(160) 1,052	NON-FERROUS METALS & PROD.
(368) 1,380	CEMENT
(79) 1,391	LUMBER
(51) 1,409	MARINE TRANSPORTATION
(136) 1,571†	QUARRY
(246) 2,372†	MINING, SURFACE
(120) 2,397	CONSTRUCTION
(198) 5,442†	MINING, UNDGRD., EXCEPT COAL
(302) 10,816†	MINING, UNDERGROUND COAL

Figure 23-2
1962 INJURY RATES, REPORTERS TO NATIONAL SAFETY COUNCIL

Source: *Accident Facts*, National Safety Council, 1963, p. 26.

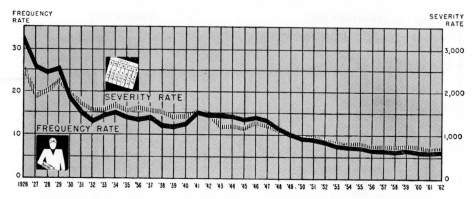

Figure 23-3

TRENDS IN FREQUENCY AND SEVERITY RATES — 1926 TO 1962

Source: *Accident Facts*, National Safety Council, 1963, p. 28.

The burden of accidents. Every work-connected injury causes obvious loss to the worker who is hurt. Shall the injured person and his dependents bear the full burden and costs — the pain and distress as well as the economic loss occasioned by the accident? Or shall some of the loss be charged to the employer or to the consuming public? Who "should" bear these costs? What is desirable from a social point of view with respect to the sharing of this burden?

These questions have long been recognized as important and difficult. Since the Industrial Revolution, we have adopted and tried several approaches in seeking satisfactory answers.

Common-Law Rules

The earliest systematic approach is represented by rules developed by courts of equity in such cases. These common-law rules distinguished true accidents — those that just happen, resulting from the nature of the work — from accidents that can be traced to someone's negligence or improper action. For the first type, no one could be blamed, and those who were injured must bear their costs. Courts sought to fix the blame for the second type of accidents and to assess their costs against those responsible for them.

In applying these general principles the courts developed several common-law rules of liability. They held that an employer must assume three responsibilities: (1) to provide a safe place to work;

(2) to conduct his business in a safe manner, and (3) to select competent employees. If he met these requirements, he could protect himself in suits for damages by three defenses. The first, the *assumption-of-risk rule*, held that employees assumed the usual risks of work when they accepted employment. Second, the *contributory negligence rule* made the employee responsible if he contributed by his own action to cause the accident. Third, the *fellow-servant rule* relieved an employer of blame if the action of some other employee contributed to the cause of the accident.

Employers' Liability Laws

In the United States these common-law rules were incorporated in statute law, generally described as employers' liability acts, and provided the basic guide during the 19th century. As a result, thousands of injured employees received no financial reimbursement for work-connected injuries. Some could not or did not undertake the lawsuits necessary to secure such recourse. Others sued but lost. Employers bought insurance to protect themselves against the claims of injured employees, much as automobile drivers buy public liability protection today. Some lawyers found a lucrative business in "ambulance-chasing," rushing injured employees into agreements in which the lawyers were assured of large portions of whatever damages they could collect.

In general, employers' liability laws appeared more beneficial to some lawyers and insurance companies than to injured employees. According to one early study, employees received only about 28 cents out of each premium dollar paid for insurance. Meanwhile, some employers, unable to afford adequate insurance, were harassed by the possibility of such severe judgments as might put them out of business. Injured employees were frequently unable to work, without funds, and hence dependent upon public or private charity.

Workmen's Compensation

In 1908 a federal law covering public employees signaled a new approach to the whole problem. It was known as *workmen's compensation* and was modeled after German legislation. The rationale or philosophy of workmen's compensation laws is sharply different from that of the common law or of employers' liability acts; workmen's compensation is based on the principle of *liability without fault*.

This newer viewpoint assumes that, except in rare cases in which an employee intentionally injures himself, the interests of society are best served by a system that provides: (1) prompt, sure, and reasonable compensation to injured employees; (2) assurance that they will not become dependent on public charity as a result of their injury; (3) assessment of accident costs as a part of total production costs; and (4) provision of employer incentives for safety programs and reduction of work-connected accidents.[35]

To attain these objectives, workmen's compensation laws specify that employers must carry insurance (or provide an adequate bond) to guarantee payment of benefits. Reports of accidents must be filed with public authorities. Employees need not sue to secure compensation, for it is automatic. They may sue if they fail to secure a satisfactory settlement. The amount of such benefits is based on statutory rules and fixed by administrative commissions or boards. Compensation is paid for a period determined by the nature of the accident and at a rate representing a specified proportion of wages.

By 1949 all states had enacted workmen's compensation laws. Each year about two million persons, including dependents, receive workmen's compensation payments in excess of one billion dollars. Some laws allow employers to elect whether to participate in the workmen's compensation program or to remain subject to employers' liability laws, without, however, the usual common-law defenses. In general, compensation laws propose benefits of 60 to 66⅔ percent of usual weekly wages, which are further limited by specified maximum weekly payments and maximum length of the compensation period. In only 6 of 50 states, in recent years, have cash benefits restored as much as 60 percent of the average weekly wage. A waiting period, typically one week, is required before benefits begin. Most laws provide for payment of medical costs. In addition, some states maintain rehabilitation services for injured workers.

Laws usually prohibit suits against employers for damages arising out of industrial accidents except as appeals from decisions of the administrative commission. Insurance is provided by private insurance companies, state public insurance divisions, and self-insurance. Several states have exclusive state funds.[36]

---

[35]For an excellent discussion, see J. G. Turnbull, C. A. Williams, Jr., and E. F. Cheit, *Economic and Social Security* (2nd ed.; New York: The Ronald Press Company, 1962), Chap. 10.

[36]See Harold A. Katz, "Workmen's Compensation in the United States," *Labor Law Journal*, Vol. 9, No. 11 (November, 1958), pp. 866–74 ff. For a legalistic but interesting discussion of administrative procedures and problems, see Stefan A. Riesenfeld,

Coverage and adequacy. Some 44 million employees (80 percent of wage and salary earners) are now covered by workmen's compensation laws. Workmen's compensation has made an important contribution to their economic security. It should not be assumed, however, that the problem is solved and that social objectives have been achieved. Current provisions of these laws are far from adequate. One source of inadequacy arises out of the tendency for maximum benefits to remain fixed while the price level and wage rates have risen. Most state laws intended to provide weekly benefits amounting to about two thirds of wages. In many states, however, maximum benefit levels fall far below this measure.[37]

In addition, public opinion is divided with respect to whether benefits should be based solely on previous earnings or should take into account family responsibilities as measured by numbers of dependents. Some states make such supplementary grants; others do not. Other unanswered questions involve the desirability of lump-sum settlements and the need for closer coordination of benefit payments and rehabilitation. In some states rehabilitation programs are available, but only a few partially disabled make use of them.[38]

Experience rating. One of the most important characteristics of the workmen's compensation approach is the use of experience rating as a basis for insurance costs. An employer or group of employers can reduce these costs by preventing accidents. These laws have thus

---

"Basic Problems in the Administration of Workmen's Compensation," *Minnesota Law Review*, Vol. 36, No. 2 (January, 1952), pp. 119–42.

[37]See United States Department of Labor, "State Workmen's Compensation Laws," *Bulletin No. 212*, Revised, January, 1964; United States Chamber of Commerce, *Analysis of Workmen's Compensation Laws*, January, 1962; Earl F. Cheit, "Medical Care Under Workmen's Compensation," United States Department of Labor, *Bulletin 244*, 1962. Provisions for government employees are described in "Workmen's Compensation Coverage of Public Employees," United States Department of Labor, Bureau of Labor Standards, *Bulletin 210*, May, 1962.

[38]It is estimated that there are more than two million physically handicapped persons in the United States who need rehabilitation in order to be employed and that each year over 250,000 additional people need vocational rehabilitation. The number with mental handicaps who need rehabilitation is even more impressive. New wonder drugs make possible the release of many additional mental hospital patients. They need vocational rehabilitation and so do employers and employees. The latter groups are very suspicious of and hostile toward employment of former mental patients. The federal-state vocational rehabilitation program aids about 200,000 persons annually. Effectiveness of placements under vocational rehabilitation plans depends upon use of differential selection and placement techniques and policies. Much more research is needed on means of improving attitudes of employers and employees, and on means of more effective placement. See George W. England, Lloyd H. Lofquist, Rene Dawis *et. al.*, "Minnesota Studies in Vocation Rehabilitation," University of Minnesota Industrial Relations Center *Bulletins 21, 22, 23*, July, 1958; also Lloyd H. Lofquist, *Vocational Counseling with the Physically Handicapped* (New York: Appleton Century, 1956).

encouraged continual attention to safety measures. They are generally credited with responsibility for much of the reduction of frequency and severity rates already noted.

At the same time, however, merit or experience rating has created some problems with respect to the employment of handicapped workers. Because employers' records and insurance premium rates, based on the claims against them, reflect the seriousness of injuries, many employers have hesitated to employ workers with partial disabilities. They have been afraid that any additional injury might create total permanent disability and thus push their insurance costs higher. To overcome this barrier, most states now maintain special *second-injury rules*, which charge an employer's record with only the specific injury incurred, as if the loss were a first injury. Additional payments to injured workers are charged to a special state fund.

Work-connected illness. Sometimes working conditions make employees sick. For example, employees engaged in painting luminous hands and figures on the dials of clocks and watches have contracted radium poisoning. Workers preparing tetraethyl lead for gasoline have become emotionally disturbed, so much so that the liquid became known as "loony gas." Tending rock-crushers under certain circumstances causes serious respiratory infections. Employees in a plant manufacturing electrical equipment developed green hair, which became a more brilliant green when washed with soap. Some of these effects are disconcerting but not disabling. Others, such as the poisoning effects of lead or mercury or the skin irritations caused by certain chemicals, may cause extensive lost time and possible permanent disability.

Security against hazards of work-connected illness is not so well established as that for industrial accidents. In part, this condition is explained by the difficulty of identifying work-connected illness. Which colds are caused by the temperature or humidity of the work place? How much dermatitis or rheumatism or backache or heart trouble is attributable to work? To what extent can the respiratory diseases that cause most absences from the job be traced to working conditions?

The current approach to the problem of work-connected illness is patterned after the workmen's compensation program for work-connected accidents. Industrial illness has been made compensable under workmen's compensation laws. The manner of providing such coverage varies from state to state and is continually changing, with an obvious trend toward making more types of illness compensable.

Workmen's compensation laws first provided protection against accidents only. Somewhat later, the term "industrial injury" in these laws was interpreted to include such illness as poisoning and silicosis. Coverage was further broadened when many laws were amended to cover "scheduled" illness, providing benefits for specific types that were recognized as being directly related to work. In recent years most laws have been modified to provide compensation for any illness that can be shown to be peculiar to an occupation and attributable to unusual hazards in the work.

Recommended changes. The adequacy of workmen's compensation would be improved were the standards met which are listed below. These are standards recommended by the United States Department of Labor, International Association of Accident Boards and Commissions, American College of Surgeons, American Medical Association, and Council of State Governments. No state law meets all of these standards; all states meet some of them. It is recommended that all states meet at least these minimums:

1. Workmen's compensation laws should be compulsory, not elective.
2. There should be no numerical exemptions (based on number of employees).
3. Agricultural workers should be covered.
4. There should be full coverage for occupational diseases.
5. There should be a rehabilitation division within the workmen's compensation agency of each state.
6. Special maintenance benefits should be provided during the period of rehabilitation.
7. Full medical benefits should be provided for accidents and occupational diseases.
8. A waiting period of not more than 3 days with retroactive benefits after 2 weeks or less should be used.
9. Benefits should be paid for permanent total disability for life or period of disability.
10. Maximum weekly benefits should be at least two thirds of state's average weekly wage.[39]

[39]See United States Department of Labor, "State Workmen's Compensation Laws: A Comparison of Major Provisions with Recommended Standards," *Bulletin No. 212, revised*, January, 1964; see also Abner Brodie, "The Adequacy of Workmen's Compensation as Social Insurance: A Review of Developments and Proposals," *Wisconsin Law Review*, Vol. 1963, No. 1 (January, 1963), pp. 57–91; J. G. Turnbull, C. A. Williams, Jr.,

Nonwork-Connected Disability

Workmen's compensation programs are designed to provide at least minimal security against on-the-job accidents and illness. As noted earlier, many accidents to workers and most illness, however, are not job-related. Such accidents and illness may destroy earning power, income, and security as surely as those that occur in or are traceable to work. What protection can be provided against these hazards?

Several types of insurance designed to reduce this insecurity have appeared. Earliest of these are benefits provided by associations of employees under what are generally described as *mutual benefit programs*. The provision of such benefits was an important activity of early guilds and unions. Many unions still maintain such benefits for their members. They have been incorporated in modern health and welfare provisions, frequently negotiated by unions and employers.

Another approach to this type of insecurity is provided by *temporary disability insurance* (TDI), now provided in four states and on the railroads. Still another approach involves the health insurance and socialized medicine provided in several other nations.

Extent and costs of disability. No careful measure of the extent to which workers and their families suffer losses in income because of illness and accident is available. Insurance company experience suggests that working men average about 4.4 days and women 6.4 days per year of nonwork-connected, compensable disability. In Rhode Island, where such losses are compensable, the average for both sexes is 6.8 days. Other estimates of losses on this account range from 2.5 days for males to 5.8 days for females. In 1960 on the average working day, 1.3 million workers were absent from work on account of accident or illness; these were 2 percent of the civilian labor force.

Income loss from nonoccupational short-term sickness was $4.5 billion in 1948, $7.5 billion in 1958, and $8.7 billion in 1961. Benefits paid under government disability insurance programs and formal paid sick leave plans replaced 29 percent of this income loss in 1961, or $2.5 billion.

The five TDI programs paid out $400 million in benefits, and formal paid sick leave plans paid out $1.5 billion. About one half of

and E. F. Cheit, *Economic and Social Security* (2nd ed.; New York: The Ronald Press Company, 1962), pp. 279–94.

the benefits are group protection for wage and salary workers in private industry; sick leave plans for government employees provide 35 percent of the benefits; and 16 percent is in the form of individual insurance.[40]

Temporary Disability Insurance. TDI programs are designed to provide benefits to replace earnings lost on account of nonwork-connected disability, principally illness.

In 1961 coverage of federal and state programs of compulsory temporary disability insurance (TDI) benefits included 11.6 million workers, an increase from 11.3 million in 1956. (In addition, approximately 18.4 million others are covered by voluntary programs.) In 1960, 25.5 million workers received temporary disability benefits. More than one fourth, 26.7 percent or 7 million, were covered by private programs under state TDI and 4.4 million by compulsory government plans.

Compulsory government programs for off-the-job accidents and illness are provided by Rhode Island, California, New Jersey, New York, and the federal provisions for railroad workers. The Rhode Island program is distinctive in that it operates through an exclusive state fund financed solely by employee contributions and is coordinated with unemployment insurance. The other state plans are financed by employer or employee contributions, or both, and permit private "contracting out" or self-insurance to provide coverage required by law. The federal plan for railroad employees is financed solely by employer contributions. Benefit maxima range from $35 to $70. A trend toward liberalization of benefits is evident. Average duration of benefits was approximately 8.5 weeks in 1961.[41]

OASDI disability insurance. In 1962, 1¼ million persons received disability benefits of $1 billion under the Old-Age, Survivors, and Disability Insurance Program (OASDI). These payments went to 650,000 disabled workers, 440,000 dependent wives and children, and 130,000 disabled since childhood. This federal disability program is similar in coverage and benefits and is related to the pension program described in the next chapter. To qualify, the worker must have social

[40]Alfred M. Skolnik, "Income Loss Protection Against Short-Term Sickness, 1948–61," *Social Security Review*, Vol. 26, No. 1 (January, 1963), pp. 10–20.

[41]See annual reports of the Federal Bureau of Employment Security, for example, "Temporary Disability Insurance: Significant Data, 1960–1961," *BES No. U-212*, September, 1962.

security credits for at least 5 of the last 10 years before the disablement occurred. Disabled workers must be unable to "engage in any substantial gainful activity." Benefits are those one would get if retired at 65; wives, children, and dependent parents can also qualify for family payments.

OASDI disability insurance is different from workmen's compensation and TDI described above. In some instances it is possible for an applicant to draw workmen's compensation payments and OASDI disability payments at the same time for the same injury. This stems from lack of correlation between state and federal laws. Such "double payments" are widely regarded as an abuse of social security programs.[42]

Union Health and Welfare Benefits

Earliest attempts to provide a measure of security against illness and accidents for wage workers took the form of employee and union benefit programs. Many early unions copied the fraternal characteristics of the guilds, including their systems of mutual aid. Paternalistic employers also frequently encouraged mutual benefit programs among their employees. The most common type of assistance provided death benefits — usually only enough to defray or partially cover funeral costs — and very limited payments to those disabled by illness or accidents. Later, unions frequently added strike benefits to aid members who were idled by a labor dispute, and some of them established limited unemployment benefits. In England, unions were permitted to operate as mutual benefit associations for many years before they were granted the right to bargain for their members. Several American unions were first incorporated as mutual benefit societies. Railroad unions have long emphasized their fraternal benefits.

While modern unions in this country are most widely known for their activities as business unions and bargaining agents, some if not much of their appeal to members is still associated with the various benefits they provide or have negotiated. Some international union

---

[42]See Earl F. Cheit, "Workmen's Compensation, OASDI: The Overlap Issue," *Industrial Relations*, Vol. 3, No. 4 (February, 1964), pp. 63–80. A similar overlap exists between OASDI payments and unemployment compensation payments. In some cases where a worker has been forced to retire, he will draw unemployment compensation for 26 weeks and then, after that time, obtain OASDI retirement benefits retroactively back to his retirement date. Thus, he gets "paid twice" for the same 26 weeks. Employers are increasingly protesting this "abuse." See, for example, *Wall Street Journal*, June 15, 1964, p. 1.

benefit programs have been prominent since the unions were organized. Union health benefits were formally instituted by barbers in 1893, by tobacco workers in 1896, by maritime workers in 1898, and by plumbers in 1903. The International Ladies Garment Workers Union created a health center for members in New York in 1919. Most of the funds for these benefits came from union dues until after World War I. In the 1930's several unions negotiated agreements providing for employer contributions to benefit programs. Since that time, negotiated health and welfare programs supported by employer contributions have become well established.

In 1926 an arbitration award gave the union of street railway workers of Chicago a system of employer contributions to provide group life insurance and sick benefits. In 1927 the same union secured similar employer contributions in San Antonio, Texas, and in Philadelphia to provide death, disability, and old-age benefits. Throughout the 1930's many unions expanded their benefit programs and increased bargaining pressure for employer contributions. Many new industrial unions found such programs essential because local company-dominated unions were already providing members with similar benefits.

Some local union programs have included contracts with hospitals and groups of medical doctors to provide for the care of members. One of the best known national programs, that of the United Mine Workers, includes provisions for old-age pensions, death and survivor's benefits, sickness and disability benefits, and hospitalization and medical care for miners and their dependents. The program is financed by a royalty paid by employers on each ton of coal and by union dues.

Employee Benefit Plans

Three principal types of employee benefit plans are now in operation. In one — *private, unilateral, employer programs* — various benefits, of which the most common are life insurance and hospitalization, are provided entirely by the employer. In a second — *unilateral, union programs* — similar benefits are provided by a union for its members. The most common of these cover death, strike, and accidental disability. A third type — *jointly administered programs* — is negotiated, operated, and managed jointly by an employer and a union. This third type has become increasingly common since

World War II, when such programs were encouraged by the wartime economic stabilization program.

All types of plans may involve the purchase of insurance and the assignment of risks to Blue Cross and other similar organizations. Purchasing insurance rather than depending on self-assurance by employers or unions has become common practice. Benefits include life insurance (average more than $1,000); weekly health and accident benefits (usually about one half of weekly earnings); paid sick leave; hospitalization for employees and their families; maternity benefits of one week's hospitalization and six weeks' health benefit; and, less common, medical and surgical benefits with specified maxima.

In 1962 private employee benefit plans covered 111 million persons — workers and their dependents — under some form of health insurance, 52 million under life insurance, and 23 million under private retirement plans. Growth in these plans is shown by the fact that from 1954 to 1962 contributions more than doubled and benefits almost tripled. In terms of employee coverage, in 1962 life insurance was the most common benefit, covering 48 million employees, 43 million had hospitalization, 23 million accidental death and dismemberment plans, 23 million retirement plans, and 13 million major medical coverage.

Employer-employee contributions for private benefit plans was $14.4 billion in 1962, as contrasted with $6.9 billion in 1954. Benefit payments were $3.5 billion in 1954 and $9.8 billion in 1962. Thus, the recent history of private benefit plans is one of growth — in coverage, contributions, and benefits. [43]

From their inception, employee benefit programs have created difficult problems of administration. In the early years of union programs, risks were frequently underestimated, with resulting drains on union treasuries. Union spokesmen frequently opposed them because of these difficulties. In current practice benefits have become so complex that most plans depend on insurance companies to forecast costs and to accept responsibility for the liabilities involved in various benefits.

Reserves in such programs are necessarily large. Their investment or the purchase of appropriate insurance is "big business" and requires expertness and special competence. Individual employees

---

[43]See Joseph Krislov, "Employee-Benefit Plans, 1954–62," *Social Security Bulletin*, Vol. 27, No. 4 (April, 1964), pp. 4–21.

cannot be expected to appraise the reasonableness of charges or the safety of funds. In recent years attention has been frequently directed to evidence of mismanagement of these funds. The temptation is powerful to favor friends in the placement of insurance and to allow a portion of the huge amounts involved to "rub off" on the hands of those who handle them. Investigations in New York state and by Senate and House committees have disclosed many questionable procedures. Evidence indicates overcharging for the risks involved, kickbacks and premiums paid to local representatives, and in some cases, the looting of funds. A Senate committee found well-managed funds in steel, autos, and the building trades; but it cited embezzlement, improper service charges, payments of large sums for promotion, and other improprieties in other programs. A House subcommittee found union domination of the trustees in some funds, high charges and careless handling of funds, collusion between insurance brokers and union officials, and insurance company "influence" payments to union officials.[44]

Five states have enacted special legislation to provide supervision for the administration of pension and welfare funds. All the laws are similar in requiring trustees to register with state insurance authorities and to file annual reports. Additional regulation by federal and state legislation appears likely and desirable.

The problem of insuring the sound administration of benefit programs, especially those involving large reserves, is of obvious and growing importance in our society. Popular concern about these funds has generally focused on the actions of union officials who hold responsibilities in this area. It is important to recognize the fact, however, that only a small portion of these plans is entrusted on a unilateral basis to union officers, less than 1 percent of the total. Jointly administered plans make up only about 7 ½ percent of the total, while more than 90 percent are administered on a unilateral basis by employers. The public interest requires that all types of plans be soundly administered and, for that reason, that all types of administration be subject to public review.

A step in this direction was taken in 1958 with passage of the federal Welfare and Pension Plans Disclosure Act. In a policy statement the act says that such plans ". . . are affected with a national

---

[44]For more detail on these findings, see *Labor Relations Reference Manual*, 1955, Vol. 35, pp. 44–48 and Vol. 36, pp. 213–15; see also Senate Report No. 1734, 84th Congress, 2nd Session, April 16, 1956, summarizing findings and seven industry case studies.

public interest; that they have become an important factor affecting the stability of employment and the successful development of industrial relations . . ." The law applies to employers, employee organizations, or both. It requires administrators of pension and welfare plans (including 25 employees or more) to publish descriptions of these plans and to make annual reports on the plan to both parties and to beneficiaries, and to file similar reports with the Secretary of Labor. The law took effect January 1, 1959. False statements and disclosures are punishable as federal crimes; enforcement is by United States district courts. The law is widely regarded as "weak" or "mild" in its requirements and especially its enforcement provisions.

The following chapter is concerned with problems of older employees, retirement programs, and public and private pension plans.

ANALYTICAL REVIEW QUESTIONS

1. Why are job rights so important in our society? How are job rights secured?
2. How are programs of prevention and amelioration distinguished? Give examples of each.
3. What percentage of GNP is represented by social welfare expenditures in the United States? What is the most costly program?
4. How is social security defined? What are its three major components in the United States?
5. What is the basic objective in social security? Is this a "full support" concept?
6. What is the principle of net advantage? How does this differ from the compensation-insurance principle?
7. What is the difference between service benefits and income benefits? Give examples of each.
8. What are the three major assignments to the United States unemployment insurance system? Differentiate the roles of state and federal governments in this system.
9. What occupational groups are not covered by Unemployment Compensation?
10. What are typical eligibility requirements for UC? Benefit requirements?
11. Why were TUC and TEUC laws passed?
12. What are the principal arguments against experience rating in UC?
13. How adequate are UC benefits? What evidence supports your position?
14. Why is it argued that quits should not bar UC benefits?

15. What determines an employer's ability to shift payroll taxes? To whom will he try to shift the burden? What may happen if he cannot shift the burden?

16. In what sense may UC taxes be considered a "wage transfer"?

17. Why should an employer seek to stabilize employment?

18. What arguments have been advanced against GAW? In its favor?

19. How do SUB plans limit the risk taken by employers as compared with GAW?

20. What are "vesting" and "funding"? Why are these important concepts? How are these concepts related to labor mobilities?

21. What determines the liability of employers under GAW plans?

22. What effects would GAW plans be expected to have on employment levels? Why?

23. What are some of the likely economic consequences of SUB plans?

24. Define accident frequency and severity rates.

25. What were the common law rules of accident liability?

26. What are the basic principles underlying workmen's compensation?

27. How are experience ratings under WC and safety programs related?

28. In what ways does vocational rehabilitation reduce economic burdens?

29. How are WC and TDI different?

30. What are the three major types of employee benefit plans?

31. What is the chief deficiency in current private sickness benefit plans?

Case 23-1

I.A.M. ACCIDENT AND ILLNESS PLAN

Local 44, I.A.M., represents production workers in a manufacturing concern with some 4,000 employees. The union has recently issued a statement outlining its demands for changes in a new labor contract to be negotiated shortly. One of them is designed to provide a measure of security for employees who suffer serious, long-term illness or injury from nonwork-connected accidents. The union proposes a clause that would make the present private pensions — provided by the employer on a noncontributory basis — immediately payable to any employee who is permanently and totally disabled either by accident or illness.

The employer has issued a comment on this demand. The firm's management regards it as ridiculous and completely unreasonable. In a newspaper advertisement the employer argues that such provisions would be so expensive that no employer could afford them. Further, they are not sensible since the employer seeks to pay for getting work done and does not pretend to be a charitable agency. Workmen's compensation benefits, it is argued, already provide security against work-connected illness and accident. In the advertisement, the employer suggests that if employees want such benefits, they should work for a nationwide public system of insurance against catastrophic illness and accidents.

• Assume that you are a member of the state's staff of conciliators. You may be called in to bring the parties together if negotiations reach an impasse. What position will you try to encourage on this particular issue?

Case 23-2

UNEMPLOYMENT COMPENSATION BENEFIT "RACKET"

As a member of the local Junior Chamber of Commerce, you have just heard a well-organized, carefully prepared speech by a union leader in which he attacked the administration of unemployment insurance benefits in your state. He cited several cases, including that of a young woman who had worked 4 years in a covered job. She had never been unemployed until she stopped work to have a child. In spite of her accumulated wage credits, she was denied benefits on the ground that she had quit her job and was not actively seeking work. In another case, a 45-year-old man who quit his job because of a nervous breakdown was also denied benefits.

• Prepare a short letter to the director of the state employment service expressing your attitude on such rulings and be prepared to read and discuss it in your next class meeting.

OLD AGE AND RETIREMENT

Everyone gets old, at an even chronological rate and an uneven physiological rate. Some people seem old when they are young, and vice versa. Individual differences in aging are the rule rather than the exception. Old age means substantial changes in our lives, for most of us build our lives around employment, and this central pillar is removed at 65 for many. Thus, an economic change in life parallels the physical.

Many of the physical effects of aging are rather apparent to all of us; the economic implications are less obvious, largely because they are complicated. On the one hand, the skilled craftsman or technician and the professional may, if they choose, become more helpful and valuable up to the day they succumb to physical frailties. Experience, continued learning, and growing insight can magnify their contributions. At the same time, in the same society, the contribution of the unskilled and semiskilled worker may follow a pattern closely following that of physical strength, growing through youth and up to the period of middle age and declining in subsequent years.

For a wealthy society built on ideals of individual freedom, the fact of aging creates many difficult questions, for example:

1. What shall be society's attitude toward the health of older workers?
2. Shall society expect individuals to build their own resources for support throughout their entire lifetime?

3. Can such a society hope to insure economic security for older workers?

4. What are the principal steps that might be taken to move toward greater economic security for older workers?

5. How can the economic effects of a comprehensive security program be evaluated in terms of gains and costs?

Answers to all such questions are difficult, largely because they require a balancing of values, especially economic, political, and humanitarian values. What may be the most desirable course for the nation in terms of its economic strength and rate of progress may be quite unacceptable in terms of humanitarian considerations. Limited economic security, especially for older workers, may be politically unacceptable, both because of their political influence and because all or most citizens may reject a political system that permits high levels of ill health and poverty among former workers.

Because a variety of values is involved, these questions evoke emotional responses. It is not easy to be objective in appraising situations that involve diverse personal values. Perceptions and appraisals not only differ but conflict. With respect to programs designed to provide a degree of economic security for the aged, sharp differences and conflicting opinions are the rule rather than the exception. For example, "Respect for Our Elders"[1] quotes historian Arnold Toynbee to the effect that "the moral tone and life span of a civilization can be measured by the respect and care given its elderly citizens." The same publication presumably speaks for a considerable segment of organized labor in its conclusion that "our elders sicken of the bitter bread of private and public charity. They deserve better than to be treated as paupers and castoffs. They want least of all to become burdens upon children who must support families of their own."[2]

PROBLEMS OF AGING

The problem of the older worker is many-sided. In part it is a problem of unemployment. Older workers constitute a disproportionate share of the unemployed. In part it is a problem of discrimination; hiring age limits often restrict opportunities for workers 45 or over. In part it is a problem of dependency; many former workers must depend on public aid to meet subsistence needs. In part it is a

---

[1]*Publication No. 45*, Industrial Union Department, AFL-CIO, undated but about 1961–62.

[2]*Ibid.*, p. 3.

problem of health; adequate medical attention and care involve costs beyond the resources of many older workers.

At the same time, the problem is not likely to solve itself; on the contrary, it can be expected to become more serious for several reasons. As noted, unusually large numbers of young workers are and will be entering the labor force (26 million in the 1960's); some 3 million women will be returning to the labor force; they will increase pressures to displace older workers. The changing industrial complex exerts a similar pressure. When the nation was predominantly agricultural, many old folks retired to the farm, where they were supported by their children. Industrialization tends to separate the generations and reduce the opportunity as well as the responsibility for such support.

Meanwhile, many firms have become reluctant about hiring middle-aged and older workers. Skills from earlier work experience may not fit; employers do not want to face the retraining problems thus created. Older workers may not work long enough to become eligible for private pensions; if they are included in the coverage of such plans, they may raise premium rates. Similarly, their inclusion in other benefit programs — hospitalization, disability insurance, and others — may raise costs.

Perhaps the most obvious reason for expecting this problem to become more serious is the prospective increase in numbers and proportions of older workers in the labor force.

Numbers of Older Workers

In 1960 there were approximately 16.6 million persons over age 65 in the total population of 179.3 million, which was about 9.2 percent of this total. This over-65 group had been growing steadily since the early years of the century. Numbers and proportions of those 65 years of age and over are summarized in Table 24-1, which also includes predictions for 1975.[3]

Several factors have contributed to this trend. People are living longer; an impressive reduction in death rates has been achieved through improved medical care, sanitation and immunization, and related public health programs. Life span has been extended. In the first half of this century, life expectancy for a male child increased

---

[3]BLS data from "Population and Labor Force Projections for the United States; 1960–1975," Labor Department, *Bulletin No. 1242*, p. 8; see also *Manpower Report of the President*, 1963, p. 10.

Table 24-1
NUMBERS AND PROPORTIONS OF THOSE
65 YEARS OF AGE AND OVER

Year	Total Population	Population 65 and Over	
		Numbers	Percent
1900	76,094,000	3,099,000	4.1
1910	92,000,000	3,900,000	4.3
1930	123,077,000	6,705,000	5.4
1940	131,700,000	9,031,000	6.9
1950	150,700,000	12,300,000	8.1
1960	179,300,000	16,600,000	9.2
1975	225,552,000	21,872,000	9.7

from 48 to 66 years.[4]   It is significant, in terms of aging, that almost one fourth of all male babies can now expect to live to be 80 years old.[5]

At the same time, changing public policy with respect to immigration has influenced the age distribution of our population, as have fluctuations in birth rates. During the first quarter of this century, as many as a million immigrants per year were admitted. They included relatively few children, so that they have helped to change the age distribution of the population as years passed. In the 1930's birth rates declined, with a similar effect.

As a result, the population 65 and over is expected to increase from about 17 million in 1960 to about 19.5 million in 1970. In the same period the population 45 to 64 will grow from 36 million to 42 million. Concern for old-age security is directed primarily at the group past 65, but the imminence of aging has a significant influence on employment of workers in their late 40's and 50's.

Work-Life Tables

In 1960 the expectancy of working life for a male worker age 20 was 43 years, and the full-life expectancy was about 50 years, indicating a 7-year period of retirement. Calculation of work-life tables, which measure past and current experience in the labor force and thus

---

[4]"The Length of Working Life for Males, 1900–1960," *Manpower Report No. 8*, July, 1963, p. 1.
    [5]*Ibid.*, p. 3.

facilitate predictions of future participation, has contributed to our understanding of the problem of old-age security — or insecurity. Such tables have been developed only since 1950 and only for men. They have been extended back to 1900.[6]

Over the years work-life expectancies have increased. From 1900 to 1950, when life expectancy for a male child increased by 18 years, work-life expectancy increased by 10 years — from 32 to 42 years. Work life does not increase as much as life expectancy because preparation for work has become more time-consuming, so that entry into the labor force is delayed, and because exit from the labor force has tended to come at an earlier age.

Increases in work-life expectancies have many implications. The young worker in 1960 can expect about 9 more man-years of potential employment than his counterpart in 1900. This adds an appreciable increment to labor supplies, which must be matched by increasing demands to provide work. Meanwhile, the earlier exits from the labor force, combined with longer life, magnify the difficulty of assuring old-age security.

Work-life tables, combined with studies of job changes, also indicate that the 20-year-old worker in 1960 can be expected to make about 6 job changes (involving shifts in employers) during his working career. Retraining achieves increased significance in this perspective, as also does the problem of relating old-age security to past employment.[7]

The decade of the 1950's was distinctive in that, for the first time in the entire period for which these calculations have now become available, the work-life expectancy declined. The decline from 1950 to 1960 was approximately one-half year — from 41.9 to 41.4 years. It results both from later entry into the labor force and earlier retirement, offsetting a one-year increase in life expectancy between 1950 and 1960. Figure 24-1 compares work-life expectancies for men from 40 to 75 years of age in 1940, 1950, and 1960. The sharp upward curve in the line representing 1960 means that, for those who continue working beyond 65, work expectancies are greater than in 1940 and 1950 because so many others have retired.

The problem of old-age security takes on meaningful dimensions when we recognize that almost one fourth of all men in the labor force

---

[6]Their development requires basic population and employment data that are not readily available for both men and women nor for all males. For details and references to earlier reports see Stuart Garfinkle, "Table of Working Life for Men, 1960," *Monthly Labor Review*, Vol. 86, No. 7 (July, 1963), pp. 820–23.

[7]*Manpower Report No. 8*, July, 1963, p. 2.

YEARS OF WORK LIFE EXPECTANCY

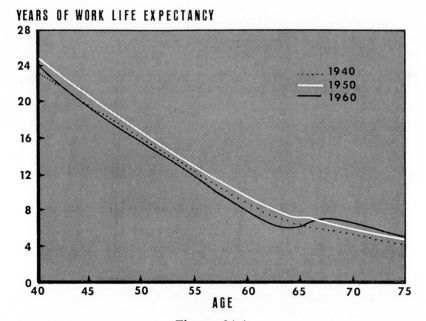

Figure 24-1
WORK-LIFE EXPECTANCY FOR MEN 40–75
YEARS OF AGE — 1940, 1950, 1960

Source: *Manpower Report No. 8, July, 1963* (Washington, D.C.: United States Department of Labor, Office of Manpower, Automation and Training), p. 5.

at age 64 retire by the time they are 65. In addition, part-time work increases from 14 percent of all those working at age 64 to 21 percent at age 65. At 85, some 8 percent remain in the labor force.

Retirement from the labor force at the 65-year mark has grown from 70 per 1000 in 1940 to 234 per 1000 in 1960. Those who remain in the labor force include large proportions of self-employed, service workers, and professionals. Occupations that have consistently employed large proportions of older workers include tailors and furriers—with 27 percent over 65—and independent shoe makers with 19.2 percent over 65. Among barbers, 13.4 percent were over 65.

Participation Rates

While older tailors, furriers, shoemakers, and barbers find it possible to stay at work, participation rates for most occupations decline rapidly with age beyond 65. Table 24-2 summarizes significant participation rates since 1947 and compares rates for those over 65 with rates for the entire labor force and for the 55–64 age group.

Table 24-2

LABOR FORCE PARTICIPATION RATES, SENIOR AGE GROUPS

Year	Participation Rates						
	Total	All Males	Males 55–64	Males 65 and Over	All Females	Females 55–64	Females 65 and Over
1947	57.3	84.4	89.6	47.8	31.0	24.3	8.1
1948	57.8	84.6	89.5	46.8	31.9	24.3	9.1
1949	58.0	84.5	87.5	46.9	32.4	25.3	9.6
1950	58.3	84.4	87.0	45.8	33.1	27.0	9.7
1951	58.8	84.8	87.2	44.9	33.8	27.6	8.9
1952	58.7	84.6	87.5	42.6	33.9	28.7	9.1
1953	58.5	84.4	87.9	41.6	33.6	29.1	10.0
1954	58.4	83.9	88.7	40.5	33.7	30.1	9.3
1955	58.7	83.6	87.9	39.6	34.8	32.5	10.6
1956	59.3	83.7	88.5	40.0	35.9	34.9	10.9
1957	58.7	82.7	87.5	37.5	35.9	34.5	10.5
1958	58.5	82.1	87.8	35.6	36.0	35.2	10.3
1959	58.3	81.7	87.4	34.2	36.1	36.6	10.2
1960	58.3	81.2	86.8	33.1	36.7	37.2	10.8
1961	58.0	80.3	87.3	31.7	36.9	37.9	10.7
1962	57.4	79.3	86.2	30.3	36.7	38.7	9.9
1963	57.3	78.8	86.2	28.4	37.0	39.7	9.6

Source: *Manpower Report of the President* (Washington 25, D.C.: United States Government Printing Office, March, 1964), p. 196.

Several of the comparisons deserve comment. It is notable, for example, that the 55–64 age group of males is characterized by unusually high participation rates. Up to age 65 it appears that almost 9/10 of all males are working or seeking work. In contrast, only about half of those over 65 were so classified in 1947 and less than one third in 1963. Meanwhile, proportions of females over 65 who were working or seeking work have grown from about 8 percent to almost 10 percent, but that proportion is only about one fourth of the rate for the 55–64 year age group.

It is quite evident from these rates that, among both males and females, 65 is a critical year so far as labor force participation is concerned. Approximately two thirds of those who preferred or found it necessary to work in the 55–64 year age group and who live on are no longer seeking work in the years following 65. Forecasts for years up to 1975 see some increase in participation rates for females in this age group and a slight decline for males.[8]

Productivity and Aging

Several immediate reasons for lower participation rates of senior workers are evident and have been mentioned. Compulsory retirement and the availability of pensions are prominent. Many employers are reluctant about hiring workers at or close to the 65-year mark; age limits and other discrimination in hiring are widely recognized. A frequent comment among workers observes that "you're better off dead than to lose your job if you're over 45."

In part such hiring policies express a recognition of reduced strength and vigor in later years. Many studies indicate that peak physical effort on the job is characteristic of the 25–34 year age group. In one of these studies, the 55–64 year group turned out about 90 percent as much. One third of the older group produced more than the average of the peak performance group 25–34, but there was a wide range of variation of individual performance in the older work group.[9] Abilities change over the years, and if workers become unemployed late in life, they may have to shift to different jobs with job requirements better correlated with their physical abilities.

Productivity appears to be much less a matter of physical strength than of appropriate training and skill. Many worker qualifications can grow with age and experience. The evidence is clear that older workers compare favorably with their younger associates in terms of accidents and absenteeism. But their skills may become obsolete in a dynamic industrialized economy. What they can do best may no longer need to be done.[10]

Unemployment and Aging

The result of such change is evident in the rate of long-term unemployment, which increases steadily by age (see Figure 24-2). Older workers resist unemployment longer in cyclical recession; apparently they gain some degree of protection through their seniority. Once unemployed, however, they are not readily reemployed. In fact, as

---

[8]"Population and Labor Force Projections for the United States," *Department of Labor Bulletin No. 1242*, 1959, p. 54.

[9]Ewan Clague, "Employment Adequacy of Older Persons," United States Bureau of Labor Statistics, October 18, 1960 (mimeo).

[10]An interesting case study describes what happened in the shutdown of Packard Motor Co. plants in Detroit. See Harold L. Sheppard and others, "Too Old to Work — Too Young to Retire," *Reprint*, University of Michigan and Wayne State University, Institute of Labor and Industrial Relations, 1959.

noted, they may be less qualified for available jobs than younger workers. Their skills may be obsolete. They may be less mobile. As a result, as the figure indicates, they are particularly susceptible to long-term unemployment, and their unemployment rates are relatively high. For example, in 1962 when men 30 to 54 years had an unemployment rate of 3.8 percent, the rate for men 55 to 69 years was 4.7 percent.[11]

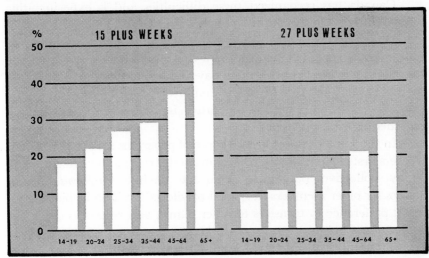

Figure 24-2
LONG-TERM UNEMPLOYMENT BY AGE
AS PERCENT OF UNEMPLOYED IN AGE GROUP — 1962

Source: "Manpower and Training, Trends, Outlook, Programs," United States Department of Labor, Office of Manpower, Automation and Training, *Bulletin No. 2*, March, 1963, p. 12.

Older workers, including those over 45, may find it much more difficult to find a new job. Those who seek to continue working must expect problems if they leave or are retired from their current employment. The concept of *multiple-job careers*, frequently mentioned in earlier chapters, has little applicability in the older age groups. The contrast between expected changes in jobs and mobilities of younger and older workers is impressive. Comparisons of *job-life expectancies* and *work-life expectancies* for younger workers with those for workers 55 and over illustrate this difference. In the early 1960's the 20-year-old male would be expected to hold 6 or 7 jobs in his working lifetime,

[11]Manpower Research, *Bulletin No. 1*, July, 1963, p. 10. See also James R. Morris, *Employment Opportunities in Later Years* (Burlingame, California: Foundation for Voluntary Welfare, 1960).

averaging about 5½ years per job. Males in the 55–64 year group faced 11.9 years of work-life expectancy. But they could expect to average less than one change of job (actually 0.6) in the remainder of their experience after age 55. The average job-life expectancy for members of this group is 7.2 years. At 65, with a work-life expectancy of 6.3 years, the male worker faced an average job-life expectancy of 4.7 years and 0.2 of a chance of changing his job.[12]

Canada has recognized these difficulties and is experimenting with a subsidy to encourage reemployment of older workers. For workers over 45 who have been unable to find jobs for six in the past nine months (and who are not drawing unemployment or pension benefits), the government may pay 50 percent of an employee's monthly wage, up to $75, if the employer provides counseling and training. The plan became operative in November, 1963, and is regarded as experimental.[13]

In the United States several types of programs seek to give senior workers first chances at jobs or to prevent discrimination against them. Many collective bargaining contracts include *preferential hiring* clauses for older members (a special privileged position in bidding for jobs), preference in transfers to other plants, and rules specifying the proportions of older to younger workers.[14] At the same time, a slowly growing number of state laws prohibit discrimination in hiring on the basis of age.[15] The federal government requires similar practice for employment financed with federal funds.

Needs of Older Workers

No doubt an important reason for the change toward shorter work life for males and toward generally lower participation rates after 65 is the fact that more workers and their dependents find public and private pensions available to them. A further reason is the compulsory retirement at the 65-year mark frequently required for eligibility in such benefits.

A major question, so far as old-age security is concerned, is the adequacy of such provisions in meeting the needs of former workers. For most former workers what they can earn after 65 seems to be quite

---

[12]"Job Changing and Manpower Training," *Manpower Report, Number 10*, June, 1964.
[13]See *Business Week*, July 13, 1963, p. 141.
[14]See Philip Taft, "Provisions Affecting Older Workers in Collective Bargaining Agreements," *Proceedings of the Industrial Relations Research Association*, December, 1962, pp. 154–62.
[15]Connecticut, Oregon, Wisconsin, Massachusetts, New York, Pennsylvania, and Rhode Island. Provisions are incorporated in fair employment practice laws.

inadequate and is becoming less adequate. In 1950, for example, half of the income of persons in the 65 and over group was from current earnings. By 1961 earnings provided less than one third. In 1961 these oldsters had total income of $35 billion, with $11 billion from private earnings and $24 billion from other sources. One fourth of the $24 billion came from private pensions, savings and investments, and life insurance. Three fourths came from government insurance programs.

Health problems are severe for this age group. Two thirds of them have a major chronic condition (heart disease, arthritis, high blood pressure, mental disorder, etc.), and half of these have limitations on their activities. Over 800,000 are institutionalized; 1¼ million are invalids. One out of every six is hospitalized each year, with a hospital and medical bill double that of the younger age group.

The BLS "modest but adequate budget" for a retired couple totals $3010, almost $500 more than average income. Possible home ownership could reduce this discrepancy by $200–$300. In 1960 about 5½ million individuals over 65, some with families, received less income than the BLS budget figure. Thus, while we are doing a better job of providing income for our retired persons than we have in the past, there is still substantial room for improvement.[16]

Family income requirements generally decline after children leave home so that the non-labor-force elders do not need as much income as in earlier years. They can and do reduce their insurance premiums and their expenditures for clothing, food, and recreation. They may be expected to contribute less to various charities. They do not need to save for the distant future. They may enjoy an income tax advantage. On the other hand, of course, they may have higher expenditures for medical attention and hospitalization. It is generally assumed that retirement income for older wage earners should provide at least 50 percent of their average wages in the most recent working years.

Some indication of the economic needs of those over 65 is available from the study undertaken by Corson and McConnell. They found that in the mid-50's about 15 percent of the workers over 65 had annual incomes of more than $2,000; 74 percent were in the less than $1,000 bracket. Only 26 percent of those who retired did so voluntarily; 56 percent retired because of compulsory provisions. Satisfaction with retirement varied with the level of retirement income.

---

[16] *The Older American* (Washington, D.C.: President's Council on Aging, 1963).

A decade later, the 1963 Survey of the Aged found that about one fourth of all those over 65 were employed at some time during 1962. More than one fifth of the men so employed held full-time jobs. They reported average earnings of $4,259. For those who worked less than full time, men averaged $2,550 and women $1,283. These earnings represented 25 percent of the total income for married couples, 14 percent of total income for married men, and 15 percent for married women.[17]

The idea of what is required as adequate income for retirement has changed. Retirees not only need more than they did in earlier years; they expect more. Some of their expenses have increased sharply; medical care is outstanding in this respect. The concept of poverty has changed; it can be applied to families with automobiles, television, and other items formerly in the luxury class. Retirees may expect more of the good life and much less insecurity.[18]

Some notion as to implications of these changes for levels of retirement income can be inferred from corporate programs for executive pensions, although such programs may be heavily influenced by other considerations, such as recruitment value. At the same time, it can be assumed that, for wage and salary workers, minimum needs may represent a higher proportion of usual earnings. The National Industrial Conference Board has surveyed pensions for top executives. They indicate that, in 1961, average pensions ranged from about 25 percent of current salaries to 46 percent. (See Figure 24-3.)

Although comprehensive information about the economic status and needs of older citizens is not available, further evidence as to adequacy is apparent in the fact that, after 65, the percentage of saving declines and dissaving shows a sharp increase.[19]

---

[17]See John J. Corson and John W. McConnell, *Economic Needs of Older People* (New York: Twentieth Century Fund, 1956), pp. 17–48; Erdman Palmore, "Work Experience and Earnings of the Aged in 1962; Findings of the 1963 Survey of the Aged," *Social Security Bulletin*, Vol. 27, No. 6 (June, 1964), pp. 3–14; also Juanita M. Kreps, *Employment, Income and Retirement Problems of the Aged* (Winston-Salem, N.C.: Duke University Press, 1963).

[18]Philip Booth, "Public Systems for Distributing Risks to Security," *Monthly Labor Review*, Vol. 86, No. 6 (June, 1963), pp. 622–29. See also R. M. Tittmoss, *Essays on the Welfare State* (New Haven: Yale University Press, 1959).

[19]For a summary, see Margaret S. Gordon, "Aging and Income Security," *Reprint No. 143*, University of California Institute of Industrial Relations, 1960, from Clark Tibbitts (ed.), *Aging and Society, A Handbook of Gerontology* (Chicago: University of Chicago Press, 1960). See also John R. Stark, "Economic Status of Older People," *Journal of Business*, University of Chicago, Vol. 27, No. 2 (April, 1954), pp. 119–30.

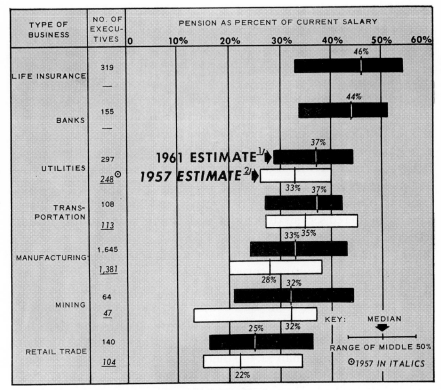

TYPE OF BUSINESS	NO. OF EXECU- TIVES	PENSION AS PERCENT OF CURRENT SALARY

[1]1961 estimated pension as percentage of 1961 salary.
[2]1957 estimated pension as percentage of 1957 salary.

Figure 24-3

EXECUTIVE PENSIONS AS PERCENTAGE OF CURRENT SALARY, 1961 AND 1957, BY TYPE OF BUSINESS

Source: "Top Executive Pensions, 1957 and 1961," *Management Record*, Vol. 24, No. 12 (December, 1962), p. 6.

Medical Care

The needs of older citizens for special, costly medical care has become a major political issue. As indicated in Chapter 23, several types of programs seek to provide health security for employed workers, notably disability and other benefits and private health insurance. A common feature of all such plans is their possible cancellation at retirement. As a result, the older former worker may be without such protection when his risks and needs are highest.

Private medical care under health insurance has grown substantially during the 1950's and early 60's. As a part of that growth, older

persons have gained added protection so that by 1960 about 46 percent of those over 65 had hospitalization coverage, 37 percent had
surgical insurance, and 10 percent had insurance covering visits by
physicians.[20] Collective bargaining has been an important factor in
expanding this coverage.

The costs of private coverage are rising. For those over 65 who are
largely excluded from group plans, hospitalization premiums average
about $125 per year for two persons. Surgical care coverage approxi-
mately doubles this amount. Nonsurgical care adds to these costs.
In several states private insurance firms have joined to provide over-
65 "major medical-hospitalization" coverage. The premium cost of
such plans is from $200–$250 per year.[21] All such voluntary plans
have encountered serious difficulties as a result of rising costs of health
services.

Federal legislation has sought to encourage and facilitate the extension of private insurance coverage of older workers. In 1960, Congress passed the Kerr-Mills Act as one means of meeting the needs of
elders through private insurance. It permits state aid with a federal
subsidy for those who meet a *means test* or *needs test*. (In one state, for
example, any individual having property worth more than $1,500 or
any couple with more than $2,400 thereby fails these tests.) Funds may
be used to provide hospitalization, physicians' and visiting nurses'
services, prescribed drugs, and post-hospital home care. Federal
grants supply from 30 to 70 percent of total costs depending on the
level of per capita income in the state. States must elect to participate;
most states have elected to do so, but several have made no appropriations to permit active participation.

The contribution of the Kerr-Mills Act cannot yet be determined;
to this time what has been accomplished appears rather meager and
grim. Benefits vary from state to state. There is no special tax to provide federal funds; time-to-time appropriations must be made from
general funds. In 1962, total payments amounted to some $288 mil-
lion, with the federal share totaling $148 million. About 88 percent of
the total federal grant went to 5 states — New York, California,
Michigan, Pennsylvania, and Massachusetts. By mid-1962 only
148,000 persons were receiving medical aid under these programs.

---

[20]Report of the Medical Care Committee to the National Advisory Health Council to
the U.S.P.H.S. reported in James P. Dixon, "Emerging Issues in the Financing of Medical
Care," *Social Security in the United States* (Berkeley: University of California, 1961), pp. 23–
35.

[21]"Who Pays for the Care of the Aged?" *Business Week*, November 23, 1963, pp. 68–69.

One stated objective of the Kerr-Mills Act was to encourage private insurance firms to develop programs that would make a nation-wide social insurance program unnecessary. Some such steps have been taken. For example, in 1963 a number of private insurance companies operating on the West Coast joined in offering a plan called *Western 65*. Similar programs were developed in Connecticut (1961), New York, Massachusetts, and Texas. By 1963 some 10 million persons were included in the coverage of a wide variety of these private plans.

Experience under the Kerr-Mills Act suggests that private programs thus encouraged require rigorous standards and inspection. Medical services can become a racket, as can hospitalization. As Dixon has noted, further extension of social insurance to cover the health of older citizens will necessitate development of quality and cost controls on a national basis.[22] In the absence of a public program, Dixon concludes that public regulation of private insurance programs may be necessary.

Unions have been active in promoting a program to provide medical care of older citizens through extension of social security (OASDI) benefits. Specifics are illustrated by the King-Anderson Bill. The law would provide hospital or nursing-home care and out-patient and home medical attention within specified limits to all those over 65 who are eligible for OASDI benefits. While it would not cover all medical expense, it would probably assume the larger share. Some protection against misuse of these provisions is included; patients must pay their share of the costs first, somewhat as in the deductible features of automobile insurance.

Funds would be provided by increasing the tax rate on both employers and employees and by increasing the tax base of taxable earnings. The program would allow a free choice of doctors and hospitals. No means or needs test is involved. The question as to whether proposed taxes would be adequate is widely debated.

Proponents of this extension of social security have named it *Medicare;* those who oppose it generally call it "socialized medicine."

PRIVATE PENSIONS

Although many expected that public pension provisions would reduce interest in private plans, exactly the opposite tendency has appeared. When the social security program was inaugurated, there

[22]Dixon, *op. cit.,* p. 32.

were less than 500 private pension plans for employees. By 1963 there were approximately 33,000 approved pension plans.

Comprehensive accounting is now possible, for practically all welfare and pension plans with 26 or more participants are covered by the Welfare and Pension Plans Disclosure Act of 1958. Most of these plans (the total reporting was 161,750 in 1963) provide two or more types of benefits. Four out of five are welfare benefit plans, while the rest are pension plans. Some 88 percent of the plans are administered by employers; unions and employers jointly manage 6.7 percent. [23]

The number of workers covered by collectively bargained pension plans increased from 5 million in 1950 to 11 million in 1960. About 60 percent of all union workers had such coverage in 1960. Thirty-one percent of all unions insure pensions for 80 percent or more of their members through collective agreements. [24] A total of almost 23 million workers were included in the coverage of private pension and deferred profit-sharing plans. Many of the profit-sharing plans are designed to increase old-age security but provide less assurance of fixed benefits. [25]

Many private plans have been established by employers on their own initiative, while others were negotiated by unions; and, as would be expected, many variations exist in the provisions of existing pension plans.

Contributory and Noncontributory Plans

Two major types of private pension plans may be distinguished. One is made up of *contributory* plans, in which funds include payroll deductions from workers' earnings. The other type is *noncontributory*, with all costs paid by the employer. Both types of plans establish minimal conditions for eligibility, generally in terms of years of employment. Pensions vary in size, depending on earnings and years of service.

Benefit Levels

Amounts paid as private pensions vary so widely that no typical or average amount is meaningful. At the executive level, pensions may

---

[23]See the reports and releases of the Office of Welfare and Pension Plans, United States Department of Labor, for details of contributions, types of plans, industry, and numbers of covered employees.

[24]"Health and Insurance, and Pension Plan Coverage in Union Contracts," United States Department of Labor, *BLS Report No. 228*, July, 1962, pp. 1–4.

[25]For details of private plans for salaried workers, see "Digest of 50 Important Pension Plans for Salaried Employees in American Industry," *Bulletin No. 1373*, Bureau of Labor Statistics, 1963.

amount to several thousand dollars per month. In most plans benefit amounts are calculated by a formula that combines years of service and the wage or salary at the time of retirement. Some plans adjust the benefit level to the total of pension credits accumulated by individual or joint contributions. Many plans permit retirement at an earlier age with reduced benefits. In some cases employees have the right to retire early if they wish; in others employer approval is required.

A common provision in private plans calculates a total pension benefit to which the retiree is entitled and makes the private plan responsible for the difference between that total and what the employee receives through the federal social security (OASDI) program (see below).

Tax Shelter

Private plans have been encouraged by public policy which provides a tax shelter for the amounts paid into plans that meet requirements for approval by the Federal Treasury Department.[26] Employer contributions to these pension funds are not taxed as income until they are withdrawn. Then, the former employee, having retired, is likely to be in a lower tax bracket.

Until 1962 employees enjoyed a distinct advantage over the self-employed in the tax shelter provided by federal law. The Keogh Self-Employed Individuals Tax Retirement Act (Public Law 87-792) became effective January 1, 1963. It permits partners and sole proprietors to treat investment for old-age pensions as if they were employees of themselves. In general, Treasury Department rules for such plans are much the same as those for all private pension programs.

These provisions permit annual contributions up to 10 percent of earned income, with a maximum contribution of $2,500, and allow a tax deduction of 50 percent of the amount committed. Employees of the self-employed who have three or more years of service must be covered. Funds may be held in a trust or custodial bank account, in special United States bonds, or by an insurer or investment firm under annuity contracts. All contributions are the property of the beneficiary, and benefits (except for disability or death) cannot be paid

---

[26] Among other requirements, approved plans must: (1) include a substantial portion of employees in any category — usually about 70 percent or more; (2) be in writing, communicated to employees; (3) be a permanent plan; (4) calculate contributions and benefits on an actuarial basis; and (5) make it impossible for funds to flow back into the company's business.

before age 59½ nor delayed later than age 70½. It is expected that the added coverage may extend to as many as 9 million.

Dependability

Not all employer contributions in these plans become pensions for the individual employees thus covered, for some plans are inadequately planned and financed, and personal eligibility is contingent on length of service. Thus, rights to a pension may be lost or reduced if plans cannot meet their obligations or if employees fail to meet minimum service requirements, frequently 10 to 20 years, or if they leave the employer before attaining the age when pensions become available.

Private plans are only as dependable as their financial planning. Many earlier plans were financed on a "pay-as-you-go" basis. Current plans are generally insured.[27] The hazards of uninsured plans are illustrated by the experience of the United Mineworkers of America. Pensions originally planned for $100 per month have had to be reduced as contributions to the Union's welfare fund have reflected declining employment. Over the years many private, uninsured plans have found it impossible to provide contemplated pensions. At the same time, individual employees have been victimized when firms changed ownership and new owners refused to accept the accrued pension liabilities.

In 1958 the Welfare and Pension Plans Disclosure Act instituted a number of federal controls designed to protect the interests of participants in private pension systems. As amended in 1962, the act requires that administrators be bonded and that annual reports must be filed for all plans covering 26 or more employees.

Vesting

Both the benefits and the costs of private pensions are directly influenced by *vesting* provisions, which specify when the right to accumulated funds becomes the property of the employee. The pension right is vested in the employee when it becomes personal and is no longer shared, as a matter of discretion or rule, with an employer.

As could be expected, vesting is somewhat related to the contributory or noncontributory nature of pension programs. When most

---

[27]Most pension funds are of two basic types — insured and noninsured; some are a hybrid. Insured funds are those deposited with insurance companies to provide individual and group annuities. Noninsured plans deposit funds in banks or invest them, with administration by a bank, company officials, or joint-labor management trustees.

private programs were contributory, early vesting was common. As the majority of plans shifted to a noncontributory basis, vesting tended to be delayed. Employers preferred late vesting as an encouragement to employees to resist competitive offers; delayed vesting tended to hold them. On the other hand, late vesting makes the promise of pensions illusory to many employees who change employers.

A persistent trend toward earlier vesting is evident in recent years. As a result, in 1963, 65 percent of 1,213 corporate pension plans surveyed by the National Industrial Conference Board vest employee pension rights before the early or normal retirement age.[28] Current union proposals emphasize early vesting as a means of increasing employee mobility. Most common provisions vest pension rights after age 40 and after 10 or 15 years of service.[29]

Portability

Some private plans have added portability features designed to facilitate transfers without loss of pensions. Among these features are some permitting early retirement and others that allow unlimited transfer within the scope of individual plans maintained by a group of employers or by a union. About one fourth of the workers in large plans are covered by multi-employer or union-managed plans, some local and some national in scope. Such plans are generally limited to a single industry or craft.

●

PUBLIC OLD-AGE ASSISTANCE

As a part of the public social security program, aid is provided for older citizens on the basis of need and is described as Old-Age Assistance (OAA). As noted in Chapter 23, public funds are available to assist the blind, those permanently and totally disabled, and a general category of the needy who are "on relief."

The Social Security Act created a program of direct assistance to the aged based on need. In the thinking of those who framed the Social Security Act, this assistance program would provide a temporary system of relief for those who could not qualify for insured pensions (see below).

---

[28]See Harland Fox, "Pension Plan Vesting," *Business Management Record* (October, 1963), pp. 41–48.

[29]Details are summarized in *Manpower Report of the President* (Washington 25, D.C.: United States Government Printing Office, March, 1963), pp. 63 and 193.

Before the Social Security Act created its federal-state cooperative system for old-age assistance, treatment of dependent older workers varied widely from state to state. Some states or counties provided assistance; others made no such provision, leaving the aged to secure such relief as they could as a part of the broader program of "poor relief."

The social security program provides federal funds to supplement state grants to needy older persons. To qualify for these grants, states must establish minimum residence requirements and include all needy older citizens who meet these requirements. Under amended provisions of these assistance programs, the federal government now provides 80 percent of the first $30 of monthly benefits and from one half to 65 percent of the rest, up to $65 per month.

On the basis of twenty years of experience, the old-age assistance program appears to be quite "untemporary." It has not been a disappearing program. In several states more than one third of all persons over 65 are now included. However, the proportion of persons over 65 receiving old-age assistance is declining gradually as more oldsters qualify for old-age insurance benefits. In 1962 about 2.2 million older persons received benefits under the OAA program. The average monthly payment was $72.55.

Levels of aid available in this program vary widely, mainly because of the "matching" provision, which limits amounts to totals determined by individual states. For the first $30 of each monthly benefit, the federal program provides four fifths of required funds. This arrangement encourages states to be generous in extending coverage, since they receive 4 federal dollars for each state dollar up to the $30 level.

Present law (since 1958) varies the amount of federal sharing in the "over-$30" per month payments according to per capita income in each state. Despite this provision, poorer states provide relatively low benefits as compared to wealthier states. As a result, benefits are related less to need than to the financial position of each state.

The aid program will presumably be continued far into the future, in part because OAA benefits may be used to supplement insured pensions provided under the OASDI program (see next section). If OAA is to serve its purpose effectively, it will require more federal intervention than at present, for poorer states find relatively little incentive to move above the 80 percent subsidy level. As a result, assistance is so minimal as to be almost meaningless in many areas.

THE OASDI PROGRAM

Many informed students of economic security regard public old-age pensions as the most successful of the programs initiated by the Social Security Act of 1935. Originally known as Old-Age and Survivors Insurance (OASI), the program was renamed Old-Age, Survivors, and Disability Insurance (OASDI) when disability benefits were added to pensions and survivors' benefits (1956). The program is nationwide, administered by the Social Security Board in the Department of Health, Education, and Welfare. No state participation is involved.[30]

Benefits (pensions, survivors', and disability) are provided on an insurance or earned basis from funds provided by a payroll tax. The tax is shared, on a 50-50 basis, by employer and employee. The self-employed may participate by paying taxes at a rate equal to $\frac{3}{4}$ of the joint employer-employee contribution ($1\frac{1}{2}$ times the employee rate).

Compulsory coverage of workers has been extended from time to time, and a concept of *voluntary coverage* has extended the opportunity to participate to employees of religious, charitable, and educational organizations; ministers; and the self-employed. Federal employees who are not covered by the independent federal program are now protected by OASDI.[31] Total coverage now extends or is available to almost all employees and to the self-employed.

Benefits are paid on a monthly or lump-sum basis. Pension benefits are paid each month to eligible participants who have reached specified retirement ages and whose annual earnings are less than a specified maximum ($1200 before age 72, no maximum thereafter). Pensions and related benefits vary in terms of average monthly wages. They are calculated as a *primary benefit* plus possible supplements, with a specified maximum. *Supplemental pension benefits* are paid if the beneficiary has a dependent spouse who has reached retirement age. Survivors' benefits are paid to the spouse or other dependents. For widows and dependent widowers 65 or over, the benefit is $82\frac{1}{2}$ percent of the primary benefit. Disability benefits (monthly) are available for disabled participants.[32]

---

[30]See Edwin E. Witte, *The Development of the Social Security Act*, University of Wisconsin Press, 1962, and also his essay in *Social Security Perspectives* (edited by Robert J. Lampman), University of Wisconsin Press, 1962.

[31]Retired employees in the federal civil service were protected by earlier legislation. Their program includes *escalated benefits*, adjusted to increases in consumer prices.

[32]As noted, pension and related benefits vary in terms of average monthly wage, age at time of retirement, and number of eligible dependents. The basic primary benefits currently range from $33 to $127.

The types and amounts of benefits paid by the program have increased since the original act created pension benefits in 1935. In 1939, added benefits included those for surviving and dependent children, dependent wives over 65, widows, and dependent parents. In 1950 the law was modified to grant benefits to dependent wives and former wives under 65 with a child under 18, dependent husbands over 65, and dependent widowers. In 1956 disability benefits were added, both for workers over 50 and for disabled children 18 or over. In 1958 benefits were added for dependent wives and children of disabled workers. In 1960 disability benefits were extended to covered workers less than 50 years of age.

Levels of benefits have risen, largely in response to changes in living costs. For specific amounts presently payable, reference should be made to current tables showing primary benefits and maxima by monthly wage classes.

Eligibility for these benefits is dependent, first, on coverage in the program and, second, on age. Eligibility also depends on the number of quarters in covered employment. A worker is *fully insured* after 40 quarters of coverage, or one fourth of the quarters since 1950, or since he became 21, with a minimum of 6 quarters. Once fully insured, he cannot lose his eligibility. A worker becomes *currently insured* if he has worked in covered employment for 6 of the 13 quarters before he dies or becomes 65. Eligibility for disability benefits is established after 20 quarters.

The normal program contemplates pension benefits after age 65, but covered workers can elect to take benefits after age 62, as can wives of covered workers, in slightly reduced amounts.[33] Average wages are calculated on the basis of the period of covered employment with a possible "drop-out" period of up to 5 years to exclude the lowest levels of earnings.

Total benefit payments under the OASDI in the fiscal year ended June 30, 1962, were $13.7 billion. Payments to disabled workers and their dependents totaled over $1 billion. Old-age and survivors' benefits were $12.5 billion. In June, 1962, 17,200,000 persons were in current-payment status. They received an average benefit of $76.03.[34]

Funds are provided by taxes on payrolls. Their level has been changed several times as the program has been expanded. These past and prospective changes may be summarized as follows:

---

[33]The reduction formula is 5/9 of 1 percent for each month before the recipient reaches age 65.

[34]*Social Security Bulletin*, Vol. 25, No. 10 (October, 1962), p. 1.

Year	Annual Wage Base	Tax Rate for Employers and Employees[35]	Combined Maximum Annual Payments
1937–49	$3,000	1% each	$ 60
1954	3,600	2%	144
1960	4,800	3%	288
1963–65	4,800	3 5/8%	348
1966–67	4,800	4 1/8%	396
1968 on	4,800	4 5/8%	444

In part because health problems are so much a part of economic security for the aged, spokesmen for organized labor and others have urged that the act be amended to incorporate benefits for medical care (see above). Proposals contemplate a higher payroll tax and a larger wage base to finance a comprehensive program of hospitalization and medical care.

To ease the economic burden of retirement, some proposals would increase OASDI benefits (usually by adding medical care) and permit retirees to supplement benefits with earnings above those presently permitted. Most private programs place no limit on supplemental earnings; proposals for changing the public program are therefore directed at raising the $1200 "retirement test" limits specified by OASDI and its rule that every dollar earned beyond $1700 reduces the benefit by that amount.

Present OASDI rules withhold benefits to balance earnings — $1 for each $2 earned between $1200 and $1700 per year and $1 for each $1 earned beyond $1700. It has been calculated that the $1700 limit could be raised to $2400 at a cost of four-tenths percent of covered payrolls. This top limit could be eliminated entirely at a cost of seven-tenths percent.[36]

RETIREMENT

Security for the aged cannot be separated from retirement policies and practice. Retirement creates an important part of the problem of insecurity at the same time that retirement programs provide income for economic security. Retirement may require difficult personal as well as economic adjustments. Many workers are not educated or otherwise prepared for it. They are so habituated to the routine of work that they contemplate retirement with fear and reluctance.

[35]The self-employed pay 1½ times the rate for employees.
[36]Robert M. Ball, "Retirement Programs and the Changing Participation of the Aged in the Labor Force," Proceedings, Fourth Annual Social Security Conference, Institute of Labor and Industrial Relations, University of Michigan-Wayne State University, July, 1962, p. 154.

Others may, for various reasons, seek early retirement if their economic security permits.

Compulsory Retirement

For many, compulsory retirement is a blow they would postpone as long as possible. Both private and public programs, however, encourage or compel retirement at a specific chronological age, most frequently 65. As noted, public pensions under OASDI contemplate retirement at 65 and reduce or eliminate monthly pension benefits to balance earnings of those who continue employment beyond that point. Similarly, private programs, including those established by negotiation, usually provide for a normal retirement age and base benefits on a formula that includes this factor.[37]

Why the requirement of retirement at a specified age? The reasons are numerous, including:

1. In situations where jobs are scarce, compulsory retirement has been favored by some younger workers as a means of limiting labor supplies and creating vacancies.
2. In executive and management jobs, older managers may appear too conservative (unwilling to venture or to change with changing times); compulsory retirement makes room for younger leaders.
3. Compulsory separation at a fixed age is the easiest means of arranging retirement because chronological age is the condition over which arguments are least likely.
4. An arbitrary rule tends to encourage both employer and employee planning for retirement.

At least as many arguments against compulsory retirement are advanced, including:

1. It is unreasonable and arbitrary, giving inadequate consideration to individual differences in abilities and skills and to the desires of workers.
2. It is opposed by many, if not most employees, who do not want to retire if they are in good health.
3. It forces employees to exist on inadequate retirement allowances or pensions, which create personal hardship.
4. Neither the individual firm nor the economy as a whole can afford the luxury of universal retirement at such ages as are now prescribed.

The issue of compulsory retirement is widely debated. It is quite clear that compulsory retirement creates serious economic problems.

---

[37]See Walter W. Kolodrubetz, "Normal Retirement Provisions Under Collective Bargaining," *Monthly Labor Review*, Vol. 83, No. 10 (October, 1960), pp. 1052.

As Ball says, "As a nation, we have not done nearly as well on (retirement) benefit levels as we have done on coverage."[38] The average monthly benefit available under the OASDI program must ordinarily be supplemented by other income. Private pensions may, if coupled with public benefits, assure adequate income. For most workers, however, they have not done so, as is evident from such studies as have been cited in preceding sections of this chapter. For the majority of workers, neither private savings nor the combination of public and private pensions assure economic security in retirement. For many of the same workers, the fear of economic insecurity is augmented by a fear of inactivity and of something like expulsion from the society of friends and co-workers.

Plans for Flexibility

Many current proposals seek to reduce both the economic insecurity of retirement and the fear of inactivity and isolation. At the same time, they propose to introduce flexible retirement that will permit many of those who wish to do so to work beyond an arbitrary pension age while, at the same time, allowing others to retire before that age when considerations may justify such early retirement.[39]

Active retirement. "Active retirement" provisions have already been incorporated in some collectively bargained plans. These provisions, first negotiated by the IBEW, allow workers 62 years of age or over and with ten years or more of company service to continue to work about three hours a day. They can earn up to the $1,200 social security limit without giving up social security benefits. In addition, they retain full union contract protection, including life insurance and hospitalization, although vacation and holiday pay are reduced to reflect reductions in hours worked.[40]

Several variations in "gradual retirement" programs are being tried. One of them provides increased vacations and reduced work time for senior employees. This type of arrangement is being used by Cannon Electric Company, Connecticut Mutual Life Insurance Company, the William Wrigley Company, Prentice-Hall, and several other firms.[41] In some, vacation periods increase one month each year

---

[38]Ball, *op. cit.*, p. 150.
[39]See Geneva Mathiasen (ed.), *Flexible Retirement: Evolving Policies and Programs* (New York: G. P. Putnam's Sons, 1957).
[40]*Associated Industries of Cleveland Newsletter*, No. 412, April 1, 1962, p. 3.
[41]See Miriam C. Kerpen, "Reducing the Work Time of Older Employees," *Management Record*, Vol. 24, No. 10 (October, 1962), pp. 2–7.

after age 55 or 60. Reductions in earnings are gradual; adjustment to retirement benefits is less traumatic. Many private plans now encourage exceptions to and modifications of the usual compulsory provisions. The National Council on Aging has suggested a *retirement index* that would combine such factors as physical and mental condition, age (with automatic increases for rising life span), the personal desire of the individual, and a variety of individual and firm economic considerations. The index would be varied to fit top management, middle management and supervision, clerical and skilled workers, and semiskilled and unskilled workers.[42]

Early retirement. Early retirement provisions make employees eligible for pensions at ages below that regarded as normal. Such early retirement may be based on the health of the retiree or on his personal wishes. He may propose to establish his own business or to change employers. On the other hand, the employer may encourage early retirement as a means of discontinuing jobs.

These provisions have achieved wide acceptance. Of the 540 larger plans analyzed for the 1963 *Manpower Report*, 447 permit such early retirement benefits. Some of these benefits are automatic, contingent only on age (usually 55 or 60) and length of service (usually 10 to 15 years). Some provisions require the employer's consent.

Many such early retirement provisions have been negotiated. In 1962, automobile industry contracts, for example, provided two levels of benefits, a higher level for those who retire by mutual employer-employee agreement and lesser benefits for individuals who make the decision without employer consent. Under these provisions auto workers with at least 10 years service who retire at 60 by agreement get double the normal benefit until age 65 (or 62 for women). Under the Steel Workers agreement workers get full benefits for retirement at age 55 (with 20 years service in steel or with 15 years in aluminum).[43]

Preparation for retirement. Plans that introduce flexibility into retirement recognize the need for supplementing flexible provisions with counseling and preparation for retirement and also for permitting

---

[42]See also Margaret S. Gordon, *Work and Patterns of Retirement*, University of California, Institute of Industrial Relations (Berkeley), 1961. See also her "Income Security Programs and the Propensity to Retire," *Reprint No. 210* (in which she notes that "there is a good deal of evidence to suggest that prospective retirement income has a highly important influence on attitudes toward retirement . . .") and her "Projecting Employment Opportunities for Middle-Aged and Older Workers," *Reprint No. 211*, University of California, Institute of Industrial Relations (Berkeley), 1963.

[43]See "Recent Changes in Negotiated Pension Plans," *Monthly Labor Review*, Vol. 85, No. 5 (May, 1962), p. 531. See *BLS Bulletin 1284* for a discussion of optional early retirement benefits See also Kerpen, *op. cit.*, pp. 2–7.

downward as well as upward revisions in the normal retirement age. Both firms and unions have provided counseling services. In some firms special courses for preretirees seek to aid them in developing new interests and avocations. The Automobile Workers maintain a center where retirees can meet and maintain friendships and contacts.

PROGRAMS IN OTHER NATIONS

As in the United States, old-age security in most foreign nations is a part of the comprehensive social security system. In European nations the share of total national income devoted to social security is considerably greater than in this country. Here, total social welfare expenditures in 1963 were estimated at about $66 billion, some 11.6 percent of GNP. They were about 9.5 percent of GNP in 1935 and 8.8 percent in 1950. Private retirement provisions cost about $2.2 billion in 1963.[44]

In the Soviet Union a system of old-age pensions was established by the National Pension Act of 1956. The noncontributory system provides benefits based on length of service, earnings, and family needs. A distinctive provision also relates benefit levels to employment hazards. Benefits vary from 50 to 100 percent of most recent earnings, plus family allowances of 10 to 15 percent. Benefits are available to men at age 60 with 25 years of service and to women at 55 with 20 years of service. Retirement is not compulsory; many continue working. Plans propose to increase levels of pension benefits.[45]

THE ECONOMICS OF OLD-AGE SECURITY

Adequate support for older citizens is expensive. Current costs of public old-age assistance and pensions, private pensions, medical care, and poor relief for the aged represent about 4 percent of national income. As has been noted, several components in these costs are likely to cost more in the years ahead. Difficult questions about each of the major social security programs as well as private pensions must be faced, and means of coordinating and introducing some rationale into the composite of answers is essential.

[44]Ida C. Merriam, "Social Expenditures and Worker Welfare," *Monthly Labor Review*, Vol. 86, No. 6 (June, 1963), pp. 687–94.

[45]See M. S. Lantsev, "Social Security in the U.S.S.R.," *International Labour Review*, Vol. 86, No. 5 (November, 1962), pp. 453–66. Also, Wladimir Naleszkiewicz, "Financing and Coverage Under Social Insurance in Soviet Russia," *Industrial and Labor Relations Review*, Vol. 17, No. 2 (January, 1964), pp. 289–301.

Some of the major questions are evident. Toward what level of economic security shall we aim, and what portion of national income shall be devoted to this goal? How shall these costs be met — by private and negotiated programs, by federal taxes, by state and local taxes, by reserves or "pay-as-you-go," or by some combination? What priorities must be established and maintained among these various programs; which shall be regarded as most important?

Each of these questions has significance in evaluating the present and future status of security for the aged. Forecasts predict increasing needs and liabilities under most current programs — a possible exception is old-age assistance. For example, benefit costs under OASDI are expected to grow from 6.85 percent of payrolls in 1970 to 11.81 percent in 2050.[46]

Mobility

The economic impact of old-age security programs is by no means limited to the costs of benefits and the purchasing power released in the form of benefits. Programs influence the mobility of manpower resources. Their reserves create a conflict of immediate and future needs and have a significant influence on investment. At the same time, these programs are a many-sided factor in the growth of the economy.

One manner in which they influence economic growth is through their effect on worker mobility. Most private plans are assumed to reduce mobility. Indeed, many employers have initiated or agreed to such plans as means of reducing labor turnover and creating a private labor pool. The costs of many private plans are justified, in the opinions of their sponsors, by these "lock-in" features.

To some degree this effect is limited by early vesting and other portability provisions. As the 1963 *Manpower Report* notes, "Plans without vesting provisions are likely to exercise much more restraint on labor mobility than those which have them, particularly among workers with longest service."[47] The same report notes that multi-

[46]Eveline M. Burns, *Social Security and Public Policy* (New York: McGraw-Hill Book Co., Inc., 1956), p. 14. See also Robert Tilove, "Social and Economic Implications of Private Pensions," *Industrial and Labor Relations Review*, Vol. 14, No. 1 (October, 1960), pp. 28–34. See also Margaret S. Gordon, *The Economics of Welfare Policies* (New York: Columbia University Press, 1963). Harland Fox has advanced an interesting concept of the corporate social security system, a private system supplementing and meshing in with public social security systems. See Harland Fox, "The Corporate Social Security System and Workmen's Compensation," *The Conference Board Record*, Vol. 3, No. 2 (February, 1964), pp. 7–16.

[47]*Manpower Report of the President*, 1963, p. 64. In this connection, however, see also Robert C. Miljus and Alton C. Johnson, "Multi-Employer Pensions & Labor Mobility," *Harvard Business Review*, Vol, 41, No, 5 (September–October, 1963), pp. 147–63, available as *Reprint Series No, 43*, University of Wisconsin, Industrial Relations Research Center, 1963.

employer and union-financed plans permit broad transfers and thus minimize the demobilizing effect. Severance pay plans may also facilitate transfers.

It should be noted that the extent to which pension plans actually reduce mobility is not at all certain. Palmer, Parnes, and others conclude it is unlikely that pensions can or will exert a dominant influence in mobility decisions. Seniority protection and the psychological comfort of a familiar workplace and community are probably stronger forces. That pensions may not be significant in worker attachment is suggested by Parnes's study in Columbus, Ohio, in 1958; in that study seniority rights were found to be the principal ingredient in job attachment.[48] The same study notes that although nonvested plans may be less directly expensive (because workers who leave take no accumulated funds with them), this saving is available only to the extent that labor turnover is involved. Since the reduction of turnover is an objective, the saving to be expected from turnover represents something of a contradiction. In addition, of course, turnover involves costs that may be relatively high.

Immediate vs. Future Needs

Funds are taken from the stream of current income and diverted into reserves for future pension liabilities. We are rather clearly committed to such reserves; pay-as-you-go plans are recognized as hazardous. To what extent do future needs deserve a higher priority than either present consumption or investment? This question can be simplified: the choice appears to be between pension (i.e. future) reserves and present consumption, since the accumulation of impressive reserves has not, to this time, had adverse effects on individual saving or private insurance purchases. Perhaps this level of saving is one important criterion for gauging the level of contributions to reserves.

Another yardstick is the extent to which we wish to redistribute current income among income receivers and over time through the combined public and private pension systems. One consideration in that connection is the possible effect of varying pension payments on prices. Presumably the pension receiver has a high propensity to spend; benefits create direct demands for goods and services. A large volume of benefit payments could exert a stabilizing influence on consumption. The accumulation of reserve funds for pensions, on the other hand, reduces current disposable income and thus exerts a

[48]See Gladys E. Palmer, Herbert S. Parnes, *et al, The Reluctant Job Changer* (Philadelphia: University of Pennsylvania Press, 1962), pp. 76–77.

deflationary pressure (except in security markets). This combination of effects may become so important to the health and balance of the economy as to require centralized regulation. That possibility is one of the reasons for proposals that public and private systems be integrated.

To the extent that increases in contributions to pension funds are popularly approved, either by negotiation or by political action, it may be assumed that continuing expansion in these benefits represents a higher marginal value to participants than its alternatives. On the other hand, however, public policy may require that top priority be given to careful protection of investment for economic growth, since greater output must be the ultimate source of expansion in both consumption and security.[49]

Such a conclusion encourages conjecture as to how much more income can be diverted to reserves before preferences change. Some current union proposals demand wage increases instead of increased fringes, which would be a reversal of the trend in the 1960's. Frequent criticisms of proposed increases in social security taxes express a similar view. As noted, tax rates have grown from a combined employer-employee rate of 2 percent in 1937–49 to a prospective rate of 9 to 10 percent in the 1970's.

Increasing rates of benefits or adding such provisions as medical care may increase these rates. (Medicare might add $\frac{1}{2}$ percent at its start, perhaps more later, depending on experience.) Some supporters and critics of expansion conclude that 10 percent is perhaps a maximum. It should be noted, however, that (1) the present wage and salary base for taxes is limited by law — it may be increased; and (2) forecasts of needed reserves do not take rising wages into full account. As a result, it has been estimated that the OASI trust fund may be taking in an annual excess over its needs of about $11 billion by 1980.

Reserve Funds

The sizeable amounts of reserves accumulated on account of pension liabilities exercise significant influences on the economy. The total of such public and private reserves amounted to some $122 billion in 1963. Of that total, federal, state, and local programs had reserves of $61.3 billion, and private pension funds totaled almost the same, $60.7

---

[49]See Gerhard Colm, "The Economic Base and Limits of Social Welfare," *Monthly Labor Review*, Vol. 86, No. 6 (June, 1963), pp. 695–700.

billions.[50] Reserves are growing rapidly. A decade before, the total was about $50 billion.

It should be very clear that reserve funds are by no means sterile. Large portions are invested. Thus, as a direct result of growing private provisions, demands for common stocks have been increased and stabilized. According to a report by the Securities and Exchange Commission, corporate pension programs increased their investments in common stocks from about $812 million in 1951 to $36 billion in 1963. State and local programs and those managed by insurance companies are also under pressure to buy such securities as a means of keeping up with the rising costs of pensions. Unions are under similar pressure. The more recent self-employed pensions now encouraged by tax shelters will add to these demands for equities. Thus, a large and growing share of pension reserves is being invested and is contributing to continuing growth.

Union Power

Some employer spokesmen have expressed fear that reserves of union-managed or union-management controlled retirement programs may give too much economic power to unions. The assets of such funds were about $1.6 billion in 1960 and are growing rapidly. By 1970 they should total between $15 billion and $20 billion. However, the portfolios of these funds indicate conservative management. Their share of investments in equities is too small a fraction of the total to justify concern on this account.

On the other hand, the provision of more generous pensions may become a divisive issue within unions. Older, senior members may find their interests opposed to those of younger participants. The latter may resent having to finance, by payroll deductions or otherwise, pension benefits whose costs cannot be met by contributions from senior participants. Younger workers may prefer more take-home pay.

That conflict of interest should, however, focus attention on the high costs of compulsory retirement. It may require a more rational approach to retirement and greater flexibility in that process.

Such large and growing reserves indicate a heavy, long-term social commitment for the economic security of our elders. The apparent determination to make that security real argues strongly for predicting more generous provisions, especially in the area of medical care. With

---

[50]State and local pension plans had reserves of $24.3 billions; the federal share was $37 billions.

a large share of that protection in private plans, and with a growing tendency to invest in equities, such expansions in the program are compatible with the goal of rapid economic growth. That consistency will become greater as programs improve vesting and portability and encourage flexible retirement. The greatest economic limitation of present programs involves their discouragement of continued worker contribution through limitations imposed on mobility and work opportunities for older (over 50) workers and through arbitrarily penalizing work after a specified chronological age.

Perhaps the most wasteful aspect of present programs is their emphasis on compulsory retirement. The costs of such provisions are so high that the trend toward flexibility is likely to be accelerated.[51]

Chapters 23 and 24 have outlined current programs designed to provide an acceptable level of economic security for workers within the framework of the free enterprise system. Our ability to develop and maintain satisfactory programs of this type in the future depends largely on the health and growth of the economy. Improved security can become a reality if the economy as a whole is successful in combining an adequate rate of growth with balance and stability. Attention turns to these objectives in the following and final section (Part VII).

ANALYTICAL REVIEW QUESTIONS

1. Show that problems of aging are complicated by varying social values.
2. Evaluate and explain the quotation from Arnold Toynbee.
3. Why is the problem of caring for older workers likely to become more serious?
4. (a) What are some of the principal arguments advanced by employers against hiring older workers? (b) Are these facts or opinions?
5. (a) What have been the gains in life expectancy in the United States since 1900? (b) How much have proportions of the population 65 and over been increasing during the same span?
6. How does age affect participation rates?
7. What are the essential facts with respect to age and productivity?
8. (a) How has the working-life span changed for men and women? (b) What are the economic and social implications of the increasing gap between life span and working-life span? (c) What is the unemployment experience of older workers?
9. What are the economic resources and annual incomes of United States families headed by those over 65?

---

[51]For continuing reports on pensions, retirement, and related problems, see *Pension and Welfare News* (New York: Dornost Publishing Company, Inc.). Vol. 1, No. 1, appeared in October, 1964.

10. What estimates can be made as to the actual needs of older workers?
11. Describe the arguments for "Medicare" programs for elders.
12. What are the essential provisions of the Kerr-Mills Act?
13. What are the major objections to medical care financed through social security?
14. How do you explain the continuing growth of private pension systems?
15. Explain the tax shelter granted to private pensions.
16. (a) What has been the growth record of private pension plans? (b) Define contributory and noncontributory plans. (c) What are average monthly pensions under private plans?
17. Explain the concept of vesting and its importance. How is it related to portability?
18. What changes were introduced by the Keogh Act?
19. Differentiate concepts, policies, and programs of (a) old-age assistance and (b) old-age and survivors insurance.
20. How many oldsters are receiving public assistance under the OAA program? Are numbers and proportions declining?
21. What are the federal-state relationships for (a) old-age assistance and (b) old-age and survivors insurance?
22. (a) Who are eligible for OASDI payments? (b) Who pays taxes for OASDI? (c) How are taxes computed?
23. (a) How are OASDI benefits computed? (b) Define primary and supplemental benefits. (c) Define drop-out provisions. (d) What benefits are available for women and dependents?
24. (a) Is the OASDI actuarially sound? (b) What economic implications does present financing hold for the future?
25. (a) What are the usual arguments in favor of compulsory retirement? (b) What are the usual arguments against compulsory retirement? (c) When given a choice of retirement or work, which do most oldsters choose?
26. Why is chronological age not a satisfactory guide for compulsory retirement?
27. Is the payment of double pension benefits to early retirees justified in some situations? Should there be a similar rule for OASDI benefits?
28. Describe plans for flexible retirement, active retirement, and early retirement.
29. (a) What are the advantages and the disadvantages of flexible retirement over compulsory retirement? (b) Which policy is least wasteful of human resources?
30. How do American provisions for old-age security compare with those in European nations?
31. What are the major policy questions to be considered in evaluating programs for old-age security?
32. What problems are created for unions by these programs?
33. Are private pension plans a major factor in reducing worker mobility?
34. Would a severe decline in the stock market have a disastrous effect on private pensions?

35. How may the question of increasing pension benefits become a divisive issue in unions?

Case 24-1

COMPULSORY RETIREMENT

In the firm for which you have been working for five years, a system of multiple management maintains several management committees or junior boards of directors. These groups discuss major management policy and problems of the firm and make recommendations for changes to the senior board of directors. You have been elected to the junior board in your division.

Your junior board has spent some time discussing the firm's present policy of compulsory retirement at age 65. Some of the members of the board think that it is a good, sound policy and favor continuing it as is. Several others, however, feel very strongly that the policy is unsound. Some of them have indicated that they would prefer restriction of the policy to hourly rated production workers. They think that managers should be considered as individuals and retired when they can no longer perform their jobs satisfactorily. Several members have argued for a highly flexible program for managers — one that would permit their retirement as early as age 50 and as late as age 80.

• Assume that you have been made chairman of a special subcommittee to consider the merits of the present provision and of alternative plans. Your assignment is to summarize the recommendations you would like to send to the full junior board.

Case 24-2

A SOCIAL SECURITY PACKAGE

You are a congressman from a state that is heavily unionized. A number of your labor supporters call upon you with the following proposition. "We have old-age insurance, unemployment insurance, workmen's compensation insurance, and disability insurance — all in separate packages. Why not cut down all of the administrative red tape and put them all together in one single economic security program. Let's throw in health insurance for good measure. And let's face the music—we pay for these things anyway. Let's have a 10 percent payroll tax borne equally by employers and employees." They ask you to draw up a bill with these provisions.

You check with employer friends, and they are outraged at this proposal. "It violates states rights, is unconstitutional, and is nothing but socialism regardless of what you call it. A 5 percent payroll tax would put us out of business. Besides most of our employees wouldn't stand for such a bite out of their checks. And the cost would be closer to 20 percent than 10 percent. The federal government would have to increase taxes on businesses to make up the deficit, and we already pay more than our share."

• You decide to analyze the pros and cons of this "one package social security" proposition with particular emphasis upon its economic effects. Be prepared to present your analysis and recommendations at the next meeting of your class.

LABOR AND ECONOMIC GROWTH

"Economic growth" has become a familiar term in preceding pages. It has been described as one of the most striking features of our national history as well as a major goal for most nations today. It is a factor in every important labor problem and an element in most solutions advanced to meet these problems. In most popular thinking growth is expected to provide both work opportunities for millions of new threshold workers and security for the older retirees and their dependents. This chapter considers the role labor plays in economic growth and the implications of continued growth for all workers and citizens.

CONCEPTS AND MEASURES OF ECONOMIC GROWTH

Economic growth has become the worldwide symbol of progress. Its implications are more than economic; growth is widely regarded as correlated with cultural advancement and, indeed, with every aspect of "the better life." The rate or pace of growth is a matter of common concern; the international Organization for Economic Co-operation and Development has accepted a 50 percent growth for the 1960's as an achievable optimum for member nations. Accordingly, wide attention has been directed to growth models and formulas that seek to identify the major factors in growth and to suggest policies and programs to insure adequate rates of growth.

Role of Labor

Every such model or formula spotlights the major role played by labor — labor's essential part in and contribution to economic growth. In a very real sense economic growth is growth of, by, and for labor. In many current models the labor force of a nation is now recognized as one of the two most critical factors. Where earlier analysis emphasized the wealth of nations in terms of their physical resources and capital-worker ratios, today's models give labor at least as prominent attention. As the *Manpower Report* of 1963 put it, "Manpower is the basic resource . . . the indispensable means of converting other resources. . . . How well we develop and employ human skills is fundamental in deciding how much we will accomplish as a nation."

Harbison and Myers note that "An initial heavy investment in human resource development is necessary to get a country started on the road to self-sustaining growth."[1] The continuing development of managers and workers is an important factor in the growth of industrialized economies.

Labor — meaning all working people, the members of the labor force — has many reasons for both interest and concern about economic growth and rates of growth:

1. Many of the suggestions for facilitating and encouraging growth propose changes in *labor inputs* — that is, in numbers and qualifications of workers, their hours, and their skills. It should be noted that both quantities and qualities of labor are involved.

2. Growth is the natural setting for more and different, more productive jobs and hence a widely approved approach to the persistent problem of unemployment. The inadequacy of demands for workers is widely regarded as a function of growth. Pressures for higher levels of employment, in the opinion of many citizens, must be generated by growth.

3. While economic growth provides the setting for personal gains (for example, in per capita disposable income), it also facilitates social gains (in education and public services and facilities) in which everyone shares. Workers, as a dominant segment of society, are a major beneficiary of these social gains.

---

[1]Frederick Harbison and Charles A. Myers, *Education, Manpower and Economic Growth* (New York: McGraw-Hill Book Company, Inc., 1964), p. 185.

Definitions of Growth

Economic growth is regarded by many citizens as synonymous with progress; it is good in itself; it is essentially "getting better." To others economic growth is essentially the same as increasing both production and productivity. To them it means that the economy is becoming more efficient.

It should be recognized, however, that economic growth is not as broad as all progress, though the two may be closely related. Neither is it the same as increasing productivity, although that is a widely recognized factor in economic growth. Economic growth is usually defined in terms of outputs in goods and services; it does not include changing social, ethical, or spiritual values. It does not include a measure of the value of leisure, for example.

Economic growth is *increased capacity* to produce goods and services for which there are demands.[2] Economic growth means a sustained increase in goods and services, or output. It can be measured in physical units (e.g., more cabbages and more trucks), but this system is too clumsy for easy generalization, comprehension and comparison. A common denominator or yardstick is needed for combinations and evaluation. For that purpose, change is usually measured in dollar (or other monetary) value, which is a product of physical units and prices. Since the value of money also changes, measurement of national growth in dollars must be corrected for changes in the price level. Such an adjustment, widely used in measures of real wages and real income, is accomplished by deflating current dollar values, using *price deflators* somewhat like the Consumers' Price Index.[3]

The Syndrome of Growth

Several growth indicators or symptoms of economic growth are widely recognized. The Committee on Economic Policy of the Chamber of Commerce of the United States has distinguished four concepts

---

[2]See *Economic Growth in the United States* (New York: Committee for Economic Development, 1958).

[3]See the "implicit price deflators" in the *Economic Report of the President* (1963), p. 179; and, for a discussion of conversions into constant dollars, see *U.S. Income and Output, A Supplement to the Survey of Current Business, 1958.* Note that the GNP deflators and the CPI include prices of both goods and services. The BLS index of wholesale prices refers only to prices of goods.

of growth.[4] A "structural" concept makes economic growth or development approximately equivalent to industrialization. An "aggregative" concept regards economic growth as increase in the gross economic product — GNP. A third or "productivity" concept considers rising per capita GNP or per capita national income as economic growth. A fourth measures growth "in terms of welfare or specifically in terms of per capita consumption and levels of living."

In 1959 the Committee for Economic Development announced a multiphase "Growth Reckoner" which includes the constant-dollar value of gross national product, an index of industrial production, increases in the labor force, per capita annual labor force productivity, and a measure of disposable income. Other indicators are sometimes highlighted — for example, the growth in jobs and employment and the rising levels of individual and family incomes.[5]

Several indicators of growth have achieved wide acceptance. Such a list includes:

The gross national product. This is the most commonly recognized indicator and the most inclusive overall measure of growth. It is a gross measure; for example, GNP can increase at the same time that real personal income falls. GNP could grow without most of the benefits that economic growth is expected to provide.[6]

Prices. Because prices modify and influence all monetary measures and because inflation often accompanies growth, indexes of consumer and wholesale prices are included in this list of key indicators. Real growth and real income must be clearly distinguished from increases reflecting dollar devaluation. Rapid price increases deflate many of the most widely used measures of growth.

Business activity. Because cyclical fluctuations can obscure longer-term growth trends, indexes of business activity are closely regarded for indications of growth. They combine various measures,

---

[4] In "The Promise of Economic Growth," 1959, especially pp. 6–32.

[5] See "Some Parts of the Economy Never Stopped Growing," *Fortune*, June, 1961, pp. 122 ff.

[6] The CEA analysis of growth has underscored the limitations of GNP as a measure. It notes: (1) the necessarily restricted concept of production, with its omission of leisure and its exclusion of such nonmarket activities as those of housewives; (2) the necessity of imputing values to goods and services that do not pass through formal markets (for example, the services of owner-occupied homes); (3) the "often tenuous distinction between final and intermediate output"; (4) questions of valuation; and (5) problems arising from changes in products. See *Economic Report of the President, 1961*, p. 56–57.

including those of production in major industries: trade (car-loadings, department store sales, business failures); retail and wholesale prices; finance (stock and bond transactions); banking; and foreign trade.

Per capita real disposable income. To translate gross growth into a measure of the impact on individuals requires some measure of personal income or purchasing power. Perhaps the most useful measure is that of family income. Since most reporting ignores the size of families, per capita real income is a desirable supplement to or substitute for the family measure.

Labor force. The labor force (and the population as its source and reserve) provides another clue to developments in the growth process. The indicator is crude; quantity may be less important than quality.

Employment and unemployment. Since the real payoff of growth to many citizens comes in the form of stable employment at rising real wages, measures of employment and unemployment deserve continued attention and are closely regarded. Perhaps the most useful single, current measure is the percentage of unemployment.

Actual and planned investment. Many economic analysts watch forecasts and surveys of business expenditures for plants and equipment as perhaps the most sensitive and critical indicators of growth. To the same end, attention may be directed to measures of personal and corporate saving, since they suggest the potential for present and future investment.

Differences in Growth Estimates

Differences in estimates of economic growth — and, indeed, arguments about rates of growth — may arise out of (1) the choice of indicators or criteria and the weights attached to each of them, (2) failure to take account of price level changes, and (3) the selection of time periods and base periods for comparisons. Also, reports of trends may be confusing because some of them describe the proportion or percentage of change in the total period while others emphasize a series of average annual rates.

Thus, crude calculations may be based on GNP in current dollars. They may, instead, use constant value dollars. They may prefer a measure of national income (or of family or per capita disposable income). They may use an index of production, which reports on dollar value of output from factories and extractive industries. They may prefer one of these measures adjusted for the growth in the labor force or changing numbers of man-hours.

For whatever indicator is selected, the time period may make a significant difference, because cyclical fluctuations are evident in many if not all of these indicators. Table 25-1 has been prepared to illustrate some of these differences. It compares rates of change in several possible indicators for the most recent two years for which data are presently available.

HISTORIC GROWTH

The general pattern of historic growth in the United States has been suggested in earlier discussions of productivity, employment, and wages. Data for years before 1900 are necessarily crude, backward-looking estimates. Although approximations of national income accounting have been extended backward to indicate the general pattern, useful comparisons and analyses are generally restricted to the years since the turn of the century. Since the whole economy undergoes continuing internal changes, the usefulness of long-term comparisons is sharply reduced as the period is lengthened. Goods and services are constantly changing, as are buying habits. Qualities of goods and services vary at the same time that quantities and prices change. National expenditures and purchases have undergone great change as the nation has paid for hot wars and cold war.

The limitations of all long-term comparisons should, therefore, be clearly recognized. What has actually happened in recent years can be assessed with more assurance and accuracy than can long-term changes in the same indicators.

In terms of *GNP* a very long-term view might look as far back as 1880 when the total, adjusted to a 1957–59 base, was about $45 billions. For 1962 the comparable figure is about $425 billions, an overall increase of more than 8 times in the 80 years. For the more recent period from 1909 through 1962, the average rate of growth has been about 3 percent; and for the past decade, 1953–1963, it has been

Table 25-1

CRUDE MEASURES OF ECONOMIC GROWTH — 1962–1963[1]

Years and Changes	Gross National Product		National Income		Disposable Personal Income		Gross Private Domestic Investment		Civilian Labor Force	GNP per L.F. Member
	Current Dollars	Constant Dollars (1963 = 100)	Current Dollars	Constant Dollars (1957–59 = 100)	Current Dollars	Constant Dollars (1963 = 100)	Current Dollars	Constant Dollars (1957–59 = 100)	(thousands)	Current Dollars (1963 = 100)
1963.........	585.0	585.0	478.4	448	402.6	402.6	82.3	77.1	72,975	8,014
1962.........	554.9	563.6	453.7	430	384.4	389.5	78.8	74.8	71,854	7,844
Difference...	30.1	21.4	24.7	18	18.2	13.1	3.5	2.3	1,121	170
Percent Change.......	5.4	3.8	5.4	4.2	4.7	3.4	4.4	3.1	1.56	2.17

[1]Data from *Economic Report of the President,* 1964.

about 3 percent annually. In the parallel index of industrial production, which emphasizes the output of factories and mines, the 1909–1957 annual average rate was 3.5 percent.[7]

Meanwhile, of course, the total *labor force* has grown from 17.4 million in 1880 to 75.7 million in 1963 so that total output has represented the contribution of an increasing number of workers and working hours. From 1929 to 1963, the civilian labor force increased from 49.1 millions to 73 millions. Its annual average rate of growth has been calculated at about 1.3 per cent for the longer period, 1909–57.

Total *civilian employment* has also grown, from 47.6 millions in 1929 to 68.8 millions in 1962. (The CED estimate found that total hours worked in 1956 were almost three times the similar total in 1880.) In both labor force and employment, rates of change have fluctuated from year to year. In depressions employment has shown sharp declines. Meanwhile, the labor force has changed with changing patterns of age distribution and participation rates. Without detailing these year-to-year variations, it is worth noting that the rate of growth in employment has slowed, from about 1.9 percent annually in the 1947–1957 period to 0.9 percent annually from 1959 to 1962.[8]

Average output, as measured by productivity per man-hour, shows impressive growth. The increase from 1880 to 1956 has been estimated by CED; the average man-hour produced five times as much at the close as at the beginning of the period. For the 1909–1957 period the improvement is estimated at an average annual rate of 1.6 percent. Investigators and estimators do not arrive at identical figures. Thus, another calculation covering the 50 years from 1909–1959 finds the average rate to be approximately 2.2 percent.[9]

As every study has noted, however, the rate of growth in man-hour productivity has shown rapid and impressive changes from one short period to another. Without repeating the discussions in earlier chapters, this situation can be reviewed by reference to Figure 25-1, which represents the findings of one recent analysis of changing productivity.

---

[7]Since GNP measures dollar values, it is worth noting that prices rose over the 1909–1957 period at an average annual rate of about 2.5 percent. The comparisons here have been adjusted for this change. For more extensive and detailed comparisons, see Robert A. Gordon, "Twenty Years of Economic and Industrial Change," *Reprint No. 222*, University of California (Berkeley) Institute of Industrial Relations, 1964.

[8]See "Industry Employment Growth Since World War II," *Manpower Report No. 5*, United States Department of Labor, January 30, 1963.

[9]See *Productivity and Wage Settlements* (Washington, D.C.: Chamber of Commerce of the United States, 1961).

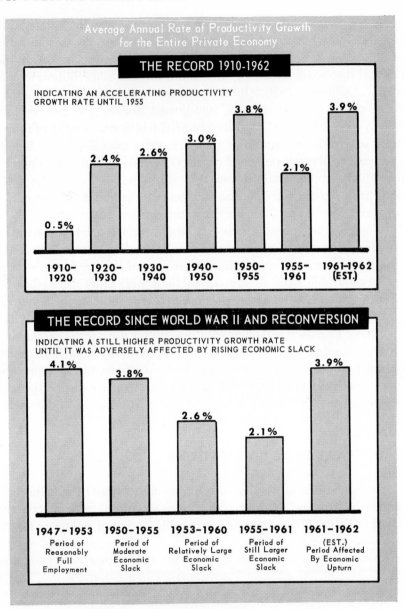

Note: Based on U.S. Department of Labor estimates, relating to man-hours worked.

Figure 25-1

**TRENDS IN OUTPUT PER MAN-HOUR
— OR PRODUCTIVITY — 1910–1962**

Source: *Key Policies for Full Employment* (Washington, D. C.: Conference for Economic Progress, September, 1962), p. 45.

Long-term comparisons of *disposable income* are particularly difficult; data on which to base historic calculations are meager and their meaning is questionable. The CED study estimates, however, that personal disposable income grew from a level of $26.7 billion in 1880 to $287.2 billion in 1956. (Both figures are in 1956 dollars.) In a more recent period and in current, unadjusted dollars, the growth from 1929 to 1963 is from $83.1 billions to $402.6 billions. Studies of shorter recent periods have found that growth in per capita disposable income amounted to about 7 percent from 1947 to 1954 and about 16 percent from 1953 through 1961. From 1939 through 1963, when the dollar totals are adjusted for inflation, the increase is about 72 percent, as compared with about 300 percent in unadjusted dollars.[10]

Figure 25-2 charts these commonly referenced measures of growth and permits visual comparisons. Data have been plotted on a semilogarithmic scale to emphasize the rate of change in each series.

Comparable rates of growth in these indicators are rather apparent from the chart, as are the more volatile indicators. Rates can be compared by sketching trend lines for each series. The civilian labor force increased rather steadily, except for the wartime reduction. Gross national product, unadjusted for the growing labor force, shows the most rapid increase. Productivity and disposable income show slower rates. It may be noted that growth in per capita disposable income has not quite kept pace with the general trend of productivity.[11]

INTERNATIONAL COMPARISONS

In the United States, popular interest in the past decade has been frequently attracted to international comparisons of rates of economic growth. Table 25-2 summarizes available data and estimates for the

---

[10]Data from *Economic Growth in the United States: Its Past and Future* (New York: Committee for Economic Development, 1958); *American Workers Fact Book* (Washington, D.C.: Department of Labor, 1960), p. 87; Solomon Fabricant, "Basic Facts on Productivity Change," *Occasional Paper No. 53* (New York: National Bureau of Economic Research, 1958); "Employment, Growth and Price Levels," *Hearings*, Joint Economic Committee (Washington, D.C.: Government Printing Office, 1959); and *Economic Report of the President*, 1964, p. 227.

[11]Morgenstern has spelled out the inherent limitations in all such estimates of growth. Since measures of gross national product are by no means free of error nor, so far as is known, subject to a uniform or constant error, measures of growth also reflect these limitations. Much depends on the choice of a base year. He concludes that inherent errors are so serious as to raise a reasonable question about the value of computing growth rates. See Oskar Morgenstern, *On the Accuracy of Economic Observations* (2nd ed.; Princeton, N.J.: Princeton University Press, 1963), especially pp. 286–97.

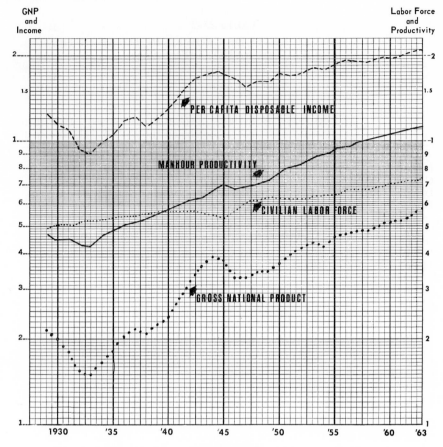

Figure 25-2
SOME INDICATORS OF ECONOMIC GROWTH,
UNITED STATES — 1929–1963

Sources: *Economic Report of the President,* 1963, pp. 172 and 191; *Economic Report of the President,* 1964, pp. 208, 209, 227, 230, and 245; *BLS Bulletin No. 1249.*

1960–70 decade. CED notes, in its comments on this comparison, that rates for several nations are accelerated because they involve recovery from the setback of World War II. Note is also taken of the obvious differences in bases; the United States began the period with a base so high that a major gain in total output amounted to only 4 percent per year in the 1950–55 period.

The Conference on Economic Progress has compared rates of growth during the 1953–59 period. For these years it estimates rates of 2½ percent for the United States; 6 to 9 percent for the Soviet Union; 6½ percent for Germany and Japan; 5½ percent for Italy; 5 percent

Table 25-2

AVERAGE ANNUAL RATES OF GROWTH IN TOTAL OUTPUT, SELECTED NATIONS (Percentages)

Nation	Total Output			Output per Capita	
	I 1950–1955	II 1950–1960	III 1960–1970 (estimated)	IV 1950–1960	V 1960–1970 (estimated)
Austria.........	7				
Belgium........	4	3.0	3.4	2.4	2.9
Canada........	5				
Denmark.......	1				
France.........	4	5.0	5.0	4.2	4.2
Germany.......	10	9.6	7.0	8.4	6.0
Greece.........	6				
Ireland........	2				
Italy...........	6	5.7	4.4	5.1	3.9
Japan..........	8				
Luxembourg....	1				
Netherlands.....	13	5.0	4.8	3.6	3.7
Norway........	4				
Portugal........	3				
Sweden........	3				
Switzerland.....	3	4.6	3.0	3.3	2.0
Turkey.........	6				
United Kingdom.	3	2.6	2.0–2.8	2.1	1.6–2.1
United States ..	4				
U.S.S.R........	7				

Sources: "Economic Growth in the United States," Committee for Economic Development, February, 1958, p. 57; "Europe's Future in Figures," *Looking Ahead* (National Planning Association), Vol. 11, No. 8 (November, 1963), p. 5. Column I computed by CED or reported by CED from OEEC, *Statistics of National Product and Expenditure, No. 2,* and from Joint Economic Committee study; data for columns II, III, IV, and V, from *Europe's Future in Figures,* by ASEPELT, Association Scientifique Europeene Pour la Provision Economique à Moyen et a Long Terme.

for Switzerland; 4½ percent for the Netherlands; and 4 percent for Sweden and France.[12]

Such comparisons have created popular concern, for many citizens have worried about our apparently laggard economy. Individuals and organized groups have been impressed with the fact that many nations now make planning for economic growth a major activity. The various Russian 5-year plans have been widely discussed. Numerous newly-industrialized nations have growth plans that exercise controlling influence on both their domestic and foreign policy.

Several European nations have experimented with similar plans. In these plans, major attention tends to be concentrated on public and

[12]*Jobs and Growth* (Washington, D.C.: Conference on Economic Progress, May, 1961).

private investment. Plans not only forecast investment; they use a variety of fiscal, monetary, and other programs and regulations to influence investment decisions. The dominant employer association in France, the *Patronat*, has favored such a public policy. The French government has established a 4-year plan, with quotas for production, investment, and consumption. Projections of spending for new facilities, research, education, housing, and highways are integral parts of this plan for growth and are combined to identify proposed inputs and outputs.[13]

Growth is a major consideration in the planning of the Common Market nations. Worldwide growth has been the major subject of analysis and planning by representatives of member nations in the Organization for Economic Cooperation and Development.[14]

In all international comparisons, rates of growth are meaningful only when related to the base from which they are calculated. Further, careful comparisons must recognize the methods of measurement and the persistent errors introduced by inflation. As has been noted, the same pressures that generate growth can have a powerful impact on price levels. Many of the high-rate growth economies are also those of drastic inflation. Thus, in the 1958 to 1963 period, while consumer prices in the United States and Canada rose about 5 percent, living costs rose 11 percent in the United Kingdom, 12 percent in West Germany, 15 percent in Sweden and Italy, and 27 percent in Japan. Much more radical changes occurred in Argentina, Brazil, and Indonesia where price levels rose from 300 to more than 900 percent.

FORMULAS FOR GROWTH

International comparisons are in part responsible for numerous proposals to increase the pace of economic growth in this country. At the same time, many of our economic problems, including labor problems, are popularly ascribed to inadequate growth. Union spokesmen have been prominent among critics of our relatively low rates of growth. The Council of Economic Advisers has given strong support to the position that we have not grown as fast as we could or should. The Council has noted that "the American economy today is beset not

---

[13]See "Europe Charts Its Business Future," *Business Week*, April 7, 1962, pp. 80–81 ff.

[14]See also "Economic Policies and Programs in Middle America," *Joint Committee Print*, 88th Congress, 1st Session, 1963; John P. Lewis, *Quiet Crisis in India: Economic Development and American Policy* (Washington, D.C.: The Brookings Institution, 1962) and his "India's Economic Future and American Policy," *Brookings Research Report No. 6*, 1962.

only with a recession . . . but with persistent slack in production and employment, a slowdown in our rate of growth. . . . Economic recovery in 1961 is far more than a cyclical problem. It is also a problem of chronic slack in the economy."[15]

The comparatively low growth rate in this country has caused critics of our public policy to suggest that we have *high-level stagnation*, meaning that we have a good standard of living in comparison with other countries and earlier time periods in the United States but that we are not increasing our standard of living as much or as fast as we should. While some critics have their own panaceas for overcoming this hurdle, the major impact of their charges has been to encourage a careful search for clues to growth. We have sought to identify desirable patterns of growth and the principal economic factors that can induce and facilitate rapid growth. As will be noted, our development and application of human resources appears prominently among these factors.[16]

The "stagnation theory," as an explanation of our growth rate, has wide popular support. At the same time, it is buttressed by some careful studies, including those relating changes in GNP to employment. Wilcock and Franke found that levels of unemployment have been highly sensitive and responsive to increases in GNP in periods of recovery. They studied this relationship in three recovery periods beginning in 1949, 1954, and 1958, respectively. They found that unemployment declined by from 3.3 to 3.7 percent for each one percent increase in real GNP in each first year of recovery. The major impact of increased productivity in these first years is on short-term unemployment. In the second year of recovery, long-term unemployment declines at an accelerated pace. In the first two of these recovery periods, each billion-dollar expansion in GNP created some 80,000 new, full-time jobs or their equivalents. In the 1958–1959 recovery the price was higher — 66,000 jobs per billion dollars.[17]

---

[15]Quoted in *1961 Joint Economic Report*, May 2, 1961, p. 60.

[16]While growth is generally considered in terms of national units, 1,400 "area development units" in the United States are concerned with regional development, sometimes described as "subnational." See "Requirements for Regional and National Economic Growth," *Looking Ahead* (National Planning Association), Vol. 11, No. 8 (November, 1963).

[17]Richard C. Wilcock and Walter H. Franke, "Will Economic Growth Solve the Problem of Long-term Unemployment?" *Proceedings, Fourteenth Annual Meeting, Industrial Relations Research Association*, December, 1961, pp. 37–49.

Major Factors in Growth

What must we do to insure an adequate rate of growth? And what are the implications for labor? What part can or must labor play in achieving a high growth rate? These questions have had growing attention in recent years.

Planning for economic growth inevitably rests upon *theories of growth;* planners must hold some explanation of the growth process. Current international interest in the rate of growth has encouraged analysis of the process and development of numerous hypotheses with respect to what may be major factors in it.

Growth inputs. Modern analysis of the growth process usually begins with recognition of two major factors or *growth inputs — labor inputs,* generally measured in man-hours, and *capital inputs* (including land). It is clear that gross quantities of both are increasing and have increased; capital has grown in total and per worker. The labor force has also grown with the growing capital-worker ratio.

At the same time, however, both have changed. Capital today is distributed among industries and regions in a manner different from that in earlier years. It is invested in different machines, buildings, trucks, railway locomotives, steamships, and other resources. Workers are different, too, with changed occupational skills and industry assignments, changed educational attainment, and changed efficiency. Capital and human resources are combined with changing *technical coefficients.*

Thus, inputs vary both in quantity and in quality. Analysis must recognize both types of variation as possible sources of growth.

Variations in inputs. Several studies have sought to discover how and why variations in these inputs have influenced economic growth in the United States.[18] They begin with data on national income, adjusted to eliminate price-level changes. Most of the studies have

---

[18]See E. F. Denison, *The Sources of Economic Growth in the United States and the Alternatives Before Us* (New York: Committee for Economic Development, 1962); J. W. Kendrick, *Productivity Trends in the United States* (Princeton: Princeton University Press, 1961); T. W. Schultz, "Capital Formation by Education," *Journal of Political Economy,* Vol. 68 (December, 1960), pp. 571–83, and his "Investment in Human Capital," *American Economic Review,* Vol. 51, 1961, pp. 1–17, and the comment on the Schultz article with a rejoinder, *American Economic Review,* Vol. 51, 1961, pp. 1026–35 and 1035–39; Moses Abramovitz, "Economic Growth in the United States," *American Economic Review,* Vol. LII, No. 4 (September, 1962), pp. 762-82 — an excellent review of Denison's book and others; B. F. Massell, "A Disaggregated View of Technical Change," *Journal of Political Economy,* Vol. 69, 1961, pp. 547–57; Twentieth Century Fund, *The U.S.A. and Its Economic Future* (New York: The Macmillan Company, 1964); For an intriguing discussion of an alternative model, see David E. Apter, "System, Process and the Politics of Economic Development," *Reprint No. 224,* University of California (Berkeley) Institute of Industrial Relations and Institute of International Studies, 1964.

directed attention to three periods in the present century: 1909–1929, with an average growth rate of 2.82 percent in national income; 1929–1957, with an average growth rate of 2.93 percent; and 1909–1957, with an overall average growth rate of 2.89 percent. Studies try to trace these increases to variations affecting both labor and capital inputs.

A preliminary conclusion notes that the quantitative increase in inputs has accounted for 1.22 of the 2.89 percentage points in the average growth rate from 1909 through 1957. In the same period, increases in output per unit account for 1.67 percentage points.

In the 1909–1929 period, when real national income increased by 2.82 percentage points, the *increased labor input* (unadjusted for changing efficiency) contributed 1.53 percentage points, and the *increased capital input* (unadjusted for increased efficiency), 0.73 points. In the 1929–1957 period, when the total increase was 2.93, these increases were 1.57 and 0.43 percentage points. Meanwhile, increases in *output per unit of input* amounted to 0.56 and 0.93, respectively. The totals $(1.53 + 0.73 + 56 = 2.82$ and $1.57 + 0.43 + 0.93 = 2.93)$ account for the overall percentage growth.

Quantitative changes in inputs are easily understood, but qualitative changes in these inputs deserve special attention. For capital, Denison notes changes in nonfarm residential structures, other structures and equipment, inventories, United States-owned assets abroad, and foreign-owned assets in the United States. For labor, he notes changes in employment, in the age-sex composition of the labor force, in hours of work, in a quality improvement related to shorter hours, in education, and in increased experience and improved utilization of women workers. At the same time, he finds that the reduction in labor input attributable to shorter hours amounted to 0.23 percentage points in 1909–29 and to 0.53 percentage points in 1929–1957.

Of special interest are the major explanations of increased *output per unit of input*, which is credited with 0.93 of the 2.93 percentage points in 1929–1957. Two major changes dominate this source of growth: "advance of knowledge" and "economies of scale — growth of the national market."[19]

---

[19]Other factors noted by Denison include: (1) restrictions against optimum use of resources; (2) reduced waste in agriculture; (3) industry shift from agriculture; (4) change in lag in application of knowledge; and (5) economies of scale — independent growth of local markets.

In summary, the simplest model of growth may be viewed as a fourfold matrix with two major types of input and two types of variation in each:

Inputs	Variation	
	Quantitative	Qualitative
Labor		
Capital		

Formulas for growth must recognize each of the major divisions on each axis. Further analysis gives more detailed attention to sources of variation in each of these divisions. Since our concern centers on the labor contribution, attention turns to conditions affecting labor inputs.

Historic labor inputs. Denison concludes that the total labor input to historic growth rates from 1927–1957 has averaged 1.57 percent, which he attributes to six changes, as follows:

1. Increased employment 1.00%
2. More and better education 67%
3. Effect of shorter hours on productivity 33%
4. Improved employment of women 11%

     Subtotal 2.11%

Less:
5. Reductions in hours worked . . . . − .53
6. Changed age-sex composition of labor force . . . . − .01

                                                       (.54%)

7. Total growth due to labor input 1.57%

Item 1, *employment*, is quantitative, measured in man-hours. The influence of item 2, *education*, is estimated from an analysis of average incomes of males by years of schooling, with age as a constant. Differences in incomes are assumed to represent rough indicators of differences in contribution. They are recognized as reflecting the influence of other modifiers, including ability and motivation, which are weighted at about 40 percent.[20]

Changes in hours of work are regarded as having both a positive and a negative influence. First, they have contributed one third of one percent to the total by improving the quality of contributions — i.e., productivity per hour worked. In the same period the total labor input is reduced somewhat more — 0.53 percent — because hours were reduced.[21]

Lesser factors — improved employment of women and the changing composition of the labor force — require no special comment, since both have been discussed in earlier chapters. Women members of the labor force have been able to improve their contribution to growth as a result of the rapid expansion of their employment opportunities. Many occupations, formerly closed to them, became accessible during the period. Meanwhile, the age distribution of the labor force changed to include much larger proportions of older workers, with a slight adverse effect on labor inputs.

Denison's analysis has been emphasized because it provides a breakdown of the labor input. Some other studies have attributed a lesser significance to labor and more to capital. Solow, for example, emphasizes the increasing productivity of new capital and suggests that growth can be accelerated by relatively small increases in investment.[22]

Future labor inputs. Models for economic growth make it very clear that what workers do and what is done to and with them have been very influential in historic patterns of growth. We may reasonably assume that somewhat similar relationships will persist in the future. The manner in which labor resources are developed, disposed, utilized, and conserved is likely to be a major factor in our success or failure in attaining desired growth objectives.

In our planning for growth, we will need to consider carefully how labor inputs can be increased and improved. Some of the choices

---

[20]Denison clearly recognizes and indicates the crude quality of these calculations. Historic data are difficult to secure; samples are small. For a critical review, see Abramovitz, *op. cit.*, pp. 770–71. For more on employment in the process of economic development, see Walter Galenson, "Economic Development and the Sectoral Expansion of Employment," *International Labour Review*, Vol. 87, No. 6 (June, 1963), pp. 1–15.

[21]Note that this analysis and most historic evidence indicate that reduced hours tend to be more productive hours. As has been suggested, there is little evidence to indicate what may be the most efficient workday or workweek. See Chapter 17.

[22]See Robert M. Solow, "Technical Progress, Capital Formation, and Economic Growth," *American Economic Review*, Vol. 52, No. 2 (May, 1962), pp. 76–86.

and alternatives we face are concerned primarily with quantities of labor, while others involve quality aspects of labor contributions. Still others involve both quantity and quality, while almost all of them are likely to influence the parallel capital inputs and contribution both quantitatively and qualitatively.[23]

Changes in quantity. The elementary significance of the labor input is clear from every analysis of historic economic growth. It is evident that attainment of national goals must seek to maintain high levels of employment as well as effective disposition and utilization of manpower resources. Perhaps the most obvious step in that direction involves reducing unemployment.

As noted in Chapter 16, one of the most promising approaches to higher levels of employment involves improvement of the labor marketing process. For that reason Wilcock and Franke suggest that programs designed to speed growth should include improved clearance among employment services in different localities, assistance in relocation, expanded retraining, and extended unemployment benefits. Similarly, the potential benefits of improved labor market information, with additional guidance and counseling about employment opportunities and working careers, all point to added responsibilities for public (and perhaps private) employment exchanges.

Improved marketing implies added labor mobility, with reduced *labor market frictions*, shorter transitional unemployment, and lessened *resistance to change*. These developments must face what is perhaps an inherent discomfort in change. It is usually less uncomfortable to avoid change, to continue as is. More rapid growth presumably means more frequent changes of jobs and employers, with movement into different industries, occupations, and regions. It means giving up the familiar patterns of work; leaving other members of the work group; moving into new climates, localities, and communities. It means joining new working groups that may include workers of different races, nationalities, and religions. For the farm worker, it may mean a move to town and the factory, filling station, or missile plant. It may generate higher costs of recruitment, selection, and training. It may require retraining, transportation and resettlement allowances,

---

[23]See Raymond D. Larson, "Economic Requirements of an Expanding Economy"; Everett Kassalow, "Problems of Wages, Productivity and Labor Costs Throughout the World"; and Joel Seidman, "Productivity, Wages and Jobs at Home and Abroad" — all in *Proceedings* of 14th Annual IRC Labor Conference, March 22–23, 1962, Industrial Relations Center, University of Minnesota, *Bulletin No. 36*, August, 1962, pp. 1–10, 31–35, and 40–43, respectively.

and improved vesting of pensions and similar portability in other benefits.

Another possible step in the quantitative direction would seek elimination of restrictive work rules. Intentional restriction of output, especially when it takes the form of featherbedding that requires the employment of workers who are not needed, can exert a significant negative impact. The elimination or reduction of these practices is an obvious challenge to the ingenuity of our society and, more particularly, of managers. Restrictions can be expected to disappear only as the reasons for them are removed. High level employment is in itself a powerful specific. Security programs can be used to reduce the pressures for restriction.

Quantitative considerations cannot ignore the question of working hours, which also has a qualitative aspect. As in the past, future reduction in hours may improve the productivity of each hour. As has been noted in Chapter 17, however, we do not know what are the most efficient lengths of workday and workweek. Moreover, what may be best at one time or in one group of occupations may be much less satisfactory in others.

As a result, the quantitative impact of change to a 35-hour week is by no means certain. We need far more understanding as a basis for sound planning on hours of work. For that reason Denison concludes that "few studies offer more promise of adding to welfare and contributing to wise decisions . . . than a really thorough investigation of the present relationship between hours and output."[24]

One possible means of increasing quantities of labor is the encouragement of immigration. In several European nations such international transfers have played a prominent part in recent growth. West Germany, Switzerland, France, Sweden, and the United Kingdom have been importers. Italy, Spain, Greece, and Portugal have been major sources. Most of this European immigration is arranged on a temporary, one-year basis.[25]

It is difficult to imagine a significant relaxation of controls on immigration in this country as long as unemployment hovers close to the 5 or 6 percent level. Indeed, some strong opposition to our temporary admission of *braceros* from Mexico has developed in recent years. On the other hand, if the growth rate rises, that change, with

---

[24]Denison, *op. cit.*, p. 39.

[25]"The Worker Goes Abroad," *OECD Observer*, Vol. 1, No. 2 (January, 1963), pp. 16–17.

reduced unemployment, could influence our attitudes and policy on immigration.

At the same time, however, our quantitative labor input is likely to be adversely affected in the immediate future by the age distribution of our population and labor force. Maximum contribution in the past has come from the 30- to 60-year age group. During the 1960's this group, as a proportion of the total, will not be as large as in the past. It is entirely possible that growth could be accelerated by admission of mature foreign workers in the most productive age groups and occupations.

Qualitative changes. Some of the measures that might increase quantitative labor inputs can also improve their quality. Better placements with improved matching of job requirements and worker qualifications through improved marketing are illustrative. Qualitative change is also very much a matter of improved management, which can plan and effect superior combinations of human and capital resources. Time study, motion study, and work simplification can assist workers to use their highest talents. Managerial leadership can facilitate motivation for superior performance. Alert managers can achieve optimum capital-worker ratios and economies of scale; they can encourage continuing personal improvement and development.

Competent management can, with energy, insight, and skill, facilitate technological change which, in turn, can expand the contribution of each man-hour. At the same time and in the other direction, fears of displacement and unemployment may readily reduce both the amount and quality of work. Measures designed to prepare employees for such changes and to increase economic security might pay high dividends if they improve the utilization and performance of workers. Similarly, vastly improved long-range forecasts of future demands for labor by industry and occupational requirements could make a major contribution.

Quality can be improved, also, by reducing discrimination in hiring and promotions so that jobs provide opportunities for workers to utilize their highest skills.

The most obvious means of improving the quality of labor inputs is continuing education, training, and personal development. One of the most impressive contributions of the studies of historic economic growth is their recognition of the importance of continuing advances in knowledge and skill. All such studies have allocated a significant role to "residuals" — factors that are unexplained by simple measures of inputs and efficiencies. For some years economists have speculated that these residuals were largely expressions of investments in education and training.[26]

In this direction the quality of labor inputs could be increased by keeping youth in school, preventing high school dropouts, and thus raising the general level of educational attainment. To the same end we might develop a program of on-the-job supplementary education in which workers who failed to finish secondary education could make up these deficiencies. Japan is experimenting with such a program, using radio and television.

The significance of continued retraining and refresher training is clear. And it should be recognized that improvements in labor inputs are appropriate for the contributions of managers as well as rank-and-file employees. "People" obsolescence is by no means limited to production workers displaced by machines, nor to technicians, engineers, or scientists. Probably no group of workers faces a greater hazard of obsolescence than managers. Managers as well as managees need to grow, to gain new knowledge and skill, and thus to improve the quality of their performance.

PUBLIC POLICY ON GROWTH

Most Americans, like the citizens of other nations, are impressed with the advantages to be gained through rapid economic growth. Political leaders emphasize the need for more rapid growth as a means of reducing unemployment, increasing individual and family incomes, and maintaining international leadership. Their proposals contemplate many of the steps suggested in the preceding section for increasing and improving labor inputs.

Critics of our progress in recent years frequently point to the losses occasioned by growth rates that are less than the possible maxima. A backward look may be impressive in this connection. The Conference on Economic Progress has pictured the employment effects of actual (as compared with potential) growth rates in the 1962–1965 period as shown in Figure 25-3. Data assume that an annual growth rate of 5 percent can and should be maintained. The figure highlights what is frequently described as the *growth gap*.

---

[26]See Schultz, *op, cit.*

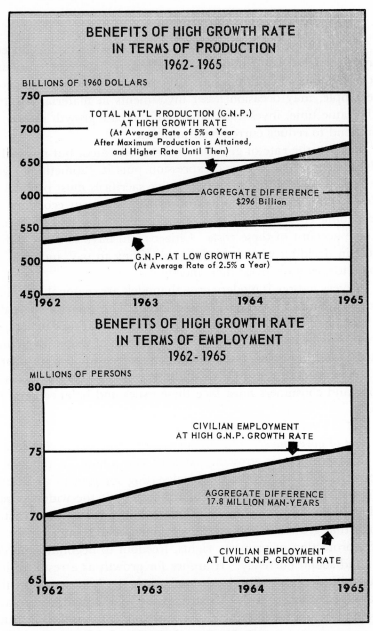

**BENEFITS OF HIGH GROWTH RATE
IN TERMS OF PRODUCTION
1962-1965**

BILLIONS OF 1960 DOLLARS

TOTAL NAT'L PRODUCTION (G.N.P.)
AT HIGH GROWTH RATE
(At Average Rate of 5% a Year
After Maximum Production is Attained,
and Higher Rate Until Then)

AGGREGATE DIFFERENCE
$296 Billion

G.N.P. AT LOW GROWTH RATE
(At Average Rate of 2.5% a Year)

**BENEFITS OF HIGH GROWTH RATE
IN TERMS OF EMPLOYMENT
1962-1965**

MILLIONS OF PERSONS

CIVILIAN EMPLOYMENT
AT HIGH G.N.P. GROWTH RATE

AGGREGATE DIFFERENCE
17.8 MILLION MAN-YEARS

CIVILIAN EMPLOYMENT
AT LOW G.N.P. GROWTH RATE

Note: 1961 is used as the project base year for this chart.

Figure 25-3

THE GROWTH GAP

Source: "Two Top Priority Programs to Reduce Unemployment," Washington, D.C.: Conference on Economic Progress, December, 1963, p. 28.

Alternatives in Plans for Growth

Models of growth make it very clear that changes introduced to improve the labor contribution to growth may have repercussions on the contribution of capital inputs. Increasing investments in people, for example, may occasion lesser investments in material resources. At the same time, investments that can increase growth rates in the future tend to reduce current consumption.

In short, the rate of growth can be accelerated, but not without costly choices. As the classic expression puts it, "something's gotta give." And some of the most impressive sacrifices must probably be made by workers. Other prices of growth represent economic and noneconomic costs to all citizens. Public policy must and presumably will take account of these costs. Citizens will have to make difficult choices in deciding what rate they are willing to pay and how they propose to spend or invest their money.

In every nation, if modern growth models are reasonably realistic, these choices must be recognized and faced. They may be more difficult in some of the newly-industrialized nations that seek to compress the maturing process into a relatively short span of years. Even in the United States, however, public policy must face unpleasant alternatives. American citizens in their multiple roles as workers, savers, investors, and consumers must face these issues and balance gains and costs.

Role of government. One major choice to be made concerns the role of government in growth. At least two schools of thought are evident. One of them sees the ideal setting for growth as based in public policies and programs designed to permit the widest possible freedom for individual action in a climate that encourages such action. It holds that growth is natural if government avoids interference and assures protection of property rights, freedom to negotiate and contract, and sound currency. It argues for growth as a result of individual initiative and effort and emphasizes the importance of individual choices and options. It stresses the market as the regulating and stimulating force in growth. As one exponent puts it, true growth "means producing goods that people want and fully choose, . . ."[27] The same spokesman suggests that any other view might regard the

---

[27]John Davenport, "The Priority of Politics Over Economics," *Fortune*, October, 1962, pp. 88 ff.

construction of "pyramids with slave labor" as an acceptable indicator of growth.

In contrast, a widely accepted view sees the maintenance and stimulation of growth as the special responsibility of government. It holds that government must constantly watch measures of growth, estimate trends, identify targets, and advance monetary and fiscal policy to encourage growth. Proponents conclude that government must almost certainly increase its regulatory functions if adequate growth is to be assured. Only government is likely to supply much of the heavy investment essential to continued expansion in space exploration and applications of atomic power. In this view only government can maintain a balance between the power of employers and unions.

The strengths and weaknesses of each of these positions may be clearer after other essential choices are recognized.

Private investment. Many popular analyses and proposals over-simplify the model of growth. Although it is clear that growth has in the past resulted from both qualitative and quantitative increases in capital and labor inputs, some investigators have singled out quantitative increases in capital as the mainspring of growth. They propose to expand supplies of money and thus ease credit, or grant tax advantages to investors, or use other means to reduce consumption and expand savings and investment. Thus, one stockholders' report concludes that "It is the allocation of resources . . . to the construction of new facilities utilizing the technology resulting from the most massive research expenditures in the world, that will create growth and provide both employment and purchasing power."[28]

Such a viewpoint frequently goes further and insists that the way to assure growth is to place more income in the hands of an "investor class" of high-income receivers. On this point it may be noted that high levels of wages and salaries now permit significant savings by wage and salary workers. They may become a major source of investment through growth bonds, somewhat as they became purchasers of war bonds.

The need for substantial profits and interest is suggested by this emphasis on private investment. One proposal sees the magic key to growth as the assurance of profits and suggests that profitability be elevated to the status of a prime national goal as an incentive to greater saving and faster growth.

---

[28]Lazard Fund, Inc., "Report for the Nine Months Ended September 30, 1962."

Employer-owner groups have used such interpretations to suggest the saving and investment hazards of union wage policies that propose "more." They argue that excessive wage demands can kill the goose that lays the golden egg by allocating income to receivers whose propensity to spend is relatively high.

It is clear that plans to increase the pace of growth must seek to augment both capital and labor inputs. More capital must be provided, and it must be mobile. Capital must move into new industries and localities; it must recognize new and different opportunities; it may also have to recognize speeded obsolescence, with related losses. More rapid growth requires the transfer of resources from less productive to more productive applications. The intention to speed the rate of growth must face and elect this choice.[29]

Consumption as the key. In sharp contrast, other sponsors of different and opposed programs see the key to growth in the expansion of consumption and demand. In their view consumption and purchasing power are identified as the starters in and sources of growth. It is frequently argued that deficient private and public consumption is at the heart of poor economic performance. "Under-consumption is at the core of the trouble. . . . Inadequate consumption prevents adequate investment."[30]

Union policy as well as the personal policies of individual workers have tended to support this underconsumption view. Few workers or unions are on record as refusing a wage or salary increase because it would interfere with capital inputs and thus hamper growth. In some foreign nations wage demands have been restrained, but the major reason for restraint has been the threat of inflation. Most unions, like individual firms, tend to assume that while the general principle of restraint in prices and charges may be sound for the total economy, special reasons make restraints inappropriate in their individual cases. Typically, the individual union argues that (1) it must secure comparatively large increases to regain some real or imagined parity and (2)

---

[29]Ranis and Fei conclude that balanced growth is largely dependent on synchronized investment in industrial and agricultural sectors, resulting in reduced supplies of agricultural labor and increased demands for industrial workers. Growth is hampered by "disguised" unemployment in agriculture (workers with little or no production). It is advanced by the rising demands and productivity of the industrial sector. See Gustav Ranis and John C. H. Fei, "A Theory of Economic Development," *American Economic Review*, Vol. 51, No. 4 (September, 1961), pp. 533–65. See also the comments and rejoinder in *American Economic Review*, Vol. 53, No. 3 (June, 1963), pp. 448–54.

[30]"Key Policies for Full Employment," Washington: Conference on Economic Progress, September, 1962, pp. 2, 23.

the industry's economic posture is such that increases can be absorbed without raising prices.

The growth hazards in wage-push inflation are widely discussed and debated. It is clear that European nations with high growth rates have experienced impressive inflation. In such nations, with low levels of unemployment and significant labor shortages, rising costs may create a significant brake on continued growth. Inflation may well be the persistent hazard in rapid growth. Labor pricing must be recognized, however, as only a part of the pricing process in which inflation develops.[31]

A balanced program. Saving levels and patterns of investment unquestionably provide an important clue to future growth. But the relationships of investment and consumption are complex. Increased investments may spark expansion. They are, however, at least as much a result of expansionary opinion and climate as a cause of these conditions. Investors invest in part because they anticipate a potential growth in consumption that can create demands for growing quantities of output. Growth requires a balance in consumption and investment; which comes first is only critical at a moment in time.

Plans to increase the pace of economic growth must recognize implicit shifts from immediate to future consumption. Savers and investors must expand their commitment of present resources to this future and shift income from consumption to saving. This may mean, for example, that the wage-earner drives his auto an extra year and uses the saving to buy equities or credit in his savings bank or public interplanetary transportation bonds.

It is one thing to recognize and plan for such choices; it is quite another to carry them out. Capital accumulation in poverty-stricken economies is a painful task. In a mature economy it requires the power to resist incessant advertising designed to stimulate consumption. The inherent conflict is sharply silhouetted by our national economic growth program as contrasted with our TV commercials.

Inadequate investment can unquestionably cripple or retard economic growth. Consumption can leave too little income for adequate

---

[31]For a discussion and extensive references, see Julius Rezler, "Economic Growth and the Price Level in the American Economy," *Reprint* (Chicago: Institute of Social and Industrial Relations, Loyola University, 1962). The "Phillips curve" (named for an English economist who analyzed historic relationships between changes in wage and price levels) suggests that wage increases tend to be smaller than price increases as long as unemployment remains at or above approximately the 5 percent level. If unemployment falls below that level, wages tend to advance more rapidly in periods of prosperity and to create pressures for higher prices.

capital inputs. Propensities to consume and save can be influenced. Consumption can be manipulated, and citizens can be encouraged to spend as well as to invest. The generosity of fringe benefits and the reduction of working hazards may de-emphasize advantages of thrift and saving. An established pattern of high-level consumption and low-level saving can create a situation in which only large income receivers or governments are in a position to invest.

Thus, government intervention is encouraged by the hazards to growth engendered by demands for higher wages and appeals for higher levels of consumption. The federal government has sought to restrain wage demands. In 1962, the President's *Economic Report* suggested that if wage increases extend beyond the guideposts of productivity, they generate pressures on prices that handicap real growth. The federal government has moved rapidly to restrain rising prices in basic industries. Many citizens and political leaders conclude that rigorous public controls must be imposed or powerful associations of unions and of employers must impose self-controls on their members and nonmember colleagues.

If inflation becomes a serious threat, that condition may generate pressures for broad price controls to supplement those on wages. Public encouragement and support of higher wage rates, take-home pay, fringes, and social insurance, can raise labor costs and restrain economic growth. Gerhard Colm, among others, argues that economic growth should be given a high priority as a goal on the theory that only growth can provide a sound base of economic security. Given adequate growth, with resultant increases in both workers' incomes and government receipts, social and private security programs can be improved. Without sufficient economic growth, he argues, we could reach levels of economic security that can actually restrict growth.[32]

Governmental intervention may take the form of tax programs designed to encourage investment and improve the climate for growth. The current level of taxes on profits, for example, places a comparatively heavy burden on both investors and workers. Both in the nations of the European Common Market and in Russia, incentives for investment present a sharp contrast to our domestic policy. Our federal government has moved in this direction by introducing provisions for accelerated depreciation and tax reduction.

---

[32]Gerhard Colm, "The Economic Base and Limits of Social Welfare," *Monthly Labor Review*, Vol. 86, No. 6 (June, 1963), pp. 695–700.

Stability and Growth

It is clear that historic growth in industrialized nations has been accompanied by wide fluctuations and persistent instability. Indeed, this cyclical variation has been so much more spectacular than growth that recession and recovery have historically attracted wider popular concern. At the same time, the assumption that growth and instability are inextricably interrelated may have been encouraged by our usual portrayal of business activity as fluctuating above and below a trend line of growth. Many public programs have been designed to curb (i.e., reduce) the amplitude of short and long business cycles. Unemployment insurance is one such program.

Current goals propose, however, to stimulate the rate of growth while, at the same time, preventing sharp fluctuations in business activity. In terms of these goals, inflation and business booms are excesses at one extreme; stagnation in prosperity is at the other.

Cyclical fluctuations in themselves may become a hazard to growth. Their expansionary phase generates pressures that lead to reluctance to invest in either labor or capital. The fluctuations of recession and depression occasion wide underutilization and waste of resources, including manpower resources. The quality of manpower inputs is adversely affected by the deterioration of skills that accompanies long unemployment. Current planning for growth, therefore, contemplates parallel programs to minimize cyclical fluctuations. The hazard that growth may include an inherent tendency to widen fluctuations must, however, be recognized.

In part this follows because growth has a built-in tendency toward increasing waste. Rapid change tends to encourage obsolescence in human resources as well as in physical facilities and equipment. Prosperity, which is associated with growth, permits managerial carelessness with respect to manpower as well as other resources. Extra managers, like extra engineers, may be stockpiled for the time when they will be needed. Direct and indirect labor costs tend to grow. Profits may suffer; private investment may be restricted as earnings ratios decline.

Critics of Growth

The goal of accelerated economic growth has wide appeal. For many it seems synonymous with progress and thus unquestionably good. There are intrepid souls who question this assumption, however.

Some basis for such criticism may be found in our tendency to give too much attention to a rather narrow economic concept of growth. Just as well-paid workers seek more than merely additions to paychecks, an advanced economy may require more than the simple challenge of more per capita GNP. Its citizens may be ready to look for gains in other types of values — broader education, more security, more leisure, more fun, and more freedom. It is possible that plans for speeding development place too much emphasis on economic targets and too little on broader cultural achievements. We can get bigger without getting better.

It can be argued that such a misplaced emphasis is the major source of stagnation. If people do not change, if their values emphasize little more than physical, material needs, stagnation may result simply because citizens feel that they already have everything. Growth — for a mature economy (and probably for those less mature) — must be a "bottoms up" process. Its roots must be nourished in social and cultural development.

In such a view the rush to outshine other nations in economic growth rates is comparable to the race to be first with a man on the moon. The economic growth competition is something of a merry-go-round. While the economic goals of rising productivity and prosperity unquestionably deserve and hold high priorities in most societies, they are not the only worthy goals. Progress in the arts (in music, the theater, the graphic arts, and others) and advancements in education and in our understanding of life (in philosophy and religion) cannot be taken for granted. Such developments may not be simply a function of economic improvement. Although they are sometimes assumed to be a sort of inevitable resultant of an economic "social surplus" (i.e., a level of income well above that needed for subsistence), their attainment also requires that they be accepted as high priority goals. Cultural advancement is thus a matter of ideas and ideals as well as of income. An affluent society may neglect rather than nurture these values.

On that basis some thoughtful observers question the whole current rationale of economic development. They argue that, in a period of rapid technological advancement, the pressures that stimulate the economy are much less a matter of satisfying needs; they tend to represent a sort of *compulsive consumption*, with major business attention directed to marketing and advertising. To the extent that the needs thus created are somewhat artificial — new colors in toilet soaps, for example — they tend to make economic activity the master rather than the servant of society.

Such critics of current programs suggest that a high level of unemployment may well be permanent, creating a new class, which Ferry calls the "liberated margin." In that case leisure may be regarded as a social goal rather than a problem. The conflict created by such a goal in a society based on wages for work may raise serious questions about the social purpose behind drives for ever greater output, keeping the machine running and accelerating its pace. Ferry argues that:

> Deliberation on the wages and the standards for getting purchasing power into the hands of the liberated margin may be the beginning of methodical social justice in the American political economy. Abundance may compel social justice as conscience never has.[33]

Optimum Growth Rates

It is entirely possible that the pattern of future growth in this country will be significantly different from earlier patterns. Popular points of view toward what are regarded as satisfactory levels of employment and leisure may be due for sharp modification as family incomes reach "prosperity" levels. There may well be limits to the extent that advertising can or will be permitted to create demands for a nation whose people have almost everything. Such citizens may settle for more stability at the price of rapid growth.

Historic standards may not, therefore, be appropriate in selecting an optimum rate. The Conference on Economic Progress concludes that the historic optimum rate is that which has been associated with maximum employment and production, but that optimum may be unrealistic for the future.[34]

On the other hand, a relatively high growth rate — in the magnitude of 4 to 5 percent — may be possible despite high level unemployment. The rising quality of labor inputs coupled with much wider popular understanding of the growth process could make such rates achievable.

---

[33]W. H. Ferry, "Caught on the Horn of Plenty," *Bulletin*, Center for the Study of Democratic Institutions, January, 1962, p. 7.

[34]"Jobs and Growth," Washington: Conference on Economic Progress, May, 1961, pp. 23–25.

Increasing numbers of today's employees recognize essentials of the growth formula and understand them. The narrowing structure of citizen sophistication, noted in earlier chapters, explains why many union members — although they still support work-spreading measures and efforts to maintain wage security — realize that persistent economic growth is most likely to assure adequate income in years ahead. They understand that economic stagnation is at least as hazardous to employees as to investors. They know that units of labor input must increase, for growing numbers of workers are already in the staging area. Today's workers can and do understand the essentials of growth. They are likely to insist on managerial as well as political policies and practices that promise persistent growth. They have the incomes to permit the savings necessary to make relatively high growth rates attainable.

At the same time, however, the growing sophistication of citizens may encourage ever more critical evaluation of economic growth and added consideration of alternatives. Value systems change as certainly if not as rapidly as subsystems in industrial relations. Citizens who have almost everything in a material sense may well pause to consider the priorities to be given the values of leisure, personal expression, and self-actualization. In such contemplation, rapid economic growth could some day come out second best.[35]

ANALYTICAL REVIEW QUESTIONS

1. How do you explain the world wide concern about national economic growth?

2. Show that economic growth is, in considerable degree, growth in and of labor.

3. What are labor inputs and how do they vary?

4. Why is economic growth not a measure of total change or progress?

5. How is economic growth generally measured and how are measures adjusted for changes in the value of dollars?

---

[35]See John Wilkinson, *The Quantitative Society or, What Are You to Do With Noodle?* (Santa Barbara, California: Center for the Study of Democratic Institutions, June, 1964).

6. What is the "growth reckoner" and how can it be used?

7. How is economic growth distinguished from increasing business activity?

8. Why is measurement of growth less accurate as the growth period is extended?

9. How do you explain sharp time-to-time fluctuations in man-hour productivity?

10. Explain the downward movements in the series charted in Figure 25-2.

11. How has this country fared in the international growth race?

12. Does this nation formally plan its economic growth? Why or why not?

13. Why is the base so important in comparing international growth rates?

14. How do you define high-level stagnation?

15. Explain what is meant by "chronic slack" and the "growth gap."

16. Distinguish quantitative and qualitative changes in labor inputs and illustrate this distinction.

17. What major changes have affected labor inputs?

18. What measures offer most promise for improving labor inputs?

19. What are some of the costs that arise out of measures designed to increase growth?

20. Summarize the major issues with respect to the government's role in stimulating growth.

21. Evaluate the contention that one essential for growth is higher levels of income for the "investor class."

22. Evaluate the argument that the basic hindrance to growth is underconsumption.

23. What is the "Phillips curve" and what are its implications for inflation in growth?

24. How are our wage guideposts related to economic growth in this country?

25. What can tax policy contribute to the prevention of prosperity stagnation?

26. Can a nation achieve a high rate of growth without wide fluctuations in business activity? How?

27. Why or how does growth have a built-in tendency toward waste?

28. If unemployment levels are to remain high or become higher, does that preclude a rapid growth rate?

29. What values may appear in the future to be more important to our citizens than rapid economic growth?

30. Examine the most recent issue of *Economic Indicators* to discover evidences of current economic growth. List what appear to be favorable and unfavorable trends. How do you evaluate the balance? Calculate at least four measures of growth for the most recent year.

Case 25-1

VOLUNTARY COOPERATION FOR GROWTH

"We can have satisfactory national economic growth and low levels of unemployment at the price of very little inflation" is the argument of one prominent economist and economic advisor. He goes on to insist that what is required is popular acceptance of and agreement on guideposts for both profits and wages. He concludes that both employers and unions can be persuaded to resist opportunities for out-of-line price and wage advances by an informed public that demands adherence to such guideposts. It is his opinion that United States citizens have become sufficiently sophisticated so that no additional laws are required to enforce such a program. He points to both employer and union restraints in the 1962–1964 period as justifying this position.

• Write a one-page evaluation of this viewpoint, explaining your acceptance or rejection.

ALTERNATIVE SOLUTIONS TO LABOR PROBLEMS

Industrial relations is concerned with work and work-connected relationships. Much of our progress toward personal and social goals is directly affected by employment and employment processes. Our system of employment relationships is new, experimental, and changing. Our ideals, goals, values, objectives, and expectations change; so do the means for their attainment through employment. Failure to attain employment, wage, and security goals results in our most obvious labor problems.

LABOR ECONOMICS AND DECISION MAKING

In Chapter 1, it was noted that labor economics provides a useful approach to the study of labor problems. Labor economics is concerned with the processes in which human resources are developed, allocated, applied, and conserved. It deals with labor markets and institutions that influence labor marketing. It is also concerned with income and wages — the pay-off for working — because they influence employment inputs and outputs.

Labor economics deals with consumer and entrepreneurial decision making that affects the development and employment of human resources; and it deals with how workers themselves contribute to such decisions and how price mechanisms facilitate and implement these

decisions. Economic analysis provides models that describe relationships — sequential, functional, and causal. These models identify
significant variables and specify the nature of relationships. They
thus provide knowledge and understanding.

Labor problems are given a high public priority by our industrial
society. We have many unresolved problems. New and different
problems are to be expected in the years ahead. Their impact can best
be minimized if they are anticipated.

Complexity and Dynamics

The complexity of employment problems, processes, policies, and
programs has been repeatedly emphasized, and this theme has been
documented in preceding chapters. Although specific parts and
chapters have dealt with partial industrial relations systems for purposes of clarity and emphasis, their interrelationships have also been
stressed. For example, though there are separate parts of this book on
wages and on employment, the two are clearly interrelated.

Consideration of partial systems and their components facilitates
analysis. Equally important, however, is synthesis — fitting the parts
back together into a cohesive, systematic whole.

Throughout the book, dynamics and change have been central
themes. Changes in values and goals, in theories, and in means of
achieving goals are the order of the day. Thus, for example, the concept that our lives might be better organized if we were leisure-
centered rather than work-centered has been discussed in Chapter 17.
Changes in mores concerning women's role in our society, responsibility for the care of the poor and the aged, and the role of government in industrial relations are other examples. Changes in value
systems and goals in underdeveloped, newly industrialized economies
in other parts of the world provide more dramatic and vivid examples.

Both the complexity of modern industrial relations systems and
the persistence of changes — many of the latter at accelerating rates —
add to the difficulties of attaining accepted goals and avoiding labor
problems.

Industrialization and technological change affect much more
than the processes of production and distribution; they have important
impacts on employment and social relationships. Industrial relations
systems that seemed reasonably adequate before such changes may
no longer be acceptable. Decisions about revisions are unavoidable.
The need for such decisions may appear as a part of the process of

planning, or it may arise out of conflict and resistance to change. In either case, appropriate yardsticks or standards are essential tools in decision making. Somehow criteria of economic value and of social and individual welfare must be developed and balanced. Creation of a conversion scale for the balancing of welfare and economic criteria represents one of the major tasks facing modern societies.

Rational decision making requires consideration of many alternatives, including value, probability, and comparative costs. In general, rational decision making seeks to maximize returns at minimal costs. Decisions to change operational systems require consideration of how the changes are to be implemented. The question as to who should bear the costs of changes, or how these costs should be shared, is always difficult. In the interests of progress, perhaps societies need a new form of social insurance that might be called "change insurance".

It should be quite clear that societies have progressed; numerous historic advances are impressive. But it should be equally clear that many old problems remain unsolved and that solutions to old problems frequently create equally difficult new problems.

The operational industrial relations system is a reality; hence an adjustment in one of its parts may "fix" that portion but cause maladjustment elsewhere. Freedom from want may come at the cost of personal freedom. Income redistribution can affect motivation. Affluence can dull incentive. Work at the expense of leisure may stifle personal and spiritual development.[1]

Decentralized Decision Making

In a free enterprise economy, heavily industrialized and specialized, the problem of interaction and choice among variables in the industrial relations system is complicated by a myriad of decision making and power centers — almost all of which are working on piecemeal decisions. These decision centers or markets are interdependent. They must have resiliency and ability to respond to "side-effect" problems that spill over into their own particular center from other centers. The results are not always successful, as we have noted throughout this volume. We still have pockets of poverty, depressed areas, and human scrap heaps.

---

[1]See Arnold J. Toynbee, *A Study of History* (New York and London: Oxford University Press, 1957), abridgement edited by D. C. Sommervill, Vol. II, pp. 332–49.

Manpower Planning

One basic form of manpower decision making in the past has been trial and error. Rather than anticipate consequences, we act and then set in motion a variety of corrective devices. If too many people are hired, they can be laid off; if employees turn out to be unsatisfactory, they can be discharged. Much of the web of rules in industrial jurisprudence is concerned with devices to prevent what is regarded as haphazard planning.

Today there is growing awareness of the need for better manpower planning, both private and public. Goals, values, and expectations can be realized more effectively through improved planning. Increased complexity of our way of life, with resulting increased interdependence, serve to make systematic planning more essential. Planning facilitates a positive and preventive approach. There is opportunity for rationalizing employment relationships as we have rationalized technical processes.

Planning, however, inevitably reflects goals and values; it is a means to the end of achieving objectives. Societies need to clarify and to articulate both ends and means. Perhaps only philosophers or theologians feel comfortably equipped to deal with problems of ultimate values and objectives, yet no one can escape the responsibility for their consideration. Ambiguity in goals and objectives leads to inefficiency in effort. It can become the source of conflict. One of the serious deficiencies of the American industrial relations system is its lack of attention to goal formulation and specification.

The importance of thoughtful consideration of social goals attracted wide attention when President Eisenhower appointed a Commission on National Goals. In late 1960, the Commission's report was published with the title: *Goals for Americans*.[2] The report identifies appropriate goals as well as programs to attain these goals in vital areas of our national life. The purpose of the report was to encourage informed discussion by the American public. Individual liberty was set as the number one goal — "the status of the individual must remain our primary concern."[3]

Goals for Americans emphasizes that people are our basic natural resource and that the first national goal should be the development of each individual to his fullest potential.[4] There are various means

[2]President's Commission on National Goals, *Goals for Americans* (Englewood Cliffs, New Jersey: Prentice-Hall, Inc., 1960).
[3]*Ibid.*, p. 3.
[4]*Ibid.*, by Henry M. Wriston, p. 53.

of pursuing this objective; for example, Clark Kerr argues that a democratic political system requires a democratic form of economic organization. He calls for as many "power centers" as possible, consistent with effective functioning of our political, economic, and social operations. These power centers should be balanced in strength, with the widest possible range of choice for individuals within such power centers. Governmental controls in the economy should be concentrated on procedural rather than substantive issues. The great challenge of our time is for us to be both democratic and effective.[5] The role of government should be restricted to areas and problems of public interest which cannot be met by private means. When need no longer exists for public intervention, or when private industry can do the job better, government should withdraw.[6]

LABOR PROBLEMS

Labor problems represent failure to attain employment goals. Major labor problem areas include employment, security, conflict-cooperation, wages, and economic growth.

Employment

A labor force has both quantitative and qualitative aspects. For the world at large, the population explosion is increasing labor supplies at a staggering rate. Not only is population tending to outrun means of subsistence in underdeveloped countries, but even more critical is the disparity between population, capital equipment, and education. In these nations investment in the qualitative aspects of manpower resources and in modern technology and equipment is imperative if they are to industrialize. At the same time it must be recognized that all of the world's current stock of education and capital are insufficient to enable the whole world to equal, in a few years, the industrial development of advanced nations such as the United States. The problem is not simply one of redistribution of capital, technology, and education. Rather, it is a problem of expansion of all.

At the same time, given the goal of industrialization, some form of control of population growth through birth control may be necessary. For developing countries the twin goals of unlimited population

---

[5]*Ibid.*, pp. 148–52.

[6]*Ibid.*, Clark Kerr, p. 160. The sections of the report discussed in the present volume do not present a balanced overview of the total document — many of the areas lie beyond the scope of this book.

growth and rapid industrialization probably are incompatible, at least for the immediate future.

Problems of capital accumulation and a corollary educational base to provide quality manpower resources require deferment of consumption and saving. This is extremely difficult in subsistence level economies. Commitment to industrial jobs and social adjustments are additional requirements. Industrial nations can aid these processes through investments and export of know-how. Aside from compelling humanitarian reasons, advanced nations may find that such export enhances their own national security.

Labor supply problems in the United States. In terms of sheer numbers, current United States labor supplies may appear to be too great in view of persistent unemployment. Solutions to labor supply problems have been suggested that call for job rationing, or work spreading among existing available supplies. The shorter workweek and double premium pay for overtime are examples. Such solutions could raise labor costs, create inflationary pressure, and threaten our balance of payments. An increase in labor costs could intensify substitution of other factors of production for labor.

Other solutions designed to ration existing job opportunities suggest the abolition of moonlighting and getting married women out of the labor market. Since a comparatively small portion of the extra jobs held by moonlighters displaces other workers and since administrative problems would be severe, this solution has grave limitations. Denying jobs to married women would be practically disastrous — removal of 15 million from the labor force would disrupt the white-collar work force. Wholesale replacement of female married teachers, for example, from the ranks of functionally illiterate unemployed males would be impossible. In general, work spreading is a measure of expediency, not a solution.

Another restrictive practice is restriction of job opportunity or of output. Control of entry to available job opportunities may take many forms. Closed unions, limitations on apprenticeships, licensing, and restriction of educational opportunities in the professions are recognized means of rationing jobs and job opportunities. Barriers to general educational opportunities aid and abet this process. Discrimination in employment is another job-rationing mechanism. Union jurisdictional devices may be added to the list. Restrictive work rules may seek to ration job opportunities. It should be noted that such efforts are not confined to union members, nor even employees in general.

Solutions to restrictive supply practices should emphasize more jobs, more personal flexibility and mobility, and qualitative improvement and upgrading of manpower resources.

Qualitative aspects of manpower resources are of vital importance in today's world. An upgraded technology requires upgraded labor supplies, not only of scientists and technologists to man the new machines but of leaders and managers. Nor should educational upgrading of the entire population be relegated to second place — a complex world requires more complex public and social policy which in turn requires a better informed and educated public.

Capital investment must be made in people as well as in machinery.[7] In this connection it is essential to recognize that we have accelerated the obsolescence of human skills as well as of machines. Manpower development is essential, not only for underdeveloped nations but also for the most developed nations.

In the future the average worker will probably not have a lifetime occupation. He will need to be "retreaded," i.e., acquire new skills several times in his multiple-job career. He will probably need more education as a foundation for future retraining. Who should pay the costs of manpower retraining? The employee? The employer? The public? At present the public heavily subsidizes education. This is regarded as a proper and sound investment in human resources. Generally, however, such public support is regarded as appropriate once in a lifetime, typically for the young entrant without heavy family and other responsibilities. We have lengthened the educational process and have added financial support to induce needed supplies of professional and graduate students. Today some graduate schools recruit and support abler students with a zeal and maintain a support program that was formerly reserved for star football players. The principle of subsidization is already established; but to date we have not extended the concept to support for a 45-year-old manager in a period of college retreading. We permit depreciation of nonhuman capital resources under our tax laws. Why should we do less for our human resources, widely described as our "most important" assets? The problem of manpower retreading may be linked to the problem of reducing hours of work. If, instead of the shorter work-

---

[7]See F. H. Harbison and C. A. Myers, *Education, Manpower and Economic Growth* (New York: McGraw-Hill Book Company, Inc., 1964).

week or shorter workdays, sabbaticals were to become the more common form of hours reduction, these sabbatical periods could be used — at least in part — for retraining and upgrading of workers' skills to meet new job requirements.

Increasing labor demands. Labor supplies are only half the story, with labor demands being the "other blade of the scissors." Even with record levels of prosperity, millions of Americans are unemployed. While we have fairly adequate data about quantities of current and future labor supplies, at least on a national level, we lack similar data series for current and future labor demands. This represents a tremendously costly gap in our knowledge.

We need improved occupational forecasting, both on a macro and micro basis. In a specialized industrial economy, jobs are specific, not general; both supplies and demands have specific requirements and lead time in matching men and jobs is essential. A first requirement would be to get the best possible estimates of labor demands — present and future. Behind these measures of labor demands lie causal variables that relate to demand, including economic growth.

Labor demand is a derived demand, effectively limited by the volume of business activity (widely defined to include all elements of GNP). When jobs are plentiful, insecurity and conflict are reduced; manpower resources are shifted more readily and put to more efficient use. Underutilization is less prevalent, as is uneconomic discrimination.

As noted in the previous chapter, we face a shortage of job opportunities relative to our expanding population and labor force. Output restriction and impediments in incentives to invest do not provide satisfactory climate for expansion. Incentives and rewards for growth-encouraging behavior must be made greater than the rewards for growth-restricting behavior. In a sense this requires substantial changes in our basic values as an essential underpinning for programs designed for economic growth.[8]

Some of our employment opportunity problems can be cured through expanding consumer demand. But employers act as interpreters of consumer demand, and their expectations are vital. We must provide adequate incentives for investments. In a free enterprise society, capital will not grow without sufficient yield. If labor,

---

[8]See Edmund S. Phelps (ed.), *The Goal of Economic Growth* (New York: W. W. Norton and Co., Inc., 1962); also his *Private Wants and Public Needs* (New York: W. W. Norton and Co., Inc., 1962).

the public, or any other group presses too hard and too successfully for current consumption at the expense of capital formation, the capital-worker ratio will suffer. The capital-worker ratio must increase to support the new technology. Increase in labor supplies requires increases in capital supplies.

Discrimination and waste. A satisfactory job provides the worker with the best form of economic security. Many workers, however, are denied jobs appropriate to their talents and merit because of discrimination in employment. Noneconomic discrimination in employment is still very much with us. [9]

An older employee out of work may find it impossible to get work because of his age, and without regard for his talents. Colored professional workers are a special minority within a minority. Women executives are the rare exception. The "haves," in the sense of those who already enjoy job rights and privileges, build barriers to insulate themselves from the competition of the "have nots."

The so-called civil rights problem is only a portion of our discrimination problem. One proposed solution, "reverse discrimination," would compound rather than decrease inequity. With reverse discrimination, minority groups would be given preference for jobs, regardless of merit, to make up for alleged past discrimination. Thus, for example, Negroes would be given first chance at jobs until proportions of Negroes and whites in major occupational groups approximate the distribution of Negroes and whites in the population. This proposed "solution" merely replaces one form of nonmerit employment discrimination with another.

Labor productivity. Chapter 3 explained our inadequacies in measuring labor productivity. These should be corrected. [10] We need to measure productivity in government and in service industries. We may and probably do need new and additional yardsticks of productivity. In government, for example, welfare, defense, and other social criteria may be as important as economic criteria. Here again the concept of a total system and balance of the parts is essential.

Labor productivity is vital because labor competes with other resources for the entrepreneur's favor. Labor can literally price itself out of the job market; relatively high labor prices invite automation.

---

[9] See Robert B. McKersie *et. al.*, "A Symposium — Minorities and Employment," *Industrial Relations*, Vol. 3, No. 3 (May, 1964), pp. 1–50.

[10] See Einar Hardin, "Measuring the Rate of Productivity Growth," Michigan State University School of Labor and Industrial Relations, *Reprint Series No. 61*, 1963–64.

Automation is a game with losers as well as winners, with costs as well as benefits. Who should get the benefits and who should pay the costs?

In general, automation is possible because consumers will pay for the products made under the new process. Automation typically increases productivity and lowers costs — i.e., produces net savings. Traditionally, these net savings have gone to consumers in lower prices, to employees in higher wages, and to stockholders in higher profits — a three-way split. A two-way split between employees and stockholders is becoming more common. But not all employees share in this net saving. Those who stay on after technological change get higher wages, but what benefits do the displaced workers get? Certainly they bear a heavy cost in their loss of jobs, employment rights, and income. It is a fair question whether or not they bear too high a proportion of the burden that we call the "risks of employment."

Few would argue that displaced employees should have a sine-cure — for example, pay them their former wages while they are at leisure. Generally they can get unemployment compensation while they seek another job. Frequently they lack marketable skills and need retraining, and perhaps relocation, and in some cases general education. When these displaced persons lose jobs through no fault of their own, and when society has the choice of a life-long dole or re-training, the course for public policy seems clear. We need to attack this problem, not as a special momentary phenomenon, but as a normal problem of an industrial society. Experimental approaches to care for those displaced by equipping them for new working careers should have a high priority.

It may well be time that we recognize and accept a whole new concept of employment — one in which we view workers as a sort of standby. Their service and contribution will involve being available when needed, like the electric power delivered to our homes. A major share of their compensation will be in the nature of a service charge, much like the charge we all recognize as part of our electric bill. Employees will be paid, not so much for the number of units they personally process, but rather for being on hand when the feedback control blows a fuse or the electronic reader encounters a flyspeck.

Labor markets. In a complex, highly specialized industrial economy with ever-increasing emphasis upon invention and change, labor markets must be responsive, anticipatory, and play a positive role. The acid test of labor market effectiveness lies in adequate matching of labor supplies and demands. This requires a minimum of frictions and a maximum of labor mobilities. So-called free labor markets are not completely free, with government regulations, union membership restrictions, company hiring limitations, and collectively bargained seniority and job rights provisions limiting the operation of competitive market forces.

Expanded information services and guidance and counseling are necessary to ensure that manpower mobilities parallel technological mobilities — that worker relocation parallels industrial relocation. We need to reexamine present hiring rules and seniority provisions to see that they provide opportunities for mobilities as well as serve their present purposes.

Employment agencies: public and private. Bureaucratic dispersion of public responsibilities for employment and manpower services have fragmented manpower planning. At the federal level over 20 agencies and committees have such responsibilities. Each of the 50 states has its own public employment service.

While these public programs are supposedly integrated, such integration is only partial. Substantial differences in performance are the rule rather than the exception. In some states emphasis has been primarily upon UC functions with employment services a residual claimant. The employment service function is important in its own right — it does and should stress prevention rather than amelioration.

Public employment service placement activities should not be confined to the unemployed and the "dregs" of the labor market, despite strong statements to this effect from private employment agencies and far Right groups. Here the essential question is not unfair competition between a tax-supported public agency and tax-paying private agencies. Instead, the essential question is: How effective are these services, public and private?

Public employment services arose in part because of the inadequacies of private employment services. Private services are still not adequate to do the entire job which needs to be done. The insistence of many private agencies that they are entitled to deal only in the "cream" of the labor market, leaving the "skim milk" to the public agencies, is a selfish rather than a sophisticated position. Private employment agencies are operated as a business service. Staff members may not have adequate professional training (e.g., in testing and counseling). Questions should be raised about the desirability of some minimum standards of professional competence for their employees.

There is a place for the private agency — a substantial place, but not an exclusive jurisdiction.

At the same time, performance of the public services needs to be strengthened. Improved staffing and budgets in the public agencies are needed. At present, public employment service operations are geared to a mass production, low quality, high quantity standard. Sufficient time and resources are not available to do a quality job. Low pay scales for personnel and political maneuvering in some states result in far from optimal placements. Federalization of employment services (as well as UC) has been suggested as a remedy; but if present federal standards are at all indicative, merely changing the management will not do the job alone. What is needed is a concept of selective placement utilizing professional approaches and techniques.

Economic Security

Another central question of our times is whether or not security can generate motivation and effort as well as insecurity can. This problem is especially relevant in an affluent society that places great emphasis upon material values, with ever-increasing demands for security from all strata of society. Given a choice between risk-taking and possible great gains, and security with small but assured gains, which viewpoint will predominate? Today many employers feel that employees are indifferent or apathetic. Some say that employees exert their greatest efforts in cashing rather than earning their paychecks. Unions complain of indifference and apathy in membership participation. Members pay their dues as a form of protection or insurance — they purchase a service from an impersonal union.

Where is the motivation to put forth extra effort in a security-conscious society? If old-fashioned virtues of thrift, effort, integrity, and honesty are out of date, with what have they been replaced? Has concern with "rights" tended to obscure concepts of responsibility and duty? Can machine-watchers in an automated society reasonably be expected to be enthusiastic about their work? Can we devise incentives that motivate? Will there have to have more emphasis upon nonfinancial instead of financial motivators?

Income and security. Wages are used to help move human resources into their most productive uses. They provide income and security to wage earners and their dependents — when working and in circumstances when they are unable to work. Our wage and economic

security systems thus reflect multipurpose objectives (e.g., to encourage output and to provide economic security). These multiple
objectives result in a multiplicity of policies and plans, public and
private, with a result that they sometimes work at cross-purposes.

Still unanswered is the problem of the bases for income distribution — productivity or need, and in what proportions? This question
becomes more difficult as a result of great advances in productivity
made possible through invention and automation. Population gains
mean more claimants on jobs and income. Productivity gains mean
fewer workers are needed to produce the same output.

Shall we end up with two classes of employees — those really
needed to do the work plus those needed to draw the paychecks?
Somehow consumption must be sustained and increased to keep up
with increased production possibilities. What of inflationary consequences if need gains greater prominence as a yardstick, with output
receding in prominence? Will conflict increase between producers
and consumers? Will subsidies replace the marketplace for most industries, not just agriculture? What concepts of equity in income distribution are appropriate for an affluent society?

Further, there are grave questions regarding appropriate mechanisms. Must it always be more government? Can labor and management devise workable substitutes? Will such solutions have to be
forced, or can we devise voluntary means? Can "suggested guideposts" do the job? Must regulations get so detailed that they stifle
freedoms — freedom of enterprise, freedom of labor mobility, and
freedom of consumer choice?[11]

As a nation, we generally find the concept of wage reductions
repugnant. We operate our wage systems like an automobile that has
only forward gears and no reverse shift. We are conditioned to expect
wage increases, irrespective of productivity considerations.

A policy of more and higher wages as a matter of "right" or custom has inflationary potential. In some countries purchasing power
wage theories have led to round-the-clock operation of currency
printing presses. Fortunately, we have slowed inflation in our recent
history. We have chosen a little bit of inflation as a reasonable
price for full employment, higher wages, and free collective bargaining. But unemployment near or in excess of 5 percent hardly can be

---

[11]See A. L. Gitlow, *The National Wage Policy: Antecedents and Application* (New York:
School of Business, New York University, July, 1964).

considered full employment. Can we say our present rate of inflation is optimal?

And what of the forms of wage payment — do more fringes provide better motivation, job satisfaction, and output? Will profit sharing prove to be the answer to increasing disenchantment with, and resistance to, incentive plans?

Problems of when we want to receive our wages (e.g., deferred versus current compensation) also require resolution. Since almost all welfare and security payments must come out of current production, can deferred portions of wages and assignment of wage rights to our beneficiaries grow to be too great a burden on the present, with its own pressing current consumption needs and desires? Can we buy more security than we can afford?

Private and public security plans. Today's economic security programs in the United States are a dubious mix of public and private plans. There are gaps in coverage and discrepancies in benefits and costs. We need to ask ourselves some basic questions about the nature and kinds of risks we seek to guard against. Do we seek catastrophic protection or complete recovery? Is it desirable to permit security plans as a basis for profit (e.g., an employee who carries several hospitalization policies so that he can make a "nice" return on his illness)? Should private plans have as a major goal pressure upon governments to install public plans? Should public plans provide minimum floors on which to erect and encourage private plan supplementation?

One of the changes needed in a philosophy of economic security is increased emphasis upon prevention rather than upon amelioration. Reduction of risk rather than proliferation of benefits might well be the hallmark. Job opportunities rather than unemployment benefits, accident prevention rather than workmen's compensation, and selective retirement rather than a compulsory scrap heap present positive opportunities.

Much of our philosophy of social insurance is based upon helping those who "through no fault of their own" find themselves victims of economic insecurity. We recognize that the individual in a complex industrial society is often helpless because of conditions or circumstances created by society over which he has no control and for which he is not at fault.

An American philosophy of economic security. The rapid expansion of economic security plans in the last three decades has involved governmental agencies, insurance companies, social institutions, and numerous employers and unions. A thorough evaluation and reevaluation of this gigantic complex is overdue. Federal programs, state programs, local government programs, and private programs have met many genuine needs but still have some grave inadequacies. Gaps in coverage provide an example. Why should a person working for a firm with 4 employees have UC benefits while a person working for a firm with 3 employees has none? Why do some plans include catastrophic protection while others do not? At the same time that we have gaps, we have overlapping protection (e.g., an injured worker under OASDI and WC). Benefits may lag relative to other considerations, such as wage and price levels. Confusion in rulings among administrative agencies needs correction.

The role of government and private plans requires careful examination. Of greatest importance is the need to restudy our purposes. The problem is not so simple as how to provide more benefits — the question of "why" deserves far greater emphasis. Again, the need for clarification and rationalization of public policy should be readily apparent.

Institutions: Conflict and Cooperation

In the quest for satisfactory employment and economic security, conflicts between and among institutions affect outcomes. Institutions are created by society as socially acceptable ways of getting things done. Institutions have a way of developing their own personalities and bureaucratic paraphernalia, and frequently seem to forget that they were created by society and not vice versa. Society giveth (institutions) and society can take away — a fact of greatest relevance for public policy in a changing world.

Institutions are not always granted clear-cut charters; many are informal. Sometimes society creates a variety of institutions to deal with the same or similar problems. In our society many employment processes are assigned to several major institutions: employers, unions, and various governmental units. The problem of coordination of rival and competing institutions is compelling; the need to trim back the branches of overgrown or outmoded bureaucracies is often forgotten. Cultural lag results in the debris of old, ineffective institutions interfering with the efficiency of new social methods.

Unions. Probably no institution has evoked as much interest and curiosity as unions. They have had a rapid growth in the United

States.   They have successfully given workers social, psychological, and economic status plus a strong voice in working conditions.   Born of depression, they have had problems in adjusting their programs to prosperity.

For several decades, from 1935–55, unions had management on the defensive.   Since then management has mounted the offensive. In each case the defensive unit has had comparatively little to offer by way of positive and constructive programs.

Today, unions in America need above all to reexamine their goals and objectives to fit the 1960's, not the 1930's.   What, for example, do they seek to maximize?   Is it wage rates, income, real income, employment, membership, or some combination of these?   Is it job security via essentially a holding operation to protect existing jobs?   Or should their goals for the 1960's center upon education, housing, international competition, civil rights, and other problems beyond the workplace?

The problem of flexibility as opposed to rigidity in work rules, job assignment, and seniority needs rethinking.   Perhaps it involves confusion over long-run versus short-run objectives and means.   Is it not likely that accommodation rather than resistance to change would be more beneficial to union members and society in the long run? Unions do not exist solely to serve their own membership — they must serve society as well if they are to survive, as must agency management, the free enterprise system, collective bargaining, and all of the many institutions concerned with employment processes.

The American public has given unions some incompatible yardsticks.   On the one hand it decries competition between and among unions which leads to jurisdictional disputes; at the same time the public denounces the absence of competition, i.e., labor monopoly. The public decries use of economic strength by unions, and a large segment is against union political activity.   Charges of compulsory unionism, and right-to-work laws, are common in a nation that says its public policy favors free collective bargaining and unionism.

The public creates institutions; it should spell out performance standards expected of its institutions.   These should be articulated with clarity.   In setting standards, legislation and regulation designed to restrict the small proportion of those who abuse their powers should not be so carelessly written and administered as to handicap the majority of unions.   On such issues as labor monopoly or collective bargaining for government employees, we need reasonable, not just political or opportunistic, standards.   More attention should be given to economic factors. Thus, in the labor monopoly issue, monopoly is essentially an economic concept. Union monopoly is regulated ultimately by product demand elasticities, substitutes, cross-elasticities, and technical production functions. The public not only regulates monopoly through laws but also has immense regulatory powers in its role of consumer.

Internally unions face new realities. Just as companies restructure their organizations to meet new and changed conditions, so should unions. Repackaging of internationals should be considered seriously — this, not so incidentally, could help resolve some of the jurisdictional problems that plague labor. Problems of leadership and management development in unions should be faced. Perpetuation of the "party in power" system is not adequate; new conditions may require new leadership of a different type. Internal union political prowess must not be the major hallmark of union officer success; anti-intellectualism may not solve employment problems adequately. Workers' education should be expanded, with education rather than propagandizing as its major function. Professional staff services must be used on an objective basis. American unions need to become more experimental, to act less as custodians of status quo and past rights.

Society must resolve the thorny dilemma of the proper balance between political and economic tools. Too much union reliance on government may mean that unions cannot demonstrate a worthwhile return for dues and can impair the role of free unions and free collective bargaining.

Employers. By and large employers in our society are given the role of experimenters, innovators, and entrepreneurs. We charge them with the responsibility for productive efficiency, for maximizing outputs from given inputs, including human inputs. Theirs is a most responsible role, and by and large they have performed it well in our society. Like unions, however, they too are a conservative force in manpower management and labor relations. Some managements dare to be experimental in handling manpower management. Others fight for status quo and management prerogatives; they seem unaware of the fact that prerogatives must be earned and re-earned. More positive, preventive, anticipative personnel and labor relations policies and programs by management are needed.

If management opposes seniority and favors productivity and merit, it has an obligation to measure and use such concepts objectively

and equitably. Management must be prepared to establish and maintain yardsticks, control systems, and feedback in use of human resources. Such experiments as "human relations" and "productivity"
joint labor-management committees are worthy experiments. Whether or not they should become a part of the collective bargaining
process may depend upon circumstances in individual labor-management situations. Despite the limited success of private automation
committees to date, they, too, should be encouraged.

Employers are assumed to be exponents of the free enterprise
system. The more problems they pass over to the various governments
for solutions, the fewer opportunities to demonstrate the viability of
the enterprise system. Employers need to realize that when the public
says problems of unemployment are our number one domestic problem area, the public means it. And so, like unions, employers must
face new responsibilities and opportunities squarely in these changing
times.

Public policy in labor management relations. Change brings not
only progress but also conflict. Cooperation is necessary to production
and security. Both conflict and cooperation are needed in our industrial relations system. Labor and management have been given joint
responsibility and authority for dealing with many employment processes. In their role of contestants they may worry too much about
who's right and not what is right. Procedure and ritual may take
precedence over substantive issues. The past may obscure the future.

The grass roots level of labor-management relations (at the plant
level) is where labor-management relations really become operational.
Such abstract concepts as security versus efficiency are given operational meaning in the workplace. Sometimes employers' associations
and big international unions appear to overlook this. Conflict over
wages and working conditions, work rules and job assignments, and
work speeds and job protection are the warp and woof of employment
processes. Here problems of rights, duties, and responsibilities are
intermingled with standards of equities and values, with many of the
latter not clearly articulated.

The absence of conflict alone is not a satisfactory social goal.
Costs must be weighed against gains; thus, for example, the cost of
man-days lost in strikes in recent years may seem to be a reasonable
price for flexibility in labor relations in a free enterprise economy. On
the other hand, if the cost of conflict becomes excessive, then conflict
must be curbed.

Cooperation, too, can be excessive. Labor-management collusion on wages and prices can result in a "gang-up" on consumers. Too much cooperation can result in dwindling job opportunities. In short, too much cooperation or too much conflict can be inimical to the public interest.

But precisely how "too much" is defined and how the "public interest" is defined and measured are difficult questions. Such concepts should be modified and changed through time to correspond with other changes in our society.

Essentially the public can seek to regulate procedure, substance, or both. In some cases the public may seek to regulate powers of the parties. Here it should not be the powers per se that are regulated — the standards should be in terms of the results of the use of power. If all power forces were equalized in a society, the society would stand still. Nor should the aim be to create a kind of game-theory situation wherein the parties seek to beat the opponent. One of the weaknesses of the bargaining theory of wages is that it presumes that the players operate in a vacuum; yet, the public provides the chips for the game.

Economic versus political collective bargaining. Employers and unions have a choice of using economic tools and pressure, or political tools and pressures, or both. The consequences of their decisions increase with the scope of the bargaining sphere. Generally the public seeks settlement of disputes as a primary consideration. To this end public intervention and pressure is used. There is a tendency in such situations for economic aspects of collective bargaining to be given too little consideration.

A collective agreement is more than a cessation of open hostilities. It is more than a dollar and cents "package." Work rules and job assignment restrictions may have a greater impact upon labor costs than the direct wage settlement. The web of rules set by collective bargaining has substantial economic implications.

These economic implications should, barring a national emergency, be given a higher priority than political considerations as yardsticks in collective bargaining. Not only the parties but the public needs economic understanding and increased sophistication if we are to have enlightened public intervention, standards, and controls in the area of collective bargaining.

In a changing society inequities often accompany change. To keep a free enterprise system, we need not attempt to regulate away all inequities but only the most flagrant and persistent ones. Market mechanisms play a vital role and require a chance to operate.

In labor-management relations we need to decide whether or not we want to handle conflict legislatively, administratively, or judicially. Increasing tendencies toward pushing more and more conflict back to the courts put employment problems in the hands of nonprofessionals. Further trends in this direction could lead to labor courts and a substantial limitation on the freedom of employers, employees, and unions.

Perhaps the most obvious failure in labor-management relations in the United States has been the increasing tendency to refuse to accept responsibility in the private area and to run to the government and the courts to protest bargaining results. This weakens the institution of collective bargaining. The parties have a choice — they can act responsibly or become wards of the government. They can produce constructive results at the bargaining table or face the prospect of further regulation.

Fortunately, however, there is and has been much successful collective bargaining in the United States. The prospect for further continuation of this success is good, granted an awareness of the need for constructive solutions. The proper balance between conflict and cooperation should be resolved at the bargaining table — it can be only apparently, and not completely, resolved by law.

Labor relations legislation. The discussion of economic security earlier in this chapter pointed out that there is substantial variation in economic security laws, with differing standards, coverage, taxes, and benefits. A similar situation is found with respect to labor relations laws. Employees in interstate commerce face different rules than those in intrastate commerce. Transportation employees are regulated by special laws; government employees come under still different regulations. The result is substantial inconsistency. Perhaps the time has come to attempt to provide more orderliness and consistency in our labor relations laws.

At the same time, since workers covered by different labor relations laws often compete in the same labor markets, labor relations laws and other labor laws (e.g., wages and hours, UC, WC, and OASDI) also require better coordination. The separation of labor relations laws from other legislation affecting labor marketing is unfortunate.

National emergency disputes. Another unsolved problem in labor-management relations is the so-called national emergency dispute. Several facts stand out in any analysis of this problem. First, no satisfactory definition of emergency disputes has been devised. In time of war, "national emergency" is easier to define. But in peacetime and in cold war such definition is elusive. Definitive and usable criteria or yardsticks are needed. Second, the present handling of emergency disputes leaves much to be desired. Under Taft-Hartley, boards of inquiry are not entitled to make recommendations; last-offer votes are not effective in settlement; after the 80-day cooling-off period, if settlement is not reached, there are no formal procedures for resolving the dispute. The public is generally apathetic and brings little pressure to bear upon the parties, and political intervention is increasingly common.

Alternative proposals should be examined for dealing with emergency disputes. There would be few foreseeable disadvantages in having fact-finding boards make recommendations. Nonstoppage strikes have been suggested, wherein employees and owners put a portion of their wages and salaries in escrow to be refunded only if they settle within a specified time period. Partial operation of an industry to provide essential production only for specified critical needs is another suggested solution. In some few cases compulsory arbitration might be necessary, although this is generally repugnant in a free enterprise, free collective bargaining economy.

Clarification of conflicting goals and values is an underlying necessity before selection of means. Essentially the balance and dividing line between priority of public interests versus private interests is the issue to be clarified. This needs to be done not just conceptually but operationally as well, which may require classification of various types of emergency disputes. Perhaps some system of specific penalties by the public against the disputing parties, if they do not settle within a reasonable time, may be needed. These penalties could be progressive as delay in settlement continued. If a dispute is clearly a public emergency with threat to public health, welfare, and safety, it appears that public rights must predominate over private rights and that private parties must yield to the public interest.

Collective bargaining for public employees. A concomitant problem is that of bargaining with public employees. Here we surely can profit from past experience with collective bargaining in other industries. At the outset we must recognize the tremendous growth in public employment — the fact that over 1 million government employees are unionized and the bewildering number and variety of governmental employing units. Generally public employees cannot strike legally, although they do strike. Further, the scope of bargaining is limited by restriction of authority granted to administrators (e.g., legislatures may specify salaries).

The problem of collective bargaining for public employees is confused for a variety of reasons, including conflicts of values and rights between "sovereign" public bodies and their employees and by a tendency to lump all types of government employees into one category. To try to decide this issue solely on the basis of "prerogatives" would be unreasonable. The effects of public employee bargaining deserve consideration. Take, for example, prohibition of strikes by government employees. In the military, police, and fire services, such prohibition might be necessary. On the other hand a strike by concession-stand government employees in public parks has different effects and consequences.

It may be possible to classify and order strikes of public employees in terms of their potential threat to public interest. Different types of collective bargaining arrangements could be provided for different classifications of government employees. For some classes the entire private bargaining policy and procedure might be appropriate. In some few classes strikes might be forbidden; perhaps compulsory arbitration could be provided in these cases so that some means of definitive conflict resolution is available.

The scope of public-employee bargaining from recognition to ultimate resolution of disputes needs reexamination. What good is recognition, for example, without a formal grievance system? Failure to solve these problems often transfers such conflict from the parties to the legislatures, Congress, and city councils. Lobbying and political advantage, rather than economic and welfare considerations and criteria, tend to be the answer. To repeat, specification and clarification of goals and effects would appear to be a more rational approach. Further delay probably will only intensify problems and conflicts.

THE FUTURE: A CALL FOR PERSPECTIVE

Many current trends will probably continue in the future. Real wages will continue to advance and more economic security will be provided. Hopefully involuntary unemployment may be reduced.

Living standards will rise and income distribution will be narrowed; pockets of poverty will be cleaned up. Working time will be reduced; more time, effort, and resources will be devoted to education, training, and retraining. The move toward a brainpower economy will be intensified.

There will be wider participation in saving and investment. More concern will be evidenced in international affairs including international wages, employment, and industrial relations. There will be more concern about and interest in noneconomic values which will be made possible by greater economic output and efficiency. Cultural values, recreation, job satisfaction, and personal fulfillment will advance in importance as objectives and criteria.

A more sophisticated public — better informed for decision making, with more time available to study and consider alternatives, values, costs, and consequences — may be able to help speed up and improve problem solving in employment relations. The parties to industrial relations (employers, employees, unions, and governments) can be most helpful in this regard. Many choices are still available; many employment and wage problems remain to be solved or re-solved.

The age-old problems of individual rights and social constraints, progress versus security, and change and resistance to change are ever with us in new settings. The tempo of industrial change is accelerating and must be accompanied by new approaches and corollary changes in social relations and employment relations. As employment and employment processes and relations become more complex, inter-dependency and congruity of the parts of the total industrial relations system become more urgent.

We need to clarify employment goals and means. We need to change institutions and keep them in alignment. When dealing with partial systems, we must keep in mind their side effects and joint rela-tionships with other partial systems. We cannot "fix" wages without considering employment, and vice versa.

We should emphasize the positive and preventive, with increased planning (private as well as public) and evaluation. At the same time, a democratic society must recognize that social dysfunction can and must be handled by democratic means. The public must be made aware of its tremendous responsibilities in industrial relations.

In listing some of our major unresolved problems, we should not become defeatists nor be discouraged. We have had many positive accomplishments in employment relations; indeed, we have been remarkably successful in this regard. But change will not permit us to rest on our laurels. Fortunately these so-called problem areas represent avenues of opportunity. Improved employment relations are not at all impossible and are indeed likely.

It is true that we need a vast increase in research in employment and employment processes, both macro and micro. We need more knowledge and understanding and the wisdom to put such knowledge and understanding to use. We need less factionalism and less special interest protection. We need to look ahead as well as back; to seek prevention rather than amelioration; to "grease the skids" for change.

These are the challenges of industrial relations in our times. If they are not met, technological change will run past its necessary social alter ego. But if we do meet the challenges, we have an opportunity for making social, economic, and moral progress to a degree never before possible on such an extensive scale to any people.

ANALYTICAL REVIEW QUESTIONS

1. How and why may labor problems be regarded as economic and social opportunities?
2. Why is synthesis as well as analysis important in the study of industrial relations and labor economics?
3. Why is it more difficult to understand a dynamic system than a static model?
4. Why is continuing decision making needed in employment relationships and processes?
5. Why is it difficult to equate welfare and economic value criteria? Why is such comparison essential?
6. How can decision making lead to conflict?
7. Can you suggest a change in employment relationships in which all affected would be winners (and there would be no losers)?
8. Should we adopt a law requiring "change insurance"? What arguments favor this? What arguments can be advanced to the contrary? How did you decide which arguments (or what evidence) should be given the most weight?
9. Why are piecemeal solutions to labor problems often undesirable?
10. Why is balance among power centers so important in an industrialized society?
11. Can trial and error be regarded as a form of manpower planning? What, if anything, is better than "experience" as a teacher?
12. How are manpower models related to values and goals? Is it true that models tell us "where we ought to want to go"?

13. What did President Eisenhower's Commission on National Goals list as our top national goal? How is this goal related to the concept of "power centers"?

14. How can we improve our capital stock of human resources? Why is retreading essential?

15. How are job rationing and job control related to problems of excess labor supplies?

16. Why should we in the United States be concerned with labor force commitment in other countries?

17. Would it be desirable for us to forbid married women to work in the United States?

18. How is job opportunity related to job and output restrictions? Does increasing job opportunity tend to ease job and output restrictions?

19. Is the United States in any sense an underdeveloped nation? Give reasons for your position.

20. Who do you think should pay the costs of manpower retraining?

21. Can we solve our unemployment problems by increasing consumer demands?

22. How are civil rights related to employment opportunities?

23. Why should we seek to maintain fluidity in employment opportunities?

24. In what sense might workers displaced by automation be said to bear too high a proportion of the burden that we call the "risks of unemployment"?

25. How is employee affluence related to employee motivation? Is this a simple or complex relationship?

26. How does increasing productivity in an affluent society create problems of income distribution?

27. Why do we have a "hodgepodge" of economic security programs in the U.S.? What could be done by way of improvement? What do you regard as the most desirable first step?

28. Should employees have rights to prevention (as well as amelioration) of economic insecurity? If you answer "yes," how might this be done? If you feel that this is infeasible, what obstacles do you foresee?

29. Why do we need a basic philosophy of economic security? What equity concepts are involved?

30. What is the "acid test" of labor market effectiveness?

31. Should we have both public and private employment agencies?

32. What are the principal objectives of American unions at the present time? Why has it been said that unions must satisfy not only their members but the public as well?

33. What performance standards have been set by the public for major employment institutions in the United States? Which of these standards are sufficiently objective to permit measurement of attainment?

34. Why is it important that unions seek balance in their use of economic and political tools? Do employers need to be concerned with this problem?

35. What types of experimental programs in labor-management relations would you recommend?

36. Why is peace, or absence of conflict, not a sufficient standard or yard-stick for labor-management relations?

37. Should the public seek to regulate the substance of labor-management relations? Is it sufficient for the public to regulate powers of the parties?

38. What constraints do economic considerations place upon "political" collective bargaining?

39. Should we seek to regulate and prevent all inequities in our labor marketing system?

40. What factors appear to be weakening the institution of collective bargaining in the United States? Do you agree that "collective bargaining has failed"?

41. Why are labor relations laws likened to a "patchwork?" Would a single federal law for all employees do the job better?

42. How should national emergency disputes be defined?

43. Should fact-finding boards make recommendations? Should they have powers of compulsory arbitration?

44. Would you prefer nonstoppage strikes or partial operation as a means of dealing with national emergency disputes?

45. Should public employees have all of the same employment rights as private employees? Should public school teachers and professors be allowed to strike?

Case 26-1

BLUE GIANT FORECAST

The economist for the Blue Giant Company was asked to speak to the Annual Industrial Relations Conference on "The Future of Industrial Relations in the United States." Actually, one of the vice-presidents of the firm, finding himself on the planning committee for the conference, suggested this speaking assignment, in part because he regarded future changes in industrial relations as one of the major elements in the firm's future. The chairman of the program committee has asked the firm's economist to make some fairly detailed forecasts and thus to answer such questions as: What is likely to happen to future supplies of employees? How will these supplies change: more men, more women, more or less skilled workers? How are industrial relations policies and practices likely to change, including both public policies and programs and those of individual firms and unions? What trends can be noted with respect to such benefit programs as unemployment insurance, workmen's compensation, disability and health benefits, and pensions? What about the future of wage rates and earnings and hours of work? What is the prospect for industrial peace?

The firm's economist welcomed the request and prepared a forecast covering these points and some others, including the probable growth of unions, their extension among white-collar workers, and the future of guaranteed annual wages. His paper was enthusiastically received, but he found himself answering questions for more than an hour following his formal presentation.

• Your assignment is to try your hand at a similar forecast. Describe in a short outline or essay the changes you would predict during the twenty years ahead.

NOTE ON INDUSTRIAL RELATIONS
SYSTEMS AND MODELS[1]

Chapter 4 provided an introduction to industrial relations systems, operational and conceptual. The material in this appendix seeks to provide additional insight into conceptual systems and their components, their relationships to operational systems, and their value as an aid to improved research and understanding.

In the conceptual sense, industrial relations may be defined as "relations between and among variables connected with employment." Understanding of these relationships is basic to understanding of employment and all of its processes.

Industrial relations can also refer to descriptions of operational relations between and among parties involved in employment (e.g., labor and management). In this sense the term connotes more superficial and less substantive understanding. Thus, for example, take the statement: "Labor negotiates with management over wages."

[1]For an excellent discussion of theory and its definition, meanings, and functions (based on a summary of the works of methodologists and logicians of science), see Calvin S. Hall and Gardner Lindzey, *Theories of Personality* (New York: John Wiley and Sons, Inc., 1957), pp. 10–15. See also R. B. Braithwaite, *Scientific Exploration: A Study of the Function of Theory, Probability and Law in Science* (London: Cambridge University, 1955); Milton Friedman, "The Methodology of Positive Economics," *Essays in Positive Economics* (Chicago: Chicago University Press, 1953), pp. 10 ff.; Joseph B. Gitler and Ernest Manheim, "Sociological Theory," in Joseph B. Gitler (ed.), *Review of Sociology* (New York: John Wiley and Sons, Inc., 1957), p. 15; K. Madsen, *Theories of Motivation* (2nd ed.; Cleveland:

This simple statement does tell us that the parties have relations or mutual dealings. But it is not nearly so powerful in its insight as the statements of bargaining theory including decision-making strategies.

OPERATIONAL SYSTEMS

As noted above, the word "system" can be used to describe a consistent order or method of doing things. This type of system exists in fact and is observable. Thus, for example, the employment selection system at the ABC Company includes the following series of events: (1) filling out application blanks; (2) analysis of application blanks; (3) interviews with those whose application blanks are satisfactory; (4) psychological tests; (5) appraisal of interviews and tests; (6) interviews with supervisors; and (7) decision to hire or reject. Obviously this system refers to only one element or phase of employment. In addition, there are training systems, compensation systems, grievance systems, work assignment systems, hierarchal and status systems, division of labor systems, and many others.

These systems may and do vary through *time*. Thus, for example, more emphasis upon matching candidate qualifications and job specifications and better techniques for man and job appraisal have resulted in better hiring systems today than were in existence 100 years ago. IR systems may also vary through *place*. In some societies wages are set by governmental authorities; in other societies they are set through labor market forces. IR systems may reflect different cultural backgrounds. They may differ for a wide variety of reasons. We can discern and differentiate and evaluate these *operating* systems through observation and comparison of facts and descriptions of relationships. Essentially such study tells us "how" these different systems work.

Some operational systems appear to us to be better than others; they seem to mirror our value systems better. For example, few Americans favor forced labor camps. Or, some systems may appear

Howard Allen, 1961); A. G. Papendreou, *et. al.*, "Problems of Methodology," *American Economic Review*, Vol. LIII, No. 2 (May, 1963), pp. 205–36; A. H. Rubenstein and C. J. Haberstroh, *Some Theories of Organization* (Homewood, Ill.: Irwin-Dorsey Press, 1960), pp. 3–11 (In the same volume see Nicholas Rashevsky, "From Mathematical Biology to Mathematical Sociology," pp. 16–18); Clair Sellitz, *et. al.*, *Research Methods in Social Relations* (New York: Holt, Rinehart and Winston, 1961), pp. 480–81; Warren S. Torgerson, *Theory and Methods of Scaling* (New York: John Wiley and Sons, Inc., 1958), pp. 1–12; James C. Charlesworth (ed.), *Mathematics and the Social Sciences* (Philadelphia: The American Academy of Political and Social Science, June, 1963); Joseph Berger, *et. al.*, *Types of Formalization in Small Group Research* (Boston: Houghton Mifflin Company, 1962); A. Ando, F. M. Fisher, and H. A. Simon, *Essays on the Structure of Social Science Models* (Cambridge, Mass.: Massachusetts Institute of Technology Press, 1963).

to be more efficient (e.g., one may get more output per unit of input under an incentive wage system than under time wages).

Whatever the reason for our feelings that one IR system is superior to another, as we probe deeper we shift our emphasis from concern over "how" to concern over "why" each system operates as it does. Knowledge of "why" makes it possible for us to understand and thus predict and control events and outcomes. Through such knowledge we can improve industrial relations in the sense that we can be more certain of obtaining desired results, and also be more certain of not obtaining undesired consequences or side effects.

If we gather all of the facts and descriptions that we can about various operational IR systems, we find that they overwhelm us. We recognize the need for classification, summarization, and abstraction. We seek to sort out unessential details and concentrate on the essential. We become interested in substantive relationships — temporal or sequential, functional, and causal.

CONCEPTUAL SYSTEMS

Through theory, we move away from raw facts and reality to concepts and abstractions. We seek principles or laws that explain relationships between and among variables. We look for causes and effects. As we generalize, we can imagine *conceptual* or logical IR systems that explain general tendencies, processes, and results. We utilize such devices as models, theories, and hypotheses. We can state our problems by reference to concepts or to facts.

Relating Conceptual to Operational Systems

For optimum knowledge and understanding (in the pragmatic sense) we should be able to specifically relate concepts to reality, and vice versa. This relationship can be clarified by a diagram such as is shown as Figure A-1.[2]

The top half of the chart (Figure A-1) is concerned with abstractions, logical and conceptual. The bottom half of the chart is concerned with the "real" world. The wavy line in the middle of the chart represents the joining of abstraction and reality through theory.

---

[2]We would record our thanks and appreciation to Thomas Mahoney, Edward Gross, Roberta J. Nelson, and David Selby of the University of Minnesota Industrial Relations Center staff for many helpful discussions and suggestions concerning models, systems, theories, hypotheses, variables, and relationships, and to the University of Minnesota Graduate School for a research grant to study these subjects.

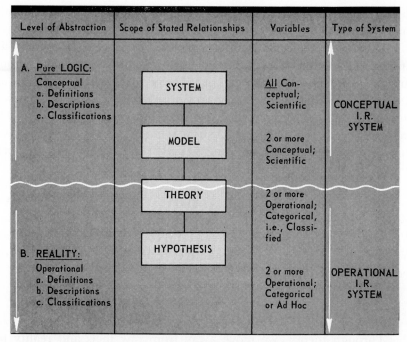

Level of Abstraction	Scope of Stated Relationships	Variables	Type of System

A. Pure LOGIC:
Conceptual
  a. Definitions
  b. Descriptions
  c. Classifications
	SYSTEM	All Conceptual; Scientific	CONCEPTUAL I. R. SYSTEM

	MODEL	2 or more Conceptual; Scientific	
	THEORY	2 or more Operational; Categorical, i.e., Classified	

B. REALITY:
Operational
  a. Definitions
  b. Descriptions
  c. Classifications
	HYPOTHESIS	2 or more Operational; Categorical or Ad Hoc	OPERATIONAL I. R. SYSTEM

Figure A-1
CONCEPTUAL AND OPERATIONAL IR SYSTEMS

The wavy line is intended to indicate that often boundaries between abstraction and reality are not clear cut nor precisely circumscribed. This is seen in the first column. It should also be noted that the following equivalent but not equal identities exist:

1. Primary statements = independent variables = input variables
2. Criteria = dependent variables = output variables

Basic Definitions in Conceptual Systems

The second column in Figure A-1 is concerned with ways and means of dealing with conceptual variables. The major components are defined below.

System. A system is a comprehensive set of variables in which all are united through some form of regular interaction or interdependence. Propositions and theorems are interrelated logically. They are deducted from definitions and postulates. The test of an abstract system is logical correctness and consistency.

General systems deal with very broad concepts and relationships. *Partial systems* are narrower in scope. Thus, a comprehensive system of employment relationships "in toto" would be a general system; a system of wage determination would be a partial system. When partial systems are combined to form a general system, typically the general system is structured around major dependent variables and their relationships. This provides a framework for locating and arranging the other variables and relationships.

Model. A model is a set of variables with specified relationships among them; it is an abstract generalization of how the relevant data are presumed to be related.

Theory. A model which is capable of being tested empirically is a theory — it has operational definitions which link the conceptual model to the real world. A theory must involve more than two variables; or put in another way, it is any statement from which we can infer two or more hypotheses. A theory must address itself to some question and try to provide an answer or explanation. It must provide a set of definitions and propositions which can be tested by observation and measurement. A theory is not judged by its truth or falsity; instead, it is judged by its usefulness. A theory is useful if its predictions or propositions can be verified through observation, and hence usable in problem solving and prevention. In short, the acid test of a theory is real-world experience.

Hypothesis. A hypothesis is a tentative explanation of the relationships between and among a few variables; a hypothesis is derived from a theory but is not a whole theory in itself. Indeed, one of the tests of a "good" theory is the number of useful hypotheses it generates. The theory predicates the relationships specified in the hypothesis. There are many kinds of hypotheses — *scientific* hypotheses are those that can be tested by appeal to empirical data; *nonscientific* are those that cannot. It should be noted that a verified scientific hypothesis becomes a fact, not a theory. In short, a hypothesis is a link between theory and fact. The proof of the hypothesis lies in observed tests and measurement — i.e., the real world.

Returning to Figure A-1, the third column seeks to show the difference in the way variables are perceived, from abstract to operational. At the conceptual stage the word "morale" may be sufficient to indicate a variable. At the hypothesis or operational stage, the word "morale" may be defined operationally as "scores obtained in the University of Minnesota Triple Audit Employee Opinion Survey, 1963 edition." Definitions of the various kinds of variables follow.

Variables. There are four major types or kinds of variables: (1) conceptual, (2) scientific, (3) categorical, and (4) ad hoc. *Conceptual variables* are regular, unchanging concepts in a system (e.g., "commitment," "morale," "effort"). These conceptual constructs give stability to the system. Without stability a system is a meaningless exercise. Thus, although relationships of morale to productivity may change, both morale and productivity are constructs that need to be related in a general industrial relations system. Conceptual variables are the elements that make up and hence define or comprise the system. These variables are postulated — i.e., given by definition or assumption. Conceptual variables are the basic inputs of IR conceptual systems. (Laws are the ultimate outputs of IR conceptual systems.)

Scientific variables are based upon deductive reasoning regarding the relationships among variables (as in a model). *Categorical variables* are those that are empirically testable, but still logically related. *Ad hoc variables* are an arbitrary grouping of variables, derived from observation and description, not arrived at by deduction (not necessarily related logically).

Returning to Figure A-1, the last column shows that conceptual IR systems are based on abstraction, and operational IR systems are rooted in reality. Conceptual IR systems are tested logically; operational systems are tested by reality.

In the explanation of Figure A-1 on page 788, reference was made to "primary statements." This is a summary title and category for the group of axioms, postulates, premises, assumptions, and principles upon which systems, models, theories, and hypotheses are based.

Dependent variables are the goals or objectives — or what we seek to explain. *Independent variables* are those which presumably provide explanation. *Intervening variables* are those between independent and dependent variables which are of sufficient importance to affect the outcome.

The different types of variables may be illustrated by the following familiar presentation from elementary psychology:

$$S \longrightarrow R$$

The independent variable S (stimulus) is followed by the dependent variable R (response). The concept of intervening variables may be illustrated by the insertion of O (organism):

$$S \longrightarrow O \longrightarrow R$$

O is an example of an intervening variable, for the type of response expected from a stimulus is in part dependent upon the organism (O) to which the stimulus is applied.

Conceptual Models

Conceptual models were defined above as a set of variables with specified relationships among them. Perhaps this can be clarified by a simple representation of a model (Figure A-2).

Each of the letters stands for a conceptual variable (e.g., morale, productivity, wage level, or employment). Arrows between letters connote a relationship and specify the direction of the relationship. Thus, A affects F — i.e., A is an independent variable and F is dependent in the relationship indicated by (1). Relationship (2) is more complicated, with A the independent, G the intervening, and B the dependent variable.

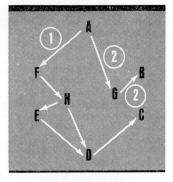

Figure A-2
**EXAMPLE OF A
CONCEPTUAL MODEL**

A relatively simple model could consist of a dependent variable and associated independent variables, with the dependent variable being the center of interest. As an example, consider Figure A-3 (page 792). Since a testable relationship must specify direction, we must specify how each independent variable affects the dependent variable.

It should be noted that Figure A-3 is a hypothetical model. It is not complete because other important explanatory variables probably should be considered. Its purpose is to make the concept of an abstract model given in Figure A-2 more meaningful.

From Systems to Hypotheses

Finally, the relationship of conceptual systems to hypotheses should be noted. This relationship is illustrated in Figure A-4 (page 792).

Note the wavy line separating abstraction from reality in Figure A-4, as it did in Figure A-1. Note also that a system may include several models, a model several theories, and a theory several hypotheses. In research, one may begin at any level within the "systems tree." One can go from hypotheses toward systems, or vice

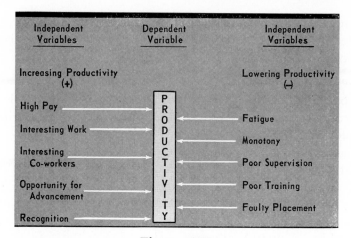

Figure A-3
VARIABLES INCREASING OR DECREASING EMPLOYEE
PRODUCTIVITY — A HYPOTHETICAL MODEL

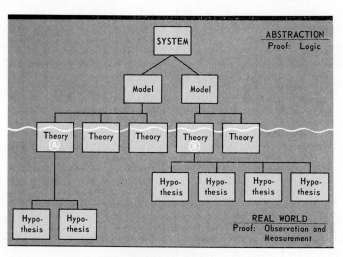

Figure A-4
THE CONCEPTUAL SYSTEMS TREE

versa. It is desirable, however, to keep in mind the systems concept. Hypotheses related to theories generally provide deeper insight. When studying one partial system, it is desirable to attempt to control or account for possible contamination effects of other partial systems. It is often said that we need more research in labor economics and industrial relations; even more urgently needed, however, is better research. To this end, a systematic approach can be most helpful.

SUPPLEMENTARY NOTES ON MARGINAL PRODUCTIVITY THEORIES

The marginal productivity theory of wages under competitive assumptions is discussed in Chapter 21, along with a brief discussion of marginal revenue (noncompetitive) amendments. Chapter 22 deals with full employment (or national income) and bargaining wage theories.

The present supplementary notes seek to expand the discussion of noncompetitive marginal productivity theories to include examples of monopolistic and monopsonistic competition and to compare these examples with the competitive models. To set the stage, and to facilitate comparison, we begin with a brief review of competitive marginal productivity wage theory.

WAGE THEORY UNDER COMPETITION

We will begin by listing our assumptions. Basically we assume a *fixed* amount of land and capital to which we can add *varying* amounts of labor. Note that labor does not have a separate product, since part of what it produces is made possible by capital. We also assume that as we continue to apply labor to the fixed factors, at some point our added returns (output) will decline or diminish.[1]

---

[1]This is known as the principle or law of diminishing returns. It could be assumed that returns would increase rather than decrease, but this violates our common sense —

It is assumed further that the units of the variable factor (that is, labor) are homogeneous and interchangeable. In other words, all labor units are equally efficient and are identical.

In the competitive situation we assume competition for the factors of production and a free labor market. This means that:

1. There are many buyers and sellers — so many, in fact, that no one buyer or seller can have any perceptible effect on price or quantity.
2. There is full knowledge on the part of all buyers and sellers.
3. Factors are mobile and will move when it is to their advantage — the principle of maximization.
4. The state of the arts is given, that is, there are no new inventions or improvements in techniques.
5. Prices are flexible.
6. There is free entrance and exit to the market.
7. Resources or factors have alternate uses.

Marginal Productivity

Total product is the total return from applying a certain number of laborers to a fixed quantity of capital. *Average product* is obtained simply by dividing the total product by the number of units of a variable factor, such as labor. *Marginal product* is the addition to total product that is obtained when one more unit of variable factor is added to the previous units of variable factor.[2]

The nature of total, average, and marginal *physical* product can be observed in Table B-1.

In this simple table, columns 1 and 2 are assumed or given. Average product in column 3 is obtained by dividing total product (in column 2) by the size of the work team (in column 1). Marginal product is obtained by subtracting the total output of a larger work team from the total output of the next smaller work team. Thus, for example, the 5-man team produced a total of 50 units and the 4-man

---

imagine potato production on an acre of land when we increase the number of laborers from 1 to 1,000. If the factors combine in fixed proportions and hence yield constant returns, it is practically impossible to determine the value of a single factor. This latter case should not be confused with the problem of "returns to scale of plant," which studies the product of variations in quantities of *all* of the factors, whereas the variable proportions problem is concerned with varying quantities of only one factor. Technically, the point of diminishing returns is reached when average physical product is at a maximum; at this point average physical product and marginal physical product are equal.

[2]Note that this is not the productivity of the last unit added, since all units of the variable factor are assumed to be equally efficient. If a 5-man team produces 60 bushels of potatoes and a 6-man team produces 69 bushels, the marginal productivity or difference *between the two teams* is 9 bushels; the marginal productivity is ascribed to the difference in *team* output, not to the productivity of the 6th man.

Table B-1
PHYSICAL PRODUCT — VARIABLE PROPORTIONS

1 Units of labor (Size of work team)	2 Total product	3 Average product	4 Marginal product
1	10	10	—
2	22	11	12
3	36	12	14
4	44	11	8
5	50	10	6
6	54	9	4

team produced 44 units; hence, the marginal productivity of the 5-man team is 6 (50–44).

It is necessary for the employer to translate physical product into monetary or revenue terms. To do this he multiplies physical product by its market price. In the short run, emphasis is upon *marginal* calculations, so the employer multiplies marginal physical product (for each work team) times product price, thus obtaining *marginal revenue productivity*.

In hiring labor the employer carefully attempts to determine whether the added cost of increasing the size of his work team by hiring one additional employee is greater or less than the value of the added marginal productivity. If the added cost is greater than the added return, he will not hire the additional laborer. If the cost is less than the return, he will hire him. He will continue to hire labor right up to the point where the added costs and added revenues are equated.[3]

The Demand for Labor (MRP)

The marginal productivity concept is important because the employer's demand for labor is based upon the revenue yielded by the marginal increments of labor, that is, the increase in total revenue resulting from the use of an additional unit of labor. His demand curve may be thought of as the *marginal revenue* he would obtain by employing different units of labor with a fixed quantity of land and capital.

The same general principle holds for all labor, that is, not just the demand of one firm but that of all firms. The general demand for labor is determined by its marginal revenue product, or the marginal revenue. This will not be a simple summation of all of the

---

[3]He also will experiment by reducing his work force.

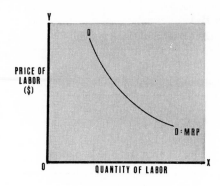

Figure B-1
DEMAND FOR LABOR

demand curves of individual firms, but instead represents the marginal revenue product for the aggregate of all firms, taking into account the interactions of all adjustments that all firms make in their attempts at maximization.[4]

This general effect is shown in graphic form in Figure B-1. The curve DD is a labor demand curve and is determined by the marginal revenues (or marginal revenue product) of various quantities of labor.[5]

The Y or vertical axis represents the price of labor (for example, wage rate per hour) and the X or horizontal axis represents the units of labor demanded.

Elasticities of Labor Demands

Elasticity of demand for labor is an important concept because of the relationship between changes in wage rates and changes in employment. The elasticity of demand for labor is not independent of the elasticity of the demand for the ultimate product. Thus, if the price of labor is raised, the effect upon employment is affected by the elasticity of demand for the product — in general, the more inelastic the demand for the product, the more inelastic the demand for labor, and hence the smaller the employment effect, i.e., the less unemployment will result. The reverse situation also holds; the more elastic the demand for the product, the more elastic the demand for labor.

---

[4]For a good brief explanation see Neil W. Chamberlain, *Labor* (New York: McGraw-Hill Book Co., Inc., 1958), pp. 331–33.

[5]The student may recall that greatest profit is realized when factors are hired up to the point where marginal revenue product equals marginal cost or marginal outlay. Firms will use all production factors until their marginal revenue products are equal to their price.

Sometimes students are confused by the difference between MRP, marginal revenue product, and VMP, value of marginal product. MRP is the difference of value of total product with N-1 variable factors (for example, labor) subtracted from the value of total product with N factors, giving the MRP for the Nth factor situation. VMP is defined as the marginal physical product multiplied by the price. Under competition VMP equals MRP, but this is *not* so under a monopolistic situation, since price is not the same as marginal revenue in the noncompetitive situation. (Price is constant and is given for each firm in the competitive situation.) Under monopoly it is assumed that increasing quantities can be sold only at decreasing price, and hence the demand curve (average revenue) decreases less fast than the MR (marginal revenue) curve.

The proportion of labor costs to total costs is another relationship that is important in wage-employment relationships. The smaller the proportion of labor costs to total costs, the more inelastic the demand for labor, i.e., the lesser the employment effects.

The fewer economic substitutes (for labor) available, the more inelastic the demand for labor. The more inelastic the supply of complementary (to labor) factors of production, the more inelastic will be the demand for labor. The more rigid and fixed the technical production coefficients, the more inelastic the demand for labor. Thus, for example, some plants are engineered to operate with rather rigid proportions of men to machines with inflexible layout of processes and production paths. They are not flexible in the technical or engineering sense, and hence small increases in wages would tend to have little employment effect.

These examples of "laws" pertaining to the elasticity of demand for labor usually relate to existing (or given) demand schedules. The marginal productivity theory is essentially static, not dynamic. But product demands do change through time, and then a different product demand curve is the basis for comparison. Thus, when business for the firm is increasing, or profits or productivity are increasing, or prices for the product are rising, the demand for labor tends to be more inelastic. Conversely, when demand for the product is declining, and profits or prices falling, the effect is to increase the elasticity of demand for labor through time.

Employers' expectations of their future competitive and profit position have a decided effect upon elasticities of labor demands in the real world. Similarly, union expectations of future business conditions, and their interpretations of factors affecting elasticities of labor demand (even if not couched in theoretical jargon) do have important effects upon wage bargains. It should be noted that unions generally have little effect upon altering elasticities of labor demands, or upon increasing demands for labor. The union label campaigns are the classical example of attempts in this direction; but by and large, as we have just noted, the forces affecting elasticity of labor demand lie largely outside the control of even the strongest unions.

Labor Supply

Here again we make the same assumptions that we did above (knowledge, mobility, free entrance, and many sellers). We assume that each worker seeks to maximize his wages, other conditions of work being equal. We also assume generally that higher rates will attract more workers and lower rates will attract fewer workers. Hence, the supply curve for industry as a whole will have an upward slope under these very simple assumptions.

Elasticities of Labor Supplies

Our knowledge of the effects of the various factors that influence elasticity of labor supplies is quite limited. As noted in Chapters 5 and 21, we know what some of these factors are, but our estimates of their influence are far less certain and objective. We do know, of course, that strong unions can and do change labor supply elasticity. They can reduce or increase effective supplies and change the shape of supply curves. An employer who had an elastic supply curve before he was organized may be confronted with an inelastic supply curve afterwards. Employer hiring policies may alter elasticity of effective supply curves (e.g., by not hiring older workers, youngsters, or members of minority groups). Labor market frictions, or forces that impede labor mobilities, may have an impact upon labor supply elasticities. While there are noncompeting labor supplies, many supplies can and do compete. Jurisdictional limitations and seniority privileges provide examples of factors that make labor supplies less elastic. Education and training and public employment exchanges can make labor supplies more elastic. As a general proposition, the supply of labor (like demand) is more elastic in the long run than in the short run. Our knowledge of the specific effects of variables upon labor supply elasticity is distinctly limited. Part of this limitation probably reflects preoccupation of wage theorists in recent times with theories that emphasize demands for labor. Increasing awareness of the importance of labor supply factors in structural unemployment may (hopefully) result in renewed attention to better models and theories of labor supplies and their elasticities.

Competitive Labor Market

In a competitive labor market made up of many firms, the forces underlying supply and demand maintain pressures for change until they are in equilibrium, that is, until there is no further reason for movement. This process is illustrated in Figures B-2 and B-3. In Figure B-2 we have added the supply curve SS to the demand curve DD we drew in Figure B-1.

In this simple diagram the price of labor (or wage rate) and the quantity of labor are determined by the intersection of the demand and supply curves at I. The wage rate is represented on the vertical or Y axis as W, and the quantity of labor employed is shown on the horizontal or X axis as Q. Because all labor is homogeneous and interchangeable, all will receive the same wage rate, OW. In this market both buyers and sellers meet all

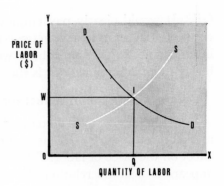

Figure B-2

LABOR SUPPLY AND DEMAND CURVES FOR A COMPETITIVE LABOR MARKET

of the competitive conditions described above. Total wages are presented by the rectangle WOQI. All labor that is willing to work for this wage is employed.

Figure B-2 represents the equilibrium position for this market; that is, there is no reason to change either the wage rate or the quantity of labor employed. A glance at Figure B-3 will reveal why this is so. Figure B-3 is made up of Figure B-2 in solid lines, plus the addition of several dotted lines representing different wage rates and quantities.

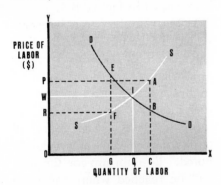

Figure B-3

ALTERNATIVE LABOR SUPPLY AND DEMAND CURVES IN A COMPETITIVE MARKET

If the price of labor were higher than OW, for example OP (or AC), the quantity of labor offered would be PA (or OC) and hence more labor would be seeking work. But note that while the price of this quantity of labor is AC (or OP), the value of what it produces (or the marginal revenue product) is only BC and hence labor would be paid more than the value of its product. This is an unprofitable condition, and hence there would be a tendency to move back to point I where DD and SS intersect.

Now suppose the wage rate dropped to OR (or GF). The price paid to labor would be much less than its marginal revenue product,

GE. It would clearly pay employers to hire additional labor until the marginal revenue product curve (DD) and the supply curve (SS) intersect, at which point there would be no further advantage in hiring more labor since this is the point of maximum return.

Competitive Labor Market for a Firm

Labor supply and demand for a firm differs from that for a market or an industry. By assumption the firm has an imperceptible effect on the price of labor. To the individual firm the price of labor appears to bear no relationship to the quantity offered. Its supply curve appears as a straight line horizontal to the X axis (infinitely elastic).[6] This supply curve is also the marginal outlay or marginal cost curve, because the firm hires so few workers (of the total labor supply) that it can get all the workers it can use without having to raise prices to attract more workers. Further, it cannot pay less than the industry or market rate because, if it did, it would not get any workers at all. Hence, the labor supply and demand situation for a firm in a competitive industry is as shown in Figure B-4.

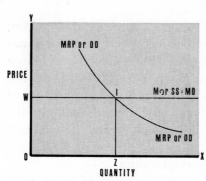

Figure B-4

LABOR SUPPLY AND DEMAND FOR A FIRM IN A COMPETITIVE MARKET

The supply curve is represented by the line WM; the firm can hire all of the labor it wants at a price of OW (determined by the intersection of SS and DD in the industry diagram). This supply curve is also the marginal outlay curve (MO) as previously noted. Equilibrium for the firm will be reached where the marginal outlay curve intersects the marginal revenue product curve (MRP or DD) for the firm. The

[6]Elasticity is the relationship between price and quantity. It is defined as the effect a relative change in price has upon the relative change in quantity.

If a relatively small change in price causes a relatively large change in quantity offered for sale, the supply of a good or service is said to be elastic. If a relatively large change in price is accompanied by a relatively small change in the quantity offered, the supply is said to be inelastic.

Elasticity is always computed in relatives, proportions, or ratios, not in absolute figures.

A line parallel to the X axis has infinite elasticity; a line parallel to the Y (vertical) axis has zero elasticity.

Elasticity is unity when the proportionate change in price and the percent change in quantity are equal.

firm will employ the quantity of labor represented by OZ at the price OW. Obviously if it hired more labor than OZ, the price for the additional labor would exceed the added revenue obtained. If it hired fewer than OZ units of labor (where revenue would exceed costs), it could continue to gain more by hiring additional labor up to the point OZ where the return of additional labor equals its cost. Employees would react also at a wage less than OW, shifting over to other employers who would be paying the market rate. Final equilibrium is reached when all labor in all firms in this market is paid at the market rate and there is no reason for additional job shifts.

NONCOMPETITIVE WAGE THEORY

Labor markets are not always purely competitive, of course, and often contain elements of monopoly, monopsony, or both. Noncompetitive wage theory is based upon assumptions that more closely approximate such deviations from pure competition. The following discussion is concerned with these noncompetitive models.

Labor Monopoly: Labor Income Maximization[7]

Now let us assume that we have a market wherein labor has a monopoly and there are many buyers of labor (the employers are competitive). Let us assume that labor is trying to maximize total income of all those in the market. The effects can be seen in Figure B-5. Here DD is the demand curve (average revenue), MR the marginal revenue, and SS the competitive supply curve.

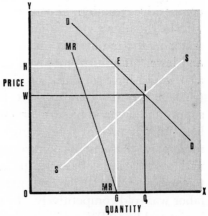

Figure B-5

MONOPOLY IN LABOR MARKET — MAXIMIZATION OF TOTAL INCOME

It can be demonstrated that total income will be maximized by selling labor at the point on the demand curve where elasticity is unity. (Price times quantity will yield the greatest total at this point.) This will occur at the point where marginal revenue is equal to zero. At any point less than this, additional labor units

---

[7]Not to be confused with monopoly in the product market.

would add to total revenue. At any point beyond G on the marginal revenue curve, no additional revenue would be obtained by using more labor units. The labor monopolist will sell labor quantity OG, where marginal revenue is zero and total return is maximized.

In Figure B-5 the point of unit elasticity is E (where marginal revenue is zero). At this point employment will be OG (or HE) and the wage rate will be OH (or GE). The total income will be the rectangle HEGO. The value of HO times OG will be greater than for any other possible price times quantity situation.

It should be noted that the wage rate and the employment for an industry in a competitive situation also can be read from this figure. The intersection of SS and DD is at point I (as in Figure B-2), the wage rate is W, and the quantity employed is Q (also as in Figure B-2).

Hence, it can be seen that in this monopoly case the wage rate is higher, and the quantity of employment is less than in the competitive situation — that is, price H is higher than W, and G is a smaller quantity than Q. It should be noted, however, that this effect stems from our assumption that point E is higher up on the demand curve than point I; the conclusion obtained in this example will hold only as long as the point of unit elasticity on the demand curve lies above the intersection of DD and SS. If the point of unit elasticity should lie at point I, the price and the quantity would be the same as in the competitive situation, of course.

In the above case (Figure B-5) where income for the use of the factor in the industry is maximized at a point of higher wage rates and lesser quantities employed than in the competitive situation, this also would have an effect on the supply price to each of the buyers (that is, the many competitive firms). In Figure B-4 we have the supply and demand picture for a firm in a completely competitive market. In our present case, Figure B-5, where the seller of labor is a monopoly, the general picture for each firm would look similar but with the following changes: the supply curve would still be horizontal to the base (X axis) for each firm, but it would be above that where labor was sold competitively. In the competitive case, supply was the horizontal line MW, and in the present instance the supply line would be higher because the market price of labor moved up from W to H in our industry diagram (Figure B-5). With the supply curve higher, it can be seen that SS would intersect DD to the left of I in Figure B-4 and the volume of employment would be reduced, being less than OZ.

Hence, generally, under a labor monopoly, a firm will hire fewer employees and at higher wage rates. This is illustrated in Figure B-8.

It should be noted that a firm faced by a labor monopoly has a situation similar to that which it faces under competition. Under competition its supply curve is horizontal, that is, it can get all the labor it wants at the market rate and cannot get any labor below this rate. The same situation holds under labor monopoly except that the market rate is higher than it is under competition.

Monopsony in the Labor Market

Now let us consider the case where we have only one buyer of labor, that is, monopsony. In this case the firm is the industry, of course. Hence, the supply curve (or the average outlay curve of labor) will be sloping upward and is positively inclined.[8] In this situation the marginal outlay curve is more steeply inclined than the average outlay curve (or supply curve). Why is this so? It is assumed that the employer must pay a higher wage rate to attract more labor. There is only one wage rate in a market, however, and since the employer in this case is in effect the market, he must not only pay the new employee the higher rate, but in addition he must pay all of the old employees the same rate (namely the new higher rate). Hence, it can be seen that marginal outlays rise faster than average outlays in the monopsony situation.[9]

We can see the effects of monopsony in the labor market in Figure B-6.

DD is the demand curve (also MRP, marginal revenue product curve) in Figure B-6, SS is the supply or average outlay curve, and MO is the marginal outlay curve. The point of equilibrium is where marginal outlay equals marginal revenue product, or where MO crosses DD; in this case it is at point T. At point T the total employment (read along the X axis) will be OR (or ZU). However, it is apparent from looking at the supply curve SS that it takes only a wage of OZ (or RU) to get this much labor. Thus, on the principle of maximization the employer will not pay more than this amount (OZ). He will not pay a wage rate of OP, for example,

---

[8]Under competition, the supply curve to the firm is horizontal and hence supply curve and marginal outlay curve are identical.

[9]There are two *added* costs to the employer when he hires an additional employee. First he must pay the new employee at a rate higher than the rate he previously paid. Second, his costs are increased by the amount needed to raise wages of his old employees to the new wage rate.

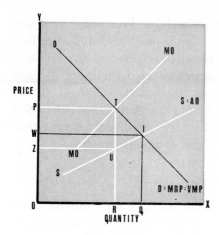

Figure B-6
**MONOPSONY IN THE LABOR
MARKET WITH COMPETITION
AMONG SELLERS**

simply because he would not be maximizing profit if he did and because labor will work for the lower price, OZ.

Since labor receives less than its marginal revenue product MRP (at point T) and does not receive a wage rate equivalent to its MRP, namely P, it is often said that labor is being exploited under these conditions.[10]

Comparison of the differences between monopsony and competition can be seen by looking at Figure B-6. Under competition, wage rates and levels of employment would be set by the intersection of SS and DD (as in Figure B-2) with wage rate OW and quantity employed OQ. Thus, it is apparent that both the wage rate (OZ) and the quantity (OR) are less under monopsony than under competition.[11]

Monopoly in the Product Market

Now let us consider the case of product monopoly, that is, one seller in the product market. It will be recalled that the competitive firm sells all its product at a uniform price — by assumption its share of the market is too small to affect the price. The monopolist, on the other hand, can and does affect price. He can sell more output only at reduced prices. In general he sets his output at a point *less* than that of the competitive firm and employs fewer workers. Thus, his reduced demand for labor is represented by a curve to the left of, and lower than, the demand curve for the competitive firm.

The monopolist, like the competitive firm, will produce at the point where his marginal costs equal his marginal revenue. His

---

[10]Such so-called exploitation will occur wherever the supply curve to the firm has less than perfect elasticity and is rising. This may not always be due to deliberate exploitation on the part of the employer but may be due to the fact that certain types of skilled labor are in extremely short supply and replacements and additions to the supply are hard to get.

[11]It will be recalled that under labor monopoly the *quantity* of labor employed was (as in monopsony) less than in the competitive situation. For *wage rates*, however, a different effect is noted. Labor monopoly wage rates are higher and labor monopsony wage rates are lower than under competition.

marginal revenue curve will be declining (sloping downward), in part because of diminishing returns (as in competition) and also (unlike competition) because he can sell additional product only at lower prices. Thus, sale of each additional unit brings in less marginal revenue, and hence marginal revenue declines faster than average revenue. To a monopolistic firm, the average revenue curve is the demand curve; the marginal revenue curve lies below and to the left of this curve. Relationships of average and marginal revenue productivity may be illustrated by Table B-2.

Table B-2

AVERAGE AND MARGINAL REVENUE PRODUCTIVITY UNDER COMPETITION AND MONOPOLY

Size of Work Team	Total Physical Output	Average Physical Output	Marginal Physical Output	Price of Product	Total Revenue*	Average Revenue Productivity*	Marginal Revenue Productivity**
COMPETITIVE FIRM							
1	30	30	—	$5	$150	$150	—
2	84	42	54	5	420	210	$270
3	120	40	36	5	600	200	220
4	144	36	24	5	720	180	120
5	150	30	6	5	750	150	30
MONOPOLY							
1	30	30	—	$5.00	$150	$150	—
2	84	42	54	4.90	412	206	$262
3	120	40	36	4.80	576	192	164
4	144	36	24	4.70	677	169	101
5	150	30	6	4.60	690	138	23

*Rounded to nearest dollar.

**Marginal revenue productivity is the increase in total revenue obtained by adding one more unit of labor to the work team.

Labor Monopoly: Profit Maximization

Now let us turn our attention to the case of labor monopoly and assume that labor acts substantially like a product monopolist, in this case seeking to maximize some hypothetical *labor profit*. (This is different from the case we had in Figure B-5, wherein the labor monopolist sought to maximize *total wage income*.)

The point of equilibrium will be reached in this case where the marginal cost curve and the marginal revenue curve coincide, since the labor monopolist will follow the same maximization principle as the product monopolist. This is shown in Figure B-7.

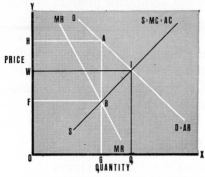

Figure B-7

LABOR MONOPOLY IN THE LABOR MARKET — MAXIMIZATION OF LABOR PROFITS — BUYERS COMPETITIVE

In Figure B-7, DD is the demand curve (average revenue) and MR is the marginal revenue curve. SS is the supply curve, and it will also be assumed to be the marginal cost curve of labor (MC).[12]

MR intersects MC at point B; hence the wage rate will be OH (or AG) and the quantity hired will be OG (or HA). Labor receives a monopoly profit of HABF, since the value of the marginal product (or marginal revenue) is only GB (or OF).

Again we can compare the competitive situation with this monopoly situation (maximizing labor profits). Under competition, equilibrium would be reached where SS and DD intersect at point I, with a wage rate of OW and a quantity employed of OQ, as in Figure B-2. For the industry, the wage rate under labor monopoly is higher (OH) and the quantity of labor employed is less (OG) than in the competitive situation.

Monopoly Sale of Labor to a Firm Buying Competitively

In Figure B-4 we considered the case of the firm buying labor competitively from competitive sellers of labor. Now let us see what happens in the firm when there is only one seller of labor (monopoly) but many firms buying (competition). For each firm buying labor competitively, the supply curve is horizontal to the base as in Figure B-4; but where the firm buys from a labor monopolist, the wage rate would be higher than OW, and the supply curve would lie above W as in Figure B-4. The supply curve would intersect demand DD or

---

[12]The more astute student may question the reality of the concept of a marginal cost curve of labor in the present situation. It is usually assumed in this case that the labor monopolist would not have to pay more money to attract additional labor since he already controls the entire supply in this market. Hence, MC would coincide with SS.

MRP to the left of point I, and hence less labor would be employed than in the competitive situation OZ in Figure B-4. This is illustrated in Figure B-8. The solid lines in that figure are from Figure B-4 and represent the competitive situation. The dotted lines show the effects of labor monopoly.[13] Under the competitive situation, the firm would hire OZ units of labor at a price of OW; its supply curve would be WM. Under monopoly, the supply curve would move up to HT, the wage rate would be OH, and the volume of employment would be OU.

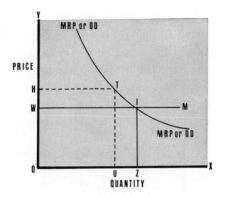

Figure B-8

EFFECTS OF LABOR MONOPOLY —
FIRM DIAGRAM —
COMPETITIVE BUYER

Monopsony and Monopoly in the Same Labor Market

The final case we will discuss is the situation where we have monopsony and monopoly in the same labor market. (In effect this combines Figures B-6 and B-7.) Here we will consider only the market diagram, and we will assume (as in Figure B-7) that the monopolistic seller is trying to maximize *labor profits* (rather than total labor income). Please note the following assumptions:

1. The supply curve of labor is the average outlay curve to the monopsonist (buyer).
2. The supply curve of labor is also the marginal cost curve to the monopolist (seller).
3. The demand curve is the marginal revenue product curve for the monopsonist (or marginal revenue curve).
4. The demand curve is the average revenue curve for the monopolist.

Thus, for the buyer (monopsonist) average revenue and marginal revenue are the same curve (DD). For the seller (monopolist) the average cost curve and the marginal cost curve are identical (SS). We have to construct a marginal outlay curve for the monopsonist as we did in Figure B-6, and we have to construct a marginal revenue product curve for the monopolist as we did in Figure B-7.

---

[13]The effect of labor monopoly in the labor market on the firm that is a competitive buyer is the same whether labor seeks to maximize total labor income as in Figure B-5 or labor profit as in Figure B-7.

In this situation either of *two different equilibriums* is possible. As we noted in our discussion of Figure B-6, wage rates for the monopsonist tend to be *below* competitive wage rates, whereas wages for the monopolist (see Figure B-7) tend to be *above* competitive wage rates. Hence, the area of uncertainty and conflict should be apparent to the student before we study Figure B-9. (The student will recall that under both monopsony and monopoly the quantity of labor taken will be less than in the competitive case, although not necessarily in the same amount.)

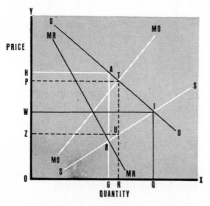

Figure B-9

**MONOPSONY AND MONOPOLY
IN THE SAME LABOR MARKET**

1. B is point of equilibrium for the monopolist.

2. T is point of equilibrium for the monopsonist.

3. I is point of equilibrium under competition.

The point of equilibrium for the *monopolist* (seeking to maximize labor profits, *not* total labor income) would be at point B, where his marginal revenue (MR) intersects his marginal cost curve (SS). The wage rates would be GA (or OH), and the quantity hired would be OG (or HA).

The point of equilibrium for the *monopsonist* would be at point T, where marginal outlay (MO) intersects marginal revenue product (DD). Employment will be OR (or ZU or PT). His wage rate will be (OZ or RU) read from his supply or average cost curve SS.

Hence, in this case the monopsonist seeks a wage rate of OZ and the monopolist seeks a wage rate of OH, the difference being the amount ZH. Since both the monopsonist and the monopolist wants his own gain to be maximum, each will try to get his equilibrium position.[14]

The quantities of employment offered will differ also; the monopolist wants to hire OG units and the monopsonist OR units, the difference being RG units of labor.

---

[14]Note that the competitive situation for an industry also can be observed in Figure B-9. Equilibrium is at point I, where SS and DD intersect. The wage rate is OW and the quantity employed is OQ, as in Figure B-2.

With the assumptions we have so far, it is impossible to predict the outcome, the wage rate being indeterminate between OZ and OH and employment between OG and OR. The ultimate outcome would depend upon the relative strengths and bargaining strategies of the two parties. This is the essence of the bargaining theory of wages discussed in Chapter 22. It should be noted, however, that: (1) once the wage rate has been determined through bargaining and (2) if that rate lies between OZ and OP for example, then it will pay the employer to expand his employment to the point where the newly bargained wage rate intersects DD or SS, whichever of these two lines it intersects first (i.e., the point of intersection which is farthest to the left, or closest to the Y axis). In this process the union also benefits from the increased employment.

A WORD OF CAUTION

The above notes are admittedly incomplete. We have aimed at providing clarity even at the expense of complete technical accuracy. The notes seek to illuminate general tendencies or relationships. No firm or industry really uses this theory as a *method* of calculating wages or employment. No real-life labor market meets completely the assumptions laid down by the theory. Real-life labor markets are full of imperfections and inconsistencies.

Despite such limitations, the marginal productivity theory can help us understand the broad basic interactions of supply, demand, and price in labor markets. It is not, however, a complete explanation nor anywhere near the final answer. Hence, the student is cautioned that the theory has limited purposes and usefulness.

INDEXES

SUBJECT INDEX

A

Ability to pay, in wage determination, 538
Abstraction, process of, 95
Accelerator effect, 416, 417
Accident rates, trends in, 676
Accidents, burden of, 676; common law rules, 676; costs and extent, 673; industrial, 673; liability for, 676; WC and, 679
Across-the-board increases, 550
"Actors" in industrial relations, 105
Ad hoc variables, 790
Adair v. *United States*, 281
Adequacy of earnings, 532
Adjustment, work, 103, 104
Administration, of collective agreements, 179
Advertising, factor in growth, 754; versus R and D as percent of GNP, 87
Affluence, and leisure, 464
AFL-CIO, changes in membership, 207; formation of, 207; officers, 210; structure, 210; views on full employment, 624
Age, discrimination in employment, 167; job shifts by, 141; of labor force, 31; legal minimum for employment, 557; mobility and, 169
Aged (*see also* Older workers), health problems of, 701; hiring policy, 692; numbers of, 693; obsolete skills, 698; occupations of, 696; participation rates, 696; productivity of, 698; retraining for, 700; unemployment of, 698
Agency management, 150, 260
Agency shop, definition, 228; legality, 304; under right-to-work rules, 293
Aggregate wages, national income and, 614
Aging, major social issues, 691; problems of, 692
Agitator theory of unions, 194
Agreement, costs of in bargaining, 631
Agreements, collective (*see also* Contracts, labor), numbers, 199; single and multiple employer, 199
Agricultural proprietorships, decline in, 553
Alliances, citizens', 267
Allocation, of labor, 122; of resources and productivity, 63; role of productivity in, 63, 606; union effect on labor force, 637; wages and labor force, 496
Allowances, family, 538
Alternative approaches to industrial relations, 100
Amalgamation of unions, 202
American Anti-Boycott Association, 267
American Federation of Labor (*see also* AFL-CIO), origin, 202
American Plan, 267
Annual earnings, white- and blue-collar, 552
Annual Economic Review, 427
Annual improvement factor, 511
Annual work time, 474

B

Backward sloping supply curve, 601
Balance, in employee and managerial rights, 103
Balance of payments, hours and, 486
Balance of power, in collective bargaining, 276
Balances, Russian manpower, 110
Bargainable issues, 314
Bargaining (*see also* Collective bargaining), arm's length, 256, 258; association, 243; attitude, 632; continuous, 356; in Europe, 243; industry-wide, 243; multi-employer, 242; positive, 258; range, 628; simple model, 628; strategy, 631; wage theory, 625; year-round, 356
Bargaining agent, defined, 178; sole, 227
Bargaining theory, levels of employment and, 633
Bargaining units, criteria, 314; defined, 178

Anticipations, of consumers and business, 615
Antikickback laws, 554
Appraisal, personnel, 260
Apprenticeship, 445
Aptitudes, employee, 144
ARA, area classification for, 398; training programs, 447
Arbitration, awards, 346; compulsory, 351; compulsory on railroads, 300; compulsory and voluntary, 346; effect on labor markets, 347; panel, 344; voluntary, 345
Area development, 437, 738
Area Redevelopment Act (*see also* ARA), 437, 447
Areas, distressed, 398; labor market, 132; redevelopment, 398, 436
Argentina, inflation in, 564
Arm's length bargaining, 258
Asia, economically active population, 28; labor force, 28; population growth, 22
Association, between variables, 98
Associations, of firms, 99; trade, 262; of unions, 99
Assumption of risk doctrine, 677
Assurance of wage payment, 553
Atomic Labor Management Relations Panel, 355
Attachment, job, 145; labor force, 375
Attitude, bargaining, 632
Authority and status system, 103
Automatic wage adjustments, 510
Automation (*see also* Technological change), and attitudes toward work, 4; burden of costs, 768; defined, 391; funds, 458; incentive wage plans and, 504
Average hourly earnings, in manufacturing, 547
Average physical output, 805
Average revenue productivity, 805

C

Canada, counterseasonal construction, 451; inflation in, 564
Capital, circulating, 578; public ownership of, 582
Capital equipment, expenditures for, 86; per worker, 86
Capitalism, downfall of, 584; private industrial, 582
Capital-worker ratio, labor prices and, 590
Careers, concept of, 103; multiple, 158, 446, 699
Cartel, 385
Categorical variables, 790
CED (Council for Economic Development), 437
Census enumeration, errors in, 48
Centers of conflict, 336
Centralism, democratic, 275
Certification, of bargaining agents, 179
Chamber of Commerce, 176
Change, insurance, 761; social and technological, 105
Charisma, 252
Chartist movement, 183

Behavior patterns, collective bargaining and, 152
Belgium, fringes in, 508
Beliefs, role of, 105, 106
Benefit and welfare programs, employee, 685; growth in, 646
Benefits, service and income, 649; strike, 237; unemployment, 653; workmen's compensation, 678
Benefits, unemployment, adequacy, 654; amounts, 653; characteristics of exhaustees, 654; wages and, 455
Big Four of Railroad Brotherhoods, 214
Bilateral monopoly, 807
Black death, and labor supplies, 573
Blacklisting, 312
Blue-collar workers, numbers, 47; wages, 551
Bonus plans, 504
Bourgeoisie, creation of, 188; in Marxian wage theory, 581
Boycott, legality, 307; Taft-Hartley rules, 290; types, 238
Braceros, 46, 744
Brazil, inflation in, 564
Brotherhood of the Footboard, 201
Budget, federal, and unemployment, 435, 624
Budgets, family, 541
Burden of accidents, 676
Burden of taxes, attempts to shift UC, 659
Bureaucratic gamesmanship, 107
Business, activity and economic growth, 728; goals of, 100; income, 501; numbers of firms, 39; organizations, 149
Business unionism, 206
Buyers, organization of, 129
Buying habits, changes in consumer, 545

INDEX OF AUTHORS AND NAMES

INDEX OF CASES[1]

---

[1]Name of case is in regular type. Issue of case is in italics, if not apparent from name of case.